Booze

Beer, booze cans, beverage rooms, bootleggers, Barleycorn, and Baby Duck: Craig Heron packs four centuries of Canadian tippling and temperance into one easy-to-open package. Booze: A Distilled History *is an informative and accessible study of Canadians who take a drink and the other Canadians who wish they wouldn't. Heron ably captures our national enthusiasm, ambivalence, and hypocrisy towards the demon drink.*

Nicholas Pashley, author of *Notes on a Beermat:*
Drinking and Why It's Necessary

Booze *is a mature decanting by a seasoned scholar. Given the importance of drink in North America's past, this book should be high octane for anyone wanting to know how we got to* AA, *a Canadian business success story, and a B.C. premier with a mug shot.* Booze *is spirited stuff, but Canadians have always been partial to a good brew. It should go down well.*

Veronica Strong-Boag, Professor of History,
University of British Columbia

Booze

A DISTILLED HISTORY

Craig Heron

BETWEEN THE LINES
TORONTO, CANADA

Booze

© 2003 by Craig Heron

First published in Canada in 2003 by
Between the Lines
720 Bathurst Street, Suite #404
Toronto, Ontario M5S 2R4
1-800-718-7201
www.btlbooks.com

All rights reserved. No part of this publication may be photocopied, reproduced, stored in a retrieval system, or transmitted in any form or by any means, electronic, mechanical, recording, or otherwise, without the written permission of Between the Lines, or (for photocopying in Canada only) Access Copyright, 1 Yonge Street, Suite 1900, Toronto, Ontario, M5E 1E5.

Every reasonable effort has been made to identify copyright holders. Between the Lines would be pleased to have any errors or omissions brought to its attention.

National Library of Canada Cataloguing in Publication

Heron, Craig
    Booze : a distilled history / Craig Heron.

Includes bibliographical references and index.
ISBN 1-896357-83-0

    1. Drinking of alcoholic beverages—Canada—History. 2. Alcoholic beverages—Canada—History. 3. Alcohol—Law and legislation—Canada—History. I. Title.

HV5020.H47 2003   394.1'3   C2003-904203-0

FRONT-COVER IMAGE: nineteenth-century brewers' poster (Workers' Arts and Heritage Centre, Hamilton, Ont.); see p.79
BACK-COVER IMAGE: Les Voyageurs bar in Montreal's Queen Elizabeth Hotel (Canadian Science and Technology Museum Corporation, CN001181); see p.328
FRONTISPIECE: Seagram's whisky and the Canadian family (unidentified photograph in the Seagram Collection at the University of Waterloo's Dora Lewis Rare Book Room)
Cover and text design by Jennifer Tiberio
Printed in Canada by Transcontinental

Between the Lines gratefully acknowledges assistance for its publishing activities from the Canada Council for the Arts, the Ontario Arts Council, the Government of Ontario through the Ontario Book Publishers Tax Credit program and through the Ontario Book Initiative, and the Government of Canada through the Book Publishing Industry Development Program.

Second printing January 2004

for
Bettina,
Anna,
&
Emily

Contents

Preface and Acknowledgements

AT THE END OF THE SUMMER OF 1919 Will Heron had many things on his mind. He had sold the old family farm in Scarborough Township east of Toronto and moved, with his wife Pearl and infant son, to a new house in West Hill. To earn a living he had cobbled together a mix of jobs while still tending a large garden and helping out on the farms of his elderly kin. Yet three times in the early fall he took time out to attend temperance meetings called to discuss a province-wide plebiscite on prohibition. On 20 October a typically terse diary entry noted that he had cast his ballot. It is safe to assume that this staunch Methodist teetotaller, who would never take a drink in his entire 108-year life, had voted to keep Ontario dry.[1]

Will was my grandfather, and his negative attitude to alcohol was part of the family legacy I inherited. My father introduced a note of ambivalence into this tradition by marrying into a decidedly "wet" family, although my mother did not drink. I am told that at my parents' wedding celebration there was no question of serving booze in front of his teetotalling kin, while my mother's more bibulous relatives insisted you couldn't have a party without it—they had to get their drinks discreetly from some hidden cache. I grew up in a household where the bottle of rye came out of the cupboard only at Christmas or similar family gatherings involving the wet side of the family. I was also legally barred from drinking until I was twenty-one, and the parties I attended right through to high-school graduation were mostly dry. It was a jolt for me, as a student worker at an American Historical Association meeting in Toronto in 1967, to find two distinguished Canadian historians sharing a bottle of gin in a back room of the Royal York Hotel. They may have been the professional role models for my later slide into long boozy nights in a pub on Queen Street West near where I lived as a graduate history student.

Over time, like most of my friends, I learned to incorporate wine into special meals and to participate in more restrained social drinking. I also took advantage of the easier access to alcohol in retail outlets and public drinking places as the provincial government loosened the controls on sales in the 1970s. In travels outside the country, I learned how differently people could incorporate alcoholic drinks into their cultures—and particularly how much less troubled most Europeans seemed to be about alcohol consumption. Later on I also had to confront the expanding role of alcohol in teenaged youth cultures. One evening, as I was knocking back celebratory libations at a friend's wedding, I found my sixteen-year-old stepdaughter happily putting down her third bottle of beer. That was before she left to go to another party with friends—the same young drinkers who were often lugging their beer cases onto our back porch in the early hours of the morning.

I must also admit that, despite my relatively relaxed attitude to drinking, I have never been comfortable with heavy drunkenness among drinking companions, or anyone else for that matter. I encountered plenty of people for whom alcohol was a problem—most visibly panhandlers on street corners in downtown Toronto (especially near the old Turner's Wine store on Queen Street)—and became aware of the abuse that heavy drinkers had inflicted on some friends' families. Like most of the rest of the Canadian public, I learned to understand this behaviour as a "sickness" and became dimly aware of extensive treatment programs available to them. I now realize that my widening familiarity with John Barleycorn, including my ambivalence, was part of a general pattern shared by many other Canadians in the decades after the Second World War.

My experience had not been a purely sensory process. I had also been reading about alcohol. I discovered some of the history of drinking and its critics in my studies of social history in Canada and elsewhere. Drinking was a theme that bubbled up in much writing about the history of the working class, the major focus of my research and writing. By the mid-1990s I was working on two book projects in which booze would appear—one a community history of working-class life in an Ontario factory town in the first third of the twentieth century, the other a wide-ranging investigation of how workers have struggled to carve out "free" time away from paid labour since the beginning of the First Industrial Revolution.

Those interests, and my sense that too little was known about the history of drinking, prompted me to propose an exhibition on the subject of workers and alcohol to the Ontario Workers' Arts and Heritage Centre, a new organization committed to showcasing the history and culture of working people. I was convinced that the exhibit would provide a great opportunity to get at the many ways in which workers engaged with alcoholic beverages: as a product that some of them made and sold, as a beverage that lubricated much of their socializing, as a source of domestic conflict, as a personal and social problem of chronic dependency in some cases, and as a source of cultural and political tension within working-class communities. In the end I became the curator of the exhibition, "Booze: Work, Pleasure, and Controversy," which ran for five months over the summer of 1998. The research I did for that project revealed a considerable amount of writing on drinking in Canada that was scattered through unpublished theses, long-forgotten company histories, and specialized journals—content that had never been brought together between the covers of one book. Given the importance that so many Canadians have attached to alcohol since the arrival of the first European colonists, this omission was surprising.

Initially I planned to prepare a short exhibition catalogue summarizing the available material, but money and time ran out. Instead I settled into somewhat deeper reflections on this fascinating theme in Canadian history, and this book is the result. It is presented as a reconnaissance and not the final word on the subject. There are gaping holes on the library shelves that can frustrate the preparation of a social history of drinking in this country. But I concluded that the issues swirling around alcoholic beverages in our national history are sufficiently important that it would be useful to undertake a mapping of the historical terrain, in the hopes of raising the profile of those issues and to stimulate further research and writing.[2] In shaping an analysis, I have benefited enormously from the work of a small band of Canadian scholars (notably Robert Campbell, Sharon Cook, Cheryl Krasnick-Warsh, Greg Marquis, Jan Noel, and Julia Roberts) and a much larger number of historians and social scientists working on the histories of the United States, Britain, European countries, and white-settler dominions in the British Commonwealth.

In my research it became clear that the huge interdisciplinary field of alcohol studies has often suffered from a narrow focus on the beverages and their immediate consequences, rather than looking for the ways in which the production and consumption of alcohol are related to much larger social and cultural processes. What follows, then, is intended not only to open up an engaging story to wider reflection but also to suggest that the issues around alcohol consumption connect to a multitude of questions that have engaged Canadian writers and scholars for some time: economic development, labour relations, consumer practices, family life and living standards, the dynamics of work and leisure, the formation of social classes, the norms and practices of gender (especially masculinities), the cut and thrust of moral reform projects, the nature of popular politics and state formation, the shaping of regional and national cultures, and, in general, the relationship between the moral and material dimensions of capitalist society. Perhaps, like so much of the vast literature in the alcohol studies field, this first stab at an overview history of drinking in Canada will help policy-makers shape their agendas with a slightly longer-range perspective. There is little that has not been tried before in attempting to grapple with booze in Canadian society.

I owe a debt to many people who helped my search for John Barleycorn. The project began as an exhibition in Hamilton in 1998, and I am grateful to the Workers' Arts and Heritage Centre for allowing me to turn such a wildly ambitious idea into reality, to Steve Penfold, James Moran, Rob Kristofferson, and Gerry O'Donnell for research assistance, and above all to Karl Beveridge, Carole Conde, Ginette Peters, and Renee Johnston for turning my stacks of notes and images into a visually stunning exhibition. At a later stage of photo research, Lorraine O'Donnell also provided valuable help.

I leaned heavily on the competent staff of many libraries and archives: the recently merged National Library and Archives of Canada, Nova Scotia Museum, Provincial Archives of New Brunswick, Archives de la Compagnie de Jésus, Bibliothèque Nationale du Québec, McCord Museum, Montreal Museum of Fine Arts, Canada Science and Technology Museum Corporation, Archives of Ontario, archives of the Liquor Control Board of Ontario, Art Gallery of Ontario, University of Toronto Libraries, United Church Archives, York University Archives and Special Collections, Central Branch of the Toronto Public Library, Special Collections Department of the Hamilton Public Library, Doris Lewis Rare Book Room of the University of Waterloo Libraries, *Tavistock Gazette*, *Windsor Star*, Glenbow Library and Archives, British Columbia Archives, Rossland Historical Museum, and Alaska State Library. Jan Noel also kindly allowed me to dip into her personal collection of images from early temperance campaigns.

Several people generously shared their research. Albert Tucker allowed me to read his delightful, dusty, unpublished masterpiece on one firm within the "Liquor Traffic." Mariana Valverde and Julia Roberts gave me a peek at unpublished papers, and Greg Marquis, Rob Kristofferson, and Steve Penfold passed on valuable details that they had uncovered in their own research.

I was able to test some of the ideas here in presentations to the history departments of York University and the University of Windsor, at the annual meeting of the Canadian Historical Association, at the North American Labor

History Conference at Wayne State University, and in front of the Labour Studies Research Group and Masculinities History Group in Toronto, all of which prompted fruitful rethinking. Along the way I also benefited from countless more casual conversations with friends who shared their thoughts and stories about booze.

I am particularly grateful to Jack Blocker, Bettina Bradbury, Steve Penfold, and Mariana Valverde, who read the whole manuscript and provided insightful commentary that pushed me back for one more substantial rewrite.

At Between the Lines, Paul Eprile swept me up with his enthusiasm for this publishing project and kept a firm hand on the editorial rudder over an intense six months of production. Robert Clarke's superb editorial prowess untangled many knots of snarled prose. Margie Adam's skilful scanning and Jenn Tiberio's design work turned the book into a thing of beauty. And Peter Steven's marketing skills were remarkable.

Above all, completing such a large project was only possible because of the constant support and encouragement of my irrepressible stepdaughters, Anna and Emily, and my loving partner Bettina. To them I raise a glass and dedicate this book.

one

In Search of John Barleycorn

No one recorded the reactions of the first humans who tasted an alcoholic beverage and experienced its effect on their bodies. It would have been well over five thousand years ago, because archaeologists have found evidence of drinking practices at least that long ago in the Middle East, Asia, and Africa. We can safely assume that those first imbibers enjoyed the experience and went back for more, given that alcohol was consumed in those regions for centuries after. Similar happy discoveries eventually made "drinking" part of human cultures everywhere on the globe. Alcohol has long been the most popular of the stimulants that humans take into their bodies to alter their consciousness and thus produce or enhance pleasure, and it was one of the first to be widely commercialized—although the reasons as to why people have sought such pleasure have varied considerably over time and between cultures.

Over the years alcohol has also often been suspect—a risk or a danger. Like many other substances we ingest, too much of it can contribute to personal and social problems. As a result it has always had a special status not accorded to other beverages or foods. State and moral authorities have rarely expressed as much interest in other pleasurable "bad habits" involving coffee, chocolate, or cola (even though excesses of caffeine and sugar in the body can result in poor health and induce negative behaviour). In part the difference lies not just in the specific psychoactive (mind-altering) impact of alcoholic drinks on the body, but also, and even more, in their association with indulgent, often hedonistic pleasures and the activities that result when people get together to share those delights. Although drinking together can often affirm social relationships, it can also be an expression of liberty and independence and therefore appear threatening or subversive.

Opposite page: *Drinking has inspired a rich heritage of paintings, drawings, and photographs that often convey the ambiguities of drinking. Did the photographer of this unidentified Québécois tippler intend to present the image of a happy-go-lucky working man ready to wet his whistle at the end of a hard day's work? Or a grizzled old drunkard, abuzz with flies, sinking into debauchery? Why was the photo taken? To commemorate an important family event? To promote abstention by inducing disgust? To sell beer by gently mocking this old-timer?* (NAC, PA-80920)

To understand the history of booze, then, is in large part to probe how various peoples have dealt with pleasures and dangers in their cultures. Canada's story is only one variant among many, and in this account of Canadians' use and abuse of alcohol I try to untangle the specific economic, social, cultural, and political strands woven through our particular approaches to pleasurable experience.[1]

Booze in the Body

Almost any natural product containing sugar or starch can be turned into beverage alcohol. Grapes, apples, pears, plums, cherries, oranges, bananas, coconuts, dates, palm sap, manioc, agave, sorghum, cactus, birch and spruce saps, sugar cane, honey, rice, potatoes, milk, corn, millet, wheat, oats, and barley—at some point in human history all of these have been transformed into alcoholic drinks. Broadly speaking, the transformation has come through two processes: fermentation or distillation. For centuries in Asia, Africa, South America, and Europe, producers turned fermented fruits or vegetables into beer (generally, though not exclusively, from grains) or wine (most often from grapes). Only during the sixteenth century did large numbers of alcohol-makers begin preparing beverages by the second, distinctly different process of heating specific fermenting liquids in a still to extract spirits (till then used mostly for medicinal purposes). They used a beer-like solution for whisky, a wine for brandy, a potato-based brew for vodka. Sometimes by combining products of the two processes they created another drink—"fortified" wines like port and sherry, for example.

The tastes and modes of preparation have changed a good deal over time, but all these drinks have a common active ingredient: ethanol (or ethyl alcohol), a chemical that has specific effects on the human body.[2] It enters the bloodstream through the stomach and digestive tract and spreads throughout the body. In most cases the body can easily metabolize the ethanol into carbon dioxide and water, mainly through the liver, at a rate of about one standard drink (twelve ounces of beer, five of wine, or one and a half of spirits) per hour, though the process depends on the ethanol content of the drink, the quantity consumed, the rate at which it is consumed, the amount of food in the stomach (to slow down absorption), the condition of the liver, and particular body characteristics such as weight or build (though these seem to be highly variable and unpredictable). When the body takes in more alcohol than it can absorb quickly, the ethanol remains in the system, affecting in particular the brain and central nervous system.

Initially ethanol is a stimulant, inducing euphoria, but as the quantity in the body increases on the specific drinking occasion, it becomes a depressant. It slows down the central nervous system and encourages relaxation. Speech can become slurred, perception dulled, and judgment and co-ordination impaired. The drinker who drinks enough gets drunk. The chance of accidents (falling down, bumping into dangerous objects, crashing a car, and so on) increases. Heavy intake can lead to sleepiness, memory loss, or blackouts, and, later, a "hangover," resulting from dehydration.

The drunkenness threshold seems to vary. The Canadian Criminal Code sets it at a blood-alcohol count of .08, or 80 milligrams per 100 millilitres of blood, but some other countries set slightly higher levels, and alcohol can affect different bodies differently. In the vernacular, some people can "hold their liquor" better than others. Attempts to explain those differences have proven difficult. There is certainly no conclusive evidence of any genetic predisposition in particular ethnic or racial groups, as people once widely believed. It does seem that women feel the effects of ethanol more than men because of their generally smaller bodies with typically more fat, less water in their system to absorb alcohol, and less of an enzyme in their digestive tract that would help to metabolize the alcohol (though older women have more and older men have less). But, for the most part, these are minor differences.

Ethanol can apparently be both bad and good for us. On rare occasions individuals can drink enough in a concentrated time period to poison themselves. More commonly, repeated heavy drinking over the long term can put a strain on the liver and heart and contribute to potentially fatal diseases of the nervous, respiratory, or digestive systems, notably cirrhosis. Among pregnant women, heavy intake poses risks to the brain development of the fetus (so-called "fetal alcohol syndrome"). Yet, across time, many alcoholic beverages have also had at least some nutritional value, providing calories, vitamins, and minerals. Recently medical researchers have been saying that one or two drinks per day of any beverage containing ethanol (and not simply red wine, as initially argued) can reduce the risk of heart disease and therefore prolong life. Moderate drinking is now seen as being most often healthier than either abstaining or heavy boozing. These claims remain controversial, but compelling enough to win endorsement by medical authorities, although a rider is always attached that the benefits can vary depending on an individual's overall health. More difficult to evaluate are the arguments that the pleasure provided by drinking beverage alcohol can have positive psychological effects, especially reducing stress, and can thereby help to promote good health. Certainly far more people today drink for pleasure than for health.[3]

Ultimately, to understand the impact of alcohol on human society we have to move beyond biochemistry, physiology, and pharmacology to a consideration of how people choose to use it in their particular cultures. We have to pursue not so much how people have appreciated the scientific properties of ethanol (which, in any case, were often seriously misunderstood in hardy folk wisdom and are still debated in medical science), but rather how, in this part of the world, people came to think about their drinks as "booze."[4]

National Peculiarities

Throughout the world, the alcoholic drinks available and consumed in any period have depended on a complex interplay of natural environment, economic development, and state policy. There has always been a close link between alcohol consumption and agriculture. Until the 1970s, for example, people living in Canada had difficulty growing grapes appropriate for good wine production, in obvious contrast to the Mediterranean world, where wine has long been the beverage of choice. Instead, in areas where grain or potatoes were grown in abundance, as in large parts of North America, Africa, and Northern and Eastern Europe, spirits and beer became more common. Early commercial distilling was closely connected to agricultural surpluses in those areas. Indeed, most countries, including poor nations, have until quite recently relied on local production, far more than on imports, for their particular beverages, and women in rural families have frequently made some kind of brew for home consumption.

The beverages available commercially have also depended on the size of the consumer market and marketing practices. As early as the seventh century BC, Etruscan merchants were importing wine into what is now Southern France. At the time, and for centuries after, the high cost of imported beverages restricted their consumption to the wealthy and enhanced the social status of wine over beer. Much later, spirits produced as an adjunct to farming proved to be a more stable, less bulky, more portable product than fermented drinks. Europeans thus made brandy and rum key components of their trade with the indigenous peoples they met in their new projects of "discovery" and colonization from the sixteenth century onward. Until mechanical refrigeration arrived in the later nineteenth century beer did not travel as well as other booze, and to be commercially viable the breweries usually needed large concentrations of drinkers relatively close by. But by 1900 in North America, much of northwestern Europe, and the white-settler dominions of the British Empire, beer had achieved something of a marketing victory over spirits, a victory built on the huge increase in urban populations that accompanied industrialization.[5]

Commercial producers of all kinds of booze were also on the cutting edge of mass consumerism, using increasingly effective systems of distribution, sales, and, eventually, advertising to promote purchases of their products. Alcohol beverages became one of the earliest mass-produced goods aimed at those able to buy them not just in more commercially oriented and industrializing regions but also in the colonized regions of the Third World, where elites often embraced the more expensive booze produced in the West in preference to traditional local drinks. Consumption tended to rise and fall with the capitalist business cycle and, eventually, with competition from other consumer goods and recreational options. The consolidation of huge, multinational booze-producing corporations after the Second World War allowed for a much wider promotion of beverage alcohol and greater harmonization of drinking patterns. Today "alcohologists" like to divide the world into three blocs based on the predominance of spirits, wine, or beer in the national consumption patterns (even though more and more countries are drinking large quantities of all three). Despite the diversity of its spending patterns, Canada still falls into the bloc of beer drinkers.[6]

As their economic power grew within some regions and nation-states, the political clout of booze producers could be considerable, and state authorities were often convinced to implement economic development programs and protective policies against foreign competition. The state also had other interests that could influence the availability of particular beverages. The British, for example, learned to appreciate port rather than French wine thanks to the international rivalries of the eighteenth century. In the same period Nova Scotians and New Englanders developed a taste for the rum delivered through the closely controlled trade with Britain's West Indian colonies. Polynesians got beer as a part of the package of Western colonial domination. Moreover, the state might promote one local beverage over another. Ethanol appears in more concentrated form in distilled spirits than in fermented wines and beers, and over the past four centuries in Canada, as elsewhere, to sway drinkers towards the less potent drink various attempts have been made to draw sharp distinctions between these categories—even, at points, to suggest that beer, cider, or wine might not be intoxicating. In France medical writers would even refer to them as *boissons hygiéniques*. By the middle of the nineteenth century, negative voices in Canada had nonetheless lumped all these drinks together as equally contemptible "booze."[7]

Drinking Cultures

Within the range of available beverages, choices about what to drink and, even more, when and where to drink were almost never purely individual decisions. In most pre-industrial societies, alcoholic beverages were seen as nutritious foods to be consumed at meals and as medicines and tonics for health, and they were often used to stimulate and reward labour. Over the years people in many societies used alcohol regularly at home (and often on the job) to wash down meals, to strengthen the body, to ward off illness, and to welcome guests.[8] At least until the mid-to-late nineteenth century, when new notions of a more protected childhood and, later, adolescence discouraged youthful drinking, the members of all age groups in the Europeanized world were familiar with the taste of alcoholic drinks.

Almost everywhere drinking has been more common among men, especially younger men, and only in the mid-nineteenth century did significant proportions of males in Western countries withdraw from drinking. Some people, of course, never touched alcohol. Although by the mid-1960s a cross-cultural survey of 139 societies found only four that explicitly forbade female drinking, the largest group of abstainers has always been women. In most societies, drinking was generally constructed as being inappropriate for women's reproductive activities, and female drinkers were often suspected of having loose morals.

Public drinking, both ritualistic and convivial, has long been as important, if not more important, than drinking in the home.[9] The consumption of alcohol has most often been a highly social act, undertaken in company with other people who share experience and social status—a particular class, occupation, religion, gender, or age group. Drinking together became an important part of creating and defining groups and classes. It was deeply enmeshed in specific cultural norms and practices that varied widely through different societies but nonetheless shared common characteristics. In some cases, alcohol was a central part of religious ritual, including early Hellenic, Japanese Shinto, Aztec, Jewish, and Christian practices. Both Catholic and Protestant churches used wine in communion services. It could also be used to cement social bonds or alliances or to conclude important transactions between individuals or groups.

The rituals of public drinking had great symbolic import in the pre-industrial world—establishing a man's personal and professional honour and his obligations and responsibilities. For centuries, drinking was also central to festive occasions in a family or community and a mainstay of more informal conviviality. Among men it was also incorporated into periods of relaxation and recreation after bouts of work. Specific spaces—usually taverns of some kind—emerged as gathering places for drinkers looking to unwind. In light of the number of alternative activities for relaxing, the overriding attraction of drinking with others in leisure time was the sociability that it made possible. Drinking together allowed men to renew social bonds and to find solace in the face of disruptive social change in other parts of their lives.

In Anglo-American drinking cultures, the seductive spirit of companionship and sociability to be found in alcohol was long ago dubbed "John Barleycorn." Early-modern Germans referred to a "boozing devil" who encouraged drunkenness. Wherever such tipplers gathered, well-understood custom would always regulate how people behaved while drinking, how much they consumed, and how quickly. That applied to such practices as toasting and treating as well as to drunken behaviour, which, anthropologists have now demonstrated, varied enormously across drinking cultures and was not necessarily disparaged.

Intoxication has proven to be a highly ambiguous category of behaviour, and English speakers have invented a rich vocabulary to convey many subtle gradations: happy (as in "happy hour"), merry, high, tipsy, tiddley, lit, buzzed, lubricated, fuddled, pickled, sloshed, soused, stewed, loaded, pissed, pie-eyed, tight, plastered, smashed, hammered, blitzed, bombed, stoned, wrecked, wasted, blotto.[10] While many drinkers slid imperceptibly into some state of inebriation, others drank deliberately to get drunk. In most cultures, this latter group participated only in occasional binges, though in hierarchical aristocratic societies drunkenness could be a mark of privileged access to alcohol. Only in the more industrialized, Europeanized world, where the drinks became cheap and widely available, did chronic, repeated drunkenness become defined as a social "problem," eventually labelled "alcoholism." In practice, even in the West, the distinction between binges and compulsive drinking proved hard to draw. Often both tendencies would be labelled "problem drinking."

In any case, drinking to a state of drunkenness never simply involved peeling away inhibiting cultural constraints and letting loose some inner "animalistic" urges in an individual. It has always followed well-understood cultural patterns and rituals concerning drinking occasions and comportment, which have taken different forms from culture to culture. Anthropologists have compared drunken comportment in many parts of the world, finding that in some cases all drunks withdraw completely into stony, somnolent silence; in many others, they indulge simply in relatively orderly (increasingly thick-lipped) toasting, singing, friendly joking, or sentimental conversation; in still other cases they become overtly aggressive and violent (though the behaviour was never completely at random and was usually narrowly focused on specific targets in patterns of conflict carried over from sobriety).[11]

Many of these societies, moreover, show marked changes in drunken behaviour over time (especially as a result of colonization) and in different contexts (for example, with newcomers or strangers). They can also place well-understood, socially sanctioned limits on the wild expressiveness that might erupt. Drunkenness most often fills a space in a culture as "time out" from normal behavioural expectations, though one bounded and scripted by social conventions. A drunk can act out mini-dramas otherwise not possible (some psychological studies suggest that men get feelings of power from this experience, though the projects have tended towards oversimplification and weak contextual analysis).[12]

The consequences of intoxication vary as well. A tiny proportion of drinkers want to repeat the sensations of drunkenness regularly and let that desire override other social obligations, especially family and work. In all societies that have undergone the transition from the relative self-sufficiency of family-based production to a reliance on wage-earning in a capitalist economy, drunken husbands can wreak financial havoc on the families that depend on their wages, or inflict violence or emotional abuse on those around them. Still, that is not a universal form of behaviour. Anthropologists have found many non-Western settings in which drunkenness is highly valued and produces none of the social disruption or "addiction" or "dependency" typically noted among Western "alcoholics." There has also been inconsistency in the acceptance of drunkenness as a valid excuse for disruptive behaviour.

Regulating Consumption

The pleasures and benefits of alcohol have long been accompanied by more formal efforts to regulate drinkers' behaviour (or "habits," as moralists might refer to ingrained patterns). In most societies religious and moral authorities have tried to stake out acceptable limits for drinking and the surrounding activities. Early Greek and Roman religious practice valued intoxication as part of the orgiastic celebrations in honour of the wine gods Dionysus (Greek) or Bacchus (Roman). But these rituals were no longer tolerated in the last two centuries before Christ or in the early centuries of the Christian era. Neither the Jewish faith nor Christianity rejected drinking, and, indeed, their sacred texts refer to the positive qualities of alcohol. The Talmud states that "wine taken in moderation induces appetite and is beneficial to health." The Bible's Psalmist saw wine as God's gift "that maketh glad the heart of man," and Paul wrote in his First Epistle to Timothy, "Drink no longer water, but use a little wine for thy stomach's sake and thine own infirmities." Yet the more ascetic, meditative, and pietistic spirituality of these religions expected individuals to exercise personal constraint and moral probity. In the emerging litany of Christian sins, drunkenness was linked to other indulgent pleasures of the flesh, including gluttony and sexual exuberance, though how much was enough remained a fuzzy area of reflection and negotiation. Sundays and holy days became occasions for drunken sprees (in England religious fund-raising events were appropriately known as "church-ales"). Religious orders regularly produced wine and beer, and in the twelfth century, for the first time in the Western world, a Christian order in Salerno distilled spirits—a practice that the Chinese had started centuries earlier.

The Protestant Reformation brought a new surge of piety, but moderate drinking was still tolerated. "Who loves not women, wine, and song,/ Remains a fool his whole life long," Martin Luther wrote. He also advised a student on fighting melancholy: "Whenever the devil pesters you . . . at once seek out the company of men, drink more, joke and jest." In practice, Confucianism, Hinduism, and Buddhism also simultaneously tolerated some consumption and discouraged excessive drinking. Islam took a different course after Muhammad reversed more than three thousands years' experience in Middle Eastern drinking practices and demanded complete abstention. The key passages in the Quran were nonetheless flexible enough to enable wealthy Muslims in some Middle Eastern countries to serve wine at their banquets and many African Muslims to follow the drinking customs of their non-Islamic neighbours. In all of these moral strictures the line between the permission to drink and condemnation of intoxication remained annoyingly difficult to draw.[13]

In the eighteenth century, "science" began to weigh in on the subject of heavy drinking, and some medical practitioners first made a case for an ailment that would eventually become known as "alcoholism." Over the years the term proved to be imprecise and unstable, combining a dose of moralism with varying amounts of frequently disputed medical opinion. The theories of the relationship between drinking and "habitual" drunkenness fell into roughly four phases, which succeeded each other chronologically and overlapped in time. In the earliest phase, alcohol was seen as a medicine and a nutritious food; drunkards' behaviour was the result not of the drink itself, but of their moral failings. A second theory, which lasted for more than a hundred years beginning in the early nineteenth century, suggested that no amount of alcohol was safe and that the slide from social drinking to disease was almost inevitable. The third theory insisted that alcoholism was indeed a disease, but that people were susceptible to varying degrees, based to a great extent on their psychological condition. Then, starting in the 1970s, a fourth theory (if it is a full-fledged theory at all) moved haltingly away from the disease theory and sought to understand heavy drinking as a complex amalgam of socio-cultural and psychological forces in particular individuals' lives. Each phase in this theoretical development brought new therapies to "cure" the problem, all requiring the intervention of medical professionals. Today alcoholism is not a recognized disease in the medical community, but it retains that status in popular consciousness and lurks in discussions of the still imprecise terms "abuse," "addiction," and "dependency." Scientific certainty remains elusive.[14]

The state has never waited for medical consensus before wading in to regulate alcohol consumption. Until the mid-nineteenth century, state authorities rarely worried about alcohol itself—indeed, almost everywhere they relied on its status as a luxury for all-important tax revenues. But, since long before Europeans began to impose themselves across the globe, gatherings of heavy drinkers had disturbed lawmakers, who always kept a sharp eye on tavern-goers and the company they kept. They worried about the criminal acts that frequenters of taverns might be hatching, the disorder they might create on the streets, and the wider political subversion they might be plotting. During the American Revolution, taverns were major forums of political debate, as they were for workers in Britain in the early nineteenth century and in France and Germany a few decades later. Laws not only frequently required tavern-keepers to curb heavy drinking and maintain order but also clamped down on public drunks. Moral concerns were generally left to religious leaders, but, at some point in the nineteenth century in most parts of the Europeanized world, the state began to intervene more aggressively to enforce a moral code of sobriety.[15]

Here again, cultural differences were striking. Most white-settler countries banned drinking by the Aboriginal populations they had colonized. Among Western nations, however, only Canada, the United States, and a few Nordic countries eventually tried full-fledged prohibition of alcohol consumption for everyone. Other countries limited themselves to some less draconian legal restraints. Many of these constraints were loosened around the middle of the twentieth century, when a new era of liberalization in alcohol regulation opened up in almost all countries. By that point, all Western nations (and many Third World countries) had laws governing where alcohol could be purchased and by whom, when and where it could be consumed, and how drinkers should comport themselves while drinking or drunk. Drinking patterns thus had to be reshaped within such legal frameworks—whether the patterns involved guzzling as much as possible before the six o'clock closing time in Australia or New Zealand, staying seated with a drink in Canadian beer parlours, sneaking out behind the barn for a swig of bootleg liquor in some dry parts of the United States, or not driving while drunk in most countries.

Drinking and Social Identities

Drinkers in Canada, as elsewhere, had not necessarily been willing to abandon John Barleycorn, and alcohol has thus provoked deep-seated conflict in our society for more than three hundred years. Drinking has been a central issue in relations between classes, genders, and ethnic groups. It was a particularly important element in the formation of the middling and upper classes in the mid-nineteenth century. Many people in these social groups rejected it at that point, and their leadership of temperance movements helped forge their emergent sense of class. At the same time, alcohol has been significant in the history of Canada's working class. By the late nineteenth century, thousands of working men had made it the centre of their social lives outside the home, despite disapproval from their families, bosses, and even workmates. The right to drink with other men became a major component in their class identity, masculinity, and, in some cases, ethnic formation. They were challenged by social forces that aimed to root out these behavioural patterns and break up their local gathering places, the saloons. These battles were at the centre of broad cultural confrontations over how to spend leisure time and how to spend money, which had become key issues in Canadian society by the late nineteenth century.

Alcohol was also part of how people established their racial identities. Whites from European backgrounds built their notions of racial superiority on contrasts between white civilization and the primitiveness of people of colour. In the Southern United States or Southern Africa, they pointed to Black drinking customs. Across North America they saw Aboriginal drunkenness as evidence of racial inferiority. When they turned Native people into the equivalent of children under the law and closed off the indigenous peoples' legal access to alcohol, they were constructing rigid racial hierarchies.

Alcoholic beverages were, therefore, a "problem" in much more complex ways than many accounts suggest. Some writers have labelled the anti-drink crusades as a project in "social control," meaning that dominant social forces aimed to use voluntary and state-sponsored programs to change the habits of subordinate groups. For good reasons, most social historians have backed away from the term, which, by assuming that one social group simply acted manipulatively on another from outside, gives an incomplete view of the dynamics at work. "Social control" implies passivity on the receiving end, but the process always involved a degree of conflict and resistance that the innovators had to engage with and respond to. Moreover, moral reformers were typically trying to create and reaffirm their own identities as much as those of others.[16]

It is certainly tempting to see the lines of demarcation in the great disputes over booze as falling along the existing fault lines of social class, gender, and ethnicity or race. As we will see, capitalists were more likely than workers to be critical of drinking, and women were certainly more negative than men. White Anglo-Celtic Protestants were more abstemious than were people of European backgrounds and raised in the Catholic faith. Yet it was never so simple and straightforward. No easy organic connection existed between particular social categories and the pro-booze and anti-booze forces. The temperance campaigns to curb or completely shut down drinking presented an ideological rationale that was pitched at (and to some degree appealed to) all elements of the social structure. The middling and upper classes were expected to reform themselves as much as were the lower orders.[17]

Temperance became a lens, a set of concepts and practices, used as a means of viewing the changing world of the nineteenth century, a way of understanding the chaos and disorder and of contemplating a different kind of future. In British North America and Canada, from the 1830s onward, it spoke directly to concerns about self-discipline and self-formation in a new bourgeois social order—concerns felt among both the emerging middle classes and some parts of the working class, especially the wives and mothers. Temperance spoke to concerns about the insecurities of life within industrial capitalism and the struggle to maintain decency and respectability.

Initially, then, regulating booze fit into larger agendas to construct a "moral dominion" in which all parts of society would learn to self-regulate, ideally in the image of the earnest middle classes. In the turn to full-scale, state-sponsored prohibition, the project took a turn towards a more blunt coercion, and, in parallel with the older assault on Aboriginal drinking, it seemed more straightforwardly a class-based attack (as it would in the tightly controlled post-prohibition era). The anti-booze campaigns focused ever more narrowly on working men, and support for prohibition in working-class constituencies waned. Yet the hold of temperance thinking on the propertied classes weakened as well over the long century after 1830, during which battles repeatedly raged over this issue. Eventually, by the early twentieth century, many among the upper classes had crafted a new bourgeois morality based on pleasure through consumption and pursued with moderation and refinement rather than constraint and denial. As a result, the temperance forces that briefly won political victories in the decade after 1915 were not the political arm of a united upper class bringing down an iron heel on the thirsty masses; they were a social bloc with a mixed following of professionals, businessmen, commercially oriented farmers, and a sprinkling of others, a bloc that attempted to consolidate its cultural hegemony over the country. In the end they failed.

Given this history, it is difficult to make definitive statements about "normal," "acceptable," or "excessive" levels of drinking. For much of Canadian history, as elsewhere, we cannot even be certain of exactly how much or how often people drank. Home brews co-existed with commercial products—state taxation systems and moral regulation encouraged both illicit brewing and distilling—and smugglers and bootleggers serviced determined drinkers. As a result the available statistics on alcohol consumption have to be treated with great caution. Much of what we know comes simply from anecdotal evidence. More important, we have to recognize that, across time among different social groups, people have had such different understandings about when, where, and how much to drink that their judgments have to be situated carefully in time. Custom and morality governing alcohol consumption could tolerate astonishingly high levels in one period and condemn the same amount as poisonously destructive in another.

Writing about Booze

Inevitably, to write about booze is to enter a minefield of controversy.[18] The word "booze" itself encapsulates the two polar opposites in the rhetorical wars over alcoholic beverages. On one hand, it was spat out of pursed lips with disgust; on the other, it rolled over smirking lips with a throaty chuckle. Throughout the literature on this topic, whether in Canada or elsewhere, there is a fundamental ambivalence about how to write about a substance that so many of us like to consume but at some level also distrust as a potential problem.

Historians of alcohol are beckoned by two loud, contending choruses. One rises out of company histories and antique collectors' guidebooks and insists that producing alcoholic beverages has been a great Canadian accomplishment and should be celebrated. A long shelf of popular histories also sings the praises of the rum-runners and bootleggers who kept the supply of these valuable goods flowing during prohibition. A merry group of consumers, just as eager to drink a toast to booze, accompanies those voices. In that crowd you will find many male historians in Canada, including those turning their hand to working-class history. At some distance are the somewhat more restrained voices of anthropologists who attempt to put drinking habits into social and cultural contexts and into larger cross-cultural comparisons, and who are more likely to point out the celebratory rituals of alcohol consumption.[19]

A second, much louder chorus thunders in condemnation. A good many female social historians have joined this choir with withering denunciations of the damage inflicted on families by male drunkards. Most historical studies of booze in Canada have seen alcohol as a problem and focused on the critiques raised against excessive drinking and the ways in which many Canadians have tried to turn off the tap. Most share their subjects' view of the "demon rum" to some degree or another. Although few acknowledge it, they get support from a large body of international literature in the enormous, interdisciplinary field of alcohol studies, where historians and social scientists mingle with medical researchers in studying alcoholism and participating in debates on public policy.[20]

Each side of this great standoff between the wets and the drys in the historiography of booze has seized on one of the two main threads in the history of alcohol consumption. The wets emphasize the sociability involved in drinking and the role of alcohol in sustaining the bonds of community. The drys focus on the results of drinking too much—the dangers for the drunkard and his (and less often her) immediate family in particular. Built into this division of opinion are two conflicting stereotypes of the drinker: the lusty, uninhibited hedonist versus the downtrodden victim of misery and social dislocation looking for escape.

The challenge is to lift the topic out of this dichotomous and too often moralistic framework, to present a broader social history of the role of alcohol in Canadian society with a more complex storyline than good versus evil, or prudery versus fun. Sociability and drunkenness are related in any culture, and they must be connected, not treated in isolation. The deep divide between them has implications for approaching the available primary sources, which are generally heavily charged discourse rather than astute sociology. Prohibitionists' statements about the social impact of drunkenness, for example, were mobilizing propaganda, not the product of careful, balanced research. Brewers' claims for the healthful qualities of beer were just as tainted. We need to untangle the ways in which activists on either side constructed and presented the "problems" they identified and the "solutions" they proposed.

The following chapters, then, survey the contours of four hundred years of booze in Canada: from the drinking practices of the pre-industrial societies through the temperance movements (and the "Liquor Traffic" that would never go away) to the effects of industrialization and, later, prohibition measures introduced during and following the First World War—contrasted with the diverse chorus of voices that opposed the repression of alcohol and defended the right to drink. We examine the regulatory regimes of "government control," the new enthusiasm for drinking and the eventual liberalization of state regulation after the Second World War, and the emergence of new approaches to dealing with heavy drinking.

What we find in all of this is that throughout most of Canadian history, drinking has first of all been a predominantly male experience. It has long been part of the process of constructing distinct masculine identities and practices, and it has been a symbol of patriarchal privilege in the public sphere. Some women drank, but they did so less often, and less publicly; far more of them had to adjust to their menfolk's demands for the right to drink. In general most drinkers saw consuming alcohol as first and foremost an important bonding experience, especially as men built all-male solidarities around combinations of class and occupation, age and marital status, and ethnicity and racial identity—although drinking could also sometimes be just a matter of celebratory imbibing.

Contrary to the interpretative blanket that teetotallers and prohibitionists have cast over the subject, people most often got pleasure from drinking moderately and responsibly, only occasionally consuming enough to get unmistakably drunk, and even then seldom posing serious long-term problems for anyone around them. In the history of drinking, drunkenness was a varied experience that could indeed become a chronic problem for individual drinkers, their families, and others in their communities, but it was interpreted (or "diagnosed") and handled in considerably different ways over time. Finally, both the rejection of booze and the opposition to constraints on drinking were rooted in more all-embracing projects of social and cultural renewal or resistance based on identities of class, gender, and ethnicity/race.

Exploring the full range of Canadians' experience with alcohol does not mean ignoring compulsive drinking as a problem, but it does mean putting it into context—just as a history of transportation would have to be about more than train wrecks and traffic accidents. It means looking for the ways in which Canadians tried, over time, to balance the pleasures and the dangers of the ever-present, ever-seductive John Barleycorn.

two

The Water of Life

WHEN INDIGENOUS PEOPLE PADDLED OUT to meet the first European ships to reach the shores of what is now Canada, they may well have smelled alcohol on the sailors' breath. All of the vessels on these long voyages carried beer or watery wine as the main beverage in place of unreliable drinking water. For the Aboriginal peoples, this would have been one of the many imponderable oddities of the newcomers, because, along with Polynesians, North America's First Nations were unique around the world in having no alcoholic beverages in their diets. They used other substances, such as tobacco, for ceremonial occasions, but not alcohol. Anthropologists have come up with no good explanation for this state of affairs. Some First Nations may have been too nomadic to take the time for brewing or distilling, but a number of the groups certainly had well-established farming practices by the time the Europeans arrived. Whatever the reason, Aboriginal peoples were not enthusiastic about the new drinks. By all accounts, they spat out the booze in disgust when it was first offered to them.[1]

In contrast, the first waves of European settlers—whether from France, Britain, or the United States—had a well-established taste for alcohol in their daily lives.[2] Throughout the colonies, alcohol was regularly consumed in the home as a beverage and a tonic, and to a degree now unimaginable it also saturated almost all arenas of work and leisure. European settlers, especially men, drank often, though only occasionally to get drunk. It was not long before producers and distributers were setting up shop in the "new world" to satisfy this thirst. From the start, booze flowed through the centre of pre-industrial, colonial life. The French called their liquor "eau-de-vie," the English drank spirits called "aqua vitae," and the Irish dubbed their whisky "usquebaugh." In all three languages, the meaning was "water of life."

OPPOSITE PAGE: *Aboriginal peoples in what would become Canada drank no alcohol before contact with Europeans, but eventually many of them developed a fondness for it. Around 1847–48 a Jesuit missionary, Father Pierre-Jean De Smet, collected this fascinating drawing by an unknown Aboriginal artist from the Pacific Northwest. This is one of the few extant depictions of the Native drinking experience. The upper half shows the acquisition of the booze, while the lower half suggests the dream-like contact with the spirit world that, Native people believed, was provided by alcohol.* (ACJ, #1602 L 1-189, no. 5)

Producers

Drinking cultures in any society take shape within roughly the same set of constraints and opportunities: most fundamentally, the material structures and relationships of daily life within which power is distributed, wealth accumulated, and production organized. In the Canadian experience, the most important factors involved not only the shifts from feudalism to capitalism and from pre-industrial to industrial economic and social structures, but also the gradual loosening of the bonds of empire. Feudalism was limited to Quebec/Lower Canada, but all the British North American colonies began as pre-industrial societies, combining the hunting and gathering and farming experience of Aboriginal peoples, the largely subsistence agriculture of the early European settlers, the production of a handful of natural products for export (fish, furs, wheat, timber), and the small-scale production of some domestic goods for sale within local communities. While some of this work involved wage-labour, much more of it was carried out by small clusters of co-operative work teams living in rural areas—usually families, kin, and neighbours—who organized and set the pace of their own work. Men and women (and adults and children) had different tasks on the farms, in the fishing villages, and in the artisanal workshops, and men were accustomed to working away from the household (during the day or for longer stretches in the fur-trading regions, in the woods, or on board ships) in predominantly male work groups. Alcoholic beverages were a regular part of this pre-industrial, colonial world.[3]

The European newcomers wanted the drinks they were familiar with, and generally got them. Beer was found on many tables (often in poorer households a weaker, cheaper "small" beer), as was some form of cider. But early French and English colonists preferred to drink distilled spirits—brandy, rum, and whisky in particular. Only as agricultural surpluses found a new outlet in the sixteen and seventeenth centuries had these more potent liquids begun to emerge from their earlier status as medicine. Such new drinks as Dutch gin, French brandy, Swedish aquavit, German schnapps, and Scottish whisky soon overtook wine and ale among drinkers in Western Europe.[4] On North American soil a preference for spirits lasted well into the early nineteenth century, especially as French brandy and West Indian rum became more widely available and local whisky production took off.

Regional differences in alcohol consumption gradually emerged in the new colonies, based to a large extent on the availability of particular drinks. French Canadians initially preferred brandy, then took up rum (they also drank a weaker homemade liquor known as "bouillon"). Maritimers were dedicated to rum from the beginning, and the settlers of Upper Canada favoured whisky, though rum and brandy were also popular with them. Since vineyards were few and far between, wine had to be imported and it remained more expensive. Aside from the earliest years of settlement in Quebec and Newfoundland, wine did not become common outside elite circles before the end of the nineteenth century. Religious or state commentators who worried about excessive drinking regularly drew distinctions among these drinks— brewed or fermented drinks were invariably discussed as wholesome and nourishing, while distilled spirits were more worrisome—but these admonitions made no serious dent in the patterns of popular consumption.[5]

Much of the alcohol consumed in New France and British North America, especially wine and liquor, was imported from the British Isles, New England, or the West Indies. Indeed, in the eighteenth century rum became a leading commodity in intercolonial trade within the British Empire.[6] Nonetheless, local production began early on. From the seventeenth century onward, many settlers throughout the colonies brewed some form of beer at home. Wealthier households sometimes had their own small breweries, which may eventually have used imported malt. In humbler homes, women made small batches for their families with their favourite combination of molasses, dandelions, ginger, maple syrup, spruce boughs, checkerberries, sassafras roots, and hops. Spruce beer became a particularly popular drink in what would become Quebec. After the Conquest, the English and American immigrants and Loyalist new-comers tended to prefer malted beer. Homemade cider was also popular, though only after pioneer farms had apple orchards. Given the relatively limited shelf life of the home brews, it is unlikely that they were available in households all year round, and they must often have been weak and watery.[7]

Commercial production emerged slowly. As they had in Europe for generations, several Catholic religious orders practised brewing off and on from as early as 1620, when the Récollets started a brewery in Quebec City. Small privately owned breweries appeared soon after. To discourage excessive consumption of hard liquor, to provide a less expensive beverage, and to promote local agriculture, the energetic intendant of New France, Jean Talon, set up a short-lived brewery in Quebec City in 1671. The royal government had hoped this would be the first of many, but it closed four years later. The colony's drinkers seemed to prefer their own home brew or, in towns, the imported *eau-de-vie*.[8]

Following the conquest of New France in 1760, English-speaking immigrants began setting up small breweries. After starting as a partner in such an enterprise in Montreal in 1783, John Molson launched out on his own in the city three years later (on the same site where beer is still being made more than two centuries later). Although at the start he was the only brewer in

Montreal, Molson was soon just one of many small-scale producers in the colonies who manufactured batches of beer for local consumption over the next half-century: Alexander Keith in Halifax, William Dow in Montreal, John Sleeman in St. David's (and then Guelph), and Thomas Carling in London, among others. Like his predecessor in New France a century earlier, Upper Canada's governor John Graves Simcoe promoted the establishment of a brewery in 1793 as an outlet for farmers' grain. Brewers got more support from the imperial government's decision to provide its soldiers with a daily allowance to buy beer, rather than dispensing it from army storehouses. Carling, for example, opened his first brewery in London, Canada West, in 1843, close to the town's military barracks.[9]

Local producers of spirits also sprang up early in the British era. Enterprising men opened rum distilleries in Halifax, Quebec, and Montreal but had limited success in the face of competition with imports of rum from the West Indies and with cheap, locally produced whisky, for which North Americans were rapidly developing a taste.[10] On the frontiers of settlement, especially in Upper Canada, farmers had trouble finding markets for their grain and therefore took their surplus to the local man with a still (an expensive item for most farmers to acquire themselves), who often ran a grist and flour milling business as well and frequently offered cash for grain to be turned into whisky. In the 1790s, Governor Simcoe tried to encourage this trade as well. The backwoods producers made American whiskey using various grains, particularly rye and corn, rather than the barley and malt used to make Scotch. The drink produced was probably much weaker than the modern product—closer to the strength of today's fortified wines—and inevitably varied wildly in quality. But a great deal of it must have been available in the new agricultural areas of Upper Canada.

Larger-scale distilling of whisky developed more slowly. In the early 1840s, a census counted more than two hundred distilleries in Upper and Lower Canada, but most of these were the tiny operations attached to local grist and flour mills. A handful, however, were among the first substantial industrial enterprises in the colonies to grow beyond the single artisan's workshop. Two of the most important were the enterprises of Molson and his sons, who began distilling whisky in Montreal in 1821, and William Gooderham and James Worts, who added a large distillery to their flour mill on the Toronto waterfront in 1837. Both enterprises dominated their local markets, selling most of their output through wholesale channels to storekeepers and tavern-owners rather than out the door to local customers. Some of the larger distilleries also built up substantial export businesses to Britain, where Canadian whisky found many new customers (Scottish and Irish whiskys were not yet as widely available to English drinkers as they would become by mid-century). The increased production of the 1820s and 1830s must have made liquor much more widely available in the British North American colonies and, as the volume of output and competition increased, the price must have dropped. "Canada is a fine place for drunkards," one British visitor wrote in 1846. "Think, my dear reader, of whiskey at ten pence a gallon."[11]

The larger distillers and brewers worked at refining their processes and producing a more consistent, commercially viable drink. Combining the key ingredients to make a reliable, palatable beer or whisky required the "art and mystery" of skilled artisans, who most likely brought into the colonies the accumulated knowledge of several generations of alcohol production in the British Isles or the American colonies.

For beer, barley had to be carefully soaked in water to promote germination, and then dried to produce malt. The maltster had to watch carefully for the perfect moment of sprouting to convert the barley's starches into sugar. The drying process took place on the heated malt-house floor and required frequent turning with special wooden shovels over several days. After the malt was ground (often by using a horse to turn the millstones, though Molson had metal rollers by the 1790s), the next step was called "mashing." In a large vat (or "mash tun"), the brewer combined ground-up malt with hot water (the purest that could be found, usually from underground springs, not lakes or rivers) to make the still-unfermented liquid he called "wort." This potion had to be filtered, flavoured with hops, boiled in a large kettle over a wood fire, and then drained through filters to remove the hops before being poured into open wooden cooling vats. Reducing the temperature was critical, and with no artificial methods for the cooling process (some brewers ran cool water through pipes in the cooling pans), the brewing season could run only through the chillier months between early fall and early spring.

Once cool enough, the wort was drained into special vats (fermenting tuns), where yeast would eventually be added to promote fermentation (that is, turn the sugar in the wort into alcohol). At the right moment (after several days, depending on the specific beer being produced), the brew was tapped into storage vats to sit for at least ten days, often longer (porter needed six months), and finally poured into kegs. Without temperature gauges or other scientific devices, making beer in those early years was a trial-and-error process that required an experienced eye (and, where available, the kind of rudimentary brewing manual that Molson brought over from England in 1786). The quality of the final product tended to be unpredictable.[12]

Although brewing had often been women's work in early modern Europe, British North America's brewery workers were all men. Owners hired one or more craftworkers for the job—maltsters, brewmasters, and brewers—all of whom generally learned their trades through apprenticeships. They also needed one or two muscled labourers to help with the lifting and hauling. All brewery owners had brewing skills themselves and worked closely with their workmen. Like many others, Molson was his own brewmaster. In the early years there was probably less specialization of tasks in these small workshops—everyone would likely pitch in when the beer had to be kegged or a wagon loaded.

Backwoods whisky stills might use "frosty potatoes, hemlock, pumpkins and black mouldy rye," as one critical English visitor noted in 1829, but producing commercial whisky involved more care. It roughly parallelled brewing beer. The grain used was often whatever was left over from the flour-milling done elsewhere on the property, though corn became increasingly important over the course of the nineteenth century, along with rye, the main flavouring grain. The grain was ground and mixed into heated water. Ground malt was then added to this "mash," which was cooked for some hours, then cooled. Yeast was added for fermentation over two to three days. The "beer" that resulted was then heated in an onion-shaped still to produce an alcoholic steam, which then passed through a sealed condenser in the form of a coiled tube ("worm") into another vessel known as a receiver. The liquid produced varied depending in part on how long the vapours had been distilling and what they were producing. By the 1830s the still-man used a hydrometer (required by law after 1846) to determine what was coming out of the condenser and how much alcohol it contained. The distillate then had to pass through charcoal filters to remove various residues before going through a second distillation.[13]

The batches of liquor produced in this way might well be in a concentrated form, with a higher alcohol content than drinkers would actually consume. The fluid might be diluted with distilled water or sold in the original strength to retailers for blending or watering before sale. By the 1830s, some of the bigger distillers were installing new "column stills" that permitted a more continuous flow of distillate whisky. All booze was stored in wooden barrels carefully crafted by skilled coopers; hardly any was bottled in British North American operations in the first half of the nineteenth century. But the distillers did not bother to let the beverage "age" for any length of time in these casks.

A distillery was generally a bigger operation than a brewery and drew together more skilled men and labourers. In the 1840s the Molson family had more than fifty workers in their distillery and only eighteen to twenty men working in their brewery (considerably more than the average). Thanks to the efforts of import merchants and many local producers, then, the supply of

Brewers and distillers relied on the skills of craftworkers like these coopers at Molson's in the early nineteenth century. (NAC, PA-125228)

beverage alcohol in New France and British North America steadily increased. But distribution and sales to customers required other commercial networks.

Retailers

Alcoholic beverages found their way to consumers throughout British North America in various ways. The earliest controversies about marketing booze involved the fur trade. From the beginning of the trade in the seventeenth century, French, and later English, traders used brandy (and sometimes rum) as the lubricant for their negotiations with the Aboriginal peoples who brought in furs to exchange for European goods. Native people insisted on maintaining their practice of exchanging gifts as a gesture of good will and solidarity in the trading relationship (and any treaty negotiations), and they came to expect brandy as an essential gift. No trading could proceed without it. Eventually they also used the value of their furs to buy brandy. As competition increased between the major fur-trading companies in the eighteenth and early nineteenth centuries, alcohol became a key factor in wooing Aboriginal people to trading posts and in allowing them to play the whites off against each other. European traders began watering the liquid down—by as much as one-third—to increase their profits. This use of alcohol faced stern criticism in the European settlements. From as early as the 1660s, Catholic bishops and missionaries in New France threatened excommunication for anyone who provided brandy to the Natives, but the royal government never seriously tried to suppress the practice. It listened more sympathetically to merchants who argued that brandy was essential to the trade and that without it Natives would shift their trade to the English and Dutch. After the conquest of New France, alcohol became even more important in the rivalry between the Hudson's Bay Company and the various traders heading inland from Montreal. It would remain a main ingredient in the fur trade well into the first half of the nineteenth century.[14]

Selling booze to European colonists was an entirely different matter. The only minor impediments were taxation and licensing, along with the obligation to police drinking behaviour at least minimally. European governments had long seen spirits as a luxury commodity that could be legitimately taxed heavily to support state business. From the earliest days of settlement importers of distilled liquor had to pay duties, which became a mainstay of colonial government finances for generations after—between a quarter and a half of government revenues in Nova Scotia by the 1830s, for example. Distillers paid a fixed duty on each of their stills, and it was only in the 1840s that the rate was shifted from the still's capacity to actual volume of production. Selling any kind of alcohol also required a licence from the government of the colony. Like the taxes, though, the licence was intended to fill government coffers and, where necessary, guarantee public order, but not to deter drinking for most colonists.[15]

Starting in New France, government ordinances put formal restraints on a tavern-keeper's business and made him responsible for keeping the peace, on the assumption that his premises were quasi-public. In New France and Louisbourg, a tavern-owner was expected to curb blasphemy and to help prevent disorder at work or in the streets. He was forbidden to give credit to his customers and could not provide drink to servants without their masters' permission. He could not serve soldiers on working days or outside mealtime, or anyone during church services on Sundays or festive occasions. Similar con-

straints were put on retailers in the first liquor acts in the Maritime colonies between the 1750s and 1780s.[16]

The soldiers' smoking room in Halifax, 1872. Supplying thirsty garrisons was the lifeblood of many local breweries. (NAC, C-58558)

By the turn of the nineteenth century, regulations on tavern-keeping in the British North American colonies put more emphasis on the character of the tavern-keepers and their ability to run an orderly house. In Upper and Lower Canada, an owner had to convince a magistrate that he was "of good fame, sober life and conversation, and that he had taken the oath of allegiance to the King." But neither the taxes nor the few enforcement officers formed any serious impediment to the production or sale of alcoholic beverages. Regulations were regularly ignored or evaded (as they often had been in England). Unlicensed stills were common, and many drinking dens operated completely outside the law, in brothels and "groggeries," in cities and the countryside. Municipal regulations requiring a specific amount of accommodation for guests were similarly ignored in many cases, even by the licenced establishments.[17]

Entering the business legally was still not difficult in the early decades of the nineteenth century. In the cash-poor colonies, commercially produced alcohol had to compete with home brew of various kinds, but the market was growing in urban areas and many parts of the countryside. The local population

A pioneer inn as painted in
1837 by writer Anna Jameson.
She had arrived in Upper
Canada from England a few
months earlier as the wife of
the colony's newly appointed
vice-chancellor. In her book on
her travels, Winter Studies and
Summer Rambles in Canada
(1838), she noted, "I found no
means whatever of social
amusement for any class,
except that which the tavern
afforded: taverns consequently
abounded every where." (AO,
Acc. 2305, S 4298)

of towns and cities could find booze readily available in general stores.
Shopkeepers were supposed to have a licence and to sell booze only in bulk
to be taken home, not by the glass. Since it was so cheap, some shopkeepers
apparently gave it away to regular customers. According to one clergyman,
most stores in early Ontario kept a pail of whisky and a tin cup by the back
door, where customers could help themselves at minimal cost. "In the numerous grog shops," he wrote, "there was no lack of drink at a penny a glass or five
cents a grunt, a grunt being as much as one could swallow in one breath." The
English gentlewoman and writer Anna Jameson noted in 1837 that, even
where licensing forbade sales by the glass in these shops, proprietors would
provide a shot of whisky "free" with the purchase of a handful of nuts. The
other source of alcohol in more and more towns and cities was the apothe-
cary shop, which dispensed numerous remedies with high alcohol content (as
did grocery stores increasingly over the nineteenth century).[18]

Much more alcohol was consumed in taverns or purchased there to be
drunk at home.[19] The French government granted the first tavern licence in
New France at Quebec City in 1648 to a cooper named Jacques Boisdon.
Within thirty years, the governor could report *une infinité de cabarets* in the
colony. In the eighteenth and early nineteenth centuries, all the colonies were
dotted with taverns, which multiplied rapidly in towns and cities and helped
to give a particular shape to the new urban life of the colonies. By the early

1830s, Saint John had one liquor licence for every 50 inhabitants, Toronto one for every 119, Montreal one for every 258, Quebec City one for every 266, and Trois-Rivières one for every 298. In 1851, across the whole region that would eventually be Southern Ontario, there was a tavern for every 478 people. This level of alcoholic service was considerably lighter than in England or France, which had far more drinking establishments per capita in this period, but there is no question that taverns were within easy reach of all colonists.[20]

The"Stag Hotel"is kept by William Dear,
Outside,the House looks somewhat queer
Only Look-in, and there's no fear,
But you'll find Inside,the best of Cheer
Brandy,Whiskey, Hop,Spruce, Ginger Beer
Clean Beds,and food for Horses here:
Round about, both far and near,
Are Streams for Trout,and Woods for Deer
To suit the Public taste, 'tis clear,
Bill Dear will Labour,so will his dearest dear

Around 1840 Captain William Charnley, a British army officer stationed in Nova Scotia, spelled out in rhyme what tavern-keepers were pitching to their customers. This signboard swung over the Stag Hotel in Preston, ten miles east of Dartmouth. (NSM, 36.70)

Alcoholic beverages were available in taverns at all times of day, seven days a week (sometimes not on Sundays), either to take home or to consume on the premises. In an age before advertising, taverns could influence drinking tastes. Customers usually found a variety of drinks there—some combination of brandy, whisky, rum, grog (a mixture of rum and water), beer, cider, wine, bitters, and a variety of spiced, fruity drinks (such as punch and sangaree). These drinks were not always cheap in comparison to colonial incomes, but were generally affordable to all but the poorest.[21]

A tavern offered much more than liquid refreshment. The first generations of settlers socialized together much more often in public than in the closed privacy of their homes, and a tavern, as a quasi-public space, was open to everyone, much like the late-twentieth-century shopping mall. Not surprisingly, by the end of the eighteenth century the building was becoming known in the English-speaking world as a "public house." In an era in which publicly accessible spaces had not become identified with specific narrowly focused activities (as they would in the nineteenth century), the tavern was often the only non-residential building in new settlements of British North America— more common than a church in the early years. As they had back home before migrating to these colonies, local residents made taverns their pivotal, all-purpose community centres. Organizations of all kinds met there. Courts held sessions, town meetings were convened, plays and circus acts were performed, and horse races were organized in taverns. Weddings, banquets, and wakes took place there, teachers ran classes, and hairdressers, wig-makers, shoemakers, dentists, and other tradesmen set up shop. Even churches held services in taverns. The first Parliament of Upper Canada met in a tavern in Niagara-on-the-Lake in 1792, and in 1820 the people of Kingston could pay one shilling and six pence to see an elephant in a tavern yard. People came to taverns to catch up on news and gossip from near and far. They could listen to travellers' stories, peruse copies of British North America's first newspapers, or while away the hours singing, dancing, gossiping, betting on horses, or playing cards or backgammon. As they had been in the American Revolution, these places could also be hotbeds of political controversy in British North America. Montgomery's Tavern north of Toronto served as the rallying point for the first ill-fated uprising of 1837 in Upper Canada (and was consequently burned down by the Tories). All these activities—official, informal, and sub-versive—usually included drinking.[22]

For travellers, the tavern (or "house of entertainment," as it was often called) was also a welcome port in the storm along the often tortuously slow transportation routes. Before the arrival of the railways in the 1850s, there was a tavern roughly every mile or two along major roads in what was to become Southern Ontario. A Nova Scotia travel guide listed twenty-nine on the busy route between Halifax and Digby. Travellers might find their coaches stopping at several of these places and could enjoy a drink at each one. Even when people came to a community for a longer sojourn, unless they had kin or friends nearby they would find no alternative to tavern accommodation.[23]

The assumption that it was appropriate for an owner to provide alcoholic refreshment along with meals for his guests would become a centrepiece of the regulation of alcohol for the next century. The parallel assumption was that only those offering accommodation should be selling booze across the bar, though this convention was regularly violated in larger towns and cities, where drinking was becoming the main activity in taverns by the 1830s and 1840s. They all provided food and shelter, but the quality of the accommodation and service varied considerably. At one extreme were the isolated country taverns far out on the edges of settlement, where, much to the disgust of British gentry who wrote travel accounts, visitors would commonly mingle in the single large room of a large log structure, and the accommodation was often no more than a common bunk room with simple mattresses on the floor. Much later in the century, as white men pushed further westward and northward, this primitive form of tavern would reappear. But in most towns and cities of British North America, these rough places were quickly replaced by architecturally more complex buildings with a variety of rooms and more comfortable furnishings. Most of them had an easily accessible barroom, fitted with little more than benches and a fireplace or stove, while further inside local customers and visitors could gather more privately in parlours, dining rooms, and bedrooms. None of this was unique to British North America. In the early nineteenth century, travellers often noted that the colonial taverns ran on the familiar principles of English alehouses and, even more so, American taverns. Many tavern-keepers ran other businesses alongside, as merchants, artisans, or farmers, and left much of the work around the place to their womenfolk. Not surprisingly, then, many widows were on the lists of licence-holders. But most tavern-keepers did not stay long in the trade—their duration was typically less than five years in Upper Canada.[24]

Running a tavern could be a challenge. Anti-social drunkenness and brawls certainly had to be prevented or dealt with, but the multiple demands made on a tavern also required careful management. The responsibilities to travellers, which governments would insist upon well into the twentieth century, had to be balanced against the expectations of the local population that made the tavern such an important part of daily life. Within that community, the tavern-keeper had to accommodate different, even competing demands on the same space from diverse social groups that showed up to carry on business, socialize, or argue about politics. Changes were afoot by the early decades of the nineteenth century. In larger centres, many taverns had begun to service a narrower slice of the local population. All the major cities (and many smaller towns) were busy ports, and drinking establishments proliferated as hangouts for transient men, especially for the soldiers and sailors in garrison towns such as Halifax, Montreal, or Kingston. Indeed, it was not unusual for tavern-keepers to be retired military men. Streets near the harbour would be lined with "groggeries" that became renowned for their rowdier clientele. As immigrants flooded into these cities after 1815, seaside taverns served a growing population of still rootless newcomers.[25]

At the other end of the social scale, a few far larger, more elegant places, taking the name of "hotel," had appeared by the 1840s in the centres of the larger cities, where they catered to the most affluent and respectable urban clientele. Montreal's Mansion House, built by John Molson, was an early example. There a well-stocked private library offered intellectual repose, and lavish dinners were held for the city's aristocratic and mercantile elite. After the hotel burned down in 1821, Molson erected an equally grand New Mansion House, later renamed the British American Hotel. Taverns had begun to be distinguished by class.[26]

By the 1840s, then, all residents of the British North American colonies, both Aboriginal and newcomer, had easy access to alcoholic drinks. Many still made their own at home or bought (or bartered) some home brew from a neighbour. But as the colonies' many independent commodity producers earned more cash from commercial transactions, more and more drinkers relied on commercially produced booze, either imported or from local breweries or distilleries, and much of that was consumed in taverns. Booze had become a major current in the flow of colonial commerce.

At Home and Work

By the end of the eighteenth century, almost everyone in the European settlements must have been tasting alcohol at some time during the year. It was a food, medicine, tonic, and stimulant, and, especially for men, it stood at the core of all ceremonies and rituals, both public and private. Men used frequent drinking to affirm bonds of all kinds among themselves. There were two distinct, though sometimes overlapping, patterns in this period down to the 1840s: daily consumption at home and work, and celebratory imbibing.

In the early years of French settlement, the *habitants* of New France, like the French peasantry, could not afford alcohol every day. Indeed, when the Swedish botanist Peter Kalm visited the colony in 1749 he noted that most settlers could not afford wine. "The common man's drink was water," he wrote. But the consumption of alcoholic beverages seems to have spread during the eighteenth century, and by the early nineteenth century, whether as food or tonic, alcohol was mostly cheap and widely available and in the cupboards of most households. In many communities, alcoholic drinks were on the table for daily meals, though they were often weak brews or watered down before drinking; and contrary to much later moralizing, they were probably consumed in the household only in relatively small quantities at mealtime and rarely led to drunkenness. People used them partly no doubt to compensate for relentlessly bland diets, sometimes as alternatives to uncertain supplies of safe drinking water, and generally as substitutes for more costly drinks.[27]

For centuries Europeans had spurned water as a healthy or convivial drink, and medical authorities seldom recommended it. In cities drinking water had frequently been polluted, scarce, and expensive. Not surprisingly, British shipping legislation required the master of a vessel to lay in at least two-thirds of a gallon of beer (about three litres) for each passenger for the trans-Atlantic voyage. Some early settlers in what is now Canada continued to harbour real doubts about water as a beverage, and many believed that it could not be drunk without the addition of spirits. William Berczy, a German aristocrat who brought a group of settlers from New York State into Upper Canada in the 1790s, insisted that his men needed "some spiritous liquors . . . in a country where it is destructive to the health for those who must chiefly work in the open air to drink constantly raw water alone."[28]

Other non-alcoholic drinks were certainly harder to get or too expensive. Until settlers had more cows, milk was scarce and when available prone to souring. Tea and coffee were costly luxuries in the colonies before the nineteenth century. In any case, popular wisdom insisted that alcoholic drinks were nutritious food and good for the health. Loyalists passing though Quebec in 1795 observed that "a glass of rum and a crust of bread is the usual breakfast of the French Canadian; the rigour of their climate is alleged as the cause of their having frequent recourse to [rum] at other times of the day."[29]

According to one Nova Scotian, spirits "were almost universally regarded as little less necessary to man's healthful existence than flesh and bread. Alcohol, it was thought, kept out heat in summer and cold in winter, supplied strength to labour, helped digestion, warded off disease, and did many other marvellous things." Many people believed, contrary to scientific reality, that alcohol gave warmth in the cold northern climate of these colonies. It was also supposed to have great medicinal value. "In many families, whiskey was served to each member of the household in the morning," one writer recalled. "It was considered to be a precaution against colds and to enable one to do hardy work." Taken straight or mixed with various herbs, alcohol was a regular household remedy for many health problems, often in the form of patent medicines. A popular remedy for cholera, for example, was Huxham's Tincture, which contained two ounces of Peruvian bark, a half-ounce of Virginia snake root, and three and a half pints of whisky. In keeping with this custom, whisky consumption allegedly rose during the cholera epidemic of the early 1830s. Doctors were more likely to prescribe brandy and wine as stimulants and tonics.[30]

Colonists in New France and British North America also drank booze regularly outside the household, especially on work sites. Unlike the regimented work world of industrial capitalism, the rhythms of pre-industrial labour followed the seasons and the tasks to be done, not the rigid structures of year-round clock time The hours of work at some points of the year could be long and demanding. As shocking as it might seem to twenty-first-century sensibilities, drinking on the job could help colonists get through the dawn-to-dusk working day—and also, along with singing, story-telling, gossiping, and debating, might help to make the experience more sociable.[31]

In the backwoods, settlers often pitched in to help their neighbours clear some bush or raise a barn. Whole communities came together for working parties known in Upper Canada as "bees," where, besides completing a major project, neighbours could gossip, discuss religion or politics, look for potential spouses, and generally have a good time. Frequently, the men who arrived to help with the heavy tasks refused to work without getting whisky. On average a host could expect to provide a gallon of whisky (about four litres) for every family that showed up. Every bee had a "grog boss" who kept the booze flowing to the workers. Drinking would continue through meals and into the merry-making after the work was completed. Susanna Moodie observed in the 1840s that "people in the woods have a craze for giving and going to bees . . . plenty of strong drink making the chief attraction." According to one London clergyman, "Many of the people came for the sole purpose of drinking and never once assisted in raising a log. Many got drunk." A traveller reported, "After the whiskey had been handed about several times they got very uproarious—swearing, shouting, tumbling down, and sometimes like to fight. . . . Many accidents happen, and lives are frequently lost on these occasions, both from accidents and quarrels." Another account told the story of a temperance supporter who refused to provide liquor at a bee. A group of eight outraged neighbours pulled down the logs on his barn as fast as they were put in place.[32]

In these early years, men who worked for wages also expected alcohol in their daily work routines, as had their forebears in Europe for centuries. Sailors in the French navy got watered wine with every meal, while their British counterparts had long been eligible for a gallon of beer a day during voyages. In both cases the drink was meant to compensate for the typically putrid drinking water (distilling equipment for treating water on board did not arrive until the mid-nineteenth century). The British seamen had also been getting a "tot" of rum every day since their country had seized Jamaica in 1655. By the time the British conquered New France more than a century later, each man was being provided with half a pint (about a quarter-litre), though commanders were instructed to add three or four parts water to one part spirits to make "grog." Work on board ships stopped at eleven in the morning and four in the afternoon for the rum issue. (The tradition of issuing rum extended to the merchant marine and carried over into the Canadian navy after 1910, ending only in 1972.)[33]

British soldiers could look forward to a similar bright spot in their otherwise dreary days. For about seventy years after the conquest of Quebec, they got a gill (four ounces, or 142 millilitres) of rum every day. They also had access to a half-gallon or more of spruce or malted beer. Officers enjoyed wine and more expensive liquors. Enlisted men might get extra rum rations as encouragement for extra effort, often as part of the pay they earned for outside work as civilian labourers. General James Wolfe claimed in 1758 that grog was "the cheapest pay for work that can be given." A year later at the battle of Quebec it was used to brace the soldiers for combat.[34]

According to artist R.C. Woodville, General James Wolfe rallied his officers with a drunken "carouse" on the night before the fall of Quebec in 1759. Wolfe is shown here leading "a drinking song," probably his own composition, entitled "How Stands the Glass Around." The song circulated as sheet music for many years after the general's death the next day on the Plains of Abraham. (NAC, C-20759)

Many men in civilian jobs expected similar daily treats as part of their wages. In 1636 the Jesuits reported that a farm labourer got "a chopine of cider a day, or a pot of beer, and sometimes a drink of wine." Five years later, the manager of the Forges du Saint-Maurice insisted that he had to provide plenty of brandy and wine for his ironworkers. Immediately after the Conquest his English successor laid in 98 gallons of rum for the workers. The English workmen who began to arrive at the ironworks insisted on whisky as part of their labour contracts. Employers in construction, logging, fishing, and the fur trade all found, in the words of a Hudson's Bay Company official, that workers had to be "bribed by Spirituous Liquors to do their duty." Among Montreal craftworkers, one writer noted, "A system of continual drinking was kept up,

Like their counterparts in the mother country, aristocratic men liked to linger over drinks late into the evening, often consuming huge quantities of port and brandy. The painter of this watercolour of five gentlemen drinking is unknown. (NAC, C-023331-bottom)

by treating on the part of the masters, and fines, footings [fines] and subscriptions, on the part of the men." Labourers digging canals broke up their long, strenuous working days with three or four gills of whisky, which, it has been argued, kept them pacified but nonetheless ready to put on a new burst of excavation with the promise of an extra booze ration. Stories of teachers drinking on the job also survived, along with those of high colonial officials who could not perform their duties after a certain hour of the day.[35]

In many cases the parallel to the modern coffee breaks took place in the late morning and mid-afternoon, when workers downed their booze. A British military officer travelling in North America in the 1820s was struck not only by the number of times a day that men took a drink, but also by the small quantities consumed at any one time. "What I did see," he wrote, "at every corner into which I travelled, north or south, east or west, was the universal practice of sipping a little at a time, but frequently." Working with alcohol in the veins was evidently the equivalent of today's reliance on the caffeine in heavy coffee consumption.[36]

In pre-industrial Canada, then, booze was obviously intended to fortify the manual worker for heavy toil, or to sustain him in carrying it out, especially out of doors. Yet there are no accounts of women regularly doing the same before tackling the laundry, feeding the chickens, or sewing a dress. To varying degrees, artisans, labourers, soldiers, sailors, and farmers built this kind of drinking into their distinctive sense of a rugged plebeian masculinity. They typically worked only alongside other men (or boys), and used alcohol to build bonds of masculine community on and off the job. But all of this happened outside the female-dominated household.

In artisanal trades, in particular, drinking rituals reinforced male solidarities among specific groups of urban craftworkers, as they had done for generations in Europe. Journeymen artisans insisted on keeping women out of their trades, and grounded their "manhood" on this right to practice an honourable craft without female participation. Apprentices learned the sinews of these fraternal relations when they were sent out regularly to get drinks for their shop mates and had to pay "footings" for various trivial infractions of craft rules, which would then be used for collective drinking.[37]

I'll Drink to That

Drinking together on and off the job was only one of several specific and intersecting drinking rituals in colonial society. For example, business deals, including in some cases hiring wage-earners, would be concluded over a drink. "Most men drank to some extent, particularly when they went to the village to do business," one local historian wrote. "It would be difficult to refrain from treating and being treated where taverns were so numerous. . . . Bargains were made and bills paid in taverns, and people considered it natural and proper to treat one another to close the transactions." Treating was widespread and considered essential to business and general conviviality. Many more drinking rituals were part of male recreational life. Almost everywhere in the colonies, outside a few intensely religious communities, men of all social classes made consuming the various forms of alcohol part of their way of socializing together, although the patterns of drinking varied. Wherever large numbers of males, especially young men, worked together—as fur traders, sailors, loggers, canal labourers, or on other jobs—they broke loose at the end of heavy bouts of work with drinking sprees. In generally less rowdy rituals, hosts of all classes almost invariably offered drinks to guests in their homes. In gentry households, men might regularly spend long evenings together consuming vast quantities of wine or port, as part of what has been dubbed "gentry masculinity."[38]

Many more people arranged to meet friends from similar social stations in local taverns. Drinking alone was rare. Men who worked together often

headed off afterwards to taverns to drink together. In Europe and colonial
America, artisans in particular made drinking after work a key part of cement-
ing the bonds of fraternal solidarity, and it seems they did the same in British
North America. For many young, unmarried men of the trades (and probably
for many other young workers as well), nothing was more important than
male-only tavern life. If they went "on the tramp" far outside their home
communities, the tavern crowd of fellow workmen was especially welcome,
both for news of work and the possibility of a good time. Around their drinking and socializing they created a social space not available to their sisters, a
space that allowed them to participate in a wider world of male association
and privilege outside their families and workshops. The absence of women
enhanced a fragile sense of independence from their masters, parents, and,
eventually, wives.[39]

The fraternal masculinity celebrated in these drinking rituals often had a
strong streak of misogyny and a veneration for bachelorhood, even after the
men married. Crucial family resources might flow out of the household into
this boozy lifestyle. When women tried to intervene to keep their families'
food money from disappearing into taverns, alcohol could become a central
issue in marital relations. The author of a temperance poem published in 1831
wanted to damn such behaviour but ended up encapsulating the attractions of
the tavern:

> *O come let us all to the grog-shop;*
> *The tempest is gathering fast —*
> *There surely is nought at the grog-shop*
> *To shield from the turbulent blast . . .*
>
> *And there will be tippling and talk*
> *And fuddling and fun to the life,*
> *And swaggering, swearing, and smoke,*
> *And shuffling, scuffling, and strife.*
>
> *And there will be swapping of horses,*
> *And betting, and beating, and blows,*
> *And laughter, and lewdness, and losses*
> *And winning, and wounding, and woes.*
>
> *O come let us then to the grog-shop;*
> *Come, father, come Jonathan, come;*
> *Far drearier far than a Sunday*
> *Is a storm in the dullness of home.*[40]

DEATH OF COL. MOODIE.

Taverns could be hotbeds of political controversy. In 1837 Montgomery's Tavern north of Toronto featured in the battles between William Lyon Mackenzie's rebels and loyalist forces. Symbolically, the tavern was later destroyed by the triumphant Tories. (NAC, C-4783)

Women worked in taverns as members of the owners' families or as servants, but otherwise the places were predominantly male spaces, where men arrived alone or in groups—a familiar pattern running back centuries in Europe. But women had always frequented taverns to some extent, and by the early decades of the nineteenth century female customers were continuing to show up, sometimes on their own (usually as travellers), more often with male escorts to spend a pleasant evening in mixed company. Women participated in tavern culture in a controlled fashion, under the protection of men, but sometimes in clusters of wives in a separate space safely out of sight of the barroom.[41]

Otherwise, in most of these establishments, all classes and social groups tended to mix freely. Despite the growing racism of white colonial society, Blacks and Aboriginal peoples were even known to frequent barrooms (though most likely only in specific establishments that catered to "less genteel" customers, like soldiers or labourers). Taverns did not dissolve important social distinctions, but they did permit a cheek-by-jowl co-existence of men of different social ranks and the possibility of dialogue and discussion among them, especially as treating and toasting broke down social boundaries and opened lines of more egalitarian communication under the influence of booze.[42]

A man's behaviour and opinion expressed so publicly in the socially mixed company of his fellow drinkers gave him and his ideas a place within wider community discourses about landholding, political corruption, republicanism, and domestic morality, among other things. In an era with few other gathering places, relatively few newspapers, and a limited franchise, taverns

In her 1849 painting "A
Country Tavern Near
Cobourg," Harriet Clench
sounds a note of bucolic
respectability. The drinking
party is made up of well-
dressed gentlemen, and the
setting is genteel, apparently
in harmony with the town life
in the distance. Later in the
century women providing this
service would become a rare
sight. (AGO)

probably filled a unique role as a limited but nonetheless important forum of male plebeian public opinion.[43]

Genteel travellers frequently complained about the rowdiness and rough equality of the inns they stopped in. In Upper Canada many of these places were run by "Yankee" immigrants. In 1817 one traveller wrote:

The kind of freedom of manner, amounting to downright impertinence, & a great mixture of rank & persons in Yankee inns or where Yankee customs are prevalent, is extremely disagreeable to an Englishman. Indelicacy too prevails, decent & even pretty girls hawking and spitting abt the room, occasionally scratching & rubbing themselves & lounging in attitudes in their chairs in a way that in Britain wd be unpardonable & throwing out more than broad hints, occasionally as to sexual intercourse.

Clearly one of the deep concerns percolating through such comments was the inherently democratic and egalitarian atmosphere of the tavern—and, ironically, it would be American immigrants who would spearhead temperance activity in the 1830s and the ultra-loyalist Orange Order that would continue to use the tavern as the centre of its social and political life. The other concern was with sexual morality and the whiff of prostitution. In Montreal, Halifax, and other major ports, prostitutes sometimes operated out of drinking establishments where soldiers, sailors, and other unattached men congregated (or in brothels on the same street). Elsewhere, though, they rarely entered the colonies' taverns.[44]

The local aristocratic oligarchs who were derided as members of "family compacts" also rarely darkened a tavern door. Like the French nobility and English gentry, they laid in or made their own supplies of booze and preferred the company of their own kind. But many respectable members of colonial society did enter. "Gentlemen in Canada appear to be much addicted to drinking," one traveller wrote in the 1820s. As the British immigrant and writer Catharine Parr Traill noted, "Intemperance is too prevailing a vice among all ranks of people in this country; but I blush to say it belongs most decidedly to those that consider themselves among the better classes of emigrant." Her sister, Susanna Moodie, complained: "Professional gentlemen are not ashamed of being seen issuing from the barroom of a tavern early in the morning or of being caught reeling home from the same sink of iniquity late at night. No sense of shame seems to deter them from the pursuit of their darling sin." To create some social distance from the lusty, freedom-loving rabble, the "better sort" might retreat from the barroom to some space within taverns where they could gather for small dinners or other social functions. At the turn of the nineteenth century, Montreal's fur-trade barons met regularly in their own closed drinking circle, which they called the Beaver Club. The forty-two gentlemen who gathered in a Montreal tavern for a banquet in 1829 consumed twenty bottles of champagne, seven of Bordeaux, fifteen of Madeira, eight of port, thirteen of sherry, along with beer and whisky. By the 1840s, in the larger cities, those who still wanted to drink were probably enjoying the pleasures of the posher new hotels.[45]

Whether in taverns or other settings, most public community celebrations also brought everyone together around alcoholic beverages. Christian churches used wine in their communion ceremonies. In a less sombre vein, some pre-industrial employers cemented their control over their workmen by breaking open a keg at appropriate moments. In eighteenth-century New France, the manager at the Saint-Maurice ironworks distributed drinks in honour of a particularly hard day's work, a job well done, or the feast of the patron saint. In fur-trade posts brandy also flowed in such convivial moments. In 1822, for example, the governor of the Hudson's Bay Company allowed his men at York Factory to unwind in a three-day drunken spree after they had finished a 126-hour workweek. Booze also lubricated festivals and fairs and annual militia musters. During election campaigns drinks were freely distributed weeks before voting began. In 1834 an open barrel of whisky sat beside one polling station near Rice Lake in Upper Canada, with a dipper for all to help themselves.[46]

All these practices involved more than a fondness for the taste of spirits or desire for the alcoholic buzz, and had little or nothing to do with a desire to escape misery or despair. In trade, work relations, and community social life, a shared drink was symbolic. It cemented mutual respect and commitment between men making a deal, an officer and his men, an employer and his workers, a political candidate and his supporters, neighbours in a town or village, members of an artisanal craft, or any other close-knit work group. Drinking together was a formal or informal ritual affirming the bonds and mutual obligations of social relationships, whether paternalistic or egalitarian. The drinkers treated each other and offered toasts as outward symbols of these connections. The few men who stood apart from communal drinking might be scorned or ostracized for their unwillingness to affirm these social ties. According to a Kingston commentator:

> It was the fashion of the times to drink, and all must drink. Drinking was the mark of hospitality, the test of friendship, the passport to respectable society. It was the watch word and countersign to all public, private, and social meetings. . . . All were invited to drink, urged to drink, compelled to drink. . . . If he would be sober, he must exclude himself from society.[47]

Booze, then, was central to the social life of pre-industrial colonists in New France and British North America, as a staple in their diets and as the central element in many social rituals. It was especially important for men, and played an important role in nurturing the distinct masculinities of gentry, artisans, and labouring men, as well as the more broad-based communitarian forms that aimed to bind together men of all social classes (and their families).

Binges

Whether in the home or the taverns, most pre-industrial drinkers were apparently orderly, relatively quiet, and more interested in pleasant socializing than in brawling. It would, of course, be naive to insist that people who drank alcoholic beverages did so simply to wash down a meal or toast the King or their patron saint. They enjoyed the chemical reaction of the alcohol on their bodies and sometimes drank enough to get unmistakably drunk. In early modern Europe, doctors had even recommended occasional "medicinal intoxication" to encourage the vomiting that would, in their eyes, purge the human system. Drunkenness was such a common experience in the trans-Atlantic English-speaking world that an English magazine found 80 different expressions for inebriation in 1770, and colonial Americans in the same period used at least 150. Yet on most occasions of heavy drinking (among European men, at least), the goal was probably not to get deliberately drunk, but rather to attempt to "hold one's liquor." Inebriation was more likely a side effect of the social event than the end sought.[48]

There were two different kinds of heavy drinking. On the one hand, lots of people in these pre-industrial societies, from various levels of the social scale, plunged into short-lived binge drinking with family, friends, workmates, or neighbours to celebrate some significant moment in their lives. On the other, some people also consumed enough on the job or during their regular visits to taverns to be somewhere on the road to serious, debilitating dependency. Some of these so-called "tipplers" became known as "habitual" drunkards. Onlookers certainly noticed a few female drunks, but men were far more likely to be publicly drunk. Women found wage labour outside the home less often and faced much sterner social conventions about their public behaviour, including intolerance of female drunkenness and suggestions of sexual impropriety. Unless they were prostitutes, they probably confined any heavy drinking to the household. Male drunkenness got more attention and was sometimes treated as a social problem, but people in the colonies tolerated forms of drunken behaviour that would not be as acceptable after the mid-nineteenth century.[49]

When communities stopped their normal business for annual festivities, such as a saint's day in Quebec/Lower Canada, drunkenness was inevitably widespread. Some male workers also used heavy drinking to turn private celebrations into public events. Throughout the colonies they often ended heavy bouts of work with lengthy alcoholic binges. Fur traders, for example, turned all the holidays on the calendar into prolonged drunken sprees. In 1735 they managed to burn down the Hudson's Bay Company post at Moose Factory during Christmas festivities. A ship's captain on the Great Lakes noted in his log on 27 December 1813: "Gave the men 3½ gallons of Rum for a Dance." The next day he reported, "No Duty Perform'd by the men this Day." Sailors who arrived in ports after weeks at sea likewise broke loose and cut a swath of wild revelry and fighting through the urban streets. Everywhere a military garrison could be found, idle soldiers flowed through tavern doors and carried their rowdy socializing into the streets. Loggers returning from the woods often amused themselves in the same way.[50]

Throughout the nineteenth century and on into the twentieth, workers on the frontiers of settlement and industry left the rigours and privations of isolated work sites for the riotous pleasures of drinking in the towns and cities. In fur-trading, canal-labouring, and urban crafts, there might well be weekend versions of these drinking bouts whenever the men got paid, beginning Saturday nights and, to the horror of the clergy, extending through Sundays. Their day of recuperation and hangover was often dubbed "Saint Monday."[51]

Later morality tales from the temperance movement probably exaggerated how frequently this kind of behaviour disrupted the tranquillity of colonial communities. In the lives of the working men these moments of drunken unwinding were generally special occasions, not everyday events. They were related not just to the seasonal rhythms of work, but also to pre-industrial attitudes to scarcity and plenty that had a long history among peasants and workers in Europe. These people never expected to be wealthy or to accumulate many possessions. After making sure that future generations of the family would be secure, they were more likely to apply any surplus generated towards their own immediate comfort or pleasure. Community-wide binge drinking was a way of sharing or redistributing any modest "savings."[52]

Drunken revels also became rituals of a rough-edged masculine identity. Drunken European men did not simply "lose their inhibitions" or set loose some bestial inner self in an alcoholic haze. Their behaviour was largely "scripted," in the sense that they used the occasion to act out familiar male theatrics of swaggering, posturing, bragging, proclaiming, and, often, fighting, usually to defend some sense of personal honour or group identity, especially ethnicity. The brawling associated with drunkenness was not a product of mere blind rage; it was invariably associated with some affront to masculine honour, dignity, or reputation and would doubtless be preceded by insults and verbal abuse. Drinking bouts, rather than causing the confrontations, more often provided the setting for provoking or settling disputes. In the early nineteenth century, Nova Scotia's famous author Thomas Chandler Haliburton described such a scene in a tavern: "The drunken man might be heard rebuking the profane, overwhelming the hypocrite with opprobrium for his cant. Neighbours rendered amiable by liquor, embraced as brothers, and loudly proclaimed their unchangeable friendship; while the memory of past injuries, awaked unto fury by the liquor poison, placed others in hostile attitude." Such fights were public performances enacted before fellow drinkers, who were neighbours, friends, workmates, and, most important, witnesses.[53]

The notion that drunken comportment in any society flows from cultural practices, not from some innate impulses, helps us to better appreciate the heavy drinking of the Aboriginal peoples who were forced to share New France and British North America with the European settlers. Given that booze flowed freely through the fur trade both as a gift to smooth trading relations and as a commodity to exchange for furs, Aboriginal people frequently got drunk at the end of trading sessions or treaty negotiations. As competition between the two fur-trading networks based in Montreal and on Hudson Bay heated up in the eighteenth and early nineteenth centuries, white Europeans supplied more and more spirits to Aboriginal traders, and reports of drunkenness increased. By that point, any First Nations groups that had signed treaties could be found enjoying drunken sprees each year when their gifts from the white governments arrived. White accounts of Aboriginal drinking both then and later assumed that the indigenous peoples were somehow biologically (that is, "racially") incapable of controlling their alcohol consumption—the so-called "firewater myth." White commentators also emphasized the destructive impact that drinking had on the lives and cultures of Aboriginal peoples, especially the violence and abuse that might take place while they were drunk.

The story is more complex than these older accounts might suggest. Aboriginal peoples did not always carry the brandy or rum back to their territories; they more often consumed it on the spot, at the end of trading or treaty-making, before returning home. In New France trading took place only in three one-week periods per year. In this sense, the Aboriginal peoples' drinking habits were not unlike white celebrations at the end of major bouts of work. Indeed, descriptions of the impact of booze on Native peoples echo William Hogarth's famous engraving, "Gin Lane," depicting London's working people besotted with gin in the 1740s, or lurid accounts of Irish shanty-town life on the Ottawa River in the 1830s. Of course, for the Aboriginal peoples, the geographical gap between home and trading post got narrower as white traders moved further inland during the eighteenth century, and some Native traders (some of them women) brought alcohol back to their villages, where it would be consumed quickly in binges. Yet most Aboriginal people would have had access to booze only occasionally, and undoubtedly drank less in total than white settlers.[54]

The white assumption that Natives "could not hold their liquor" was also an insensitive misreading of what was happening when they drank. Aboriginal peoples used alcohol consciously and purposefully. In part, their use was rooted in their sense of spirituality. As many worried missionaries reported, Aboriginal peoples drank not to enjoy the taste, but simply to get drunk. The Jesuit Paul Le Jeune reported the pattern that whites observed repeatedly: "Give two Savages two or three bottles of brandy, they will sit down and, without eating, drink, one after the other, until they are emptied." If there was a limited quantity of alcohol available, the Natives would choose one or more among them to drink it all and thus become thoroughly drunk. According to an English fur trader, they drank "not from absolute sensuality, nor for the sole pleasure of drinking that the flavour of liquor creates such an irresistible craving for more; they merely seek in their orgies a state of oblivion, of stupefaction, and a kind of cessation of existence, which constitutes their greatest enjoyment." It became clear that Aboriginal peoples experienced drunkenness as an extension of their established spiritual beliefs and, perhaps, their faith in the power of dreams. They believed they were entering an enhanced, dream-like state of consciousness in which they could feel more powerful, more perceptive, and free from responsibility for their actions.[55]

The "spirit" in the spirits was powerful enough to take them outside themselves—and outside any guilt for anything they did while drunk, since the alcohol was to blame, not the individual. In this state, they might remain relatively quiet and calm (heavy drinking was sometimes integrated into rituals of hospitality or mourning the dead), or break loose to dance and sing. But, in some cases, they could also become violent and destructive (though rarely against Europeans and usually within well-understood limitations). In the dramatic language of an early Sulpician missionary, François Vachon de Belmont:

> Once inebriated, they throw off their clothing, or let it drop, and, running about town naked, they beat one another. They bite each other's noses and ears so that there are few whole, entire visages remaining. They run about howling with knives in their hands; they delight in seeing their women and children fleeing before them, as if they were masters of the World.

De Belmont's account provides a grisly list of the deaths and destruction that allegedly resulted from such binges. Most often the drinkers in these accounts of Native binges were men, though women occasionally joined in the drunkenness. Many Natives came to believe that nothing else gave them such an intense high, and they therefore adjusted their trading patterns to get access to more and more booze, even if only for brief binges. There was no question of encouraging more "temperate" habits, because they wanted the drunken experience and would drink until they had consumed all that was available.[56]

Although Aboriginal groups had some practice of expressive "time out" before the arrival of Europeans and their alcohol, the wildness and violence seem to have been new forms of behaviour and may well have been learned from the drunken antics of the fur traders. They may have used this new kind of public posturing to act out more individualistic impulses that, under cover of drunkenness, did not threaten the social cohesion of their communities. At the same time, these could be acts of defiance against European authorities— some Native peoples apparently feigned intoxication just to be able to play out their drunken performances. White European moralists misunderstood all this behaviour as evidence of an inherent lack of willpower among Aboriginal peoples, as evidence that they could not control themselves. But the drinking was more structured and contained by culture and belief than it appeared, even if increasingly more destructive within Native communities.[57]

Drunkards

In the pre-industrial world before 1840, "binge" drinking among both Native people and whites was seldom a daily occurrence, but some people drank heavily much more often than others and became known in their communities as habitual drunkards. Most often they were men.[58] Large quantities of alcohol in the system could leave people physically disabled—staggering, swaying, falling down, slurring words—and capable of hurting themselves (falling, drowning, freezing to death). In some cases the periodic fits of violence that accompanied the drunkenness would endanger family members, workmates, and public order.

The drinking could also interfere with men's ability to work. During the construction of Gooderham and Worts' new flour mill in Toronto—the site of what would eventually be one of the country's largest distilleries—a master bricklayer was disgusted to find a journeyman at various points "partly drunk," "drunk half a day," "sleepy drunk," "dead drunk," and "drunk as David's sow." Ships' masters often faced the same problem with sailors too hopelessly drunk to get their vessels out of port. Those in charge of workers could hit the bottle hard as well. A group of Hudson's Bay Company employees reported on an officer:

> He drinks 'till he is not able to walk nor set, and there he lies on the Floor, which it is pitiful to see, and if it was not for his Wife he would set the place on Fire, never blows out his Candle, lies in Bed, and drinks 'till he loses his

*Among his many colourful
paintings of daily life in
nineteenth-century Quebec,
Cornelius Krieghoff produced
this image of a habitant
apparently well into his cups.*
(NAC, C-005994)

Senses entirely; Sunday morning, Beastly drunk, Cursing and Blasphemy, for
every person, and for you Sir in particular.[59]

There are no reliable statistics to measure how many people in the eighteenth
or early nineteenth centuries were what we might now call "problem
drinkers." For one thing, there was no systematic approach to dealing with
them. Heavy drinking was widely enjoyed and tolerated, and onlookers might

only wink at some level of intoxication. Drinking companions undoubtedly tried to keep each other's consumption within limits, and tavern-keepers were ready to intervene to maintain order in their premises, sending the drunk home or putting him to bed. Popular music recounted how wives tried to rein in drunken spouses, as in one early Quebec ditty, "Au Cabaret":

> *The morning that followed my wedding day,*
> *My good wife wanted to beat me.*
> *I made my way toward the cabaret,*
> *Where my friends were drinking, drinking,*
> *Everyone was drinking,*
> *Everyone was drinking,*
> *Everyone was drinking, drinking.*
>
> *"Friends let me warn you not to drink so much,*
> *For I see my wife a-coming.*
> *Look where she comes, I see her in the offing.*
> *Can't you hear her scolding, scolding? . . ."*
>
> *Quickly she found us in the cabaret.*
> *"Get out of here you drunkard!"*
> *"I won't delay to leave the cabaret,*
> *When I'm finished drinking, drinking. . . ."*
>
> *"Husband of mine, if you continue so,*
> *You'll destroy your loving fam'ly!*
> *One shoe is on, the other is missing.*
> *Get you to your home you drunkard!"*[60]

Drunkenness could face penalties if it posed dangers to others. Drunks crossed a line if they were too quarrelsome, started a brawl, or damaged property. If a husband's habitual drinking interfered with family production or wage-earning, a wife might appeal to a magistrate to stop her husband from threatening the family with poverty, and local officials might be sympathetic if the man's devotion to alcohol was forcing his family onto some kind of poor relief. The army and navy had the most severe response: men could be flogged for drunkenness on the job. Other employers in pre-industrial society, like the managers of the Saint-Maurice ironworks or the Hudson's Bay Company, might discipline drunkards with fines or even imprisonment. Eventually, once the pool of wage-earners got large enough, the men who drank too much on the job would simply be fired. In both the French and British regimes, a drunk in the street could face criminal charges before a judge or magistrate and be fined or flogged or put in stocks in a public square. In Upper Canada some towns might sentence drunks to clearing stumps.

Much drunkenness went unpunished, however, unless it was combined with other unacceptable behaviour. Town constables were amateurs and few in number, and drunken soldiers, the ostensible forces of order, were often among the worst offenders of the peace in pre-industrial streets. Moreover, until the 1830s, if imprisoned for a serious offence, a drunkard in Nova Scotia or Upper Canada could buy more liquor from the jailer.[61]

Perhaps most important, in popular usage, there was no widely accepted notion of "alcoholism" as a serious social problem or a distinct disease requiring medical intervention. Indeed, the word itself had not yet been coined, and there was no other term to apply to serious alcohol dependence beyond the phrase "habitual drunkenness." In the limited medical research on the subject in the eighteenth century, heavy drinking was not seen as a medical condition in its own right; rather, it was more often seen as the cause of other maladies, including mental illnesses. Although by the turn of the nineteenth century a few medical writers in the English-speaking world, notably Dr. Benjamin Rush in the United States and Thomas Trotter in Scotland, were publishing their learned opinions that habitual drinking was a disease, there is no indication that anyone in British North America paid much attention to their ideas before the 1820s and 1830s.[62]

Colonial officials and clergy condemned serious drunkenness simply because it was disorderly and disruptive. Like most of the rest of the population, they believed that a propensity to drink was a personal, and controlled, choice for pleasure, not an uncontrollable addiction. Since medieval times, drunkenness had been seen as a sin in the same category as gluttony, and the problem lay with the individual, not with the alcohol—though some drunks inevitably blamed the booze itself for their behaviour, and courts sometimes accepted this excuse. Critics were more likely to blame the atmosphere of the tavern for encouraging men to drink to excess, avoid work obligations, and engage in sundry disorderly, immoral, and even illegal acts—blasphemy, philandering, theft, and the like.

In these early years, drunks were treated more as a nuisance than as a grave public danger. The figure of the drunkard was ridiculed without particular harshness in song and verse. Perhaps the behaviour was less contemptible because men from all social classes regularly got visibly drunk. "It was no unusual thing to see gentlemen join a company of ladies in a state of intoxication, which would now be deemed very disgraceful, but which was merely laughed at by the ladies themselves," Thomas Haliburton later wrote. These were long-standing patterns, and seldom did anyone suggest that this kind of drinking should stop altogether.[63]

Before the 1830s, then, most people in the territories that would become Canada drank alcoholic beverages happily and without remorse. They drank because they believed booze was good for them in several ways and because it brought them together for a good time. In the often harsh social conditions of colonial life, people used alcohol to mitigate their hardships through the sociability around drinking, rather than simply sliding into a personal alcoholic haze. While some of the earliest peasant farmers who settled in New France may have found booze affordable only on special occasions, it seems to have become more accessible and more regularly consumed in all the colonies over the course of the eighteenth and early nineteenth centuries, as the supply increased, distribution improved, and prices dropped. The drinks that appeared most often on colonial dinner tables may have been weak or watery. Those poured down parched throats on working days may have been somewhat stronger. Per capita consumption was probably much higher than it would ever be again after about 1840, but most of the drinking was done by adult men.

There could certainly be conflict over drinking, including violence on the job, in the tavern, or at home. Some men's compulsive drinking certainly brought misery and suffering to their wives and families. Yet however much drunkenness may have been denounced from pulpit or magistrate's bench, people did not bind themselves together in voluntary associations to stop it. Most of the time, people in pre-industrial society were apparently ready to tolerate deviant behaviour influenced by alcohol in the bloodstream, especially among the male population. Heavy drinking, most often done by men, was generally limited to special occasions. Getting drunk, or at least tipsy, was common at those times—indeed, expected. Drink may have tasted good, promised sound health, and helped drinkers to relax, but above all drinking was typically a public and an intensely social experience—a set of rituals, including the drunkenness, that brought people together around their shared values and interests. More correctly, it brought together men, who used alcohol and the social time spent consuming it to affirm various kinds of bonds among themselves. Drinking was thus deeply enmeshed in the social relations of pre-industrial colonial society.

PROBLEMS FOR THE WISE.

A thirsty man, with an empty pocket, opposite a fountain: Result—A hearty drink, a clear head, a healthy stomach, pocket as before.

A tippler, with a shilling and no thirst, opposite a bottle of whiskey: Result—Stupefaction, fever, dyspepsia, and an empty pocket.

three

Taking the Pledge

Opposite page: *From* Canadian Illustrated News, *9 September 1871.* (NLC, C-56484)

IN THE HALF–CENTURY BEFORE Confederation, many Canadians did some serious rethinking about the place of booze in their daily lives. Initially a campaign gathered steam to encourage moderation in drinking and abstinence from spirits, though not beer or wine, but by 1840 many more people were rejecting all alcoholic beverages and urging others to do the same. The drinks were soon banned from workplaces and relegated to after-hours consumption. Public drinking rapidly lost its respectability. In this process, "drink" became a central issue in the construction of a new social and economic order in mid-nineteenth-century Canada. It would be on the country's social and political agenda for the next hundred years.

What prompted this rethinking of the place of alcohol in colonial society? For one thing, in the early decades of the nineteenth century, although hard statistics are impossible to find, the volume of alcoholic beverages consumed was apparently on the rise. Perhaps even more troubling was the clear preference for "spiritous liquors." In British North America, as in the United States and several Northern European countries, people were increasingly drinking distilled spirits that had a much higher alcohol content than did the fermented drinks of the day. Importers had increased the flow of cheap West Indian rum into the Atlantic colonies and Lower Canada. From 1768 to 1783, for example, ships arriving at Quebec City carried an average of 275,000 gallons of rum per year; after 1810 the annual total was regularly over 800,000 gallons (some of it destined for the fur trade and the armed forces). Local merchants helped to spread this liquor widely throughout the countryside. As farmers disposed of their surplus crops, the rapidly growing number of distilleries in Upper and Lower Canada also made whisky much more easily accessible and probably cheaper by the 1820s and 1830s. Upper Canada's decision to start licensing wholesalers of spirituous liquor in 1818 suggests how increasingly well organized this trade was becoming. There were far more taverns where all this alcohol could be consumed.[1]

Other than the undoubtedly exaggerated commentaries of upper-class travellers and memories of temperance activists, little hard evidence exists through which we can determine the extent of regular intoxication, but the wider availability of more potent booze and what we know about drinking patterns suggest that serious drunkenness may have been increasing, especially in urban areas, and that families and communities may have been suffering more as a result. Certainly that was the central message of a widely read U.S. tract by Dr. Benjamin Rush of Philadelphia, who argued that "ardent spirits" would do serious harm to the body and create an uncontrollable addiction. Perhaps just as important, in the larger cities more drinking was taking place among workmates and strangers in new commercialized settings, further from the context of home and family. These much maligned "groggeries" made no pretense of doing much more for customers than selling them drinks. In this context binge drinking was probably becoming more regular and more troublesome, following a pattern that had already caused concern among authorities in Britain and the American colonies in the eighteenth century.[2]

European societies had previously seen waves of heavy alcohol consumption without a broad-based, well-organized backlash building up against the drinking. Moreover, in some Western countries (Russia and Poland, for example) people drank large quantities of liquor in this period, and in others (Spain and Italy) people consumed even higher levels of absolute alcohol through winedrinking, but without any significant social movement to curtail that behaviour taking hold.[3] In nineteenth-century British North America, though, alcoholic beverages were being cast in a new light. By the 1830s drinking there was facing a new, more widespread scorn. Many more people were eagerly listening to a new message emanating from the United States, and as a result were quickly establishing independent movements of their own. John Barleycorn was under attack on a scale and with an intensity never before seen.

The Cold-Water Army

Before the 1820s few efforts had been made to encourage, or force, white settlers in colonial Canada to stop drinking booze. No major religious group had demanded complete abstinence. Methodists bought liquor and beer outside their camp meetings in the early nineteenth century, and the publications of Anglicans and Presbyterians continued to take advertisements for booze as late as the 1840s.[4] Government regulation came only in the form of the licensing and taxing of purveyors of alcohol and, to limited degree, constraining public drunkenness, without any attempt to modify drinking habits in any fundamental way. Then, in the late 1820s, a new social movement began to urge British North Americans to be more "temperate." The movement soon had a large following, and Canadian society would never again be the same.[5]

Temperance was an American export industry in the 1820s and 1830s, reaching north into British North America and across the Atlantic to Scotland, England, Ireland, the northern German states, and Scandinavia, and eventually further afield to Australia and New Zealand. The American temperance movement had begun in 1808 and was consolidated in a national organization, the American Temperance Society, in 1826. U.S. speakers visited and lectured in the British North American colonies in the following decade, and U.S. temperance literature, especially the early pamphlets of Benjamin Rush and the published sermons of the New England Congregationalist Lyman Beecher, circulated widely. In 1826–27 temperance societies began to appear across British North America. Support in Lower Canada outside Montreal would be insignificant before 1840, but elsewhere societies blossomed in profusion. In Upper Canada alone, one hundred societies with 10,000 members were in place by 1832, and in Nova Scotia eighty societies with 30,000 members by 1837.[6]

These were decentralized, grassroots organizations sustained by local enthusiasm rather than centralized direction. They kept in touch through the visits not only of temperance agents paid by the larger societies, such as those in Halifax and Montreal, but also of accomplished speakers, who travelled about addressing meetings in community after community. Eventually provincial organizations emerged to co-ordinate these efforts. Specialized newspapers with large readerships also helped to sustain the momentum. The widely circulated *Canada Temperance Advocate* began publication in Montreal in 1835 and claimed to have more than 30,000 readers throughout Upper and Lower Canada by the early 1840s. The weekly *Temperance Telegraph* had similar success among New Brunswick's teetotallers. Local organizations pumped out a flood of temperance writings—Montreal's Society for the Promotion of Temperance distributed 65,000 pamphlets in 1836 alone. The number of converts exploded in the early 1840s, as temperance campaigners spread the word through the backwoods of Canada West. At that point too, Catholic crusaders for temperance won widespread support among the francophone population in Canada East.[7]

Initially the temperance societies promoted only the moderation and avoidance of distilled spirits, but not fermented drinks—beer, cider, and wine—which were still considered healthful if consumed in moderation. The

(Courtesy of Donna Hall, Calgary)

Montreal Temperance Society, whose influence was enormous throughout English-speaking regions of the Province of Canada (Ontario and Quebec), used what has been called the "short oath," affirming "that we will not use intoxicating liquors as a beverage, nor traffic in them; that we will not provide them as an article of entertainment, nor for persons in our employment; and that in all suitable ways we will discountenance their use throughout the community."[8]

From the mid-1830s onward, however, a new phase in temperance agitation emerged, as some advocates began to demand that converts take the "long oath" to become complete—"teetotalling"—abstainers from all alcoholic beverages. Water was to replace alcohol as the beverage of choice (a risky choice, in an age of frequently polluted urban water supplies, unless the water was boiled). This demand quickly alienated many moderate supporters, especially Anglicans, Catholics, and more cautious Presbyterians, including wealthier supporters who had not been bothered much by a call to put down the whisky bottle but resented having to abandon the sociability of wine drinking. The controversy split some societies, and in many communities "total abstinence" societies grew up alongside the original temperance groups. Some churches also became embroiled in bitter controversies over the biblical basis for fermented wine in communion services. But by the early 1840s "moderationists" from the initial phase of organizing had mostly either embraced teetotalism or dropped away.[9]

More than half a million colonists—including somewhere between a quarter and a third of the population in the Province of Canada—had taken the pledge to stop drinking by 1855. Nevertheless, teetotallers remained a minority in their communities. In Peterborough in 1845, for example, the local temperance society had no more than 150 members, while the town's population of only two thousand still supported twenty licensed taverns, one brewery, and three distilleries. Yet, by anyone's definition, the temperance campaign had become a mass movement.[10]

This new "cold-water army" did not focus its energies narrowly on the heavy drinkers. It aimed at educating the whole drinking population about the moral and health-related problems of excessive alcohol consumption. In part, its efforts presented a warning to the moderate drinker to steer clear of the dangerous drug; in part, they were reaching out to the drunkard to reform his habits. There was no safe quantity, activists argued, and moderate drinking was a dangerous sham. Every drinker risked the slide towards habitual drunkenness, "and then poverty and discord and wretchedness [would] become inmates in his dwelling." Alcohol, the temperance forces argued, released destructive impulses that normally be kept under control, impulses that prompted the drinker to commit immoral and anti-social acts. Drunks became paupers, criminals, and threats to the well-being of their families. Regular heavy drinking inclined individuals towards such behaviour whether or not they were actually drunk—a condition labelled "intemperance." Not surprisingly, teetotallers urged supporters to have nothing to do with anyone who trafficked in booze.[11]

In these early years the movement's methods were moral suasion through example and education, not legal coercion. To support their attacks on booze, temperance orators brought to the teetotal platforms whatever "expertise" they could claim. Clergy worried about the soul of the drunkard, magistrates drew lessons from cases in their courtrooms, doctors decried the effects on the body. In "scientific" flourishes, speakers would ignite the alcohol extracted from liquor, or show lantern slides of stomachs "defiled and injured" by alcohol. One doctor described the "spontaneous combustion" of a habitual drunkard. The most powerful messages came from the converts, who narrated sentimental tales about their lives as drunks and their new happiness as teetotallers. A few reformed drunkards became popular entertainers on the temperance speaking circuits across North America—one of them was the rough-edged crowd-pleaser John B. Gough, a former printer turned orator. Unquestionably, temperance orators got their rhetorical inspiration from the evangelical movement in the Protestant churches and, in Canada East, from the new Catholic spiritualism of the 1840s.[12]

Frequently the excitement and commitment waned soon after the crusade passed through a community, and the movement soon recognized that backsliding was easy when alcohol filled such an important place in social life. Temperance societies hoped to gather in and protect the temperate. In some cases, small societies were constituted as a kind of affinity group within a local community. But, to consolidate their victories, teetotallers realized they had to create booze-free zones of sociability outside the orbit of taverns, with alternative recreation for teetotallers. In Saint John in the 1830s they organized soirees with tea and coffee as alternatives to the large, boozy public feasts that the city sponsored in honour of such events as Queen Victoria's coronation. Temperance sailors' homes were also opened in many ports to give the single men a place to relax away from the tavern and the brothel. In some communities, "temperance hotels" offered accommodation for travelling teetotallers (though few of them made much money). For the more settled population, the societies built temperance halls as alternative social centres. To stimulate the wholesome fun that was expected to animate these places, temperance organizations distributed journals, books, and songbooks far and wide. Striking up anti-drink tunes would replace what the *Canada Temperance*

Temperance enthusiasts organized social spaces free of booze for those who signed the pledge. They set up lodges of fraternal societies, several of them harkening back to the medieval Knights Templar, who undertook to protect Christians in Jerusalem. (AO, C287-2-0-55)

Advocate called "the Bacchanalian rants which are so common" in taverns. The increasingly respectable venues for temperance social activities soon attracted more of the "higher classes."[13]

To organize a separate social life, late in the 1840s temperance advocates created teetotalling fraternal orders modelled on the Masons and Odd Fellows. They set up meeting halls and ran a range of recreational outlets for the abstainer: educational evenings, libraries, music and plays, public-speaking contests, picnics, and parades with marching bands, elaborate uniforms, and banners. Members quenched their thirst at these events only on water, tea, or other non-alcoholic beverages. The organizations also operated mutual benefit funds to help members deal with financial hardships. These fraternal orders included the Rechabites, the Independent Order of Good Templars (which eventually drew in thousands of members on three continents), and the Royal Templars of Temperance, but the first and most influential was the Sons of Temperance. This society began in the United States in 1842 and had its first British North American branch five years later at St. Stephen, N.B. Hundreds more soon sprang up throughout the colonies, with thousands of members. The order put down particularly deep roots in the Maritime colonies.[14]

By mid-century women had a prominent role in many temperance organizations, even as speakers and organizers, and sometimes had their own branches, such as the Daughters of Temperance. They were regularly included in the many public activities of the temperance movement to set a higher moral tone and to keep male excesses under control. By the early 1840s women were running benevolent societies to assist the families of drunkards, and they were submitting their own petitions to the legislature. But they were never permitted any leadership roles in the movement. Among the dry fraternal societies, only the Good Templars admitted women to full membership in these early years (the Sons of Temperance waited until 1868, when they also agreed to admit Blacks). A zone of women's activism that might otherwise have challenged the central assumptions of gender roles in this mid-nineteenth-century world was thus carefully circumscribed within the limits of support for menfolk and quiet moral suasion at home. Children too had their own organizations. Groups like the Cadets of Temperance, Coldwater Army, and Bands of Hope were intended to provide them with carefully protected fun and games, far from the evil influences of the streets.[15]

The Teetotallers' Progress

In British North America, as in the United States and the British Isles, temperance was a campaign fired by a powerful synthesis of two leading passions:

By the 1850s women had their own teetotalling societies, most notably the Daughters of Temperance. (BHC)

intense Christian conviction (first, evangelical Protestantism, then pietistic Catholicism as well) and economic "improvement." While religious conviction was important in kick-starting the movement, it was the blend of the two that drew in a mass membership. In part, concerns about drink emerged from the changing conditions of colonial life; in part they arrived as a piece of the cultural baggage brought in by some of the many new British and American immigrants.

Like their British and American counterparts, the various evangelical churches were emerging from a period of intense revivalism and looking to establish more orderly institutions. Within their own congregations, Methodists, Baptists, and many Presbyterian preachers put new energy into exhorting their members to give up alcohol and to refuse to engage in the liquor trade. Local church disciplinary committees turned up the heat on unregenerate tipplers and sometimes expelled them.[16]

Increasingly after the 1820s, though, evangelicalism was spreading beyond the confines of specific church membership into voluntarist, secular organizations dedicated to using direct moral suasion to eradicate such evils as gambling, swearing, consorting with prostitutes, violating the Sabbath, and, above all, drinking to excess. For all its Christian rhetoric and evangelical style, then, the English-speaking temperance movement arose outside the churches themselves, as a non-denominational, non-sectarian campaign intended to unite people of all faiths. In this way the temperance societies with their public meetings, parades, and vast outpouring of printed literature were an important part of the new practice of attempting to mobilize public opinion and action outside the state for various forms of moral reform—to create "civil society"— a practice evident in the English-speaking world on both sides of the Atlantic.[17]

Evangelical clergymen nonetheless played key leadership roles in the movement's early days, with Methodists and Baptists in the front ranks. Their religious competitors—Anglicans, Catholics, and many Presbyterians—often held back, suspicious of the revivalist spirit that bubbled through in temperance-movement practice. Protestant temperance enthusiasts took for granted the evangelical assumption that all souls were equal in the eyes of God and capable of personal redemption—a doctrine that undercut the hierarchical principles of the older churches and could be interpreted as undermining the authority of the established clergy.[18]

The connection between temperance and economic development was less directly obvious. The colonies were not yet caught up in the kind of Industrial Revolution that had already begun to rip apart British society and was taking shape in the United States, although many newcomers to British North America undoubtedly brought with them a familiarity or even an experience with those transformations back home. There was not yet any coherent social grouping that could be called a "working class," because waged employment was still typically a temporary stop on the road to self-directed labour in a family production team of independent commodity producers: farmers, fishers, artisans, or, in the case of women, housewives and mothers.[19] Yet a major social and cultural transition was nonetheless underway within Britain's North America colonies, and the new critique of alcohol was an important part of it. By the 1820s the political, economic, and cultural forms of the pre-industrial *ancien régime* were facing serious challenges. Successful merchants in every region were making commerce a central concern of colonial policy-making, and farmers were turning more and more of their production to the market. New political parties were shaking up established notions of governing with new theories of liberalism. Protestants in the Methodist, Baptist, Congregational, and other "dissenting" faiths were demanding the end of privileges for the state-supported Church of England and the complete freedom of religious expression.

At the heart of this ferment was a new emphasis on the independent, self-directed, self-regulating individual. More correctly, since women, children, Aboriginal people, and the poor were not considered capable of independence, it was the white male property-holder who mattered; increasingly he would speak of the new sense of self that was expected as his "manhood." In religion, business, and politics, a man was to take responsibility for his own interests—his soul as much as the economic well-being of himself and his family. Self-control and self-improvement became primary concerns. This approach would mean no degrading dependency on the paternalistic aristocrats of the various "family compacts," no state interference in religion, complete freedom of contracting in trade or employment, and a taming of the unruly "animal instincts" of the body, which, it was assumed, could be set loose by alcohol. Better to be sober, rational, orderly, and literate. In these ways a man could "improve" himself and "get ahead." As a Methodist magazine suggested in 1838:

> Temperance is a virtue of very extensive application, and implies not only that bodily appetites are properly controlled, but that all the powers and affections of the mind are properly regulated. The truly temperate man desires to eat and drink as much as will render his body strong and healthy, and his mind active and cheerful. His desires after any worldly goods are moderate. He is patient under afflictions, and submissive to all the dispensations of Providence.

Those who preached this new culture of responsible individualism promised that the personal rewards would be spiritual salvation, material prosperity, and social acceptance—that is, "respectability." By the 1840s the benefits of this new way of life for the whole society had been dubbed "Progress."[20]

Temperance had become a cornerstone of emerging middle-class identities through which, by mid-century, growing numbers of professionals, businessmen, white-collar workers, master artisans, and their families differentiated themselves in various ways from the rougher elements of the manual workers below them and the decadent aristocracy above. It was also the leading example of how the middle class did not simply create itself through living sober, industrious, and respectable lifestyles, but, far more important, drew together in voluntary associations to advance its key concerns. Its members were not simply creating a narrow class culture, as the older aristocracy had done. The middling classes' promotion of and support for this ideology of self-improvement became part of a hegemonic way of viewing the world, an approach intended to suffuse the whole social and economic structure and influence its development.

Rather than rely on a set of external constraints—family, church, community, law enforcement—to control behaviour, the proponents of this new culture expected individuals to learn to regulate themselves through deeply ingrained self-control. They were immensely optimistic about the perfectibility of people and the bright future that lay ahead. They were also pushy. Others had to be convinced, and in the context of the broader changes underway many British North Americans were ready to listen. The campaign to change drinking practices, then, was not defensive or backward-looking, as later writers sometimes suggested; rather, it was at the cutting edge of a cultural revolution underway in the first half of the nineteenth century, a revolution that was creating a bourgeois social order based on new principles and practices.[21]

The evangelicalism sparking the temperance cause bridged easily to a commitment to commercial success. Indeed, the evangelical teetotaller's sense of righteous purpose gave a moral edge to the process of self-improvement in the material world. In the words of a member of the Queen's County Temperance Society in Nova Scotia in 1834, alcoholic beverages were "highly injurious and detrimental to our prosperity in as much as their use were calculated to disturb the harmony of the community, to paralyze the energies of industry, to lead to misapplication of the produce of our farms and forest and in short to plunge us into a deplorable state of moral and physical degradation." Spiritual and material hopes were tightly woven into the new aspirations and identities of class, gender, and race.[22]

Remaking Culture

The role of temperance in class identities was complex, and we should be wary of making quick and easy assumptions. Some writers have argued that temperance was mainly imposed from above by a dynamic capitalist class eager to make its businesses more efficient by disciplining its workers.[23] By mid-century the movement did include many men with this goal, but their plans lacked such stark simplicity, especially at the outset. The temperance forces were always a coalition of diverse interests and perspectives.

At the beginning some respectable businessmen were involved, notably in Montreal and Saint John. Still, British North America probably lacked much of the earlier paternalistic version that had emerged in the Northern United States before the 1820s to convince "gentlemen" of power and influence to change the habits of their employees and dependants. Far more of the earliest teetotallers in what was to become Canada were more common folk: farmers, artisans, shopkeepers, doctors, journalists, and other self-employed men who saw advantages in a more sober, orderly life. One U.S. historian has aptly characterized these participants as "improvers." They did not have to aspire to be rich capitalists to be convinced that they might well be able to enjoy greater security and comfort if they tried to run their farms or workshops as more orderly commercial enterprises. Drunken binges could endanger that prospect, especially when farm families were struggling to move beyond backwoods pioneering to more productive homesteads. In Nova Scotia temperance societies often appeared in communities where agricultural societies had already emerged to promote more effective farming. In Upper Canada as well, their greatest support sprang from long-settled, more commercially successful rural areas. In town and cities, they fed on the same enthusiasm for "improvement" that led to the creation of such voluntary associations as mechanics' institutes.[24]

The ruling Tory, Anglican oligarchies would have nothing to do with these organizations. The richest and most powerful gentry of the old colonial regime cast scorn on these "damned cold-water drinking societies" and suspected them of subversive American and overly democratic tendencies. In the words of the Anglican magazine *The Church*, temperance was "the mere tool of intriguing politicians and religious anarchists." There was more than a little truth to the charge. In the Canadas of the 1830s, many prominent teetotallers were Reformers bent on transforming the politics of the colony—men like John Rolph, Jesse Ketchum, and Robert Baldwin in Upper Canada, and John Neilson and Joseph Bédard in the lower province. The same was true in New

Brunswick, where the leading temperance campaigner was the Liberal politician Leonard Tilley.[25]

The old-style Tory oligarchs would soon be left behind in the great transition. Symbolically, the governor general of the Canadas, Sir Charles Metcalfe, pledged his personal support for the temperance movement in 1844 and donated £100 to the Montreal society. As the commercial economy expanded in the first half of the nineteenth century, many members of the new capitalist elites of merchants and industrialists in all the colonies embraced either evangelicalism or the new stern, ascetic version of Catholicism, and they made temperance part of their efforts to rebuild society on new bourgeois principles. In Montreal leading businessmen controlled the main temperance society. In other parts of British North America, they rallied to the temperance cause somewhat more slowly, but, by the end of the 1840s, had similarly moved to centre stage and managed to give the movement a much more secular, materialist cast. Now the arguments paid more attention to productivity, efficiency, work discipline, and "Progress."[26]

As part of their optimistic belief that everyone in society would benefit from this culture of self-restraint and self-improvement, these businessmen hoped to be able to convince workers and everyone else to maintain a sober life off the job as well as on. A poem published in the Kingston *Chronicle and Gazette* in 1842 under the title "The Effects of Teetotalism" caught the spirit:

> *More of good than we can tell,*
> *More to buy with, more to sell,*
> *More of comfort, less of care,*
> *More to eat and more to wear,*
> *Happier homes with faces bright,*
> *All our burdens rendered light,*
> *Conscience clear, minds much stronger,*
> *Debts much shorter, purses longer,*
> *Hopes that drive away all sorrow,*
> *And something laid up for tomorrow.*

Five years later a teetotaller's manual presented a vivid before-and-after portrait of how temperance could transform the workplace:

> Tradesmen who before had squandered their week's wages in drunkenness and debauchery, on Saturday night and Sunday, abused their wives when they came home, and been sick all Monday, Tuesday, and perhaps Wednesday, were now working diligently from Monday morning to Saturday night. . . .

Indeed, master workmen could now get as much done by seven men as they could before by thirty, and the men were saving money fast.

By the time these men were pushing the colonial societies towards more industrial growth after the arrival of the railways and wider markets in the 1850s, the cultural expectations of the new industrial order were widespread. In assessing the credit risk of customers, financial agencies now took careful note of their "sober and careful habits."[27]

Temperance was only part of a broader bourgeois agenda extending beyond business and the economy. Habits, ideas, and desires were under reconstruction in many ways. The project to establish a liberal order of individualism in all social relations gave birth to sundry new programs and agencies designed to balance liberty with self-discipline: revised laws governing property, marriage, and much more; remodelled penal, social-welfare, and health-care institutions (penitentiaries, "houses of industry," and "lunatic asylums"); voluntary adult education initiatives (mechanics' institutes, scientific and literary societies); and, perhaps most important, a much-expanded public school system, where the future citizenry could learn what was expected of them in liberal-capitalist society. An overhaul of the state itself swept away old aristocratic paternalism and implanted the principle of self-government (enshrined in our national heritage as "responsible government") and the political rights of equality and liberty, at least for white male property-holders.[28]

Unquestionably, however, the general optimism and hope that lay behind the temperance message and the wider project of liberal reform had begun to slide into a larger sense of social crisis by the 1840s. Thousands of new immigrants, large numbers of them from Ireland, washed up in British North America in these years. Along with their worrisome fondness for whisky, some brought epidemic disease. The growing insecurity of an emerging capitalist labour market was also leaving these newcomers, and many others, in acute poverty in many towns and cities. Respectable burghers were convinced that crime was rising (even if it was not). Frequently, angry crowds were taking to the streets to fight openly for their interests—the Irish in their Green or Orange factions, lumberers, canal labourers, and many more. Moral reformers looked over their shoulders at the upheavals of 1837–38 and, through lenses borrowed from the metropolitan centres of London or New York, began to fear the public disorder of the "dangerous classes" that they believed were emerging in their midst. For temperance men and women, booze still seemed to be the nub of the problem, and it was not going away. The thrust of their critique was shifting from damage caused to individual lives to the dangers that alcohol posed to the whole society. Self-reform began to expand to social control.[29]

Indeed, booze worked well as an explanation for all the social ills of a society in transition to industrial capitalism. The allegedly "scientific" message of the temperance movement made drink the central cause of poverty, insanity, and crime. "One half of the crime annually committed, two thirds of the cases of insanity, three-quarters of the pauperism are ascribable to intemperance," a parliamentary committee concluded in 1849, with a flourish of statistics. Temperance was the simple panacea that would cost far less than poorhouses, prisons, and the like and that shifted attention away from the social forces responsible for the economic and social transformation underway by that point—social forces that temperance supporters generally applauded.[30]

Sobriety and Resistance

Members of the working classes, only just emerging in the 1840s and 1850s as a distinguishable part of the social structure, got more attention in the temperance campaigns than anyone else. In the words of the Toronto *Examiner*, "It is only when we descend the scale of wealth, so far as to get within the line of penury and want, that the vice (intemperance) presents itself in a noticeable form." The most common symbol of the degradation caused by alcohol was the suffering family of the working-class drunkard who drank up his wages, left his children starving, and beat his wife. Indeed, the image of chronic drunkenness almost always had these thinly veiled class dimensions. Again and again, the pressure to change drinking habits seemed to be aimed primarily at working men. Before-and-after portraits of the reformed drinker's household—degradation versus domestic bliss—were standard features of temperance propaganda. (Concerns about female drunkenness were heard, but much less often.)[31]

It would be too simple, however, to see temperance simply as clear-cut class oppression aimed at the emerging working class. As in the United States and Britain (where temperance principles percolated through the radical Chartist movement), in British North America some wage-earners, particularly those in more skilled jobs, joined the cause. The ranks of Saint John's tee-totallers, for example, were filled with artisans and tradesmen, both masters and journeymen, and, over at least the next half-century, Southern Ontario's temperance societies had a similar composition. As proud producers, these participants in the cause might use the lens of temperance to underline the value of honest toil and to cast aspersions on upper-class decadence—"the

liquor loaded tables of the rich and the drinking usages of so-called fashionable society," evidence of a "selfish genteel class." Like farmers and other petit-bourgeois elements in society, these working men (and their spouses) also saw in temperance a means of finding more economic security and respectability for themselves and their families in the new bourgeois order. Drunkenness took on a new meaning for these workers as the world changed around them. Drunks seemed to be doomed to poverty and degradation in the emerging capitalist labour market and the uncertainties of urban life. Far from merely mimicking middle-class ideas about upward social mobility, working-class tee-totallers believed they could assert more self-respect and independence as workers in relations with their bosses and other men of authority if they stayed sober. They could also devote themselves to more "rational" leisure pursuits, such as a night at the mechanics' institute or the fraternal lodge. Of

On Sunday mornings in 1877, chronic drunkards in Toronto could get breakfast and a stirring lecture from the Gospel Temperance movement. Line engraving by W.W. Cruikshank, from Canadian Illustrated News, *25 August 1877.* (UTL)

course, by embracing these new cultural values, the working men were creating severe tensions in their communities over class and gender identities, between earnest, responsible sobriety and the old-time pleasures of lusty drunken revelry.[32]

One branch of the temperance movement was explicitly created to reach out to working-class drunkards to help them find their feet again. A number of short-lived societies drew their inspiration from the so-called "Washingtonian" movement in the United States. In the early 1840s societies with that name swept up thousands of American artisans, shopkeepers, working men, and their female family members, both former drunks and confirmed teetotallers, into self-help and mutual support networks for kicking the habit. Few self-improving entrepreneurs went near these organizations, whose target audience was primarily the habitual drunkard of the lower-middle and working classes. As in the United States, this strain of temperance activity seems to have been absorbed into other organizations, especially the large Sons of Temperance but also the more plebeian Rechabites and Good Samaritans. Yet by the 1870s a similarly rough-edged organization with a substantial working-class membership burst on the Canadian scene as the Gospel Temperance movement. Also known as the Blue Ribbon movement, it was headed by the Irish-born Francis Murphy and took in thousands of members in the late 1870s. One of its most powerful orators, D.I.K. Rine, a former drunkard, drew huge crowds in Canada. Gospel Temperance groups could still be found in Canadian cities in the early twentieth century. The Canadian Temperance League, founded in 1889, carried on much the same work, including running a coffee house for working men.[33]

Participants in these self-help organizations worked out their own culture of redemption, separate from the more sedate middle-class temperance organizations, which viewed this working-class temperance activity with discomfort and suspicion and found some of its practices "vulgar." The frequent meetings of these movements featured not sedate lectures by learned temperance orators but lurid, emotion-charged confessions by ordinary folk, lusty singing about the depravity of drunkards' lives, and exuberant socializing in excursions, concerts, dances, picnics, and processions. For men they helped to provide a social life apart from the "rough culture" of the tavern, but kept as many familiar ways of socializing as possible—the taverns without booze. For women they provided a network of solidarity and support among housewives and mothers so that they could help each other sustain the working-class family materially and morally. Mutual aid—psychological, cultural, and material—was central to this distinctive, admittedly much smaller, and little-studied plebeian current within an increasingly middle-class movement of top-down moralism.

THE RUMSELLER'S TRICK—THE BOTTLE IS INTRODUCED—THE HUSBAND INDUCES HIS WIFE "JUST TO TAKE A DROP."

Temperance was also about gender identities. The new bourgeois culture into which temperance was woven also addressed the family and relations between the sexes within it. Many workplaces were now far removed from the household, which was reconfigured as a protected haven of domestic comfort and support. Much more rigidly defined gender roles were pushing women out of public life and into full-time responsibility for maintaining harmony and prosperity in the home. Ideal femininity was now rooted in the nurturing activities of domesticity—of supporting husbands and raising morally sound children. Men too had to learn new ways of being masculine. Husbands now shouldered full responsibility as breadwinners for their wives and children, who appeared to be more fragile and dependent. In their time away from work males were also expected to become family men, to turn inward to the private world of the family rather than to more public spaces such as taverns. Bourgeois life was lived in a closed, privatized world. The public life of the streets was disreputable and dangerous. Although there is no research in Canada on how fully working-class men bought into this new, more

This 1851 engraving was part of a series depicting the destruction of a family by rum. Here the husband and wife first develop a taste for booze. From Canada Temperance Advocate *(Montreal), 1851. (Courtesy of Jan Noel)*

domesticated masculine identity at mid-century, there is good reason to believe that, as in Britain and the United States, working men drawn to the message of respectability through sobriety developed their own working-class version of manhood, based on the dignity of manual skill and the self-respect of responsible breadwinning.[34]

Of course, the domestic ideal could go sour, and the temperance movement cast a more intense searchlight on any breakdown. Women and children needed to be protected from the violence of drunken men and the financial irresponsibility of breadwinners whose fondness for drink threatened their families' well-being: the farmer who neglected his crops, the artisan who lost customers, the wage-earner who could not keep a job or drank up his wages. Responsible manhood and endangered womanhood became central themes of the temperance propaganda. A group of temperance women in Chatham, Canada West, apparently won over some men by parading through the streets beneath the banner "Teetotalism or No Husband."[35]

Ironically, teetotalling masculinity, whatever its class content, remained somewhat contradictory, in that the temperance movement made concessions to well-established modes of all-male socializing by creating teetotal fraternal societies. Although these single-sex organizations played a prominent role in promoting men's responsibility for domestic bliss, the men in them were "sons" of temperance, not fathers. Most of them met apart from women to carry on the "brotherhood" of tavern life without the booze. Only a few men attempted to resolve this contradiction by including women equally in their social and organizational lives.

The claims to moral and economic "Progress" that arose from the temperance movement also had ethnic and racial dimensions. The white Anglo-Celtic proponents confidently asserted their racial superiority and saw temperance as a mark of civilization not reached by "inferior" races. Yet other ethnic groups in British North America staked their own claims to temperance principles. Many Irish Catholics in the colonies were drawn to temperance, most often as efforts were made to carry over from Ireland the fervour of the anti-alcohol crusades led by the charismatic Father Theobald Mathew, a priest who had worked extensively with the poor in Cork. In the late 1830s and early 1840s, his emotional preaching brought some six million pledges from the lowest reaches of the Irish social scale and left a trail of new local temperance societies across Catholic Ireland. A cultish figure to his followers, he also distributed a flood of temperance medals among converts, who were reported to treat them as magical talismans. Across the Atlantic, his work inspired campaigns among Irish Catholics in many parts of British North America.[36]

Father Mathew toured the United States in 1849, but on both sides of the ocean his crusade was faltering and soon collapsed. His impact had nonetheless been powerful. The Irish-Catholic temperance crusade had reached out to an oppressed group under English rule, a group facing new economic pressures, and urged the Irish to flex their ethnic pride through moral commitment and renewal. Indeed, in Ireland, the burgeoning nationalist movement for repeal of the union with England had effectively taken the reigns of teetotalism by 1843. In British North America, the Catholic hierarchy eventually replaced Father Mathew's emphasis on individual conversions with clerically controlled, parish-based temperance societies, largely for men, which never did attract the same numbers in the later nineteenth century.[37]

Starting in the 1840s, the Catholic Church in Quebec sponsored a series of temperance campaigns.

In a similar way, the francophone countryside of Canada East (Quebec) proved to be surprisingly fertile ground for the cause. Here too the Catholic Church provided the leadership, as part of a great burst of "ultramontane" renewal, reorganization, and revivalist evangelizing in the colony in the 1840s. The clergy who carried this new temperance message injected a strong dose of nationalism in an effort to redirect ethnic identity away from the liberal channels that it had flowed through before and during the insurrections of 1837–38. In the uncertain years of the early 1840s, when French Canadians faced both economic insecurity and overt efforts by the British authorities to submerge their ethnic culture, the Catholic Church hoped to use the ideology and organizational structure of a clerically controlled temperance movement to rally its flock. To make the connection clear, they made the French Canadians' patron saint, Saint Jean-Baptiste, the patron of this new movement. For these clergymen, drunkenness was "the foremost evil in this land, threatening wealth and religion." Clean up your lifestyle so that you can preserve a vibrant, prosperous, Catholic *patrie* capable of withstanding the English, they argued.[38]

The initiative came from several points and was woven into the new *missions populaires* of the early 1840s, which featured highly dramatic, hell-and-damnation preaching by outside missionaries that aimed to disrupt the moral complacency of daily life and anchor a new morality in the parish temperance society. In the diocese of Quebec, the first such organizations were built on the enthusiasm of local priests and the inspiration provided by a French prelate, Monsignor Charles de Forbin-Janson, who brought Father Mathew's message when he arrived in 1839 and went on to hold many retreats and rallies throughout the colony. In Montreal the new bishop, Ignace Bourget, consulted the Irish priest about his work and set in motion a vigorous campaign to organize such societies throughout his diocese with the assistance of the newly arrived Oblate Order. Eventually, the most compelling spokesman for the cause was Father Charles Chiniquy, a spellbinding preacher from Beauport. Inspired by Father Mathew, Chiniquy set up the colony's first Catholic temperance society in 1840. Four years later he consolidated his message in the widely read *Manuel de la Société de tempérance*. In 1848 Bourget recruited him to promote temperance work in his diocese, and, as Chiniquy barnstormed through rural parishes over the next few years, his charismatic appeal prompted the establishment of many more temperance societies and elicited more than 160,000 pledges. His personal popularity was enormous. He was revered and feted everywhere he travelled.[39]

Earlier in the decade, converts had been called upon to renounce drunkenness, cabaret life, and "strong" drinks, but Bourget and Chiniquy preferred complete abstinence from all alcohol. Temperance society members got special indulgences and sometimes medals to display their commitment. The heads of families who took the pledge got three-foot, black wooden crosses to hang on the wall at home as visible symbols of their abstinence (the black cross remained the central symbol of temperance appeals for decades after). Colourful temperance banners honouring a local patron saint were also unfurled at religious festivals.

In 1851 Bishop Bourget abruptly pulled Chiniquy out of these campaigns in response to well-founded reports about sexual indiscretions with some of the female converts. Bourget shipped the priest off to Illinois, where, five years later, under another cloud of allegations, Chiniquy was excommunicated. He later converted to Presbyterianism and turned his oratorical skills against the Catholic Church.

The original scandal was kept under wraps, but, while the clergy's temperance propaganda continued, the movement was slumping by the end of the 1850s. Many converts forgot their pledges and temperance societies folded. Bourget blustered, "Drunkenness [has] returned more hideously and more boldly than ever." A parish priest reported in 1870 that, although almost every household had a black cross on the wall, drinking and drunkenness were common. The Catholic Church in Quebec would continue to promote moderation in drinking through parish branches of La Société de la Croix, run by the local priest, but Catholics would have little to do with the mainstream temperance movement. For both French and Irish teetotallers, ethnic confrontations with the English and the evangelical contempt for Catholicism that their communities faced made co-operation with the Anglo-Canadian Protestant temperance forces virtually impossible.[40]

Temperance also became a powerful force within the colonies' smaller African-Canadian communities, where liberation from the "slavery" of alcohol was closely linked to the abolition of slavery in the American South and the settling of fugitives from that regime in the British North American countryside. Like white temperance activists, Black teetotallers linked abstinence from alcohol with independence and self-reliance. By the 1850s the charismatic journalist and activist Mary Ann Shadd was writing regular columns in the African-Canadian press denouncing intemperance. Racial prejudice, however, kept these teetotallers in their own segregated societies, shut out of the dominant organizations. Shut out as well were the few Aboriginal peoples who had taken the pledge.[41]

Abstention from alcohol, then, became a key part of the new bourgeois culture that regulated social relationships and shaped economic, social, and political behaviour. Temperance was nonetheless a flexible ideology embraced by diverse groups in mid-nineteenth-century Canada. Many in the self-confident, expansive middling classes built it into their emerging class identities, as did, for different reasons, at least some within the less secure working-class population. It also became a central element in the script for new notions of "manhood" in these classes. In mid-century debates about race and ethnicity, temperance both fuelled the dominant Anglo-Celtic sense of racial superiority and allowed subordinated populations of French, Irish, and African Canadians to claim dignity. Working men and ethnic or racial minorities, however, increasingly found their versions of temperance overwhelmed by the discourses and practices of the dominant white, English-speaking, bourgeois forces.

Drinking Carries On

By the middle of the nineteenth century, teetotallers had much to celebrate. Their measure of success was first and foremost the widespread acceptance of the idea that consuming alcohol was a social and moral evil. They could also point to a near-revolution in drinking practices that, from the 1840s onward, made alcohol a more and more disreputable pleasure, even among those who never took a pledge.

Alcohol steadily disappeared from the tables of many of the rich and powerful. It was banned from most workplaces. The Hudson's Bay Company drastically cut back on the liquor provided to its men. Lumbermen forbade drinking in their camps. Canal companies ordered their contractors to stop supplying alcohol, and they set fines for drunkenness on the job. Governments banned booze from public work sites. Railway operators threatened to fire anyone caught drinking. Mine-owners barred any drinking establishments from the immediate vicinity of their mines. New factory owners, who were installing more complex, increasingly mechanized production systems, cracked down on drinking as dangerous and inefficient. Even the British navy slashed its daily rum ration in half and offered more wages to those who gave up the rest. From about 1850 onward, drinking was clearly an off-the-job, leisure-time experience, part of the new, more rigid distinction between work time and non-work time that came with industrial capitalist management. Henceforth controversies over alcohol would be disagreements about the use of leisure time.[42]

Booze also disappeared from many rural social events, including "bees." The most abiding contempt for John Barleycorn took root in the countryside, but even in urban areas drink was under attack as an after-work indulgence. Some fraternal societies such as the Odd Fellows and Knights of Pythias barred anyone in the booze trade from their membership. The defence of alcoholic beverages as healthy tonics was drowned out by a chorus of voices decrying the social devastation that the drinking allegedly caused. The tavern also increasingly played a less central role in community social life. In the 1850s and 1860s, new government buildings, halls, theatres, billiard parlours, and sporting facilities provided alternative locations far from John Barleycorn. In the 1870s and 1880s even many unions stopped meeting in taverns. Across the country sales of alcoholic beverages slumped at mid-century, and some distilleries and many taverns closed, especially outside the cities. Perhaps most significantly, the per capita consumption of distilled liquor began to plummet—a long-range pattern that would combine over the second half of the nineteenth century with a steady shift to beer, the cheaper, less alcoholic, somewhat less disreputable drink favoured by working men.[43]

Some of these patterns were evident in other parts of the Europeanized world, especially the shift in beverages, but along with the U.S. teetotallers who provided so much of the inspiration and ideology, Canadian temperance activists were far more successful in discrediting booze and setting new standards of conduct. More broadly, by the 1850s, a new culture of sobriety, rationality, and restraint—symbolized by the mechanics' institute reading room, the Sunday school, and the temperance hall—loomed large over such older pleasures of popular culture as gambling, fighting, blood sports, and sexual dalliance.

Yet in some ways the impact of temperance agitation had its limitations. For booze producers, the mid-century setback proved short-lived. Their troubles seem to have had less to do with the flight of drinkers into total abstinence than with disruptions in the colonial economies in the late 1840s, as the British Empire lurched into free trade and business went into a depression. Firms like Molson's bounced back quickly in the 1850s; that family even opened a large new brewing and distilling complex at Port Hope in Canada West in 1851. Two years later, the Carling family massively expanded their brewery in London, and their local competitor, a company owned by John Labatt, continued to prosper. The principal brewers were also joined by many new beer manufacturers, among them John and Sarah Oland in Halifax, James Ready in Saint John, Patrick Cosgrave in Toronto, Harry Brading in Ottawa, Edward Drewry in Winnipeg, and William Steinberger in Victoria. In Canada West the hundreds of miles of new railway lines laid down in the 1850s opened up wider regional markets that allowed breweries to boost production and sell their larger volume of beer through agencies in distant communities.[44]

At the same time the era of the backwoods distiller who processed surplus grain or potatoes was largely over, as the new canals and railways opened up easier routes for agricultural exports. The temperance-driven disruption in demand probably accelerated the consolidation of the distilling industry into a smaller number of much larger manufacturers capable of producing a huge supply of liquor. The distillers even perfected an associational understanding that brought effective price-fixing and marketing agreements. Moreover, the closing of taverns probably had more to do with major structural changes in servicing travellers, changes triggered by the much faster railway journeys. Far fewer stops were needed along transportation routes to provide rest and refreshments than in the era of the stage coach.[45]

Thousands of taverns and liquor shops did remain open, especially in towns and cities. Indeed, in 1851 the region that would become Southern

Ontario still had about one of these retail outlets for every 250 people—the same proportion as a half-century earlier. In the same year the population of that region was quaffing an estimated three and a half gallons of legally distilled spirits and wine per capita (compared to just over three gallons a year in the 1970s, a post-prohibition high point). That figure would be considerably higher if only adult males, the most likely drinkers, were counted.[46]

Furthermore, the teetotalling movement had sailed into stiff gales of resistance and opposition. Temperance meetings had often been disrupted by hecklers or pranksters or interrupted by articulate tavern-owners or distillers ready to argue the merits of drink. Teetotallers would sometimes find themselves an isolated and vulnerable minority in their communities. In Canada West, two barrels of cold water were poured from the ceiling over members of the Trent Village Temperance Society, and a meeting in Oakville in 1843 was "most shamefully disturbed by a mob, throwing in chips, broken glass, and even breaking the windows." In 1852 the window of the Sons of Temperance Hall in Goderich was smashed. Occasionally the local liquor interests formed their own "intemperance" or "anti-abstinence" society.[47]

Moreover, victory for the temperance forces was certainly far from complete, especially in larger cities (notably ports like Halifax) and rural settings dominated by marginal agriculture—in places where the rhythms of life had not shifted from the irregularity of seasonal industries and where large numbers of unattached single men continued to congregate—in seafaring, the army, the fur trade, unskilled labouring. In 1856 a settler in what would become Manitoba argued in a public meeting that all men should drink whisky: "It makes better neighbours, better farms, better mechanics. . . . Every man ought to have your bottle on the table to treat a friend when he comes in."[48]

Even in the long-settled parts of the country, drinking carried on. Years later the head of the Ontario Agricultural College remembered sharing with farm hands a bucket of beer that his father had brewed. Industrial paternalism still sometimes involved drinking: in 1864 Hamilton's leading boot and shoe manufacturer, Robert Nisbet, provided champagne for the toasts at his employees' picnic; and three years later, just before the city's parade to celebrate Canadian Confederation, the Wantzer sewing-machine manufactory was thrown open to visitors to see the firm's production processes while "quenching their thirst with a draught of excellent ale."[49]

The population was also expanding with outsiders who had not heard or had chosen to ignore the teetotallers' message back home. In particular, like many other newcomers from the British Isles and Northern Europe, thousands of the new Irish immigrants who poured into the colonies in the 1840s had little interest in Father Mathew's message and were firmly attached to

their whisky. The "rough" lifestyle of the large numbers of these newcomers who found work in canal and railway construction in the 1840s and 1850s made their indifference (and hostility) to temperance highly visible and troubling.[50]

Nor had all the elements of the new middle and upper classes bought into the dry life. Within bourgeois culture another, less prudish, less pietistic, less interventionist stream was in motion, which represented much more than the overflow of the pre-industrial gentry's version of class and masculine lifestyle. The men involved, most of them Tories with connections to the Anglican, Presbyterian, Lutheran, or Catholic churches, were more likely to include wealthy merchants or lawyers than industrial employers. They worried about the threat of teetotalism to property rights and distrusted the American-inspired radical individualism and egalitarianism of the temperance zealots and the implicit threat to the deference expected within hierarchical social relations. They saw no strong need for the excessive degree of personal restraint that the evangelical improvers demanded, being quite prepared to accept such vices as drinking, smoking, gambling, and other moral indiscretions provided that those pleasures were not excessive or socially dangerous. These men

In 1873 the upper-class patrons of the Russell House in Ottawa still enjoyed wine with their dinner. From Canadian Illustrated News, *5 April 1873.* (NLC, C-008176)

At the 1879 Conservative Party banquet in Ottawa, the alcohol flowed freely. From L'opinion publique, 11 December 1879. (BNQ, 3801)

LE GRAND BANQUET DES CONSERVATEURS A OTTAWA
LA SANTÉ A L'HÔTE DE LA SOIRÉE

cultivated a lustier form of bourgeois masculinity than that displayed in the earnest, righteous version of the teetotaller. They continued to enjoy their more expensive drinks in private clubs and posh hotels. Ottawa's Russell House became the favourite watering hole of the city's political elite. A clerk in the Department of the Surveyor-General at Kingston, Harry Jones, left a journal running from the 1830s into the 1880s that is littered with references to evenings spent at such places in the company of "merchants, bankers, Lawyers and gentleman farmers."[51]

At home their wives still set out dinner tables with wine glasses and kept the dining-room liquor cabinet stocked (a senior Ottawa civil servant complained in his diary in 1867 that his cook "was drunk on whiskey taken out of my wine closet"). Mass-market cookbooks provided recipes for almost every imaginable alcoholic beverage. Per capita consumption of wine stood at between one-fifth and one-quarter of a gallon in the early 1870s before falling quickly to around a tenth of a gallon, where it would remain until the arrival of wartime prohibition. Vice-regal balls in that period were far from dry occasions. A mammoth costume party hosted by Lord Dufferin in 1876 had three wine glasses at each place at the table. Nor was the business world exempt: a stash of liquor was uncovered in the Canadian Manufacturers' Association offices at the Toronto Industrial Exhibition in 1893. John A. Macdonald's infamous drunken escapades made the wet alternative clear to all. "I know enough of the feeling of this meeting to know that you would rather have John A. Macdonald drunk than George Brown sober," he is reputed to have told an audience. Far less flamboyantly, Macdonald's minister of justice (and future prime minister), Sir John Thompson, liked his glass of claret and got advice about where to obtain it by the barrel in Ottawa.[52]

Upper-class bachelors enjoying beer on their picnic. (NAC, PA-119075)

Among the wets in the upper and middle classes, however, the demands of polite respectability redefined "acceptable" drinking practices. A new model of moderate consumption in genteel surroundings could be constructed as a version of bourgeois self-restraint and posed as an alternative to the excesses of both the undisciplined plebeian tavern and the temperance fanatics.

Temperance forces might take heart from one development: at least this drinking was now more likely to be out of sight, because new definitions of respectability and an increasing elitist exclusivism were driving people from taverns. Of course, some, especially young men, might simply lead a double life, from time to time slipping away from bourgeois propriety to the sensual pleasures that still flourished in working-class saloons, for some "time out" from the tight control over impulses and desires. Teetotallers would continue to decry these secret vices, but what continued to go on behind the closed doors was of less concern than the highly visible drinking that still took place in public, where working-class men in particular continued to find pleasure. More and more, the debate over drinking would be about male working-class culture.[53]

four

The Reign of King Alcohol

PERMIT ME TO INTRODUCE a different character, who comes to the court of King Majority as chief ambassador from the empire of his Satanic Majesty. Behold! I show you the skeleton at our patriotic banquet. It has a skull with straightened forehead and sickening smile; but bedecked with wreaths of vine, clusters of grape, and heads of golden grain—King Alcohol, present at court in radiant disguise. With foaming beer-mug at his lips, he drinks the health of King Majority.[1]

As the imagery used by Frances Willard, a prominent American anti-drink crusader, suggests, temperance activists saw their enemy in a new, more menacing light in the years between 1850 and the First World War. Up to that point they had made great strides in putting drinkers on the defensive, but, to their great chagrin, they had not succeeded in stamping out drinking throughout Canadian society. The markets for alcoholic beverages grew steadily in the second half of the nineteenth century, along with the growing urban workforce in the First Industrial Revolution that got underway in British North America in the 1840s and 1850s. Teetotallers watched in horror as the making and selling of booze expanded and changed to satisfy that relentless thirst.

Now, in place of the dispersed, decentralized structure of production in the pre-industrial era, much larger, more concentrated industries of brewing and distilling took shape. Aggressive entrepreneurs created more productive industrial-capitalist enterprises to turn out much more booze and several more kinds of alcoholic beverages. By the turn of the twentieth century, these operations had become a powerful economic force in the emerging consumer economy. Up and down streets in the heart of Canadian towns and cities,

OPPOSITE PAGE: *Towards the end of the nineteenth century brewers and distillers began to promote their products with much flashier advertising. Posters like this were intended to hang on saloon walls. Such ads often featured alluring women to appeal to the all-male clientele.* (WAHC)

drinkers could still find numerous stores and taverns retailing beer and spirits. Public drinking cultures remained alive and well in working-class neighbourhoods. Many families suffered as their chief breadwinners drank up their wages and inflicted violence and emotional abuse.

As they watched these developments, worried teetotallers were aghast at the apparent power of what they took to calling "King Alcohol."

Drink and Drinking

Although the thirst for alcoholic beverages had by no means dried up, the patterns of where drinkers got them, when they drank, and what they chose to drink were changing considerably. Home production of booze was becoming much less common in the towns and cities than it had been (and continued to be) in the rural countryside. In 1868 federal Inland Revenue officials seized thirty whisky stills in Montreal, but, along with the keeping of livestock and gardening, this kind of production in the city went into decline; in 1892 the Inland Revenue inspector for Montreal reported that department staff had uncovered only four or five stills over the preceding two years. Working-class families gradually consumed more and more of their wage income in buying commercially produced goods—from ready-made clothing to bakery bread to draft or bottled beer. Between the mid-nineteenth century and the First World War, brewers and distillers expanded production. They also guaranteed a purer, more consistent drink than the backyard producers were able to provide, although adulteration at the retail level remained a problem.[2]

Canadians were also changing their drinking preferences. By the last third of the nineteenth century, like the British and Americans, they were generally drinking less liquor and more beer. If every man, woman, and child had consumed the same amount of liquor in 1874, they would have downed nearly two gallons each over the year, but that was seemingly a high-water mark. Rarely over the next thirty years did the annual total of spirits consumed reach one gallon (the average from 1880 to 1916 was .843 gallons, or about three litres), although a marked increase occurred again after 1900. Per capita beer consumption was only 2.2 gallons in 1870, but within a few years it had risen past three gallons before hitting five in 1902 and seven in 1913. In part this trend reflected sharply increased taxes that made spirits more expensive in a period of relatively stable retail prices.[3] In part it reflected new marketing opportunities that brewers aggressively pursued. As a bulkier drink that was more expensive to transport and more prone to spoilage, beer was predominantly an urban beverage. Its growing popularity reflected both the expansion of the urban (especially working-class) population and therefore the concentration of more drinking in towns and cities—in some cases, no doubt in response to still uncertain supplies of drinking water. It may also have been that the immigrants arriving in great numbers from British cities brought with them their taste for beer, which had become a staple in their lives back home.

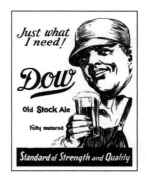

Despite the temperance movement's anxieties, then, much more of the alcohol entering Canadian bodies was doing so in the less harmful, less debilitating form of beer. Moreover, thanks to the lower alcohol content of beer, the actual alcohol intake per capita dropped between the 1870s and 1890s. Ironically, the temperance movement may have contributed to the marked resurgence of spirits consumption after 1900, because as more retail outlets were closed, persistent drinkers may have been forced to turn back to the more portable bottle of liquor, which was available through the legal mail-order business and illicit bootlegging and moonshining operations.[4]

Many working men believed that beer was good for them. Brewers often picked up on this theme in their advertising. From Gazette (Montreal), *5 September 1927.*

National patterns masked important distinctions. Regional variations in drinking preferences were still striking in the late nineteenth century. Compared to the national average, drinkers in Ontario and Manitoba consumed far more beer and less liquor, while those in Quebec took in more liquor and less beer. The drinkers in British Columbia consumed more of both (though their whisky was more often Scotch than Canadian rye), while drinkers in the three Maritime provinces drank considerably less of both major beverages than did drinkers in the rest of the country. Beer was evidently most popular in the more urbanized provinces with large new English-born, working-class populations, while the long-established taste for spirits survived where population change was less dramatic, notably in the Maritimes and Quebec outside Montreal (though, arguably, the residents of these generally more rural regions may have obtained much of their booze from unlicensed vendors whose products bypassed the Inland Revenue officials).[5]

After the turn of the century, as new immigrant neighbourhoods began to appear in the larger cities of Central and Western Canada, ethnic differences in alcohol preferences also became more marked, as Southern European drinkers renewed their taste for wine and Eastern Europeans their fondness for spirits. The arrival of much larger numbers of immigrants from societies where drinking alcoholic beverages faced no serious criticism might also help to explain the increase in overall Canadian consumption in the decade before the First World War.

In general, the Royal Commission on the Liquor Traffic noted, Canadians drank somewhat less per capita than Americans did, and much less than many European nationalities. The difference in beer consumption was striking: according to statistics presented to the Commission (statistics that, for some unknown reason, did not conform to Inland Revenue figures), Canadians drank 8 gallons of beer per capita in 1892, while the Americans quaffed 9, the French 11, the Germans 18, the British 27, and the Belgians 28.5. A British study from the same period put the consumption of absolute alcohol from wine, beer, and spirits at .54 gallons in Canada, alongside 1.16 in the United States, 2.05 in the United Kingdom, 2.09 in Germany, 2.81 in Belgium, and 3.72 in France (where absinthe had recently become extremely popular).[6]

Booze was also increasingly less likely to be on the table at mealtime and more often consumed as a purely leisure-time drink. Families now more often started their day and washed down their meals with other more affordable beverages. Milk was widely available in towns and cities, and in the last quarter of the nineteenth century the price of tea dropped, so that now thousands of families at all levels of society could brew it daily (as people in Britain had been doing for a hundred years). By the end of the century, far more Canadians were also enjoying coffee with meals. Booze therefore became much more a purely recreational drink, often consumed outside the family home. Men were far more likely to do that kind of drinking, because women's domestic responsibilities tied them down at home. Private drinking continued in some households of all social classes, even with meals and especially on festive occasions, but it seems that most wage-earning men got their booze in nearby taverns.[7]

Meanwhile, alcohol consumption had yet another new dimension: the narrowing of the time available for drinking. Even though booze had been banned from most workplaces, many workers continued to believe that alcoholic beverages were nutritious, healthy, and thirst-quenching and could help them through arduous labour in a smoky foundry, steel plant, or glass works. "One old timer always prepared for his day by downing a tumbler of green rye whisky and then ate nothing until he was through at night," the historian of the Montreal Rolling Mills later wrote. "Most men brought their two meals in the top of a large bucket, with half a gallon of beer, officially recognized as 'tea,' sloshing in the bottom." A foreman at the Hamilton Steel and Iron Company (later Stelco) told a parliamentary committee in 1910 that "if he stopped the men from drinking during working hours . . . half of them would walk off the job."[8]

Drinking on the job was a common experience for the 600,000 Canadian men who enlisted in the Canadian armed forces during the First World War. At the front, officers issued rum rations at dawn and dusk and extra drinks before and after battles. "Under the spell of this all-powerful stuff," one soldier claimed, "one almost felt that he could eat a German, dead or alive, steel helmet and all." For many, including many former teetotallers, rum became the forti-

fier that made the strain and pain of life in the trenches more bearable. One soldier told his mother that rum could "be regarded more as a medicine than a beverage" since it was "absolutely invaluable to put men to sleep when they are wet and cold." Few men spurned the booze made available to them. "The individual is in all cases free to refuse the issue of Rum if he so desires," a cabinet minister was informed, "but this option is only exercised in a few instances." Not surprisingly, many of these men came home from war with a strong attachment to alcohol.[9]

Yet, for the most part, drinking at work was difficult in the late nineteenth and early twentieth centuries. Those drawn into the new factories and mines in the second half of the nineteenth century found their daily lives more rigidly structured by fixed working hours marked off by the clock and the factory bell. On the job their bosses insisted that the work was to have

Drinking on the job was universally forbidden by the late nineteenth century, but it often continued illicitly. In 1894 these construction workers in Tavistock, Ont., paused to enjoy a glass of beer more openly. They were building an addition to the Commercial Hotel, and the owner of the premises provided the drinks. (TG)

Like this painter in Midland,
Ont., around 1900, some
working men slipped into a
saloon for a quick drink and a
chat during their working day.
(NAC, PA-178789)

their undivided attention, and socializing or merrymaking—including drinking—would not be tolerated. In their efforts to speed up work and push up
productivity, employers insisted that workers keep their noses to the grind-
stone, a condition eventually backed up by the stopwatches and assembly lines
of "scientific" management that arrived in the country's Second Industrial
Revolution after 1900.[10] As moments of pleasure were squeezed out and the
working day became more demanding, the more clearly demarcated "free"
time after work took on new meaning for many working men.

Wage-earners who laboured in poorly paid, less skilled, seasonal jobs—
loggers or longshoremen, for example—often put in excessively long hours
for intensive periods and then faced long bouts of unemployment. They saw
little that made much sense in the teetotalling culture of sober self-improvement, and viewed drink much as their forefathers in pre-industrial times had
done. The physical demands and seasonality of their jobs encouraged bursts of
binge drinking at the end of heavy bouts of work. In contrast, workers in the
more regularized, regimented routines of industrial capitalist production had
to arrange their leisure time around the daily and weekly hours of waged
labour.

Despite the general failure of the impressively large nine-hour movement
in Central Canada in 1872 and of later efforts to get even shorter working

days (efforts persisting until the middle of the twentieth century), most wage-earners worked a ten-hour day from the 1870s to the First World War—which was considerably less than the more open-ended pre-industrial working days, which often ran to twelve or fourteen hours in busy seasons. There were exceptions—textile, lumber, and rolling mills still tended to run twelve-hour shifts, and by the early years of the new century's first decade a few groups of well-organized craftworkers were enjoying an eight-hour day. In most cases the workweek lasted a full six days—that is, sixty hours. Before the First World War a small proportion of the workforce were enjoying their Saturday afternoons off, usually only in the summer months. Most waged workers had to squeeze their leisure into evenings and Sundays (which the Sabbatarian movement was campaigning flat out to shut down as fully as possible). Outside Quebec, work rarely stopped any more for religious or folk festivals, and other one-day public holidays were few and far between. Drinking now had to fit into a much smaller slice of most Canadians' daily lives.[11]

"Under present circumstances," a working man told the Royal Commission on the Liquor Traffic in 1892, "I believe that liquor is a necessity. A man working sometimes, nine, or ten or eleven hours in front of a furnace or fire, and who has got to be at work the next day is unnerved, and unless he has some stimulant, ofttimes he will suffer from insomnia." For thousands of working men, stopping at a saloon on the way home was a moment of transition, an opportunity to unwind at the end of a long working day. Alcohol became the lubricant for the passage between wage labour and leisure, and the moments spent with workmates or neighbours rekindled the sociability that the capitalist workplace had repressed. A study of drinkers in saloons in the Ontario municipalities of St. Catharines, Thorold, Merritton, and Port Dalhousie in 1915 noted how the numbers swelled in the late afternoon and early evening. Many men did not linger long in the saloon because family responsibilities awaited them (married working men had numerous gendered domestic responsibilities, including gardening, splitting firewood, repairing and building their houses, and even, when they were willing, helping with child care). Saturdays and paydays always saw bigger crowds of men lingering in front of the bar, but even on weeknights a good number either stayed or returned later in the evening. In the compact houses that working-class families normally occupied in Canada's industrial centres, family members had little space to themselves and no room for entertaining. For men facing seasonal unemployment, hanging around barrooms was a common way of killing time.[12]

Alcohol also had to find space in household budgets. When working-class communities began to take shape in industrial centres after the 1850s, at first beer and whisky, along with tobacco, were among the only widely available

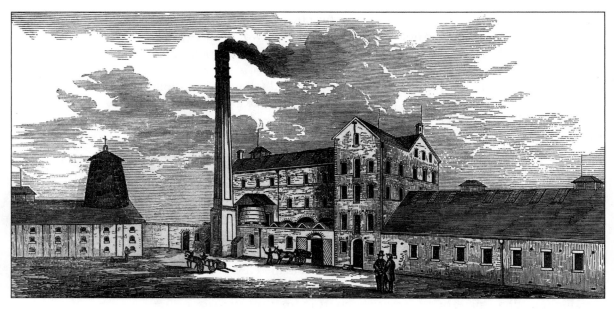

In 1861 Gooderham and Worts opened a large stone, state-of-the-art distillery (in a building still standing) on the Toronto waterfront. From Canadian Illustrated News, *25 April 1863.* (NLC, C-134294)

consumer goods. Gradually, over the last quarter of the nineteenth century, such commercial ventures as vaudeville houses, dance halls, roller rinks, baseball games, and amusement parks joined taverns in offering cheap leisure-time pleasures. Working people could also enjoy such inexpensive consumables as mass-produced candies, soft drinks, or ice cream. Working men could invest in a baseball, bat, and mitt for after-work games with workmates. They could buy a second-hand bicycle for heading out of the city, the regalia for a fraternal society's meetings, or an outfit of ready-made clothes for respectable holiday outings. As those options proliferated, booze became only one of several possible outlets for the consumer dollar spent on leisure. It also became a discretionary expenditure that would be sacrificed if workers faced severe unemployment, as most did regularly in the late nineteenth century—and the rise and fall of per capita consumption figures generated by the federal Department of Inland Revenue each year indicate that drinkers did curtail their tippling in hard times. The royal commissioners noted that per capita consumption and arrests for drunkenness were dropping off in the late nineteenth century, especially in the economic slump of the early 1890s. Indeed, the lower level of alcohol consumed by Canadians compared to that downed by American, British, or European drinkers may point to a harder life and a lower standard of living for the workers of the Dominion.[13]

The Liquor Traffic

In 1892 the Canadian government sent a royal commission of five men out across the country to investigate what had become widely known as the "Liquor Traffic." That meant looking into the making and selling of alcoholic beverages of all kinds and their impact on society. That the government should apply the term "traffic" to a large and flourishing complex of businesses indicates that the enterprises were seen as something more than just another industry in Canada by the close of the nineteenth century.

In their final report three years later, the commissioners admitted that finding precise information on how the industry operated was not easy. "Inquiries into the effects of the liquor traffic upon the communities where it is carried on have been met everywhere by an almost entire absence of systematized statistics and information," they complained.[14] A century later it is still not much easier to find evidence because surprisingly little systematic research has been done on the industry in Canada. It is certainly clear, however, that the two main branches of the industry—production and retailing— were standing fast in the face of the temperance storm and providing large quantities of liquor and beer to Canadian drinkers.

To get their own sense of the industry, the royal commissioners must have strained their eyes pouring over the long columns of tiny figures published every year by the Department of Inland Revenue. Since just after Confederation, civil servants in the department had been keeping tabs on alcohol producers and their output to make sure that the excise duties so important to government coffers were paid. Their reports revealed two distinct trends: fewer producers but higher output, most of it for the domestic market. Their tabulations also revealed that vintners—people who made or sold wine—were still engaged in a marginal, commercially insignificant venture in Canada, and that distilling was taking a somewhat different course from brewing (a small number of independent firms continued to make malt for both the liquor and beer industries, but far more malting was now being done inside each distillery or brewery). In 1870, twenty-eight distillers got licences; yet ten years later only twelve were licensed, and in the later years of the century the annual total often dropped as low as nine or ten. Almost all of the country's distillers, including the largest, were in Ontario, notably Belleville's Henry Corby, Prescott's J.P. Wiser, and Walkerville's Hiram Walker (all of whom started up in 1857-58), Waterloo's Joseph Seagram (who took charge of an existing distillery in 1883), and the country's biggest, the venerable Toronto firm of Gooderham and Worts, which dated back to the 1830s. By 1902 production in the Toronto giant's plant alone peaked at two million gallons a year. The operations in other provinces were generally much smaller and prone to closing in economic slumps. The early-nineteenth-century connection of distilling with flour milling had been broken, and the leading producers were now highly capitalized enterprises capable of much larger output. The production of spirits rose and fell, but the much smaller number of distilleries was still capable of turning out as much in the early part of the century as in the early 1870s: more than five million gallons a year, almost all of it whisky.[15]

The industrial map of Canadian brewing was noticeably different. The total number of licensed breweries hit a post-Confederation peak of 166 in 1874 and then declined as the economy slid into depression. From 1880 to 1916 (the year prohibition began to arrive), an average of 128 breweries were licensed each year. In prosperous years there might have been as many as 134 to 139, but the total dropped to below 120 after 1910. Brewing was far more decentralized than distilling, mostly because, before mechanized refrigeration, beer was not as easy to transport without spoilage. Almost every decent-sized town had a brewery in the late nineteenth and early twentieth centuries. Some of the smaller operations might be extensions of a hotel and tavern business. Ontario always had the most (though the total fell steadily from 119 in 1871 to 78 in 1891 to 48 on the eve of prohibition in 1916). Quebec had 15 to 20, and the Maritimes only a sprinkling of 7 or 8. There were always 10 to 12 on the Prairies in this period and a rapidly expanding number in British Columbia, peaking at 37 in the early twentieth century.[16]

The volume of beer flowing out of all these local enterprises continued to rise—from under ten million gallons a year in the early 1870s to well over twenty million at the turn of the century. The average brewery was also able to produce much more. In 1874 the country's 119 licensed producers brewed roughly 11.6 million gallons of beer, or an average of 97,000 each; in 1914, 117 breweries poured out more than 56 million gallons, or 480,000 each.[17]

Some breweries were huge enterprises producing far more than the statistical average. In 1896 John Labatt (son of the original owner) made his own list of the leading seven breweries based on output: Dow and Dawes of Montreal, Carling of London, and Sleeman of Guelph were far out in front, while Labatt placed his firm in a second tier just behind O'Keefe and Dominion, both in Toronto; no other breweries in any other provinces, including Molson's, were in the same league. Typically these industry leaders had started in bigger cities where the drinking population was large enough to allow them to invest in big facilities and reach out to wider regional, and even national, markets. Their prosperity was visible in the huge, architecturally stunning factories they erected (and often had to rebuild after devastating fires).[18]

Gooderham and Worts's steam-powered mixers and huge stills put the distillery in the forefront of Canada's First Industrial Revolution. From Canadian Illustrated News, *25 April 1863.* (NLC, C-134290, C-134291)

In 1882 Carling became one of the first joint-stock companies in the industry. More followed in the 1890s, along with the first merger. In 1895 a British syndicate bought five Maritime breweries, including Oland's in Dartmouth and a plant in Charlottetown, and ran them as Halifax Breweries

Limited. Over the next two decades, four British Columbia companies in Victoria, New Westminster, and Kamloops folded into Coast Breweries, and four more in Vancouver, Cumberland, and Nanaimo merged into British Columbia Breweries Limited. In Hamilton three firms became the Hamilton Brewing Association, and the Sudbury Brewing and Malting Company Limited bought up plants in Sault Ste. Marie and Fort William. On a much more spectacular scale, in 1909, as part of a wave of merger mania that was sweeping through Canadian business in the half-decade before the First World War, National Breweries Limited pulled together virtually all the breweries in the province of Quebec into a large new corporation, with the goal of rationalizing and modernizing the many small operations. Molson's stayed out, and watched as half of the fourteen plants involved in the merger, including all but two of its competitors in Montreal, Dawes and Dow, were shut down in the reorganization. Although the large British brewing companies had already shown some interest in moving into Canada, they got no further than Nova Scotia. Their discussions first with Carling and Labatt and later with Labatt and O'Keefe went nowhere. U.S. producers could never get a toehold either, and the brewing and distilling in the country remained solidly Canadian. By the turn of the century, the men at the head of leading firms were also highly respected corporate capitalists, men of power and substance, and well entrenched in the bourgeois elites of the period.[19]

Increasing productivity reflected significant changes in production. As in so many other branches of Canadian industry in the second half of the nineteenth century, the processes for making booze were changing, though unevenly—distilling more dramatically and quickly than brewing. In spirits production, Gooderham and Worts was setting the pace. When the firm opened its new plant on Toronto's waterfront in 1861, it was clearly on the cutting edge of the First Industrial Revolution. A year later, a wide-eyed Toronto *Globe* reporter wrote: "In scarcely any other establishment in Canada is there so much accomplished without the aid of manual labour. From the time the corn is received at the door until it is 'racked' or drawn off into barrels, as whisky or spirits, it is not handled by human hands." Everything in the factory was larger than in the past, but the really vital difference was the hundred-horsepower steam engine that powered new machinery for moving, mixing, and processing raw materials and end products. The reporter described how the various grains used were transported mechanically to the top floor of the building and deposited in hoppers. From there they were drawn for grinding mechanically, then elevated again to the top floor to different hoppers immediately over the "mash tuns." Once dropped into those large vats, they would be mixed with water pumped up by the huge engine, and then stirred regularly by machinery. After a few hours the liquid would flow down into fermentation "tuns," and after four days the result would be pumped up to the still. No longer onion-shaped, the so-called "column" stills had been designed to allow for continuous, rather than batch, production. Here steam heat, rather than wood fires, now produced the distillation process, and the product of that stage would be run through a charcoal filter to produce "common whisky." (Wastes from the distillation process were pumped to outside containers to be used as cattle feed.)[20]

The "common whisky" could be barrelled or, for higher grades, passed through another distillation to remove more of the oils. This product could be sold in that pure form or be diluted with distilled water and flavoured and coloured appropriately to produce the firm's popular "Toddy" or "Old Rye Whisky." Although the name "rye" would increasingly stick to the whisky produced in Canadian distilleries, most of the raw material used in its production was now corn; the distinctive flavour was produced through blending with small quantities of rye whisky.

Aging the spirits in their barrels was still limited, but the federal government would soon step in to require at least two years for that stage, thus helping to ensure a high-quality product that would generate good tax revenues. The maturing process in huge warehouses eventually came to be understood as being important to the taste, because the tannins in the oak of the barrels added subtle flavouring. By the end of the century the blending of different whiskies and the addition of flavouring and colouring had become the final steps in the process—and the most closely guarded secrets from competitors. By that point too, the larger distillers were using more chemical analysis in laboratories for quality control. At that stage the liquid was ready for bottling, where no further maturation would take place.

In 1862 Gooderham and Worts employed 150 men to run their plant. A decade later census takers found that the company's output was worth more than that of any other industrial enterprise of any kind in Ontario, that the value added through production was also the province's highest, that its capitalization ranked seventh—and that the company still needed only 150 men to produce the whisky.[21]

In breweries, in contrast, much of the labour process still required the muscle, dexterity, and skill of the workers, as in many other industries in this period of uneven industrialization. In the numerous small breweries, men had to lift and heave and lug and tote the raw materials and the barrelled beer. Workers filled bottles using hoses connected to barrels, and then corked the bottles by hand. Above all, making good beer still required the knowing touch of the maltster, the brewmaster, and his brewers, who had to regulate the

*Brewery workers at
J. MacCarthy and Sons in
Prescott, Ont., were still filling
beer bottles by hand in 1910.*
(NAC, PA-107328)

quality at each step of the way. Labatt's future brewmaster, Denis Mason, signed an indenture of apprenticeship with John Labatt in 1870 and stayed with the firm for more than forty years. Mason and the others were proud craftsmen who could still learn the "art and mystery" of their trade through apprenticeships.[22]

In the last decades of the nineteenth century machines gradually replaced some of the manual labour. Steam power was applied to hoisting the grain, grinding the malt, and pumping water, wort, and beer. It was used to stir the barley in the malt house and the malt in the "mash tub," to heat the brew, and mix the yeast into the "wort"—all of which helped to speed up production and create more consistency in the quality of the beer. As in the distilleries, the brewing workforce thus came to include skilled stationary engineers and their helpers. By the 1890s, fairly simple bottling machinery was also available. Brewing could also stretch over more of the year. The use of huge blocks of ice cut from nearby rivers and lakes during the winter and stored in large ice houses at the breweries now made possible the cooling of the wort through more of the warm weeks in spring and summer.[23]

Innovation probably came more slowly in Canadian brewing than it did among U.S. brewers, as the smaller Canadian market and the prolonged depression of the late nineteenth century made economies of scale difficult. By the turn of the century a few of the larger Canadian producers were nonetheless edging towards the kinds of changes in production that would give the period the status of a Second Industrial Revolution. They began to pay attention to

the more systematic science of brewing chemistry, including the new discoveries of the scientist Louis Pasteur about the fermentation process. In the 1890s, a young member of the Molson family was sent to a technical school in New York known as the United States Brewing Academy, as was John Labatt's son some years later. Others followed new scientific developments in trade journals. The expanding mechanization of the industry included new refrigeration processes (ice-making equipment and ammonia-based refrigerators, especially for lager production) that permitted year-round production. Machinery for filtering the beer under pressure speeded up the whole process. In the larger plants, bottles were no longer filled by hand, but moved through sterilizing equipment and along conveyor belts to be filled and sealed automatically with the familiar "crown" cap (invented in the United States in 1892). Cheap electricity to replace steam power brought more flexibility at many points in production. In the boom of the first decade of the century,

By the 1920s Toronto's large O'Keefe brewery had mechanized bottling and an assembly-line operation more typical of the Second Industrial Revolution. (NAC, PA-068062)

By the end of the nineteenth century women's involvement in booze production was limited to labelling and packaging spirits in distilleries. In the 1920s these women at the Seagram's plant in Waterloo, Ont., were packing bottles of whisky. (UWL, Seagram Collection)

several Canadian brewers would follow the U.S. technological and managerial lead and position themselves to withstand the impact of prohibition after 1916.[24]

Many of the men who worked in the larger establishments still had the crucial know-how that enabled them to judge the timing and quality of distilling and brewing. But the workers in the larger firms' much-expanded labour force generally had more narrowly focused, specialized jobs and included many more less-skilled workers who simply applied their muscle power at various points along the way, from malting to bottling. As in so many other parts of industrialized production in this period, women had no place in the labour process of either distilling or brewing, with one predictable exception. In some of the largest firms, the division of labour brought young women into the bottling, labelling, and packing departments (where they could also often be found in other light manufacturing such as food-processing). Molson's had three female bottlers in 1879 and twenty-nine some ten years later. Initially they had to wash, fill, and cork the heavy, dark-green bottles by hand, watching all the while that no mice had crawled out of the straw packing and found their way into a bottle waiting to be filled. Presumably, in the characteristic gendering of paid work, these tasks could be construed as "women's work," because they were similar to what the women did in their own kitchens (even though most small breweries, with a less severe division of labour, confused such gender identities by using men to do the bottling). Some breweries, like Labatt's, avoided using females by hiring boys instead. After bottling machines replaced manual labour in the larger firms, women often still sat in large numbers at the end of the line, checking the appearance of the bottles and packing them for shipping.[25]

Beverage alcohol production had thus burst out of small-scale artisanal workplaces and embraced the new operational principles of capitalist industrialization. Marketing would have to make the same kind of leap into new commercial practices.

Reaching Customers

Starting in the 1870s and 1880s, booze producers worked harder to cultivate the trust and allegiance of drinkers and to reach as many more of them as possible. In part this involved new products to meet varied drinking tastes; in part it involved much more aggressive marketing.

The distillers refined the quality of their liquor through blending different whiskies, and, in contrast to brewers, promoted an export market for the distinctive Canadian taste that resulted. To cater to more tastes, brewers diversified their product lines. In the last third of the nineteenth century, several breweries began making a new drink known as "lager." It was a "bottom-fermenting" product made with a different yeast and was clearer and lighter in taste than the well-established English-style ales, porters, and stouts. First made around 1840 in Germany, lager was brought to North America by German immigrants, such those who began brewing in Grey, Bruce, and Waterloo counties in Ontario in the mid-nineteenth century. By the turn of the century a third of all Canadian beer produced was lager. A drink served ice-cold rather than simply cellar-cooled, it was a hit in hot summer weather. In 1879 the management of the Toronto Industrial (later the Canadian National) Exhibition decided it would be a fine drink to sell from booths on the exhibition grounds during the event, held in late August (after a few years of uncertainty, the provincial government shut them down). Nonetheless, however much lager may have appealed to many palates, most Canadian beer drinkers in this pre-war period continued to prefer ales—both the more traditional heavy ales and, for growing numbers, the lighter pale and amber varieties, which were also gaining favour in Britain. That preference set Canadians apart from the bulk of U.S. drinkers. India Pale Ale, more bitter and slightly heavier than lager, was particularly popular.[26]

When the booze producers found that higher profits came from expanding and consolidating their market share, they began to promote their products more aggressively in an increasingly competitive industry. Rather than getting a generic whisky or beer from a barrel, consumers were now encouraged to choose a specific, well-labelled product—Carling's Imperial Club Lager, Labatt's Extra Stock Ale, Walker's Canadian Club, or Seagram's '83, for example— and to stick to it exclusively. Over time customers would develop intense loyalties to the brands they chose, and the labels on bottles became distinctive and colourful. To keep the brand name in the public eye, breweries distributed posters, show cards, and calendars for display in saloons, along with lighters, matchbooks, serving trays, shoeshine brushes, and other novelties featuring their product names. By 1915 moral reformers in London, Ont., were complaining that "much of the best bill board space in the city is used to increase the consumption of liquor."[27]

Relatively simple notices had also run in newspapers since at least the 1850s, but, by the 1880s, more eye-catching advertisements for various kinds of booze reached out to readers of the daily press and magazines, sometimes reinforcing the message by reproducing the new label images from their bottles. Many ads used superlatives like "finest, purest, and best"—Labatt in particular liked to flaunt the medals his beers had won in international competitions—and trumpeted the modern efficiency of their production facilities. They also featured the healthy qualities of their beverages. Sleeman's beer was alleged to be "the most efficacious remedial agent of its kind for Indigestion, Dyspepsia, Loss of Appetite, General Debility, Nervous Exhaustion, Sleeplessness, Coughs, Colds and other maladies that may result from an impaired constitution" and could be "especially adapted to nursing mothers, weak and delicate children, convalescents and invalids." Carling proudly proclaimed that his ale, porter, and lager were "highly recommended by the medical faculty." By the turn of the century the ads were incorporating more dramatic artwork that placed the consumption of booze in familiar settings, especially the home, and associated it with positive life experiences, from good health to respectability to discriminating taste. All of these were familiar themes in an emerging advertising industry aiming to encourage consumers to believe that purchasing the product could bring happiness, success, renewed vigour and vitality, or greater meaning in life.[28]

Producers also put more of their beverages in bottles to encourage home consumption—a trend, as the royal commission learned, that accelerated after

Most breweries served only local markets. Here barrels of Victoria-Phoenix beer are shown arriving at Victoria's Retreat Saloon in the 1890s. (BCA, D-00334)

1878 when the so-called Scott Act opened up the possibility of local prohibition zones. Robert Davies of the Dominion Brewery in Toronto explained: "When that act came into force it changed the whole shape of our business. . . . We could not ship our goods into the country because everybody would see it, and the orders would come in for them to be delivered in bottles, in flour barrels, in packages without any labels on." As a result, four to five dozen bottles would be sewn into burlap bags and packed in flour at the breweries. Open sales of bottled booze increased as well. At the turn of the century, one-third of Canadian beer was sold in bottles. By 1911 Molson's was selling four-fifths of its output in quart bottles.[29]

Although some brewing firms built huge new factories, before the 1890s most brewers found that there was not much to be gained through larger operations. Production processes were still too labour-intensive and markets still mostly local. Most of the small, local breweries simply sent their horse-drawn wagons of beer kegs around to nearby liquor shops and hotels. The larger producers, however, sent commercial travellers far and wide to promote their beverages among local merchants and hotel-keepers. Some brewers expanded production by setting up branch operations in other towns (Sleeman had five plants by 1889, Waterloo's Kuntz family four by the turn of the century). But it was the expansion of railway lines and the eventual introduction of refrigerated railway cars that helped the larger producers reach "agencies" (the equivalent of modern franchisees) and branch bottling operations far from the brewing plants. By 1900 Labatt was sending two-thirds of his production out of London by train to bottling units in distant cities. The

Booze was sold in grocery stores across the country in the 1860s. This early photo was taken in a mining camp on Leech River in British Columbia. (BCA, A-04473)

biggest brewers were reaching out to regional and, where possible, national markets. Their access to U.S. markets was blocked by high tariffs.[30]

By the late nineteenth century, depending on provincial regulations, alcoholic beverages could still be sold in a variety of outlets: licensed grocery or liquor stores, "wholesalers" (where booze could be purchased in bulk), free-standing saloons, restaurants, steamboat and railway cars, private clubs, and taverns in hotels. But a growing thicket of licensing restrictions meant that the most likely spots to find whisky or beer were handfuls of specialized liquor stores or, far more commonly, urban taverns located in hotels, typically known as "saloons." In the 1880s some brewers began to give financial backing to individual saloon-keepers to ensure a reliable outlet for their beer. They regularly extended generous terms of credit to help keep the retailers afloat. Whether brewers and distillers came to control saloon-keepers as effectively as their counterparts did in the United States and Britain is difficult to determine. When as proof of the growing commercial power of the liquor traffic the temperance movement targeted the so-called "tied house" that resulted from this relationship, the industry became understandably tight-lipped about how it worked.

In the early 1890s the Royal Commission on the Liquor Traffic tried to untangle what was going on. It heard evidence that suggested that many retailers held loans and mortgages from brewers, presumably to pay for the

equipment and furnishings needed for a saloon. One Hamilton brewer admitted that his company had such links to thirty-one of the city's eighty-five licensed hotels. A temperance journalist in the same city insisted that one "distiller" (probably a loose term) controlled forty hotels and was in the habit of replacing saloon-keepers who proved unacceptable. A special investigation in Toronto in 1907 revealed that seven brewing companies held 138 loans on 146 hotels worth nearly $600,000. Abe and Harry Bronfman had got similar help from a local brewer when they bought a hotel in Emerson, Man., a few years earlier.

Some Canadian saloon-keepers used this kind of support to provide free lunches as an enticement to drinkers. Perhaps because Canada had a much smaller number of large breweries than did Britain or the United States, the tied house was less common here. The temperance movement nonetheless argued that it was a widespread problem, and some provincial governments would make a point of banning the practice when public drinking returned

By the close of the century alcoholic beverages were available only in saloons or in licensed, privately owned liquor stores. (UWL, Seagram Collection)

after prohibition. Whatever the details of the relationship, a close link undoubtedly existed between producers and retailers.[31]

Workers and Bosses

Relations between bosses and workers were also close. In different ways,
industrial relations in the two branches of booze production were highly
paternalistic.

In distilling, the owners were patriarchs who watched over their extensive
production setups and large workforces with a keen eye. In 1863 Gooderham
was living right on the site of his large new plant in Toronto, and Hiram
Walker later built a whole industrial community around his distillery—
"Walkerville"—where he provided workers with a church, school, fire company, music hall, and reading room.[32]

Industrial paternalism worked somewhat differently in brewing. The small
scale of most of the breweries and their continuing reliance on their workers'
skills encouraged brewers to cultivate close bonds with their workmen. Craft
identities were strong because the owners were themselves generally skilled
brewmasters who watched closely over production. Also strong was the proud
assertion of artisanal masculinity, which kept women out of brewing work
throughout the period before prohibition. Sometimes ethnicity also provided
the social cement, because many brewers were German. Some consciously
built up their rapport with their workmen through company picnics or baseball teams. In Guelph, for example, George Sleeman sponsored his own factory team and presided over the town's leading ball club, the Maple Leafs.
Even in the largest breweries, where the artisan-owner had become the more
distant industrial capitalist who was far less likely than in the past to roll up his
sleeves and work alongside his men on the malting or brewing floors, company executives strived to maintain good relations with their staffs.[33]

By the close of the century many of these workers were no longer content with the brewers' paternalism. They played no major role in labour's
"great upheaval" of the 1880s, although a few independent brewery workers'
unions appeared in the 1880s and 1890s, including a local assembly of the
Knights of Labor in Toronto. Far more important was the first stable union in
the industry, the United Brewery Workers, organized in the United States in
1886. Its leaders were German socialists who insisted on taking in everyone
who worked in a brewery, regardless of skill—a stark contrast with the more
restrictive mode of organizing among craft unions in the period. In 1901 the
union chartered its first Canadian local in Victoria, B.C., and within a year had

seven more. Initially, members of the Brew Masters Association of Ontario vowed to sign no agreements with the new union, but the Toronto companies agreed to union demands for higher wages in 1903. Then, when workers at Toronto's O'Keefe and Reinhardt operations struck to back up new demands a year later, the other five breweries locked out their employees in the hopes of crushing the union (in the spirit of union-busting then promoted by the Toronto Employers' Association, which included the brewers). The companies threatened legal action when union members, supported by the local trades and labour council, proposed a boycott of the companies' beer.

The city's Licensed Victuallers' Association (the saloon-keepers) intervened as mediators, and the union eventually won recognition. Regular collective bargaining and signed contracts thus became part of the industry in Toronto and Hamilton. Labatt held out until a union boycott of his products in London convinced him to sign on to this new labour-relations regime. By 1912 there were twenty locals across the country, ten of them in Ontario. Two years later, however, brewery workers at Montreal's Frontenac Breweries lost a bitter fifteen-month struggle to bring a union into Quebec's completely non-union brewing sector.[34]

Distillery workers generally exercised less skill in the labour process and had less independence from the paternalistic management of their large corporate employers. They apparently found it harder to mobilize collective resistance and had no unions before prohibition. Bartenders, though, were a different story. In 1891, although barred from membership in the Knights of Labor, their U.S. counterparts had founded the Waiters and Bartenders National Union, a craft union affiliated with the American Federation of Labor. In 1898 the union changed its name to the Hotel and Restaurant Employees International Alliance and Bartenders International League of America. The first Canadian local was formed in Brantford, Ont., in 1899, and by 1915 twenty-eight more had appeared across the country. The Canadian organizations were made up exclusively of bartenders, without any of the cooks, waiters, and dishwashers who worked on the same premises, or any women. In 1915 some delegates to the international convention even proposed splitting the bartenders from the rest and merging them with the brewery workers' union. Prohibition put an end to this discussion.[35]

In their contract negotiations from the start, workers in both breweries and barrooms demanded that employers display a union label as a sign that their workers were unionized. This was a strategy to use the popularity of beer among working-class drinkers as a lever on the brewers and saloon-keepers. Those who agreed would be rewarded with guaranteed sales among sympathetic working men, and unionists themselves would promote the consumption of

*In 1894 the owners and
workers of the Kuntz Brewery
in Waterloo, Ont., gathered
amid their tools and products
and faced the camera with
sober respectability. The
photo captures the pride in
the product that could unite
owners and workers.* (AO,
F 1405-17-21, MSR 1929)

union-label products and services through Union Label Leagues (jointly sponsored by other unions in consumer-goods industries, such as garment workers, bakers, broom-makers, and printers). Otherwise, union leaders warned,
consumers would be urged to boycott non-union products. Sometimes this
strategy required strikes to back it up, but not often in Canada. With the
important exception of Quebec, most brewers and saloon-keepers in the
larger centres accepted the union label.[36]

In the large cities almost all local bartenders and brewery workers were
unionized before the First World War. The particular market for beer and the
leverage available to the men who made and sold it had thus produced a
remarkable crossover of industrial relations and marketing strategy.

Taking Stock of King Alcohol

Reviewing all this information, the royal commission concluded that the
liquor traffic had deep roots and many spinoffs. It was a multi-million-dollar
complex of industries that could not be shut down abruptly without significant economic disruption in many parts of the country. Farmers supplied
barley, hops, and corn. Cooperages made the innumerable barrels, and glass-
works produced the bottles. Teamsters, railways, and ships transported all the

goods and supplies. Wholesalers distributed the product. Printers and publishers provided the flood of advertising. Furniture manufacturers fashioned the ornate saloon furnishings. Tobacco companies relied on selling cigars over the bar.

In the early 1890s the distillers and brewers had a capital of nearly $16 million invested in their production facilities, and they paid out more than $5 million a year for various supplies and services, including $1.2 million in wages to their roughly 2,400 employees. The retailing end of the trade had some $38 million invested in real estate, and paid perhaps as much as $10.5 million in wages to bartenders, warehousemen, and others. The majority report of the royal commission, noting that "these interests are very extensive," concluded that "any serious interference with the traffic must necessarily depreciate the value of a large amount of property—a property which . . . is equal to, or rather in excess of the whole of the chartered banks of the Dominion." Any disruption "would interfere, for a time at least, to no inconsiderable extent with the general business of the country."[37]

Lest politicians had forgotten, the commissioners reminded them that in the early 1890s the federal government was raking in some $7 million in excise and custom duties and licence fees for brewing and distilling, while provincial and municipal governments took in around $1.5 million in retail licence fees and fines. Indeed, from Confederation to the First World War, when customs duties and excise taxes filled up more than three-quarters of

Calgary's brewery workers were not alone in using a Labour Day parade to urge working men to drink only union-made beer. (GA, NA-3164-380)

the federal government's coffers, imported spirits and wine contributed between 10 and 13 per cent of customs revenue, and all alcoholic beverages (but preponderantly spirits) made up between half and two-thirds of excise revenue. Small wonder that federal excise officers were stationed in each distillery to monitor the entire distilling process, which could not proceed without their presence. Arguably, before the arrival of income tax in 1917, these indirect levies were the way that working-class drinkers massively underwrote state expenditures. As the hostile armies of teetotallers moved against them, both the producers of booze and the hotel-keepers would regularly band together to use such arguments to remind legislators and voters of their importance to the economy and the state.[38]

What the commissioners quietly sidestepped in their report was the liquor traffic's place as a fixture of the Canadian political process. Booze producers and retailers maintained close links with governing parties and were not shy about entering politics through a seat on city council or other legislative chambers. Political parties also recognized that retailing licences and inspectorships were lucrative patronage plums for the party faithful. This role became much more important as the vote was extended in the 1880s and 1890s to most adult men resident in a community. At the ward level, saloons remained vital to marshalling voters on election day. John A. Macdonald turned the tavern near his law office in Kingston into the local Tories' rallying point, and at the turn of the century an urban politician's evening campaign trail could often still be traced along the route between such drinking spots. The saloon-keepers could be useful too. "One popular tavern keeper can often do more than a score of worthy citizens in the way of influencing votes," a federal cabinet minister later wrote. Whether or not it was always justified, an odour of electoral corruption often hung around the taverns. No one was completely surprised when Sam Bronfman and several other Winnipeg hotel-owners got into hot water in 1914 for fraudulently registering voters in their saloons to support Manitoba's Conservative government. It was the importance of the liquor traffic for the party machinery, along with the revenues for state coffers, that would bring the federal and provincial governments into open conflict over constitutional control of the industry.[39]

The liquor traffic of the later nineteenth and early twentieth centuries, then, had evolved and changed considerably since the temperance movement had first confronted it before 1850. The numbers of producers had steadily shrunk, and while small-scale enterprises survived, especially in brewing, the liquor and beer industries were dominated by handfuls of large capitalist enterprises that had thoroughly industrialized their production processes and were aggressively promoting consumption of their products. In contrast, the

retailing end was largely in the
hands of hundreds of independent
shopkeepers who ran the local
liquor stores, hotel taverns, and
free-standing saloons in the face of
ever tighter government regulations on their businesses.

The liquor traffic was also a
complex set of social relationships.
Businessmen caught public attention, but workers were also unquestionably at the centre of it—as
proud producers, trusted bartenders,
loyal consumers, and citizen-voters.
What complicated the picture still
more was the central importance
of the saloon to the social life of so
many working men.

*When John Davis arrived at
the William Notman photo-
graphic studio in 1868, he
brought along the tools of his
trade as an excise officer. Like
other such employees of the
federal government's Excise
Department, Davis worked
inside a distillery, watching
over the whole process of
spirits production. His job was
to protect the government's
tax revenue by making sure
that the booze was made
properly.* (MM, I-30178.1)

Saloon-Keeping

From the mid-nineteenth century until the arrival of prohibition during the
First World War, hundreds of local taverns across the country formed the core
of public drinking cultures in Canada. The royal commissioners had difficulty
counting the total because licensing in most provinces was at the municipal
level, and in those cases the provincial civil services did not keep centralized
statistics. As early as the 1850s, in their efforts to make their premises more
attractive to paying customers, some tavern-keepers began to use the name
"saloon," hinting at the grander spaces on board ships. Whether or not inscribed
on a sign over the door, the name stuck as the generic term for the public
drinking house in Canada and the United States down to the First World War.[40]

Photographers were entranced by the turn-of-the-century saloon. Dozens
of surviving photos provide wide-open windows on these popular local
drinking establishments. They reveal the decor, the jaunty owner and his staff,
and the motley assortment of drinkers gathered in front of the bar. Although
the drinkers probably catch the eye first of all, temperance forces zeroed in on
the goal of that solidly built man in the sparkling white shirt, tie, and vest
behind the bar: to make money by selling large quantities of beer and spirits.
By the end of the nineteenth century, he was boxed in by the power of the

booze manufacturers and increasing state regulation, and he knew he had to keep excessive drinking from overflowing into disorderly behaviour. But he was also always interested in providing an environment where men—especially working men—would want to spend time and money. The commercial dynamic was central to the shape of saloon life in the half-century before prohibition.[41]

Until at least the 1870s, becoming a saloon-keeper was relatively easy. Licence fees were modest, and otherwise regulation was light. Typically a saloon-keeper left some kind of waged job to open a "groggery" in a working-class neighbourhood. Widows and other needy women might open small neighbourhood drinking places off their kitchens. Many unlicensed places (sometimes grocery stores) operated alongside the legalized premises. In the 1860s, for example, Halifax had between 30 and 120 illegal drinking spots amid its two to three hundred licensed taverns and shops, while Montreal probably had some eight hundred illegal watering holes, more than twice the number of licensees. Starting in the 1870s, however, temperance agitation and stricter licensing systems pushed out the smallest sellers, including most women. Female sellers were henceforth more likely to be bootleggers. Higher licence fees, more careful scrutiny of applications, and requirements that drinking establishments be part of hotels raised the stakes for getting into business. Like many shopkeepers in working-class neighbourhoods, most saloon-keepers nonetheless came from modest backgrounds. They lived alongside workers and shared more in the rhythms and values of working-class respectability than in the prim prudery of the middle class.[42]

The personality of the saloon-keeper helped to define the place. Joe Beef's Canteen in Montreal, one of the country's best-known establishments in the late nineteenth century, got its reputation in large measure from its remarkable owner, Charles McKiernan, an exuberant Irishman and former soldier with a generous hand for those in need and a sympathy for organized labour. He also had a penchant for poetry, which he both recited for customers and published in local newspapers. A few blocks away, another saloon-keeper was also known for his generosity: "Many a starving man who is on his feet to-day can say that he got a helping hand when down on his luck from the neatly dressed, hard-smoking owner of the Suburban," a Montreal journalist wrote in 1889. A quarter-century later, some saloon-keepers were still known to act as bankers for workers, to help them find work, and to contribute to such charitable institutions as the Salvation Army or the local sailors' home. "Cases are common of their paying a man's fare to a new job, giving meals and lodging," a Vancouver social survey reported in 1913. If they were members of an ethnic or racial minority, they doubtless played an important role as mediators and facilitators for their fellow countrymen in the city.[43]

In male-dominated frontier settings, such as Donald, B.C., in the 1880s, prostitutes might ply their trade in saloons, but elsewhere proprietors kept them out. Otherwise women were rarely seen in public drinking establishments in Canada by the end of the nineteenth century. Photograph by the Smyth Brothers. (GA, NA-782-2)

The space itself might not promise much. Typically these drinking establishments had little furniture beyond the big bar itself and perhaps a few wooden chairs and tables. Most men stood up to drink. Sometimes a pool table could be found in one corner, sometimes a small bowling alley. The air was invariably thick with smoke because many customers puffed on cigars and pipes while they drank. Many barrooms were grim, plainly built places with dank sawdust underfoot and little or no decoration. They smelled of stale beer, tobacco juice, and the unwashed bodies of working men. These places were particularly common on the waterfront or in frontier towns, where, as in pioneering days back east, there might be no other social centre in the town. A British journalist claimed to have found "more drinking saloons and bowling alleys than dwelling houses" in Victoria in the 1860s, and Winnipeg had eighty-six hotels cheek by jowl in the centre of the city in 1882, at the peak of its first boom.[44]

By the turn of the century the working man with a penchant for respectability was most comfortable in the many hotel barrooms in the larger centres—in places fitted up with ornate woodwork, huge mirrors, elaborate bottles and glassware, bric-a-brac, brass spittoons, and the inevitable brass foot-rail in front of each bar. The rooms were modelled, it seems, on the English "gin palaces," which had begun to incorporate such glamour back in the 1830s. As many photographers in this period realized, these accoutrements gave the two or three bartenders in each saloon the appearance of actors on an elaborate, brightly lit stage that dominated the whole barroom. Moreover, however dirty their work clothes, the drinking men could cockily lean back

On the industrial frontier, saloons like this one in Horsefly, B.C., were typically built simply and plainly furnished, but were nonetheless homey for men looking for good company after work. (BCA, C-09619)

against the bar, one foot on the rail, one hand on hip, the other clutching their drinks, and enjoy their own elegant appearance in the huge ornately framed mirrors behind the bartenders. Wiping the foam from their mustaches with one of the towels hanging along the bar front, and expectorating into one of the numerous brass spittoons at their feet, they could shift their gaze upward to the walls and the images there celebrating "manly" interests: pictures of scantily clad women, scenes of hunting trips and sporting events, or large stuffed animal heads. Across the great mahogany surfaces of the bar passed little but beer and whisky. At the turn of the century, beer cost five cents a glass and whisky ten cents a shot.[45]

Saloon-keepers provided working men with much more than drinks. On the industrial frontier in the north and west, their hospitable buildings were multipurpose community centres, just like the taverns back east in pioneering days. Elsewhere, saloons provided a space for socializing that the compact, four-to-five-room working-class houses of the period could not easily accommodate. Saloons might be the gathering places of workers from particular factories or railway yards. There men could pick up tips about jobs, and maybe even buy a foreman a drink to get hired. They could pass on news and gossip about the companies they worked for, the unions that might be started, the politicians that represented them, the local baseball teams, or their neighbours' philandering. Some men could find accommodation for a night or longer—sometimes in the nineteenth century only in the corner on the floor, but more often in small rooms upstairs. Most provinces eventually required that saloons be connected to hotels and provide rooms and food for at least some

travellers. Many of the "hotels" paid only lip service to these regulations and never actually accommodated visitors. Food was sometimes available, and some places provided free lunches to attract customers—though this was apparently done far less often than in the United States. Social survey investigators found none in any Vancouver saloons and scarcely any in Fort William and Port Arthur, Ont.[46]

Transient workers often used saloon quarters as their temporary home away from home. "Some of the lower class places are sanctuaries from arrest for vagrancy for characters who would otherwise find their way to jail if not provided with a refuge," a Regina superintendent of the North-West Mounted Police reported in 1899. Pay cheques could be cashed after banking hours. A tavern might also have the only available telephone or washroom. Politicians saw the advantages of hanging out in these places during election campaigns and buying rounds of beer for potential voters. The meeting rooms for rent in these establishments were convenient for a variety of organizations, although far fewer groups than in the past now made use of them, including unions, which preferred to meet in their own or fraternal-society halls.[47]

At the close of the nineteenth century, a New Brunswick songster advised men to head for Duffy's Hotel in Boiestown if "you're looking for fun

Photographs are the best surviving records of turn-of-the-century saloons. This shot of the Hoffman House barroom in Rossland, B.C., in the 1890s shows the adornments intended to appeal to the male customers, from the long mahogany bar to the spittoon on the floor and the huge painting of the seductive female hanging above the bottles. The notices about cheque-cashing and laundry point to the practical services available to the town's miners. Men could feel comfortable wandering in wearing their work clothes, and the two Black men at the end of the bar would not be excluded. (BCA, B-04642, from RHMA, 13-117)

By the 1870s many urban taverns offered some kind of entertainment. Montreal's most colourful example was Joe Beef's Canteen, run by Charles McKiernan. The customers could listen to McKiernan reciting his own poetry, watch an occasional minstrel show, or goad Jenny, the alcoholic bear, to have another pint. By the end of the century new regulations had pushed most entertainment out of Canada's saloons. From Le Canard, *29 April 1874. (NLC, NL 8707)*

Joe Beef's Canteen, Montreal.
Take away the Beef and Beer from the British Army, and England is no more!

—o—
JOE BEEF'S ORIGINAL GENIOUSES

Citizens, we eat and drink in moderation ;
Our head, our toes, and our noses are our own,
And all we want is to be left alone !
We eat and drink what we like,
And let alone what we dislike !

and enjoyment or inclined to go out on a spree." The places always offered plenty of entertainment. When customers at Thomas Lloyd's Tavern in Oakville, Ont., got bored with his raccoons and other captured animals, they could watch the owner feeding a live pig to the black bear chained to a pole in the backyard. Some Toronto taverns offered dog and cock fights and bull-baiting in the 1850s and 1860s. In Montreal Joe Beef's tavern featured Jenny the alcoholic bear and a menagerie of other creatures from the wild, including a live buffalo.[48]

Saloons also nourished a healthy respect for physical strength and athletic prowess, and for a time featured boxing or wrestling matches as spectator sports, until the law came down hard on these events. Saloon-keepers might also have facilities for playing pool or a game of cards (gambling was banned). In a few saloons, mostly in the north and west or among the most disreputable dives in cities, prostitutes might offer their services upstairs, but by the end of the nineteenth century local police had made this a risky business for saloon-keepers.[49]

In the 1850s some saloon-keepers began installing small stages for musical performances and variety shows, the forerunners of vaudeville and burlesque houses. In Toronto's Apollo Tavern the entertainment included blackface minstrel shows. A few made space for dancing. In Montreal's Horseshoe Saloon, located near the waterfront, men often entertained each other with song or dance on a small wooden stage, to the accompaniment of a resident piano player—a practice well known in England as a "free and easy." A Hamilton newspaperman later recalled similar gatherings:

In the second story above the majority of saloons were large assembly rooms that would accommodate from seventy-five to a hundred persons. Down the center of the room was a long table, and comfortable armchairs on each side of the table. Each saloon had its own regular habitues, and almost promptly on the hour when the chairman would call the assemblies to order every seat at the table was occupied. The first thing in order was to call for one's favorite beverage—whisky or beer—and the program opened with the song, God Save the Queen, in which all heartily joined. After this loyal preliminary, each guest was expected to tell a story or sing a song, at which most of them were quite clever; and on special occasions the landlord would furnish a trained glee club at his own expense to add to the pleasure of the evening. They were a jolly crowd that attended those free and easy entertainments, and as every guest was expected to keep his glass filled, they were a source of great profit to the landlord.[50]

Drinkers sometimes amused each other with stories, off-colour jokes, or recitations of popular poems such as Robert Service's "The Shooting of Dan McGrew." They might break into lusty choruses of popular songs, most of them apparently sentimental reflections on mothers and fallen women or hearty celebrations of the working man. Occasionally tempers would flare into fights, which became another spectator sport. A fight could erupt in response to insults ("coward," "cur," or whatever) or wounded honour ("your wife's a whore"), or through competitive challenges, such as a drunken claim to be able to "whip any man" present. Saloon-keepers who wanted to keep their licences would break up these fracases quickly or send the pugilists out into the street.[51]

By the end of the century, outside frontier settings like the Klondike, most of the informal and commercialized performances had moved out of the saloons under pressure from licensing authorities (such as those in Halifax who banned skittles, board games, music, and dancing in the 1860s) or in the hopes of attracting a wider audience that included women and even children. In 1893 the manager of Montreal's Lyceum Theatre told the royal commission that his was the only theatre licensed to sell alcohol left in the country. Canada would thus not have the equivalent of the British music halls, where booze was available.[52]

Still, saloon-keepers made a modest living providing an attractive, entertaining space for the many working men who were not willing to throw in their lot with the temperance movement. They were also prepared to band together to protect their business interests from the attacks of the dry forces.

Like many other saloons, the Royal Hotel barroom in Nelson, B.C., offered space for working men to amuse themselves, in this case with a game of cards or pool. This photo was taken around 1898 by G.W. Millar. (BCA, B-03169)

A Man among Men

The people who gathered in barrooms had their own ideas of what was supposed to happen there. Ultimately, for most of the time spent in public drinking establishments, the unwritten code of sharing seems to have been more important than competition, and even proving one's manhood by drinking to excess does not seem to have been typical. Together the saloon frequenters created a distinctive set of well-understood informal practices and modes of behaviour based on the particular mix of gender, class, and age that the rooms attracted—what some contemporaries referred to as "the working man's club."

The customers elbowing up to the bar in this period were almost entirely wage-earning men. Some women continued to help their husbands run hotels with saloons or (usually as widows) owned them outright, but they were rarely seen in the barrooms. Thanks to provincial laws and emerging custom, even barmaids were unknown in Canadian drinking establishments, in contrast to tavern management practices in Britain, Australia, or New Zealand. Women customers were just as scarce. The once common side entrances into somewhat quieter spaces for female drinkers generally disappeared. In the late nineteenth century a few liquor licences were issued for dance halls or parks,

A DRINKING "BEE" AT WHITE CHAPEL, DAWSON.

where men might be able to socialize with women, but, from the 1870s onward, the saloon was almost always a space without women. Even the Yukon Council banned dancing in licensed premises in 1901. Among the hundreds of drinkers that social survey investigators tallied up in St. Catharines and London in 1915, they found a total of only ten and twelve women in each city, all of them partially concealed in side alcoves. In Hamilton they spotted none. The small number of women willing to flaunt dominant bourgeois assumptions about the feminine ideal by enjoying the pleasures of booze in a public tavern faced harsh denunciations as "bad mothers," "fallen women," or prostitutes (though, other than in frontier environments like the Klondike, prostitutes were still seldom found in saloons). Aboriginal women who visited barrooms were particularly vulnerable to such charges, and to sexual abuse from men who identified them as "loose" women. Children were just as rarely

These Dawson women were brazenly flouting gender conventions for this carefully staged, turn-of-the-century photograph, but they remind us that some women did drink, sometimes in sociable groups, though typically outside saloons. (ASL, 41-53)

seen in saloons, unless they arrived with a pail or jug to pick up beer for a
parent, or slipped in with newspapers to sell.[53]

Saloon life contributed to a vigorous form of working-class masculinity.
Working men came together in a saloon as part of their gendered right and
privilege not only to participate in the public sphere in a way effectively
denied to females but also to leave most domestic concerns to the womenfolk. And here they cultivated the well-understood attributes of a hard-edged
"manhood." At least a few Canadian saloons even incorporated the ultimate
symbol of single-sex socializing: urination troughs in front of the bar.[54]

These drinkers also shared a working-class identity. After 1850 the tavern
had become more and more a social centre primarily for working people. In
the larger cities in particular, most businessmen and professionals were either
giving up the bottle or retreating behind the closed doors of private clubs,
where they could drink with their own kind, far removed from the rough-
edged rabble. Young middle-class men might slip away from bourgeois constraints to join the fun in a saloon, but the tone was decidedly proletarian.
Saloon-goers thus shared an experience of selling their labour power for
wages, which included their relations with their bosses but also the bonds
among workmates. From the work world they brought in a respect for manual
labour and physical strength, a specific occupational competency, and a pride
both in their personal accomplishments and in the value of working men to
industrial life. They also brought individual or collective resentments at any
insults or degrading treatment on the job.

Not surprisingly, then, the saloon might be the place that a spontaneous
strike was organized for the next day or that the need for a union got aired.
More often, it was a place to forget how the changing work world of capitalist
management was eating away at their independence, creativity, and dignity on
the job, and to find other ways of building working-class masculine identities
in their leisure time. Their discussions could range over activities that were
exclusively male—hunting and fishing, sports, or politics, for example.
Inevitably, relations with women were a central theme. In the saloon, these
men could smoke, spit, swear, fart, tell off-colour jokes, laugh and shout boisterously, ridicule women, and generally ignore the civilizing constraints of
domesticity. Social surveyors in 1913 were horrified to find "lewd and profane" and "coarse" language in many of the saloons they visited. Although the
sentimentality of song and storytelling might erupt into an appreciation of a
wife's fine qualities, drinkers were just as likely to fill the air with complaints
about nagging wives, warn each other about the dangers of designing women,
or extol the virtues of bachelorhood. Young men in particular made saloon

culture a symbol of their freedom from their mothers' apron strings and the shackles of marriage.[55]

A Brandon clergyman remarked on how many young men thronged the barrooms as he walked by, and, indeed, young bachelors probably made up the majority of a saloon-keeper's customers. Throughout this period they had enough time, money, and relative freedom to enjoy public drinking and set the pace of saloon culture. The life cycle of working-class males in Canada before the First World War included a long period of relative freedom in early adulthood. Until the turn of the century, boys typically left school to start work

Many men posing for studio portraits created vivid tableaux in which their shared booze symbolized both their comradeship and their defiant masculinity. The bonds revealed could be sexually charged. These young miners in North Wellington, B.C., seem to have turned their bottles into phallic images. (AO, F 1405-15-127, MSR 8361, File 48, Photo 1079)

around age twelve; after that point, new legislation and the appointment of more truant officers began to push the age up to about fourteen (Ontario took the lead in extending schooling, but other parts of the country tended to move more slowly). Since the average age of marriage for men remained in the late twenties until well into the twentieth century, these young men had ten to fifteen years with minimal domestic responsibilities. Initially their wage-earning was carefully under the watchful eye of parents, who expected all earnings to be contributed to the family coffers. But by their late teens and early twenties they were often able to negotiate to keep a larger chunk of their wages for their own use. They were also seldom expected to help out at home, as their sisters were. So, with cash jingling in their pockets, they could leave the household at night looking for fun and companionship. In their teens some boys joined informal gangs of boys who, when not skirting the edges of the law with some kind of petty theft or property damage, kept up an informal social life in poolrooms and on street corners, smoking, joking, and bantering with young women out for a stroll. By their late teens, they were slipping into saloons.[56]

Eventually the more adventurous among them might take off for months or years at a time to travel and work far from home, where they might spend their limited domestic time in urban boarding houses or bunkhouses in mining or logging camps. In the early twentieth century Canadian cities were

Each saloon developed its own flavour. In 1913 the Vendome Hotel in downtown Toronto apparently catered to a fairly respectable clientele. Yet the trough at the base of the bar, probably designed to carry away urine, reminds us that this was an exclusively male space. (CTA, SC 656-3)

overrun with newcomers in this young–adult age bracket. Many of them (especially those from continental Europe and Asia) carried their families' expectations that they would send home their earnings, but many also had limited contact with families. The big corporations opening mines, logging camps, or railway construction camps leaned heavily on this young, male, transient, immigrant labour. The Industrial Workers of the World, the militant new workers' movement that swept through Western Canada in the decade before the First World War, built its organizational strength and creativity on these young men. Among the skilled trades, young "boomers" brought a similar spark to many urban workplaces. Many of them, far from home, found the saloon the only place to socialize outside the tightly packed boarding houses or crowded family homes where they slept. In small-town Ontario in the late nineteenth century, single men bulked large among those arrested for drunk and disorderly offences. It may well have been the growth of this young, mobile element in the population in the decade before the First World War that accounted for the rising rates of per capita alcohol consumption and of public drunkenness.[57]

Whether living at home or hitting the road, these young, unmarried male wage-earners built a bachelor subculture that included vigorous sports, gambling, fighting, and sexual pleasures. At the centre of it all was the saloon. Some of them would find this lifestyle attractive enough to remain lifelong bachelors, but, at some point, most would marry. They then faced the hard decision about how far to distance themselves from the realm of John Barleycorn. Married men were expected to direct their energies to the serious business of supporting a family and to shift the focus of their time off the job to the domestic sphere. We have no quantitative measure of how many completely abandoned their youthful pleasures, but, in the face of family pressures and powerful bourgeois discourses linking respectability to family and home, most husbands and fathers probably cut back on their drinking. Some men were able to continue the bachelor lifestyle when they had to leave their families behind and travel far from home to find work. Yet even among those who stayed put, the world of the saloon remained a pole of attraction.[58]

Sometimes workers would show up in barrooms alienated and depressed, hoping to "drown their sorrows" quietly in a corner. A Montreal machinist reported to the Royal Commission on the Liquor Traffic that "here around Griffintown and Point St. Charles, if the people get little wages, it seems a hopeless task for them to live decently; they cannot take enough money home to live properly, and they live for an hour or two on liquor." But the drinking places did not in effect make much room for the solitary drinker, especially the unemployed man who had no money to pay for his drinks. As a Toronto journalist explained about the unemployed tramp in the 1880s, "Occasionally they invest the barroom to thaw themselves out in cold weather, and with a faint hope that someone will 'set them up,' but they seldom stay long, for they know they are not wanted by the proprietor."[59]

For most customers, saloons were much more convivial places—an "oasis of good cheer," according to a U.S. commentator. Whatever their state of mind, most workers swung through the saloon doors in search of good company among people of their own kind—workmates, neighbours, fellow countrymen, and, above all, other men. "The spending of money unnecessarily on, and the over-indulgence in liquor among the working classes . . . frequently result, not so much from a love of liquor, as from the love of sociable society; and in the comfort that is found in the places where the sale takes place, but often is not to be met with in their own homes," the royal commission concluded in 1895 (predictably, the commissioners' remedies were better housing and better "domestic economy" by working-class women).[60]

In an age in which respectable families put a premium on privacy, the saloon was probably the largest, most accessible indoor meeting place in a neighbourhood. By the 1880s, most of them were open from early morning until ten or eleven on weeknights and seven on Saturdays. Despite liquor legislation, many saloon-keepers apparently let drinking continue after the doors were officially closed. At almost any time of day or night except on Sundays, a man could wander in without being invited and join in casual socializing. Few men were kept out unless they made a serious nuisance of themselves, but some, especially people of colour, could be made to feel unwelcome. Most saloons had a regular clientele who provided the particular atmosphere of the place and eyed strangers cautiously. The crowds inside were not huge: during brief visits in 1913 and 1915 researchers found an average of sixteen to twenty-three customers in smaller cities' saloons (often many fewer) and thirty-one in Hamilton, where only five of the fifty-seven barrooms had more than fifty customers. Some drinkers might float between barrooms, but most of the places developed a distinctive flavour, and clientele, of their own. One room might be a favourite hangout for workers from a specific factory or trade. Another might reinforce that pattern by catering to a specific ethnic group—an increasingly important form of segregation as the numbers of Southern and Eastern European migrants increased after 1900. Still another might be simply the favourite gathering place in a particular neighbourhood.[61]

A specialized clientele also shaped the life of particular saloons. In Montreal in the 1880s, for example, sports enthusiasts flocked to the Suburban, militiamen frequented the Oxford, which was close to the city's armouries, and the horse-racing fanatics hung out in the Turf House. Most saloons built reputations for being quiet, lively, or "tough"—meaning mostly that the places were dirty, poorly furnished, and located near such other disreputable enterprises as brothels or gambling dens, and that the customers were probably poorer, more shabbily dressed, and prone to serious drunkenness and fighting. Transient workers undoubtedly learned where they could fit in from workmates or boarding-house companions.[62]

Once accepted in a saloon, a man was on an equal footing with everyone else. Whatever its condition, a tavern was a democratic space. The president of the American Federation of Labor, Samuel Gompers, later recalled that conversations in saloons "had a peculiar freedom from formality that engendered good fellowship and exchange of genuine intimacies." The continuing ritual of treating each other to drinks symbolized the bonds of mutuality and intensified the camaraderie. "There is a great deal of 'standing treat' among miners, and very expensive work it often proves, in more ways than one," a visitor to British Columbia wrote in 1863. According to a later reminiscence:

Drinking bouts for the whole night were then very common. Usually a party of boon companions—say eight or ten of them—would assemble in the sitting room of the hotel, next [to] the bar, and someone would at once "stand the treat" all round. This having been partaken of, one of the number would sing a song and then provide a drink all round. Probably a story would follow, succeeded by another drink; then another song and another treat, as a matter of course, and so the song, story and glass passed around until everyone had treated.

With these communal traditions, working men made the tavern a thriving centre of a value system that formed an alternative to the one they met on the job every day—a value system based not on the cold, market-driven relationships of wage labour, the restraints and delayed gratification of industrial discipline, or the narrow individualism and privatization of the dominant culture, but rather on comradeship, equality, and (particularly as the alcohol levels in the blood rose) raucous fun that flew in the face of prim bourgeois conventions. This was not a clearly articulated alternative, with an activist social or political agenda. It was a completely informal culture without any organizational structure that could be easily mobilized for larger social goals. Canadian saloons never did become hotbeds of left-wing organizing, as in some European countries. Although collective action on the job might be discussed, unions typically met elsewhere. A saloon was simply a refuge, a port in the industrial storm, a place where working men could informally nurture a different way of thinking and behaving within industrial capitalist society.[63]

This would be an unlikely place for anyone to stake a claim to manhood on the basis of being a breadwinner, as one might in negotiations with employers over wages. If the saloon's social relationships were at all family-like, it was as a world of brothers, in which the saloon-keeper played the only parental role as the father figure. Building bonds with other men was what really mattered, and storytelling, joking, singing, and, above all, treating were the critical elements. The customers did not rely upon open gestures of affection but bonded indirectly through playful, competitive jostling and joking that could overflow into fighting if personal boundaries were crossed. A young blacksmith from Ingersoll, Ont., who converted to the Salvation Army in the 1880s listed the barroom activities that he had abandoned and that must have filled the leisure time of many other young saloon-goers: "drinking, swearing, and telling yarns and sometimes fighting."[64]

Most likely this behaviour was not unique to the saloon, but was typical of the (little studied) informal interactions among working men every day on

Many working-class women must have shared the view of Ontario's prohibition newspaper that male drinking undermined family budgets. From Pioneer *(Toronto), 9 July 1909, 19 September 1919.*

Liquor Taxation

The way it is paid and earned

BREWER

PAY ENVELOPE

WIFE

HOME BREAKER

HOME MAKER

Which Will You Vote To Give It To?

the shop floor. The key difference was that socializing in the workplace was limited to times when the foreman was not watching, whereas in barrooms it lacked that authoritarian constraint. Emotionally and psychologically, the warm, supportive relationships created in this free-time, all-male environment could be as important as those found within families. Working men thus used the saloon and the associations within it to nurture a rewarding social life with other men like themselves and a culture of male solidarity that would help them cope with—or perhaps avoid—the demands of work and family.[65]

For much of the late nineteenth century, the main alternative to the saloon in most communities was the church (though ironically, in the decade before the war, some fundamentalist evangelical preachers found that they had to hold many of their revival meetings aimed at working men in saloons). But by that time, too, other commercialized space was opening for public socializing. Some of it—notably the poolroom, the sports stadium, and the lodge meeting room—merely extended the realm of male camaraderie. Other places were sites of heterosexual courtship—dance halls, roller rinks, skating rinks, steamer cruises, amusement parks, vaudeville houses. Yet, however much young women might coax their male friends to take them out to these new spots, the saloon never lost its standing as a mecca for countless working men. Only when the temperance forces managed to mobilize state power was it completely forced out of working-class neighbourhoods.[66]

A Menace to the Home

Temperance activists—and no doubt many working-class wives and mothers—had a much different view of the saloon than did the men who gathered there. The moral reformers talked about how the saloon drained scarce family income and promoted loutish drunkenness that flowed out into the streets and in the front door of family households. They tended to cast all working-class drinkers as degenerate drunkards, and repeatedly insisted that public drinking was the root cause of working-class poverty. They argued that men's earnings that should have gone to feed and clothe their families were wasted in the saloon. Police-court columns in the daily press provided regular examples of women publicly denouncing their drunkard husbands for failing to provide.

Yet although public drinking was an almost exclusively male activity, not all men who drank got drunk, and only a distinct minority posed serious problems. There is also good reason to doubt that drinking was a significant contributor to most poverty. In Britain highly impressionistic contemporary estimates of the portion of working-class income consumed in drink ran as high as one-third; but more careful calculations later found a peak of only about 15 per cent of British working-class expenditures in the 1870s and a steady decline to less than 9 per cent by 1910 (a U.S. study of British workers in the iron and steel and cotton industries in 1890 found less than 5 per cent). German studies in 1904 and 1909 found that the proportion of income spent on alcohol ran between 4.8 and 6.7 per cent. In the United States, contemporary investigators set the percentages even lower. In 1891 the U.S. Commissioner of Labor published the results of a large survey of nearly 1,300 working-class families. Among the nine occupational groups studied, glassworkers and steelworkers reported the highest expenditures on alcohol, at only 6.38 and 3.99 per cent of family income respectively; the other groups were in the range of 2 to 3 per cent (although individual cases could be dramatically higher). In 1903 the labor commissioner reported that only half of the working men surveyed spent anything at all on alcohol. British, German, and U.S. studies all indicated that spending on booze rose as income rose and that the poorest workers drank least (a now famous British memoir about growing up in the "classic slum" argued that in the early twentieth century many men could not afford to go drinking and simply hung around the house after work).[67]

Despite the limited availability of studies of Canadian working-class expenditures in the late nineteenth and early twentieth centuries, a few general patterns in the "drink bill" for Canadian workers' families are evident. As the mark of their status as chief breadwinners, most husbands and fathers regularly held onto, or negotiated from their wives (the families' financial managers), a small portion of their wages as their weekly pocket money to cover street-car fares, hair cuts, shaving cream, and other incidentals, as well as luxuries such as tobacco and alcohol. That small sum probably allowed at most only a few drinks a week (in the late nineteenth century the Toronto Police Court saw its fewest cases of drunkenness on Fridays, when "the boys are short of funds"). One working man wrote to the Toronto *Telegram* in 1886 to express the sense of entitlement to this kind of recreational drinking:

> Why should a poor man going home to his family, with $5 or $6 in his pocket (by his stipend for a week's hard toil from early morn till dark night), be arrested, dragged before the Magistrate and fined $1 and costs (in all about $4—nearly all he possesses), for simply taking a few glasses of liquor, or being unable to walk straight on the streets, but who nevertheless, if let alone, would reach his wife and children with most of his wages.

Most working-class families no doubt fatalistically accepted this male privilege as the right of the chief breadwinner, although it could certainly be a source of conflict if the family's income shrank as a result of unemployment, illness, or some other interference with male wage-earning. Given that alcohol consumption tended to drop in times of economic slumps, most men, it seems, were willing to cut back or give up drinking when the family budget got tight.[68]

Most likely, as in Britain, two versions of working-class masculinity co-existed: the "good" husband who accepted responsibility for limiting his drinking in the face of family need, and the "bad" husband who still seemed more attached to the bachelor lifestyle and indulged his thirst no matter what. Whatever the economic conditions, tensions would flare if a "bad" husband spent much more than the agreed-upon amount in the saloon and thus forced his wife to stretch the family's meagre resources. Some men refused to hand over much of anything to their families and drank up much of their earnings, forcing their wives and children to find other ways of making money. To make ends meet mothers might take in sewing or laundry, boys might sell newspapers or shine shoes, and other children might scavenge for food or fuel. Some women took their drunkards to court to get them legally barred from drinking establishments—a procedure popularly known as putting them on the "Indian List." A saloon-keeper could be charged if he served anyone on the list.[69]

Unquestionably many working-class families suffered severe deprivation as a result of the self-indulgent drinking habits of the male breadwinner. Winnipeg journalist James Gray has provided one of the best-known accounts of such a man, his father, whom he often had to retrieve from a barroom. Yet it seems likely that only a distinct minority of husbands in working-class communities were ever that dissolute and irresponsible.[70]

Chronic drunkenness was a more complex issue. Many men did get drunk, perhaps as a regular Saturday-night ritual, perhaps more often. Drunkards also spilled out onto the streets of Canadian cities, where they often upset standards of public order. Policemen often found men who had developed too great a fondness for alcohol spewing profanities at full volume and swinging fists at their drinking mates or lying in drunken stupors on the sidewalk. With the help of friends or family, the officers most often saw them home. Police magistrates nonetheless dealt with legions of these men, often as repeat offenders. At the turn of the century the number of convictions for drunkenness began to rise steeply; after hovering around 10,000 to 12,000 convictions a year across the country in the 1880s and 1890s, the annual totals had more than doubled by 1906 and hit nearly 61,000 in 1913.[71]

If, as the rising number of convictions seems to suggest, drunkenness was on the increase, that change was at least partly due to migration and its related effects: many more young, single men were moving into cities from the countryside and abroad, and once there they no doubt made full use of the barroom as a stage to play out their familiar rituals of boisterous braggadocio. Younger men were certainly overrepresented in the jail cells into which drunks were thrown. As well, the sharply reduced hours of drinking that licensing authorities were imposing on saloons, especially on Saturday nights, arguably encouraged men to drink as much as possible as quickly as possible, rather than pacing their drinking over a longer period. The shorter hours (and the closing of so many drinking establishments through licence reduction or local prohibition) may also have turned more committed drinkers to the whisky bottle available from a bootlegger and away from the less intoxicating glass of beer.

Then too, the staggeringly large increase in convictions for drunkenness may well have resulted more from population growth and heavy-handed policing than from a substantial change in "criminal" behaviour. The Canadian population grew by leaps and bounds after 1900, and those convictions still added up to only about one-third of all summary convictions across the country— the same level they had been since the 1880s. Perhaps most important, as a percentage of the adult male population, the convicted drunks still amounted to a tiny fraction of drinkers. "The drunkard, after all, important though he is, does not fill the whole sky," wrote humourist Stephen Leacock.[72]

Other evidence suggests that the menacing drunkard who loomed large in temperance literature was not the typical drinker. Two Montreal working men testified before the Royal Commission on the Liquor Traffic that, among the hundreds of workers in the factories where they worked, no more than three or four men were chronic drunkards. A unique glimpse through some barroom windows in 1913 and 1915 gives the same impression. In those years Canada's Methodist and Presbyterian churches undertook a set of preliminary social surveys of several Canadian cities, including assessments of the local "liquor problem," and produced the only available statistical snapshots of the relationship between drinking and drunkenness in the early twentieth century. Teams of investigators slipped into all the saloons in six cities for brief fifteen-minute visits to tally up the number of drinkers and drunks. These squeamish teetotallers lurking in the corners of the smoky dens of iniquity and nervously clutching their notebooks might well have had some difficulty distinguishing a drunk from an extroverted personality, but their reports do suggest that, for the vast majority of working men, drinking did not necessarily mean getting intoxicated.

When the investigators visited Hamilton's fifty-seven bars in the last hour before closing at seven o'clock on a Saturday night in 1913, they found only 217 of the 1,775 they counted who could be identified as intoxicated. In Port Arthur, a sweep through all the barrooms found only 29 drunken patrons among 224. A similar investigation in St. Catharines two years later found only 44 drunk out of 311 in the three hours before closing. In London that same year another group of spies spotted 195 out of 561 who were "apparently intoxicated." In four London saloons where "the evils and abuse of the business were most glaring," 67 out of 187 were alleged to be drunk.

Most of these observations were made late on Saturdays, when drunkenness was more likely to be a weekend celebration than an indication of chronic dependency. The many surviving photographs from the turn of the century also point to the likelihood that working men stopped only long enough for a brief period of imbibing.[73] The photos show almost everyone standing, with few chairs available for settling into prolonged boozing.

Whether on occasional binges or through compulsive drinking, some men unquestionably used drunkenness as an excuse to inflict violence on family members, particularly their wives. Women regularly presented their bruised and bloodied bodies to police magistrates as evidence of their husbands' drunken excesses. Courtroom testimony, however, usually revealed that the incidents were not a matter of irrational behaviour unleashed by the booze, but part of continuing patterns of conflict within the household, actions based on a husband's alleged failure to provide, or a wife's alleged inadequacies as a housekeeper, her assumed marital infidelities, or her own drunkenness. The confrontations often erupted in periods of unemployment for the breadwinner or inadequate wage packets for family upkeep. Yet, besotted with alcohol, a man might simply be acting on popular assumptions about the ups and downs of marriage, assumptions that allowed

Temperance propaganda often emphasized male violence against women and children. From Herald *(Halifax), 23 October 1920.*

for a husband's patriarchal right to "correct" his wife's slovenly, lazy, or disrespectful behaviour with mild corporal punishment (though in the process he might well go too far into excessive brutality). A drunken man's actions in the home could also be just as much a performance as they were in the barroom or on the street—for example, smashing crockery and furniture in symbolic aggression against his wife's domestic domain. The number of these cases that surfaced in courtrooms was small, but we can easily imagine that many more wives suffered in silence, especially since it would have been clear in newspaper coverage that magistrates most often urged reconciliation.[74]

Yet however much the patriarchal script of wife-beating was familiar across working-class (and, for that matter, middle-class) neighbourhoods, the temperance forces' claims that drinking inevitably led to this kind of domestic violence undoubtedly exaggerated a complex but most likely more limited experience. The urge to live a more respectable lifestyle must certainly have given many working men pause before using their fists on their wives, and wife-beaters would receive harsh words from male neighbours and relatives.

Although the saloon could certainly threaten working-class economic and physical well-being, most of the married men who dropped in for their pint probably had their families' tacit, perhaps grudging, consent to this compensation for the demands (and privileges) of wage-earning. Stephen Leacock urged his readers to realize "just how much a glass of ale and a pipe of tobacco means to a sober industrious working man—not a picture-book drunkard—after his hours of work. It puts him for the brief moment of his relaxation on an equality with kings and plutocrats." Many working men exercised a degree of self-control, whether to protect the family economy or, perhaps, to direct their money and energy into other consumer expenditures—a ticket to a baseball match, membership fees for a fraternal lodge, or even a downpayment on new furniture for the family home. Alongside the sober working-class teetotallers and the more dissolute heavy boozers, then, stood what was probably a much larger group of moderate drinkers. For those men, occasionally sharing a few drinks with friends (and perhaps, but not necessarily, occasionally ending up inebriated) fit into their sense of an acceptable standard of living and, despite temperance charges to the contrary, could co-exist with what they understood to be a respectable lifestyle. The efforts of saloon-keepers to provide a more refined atmosphere with gleaming mahogany and sparkling glass undoubtedly played on precisely this desire among many working men to reconstruct their drinking cultures as less disreputable leisure pursuits within industrial-capitalist society, rather than as some marginal remnants of a debauched pre-industrial past.[75]

Then again, the saloon was not the only site of drinking between the mid-nineteenth century and the First World War. Many people enjoyed alcoholic drinks in more private settings. Wealthy men sipped their claret or port in their exclusive clubs or hotels. Many upper-class women continued to keep a liquor cabinet stocked for entertaining at formal dinner parties. Some working men brought bottles home on Saturday night to be able to drink through Sunday, and sometimes their wives and neighbours joined in. Local bootleggers could expect brisker business after public drinking shut down. Moral reformers expressed horror at the intoxication that sometimes resulted in the family household. On special occasions, particularly for small celebrations with family or friends, working-class men and women might decide to pick up a bucket of beer at the local saloon (a take-out practice dubbed "rushing the growler"). Women in these families might occasionally join small, furtive female gatherings on back steps with a bottle from a discreet grocer or a local bootlegger or a pail of beer from a saloon.

When Toronto's new licence commissioners visited all the city's drinking establishments in 1905, they were "struck with the number of women who were served through side-door entrances." One labour leader worried that some working-class women got liquor while shopping: "They can go into grocery stores on the pretense of purchasing groceries and buy liquors at the same time, and the men will know nothing about it until their wives are to such an extent controlled by the use of liquor that they are past redemption." Some women in all social classes no doubt sneaked a sip or two from one of the bottles of high-alcohol patent medicine that sat in so many family cupboards. Lydia Pinkham's "Vegetable Compound," roughly 20 per cent alcohol, was wildly popular. When they drank, however, women seem to have been far less likely to engage in the binging and boisterous public drunkenness that was mixed into male drinking cultures.[76]

Some restraint was also necessary among the new European immigrants arriving in the early twentieth century. They still expected wine or liquor with their meals, and their fellow countrymen who ran boardinghouses evidently tried to provide it, sometimes in the face of police harassment with charges of "bootlegging." Growing numbers of Italian newcomers began producing their own wine. Booze had certainly not disappeared from the private lives of countless Canadians.[77]

John Barleycorn's reach into private life brought criticism from temperance forces, but the stalwarts of that movement generally left individual households alone (at least until prohibition was in place). The focus of greatest controversy was public drinking, and the space that had become a kind of "working man's club" was the central issue. The saloon was unquestionably a mixed blessing for the Canadian working class. On one hand, it was an important centre of male fellowship in lives that usually had few bright spots; on the other, it was a central institution of male privilege that drew men away from their families and drained away money often needed in the family household. It seems that there were many ways for working men and their wives to confront and negotiate these issues, with varying degrees of satisfaction. For the temperance movement, however, there were no subtleties or ambiguities. The glistening mahogany bar symbolized all that was wrong with the liquor traffic, and, as far as the teetotallers were concerned, it had to go.

Far back in the eighteenth century, then, alcoholic beverages had been one of the first products marketed commercially for mass consumption in British North America. By the end of the nineteenth century the purveyors of alcohol had made their products a leading item of discretionary expenditure among the growing number of people who relied on wages paid in cash. Indeed, workers with any excess cash were likely to fall back on these old, familiar items of consumption before they were coaxed into following new consumerist paths.[78] Distillers and brewers not only improved the quality of the liquor and beer they sold and made them more widely available, but also aggressively promoted consumption through increasingly sophisticated advertising. Their success, however, rested heavily on the ways in which working men used these products and the public spaces in which the drinks were available—the saloons—to nurture the warm glow of male working-class camaraderie outside the domestic household. The smallest-scale businessmen within the liquor traffic, the saloon-keepers, did their part to support both alcohol consumption and male bonding. King Alcohol, then, ruled over a kingdom of powerful capitalists, shrewd publicans, and thousands of willing working men.

THE CURSE OF CANADA.

IS THERE NO ARM TO SAVE?

five

The Long Arm of the Law

Opposite page: *The evil King Alcohol was featured in much of the imagery of the temperance movement, such as in this cartoon by J.W. Bengough, the leading Canadian artist in the cause. From Bengough's* A Caricature History of Canadian Politics *(Toronto: Grip Printing and Publishing, 1886).*

THE FEASIBILITY AND NECESSITY of Legislative interference and action on this subject can hardly be denied. As to a man's religious belief and modes of worship, no authority ought to stand between him and his God. But here is a question of public economy, public morals, public life.[1]

As early as the 1830s some temperance advocates, like this Methodist editor, were arguing that the state had to be mobilized to assist in the promotion of a "dry" society, but few had listened. In those early, optimistic days of anti-drink agitation, most activists had been confident that individuals could be convinced to give up drinking alcohol and that alternative social institutions such as dry fraternal societies would support these new resolutions. By 1850 many teetotallers were having their doubts about this proposition. John Barleycorn still stalked too many communities, subverting their victories and winning back converts. Now, temperance advocates believed, the state would have to step in to impose discipline backed by the power of the law. That meant measures aimed at both restraining drunkards and shutting down the liquor traffic. Legislatures had to be convinced to enact new laws, and police and courts had to enforce these laws. To that end, public opinion had to be mobilized through petition campaigns and plebiscites.

Still, temperance forces would have to live through decades of frustration and halting progress before being able to use the unusual atmosphere of a world war to make Canada "dry." In this long campaign much more was at stake than a glass of beer. As in the past, the anti-booze crusades of the late nineteenth and early twentieth centuries articulated a social and cultural critique with much wider implications. In essence, they still wanted to implant self-control as the central dynamic of behaviour and social relations at all levels of Canadian society; yet the times were changing. Canadian social and economic life had begun to revolve much more around wage labour in an urban, industrial capitalist society, rather than around the independent production that framed the horizons of the temperance pioneers of the 1820s and 1830s. Rather than tackling the remnants of pre-industrial popular cultures, as the earlier teetotallers had done, temperance forces were responding to the new place of booze in an industrializing society.

In the broadest sense, the activists were not only proposing a simple solution to social problems and conflicts—poverty, disease, crime, strikes—but also struggling to sort out how Canadians should best spend time and money in this new economy. They wanted to fashion morally appropriate ways of using the newly constructed "free" leisure time, now so sharply separated from paid work, and of participating in a consumer society, where so many more products, including leisure-time amusements and entertainments, could be purchased.

Temperance was part of larger cultural critique concerned about an apparently rampant lack of self-control and frugality and a disregard for "higher" forms of cultural expression: reading an instructive book, attending a lecture or concert, or taking a stroll in a public park. Curbing saloon life and rougher forms of popular culture would contribute not only to more "rational" recreation, but also to the disciplining of consumers. It would help people make more refined, morally sound uses of their disposable income, pulling them away from the pool halls, vaudeville houses, amusement parks, roller rinks, and brothels. The late-nineteenth-century movements to establish new urban parks, public libraries, amateur sports clubs, and the Young Men's (and Young Women's) Christian Association were all in the same moral-reform ball park. These were issues for middle-class Canadians as well as the working men they so often targeted, especially since the middle class had the time and resources that working-class families would not have on the same scale until after the Second World War.[2]

At root, then, a good deal of the recurring debate about booze between the 1850s and the 1920s was about the nature of leisure in an increasingly consumerist society. Of course, it was largely men's leisure pursuits that preoccupied the reformers, and temperance enthusiasts continued to assert their preferred version of masculinity—earnest and responsible, sober and restrained, purposeful and productive. With booze out of their reach, they believed, men would meet these expectations.

Locking up Drunks

The 1840s marked a sharp turn in official attitudes and policy towards heavy, and open, drinking. For generations public drunkenness had been tolerated to some degree as part of the familiar flow of social life. Drunks who became particularly disorderly or violent might expect a magistrate to punish them, but most drunken behaviour went unchecked. By the 1840s this kind of "rough" behaviour was beyond the pale of the more orderly, sober bourgeois society that was starting to take shape.

Where once the local gentry or leading employers had joined in celebratory binges in taverns and streets, now many in the upper and middle classes were drawing back and retreating into more exclusive, private lifestyles, distant from other social classes. Meanwhile, many plebeian men still indulged in binge drinking at the end of seasonal work or, increasingly, on weekends. For some, heavy drinking was a regular, compulsive behaviour displayed loudly and rudely on street corners. But all these drinkers soon discovered that Victorian culture was drawing a firm line that placed alcoholic revelry outside the bounds of bourgeois respectability. Drunken behaviour also seemed more threatening when combined with the influx of the thousands of new immigrants who flooded into the colonies in the years down to 1850.

Patterns of violent popular protest were causing concern as well. People were regularly forming themselves into angry crowds and surging through the streets to challenge other social groups or unpopular public policies. The respectable elements of British North American towns and cities were deeply concerned that they were facing a crisis of disorderliness arising from what they were calling the "dangerous classes." Special measures had to be devised to combat the crisis, and as the private household became the preferred space in bourgeois society, the use of public space became increasingly criminalized. The confrontation would follow sharp lines of race, class, and gender.

The first attacks on heavy drinking involved Aboriginal peoples. Clergymen had blustered against fur traders using booze in their transactions with Native peoples since the early days of the French regime. The royal government had tried to stem the flow, without much success, and, under British rule, no effective state power extended into the Western interior. The trading companies were the only centralized authorities, and they deferred to the fur traders' argument that the booze was necessary for keeping the furs flowing in, as long as competing traders were supplying it to the Natives. By the turn of the nineteenth century, some Aboriginal leaders themselves also saw the dangers and petitioned the authorities to ban booze from the trade. These pleas came in part from newly converted Christians in Aboriginal communities,

The Royal North-West Mounted Police clamped down on whisky smuggling on the Prairies, especially by Métis like these men. (NAC, PA-201330)

as well as from leaders anxious to rally their people against white incursions into their territories and societies. They had limited success at best—too many of their people wanted booze and could get it easily.[3]

Eventually even fur-trade company officials began to worry about the drunken binges occurring regularly around the trading posts. But only after an 1821 merger eliminated the competition did the Hudson's Bay Company undertake to suppress the use of alcohol in the fur trade. West-coast Natives were nonetheless still finding their way to illegal supplies of potentially poisonous rotgut in the 1850s, and by the early 1870s U.S. traders were peddling great quantities of whisky in Native communities on the Prairies, with devastating consequences.[4]

By that point, white Europeans were demanding a new, more constrictive relationship with the Aboriginal peoples as settlement replaced the fur trade throughout most of British North America. The new Indian acts passed in the British North American colonies in the early nineteenth century gave Natives the legal status of children and prohibited the sale of alcohol to them. This was part of the process of marginalizing and segregating them on reserves, where white missionaries and others wanted to reshape them into sober, settled, industrious—that is, "civilized"—citizens. Colonial legislators were determined not only to curb their consumption of alcohol, but also in effect to deny them access to the social life of white drinking establishments. When the Canadian government purchased the Prairies and the North from the Hudson's

Bay Company in 1869 and brought a large Aboriginal population into the new Dominion, it banned alcohol from that huge land mass, renamed the North-West Territories. Under the first federal Indian Act of 1876, Aboriginal peoples everywhere within the Dominion were denied access to alcohol—a law changed only in 1951.[5]

In many ways these constraints on Aboriginal drinking became models of public policy to which legislators would turn in clamping down on white drinking—which is why, eventually, anyone barred by law from buying booze was said to be on the "Indian List." White bourgeois culture had no tolerance for racial groups with a fondness for drinking heavily in public.[6]

This Sarcee man in Calgary, perhaps a cowboy, was violating the Indian Act's prohibition on Aboriginal drinking. Photograph by Arnold Lupson. (GA, NA-667-514)

The ban in all the provinces pushed Aboriginal drinking into the shadows, but did not eliminate it. Bootleg liquor found its way onto reserves, and sometimes was even produced there. Moreover, the many Native peoples who drifted into towns and cities found ready suppliers. Especially in Western Canada, courts regularly levied heavy sentences on First Nations people who were found drunk and on the people who had supplied them with alcohol. A new stereotype of the "drunken Indian" gradually emerged in urban Canada.[7]

Drunkenness was also under attack among whites. In the 1830s and 1840s moral reformers looked to a variety of new state-funded initiatives that would teach sober self-discipline to various deviants: "houses of industry" for the helpless poor, public schools for untamed youth, mental hospitals for "lunatics," and new penal institutions for various categories of criminals.[8] Men and women who drank enough alcohol to "lose control" increasingly found themselves targeted as problems to be solved by the new social engineering. By mid-century they were falling into the clutches of two new disciplinary forces, the law and the medical profession, both with their own solutions.

To strengthen the existing English common law, provincial governments and many towns and cities began passing laws to clamp down harder on public drunkenness, rowdiness, and vagrancy. Behaviour that was once merely annoying was now criminal. The Province of Canada passed its first Lord's Day Act in 1845 to eradicate various forms of public popular culture, including drinking, on the Sabbath. Most of these measures were consolidated into the new national Criminal Code after Confederation. At mid-century municipalities also began organizing new paramilitary departments of full-time, professional policemen to bring order to urban public space. A large part of their time on the job involved rounding up those found drunk and disorderly on the street. Some of the offenders were charged with the loose catch-all of "vagrancy." Police courts with full-time magistrates tried offenders on a daily basis.[9]

For ever larger numbers of the poorest working people, "drunk-and-disorderly" behaviour led to incarceration. Jails and prisons had been slow to emerge in British North America, and it was only in the early decades of the nineteenth century that jailing lawbreakers became the norm, rather than publicly shaming them with whippings, branding, or exposure in the pillory or the stocks. In the 1830s and 1840s, legal reformers gave new meaning to the locking up of convicts by convincing colonial legislatures that the experience should aim to reform their characters with Christian instruction and hard work, so that they would be less likely to commit the crime again. The state could address the specific problems of criminals through careful "scientific" classification and separation. Ideally, the drunkard committed to this reformed penal system would learn how to live a more sober, orderly, respectable life. In practice, the many new local jails and prisons fell far short of the reformers' expectations and remained crowded, dirty, damp, underfunded holding tanks with no services to help the impoverished workers who washed up there get back on their feet.[10]

The most common mode of dealing with what would later be called "problem" drinking among working people in late-nineteenth-century Canada thus became locking up the offenders. Although many police officers grew sceptical about the value of legal coercion (and often simply sent the less obstreperous drunks home), local jails became filled up with drunkards dragged in off the streets. In Halifax, Saint John, Toronto, and Hamilton, roughly half of those brought before a police magistrate from the 1850s to the end of the century faced charges of drunkenness and/or disorderliness. The

HAMILTON. AUTUMN MANŒUVRES.

largest number of men caught in this tightening web were unskilled labourers, many of them recent immigrants, especially from Ireland, and, in ports, sailors. Most of the alleged offenders had uncertain employment and were often on the move in search of work. They were still tied to the seasonal rhythms of work and recreation that gave them the time, space, and inclination to drink to excess. The much smaller numbers of women arrested for drunken and disorderly behaviour were also most likely Irish immigrants struggling with a life of poverty, sometimes working as prostitutes, and they tended to get more severe punishment for the violations of bourgeois gender expectations.[11]

Many of these men and women could not afford to pay fines when convicted and therefore often ended up behind bars for a week, a month, or more. A small but highly visible minority were repeat offenders who were in and out of jails and prisons on a regular basis. Some desperate people got themselves locked up regularly to avoid harsh winters on the street. Their

In the early 1870s, as this cartoonist documented, the police constables and magistrate in Hamilton, Ont., cracked down on public drinking. In this case both men and women were caught in the act. From Canadian Illustrated News. *(NAC, C-062942)*

significance in the prison population was usually exaggerated, as bourgeois Canada agonized over "habitual criminals," members of a permanent underclass.

The people arrested repeatedly for drunken and disorderly behaviour or vagrancy lived in working-class communities and were least able to hide their behaviour from public view. Their appearances before magistrates provided popular theatre for the many spectators who haunted city police courts and for readers of city newspapers, whose police-court columns regularly featured stories such as this report in the Hamilton press in 1872:

> The incorrigible Peter Kane was again brought into court, he having been arrested . . . last night on John Street, where he was very drunk and boisterous and using bad language. Peter was sent to jail for ten days without the option of a fine. Upon being removed from the dock, Peter cried like a baby, and would not stir until he was forced, pleading piteously to be fined and not to be sent to jail, but His Worship turned a deaf ear to his entreaties, as he had on so many times previously made faithful promises to abstain from liquor.

The Royal Commission on the Liquor Traffic was not amused. It found such treatment of drunkards "not only inefficient, but, as a general rule, demoralizing. . . . The associations and experiences of the common jails of the country cannot be considered to have a deterrent or elevating influence upon such persons." Hardly anyone was listening.[12]

Putting heavy drinkers behind bars was not simply a matter of the rich ganging up on the poor. Working-class drunkards were most likely to harm the people in their own families and neighbourhoods. In the second half of the nineteenth century, some families also took their drunken relatives to court to stop their abuse and violence. After failing to extract their husbands from barroom indulgence, with the family income being all drank up, wives might haul the men into police court and have them charged with criminal non-support or vagrancy. Provincial governments also provided new legislation empowering the courts to deny errant husbands the right to buy alcohol by putting them on an interdiction list (the "Indian List"), which would be circulated to all saloon-keepers with a warning about fines for serving such men. In 1887 British Columbia went one step further with a new (but rarely used) Habitual Drunkards Act, which permitted wives to petition to have their husband's property rights suspended and placed under the control of a trustee appointed by the courts (typically the wife).[13]

Working-class families could thus turn to the legal system for support in resisting the impact of drunkenness on their personal and domestic well-being. In many cases they found the police and courts unreliable allies because the enforcement of interdictions was predictably difficult. A "habitual drunk-ard" only added more harshness and insecurity to the lives of the urban work-ing poor in Canada's emerging industrial-capitalist economy.

Finding a Cure

Not everyone was content to let the courts handle drunkards. Many doctors thought they had better solutions. They tried to bring their professional expertise to the problem of excessive drinking, that is, to "medicalize" it. In this way, alcohol became part of the medical men's efforts to win a more secure status in urban industrial society by turning many human conditions into scientifically defined "diseases" that required their specialized knowledge and practices to cure. To carry out this agenda they required state support, as they did with their other projects in public health. A sceptical public needed to be convinced.

The mainstream medical profession in nineteenth-century Canada was ambivalent about booze. Some physicians mounted temperance platforms to point out the dangers to the body. Since medical research on alcohol was still limited, they drew heavily on the early writings of the American doctor Benjamin Rush, whose popular 1784 pamphlet, *An Enquiry into the Effects of Ardent Spirits on the Mind and the Body*, warned about the physiological dan-gers of alcohol consumption and connected it to various diseases, including outright insanity, as well as to anti-social behaviour. The "craving" for alcohol, Rush argued, was a disease in itself. Pro-temperance doctors denounced alco-hol in any quantity as a poison that led to physical and mental deterioration. Abstainers were alleged to live longer—and eventually, later in the century, they got better deals from insurance companies (which earlier had charged them more on the assumption that abstinence was abnormal).[14]

Temperance groups latched onto such ideas as scientific proof of their position and continued to agitate to have these views more widely accepted. By the end of the century the school curriculum in many provinces had incorporated "scientific temperance" classes to teach the harmful effects of alcohol. For a while in the 1890s, Ontario's public-school students had to read William Nattress's *Public School Physiology and Temperance* in their hygiene classes, where they learned that alcohol would rot their stomachs and endan-ger every organ of their bodies. The 1895 winner of the student scientific temperance essay competition in Toronto had heeded the lesson: she argued that booze "injures the body, causing scurvy, apoplexy, epilepsy, and harming each of our senses." Nova Scotia's high-school students learned from H. Newell

Martin's 1892 physiology textbook, *The Human Body and the Effects of Narcotics*, that "one of the worst features of the poisonous characteristics of alcohol is its power even in small quantities to create a craving for itself that often becomes irresistible." Teachers in training at the normal school got instruction on how to teach these issues, and temperance questions began to appear on provincial examinations.[15]

Plenty of doctors nevertheless continued to believe in the nutritious qualities and healing power of alcohol. Temperance activists were shocked to discover in the 1850s that the latest medical research was arguing that alcohol taken in moderation was not destructive, and within a decade alcohol had bounced back as a respectable part of evolving medical therapeutics, to be used as a valuable stimulant. The doctors' mid-century change of heart fitted into the shift in medical practice away from the "heroic" treatments of bloodletting and purging towards an emphasis on stimulation and nourishment. One physician responded to a House of Commons Select Committee inquiry in 1874 by arguing that "moderately used, not oftener than thrice a day at meal times, it is with many conducive to health, strengthening both the mental and physical powers." Another suggested that alcohol "is a food exalting both mental and physical force." Many medical practitioners prescribed various kinds of it to their patients (who seemed to expect it as regularly as twenty-first-century patients look to antibiotics as cure-alls). By the turn of the century, some physiologists were emerging from their laboratories to challenge the central tenet of "scientific temperance" education—that alcohol was a poison (their critique would help to push temperance into the broader subject of "school hygiene"). In effect, the medical profession was narrowing its positive assessment of booze from its nutrient qualities as a food to its healing power as a specialized remedy administered by properly accredited doctors (just as they were doing with opium and other drugs in the same period). Staking a claim for its curative powers as rooted in scientific research helped to bolster public appreciation of their professional status. Ironically, in daily practice doctors' prescriptions for alcohol (along with their patients' use of the potent patent medicines of the period, which could be up to 50 per cent alcohol) undoubtedly facilitated excessive drinking, especially among women, who could not comfortably enter saloons.[16]

Administrators of "lunatic asylums" also argued about the value of alcohol for their inmates. Many said that they could not run their institutions without it, while some shared the fears of a Kingston asylum superintendent: "Some physicians . . . prescribe it as a restorative, and assert that in wasting diseases it is useful in . . . preventing waste of tissue, neither of which effects I am quite positive it possesses." He insisted that it was "the most destructive agent to every organ or tissue of the body either in a state of health or disease." This division of opinion in the profession surfaced again when the Royal Commission on the Liquor Traffic surveyed Canadian doctors in the early 1890s. Of the 1,457 who replied to the commission's questionnaire (one-third of those surveyed), 90 per cent still prescribed alcohol as medicine. Yet three-quarters of them believed that total abstinence would create a healthier population, and three-fifths thought that moderate drinking was harmful to health (needless to say, the pro-temperance doctors were probably more likely to reply). There was nonetheless a strong current of opinion among doctors that objected to any proposals to take this question out of their hands through government-imposed prohibition. State intervention, they believed, should come only in the form of financial support for institutions and programs controlled by physicians.[17]

If alcohol as medicine was controversial, the issue of "habitual drunkenness" was scarcely less so. In the second half of the nineteenth century, many medical researchers began to call that condition a disease—"inebriety" (or sometimes "dipsomania")—that required the careful intervention of medical practitioners. Some joined the American Association for the Cure of Inebriates founded in the United States in 1870. Many no doubt thumbed the pages of its *Quarterly Journal of Inebriety*, which began to appear a few years later. They could also follow the work of the high-profile British society with a similar name founded in 1884. The new disease provoked widespread discussions in Western Europe as well. The "research" into this newly defined ailment consisted mostly of clinical studies of narrow slices of the population, many of them inmates of lunatic asylums or penal institutions.[18]

The medical definition of this disease was extremely fluid, sliding back and forth between the moral and the physical. Alcohol as a chemical was seen as physiologically destructive and addictive, but overcoming or resisting it required an act of determination. Heavy drinking was most often seen as a "disease of the will," an inability to exercise self-control akin to lying, stealing, and other immoral acts—a position that allowed sceptics inside and outside the medical profession to argue that naming this behaviour a disease was to give drunkards an easy rationale for their vice. By the 1880s the inebrietists' essentially moralistic diagnosis was folded into the new notion that heavy drinking resulted from a physical disease of the nervous system and was therefore a form of insanity. Booze was not the cause—it merely triggered the pre-existing lunacy. "Inebriety is a lesion of the brain which has gone so far as to affect the will-power," a writer in Canada's leading medical journal explained in 1889.[19]

The alleged causes of this "psychological" condition ran the gamut from emotional traumas to physical accidents, but growing numbers of specialists began to argue that it resulted from degeneration through inheritance. A debate thus opened up on the terrain of the emerging field of psychiatry. In 1911, seemingly unaware of its theoretical confusion, the *Journal of Inebriety* explained that its policy had always been "to keep prominent the fact that inebriety is a neurosis and psychosis and that alcohol is both an exciting and contributing cause as well as a symptom of conditions which existed before."[20]

Given the uncertainties about the origins of the "disease," plenty of ink was inevitably spilled over how to cure inebriety. There was agreement that the moral exhortation of the temperance movement alone was not enough, but less agreement on the relative importance of environment and heredity. The environmentalist minority believed inebriates could be cured if they were not only isolated from the "unhealthy" conditions that engendered the disease but also placed under the close care of medical practitioners. The most committed of these doctors proposed the creation of "inebriate asylums," modelled on the new lunatic asylums that were being built in mid-nineteenth-century British North America, as in many other parts of the Western world. Families could send their troubled members to them, and judges could compel chronic drunks to enter them. As in the United States and Britain, Ontario's Inebriate Asylum Act of 1873 and Nova Scotia's Habitual Drunkards Act of 1875 would make such committals easier, though ultimately funds were never provided for a specialized asylum. The "therapies" proposed were much like those applied to people with nervous disorders—isolation and a strict regimen of food, rest, and hygiene under careful, gentle supervision—and essentially aimed at a gradual withdrawal from compulsive behaviour. Otherwise the most common treatment was hydrotherapy—prolonged soaking in warm baths. The therapists assumed separate care for men and women and for different social classes. Upper-class inmates would live in separate wings and be exempt from the heavy labour that working-class inebriates would be expected to perform. Asylum enthusiasts often expressed contempt for the rough types who ended up in police court and eventually proposed separate "industrial hospitals" that sounded all too much like the "houses of industry" that many cities and rural municipalities had already set up.[21]

When, in 1891, Ontario's Prison Reform Commission recommended such an industrial reformatory for habitual drunkards, the government decided it would be too costly. Four years later the Royal Commission on the Liquor Traffic agreed that specialized institutions might have a better chance of reforming the inebriate than would common jails, but, in the end, few local politicians could be convinced that this treatment would be fundamentally different or could actually cure drunkards. Consequently, despite major efforts by a few doctors and the example of inebriate homes and asylums in the United States, Britain, Australia, and Europe, no such state-funded specialized institution for drunkards ever opened in Canada. The one built for this purpose in Hamilton in 1873 was quickly converted to a lunatic asylum. A city-wide plebiscite in Toronto in 1889 decisively rejected any expenditure on an inebriate asylum, revealing how little popular support could be mobilized for such a project. Rather, the work these places might have done was carried on within the more all-purpose, and increasingly overcrowded, institutions designed for the mentally disturbed. Between 1883 and 1920, for example, a third of those admitted to Guelph's privately run Homewood Retreat were inebriates. Overwhelmingly these were middle-class patients who could afford the high fees. When a male worker might be bringing home no more than $10–12 a week, no working-class family could pay the rates charged in 1894: $12 a week for more than twelve weeks, $30 a week for staying only a month. This class bias made it hard to argue for state support, because the large numbers of highly visible working-class drunkards would remain largely untouched.[22]

The growing numbers of physicians who believed inebriates had inherited their "craving" for alcohol shared the environmentalist concern that these degenerates be confined under medical care at an early stage, in the hope of weaning them from their destructive habit. Yet most of those in the medical profession who believed in the crucial importance of heredity saw little hope for drunkards in the end and took limited interest in them. Doctors' optimism about institutional treatment for any kind of mental-health problem was waning by the end of the nineteenth century. Prevention became more important than cure. Habitual drunkenness was only part of the generalized "degeneration" that medical men theorized about in the late nineteenth and early twentieth centuries. Under the rapidly expanding influence of the new "science" of eugenics, they worried about drunkards passing on their bad habits to their children, and argued that inebriate marriages had to be stopped. Over time heavy drinkers would tend to be lumped with the "unfit" and "feeble-minded," and concern would begin to shift to a focus on healthy mothering to prevent such progeny. Their pessimism about curing "inebriates" probably helped to undermine their colleagues' more optimistic projects for reforming heavy drinkers under medical care.[23]

Within their private practices, some doctors were ready to recommend chemical cures for the propensity to excessive drinking or, more often, for helping a person withdraw from the habit. This brought them onto the shadowy terrain of patent medicine, where numerous products were available. In

HER FATHER WAS A DRUNKARD

A Plucky Young Lady Takes on Herself to Cure Her Father of the Liquor Habit.

STORY OF HER SUCCESS.

A portion of her letter reads as follows: "My father had often promised mother to stop drinking, and would do so for a time but then return to it stronger than ever. One day after a terrible spree he said to us: 'It's no use. I can't stop drinking.' Our hearts seemed to turn to stone, and we decided to try the tasteless Samaria Prescription, which we had read about in the papers. We gave him the remedy entirely without his knowledge, in his tea, coffee, or food regularly, according to directions, and he never knew he was taking it. One package removed all his desire for liquor, and he says it is now distasteful to him. His health and appetite are also wonderfully improved, and no one would know him for the same man. It is now fifteen months since we gave it to him and we feel sure that the change is for good. Please send me one of your little books, as I want to give it to a friend."

FREE SAMPLE and pamphlet giving full particulars, testimonials and price sent in plain sealed envelope. Correspondence sacredly confidential. Enclose stamp for reply. Address THE SAMARIA REMEDY CO., 23 Jordan street, Toronto, Canada.

L'ALCOOL, VOILA L'ENNEMI!!

Victimes de la boisson
Voulez-vous vous guérir ?
Si oui Prenez le
REMEDE VEGETAL DIXON

Le seul Spécifique infaillible qui rende contre l'alcoolisme.

Traitement raisonnable, dé par nombre de médecins et amateurs des effets merveilleux. Non préférable à tous les "Gold Cures" en poudre.

Guérison garantie dans tous les cas et argent remis.

Peut être pris après un repas sans perte de temps, sans publicité, sans danger.

Une visite à notre bureau sollicitée aussitôt les plus incrédule.

J. B. LALIME, 572 Rue St Denis, Montreal.

Canadian newspapers regularly carried advertisements for drugs, presumably substances that made the drinker nauseous, to cure heavy drinking. From Spectator *(Hamilton, Ont.), 4 December 1902;* La Presse *(Montreal), 31 August 1901.*

the 1880s, the leading Canadian medical journal briefly gave favourable coverage to injections of bichloride of gold as a possible cure. This so-called "gold cure" was promoted widely through the ninety-two private clinics set up across North America as franchises by an entrepreneurial U.S. physician, Dr. Leslie Keeley. The men who checked into one of the Keeley Institutes for the three-week program (few women were admitted) subjected themselves to a kind of aversion therapy. Four times a day they were given a hypodermic injection of the "gold" (mostly strychnine) and every two hours a swig of a chemical cocktail that included atropine, a drug that eventually made the taste of alcohol abhorrent. Later, another injection of a strong emetic induced vomiting. Less well publicized was the regime of rest, good nutrition, pleasant socializing, and patient solidarity.[24]

Some doctors, even those running asylums, readily recommended the Keeley method, but medical journals eventually denounced the gold cure. The treatment nonetheless became immensely popular, especially among men who associated the physically demanding "cure" with a more vigorous masculinity than that offered by the temperance movement. All customers could take heart from the therapeutic optimism that insisted that the inebriate was not a prisoner of his or her heredity, as so many doctors claimed. Graduates of the program even formed their own B-Chloride of Gold Clubs as mutual-support agencies. Inevitably, many imitators and competitors appeared to capture some of this lucrative market. But too many of those "cured" by Keeley and other "quacks" slid back into drinking, and most of the "institutes" closed within a few years amid financial difficulties and medical scorn. The Keeley cure died out without delivering on its promise of the medical silver bullet for habitual drunkenness.[25]

Canadian doctors liked to speak with authority about alcohol abuse, and, to some extent at least, had won respect for their "expertise" by the end of the century. Yet, ultimately, like their counterparts in Europe and the United States, they could not reach a consensus about whether "inebriety" was actually a disease. The medical superintendent of the Toronto Asylum must have helped to muddy the waters when he testified before the Royal Commission on Prison Reform in 1890 that drunkenness was a "deterioration of character, not a disease." Some physicians maintained a class-based moral distinction that saw inebriety as a real disease growing out of a genteel existence, in contrast to simple "intemperance, the vice," which was allegedly rooted in rough working-class culture. Even without this class analysis, many doctors continued to believe, along with thousands of other Canadians, that drunks were simply moral degenerates who should be able to shake their bad habits through their own willpower. Such a diagnosis was saturated with the

Protestant evangelicalism of the period. It was therefore hard to proclaim such a condition a scientifically based disease and to "medicalize" it convincingly.[26]

In any case, by the end of the nineteenth century heavy drinkers had been targeted as a serious social problem. The term "inebriety" (and sometimes "alcoholism") was coming into wider use to describe their behaviour, but it lacked precise definition. It could be a description of the effects of frequent drunkenness on the body, or an attempt to explain its causes. There were no firm distinctions made between frequent drunkenness and alcoholism as some kind of chronic dependency. The medical community had failed to define the problem, and police constables and magistrates paid little attention to such subtleties as they rounded up the "habitual drunkards" and fined them or sent them back to jail. Although in the second half of the nineteenth century the legal and medical professions had appropriated much more responsibility for dealing with chronic drunks as individual "cases," they were not pursuing a common agenda of moral regulation. Before putting a man on the Indian List, magistrates never bothered to consult medical opinion. Medical specialists in "inebriety" had failed to draw these working-class inebriates into their professional care; many had never wanted them in the first place. Policing authorities seemed more concerned with public order than with personal reformation. In the end, the organization that took a leading responsibility for helping public drunks was the Salvation Army, which ran hostels in most Canadian cities after 1890.[27]

There is little indication that compulsive drinking declined, and for many working people, especially women and children, the inebriate who spent all his wages at the tavern or beat up members of his family remained a daily challenge. Meanwhile, the criminalization of public drunkenness provided temperance advocates with mountains of statistics allegedly proving the social costs of booze to Canadian society, adding new ammunition in their war on King Alcohol.

Battling the Bottle

The temperance movement made good use of statistics on drunkards' arrests, but it did not put much organizational energy into campaigning for this new criminal and medical regime. Helping the drunkard shake his bad habits had been a central feature of the early years of the campaign, but increasingly after 1850 anti-booze activists lost interest in personal contact with such individuals (other than perhaps their own family members). Analytically, their focus shifted to the supplier of alcoholic beverages—the "Liquor Traffic," "King Alcohol"—and, strategically, to state intervention.

The state had long kept a close eye on the production and consumption of alcohol, more so than on most other commodities in European colonial society, mainly to generate tax revenues and to maintain a modicum of public order in and around the taverns. From the earliest days of settlement, provincial governments licensed distillers and brewers and generally left municipal officials to regulate retailers. Provisions for inspection were typically poorly enforced before the mid-nineteenth century. Prosecutions were rare and convictions difficult, because few witnesses would testify against tavern-keepers.[28]

Temperance forces called for a much more aggressive use of state power to curb and ultimately shut down the liquor traffic. The demand marked a perceptible shift, both from the individual to the industry that supplied him and from the religious to the secular within the movement. "The cursed traffic has its grip upon the city's throat and is stifling it," a Montreal journalist wrote with a typical flourish in 1889. In parts of the temperance campaigns, the original emphasis on self-help—on convincing individuals to "take the pledge" and helping them find a new life—carried on, but, from the 1870s onward, that approach was increasingly overshadowed by the commitment to legislated repression. Now the reformers considered it necessary to protect weak people from the influence of the booze pedlars by completely cutting off the supply. As in so many other late-nineteenth-century social movements, the blame for personal and social problems was now laid at the door of a bad moral environment.[29]

Indeed, by the turn of the century the old teetotalling fraternal societies had slumped into a long-term decline from which they would never completely recover. As the head of the Royal Templars of Temperance told the Ontario Grand Council in 1902, their work had "partially changed, in character, from individual to Parliamentary and, in aim, from total abstinence to Prohibition. The old-fashioned lodges and local work [are] in some measure things of the past."[30]

Such arguments ran headlong against the general distrust of state intervention embedded in nineteenth-century liberalism, and required a theoretical reformulation of liberal thought. Temperance activists now emphasized the need to provide order and a proper moral framework for a society to work along liberal lines. They emphasized community responsibility over individual rights, when the two came into conflict. But they also argued that, for individual citizens to be self-sustaining and to exercise rational, independent political judgment, they needed to be protected from the demoralizing influence of alcohol. Liberty was impossible in a state of drunkenness. In keeping with liberals' antipathy to entrenched interests with undue power over governments, the liquor traffic was thus construed as an enemy of liberty and a corrupting influence within the body politic of a truly democratic society. "If the Liquor Traffic embrutes men, destroys homes, blights lives, degrades character, breaks hearts, ruins bodies and damns souls," one campaign leaflet argued, "then in the name of liberty we must overthrow the Liquor Traffic and give fuller freedom to body, soul, heart, life and home." It went on to quote a U.S. clergyman:

> The man who has not his mind is as much worse than the slave as is the brute. It is the brutalizing of the man, and hence the imposing upon him of the brutish fetters of slavery, that makes the slavery of drink; and the slavery-making of the drunkard-maker is the most detestable, hateful, and deadly that is known. Liberty? Liberty forever—the liberty of the man; the liberty of the citizen; the liberty of conscience; the liberty of religion; always, forever; more of it, in greater and deeper draughts, that liberty may enter into our very blood, that there may be less restraint upon the free limits of every man born in the image of God, but no liberty to do wrong, deadly wrong; no liberty to make slaves; no liberty to poison liberty; NO LIBERTY FOR THE Liquor Traffic.[31]

By the 1870s and 1880s the context for this analysis was changing rapidly. While the early temperance movement had ridden the tide of optimism that ushered in a liberal and more commercial social order, the blossoming of industrial capitalism in the second half of the century brought disturbing new class tensions in towns and cities across Canada. Charity workers found serious poverty. Doctors proclaimed the dangers of poor housing and sanitation. Urban wage-earners themselves found their jobs in the new capitalist workplaces changing disarmingly quickly and their ability to provide adequately for their families at risk. By the 1880s large numbers of them were organizing independent working-class bodies—craft unions, miners' lodges, and local assemblies of the Knights of Labor—to resist these new tendencies towards working-class degradation and to promote a social order that respected working people. The new temperance ideology offered a clear, compelling explanation for deteriorating living standards, political corruption, and social conflict in Canadian urban life, especially for the many prohibitionists firmly rooted in the middling and propertied classes. One evil force was at work—the liquor traffic—and suppressing alcohol would be the quick fix. What the temperance enthusiasts chose to ignore was that alcohol consumption in the country was not undergoing any dramatic expansion—indeed, many drinkers were shifting

Prohibitionists frequently placed the risks to boys, and the development of appropriate masculinity, at the forefront of their propaganda. From Pioneer (Toronto), 18 July 1902.

WHICH WILL YOU CHOOSE

For your bright-eyed boy, who stands to-day at the parting of the ways? Which road will your personal example induce him to take? The temperance way leads to usefulness, honor, peace and joy. The way of indulgence leads to ruin, sorrow, sin and shame.

"The crisis is upon us!
Face to face with us it stands,
With solemn lips of questioning,
Like the Sphynx in Egypt sands.
This day we fashion destiny,
The web of life we spin.

"This day, for all hereafter
Choose we holiness or sin.
Even now from misty Gerizim,
Or Ebal's cloudy crown,
Call we the dews of blessing
Or the bolts of cursing down."
—Lowell.

away from spirits, and even per capita figures on beer showed only modest growth.[32]

To point to booze as a convenient scapegoat is not to suggest any lack of sincerity among prohibition forces; many middle-class prohibitionists undoubtedly saw themselves as highly principled radicals involved in a major struggle to create a moral utopia. The new construction of the "Traffic" as a powerful economic force and the critique of profit-making in alcohol production and sales resonated with other new social critiques that attacked monopolies and "trusts" of all kinds and thus opened up possibilities of winning over wider support for their campaigns. Yet the temperance analysis made no frontal attack on the social order, and allowed thousands of Canadians to believe that sobriety was the simple remedy to most of the alleged ills of their society. There was a kind of complacency about critical social problems in such an analysis. Arguably, for example, once alcohol was banned neither low wages nor wife-beating could realistically be expected to disappear completely.

Both this analysis and the strategy of legal coercion reflected the social complexion of the movement. The wealthier and more powerful men drawn to the temperance cause were now solidly in the saddle of the movement. It would remain an alliance of diverse social forces, including large numbers of farmers, shopkeepers, self-employed businessmen, and some workers who aspired to respectability, many of whom would eventually tie their temperance principles to broader programs of social and political reform. But, from the mid-century onward, the key strategists and the commanding voices were drawn from families of professionals, businessmen, and others with a solid stake in the emerging liberal-capitalist order or, in the case of the many Protestant clergymen involved, who assumed that support from the propertied classes was essential.[33]

But class identity remained only part of the explanation for prohibition support. Evangelical Protestantism still saturated the movement, and temperance meetings were still punctuated with prayers, hymns, and invocations of missionary zeal. Those elements of the respectable propertied classes that embraced this fusion of the religious and the secular would sustain the prohibition cause. Others in similar class locations might remain aloof or, eventually, become overtly hostile to such moral fervour.

The message had to get out, and the temperance movement became an increasingly prolific propaganda machine, spewing out huge quantities of literature as news-sheets, pamphlets, posters, songbooks, poetry, playlets, and recitations. Well-advertised public meetings featured travelling lecturers (both men and women) and local drama and musical groups who took to the stage to entertain, educate, and organize. Temperance events were relentlessly earnest and didactic: "Every recitation, dialogue or song rendered, even by the youngest of the crowd, inculcated some strictly moral or temperate sentiment," one activist recalled. "Nothing merely comic was ever tolerated, so that the entertainments never degenerated, as is sometimes the case, into mere buffoonery." The arguments were often given a scientific cast, with a flurry of statistics on such subjects as the number of inmates of poorhouses, prisons, or lunatic asylums who allegedly drank, but the correlations were crude and unconvincing. Prohibitionists rarely did systematic social investigation, and seldom did the figures they flourished prove definitively the causal connections between drinking and poverty, crime, or insanity that they were alleging—nor did the available data on these issues in dry municipalities provide convincing proof that state repression of beverage alcohol sales had brought any significant social progress.[34]

Far more important was the use of dramatic parables to implant in public consciousness the powerful imagery of moral danger. On her wide-ranging travels, for example, Canada's leading female prohibitionist, Letitia Youmans, regularly delivered a lecture entitled "Haman's License," which compared the Old Testament story of a man licensed to slaughter Jews in return for silver to the modern liquor traffic. In the text and graphics of temperance publications, the "Traffic" came to life as reptilian beasts, serpents, or menacing birds of prey, often drawn from the imaginative realm of folk and fairy tales (there was far less interest in the apparent realism of photography as an educational tool). Much of this was home-grown propaganda—the prolific cartoonist J.W. Bengough was a stalwart in the movement—but much flowed across the border from the United States. Literature was imported in great quantities, and was frequently reprinted on Canadian presses. Articles from U.S. writers and news of U.S. struggles appeared regularly in Canadian temperance papers. U.S.

THE PROHIBITION YOUTH AND THE LIQUOR TRAFFIC GOLIATH

A CRIME PRODUCER

ABOVE LEFT: *Temperance propaganda drew on familiar imagery. Here the biblical story of David and Goliath is overlaid with the reptilian menace of a fairy tale. From* Pioneer *(Toronto), 31 October 1902.*

ABOVE RIGHT: *The saloon-keeper was often presented as a dangerous creature. From* Pioneer *(Toronto), 17 July 1903.*

temperance leaders were invited to Canadian podiums. Classics of U.S. temperance propaganda, such as the ubiquitous recitation "Father, Dear Father," about a child's fruitless efforts to convince his father to leave the saloon, and Timothy Arthur Shay's immensely popular play *Ten Nights in a Barroom*, were widely and repeatedly used to dramatize the cause. Perhaps most important, the tactics of mobilization and agitation owed a great deal to inspiration from south of the border.[35]

All of this activity could help to build support, but the central question for prohibitionists was how to get a law suppressing the liquor traffic on the statute books. They approached the seamy bear pit of Canadian politics with caution and disgust. For the most part, they refused to taint their noble cause by jumping into a partisan alliance with any political party. Instead, prohibitionists became the leading practitioners of a form of extraparliamentary pressure politics that would be taken up in the late nineteenth and early twentieth centuries by more and more social-reform organizations dealing with Sabbath observance, public health, prison reform, child welfare, and women's suffrage, among other causes. They positioned themselves as a morally superior grouping of concerned citizens capable of shaping public opinion and bringing it to bear on politicians. They were open and uncompromising, using their organizations to broadcast compelling arguments through speeches and lectures, newsletters, and pamphlets, to demonstrate the numerical strength of their support through large public meetings, mass demonstrations, and voluminous petitions, and to marshal large delegations to meet with politicians, especially premiers and their cabinet members.

By the end of the nineteenth century temperance leaders would prefer to avoid electoral politics in favour of direct appeals to voters through plebiscites, but, at the local level, they often still put pressure on candidates in election campaigns to support prohibition. They would attempt to be rigorously non-partisan, but there is no question that from the 1850s onward they knew that they could generally find more support among Liberals than Conservatives (even though both parties always had wets and drys).

SIR JOHN SURRENDERS HIS SWORD.

Prohibitionists believed that political leaders were under the control of the "Liquor Traffic." Here J.W. Bengough was denouncing Sir John A. Macdonald for weakening the Canada Temperance Act in 1883. From Bengough's A Caricature History of Canadian Politics *(Toronto: Grip Printing and Publishing, 1886).*

The Politics of Prohibition

Over the years prohibitionists succeeded in building a measure of public support for their cause and in compelling political leaders to take them seriously. But in their righteous distancing of themselves from the nitty-gritty of legislative politics, they watched in horror and frustration as their concerns were repeatedly sidelined, ignored, or watered down. Their crusade would stretch over seven decades before finally reaching the dry utopia that the movement dreamed of. It passed through four phases of renewed organizational strength and political influence, spaced out roughly at twenty-year intervals (the 1850s, 1870s, 1890s, and 1910s), each separated by setbacks and disappointments, until the arrival of a full-fledged, countrywide prohibition by the end of the First World War.

In the 1850s turning to the state was not a completely new idea within the movement. Some of the earlier temperance activists had tried to give state regulations more teeth to restrict retail sales. In the early 1830s, for example, the Nova Scotia legislature began receiving a steady flow of petitions asking for at least some restrictions on licences, usually through higher fees, as well as stiffer taxes on imported booze and controls on the appointment of local officials to limit the influence of liquor dealers. Under similar pressure, the Lower Canada and Upper Canada assemblies both enacted regulations, in 1831 and 1836 respectively, to impose minimum standards on taverns. Yet without adequate enforcement provisions, these controls remained mostly wishful thinking. More than one temperance petition hinted that the government should consider cutting off the liquor traffic completely. Although the Nova Scotia legislature alone set up special committees to study the issue seven times between 1834 and 1848, colonial governments were certainly not eager to take action against such a major source of revenue.[36]

After 1850, prohibitionists put increased pressure on all levels of the state. They often found that local battles were the easiest to win but the least effective in stopping the liquor traffic. A new era of British North American politics had just opened under the banner of "responsible government," and reformers in the new colonial governments were bringing in state measures to promote key elements of the new liberal order: public education, transportation development, legal reforms, and much more. In a similar vein, when special committees of the legislatures of Nova Scotia and the Province of Canada looked into the drink question in 1848 and 1849, their reports spoke bluntly about the urgent need to restrict the sales of alcoholic drinks.

Prohibitionists took up the cry. With unprecedented passion and a considerable degree of support, they demanded that the colonial legislatures ban the production and sale of alcoholic beverages across each province. Their inspiration was the state of Maine, which had brought in a weak prohibition measure in 1846 and a much tougher law in 1851 (soon known in temperance circles as the "Maine Law"). Some twelve other U.S. states and territories had followed suit by the mid-1850s. North of the border, under the driving leadership of the Sons of Temperance, the prohibitionists were remarkably successful. Their agitation brought huge petitions to the floors of the legislatures, many of them signed or sent by women, who legally could have no other input into the political process. In the Province of Canada a prohibition measure with solid support in the Assembly was defeated in 1855 only after the speaker rejected it on a technicality. In Nova Scotia a similar measure passed the Assembly but was defeated in the province's upper house. In New Brunswick an ineffective 1852 measure meant simply to stop importation was repealed in 1854, but later that year the so-called "smashers" won the election over the "rummies" and introduced the first prohibition act in British North America, which came into force on 1 January 1856. Riots broke out against the legislation, as they did on similar occasions in the United States, and the law proved generally unenforceable. Concerned that the prohibitionist government lacked a mandate for such a controversial measure, the British governor dismissed it and called new elections. A new government promptly repealed the act. Along with major setbacks in the United States, where prohibition was rolled back, rejected by the courts, or severely weakened in all but five states after 1855, the failure in New Brunswick took the wind out of the prohibitionists' sails and convinced many politicians that such a measure was unworkable in the face of such deep-seated opposition.[37]

Sobered by their setbacks, the prohibitionists regrouped and continued to demand government action. The second phase of prohibitionist agitation took off again in the 1870s. Organizationally, the movement had two important new dimensions. First, and perhaps most important, a new element joined the anti-booze forces: an independent women's organization known as the Woman's Christian Temperance Union. Concerned women had concluded that leaving the initiative to the men had not worked and that they needed to take up the cause on their own. Originally founded in the United States in 1874 in the wake of a remarkable surge of independent, grassroots women's agitation against liquor retailers, the WCTU had its first Canadian branches in the Ontario towns of Owen Sound and Picton later that year and formed a national organization in 1883. It was the first Dominion-wide, non-denominational women's group in Canada. It quickly grew into a mass movement among middle-class women. Some wives of skilled working-class men joined, but they were swamped by the wives and daughters of doctors, clergymen, and merchants. Some ten thousand of them wore the organization's white ribbon by the turn of the century, and nearly 17,000 by 1914, spread through cities and towns across the country.[38]

The women drew strength from the knowledge that they were part of an international movement with nearly one million adherents in branches and national organizations in the British Isles, all the white-settler dominions of the British Empire, Scandinavia, India, and China, all affiliated to the World's Woman's Christian Temperance Union (founded in 1891). For many years the Canadians' energetic leader was Letitia Youmans, who carried the temperance message in lecture tours across the country. By the turn of the century the organization had a paper—first *Canadian Woman*, later *Canadian White Ribbon Tidings*—to bind members together and promote their cause.[39]

Combining a fervent Protestant evangelicalism and a commitment to secular social reform, these female prohibitionists were determined to attack all the forces in their society that they believed threatened the home. With the all-encompassing slogan "Do Everything," coined by the U.S. WCTU's charismatic leader Frances Willard, they campaigned on many fronts. They took a particular interest in children, whom they attempted to organize into Bands of Hope or Little White Ribboners and to reach through "Scientific Temperance Instruction" in schools. They also worried about grown-up sons who were vulnerable to the attractions of the rougher male leisure activities in pool rooms, saloons, or brothels. Booze was a key concern, but they also attacked tobacco, child neglect, and the moral dangers to working women, and launched support programs for working-class mothers and children. Ultimately, they saw women as the chief victims of excessive drink.

The WCTU's earnestness and moral righteousness gave the whole temperance movement a new energy and renewed the sense of mission to purify society. It also gave many women across the country the opportunity to learn organizing and speech-making skills and to plunge into public agitation. Much of the time they were simply distributing literature and lobbying individual politicians, teachers, doctors, labour leaders, and many others to support their cause, but during the 1880s some WCTU activists contemplated a political program with broader dimensions of social and political reform. Starting in 1889, the organization regularly called for votes for women to give them the chance to implement their moral vision via the so-called "Home Protection Ballot." As a verse suggested, they were tired of men's approach to politics:

> We women pray for better times,
> And work right hard to make 'em;
> You men vote liquor with its crimes,
> And we just have to take 'em.

There was a relentlessly anti-male tone to much of the propaganda: men were weak, women were morally superior. These activists were feminists of a kind, not looking for radical changes in male and female social roles, but concerned to get men to respect women and their needs within the family and determined to enter public life to defend women and their domestic sphere against the abuses they faced in a male-dominated society.[40]

The second major development of the 1870s was the consolidation of a national prohibition organization. Provincewide groups had appeared in the 1850s, but in 1875 sixteen prohibitionist Members of Parliament convened a large gathering of temperance activists in Montreal to consider a countrywide force. An interim Dominion Prohibitory Council undertook to bring together the several arms of the movement under a new umbrella organization, and early the next year launched the Dominion Alliance for the Total Suppression of the Liquor Traffic (usually shortened to the Dominion Alliance, a named modelled on the United Kingdom Alliance formed in 1853). Branches soon

By the turn of the century the Woman's Christian Temperance Union had thousands of members across the country. Here the delegates to a regional convention pose on the steps of a Baptist church in Red Deer, Alta.
(GA, NA-5395-2)

appeared in all the provinces. The Alliance included the leading evangelical Protestant churches—the Methodists and Presbyterians—which had held back from formally endorsing this secular movement for decades. By the end of the century the churches had made curbing alcohol consumption central to their broader social-reform program, later known as the Social Gospel. This confrontation with the real-world issues of "intemperance" contributed to the increasing secularization of the evangelical churches. The Methodist Church once again set the pace when in 1898 it transformed its Committee on Temperance into the Committee on Temperance, Prohibition, and Moral Reform (later renamed the Board of Moral and Social Reform). Clergymen continued to be prominent spokespersons for the movement, and at the local level churches were often the organizing base of temperance campaigns. Churches also provided an increasing proportion of the funding base of prohibition organizations.[41]

The limitations of the prohibition alliance and its constituent parts were also clear. The members of evangelical religions who were drawn to the movement were "pietists," who believed in the importance of personal conversion and of establishing a rigid moral framework within society to sustain morally correct behaviour. In contrast, those who practised the more liturgical faiths (Catholics, Anglicans, German Lutherans, and Orthodox Christians in particular) relied on belief rather than action, and mediation by clerical hierarchy rather than state intervention. Not surprisingly, then, Anglicans played an extremely limited role, ultimately withdrawing from the Alliance's council. "The Church's work is to teach temperance on the basis of the moral, not of the civil law," the *Church Record* insisted in 1901.[42]

Roman Catholics stayed out completely, generally preferring to teach temperance and moderation through branches of their own League of the Cross or Catholic Total Abstinence Society. The divide had widened by the late 1880s, as the prohibition movement became overtly anti-Catholic and implicitly anti-French. Over the next thirty years, temperance activists could be heard to denounce the liquor traffic in one breath and Catholic schools in the next. After the turn of the century, the movement also showed massive intolerance of the new European immigrants, the bulk of them Catholics. The leadership of the prohibitionist crusade of the late nineteenth and early twentieth centuries had white skin, spoke with Anglo-Celtic accents, and glowed with evangelical Protestant righteousness.[43]

By that point the Dominion of Canada had been created from the merger and absorption of the various British colonies and territories across the northern half of North America between 1867 and 1873, and a new division of state power had emerged between federal and provincial authorities. There was plenty of confusion in the air about which level of government should be acting on the issue of alcoholic beverages. The British North America Act was ambiguous enough that both federal and provincial governments could (and did) claim constitutional responsibility (and thus access to tax revenues and patronage advantages). Sir John A. Macdonald's aggressively centrist government in Ottawa saw booze falling within both its control of trade and commerce and "peace, order, and good government," while the provinces argued that it fell within their specified responsibility for "property and civil rights." Regulating and even prohibiting the production and sale of alcohol thus emerged as a central issue in the growing confrontation between the provinces (especially Ontario) and the federal government from the 1870s to 1890s.

The country's highest court, the Judicial Committee of the Privy Council, passed judgment on booze-related questions several times. In 1882, in *Russell v. the Queen*, it ruled that the federal government could take action to prohibit the retailing of booze in maintaining "peace, order, and good government." But three years later, after the Macdonald government upped the ante by passing the so-called McCarthy Act to allow it to license retail outlets, the court ruled in *Hodge v. the Queen* that this legislation was ultra vires because licensing was exclusively provincial terrain. It seemed that both levels of government had some jurisdiction over booze, but the court had left an uncertainty about whether or not the provinces could also pass prohibition legislation.[44]

A decade later, under pressure from the temperance movement to act, the Ontario government wanted clarification, and the federal government eventually agreed to submit a set of questions to the courts. The outcome recognized that regulating booze would remain a shared responsibility. The Judicial Committee's historic ruling in 1896 (and further confirmation in 1901) gave the provinces wide powers to act within their borders, including control over most aspects of alcohol retailing, while Ottawa retained jurisdiction over manufacturing and interprovincial distribution—a decidedly awkward compromise for the prohibition movement.

On the Attack

Prohibitionists had not waited for this settlement of legal niceties before attempting to prod governments into action. They targeted the liquor traffic in its broadest sense, but in practice the powerful booze manufacturers got much less attention than the more vulnerable retailers—the tavern-owners and shopkeepers. At a point when the urban saloon was becoming more and more a hangout for working-class men, the temperance movement began to show a more blatant class bias.

The revitalized movement carried its campaign forward on a number of fronts. At the local level prohibitionists pressured municipal councils and provincial governments to reduce the number of licences handed out to taverns and stores. Partisan politics could be an obstacle in this endeavour. Invariably the positions of licence commissioner and inspector were patronage appointments for the party faithful, and licence holders were likely to feel pressure to fall into line with the party in power as well. As a result the goal of licence reduction could easily get bogged down, although the temperance groups never tired of demanding a vote on a local ballot to force the hand of the licence commissioners. Outside Quebec and British Columbia, their agitation eventually had considerable effect; the number of licensed drinking establishments plummeted abruptly. Several provinces set a ratio of licences to a specified number of people in cities, towns, and rural areas. Provinces made getting into the business much harder by implementing sharp increases in licence fees—generally $150 to $250 for a saloon or hotel in a city by the 1890s, and occasionally as high as $500 (Vancouver) or $800 (Montreal), compared to only $50 in Ontario and Quebec in the mid-1870s. The main casualties were small taverns, often run by women. The heavy pressure to eliminate shop licences also hit some female grocers, and as the WCTU had intended, further separated off alcoholic beverages from food consumption and domestic space.[45]

Under new laws, residents could also petition to keep drinking establishments out of their immediate neighbourhood. In the larger cities, many barrooms were thus squeezed out of residential areas, especially middle-class neighbourhoods, and they became concentrated instead in commercial districts or near downtown working-class neighbourhoods. Public drinking in most cities thus came to have a narrower geographical focus. By 1915, for example, London's twenty-six bar licences, and three shop licences, were all located in a half-mile square in the centre of the city, including a cheek-by-jowl cluster along one street that went by the name of "Whiskey Row" or "London's Bowery."[46]

The temperance movement's campaign also included attempts to convince provincial governments to enact tighter regulations on the selling of alcohol—hours of operation, provisions for travellers, spacial arrangements—and more effective policing mechanisms. These changes came in a wave of new legislation governing retailing in the 1870s and 1880s, notably through major consolidated acts passed in Ontario (1876), British Columbia (1878), Nova Scotia (1886), New Brunswick (1887), and Manitoba (1889). Sale by the glass or the "grunt" from the open liquor barrel was banned from grocery stores. In several provinces, licensed premises could sell only alcoholic beverages and tobacco products. Sales to minors (under age eighteen) were prohibited. New laws set fines for a saloon-keeper for serving a drunk, and made the owner legally liable if anyone died in an intoxicated state as a result of the service. To make taverns less attractive spaces for casual socializing and amusement, legislators gradually squeezed out gambling, pool, boxing, and other forms of entertainment. They more clearly specified and gradually restricted hours of operation, including a move to early-evening closings on Saturdays. Free-standing saloons were phased out in favour of those attached to hotels that had at least a few rooms for guests. In some provinces, licence-holders were forbidden from holding public office in a municipality.[47]

Starting in the 1870s and 1880s, Ontario, Manitoba, Prince Edward Island, and the North-West Territories (soon to be Saskatchewan and Alberta) all decided to take the administration of these regulations away from local governments and to appoint a board of commissioners for each municipality to administer the liquor licences and monitor local hotels and saloons. Each board had its own inspector separate from the local police force, as did some municipalities in other provinces. In Nova Scotia these inspectors had to be members of temperance societies. They got help from temperance enthusiasts who volunteered as informers, snooping about towns on the lookout for violations of liquor regulations in the hopes of getting a tavern-keeper's licence

CLOSING THE BARS ON SUNDAY.

Prohibitionists were frustrated that, although tighter regulations were often passed, enforcement remained a problem. Barrooms often still served customers on Sundays, in violation of the law. From Canadian Illustrated News. *(NLC, C-067667)*

withdrawn. Their success was uneven, and many regulations were poorly enforced, especially restrictions on hours of operation. Thanks to the temperance activists' pressure, however, public drinking had begun to be snarled in a growing web of regulations that brought an end to the free-and-easy access of the past.[48]

Never content to let John Barleycorn survive even in this more limited way, the temperance forces kept up the battle on yet another front: total prohibition. After failing in this regard at the provincial level in the 1850s, they pushed for, and got, provincial legislation to allow for what became known as "local option"—the right of residents in one town or county to vote for prohibition in their own community. In 1854 the Province of Canada had first authorized city councils to cut off all licences after a positive vote in a local referendum. Other provinces eventually gave municipalities this weapon. In 1864 the Province of Canada passed a more generalized law to shut down the liquor traffic by local option, putting in place a much more stringent measure popularly known as the Dunkin Act after its sponsor, Christopher Dunkin. After a committee of investigation appointed by the Liberal government in Ottawa supported prohibition in 1874, the national temperance convention in Montreal the following year demanded complete countrywide prohibition. In 1878, a year after the Supreme Court ruled that Parliament could act on these

ABOVE: *Even after a successful fight in a local-option referendum, temperance forces such as those in Napanee, Ont., in 1877, organized to ensure that the law was enforced.* (AO, C 233-1-4-2-54, 412)

OPPOSITE PAGE: *The 1864 Dunkin Act allowed for referendums in individual municipalities to shut down the retailing of alcohol. In 1877, at a point when the secret ballot had not yet replaced open voting in these contests and voting lasted several days, Toronto streets erupted in confrontations between wets and drys. The wet triumph prompted a boisterous victory parade. Line drawing by W. Cruickshank, from* Canadian Illustrated News, *15 September 1877.* (NLC, C-066046)

matters through its constitutional responsibility for trade and commerce, the federal government sidestepped the issue by enacting the Canada Temperance Act. Popularly known as the Scott Act (after its sponsor, R.W. Scott), the act gave all parts of the country the opportunity to exercise local option. Under this legislation, a quarter of the electors in a town or county could demand a vote on prohibiting the retail sale (but not the production) of alcoholic beverages within the municipality's boundary. The results of such a referendum, whether positive or negative, would be decisive and could not be challenged for three years. Fredericton became the first municipality to vote itself dry under the new legislation in 1879. Over the next twenty years, several provinces added their own versions of this legislative model, which co-existed with the Scott Act.[49]

As in the past, there was some voter support for the dry option in larger towns and cities, within respectable middle-class circles and among some working men. But the prohibitionists scored their earliest and most lasting triumphs in the rural areas of Ontario, Manitoba, and, above all, the Maritimes, where the Scott Act was used more often and more successfully than anywhere else in the country. By 1900 two-thirds of that region's municipalities, covering 70 per cent of its population, had voted themselves dry, and rarely was a decision in a rural constituency ever reversed. In the Quebec countryside, some of the local Catholic priests, who were otherwise opposed to state-imposed prohibition, also supported local option as part of their efforts to promote abstinence under clerical supervision. Across the country, as small-scale producers still committed to independence and self-respect, farmers formed the solid base of rural prohibition sentiment.[50]

Not all campaigns bore such fruit, however, and in many communities local victories were never fully secure. The decentralized local option strategy was slow and tortuous because, in practice, the results created a patchwork of dry and wet areas. Temperance forces had to fight back a new challenge in 1885 when the Canadian Senate passed an amendment permitting the sale of beer and wine in dry areas (the House of Commons rejected the bill). The campaigns for local option could be rough-and-tumble confrontations that pitted prohibitionists against angry crowds of young men who liked their beer or whisky. In 1877 the one attempt to close all taverns in Toronto by local option saw hundreds of rowdy working men challenging prohibitionist voters who approached the polling platform. The measure was defeated, and ten thousand people joined a torchlight parade to celebrate. In the same year George Sleeman led a parade through the streets of Guelph behind a float with a figure of Gambrinus, Greek god of beer, to celebrate a similar victory

TORONTO.—SCENES DURING AND AFTER THE MEMORABLE VOTE ON THE DUNKIN ACT.—FROM SKETCHES BY W. CRUICKSHANKS.

over prohibitionists in Wellington County. Of the eighty Scott Act plebiscites fought between 1879 and 1898, fifty-one were defeats for the drys.[51]

Moreover, many communities repealed local prohibition after a disappointing trial period. In 1888–89 alone, twenty-nine dry counties voted to end the Scott Act local option, including all of those in Ontario. Five years later the Royal Commission on the Liquor Traffic found only twenty-seven municipalities in the whole country covered by the Scott Act (and one in Quebec under the old Dunkin Act), all but two of them in the three Maritime provinces. Perhaps most important, most cities and large towns voted down local prohibition and stayed wet until the First World War. In Nova Scotia, Halifax remained a wet oasis surrounded by complete prohibition in the rest of the province. Even in Quebec, the wettest province, half the licences issued were in the Montreal district alone by the 1890s.[52]

Beyond their obvious failure to drive John Barleycorn from the bastions of boozing, the prohibitionists particularly resented how much alcohol was transported from the wet areas to be sold in the dry municipalities, legally by mail order to private households or illegally in unlicensed drinking establishments popularly known as "shebeens" or "blind pigs." In the early 1890s, F.L. Fanshawe, a British writer, visited the Maritime provinces and found, "In some, if not most, of the towns drink is obtainable by anyone who wishes for it." The Royal Commission on the Liquor Traffic heard repeatedly how the illicit watering holes proliferated after the licensed places were closed. Local law enforcement was often haphazard and unenthusiastic, especially since local residents often refused to testify against lawbreakers. Fanshawe heard that in Ontario's Halton County, a model of prohibitionist victory, "Such a revulsion sprang up in popular sentiment that it became impossible to obtain convictions. The inspector might walk into a place where liquor was being served and drunk before his eyes; [but] when the case came before the magistrate, witnesses would swear positively that no liquor was sold. Perjury was naked and unashamed." The prohibitionist victories remained hollow when the liquor traffic was still alive and well inside the many outposts of temperance purity.[53]

The situation on the Prairies was particularly disturbing. In the North-West Territories, the former Hudson's Bay lands west of Manitoba, prohibition had been firmly implanted as government policy. This was a beefing up of the long-standing policy to cut off the supply of alcohol to Aboriginal peoples, which would be expanded in the Indian Act of 1876. The new Royal North-West Mounted Police (RNWMP) had been sent out to enforce such Dominion regulations, and had some initial success in curbing the flow of liquor, especially from the nefarious "whisky traders." Yet, by the 1880s, as more white settlers arrived, the law had become a farce in practice, openly flouted and ignored. Whites could easily get a permit to import liquor for their private consumption, and smuggling reached huge proportions. Long drunken binges were common. "If a man had a permit for five gallons of whisky all his friends called on him," a Brandon journalist told the royal commission, "and there was what was called in that country a general jamboree until the liquor was finished." Hotels had no qualms about selling booze openly across the bar. The alcohol available might be adulterated rotgut, and one Brandon doctor said he had difficulty getting good-quality liquor to use in his practice. To the horror of those committed to racial separatism, "mixed-bloods" regularly spirited booze onto Aboriginal reserves.[54]

The RNWMP found effective enforcement of this odd legislation impossible and repeatedly complained to Ottawa. In 1888 the new lieutenant-governor tried to channel consumption along safer paths by allowing the open sale of 4 per cent beer, but the result was only more legal confusion. The federal government finally repealed its prohibitory law in 1891 and enabled the territorial council to bring in a year later a new act allowing for licensed saloons and regulations like those in other provinces.[55]

Modernizing the Movement

By the close of the nineteenth century, then, prohibitionists had little to cheer about. The voluminous evidence presented to the Royal Commission on the Liquor Traffic in the early 1890s had confirmed their worst suspicions: under both the licence system and the patchwork prohibition of local option, enforcement was lax, and alcohol still flowed out to thirsty drinkers from druggists, bootleggers, moonshiners, out-of-town mail-order services, and far too many licensed retailers. Something more had to be done.

The prohibitionists not only needed a new strategy, but also found themselves on shifting ground. Beginning in the 1890s, and over the next thirty years, the Canadian economy was shaken up by the arrival of huge new industries—wheat, pulp and paper, hydro-electricity, hardrock mining, steel and auto production, and much more—and a new form of business that reached out across the continent—the corporation. Immigrants poured into the country in record numbers to provide much of the muscle for this booming economy. The largest number of them came from the British Isles, but an unprecedented proportion migrated from outside the British Empire, notably from some previously untapped regions of Southern and Eastern Europe.[56]

In their jobs these newcomers and the Canadian-born found that corporate administration of business was shaking up the world of work with managerial and technological innovations that ultimately added up to a Second Industrial Revolution. Spiralling retail price inflation began to threaten real wages. The country's growing cities soon faced problems of overcrowding and inadequate transportation and health facilities. The Canadian state confronted new pressures at the national level: internally, the need to accommodate population growth by creating two new provinces on the Prairies (Saskatchewan and Alberta), and, externally, the push to participate in the politics and defence of a more integrated, aggressive British Empire.[57]

All of these developments proved controversial for large groups of Canadians, who forged new social movements of diverse kinds to resist them or smooth out the rough edges. Groups of businessmen looked for bureaucratic models of state regulation that could bring more order to the marketplace. Municipal reformers pushed for new kinds of urban planning. Revitalized farmers' organizations questioned the economic priorities of governments and corporations. New unions and working-class political organizations challenged the impact of corporate decision-making on the workplace. Various organizations targeted urban slums, public-health issues, and education and child-welfare problems. Women's organizations demanded fairer treatment for females. Moral-reform societies tackled "white slavery" (prostitution), gambling, juvenile delinquency, and other forms of disreputable behaviour, along with drinking, using new provincewide umbrella organizations known as Social and Moral Reform (later Social Service) Councils. Ethnic tensions boiled over into politics as enthusiasts for Anglo-imperialism promoted closer attachment to the Empire and worried about the dilution of the "racial stock" by many of the new immigrants, while francophone Canadians organized to defend their ethnic heritage and resist the pull of imperial entanglements.[58]

There was no single "Progressive movement" to which all these groups rallied. Each of them organized around its particular concerns and had its own constituency and specific agenda. Yet they were not completely isolated from each other, and there was often considerable overlap in personnel and program. Most shared both a faith in science, rationality, and (the new business buzzword of the period) "efficiency" on the one hand and a sense of moral earnestness and renewal on the other. Protestant and Catholic churches encouraged that link by turning their attention to questions of social and moral reform in what would become known as the "Social Gospel" and "Social Catholicism." They promoted new "sociological" investigations, including the social surveys of 1913 and 1915, to "prove" the impact of alcohol on Canadian societies.

Not surprisingly, participants in many of these diverse movements supported prohibition as part of a loose agenda of reform measures aimed at restoring order and direction to Canadian society. One of the activists, for example, was Frank Spence, perhaps the best-known prohibition propagandist in Canada before the First World War. As a prominent member of Toronto's city council for two decades before the war, and ultimately a member of the Ontario Municipal Association, Spence was also an active campaigner for female suffrage, public ownership of utilities (including Ontario Hydro), and city planning (notably the development of Toronto Harbour). Just before the war a Saint John schoolgirl captured the range of this kind of reform vision in a prize-winning essay on civic improvement. She highlighted prohibition as the most pressing need, but tied it to the importance of a public library, playgrounds, better policing, a chemistry lab in her high school, and the new centralized form of municipal government known as a board of control. Her ideal city would be orderly, rational, Christian, and free of alcohol.[59]

The social complexion of the temperance movement from the 1890s onward was still broad and mixed, but arguably less inclusive than it had once tried to be. The dominant voices and the mass of the active membership came from two distinct locations in Canadian society: some (and by no means all) elements of the urban Protestant, Anglo-Canadian upper and middle classes (businessmen, lawyers, doctors, journalists, clergymen, and others of the respectably self-employed), along with their francophone Catholic equivalents in Quebec; and the more commercially engaged farmers and other respectable folks in the countryside. Each of these groups enjoyed a measure of success in the rapidly changing social order of early-twentieth-century Canada, and each had broader concerns about how their society was evolving—and booze was only one part of those concerns.

In cities prohibitionists might still attract some working-class support, but overwhelmingly the adherents were drawn from the middle and upper classes. For urban activists and supporters of the turn-of-the century prohibition movement, attacking drunkenness was often part of the pervasive "Progressive" agenda of modernism and its fascination with the organizational imperatives of the new corporations. The much older identification of temperance with economic "progress" was now recast in new terms.

"Temperance work today is very practical as compared to the sentimental exhortations of yesterday," the president of the Winnipeg District WCTU stated in 1913. "These are days of efficiency." This speaker can be forgiven for failing to notice how much of the older sentimentality survived, but a new layer of arguments did try to emphasize how suppressing alcohol was part of the larger project under discussion inside business management, municipal government, public health and education departments, and many more circles—a project to reshape society according to the dynamics of a more centralized, bureaucratized, corporate-capitalist economy. Prohibition would help to impose rationality and order on social and economic behaviour and to make people more ready to participate in the new capitalist order of "efficiency" and "modernity."[60]

The business idiom became commonplace in prohibition campaigns. Activists liked to cite the prohibitionist ideas of Henry Ford, who connected sobriety with managerial innovations such as his automobile assembly line. Ontario's Liberal leader, Newton W. Rowell, made the same case: "Modern science and industrial investigation show that the use of alcohol impairs and injures human efficiency, lessens the capacity of the worker and produces social degeneration." While some of the prohibitionists' contemporaries might hear vaguely anti-business, or at least anti-monopoly, sentiments in their attacks on the liquor traffic, the critique made no fundamental assault on the prevailing economic system and instead strongly identified with its main dynamics.[61]

Support for prohibition in the countryside was similar but different. As in the more distant past, rural temperance supporters were among the most commercially oriented in their farming communities. In Ontario the strongest rural support came in a band of Southern Ontario counties surrounding the major cities, and in Manitoba in the southwestern region of the province. Across the country it was the small towns in such rural areas that harboured the hard core of leading temperance activists. Although Canada still had many marginal farms where families combined subsistence agriculture with some form of wage labour, more and more farmers were running commercially viable farms that required sober hard work to succeed. By the early twentieth century, they were also concerned about how booze might harm the operators of the new machinery on their farms. "This is an age of power machinery and fast transportation," the *Farmers' Magazine* argued. "It demands clear heads and kindly hearts. Befuddled brains must assuredly be responsible for hurling many a monkey wrench into our delicate social machinery when liquor is openly sold."[62]

In these ways rural prohibitionists were much like urban temperance supporters. Yet they tied their concerns about drinking to a deeper critique of developments within the evolving industrial-capitalist society. In Eastern and Central Canada, they worried about the large-scale outflow of population from rural communities. In all parts of the country they viewed the burgeoning industrial cities as threats to all the core values of rural life. A series of huge agrarian protest movements—from the Grange and the Patrons of Industry in the late nineteenth century to large regional farmer organizations after 1900—undertook to mobilize a rural alternative to the economic and political degradation that they perceived in Canada. Booze stood out as a central symbol of that general social decay.[63]

In 1914 the Alberta farmers' organization declared, "The practice of treating at public bars and other places of intoxicating and alcoholic liquors is proving demoralizing and a public menace and a national calamity." Treating "causes moral and physical degeneracy, personal and public poverty, and indebtedness," the farmers said, while insisting, in contrast, that agriculture was "the mistress and school of sobriety, temperance, justice, religion and in short all virtues." On the Prairies the Manitoba and Saskatchewan Grain Growers' Associations and the United Farmers of Alberta all proclaimed their support for prohibition.[64]

Making the saloon the central focus of prohibitionist agitation united diverse groups, including these Presbyterian Sunday School students in Calgary. (GA, NA-1639-1)

These rural voices brought a democratizing current into temperance campaigns, attacking political corruption (to which the liquor traffic was identified as a major contributor) and linking prohibition to political reforms such as proportional representation, direct legislation, and women's suffrage. Small wonder that, in the 1914 Manitoba provincial election, the ruling Conservatives denounced the reformist, prohibitionist Liberals as the party of "degenerate republicanism."[65]

Democracy had more resonance, it seems, among rural prohibitionists than among their city counterparts. In practice, many urban prohibitionists were a good deal more suspicious of democracy, especially when votes went against them. They could only understand this kind of electoral behaviour as manipulation, and never made the same claims when the outcome of pathetically small votes brought victory to them. For much of the leadership of the movement, like so many "Progressives" of this period, democratic procedures were a means to an end rather than a goal in itself.

In an age when the British Empire loomed much more prominently over public life, most prohibition supporters in city or country also shared a concern about nation-building and insisted that sobriety was a central feature of either Anglo-Celtic or French "civilization." They worried that the new European immigrants in particular represented a growing bloc of resistance to the anti-drink cause and that the cultural virtues of the "race" were therefore in jeopardy. By 1909 a Toronto temperance leader would regret the "influx in the last few years of many foreigners still far behind our glorious land in moral development." Winnipeg's J.S. Woodsworth believed that some Eastern Europeans were "addicted to drunken sprees." In the eyes of the Dominion Alliance, it was essential to make Canada "the land which is to give the world a civilization embodying the best features of older civilizations without their drawbacks." Temperance became a matter of "good citizenship." "Do you belong to the British Empire?" the editor of the WCTU's magazine asked in 1915. "Then you belong to the blessed race, the blessed Empire—God's chosen rulers of the world."[66]

The revived temperance forces in francophone Quebec did not embrace such imperial sentiment (and indeed were, in part, rallying against it), but nonetheless linked abstention from alcohol with the survival of the French "race." A Catholic temperance congress saw intemperance as "one of the worst enemies of our religion and nation," while Monsignor Paul Bruchesi denounced it as "a real national curse."[67]

In all these ways, then, the prohibition movement shared ideological space with the "Progressivism" of the period, but its central focus put it at the crustier, more rigid end of the continuum, in company with "social purity" activists and other moral reformers. Progressives generally looked to the state for one of three forms of intervention: reformation of character through specially designed institutions (schools, playgrounds, juvenile courts, social-settlement houses, medical clinics), regulation through new agencies (commissions or boards), or outright legal abolition backed by strict policing. Most prohibitionists had abandoned any faith in using institutions, whether self-help temperance societies or inebriate asylums, to reform drinkers. They were fundamentally opposed to merely imposing a tighter regulatory regime on the liquor traffic—that would be an unacceptable compromise with evil—and so they clung to the least flexible and most authoritarian option. They put no faith in the rule of the "experts" extolled by so many "Progressives," and instead expected heavy-handed policing to maintain public morality. In this sense, their project set them apart from the more administratively innovative approaches to the state in the period. Their ultimate success would require the authoritarianism of the wartime state.

Let the People Decide

In the face of numerous setbacks, prohibitionists had begun a third phase of organizing by the early 1890s. In that decade they mobilized once again for a single piece of legislation at the national level or, failing that, in individual provincial jurisdictions—a direction that the U.S. movement had been following with renewed vigour since 1880 (the new departure in the United States was to use plebiscites to try to get anti-booze amendments incorporated into state constitutions).

A large national convention called in Montreal in 1888 to discuss political action had divided on the best way to get a prohibition act. A minority group wanted independent political action modelled on the Prohibition Party launched in the United States in 1869, which had won 250,000 votes in the presidential election of 1888 and would continue to be active well into the early twentieth century (in fact, it still exists). A radical wing of the Canadian movement in Ontario walked out of the Montreal meeting and established its own national Prohibition Party in 1887–88 to carry the fight into legislatures. A separate Maritime Prohibition Party appeared in Nova Scotia in 1889. Each was soon organizing in local ridings and publishing its own newspaper. In the early 1890s this current in the movement dubbed themselves "Advanced Prohibitionists" and continued their political organization outside the Dominion Alliance. Independent prohibition candidates also ran in the Ontario and Manitoba provincial elections in 1902 and 1903.[68]

But none of these political projects managed either to convince enough temperance supporters to join or to make any dent in the electoral process. At the 1888 convention, the Alliance had adopted instead a non-partisan political strategy of organizing outside party structures and supporting prohibitionist candidates of all political stripes. Between elections, that also meant amassing signatures on petitions and sending large delegations to meet with provincial and federal politicians regularly and persistently. At the forefront stood the Alliance's irrepressible national secretary, Frank Spence, followed from 1907 by his equally dynamic brother Ben. At points over the next quarter-century, prohibitionist organizations in some regions of the country would become the most powerful extraparliamentary force in Canadian politics outside the business community.

Like the Anti-Saloon League organized in the United States in 1895, the Alliance also had a much narrower political agenda than did the Prohibition Party—suppressing the "Traffic" was limited to closing commercial outlets and not embedded in a wider program of social and democratic reform. The mantra of prohibitionist organizations for the next three decades became, simply, banish the bar, abolish the treating system among drinkers, and close the club—and the last of those was a marginal theme because there were relatively so few clubs, and their activities were more or less concealed from public view. "The open saloon, the public bar, where treating for the sake of good fellowship goes on, the brilliantly lit and attractive bar-room, these are the temptations we have to fear," the Toronto *Star's* editor wrote in 1898. Prohibitionists made the glistening bar the central image of their demonology, the symbol of the commercialized vice that they were determined to root out.[69]

These more limited goals aimed at public drinking could shore up support among middle- and upper-class Canadians by turning the heat primarily on working-class men and their allegedly disreputable social lives in saloons. In these bourgeois circles, a moral-reform thrust that targeted proletarian drinking cultures was a non-threatening response to distressing social problems and conflicts. It also formed an alternative to the equally disturbing voices coming from the new labour and socialist movements, which were trying to make class a more divisive flash point in Canadian society. Moreover, although total abstinence was still the goal, the prohibitionists' shrewd political strategy was to target the legalized sale of booze and public drinking, not private consumption at home. Building momentum to close the saloon was politically a far more realistic goal than proposing to invade family households (especially the wealthier ones with well-stocked wine cellars). A focus on banishing the bar ran the risk of alienating citizens from working-class, Catholic, or European-immigrant communities, but in any case those were not the movement's prime constituencies.[70]

In contrast to their U.S. counterparts, Canadian prohibitionists could not as easily target individual politicians to win over legislatures. Local groups might try to pressure candidates in legislative or parliamentary elections, but stronger party discipline in the Dominion made it necessary to deal directly with governments. Although both the major parties were tainted by association with the liquor traffic, the Liberals still offered the best hope (Frank Spence remained an active Liberal). Wilfrid Laurier, leader of the Opposition in Ottawa by the early 1890s, and his counterparts who held power in several provinces were under relentless pressure. Laurier confessed to an Ontario friend that he was "more in dread of Temperance than of Senate reform." He worried that "some friend, saturated with temperance, but intemperate of language, will propose as part of our platform, some temperance notion, which it will be impossible for the party to agree upon." An Ontario Liberal cabinet minister explained to Laurier how his party was caught "between two fires— the temperance party on the one side and the liquor party on the other." A pattern emerged in which these politicians made vaguely supportive statements, but tried to deflect such a hotly controversial topic into channels that would avoid having their parties stick their necks out.[71]

In 1892, under the weight of 2,626 new petitions with over 300,000 signatures, the Conservative federal government responded to the prohibitionists much as it had to labour leaders a few years earlier, by trying to bury the issue in a royal commission. The five-man Royal Commission on the Liquor Traffic in Canada held hearings across the country (and in the United States) over the next year and a half, and heard from a parade of municipal officials, law officers, clergymen, employers, and sundry other self-styled experts on alcohol consumption. Although not a member of the commission, Frank Spence was allowed to question witnesses on behalf of the prohibitionists, as was lawyer Louis Kribs for the "liquor interests." The commissioners heard a sprinkling of wet voices, mostly producers and retailers (significantly, no mere consumers), but most witnesses argued that booze was bad for individuals and society to some degree. No clear consensus emerged, however, on the benefits of prohibition in theory or as experienced either under the Scott Act or in the North-West Territories. The commission's two reports, released early in 1895, criticized much about the liquor traffic, but, to the disgust of the temperance movement, the majority report, signed by four members, recommended no more than tighter regulations and explicitly rejected full-fledged prohibition (the teetotalling clergyman on the commission appended his dissent). In effect, the commission identified the two options that would be argued out over the next twenty years: more rigorous regulation of licensed retailers versus a complete shutdown of the "Traffic." Prohibitionists all shared the view of Winnipeg's Young Men's Prohibition Club, that licensing was a completely unacceptable "compromise with the powers of darkness."[72]

Meanwhile, provincial governments had turned to a device rarely used beyond the municipal level in Canada to settle major disagreements about public policy—the plebiscite. Putting the issue to a vote of all electors allowed governments to avoid taking the lead, or to take no action if the results were negative or ambiguous. Although the Judicial Committee of the Privy Council would rule in 1901 that legislatures could not delegate lawmaking powers to such direct votes, the political hot potato of liquor policy would be thrown to voters in provincial and federal plebiscites thirty-four times over the next half-century, far more than any other single issue in Canadian public life. The first votes were held in Manitoba in 1892, Prince Edward Island in 1893, and Nova Scotia and Ontario in 1894. Each registered large majorities for turning off the tap, but in each case low turnouts gave cautious governments cause for delay, as did the lingering constitutional ambiguities about which level of government could act. The turnouts were not surprising, because many newspapers had reported widespread apathy during the run-ups to the vote. The results also confirmed the depth of support in rural constituencies (unless they were Catholic and French) and the much narrower margins of support in urban areas (where turnouts were lowest).[73]

Nationally, the strong prohibitionist forces in the Liberal Party convinced Wilfrid Laurier, now prime minister, to follow through on promises made in the 1893 Liberal policy convention and 1896 election campaign to hold a national plebiscite on prohibition. This was the first time that this procedure had ever been used at the national level (voters had not even been asked to express an opinion about the Confederation agreement in 1867). Putting the Prohibition Plebiscite Act through Parliament provoked extensive debate about whether there was room for such a vote in a British parliamentary system of representative, not direct, democracy, and about how the government intended to interpret (and act on) the results. The measure passed nonetheless, and on 29 September 1898 eligible Canadian voters (all men) had the opportunity to express an opinion on the question: "Are you in favour of the passing of an Act prohibiting the importation, manufacture, or sale of spirits, wine, ale, beer, cider, and all other alcoholic liquors for use in beverages?" The Dominion Alliance turned on the heat. It blanketed the country with attacks on alcohol and the "Liquor Traffic" in nearly nine million leaflets, forty thousand cartoons, and ten thousand posters.[74]

The outcome was a slim majority of 51.3 per cent in support of the question asked, but, with only a 44 per cent turnout (lower than in the earlier provincial plebiscites), Laurier could argue that only 23 per cent of the electorate had endorsed prohibition. In Manitoba and British Columbia only three eligible voters out of ten turned out, and in the North-West Territories fewer than four in ten. Arguably many anti-prohibitionists had stayed away from the polls. Laurier also recognized the divisiveness of the issue. Not only did most of urban Canada reject prohibition (all but a handful of the largest cities voted wet), but regional differences were also marked. The Maritimes' results were a resounding endorsement of prohibition—82 per cent in favour, and only three of thirty-six municipalities opposed—while British Columbia had a scant majority of under one thousand votes. Most important for Laurier, Quebec's predominantly francophone voters were overwhelmingly opposed, as were most constituencies with large French Catholic populations

CITIZENS AWAKE AND ACT

Prohibitionists turned up the political temperature in provincial and national plebiscites in the 1890s and early 1900s. In the 1902 Ontario campaign, voters were presented with terrifying images of the degradation that saloons brought. From Pioneer *(Toronto), 24 October 1902.*

in the Maritimes, Ontario, and Manitoba. As a politician dedicated to avoiding this kind of ethnic split, the prime minister refused to take any action.[75]

Defeat at the national level set Canada's prohibition movement on a different course from its U.S. counterpart. South of the border, as state prohibition experiments were failing and the Supreme Court reinforced federal powers to intervene on this issue as an aspect of federally controlled interstate commerce, prohibitionists looked to Congress for action and then, in 1913, decided to seek an anti-booze amendment to the Constitution. In contrast, the Canadian movement turned decisively back to the provinces, where members would concentrate their energies for most of the next three decades. Canada's highest court helped shape that strategic direction with its 1896 and 1901 declarations that prohibiting the sale of booze within the boundaries of one province was a solidly provincial responsibility (although the federal Scott Act was still valid as well). Both Manitoba and Prince Edward Island had passed acts in 1900, but had waited for the final court decision. Prince Edward Island then became the first province to take the plunge into total prohibition in 1901, by shutting down taverns in Charlottetown, the last wet holdout (and in 1906 the provincial law was extended to the whole island in place of the Scott Act).[76]

That move in the country's smallest province created no momentum else-where, however. New plebiscites on the issue in Ontario and Manitoba resulted in one victory and one defeat, again with small turnouts. In Manitoba the prohibitionists were angry that the government was holding another bal-lot on the question and for the most part urged voters to boycott the vote. Both provincial governments refused to act, and New Brunswick and Nova Scotia explicitly rejected prohibition petitions that year. In the remaining years before the First World War, opposition parties (including, occasionally, some politically opportunistic Conservatives in Nova Scotia) might promise action to cut off booze, but most provincial administrations still recognized the deep divisions in public opinion, especially in the cities and among fran-cophone communities, and the practical problems of administering total pro-hibition. Even Ontario's Liberal premier, George Ross, a long-time temperance crusader, was not prepared to move ahead too quickly. "Prohibition was not a matter of force but one of persuasion, education and instruction," he told a temperance convention in 1901. "Parliament could not make laws that could not be enforced because someone would carry their repeal."[77]

Although they rarely admitted so in public, these provincial politicians were also reluctant to sacrifice the licence revenue from the liquor traffic or the vital link to patronage. Outside Prince Edward Island, they all held back from any provincewide measures.

Banishing the Bar

A climactic moment had passed by 1902. The prohibitionists were furious and soon demoralized. The Ontario organizer for the Royal Templars of Temperance was convinced that "a condition of apathy existed amongst the people regard-ing Temperance matters." He threw in the towel, and left for the Prairies. Some provincial temperance organizations slumped badly and had to be rebuilt a few years later.[78]

Still, new provincewide coalitions appeared in Nova Scotia (1904), Prince Edward Island (1905), New Brunswick (1906), Manitoba and Alberta (1907), and British Columbia (1908). At that point in most provinces, the Protestant prohibitionists began to participate in broader Social and Moral Reform Councils. The goal of full-fledged prohibition was still paramount, but in practice over the next few years these organizations turned their energies to badgering the provinces into tightening regulation and enforcement and per-suading municipalities to cut off licences and bring in local option. They got uneven, sometimes frustrating responses.[79]

For some of these measures they had support from a new Catholic temperance movement in Quebec. In 1905, as part of the emerging Catholic nationalist agenda for social action, Montreal's Monsignor Bruchesi spearheaded a renewed campaign to promote abstinence. The Franciscan Order was given special responsibility for the crusade, and within a few months bishops across the province of Quebec joined in. Early in 1907 a new lay Catholic temperance society, the Ligue anti-alcoolique, was founded and within a year had enrolled 80,000 members. The Ligue flooded the province with temperance literature, including copies of a new journal, *La Tempérance* (which had a circulation of 39,000 by 1918), and staged large conferences to promote the cause. For the most part this movement steered clear of the English-language, evangelical, prohibitionist platform and resurrected the old "short pledge" of swearing off only distilled drinks and consuming fermented beverages in moderation. It concentrated on anti-alcohol education, including instruction in schools, and on reducing the number of retail outlets of alcohol sales at the municipal level. The Ligue's pressures on municipal councils led to many more dry zones in rural Quebec just before the war, in effect consolidating the parish priest's supervision of local moral standards. At the same time, however, as Ben Spence bitterly complained, "The Church has been opposed to having the issue voted upon in the province as a whole, fearing it would militate against its spiritual and material prosperity."[80]

In response to prohibitionist lobbying, between 1906 and 1913 all provincial governments amended their legislation covering alcohol consumption. The measures varied, but followed general patterns. One major approach was to make public drinking places more respectable and thus reduce the grounds for criticism. In most provinces, licence fees were cranked up (in Ontario the fee for a city tavern hit $1,200 in 1906), the number of licences was reduced, or licences were made more difficult to obtain. Various provinces required all bartenders to be licensed, forbade women to work in barrooms, and further curtailed hours of operation (including some public holidays). Some of them raised the legal drinking age to twenty-one and banned cheque-cashing. Manitoba prohibited free lunches and any "singing concert or entertainment." Ontario's premier also blustered about legally abolishing the "ridiculous and disgusting" custom of treating, but nothing to that effect ever appeared on the statute books before the war (even the WCTU thought such a measure would be unenforceable). Some provinces also tried to curb the flow of alcohol from the wet districts to the dry and set more severe penalties for lawbreakers.[81]

There were a few contrasting trends. Nova Scotia passed new regulations governing Halifax, the province's wet stronghold, which, to the disgust of prohibitionists, brought back licensed drinking in hotels. The Ontario government also extended legalized drinking places to vessels (like steamboats on the Great Lakes) and railway dining cars, and both Manitoba and Saskatchewan began licensing clubs. Both New Brunswick and Quebec set special royal commissions to work to investigate the administration of alcohol regulations, although no significant changes resulted from their reports.[82]

As with so much other social legislation in Canada that lay in the hands of the provinces, the result was an uneven, irregular patchwork—Quebec and British Columbia were always more permissive, the Maritime provinces far less so—but, outside Prince Edward Island, there was a broadly consistent pattern of restrained tolerance for some kind of legalized sale and consumption of beverage alcohol, mostly in urban areas. For die-hard anti-prohibitionist premiers like Nova Scotia's George Murray, Quebec's Lomer Gouin, Ontario's James P. Whitney, Manitoba's Rodmond P. Roblin, and British Columbia's Richard McBride, cleaning up the excesses of public drinking with an effective licensing system was a politically (and personally) more palatable alternative to full-fledged suppression. The approach also fell into the conservative state-regulatory model that they and others were using to deal with other controversial questions surrounding railways and public utilities, city government, workers' compensation, or environmental conservation (usually placed in the hands of an "impartial" commission of "experts" headed by professionals and businessmen). Ontario made the connection explicit in 1915 when it created a powerful provincewide License Board under the chairmanship of the respected Toronto businessman Joseph Flavelle. The temperance movement never agreed that regulation was enough.[83]

Just before the war, in provinces where the Liberal Party formed the Opposition in legislatures, prohibition became a more partisan issue. The Liberals attacked the Tories' regulatory approach, to the eager applause of the temperance movements, but soon found that their staunch anti-booze position did little to improve their chances for success at the polls. In 1912 and 1913 the B.C. and New Brunswick Liberals who pledged themselves to prohibition were all defeated. After numerous by-election defeats, the Ontario and Manitoba Liberal parties also went down to crushing defeats in provincial elections in 1914, when they ran on flat-out "Banish-the-Bar" platforms. Later that year, the Saskatchewan government abruptly refused to hold the prohibition plebiscite it had been planning in consultation with the province's Banish the Bar Committee.[84]

By the outbreak of the First World War, prohibitionists nonetheless were taking heart from more limited accomplishments. In most provinces they had managed to keep their issue and their slogan "Banish the Bar" at the forefront of Canadian politics, and as a result of renewed campaigning for licence reduction and local option prohibition they could point to more dry areas in many parts of the country, mostly rural constituencies. Indeed, they liked to publish maps showing how extensive their victories were, though the details were often misleading or inaccurate. The Ontario branch of the Dominion Alliance ran a particularly impressive centralized organization with a well-staffed office of twenty-five to thirty full-time employees, campaign war chest, speakers' bureau, literature distribution service, and weekly newssheet, the *Pioneer* (which had a circulation of 22,000 in 1913). It co-ordinated an effective network of constituency organizations across the province, and between 1905 and 1914, despite a 1906 law requiring a three-fifths majority in the votes, it had brought 288 municipalities, most of them rural townships and small towns, into the dry fold. In contrast to the 1880s and 1890s, far fewer local votes resulted in repeal.[85]

The results in the other eight provinces were less stunning, with clear signs indicating that the movement had reached the limits of its capabilities and could expect to make few more inroads in the near future. "During the last four years not one single bar-room has been closed by Local Option," the Manitoba Methodists complained in 1914. British Columbia still had no local option law, and no breakthrough to complete prohibition was in sight anywhere outside Prince Edward Island. The country was still deeply divided over the issue. The Scott Act and its provincial counterparts had still not touched most of the major cities across the country. When the Ontario local option battles in January 1916 again produced defeats in several urban centres, the authoritative *Canadian Annual Review* concluded, "It looked rather as if the movement had expended itself as a sweeping force."[86]

Moreover, although the number of liquor licences had been slashed, drinking had not stopped, especially in urban areas and among working men. Bootlegging and unlicensed "blind pigs" still flourished. Boatload after boatload of British and European immigrants with a fondness for alcohol continued to arrive to swell the wet population of Canada's cities. By 1914 each Canadian was consuming, on average, over seven gallons of beer a year (a 65 per cent increase since 1900) and roughly a gallon of spirits (a 50 per cent increase)—not counting the illicit booze that avoided federal excise officials.[87] By the time hostilities broke out in Europe, prohibitionists still found themselves with little cause for celebration.

How Dry I Am

The war changed everything. Reticence about state intervention receded as the federal government slowly moved beyond military mobilization into wider and deeper regulation of economic and social life, and Canadians got used to a press censor, food controller, and cost of living commissioner. The new rallying cry in public life became service and personal sacrifice in support of the common struggle. Drinking could now be cast as an unacceptable indulgence. Even King George V agreed to abstain for the duration of the war, and a new pledge-signing campaign started up to commit people to stop drinking until the war was over. Allowing valuable foodstuffs to be directed to booze production was wasteful, it was argued, and money spent on booze should be redirected to savings in Victory Bonds.[88]

These old moral arguments, however, were overshadowed by much more compelling appeals to economics and nationalism. "Efficiency," the new watchword of industrial management, became the standard for evaluating all contributions to the war effort. "National efficiency" demanded control of all human and material resources. According to Ontario's new teetotalling Conservative premier, William Hearst, the war placed new obligations before the people "and emphasized the duty of economy and efficiency that did not exist before." Drunkenness was no more acceptable on the home front than in the trenches, stern voices argued.[89]

Prohibitionist sentiment also played on wartime jingoism. The president of British Columbia's WCTU was pleased that governments had finally realized "no drinking nation can be 'fit.'" The implicit racism of the prohibition movement also got more explicit, as beer in particular was equated with alien, militaristic "Kaiserism." In the words of one New Brunswick temperance spokesman: "While our armies are fighting the German Kaiser of frightfulness, we are fighting the Alcohol Kaiser of life, and our fight will still be on when the other Baby Killers are put out of business and there will be boys and girls to guard against the ravages of King Alcohol when Kaiser William shall have gone to his ultimate destiny."[90]

Booze was presented as un-British and therefore un-Canadian. "Anyone who will vote in favor of liquor might as well enlist under the Kaiser," one Prairie paper insisted. Saskatchewan's prohibitionist *Banish-the-Bar Crusader* saw disloyalty lurking in the saloons: "Some of the bars are meeting places for our Empire's enemies and breeding-centres of sedition. Surely the province cannot continue to license convenient centers for spys [sic] and plotters against the country's peace." Much of this reasoning was intended to support prohibition only while hostilities in Europe lasted, but moral reformers of all kinds saw this widening consensus about purity in public life as the crucible of more permanent changes in the nation's culture—a way of making a society "fit for heroes."[91]

In this context the seasoned temperance troops found new and important allies stepping forward. Among them were the large numbers of prominent businessmen who began to take leadership roles in new bipartisan organizations dedicated to cutting off booze during the war. For the first time, too, they were joined by the upper echelons of the Anglican Church. In Ontario, Saskatchewan, and British

Decorating His Chief Ally

THE KAISER: My dear friend, in recognition of your magnificent work in undermining the strength of our enemies, it is fitting that I should decorate you with the Iron Cross. Let the good work go on.
HINDENBURG: Hear! Hear!

During the First World War, prohibition campaigns denounced booze as unpatriotic and dangerous to the Allied cause. From Pioneer *(Toronto), 22 June 1917.*

Columbia, respected businessmen and politicians organized a Committee of One Hundred outside the established parties to spearhead the drive (in 1913 U.S. prohibitionists had orchestrated a Committee of One Thousand to launch their campaign for an anti-booze amendment to the U.S. Constitution). Each of these committees was linked to a network of activists in local constituency groups (the Ontario committee had some 35,000 volunteers at work). In all provinces they organized huge demonstrations and brought in prominent speakers like the U.S. temperance orator Billy Sunday and Canada's own Nellie McClung. Petitions with thousands of signatures poured in. Newspapers offered almost unanimous support, and provincial governments began to capitulate.[92]

In March 1915 Saskatchewan's government became the first to do so when it abruptly announced the closing of all drinking establishments and the sale of alcohol only through government stores in municipalities that had not voted themselves dry—and in late 1916 the government outlets too were shut down following a plebiscite. As a result of pressure from the farmers' movement and others, the issue was put to voters in Alberta and Manitoba in 1915 and then in British Columbia in 1916. The results of the B.C. plebiscite were controversial, because the votes of soldiers overseas overturned a previously announced victory and had to be sifted for alleged irregularities by a royal commission, which ultimately declared a victory for prohibition. In each of the three Prairie provinces, the majorities for prohibition were substantial (though generally still not in settlements of francophones or recent European immigrants).[93]

In March 1916 Ontario's William Hearst agreed to introduce prohibition legislation after 15,000 people paraded to the provincial legislature with three wagons laden with petitions containing 825,000 signatures (including 350,000 eligible voters). The governments of Nova Scotia and New Brunswick capitulated the same spring, also without holding plebiscites. Out on the North Atlantic coast, the self-governing Dominion of Newfoundland voted itself dry the same year. In the northwest, after an indecisive plebiscite, the federal government made the Yukon dry by order-in-council in March 1918, effective 1 May. Quebec moved much more hesitantly: early in 1918 the provincial legislature endorsed complete abolition of retail sales to start on 1 May 1919, but taverns and licensed stores would remain open in the interim. Then, under pressure from the province's brewing interests to hold a plebiscite in April 1919, the government cut off only spirits and allowed lighter beer, cider, and wines to be sold.[94]

Since the provinces had no jurisdiction over interprovincial trade, it remained possible to import alcohol from wet areas (and manufacturers quickly arranged for delivery). But John Barleycorn's death seemed assured when on 22 December 1917, under an organized prohibitionist pressure not seen at the national level in twenty years, the newly elected Unionist federal government used a flurry of orders-in-council (later consolidated into one on 11 March 1918) to order a halt to importation (effective immediately) and to production and interprovincial trade (effective 1 April 1918) until one year after the end of the war (in effect, the end of 1919). Although, to sustain morale in the trenches, the soldiers' rum allotment was not cut off, Canada itself was as close to completely dry as it would ever get.[95]

"Dry" meant the same constraints on personal behaviour that had been written into all Canadian prohibitory legislation over the previous half-century (most of the wartime acts were modelled on Manitoba's 1900 law, which had never been put into force). The main attack was on public drinking. All saloons and clubs were closed, and alcohol was banned from hotels, boarding houses, and businesses. All retail liquor shops were closed. Private consumption at home remained legal, although people could not keep large quantities in their residences. Most provinces set no specific amount for this personal stock, but in Alberta the limit was fixed at one quart of spirits and two gallons

Prohibition forces in Ontario organized a mass petition to convince the provincial government to shut down the liquor traffic. In March 1916 they marched through downtown Toronto and presented the fruits of their labours to Premier William Hearst, who promptly introduced prohibition in the province. (NAC, PA-072527)

of beer. Booze could be purchased legally only from properly licensed whole-salers or, more commonly, from official government-run dispensaries and only for "medicinal, mechanical, scientific and sacramental purposes." Ontario allowed local wineries to continue selling, but federal regulations set the limit at beverages containing no more than 2.5 per cent proof alcohol (roughly 1.5 per cent by volume)—the standard legal definition of intoxicating drinks (New Brunswick used the lower British standard of 2 per cent). Hotels and some other outlets could sell so-called "near beer"—sometimes dubbed "temperance beer"—which had an alcohol content below that line.[96]

Looking back over the long march from the first prohibitionist campaigns of the 1850s, one is hard-pressed to say definitively when prohibition had started in Canada. Booze had been banned in the North-West Territories in 1873, but legalized under a licensing system twenty years later. At the same point, some municipalities had used the old Dunkin Act to shut down public drinking. In 1879 Fredericton had become the first of many jurisdictions to use the federally sponsored version of local option under the Scott Act, but many of the initial experiments with this model had been repealed by the early 1890s. Then a new wave of local option victories hit the country in the decade before the war through a combination of federal and provincial legis-lation. The Maritimes had shown the greatest support, and, not surprisingly, it was the Eastern province of Prince Edward Island that in 1901 brought in the first provincewide shutdown of booze retailing. Only in 1916–18 did the other provinces follow suit, though in reality the wartime legislation was largely aimed at the patchwork of wet areas, most of them cities, that had

Beer or the Boy?

The Referendum Places the Alternative Squarely Before Every Parent in Ontario

The plebiscites on continuing prohibition after the war featured familiar themes. From Spectator *(Hamilton, Ont.), 17 September 1919.*

consistently resisted local-option prohibition (in the still awkward constitutional split, the new provincial acts generally extended only to those areas not already covered by the Scott Act).

What made these final steps more impressive was that for the first time legislation covered all jurisdictions simultaneously and that in 1918 the federal government finally stepped in to shut down the liquor traffic completely. But it was a peculiarly Canadian compromise. In contrast to the United States, Canada closed down retail outlets and restricted shipment of booze, but allowed the brewers, distillers, and wine-makers to continue making and selling their products for export.

Popular support for this sea change in public policy is hard to measure. Three of the four Western provinces had seen solid pro-prohibition majorities in their plebiscites, but the outcome in British Columbia was clouded in controversy. The problems with tallying votes there made clear that the decision of the other three provinces not to include soldiers serving overseas in the vote had silenced thousands of young men who had always been the backbone of Canada's public drinking cultures. The other four wet provinces (Ontario, Quebec, New Brunswick, and Nova Scotia) had not put the question of prohibition to the electorate before passing a law.

The Canadian prohibitionists were nonetheless determined to hold onto their triumphs after the war. In 1920 they rekindled their national links in a new Dominion Committee on Liquor Legislation, renamed the Prohibition Federation of Canada three years later. Provincial federations would nonetheless remain the real armies in the struggle. They were counting on the many women voters who had for the first time been added to the voting lists during the war (in all provinces but Prince Edward Island, which added them in 1920, and Quebec, which waited till 1940). Indeed, the first woman elected to a provincial legislature was Louise McKinney, president of Alberta's WCTU.[97]

Prohibitionists were delighted and relieved when positive plebiscite votes in Ontario in October 1919 and New Brunswick in July 1920 made wartime legislation permanent and thus guaranteed that the prohibition on booze would extend indefinitely in most provinces. Only Quebec, in April 1919, and British Columbia, in October 1920, rejected complete prohibition. The attack then shifted from the saloon to the home. The drys had hoped that federal importation controls would be entrenched as well, and in the spring of 1919 they convinced the Canadian House of Commons to pass such legislation. But, to the prohibitionists' disgust and horror, when Quebec voted that April to permit the sale of beer, cider, and wine, the Canadian Senate rejected the federal bill. The following November the federal government enacted a compromise, whereby a plebiscite of residents of any province could trigger a ban on importation of alcoholic beverages from outside their borders for personal use (simple possession would still not be a crime). On 25 October 1920, Nova Scotia and the three Prairie provinces voted to ask Ottawa to end imports. Ontario followed their example the next spring, New Brunswick in the fall, and Prince Edward Island in January 1923. The Quebec government also decided to ban exports to prohibitionist provinces. In 1921 the federal government also doubled the duties and sales tax on alcohol. A new era of enforced sobriety had been proclaimed in seven provinces, and supporters of the dry cause were soon trumpeting the sharp decline in public drunkenness. "Intoxicated men are rarely seen upon the streets of our cities, towns, and villages," Ontario's Board of License Commissioners proclaimed in 1921, "and countless families, whose breadwinners formerly wasted their earnings on drink, are now able to live in comfort."[98]

Starting in 1920 several provinces held plebiscites on cutting off the importation of alcohol into dry areas. This had allowed wealthier citizens to stock their wine cellars and bootleggers to get their supplies. In all cases the prohibitionists won, though voter turnout was small. (NAC, C-056167)

Prohibitionists were also jubilant about the international prospects, especially when the United States weighed in with a constitutional amendment enshrining prohibition effective 16 January 1920. They saw themselves as part of a worldwide movement that had also brought various wartime restrictions on drinking in England, Scotland, France, Belgium, Denmark, Norway, Holland, and New Zealand (though they seldom stopped to notice that Canada stood alone with the United States, Finland, Iceland, and post-czarist Russia in introducing full-fledged prohibition). Indeed, decades before the war, both the Independent Order of Good Templars and the WCTU had spread into European countries and British white-settler colonies. In 1919 the Dominion Alliance joined forces with the Anti-Saloon League in the United States to launch the World League Against Alcoholism, and three years later it hosted the League's first international conference in Toronto. This new organization was a clearing house of information, propaganda, and speakers (notably the renowned American "Pussyfoot" Johnson, who became the League's organizing secretary) for spreading the prohibitionist message to such "underdeveloped" countries as South Africa, India, and China, and to support dry campaigns in Europe against the powerful wine and whisky interests. It was brimming with a crusading zeal to identify its central project of eliminating alcohol with the notions of "civilization" and "modernity" and to make this culture dominant throughout the world. Despite setbacks in most of these efforts after the early 1920s, Canada's WCTU president Sara Rowell Wright confidently proclaimed in 1925 that "the world is going dry."[99]

But there were clouds on the horizon. A closer look at the postwar plebiscite results across Canada would have alerted the drys to some hoary old patterns. Turnouts were often light (barely half of the potential voters in Saskatchewan and Manitoba, less than half in Alberta, only 40 per cent in

Nova Scotia, less than a third in New Brunswick), and the sharp regional, rural-urban, class, and ethnic differences over this issue had reappeared. Moreover, the prohibitionists themselves were threatening their base of support by pushing beyond their prewar focus on saloons to target liquor in the private household.

In 1922 the Ontario branch of the Dominion Alliance met with Premier E.C. Drury to urge that "every person be compelled, if desired by the Police, to submit a detailed return of the liquor held in his house and if such a return were not made or if an abnormal shrinkage took place in his stock from year to year, it should be made an offense under the Act." The organization also proposed that "it be an offence to give liquor in a private house where more than three persons—other than the family—were present." Although a staunch prohibitionist, Drury, like provincial leaders in other provinces facing similar pressures, recognized that this step would be going too far. By that point active campaigns of resistance were underway in the shadowy world of illegal commerce and the open arenas of politics. The dry utopia was far from secure.[100]

The triumph of prohibition had been a convoluted affair. As a social and political project, it had brought together a bloc of Canadians who were for the most part solidly rooted and successful in the liberal-capitalist order and convinced that legislated repression of drinking was essential to shoring up a morally sound, productive, and civilized nation. They had constructed a cultural package for bourgeois society that folded together an evangelical Protestantism (or, in Quebec, Social Catholicism), economic rationality, and ethnocentrism that they hoped to make into collective "common sense" for Canadians. They did succeed in casting booze as a social menace, but they repeatedly failed to make their vision of legislated morality hegemonic until the country was in the throes of a "Great War"—which indicates that, even for many of the wealthiest and most powerful Canadians, the zeal of this bloc bordered on a kind of discomforting and unrealistic fanaticism.

The campaign was thus not a straightforward project of a dominant class attacking a subordinate class—capitalists against workers—because not all capitalists would climb on board the prohibition bandwagon. Yet in attempting to rally the respectable, propertied elements to their cause, prohibitionists turned their crusade into a narrowly focused attack on the public drinking cultures of urban working men. They also expressed intolerance of the cultural preferences and drinking habits of those Canadian residents whose first language was not English, and many of those people were in the working class.

The real victory of the 1916–18 period, then, was the turning of those class and ethnic biases into state policy backed by powerful legal constraints. For a few years after 1915, prohibitionists managed to make their vision the "common sense" of their society, part of the still potent sense in the immediate postwar world that the more aggressive use of the state to oversee and regulate many aspects of social and economic life should continue into the era of "reconstruction." It remained to be seen how long that consensus would hold.

Thanks to this relentless crusade, consumers of alcoholic beverages found the long arm of the law reaching deeper into their lives after 1850. If they were members of one of Canada's First Nations, they would find themselves completely shut out of legal drinking cultures. Whatever their race, if they drank enough to get decidedly drunk, they would face beefed-up police forces and stern magistrates who might lock them up for public drunkenness or curtail their liberty for neglecting their families. If their families had them committed to the care of doctors in state-supported mental-health institutions, they would find their habits now defined and treated as a disease. If they simply wanted to enjoy a drink with friends in a public space, they found that the available watering holes were far fewer in number, more concentrated in specific zones of towns and cities, and open for fewer hours. In many places before the war, and everywhere outside Quebec by the Armistice in 1918, governments shut down all drinking places and retail shops. Perhaps most disturbing for those who enjoyed their pint of ale or shot of whisky was the saturation of public discourse with the evils of alcohol. Would no one speak out for the drinker and his friend John Barleycorn?

six

Wet Voices

 "I AM A PROHIBITIONIST. WHAT I propose to prohibit is the reckless use of water."[1] Bob Edwards, the sharp-tongued editor of the Calgary *Eye-Opener*, was not a voice in the wilderness when he penned this line in 1904. Repeatedly, since the 1850s, larger numbers of Canadians had made it clear that they wanted nothing to do with prohibition. Most booze-swilling friends of John Barleycorn scoffed at the temperance enthusiasts, but never created a solid oppositional movement based simply on their fondness for alcohol. They might pen an occasional bit of doggerel, such as "A Reminiscence of Cariboo Life," which opened with the memorable lines "Oh, I love to snore / On a bar-room floor / And sleep a drunk away!" Or they might launch into a few verses of drinking songs like "How Dry I Am" or the 1904 Canadian classic "Give Me a Song That's Gay." But the popular drinking cultures in the country's hundreds of taverns and saloons remained mostly defensive and inward-looking. The chorus of the 1904 Canadian song suggested their limited horizons:

> Give me good wine and sparkling,
> Give me a song that's gay.
> Give me a life free from care,
> Long as I have to stay.
> Fighters may take the glory
> And candidates gather the fame.
> I'll take a farce, a lass, and a glass,
> That's if it's all the same.[2]

OPPOSITE PAGE: *At the end of the nineteenth century, Saskatchewan farmers were still taking a beer break.* (NAC, C-89660)

Sheet music like this composition from Bala Falls, Ont., helped to spread the wet message, in the face of a torrent of temperance song sheets. (TPL, 1904, Music, CSM, S)

There were moments of greater aggression. In the last gasp of open voting, in Toronto in 1877, crowds of "Anti-Dunkinites" attended rallies and surged around the polling platform to block prohibitionist voters, but the secret ballot used in all later campaigns never ignited such public solidarity. Most often, when given the opportunity to vote on the issue, large numbers of drinkers never bothered to go to the polls. They never presented themselves to the Royal Commission on the Liquor Traffic to explain or justify their taste for alcohol. At most, the more defiant and militant defenders of booze engaged in sporadic local campaigns of guerrilla warfare against prohibitionists.[3]

In Brantford in 1877 two hotel-keepers charged with liquor violations led a gang of supporters to rough up two whisky detectives. They pelted the detectives' boarding house with rocks and sent them scurrying out of town. A few years later in Ontario County, witnesses flooded trials of local hotel-keepers to protect them from prosecution. One temperance advocate in the county had his orchard chopped down, and two prohibitionist "spotters" were roughed up in a roadside attack. Temperance supporters in Huron County had their property damaged by arson; a prohibitionist in Sarnia had his house dynamited; another in Peterborough had his store window smashed. On the eve of prohibition in Ontario, as the temperance forces assembled on Toronto streets in 1916 for their march to Queen's Park, soldiers and other bystanders sang lusty drinking songs, pelted the marchers with pieces of ice, and destroyed their half-mile-long banner. Ultimately, this kind of direct action was more the extension of masculine barroom bravado than a serious strategy to deter the prohibitionists or win the support of politicians and a wider public.[4]

For much of the period before the First World War, these wet voices remained unorganized. But as the prohibitionist challenge got more serious, various groups rallied to defend the right to drink alcoholic beverages, or at least to oppose state intervention as wrong-headed. By the early 1920s their collective critique of prohibition was gathering support and giving many politicians the push to rethink the regulation of booze.

The Traffic Fights Back

The actual producers and sellers of booze had to proceed more cautiously than the lusty drinkers. Unquestionably they had the most at stake. Privately they reminded governments repeatedly that they were legitimate business interests that contributed significantly to the Canadian economy. By the end of the nineteenth century, however, they recognized that the temperance movement's construction of them as the "Liquor Traffic" cast a shadow over their operations that had to be dispelled. As concerned businessmen, they mobilized against prohibition quietly, avoiding the highly visible organizational presence and loud public agitation of their critics. Their first step was to band together for common defence. They had much more difficulty in showing solidarity than their prohibitionist foes liked to believe.

In the late nineteenth century, the retailers' city-based associations, the Licensed Victuallers' Associations, had eventually linked up in provincewide bodies and, by 1901, a Dominion association. One cabinet minister admitted that it was impolitic "to offend a powerful and well-organized body like the Licensed Victuallers." For the most part, the large brewers and distillers tended to unite separately from the more plebeian tavern-keepers and most often from each other as well. They also created their own provincial and national associations. The Canada Brewers and Maltsters' Association was formed in 1878 in response to the Scott Act and presumably to help fight local-option battles (though it seemed to function as an Ontario organization). The members also used price-fixing to reduce competition among themselves. In the prewar battles against prohibition, beer-makers were probably complacent about sales and how they could distant their more benign product from distilled spirits (even casting beer as a "temperance drink") and from the poorly run saloons and "groggeries" that were the real source of concern. In 1885 the brewers' national organization lobbied the Senate to pass an exemption to the Scott Act allowing for the sale of beer, wine, and cider, but lost out when the House of Commons balked at the measure. Similarly, in response to the wartime prohibitionist legislation, brewers' associations in several provinces argued for special treatment for beer. For their part, distillers may have assumed that they were safe from attack as a result of the high revenues they provided to the state. They may also have recognized that, unlike the brewers, they would probably have customers even under prohibition, since their whisky was less bulky and easier to transport to wet households in dry communities.[5]

As the branch of the liquor traffic with the most to lose in prohibition battles, the various Licensed Victuallers' Associations were thus generally left to carry the ball in challenging prohibition legislation in the courts and in lobbying efforts with governments. Their large petitions often carried thousands of signatures (presumably gathered in saloons). At key moments a common front with the producers was possible, though usually ephemeral. In the 1850s all branches of the "Traffic" had banded together and hired a paid secretary to represent them in the first battles with the prohibitionists in the legislature of the Province of Canada. Four decades later they jointly hired a lawyer to represent them in higher-court constitutional cases and paid a journalist, Louis Kribs, to travel with the Royal Commission on the Liquor Traffic and

OPPOSITE PAGE: *O'Keefe was*
one of the many producers of
beverage alcohol that used its
newspaper and magazine
advertising to promote the
healthful qualities of its
drinks. From Saturday Night
(Toronto), 11 January and
1 February 1913.

question witnesses. In 1902 Toronto's Eugene O'Keefe led a huge delegation of over one thousand brewers, distillers, and retailers to the Ontario legislature to forestall prohibitory legislation and demand compensation should any such measure be enacted. By the time of the 1916 plebiscite in British Columbia, all these groups were co-operating again inside a single Merchants' Protective Association. Yet such alliances seemed to be fragile and fleeting.[6]

Before the war the various industry organizations were all shadowy groups that repeatedly refused to engage in public debates with prohibitionists and rarely convened rallies of supporters. "The campaign against us was a still one," a Saint John clergyman wrote in 1909. "They held no public meetings, nor did they appear at our meetings." In the daily press the referendum campaigns often seemed curiously one-sided as a result. Pro-drink forces concentrated instead on printed propaganda, setting out their arguments against the alleged injustice and ineffectiveness of prohibition in numerous leaflets and advertisements. Their short-lived journal the *Advocate*, edited by Kribs, hit the streets in Toronto and Montreal just days before Ontario's 1894 vote. During referendum campaigns producers and retailers funnelled money into the anti-prohibition camp to cover organizers' salaries and advertising, and they mobilized newspaper editors and sympathetic community leaders to support a wet vote. Two days before the voting on Ontario's 1902 plebiscite, they used the press to unfurl a public manifesto urging voters to reject the proposed prohibition act for the province. The statement was signed by 244 high-profile bankers, stock brokers, manufacturers, and professional men in Toronto and Hamilton. The industry also sent delegations to lobby governments to head off unfavourable legislation. Some six hundred representatives descended on Ontario's Premier James P. Whitney in 1906, and three hundred on Manitoba Premier Rodmond Roblin three years later. As the battle intensified between 1914 and 1916, the producers and retailers finally began to sponsor prominent speakers to attack prohibition and presented provincial governments with petitions containing thousands of signatures. Nonetheless, in the efforts to get the message out, paid advertising remained far more important than popular mobilization.[7]

Industry associations put at least as much energy into trying to get their memberships to clean up their act. Licensed victuallers urged their fellow tavern-keepers to improve the standards of their businesses and thus their public image—in the words of the Territorial Licensed Victuallers' Association, meeting in Regina in 1905, "to give the business a better reputation than had clung to it in the past . . . to elevate the business." To this end the organizations supported government measures such as high licence fees, which would help to crack down on the loosely run dives. In 1899 the B.C. Licensed Victuallers'

Association called on Vancouver's police to shut down illicit Asian drinking places. Some fifteen years later their Montreal counterparts even publicly denounced six cabarets as "a menace to public morals" and urged the cancellation of their licences.[8]

The booze manufacturers also used a far more subtle but perhaps more effective method of winning over public opinion—their product advertisements. Every day sprinkled through their newspapers Canadians found reassuring statements about the nutritious and healthy qualities of alcoholic drinks. O'Keefe's Special Extra Mild Stout was touted "as rich and nourishing as fresh cream," and, as for the firm's Imperial line of ale, lager, and stout: "Thousands of people have found in these brews the tonic they have so long needed; one that renews the old-time vim and vigor, that banishes the strain of work, and satisfies the craving for a delicate delicious, satisfying drink." Vancouver Breweries' Cascade beer was "as truly a food as the bread you eat," and "not only a drink that refreshes, but one that tones up the system, builds body strength and brain efficiency." White Horse Cellar Scotch was promoted as a "certain cure for indigestion," and a Dr. Paget, "the famous English practitioner," recommended it with all meals. Hennessy Brandy was promoted as "a life-saver in summer," to combat "a case of threatened sun-stroke, or indigestion with colic, or a fainting spell, or exhaustion from fright, or rescue from drowning, or a weak heart action." Testimonials helped: Mrs. Albert Mathews wrote that she was "completely cured of Grippe and Stomach Trouble by the use of Duffy's Pure Malt Whiskey. . . . It brought back restful sleep and health." All of this commercial propaganda tried to sidestep the issue of public drinking and the evils of the saloon by focusing readers' attention on the product itself and on home consumption.[9]

These issues eventually spilled over into the referendum campaigns during and after the war, as wets and dries debated the merits of drinking alcohol and the impact of so-called "light beer" on the human body. The brewers ignored distilled liquor and struck out on their own in a vigorous defence of beer as a healthy, beneficial drink. The medical profession generally provided little support for this kind of pseudo-scientific propaganda. Although opinion in their ranks remained divided, the few doctors making public statements usually supported prohibition.[10]

By the First World War the "liquor interests" recognized their need for allies in heading off prohibition. In most of the provincial referenda of 1915–16 they had no army of volunteers to support their cause and had to rely on newspaper advertising to make their case. In the next round of referenda starting in 1919 they were better able to build broader coalitions in most provinces.

Good Health will be yours if you drink O'Keefe's "GOLD LABEL" ALE

YOU can almost FEEL your strength coming back, as you enjoy a bottle of this rich, creamy, old ale.

Before meals, with meals and after meals—take it as you prefer. It will do you good anytime, and all the time.

Your doctor would recommend it

PROF. Gaertner, in his "Manual of Hygiene" states that *one* quart of *beer* is equal in *food value* to three and one-tenth *pounds* of bread (as to the quantity of carbohydrates), and to two ounces of bread, or nearly one ounce of meat (as to the quantity of albumen).

O'Keefe's Special Extra Mild Ale

is strong in stimulating food values—rich in nutriment— yet so light and mild that everyone may enjoy it.

The Great Protector of British Freedom:

"YOUR pretended fear lest error should step in is like the man who would keep all wine out of the country lest men should be drunk. It will be found an unjust and unwise jealousy to deny a man the liberty he has by nature upon a supposition that he may abuse it. When he doth abuse it, judge."

—Letter from Oliver Cromwell, September 12, 1650, to the Governor of Edinburgh Castle for leave to Ministers of Religion.

Vote for Moderation
Temperance and Freedom

The anti-prohibition forces reached back in history to find support for their cause—to the Magna Carta and, in this case, to Oliver Cromwell. From Sun *(Vancouver), 15 October 1920.*

By that point many other Canadians had their doubts about the advantages of a dry country and were prepared to join actively in the campaigns.[11]

The Politics of Moderation

For many outspoken Canadians, prohibition was an unacceptable invasion of state power into their private lives. They spoke out in defence of liberty, both personal and, among certain religious and ethnic groups, collective. By the end of the war some of Canada's most prominent citizens had put themselves at the head of broad-based coalitions that recast the libertarian perspective into a more expansive ideology of "moderation."

The defence of personal liberty, the sharpest, angriest argument against prohibition, reverberated through many sectors of the male population. The "right" allegedly being violated was not simply that of being able to drink publicly but of being able to do what a man wanted to do in private. As Dr. R. MacNeill of Charlottetown complained, "Parliament has no right to deny a sober respectful man of his civil liberty—such a man has a right to choose what he shall eat or drink so long as he behaves himself and does not become a nuisance to his fellow man." This civil-libertarian argument had been marshalled by the turn of the century, but in the years just before the First World War it became a major preoccupation. In 1913 the liquor interests in Ontario helped to pull together a Personal Liberty League modelled on similar organizations in the United States. "Whether men shall or shall not drink is a minor question," a League ad insisted in 1916.

> The real point is whether there is any personal freedom which the majority is bound to respect. For if such majority can decree what men shall and shall not drink, why not what they shall and shall not wear, how they shall and shall not vote, and how they may and may not worship God?

London's Roman Catholic Bishop Michael Fallon agreed: "It is the battle for liberty against State omnipotence. . . . I am afraid of the orgy of collectivism, whereby the State regulates the private conduct of the people."[12]

Humourist Stephen Leacock, also solidly in this camp, denounced prohibition as "social tyranny" and told a Toronto audience: "They are putting their trust in coercion, in the gaol, in the whip and the scourge. They are done with the moral appeal. They are finished with persuasion. They want authority and to be obeyed under the fear of the criminal law." For him the "moral issue" involved was "the spirit of human freedom struggling against bondage. The age-long spirit of liberty that the chain can never bind, that the gag can never silence."[13]

This kind of defence of individual rights was harder to sustain in the face of wartime propaganda about sacrifice and service, but the wet discourse soon broadened out into a defence of British citizenship and thus competed with prohibitionists for patriotic turf. In 1916 British Columbia's anti-prohibitionists labelled that province's proposed prohibition legislation "Un-British" and warned that it "provides that any constable, without an order or warrant, may forcibly enter your home at any hour of the day or night, on the mere suspicion that you have liquor in your possession, and break into any room or closet in the house in prosecuting his search." The wets pointed out that prohibition "was rejected by Britain as being fundamentally contrary to traditions of individual liberty and responsibility." Seizing on the common coin of wartime rhetoric, the widening coalition of anti-prohibitionists in Ontario rechristened themselves the Citizens' Liberty League in 1919, and a similar group in Nova Scotia became the Citizens Committee the next year. Over the next few years the increasingly invasive powers of the state to raid and search private premises and the loosely violent practices of enforcement officers became a great cause of concern. The personal-liberty argument had a particularly strong resonance among returned soldiers, who quickly showed plenty of collective resentment about the undermining of the rights that they thought they had been fighting for. Branches of the Great War Veterans' Association (GWVA) and other veterans' groups quickly joined the chorus against prohibition.[14]

"Personal liberty" could, of course, be a mask for male privilege, and a persistent current in the anti-prohibitionist arguments derided the meddling of female prudes, including the recasting of the Woman's Christian Temperance Union as "Waggling and Critical Tongues United." Veterans paraded through Toronto streets on WCTU tag day in 1919 to denounce that organization for trying to close wet canteens and cut off rum rations and tobacco shipments to the troops. The Parkdale branch of Toronto's GWVA passed an angry resolution in 1919: "Having resisted the tyranny of Wilhelm, [we do not] propose to submit to the meanest of all tyrannies, the tyranny of petticoat government." A B.C. veteran argued: "Drinking is a social custom of man, just as tea drinking is a social custom of women. We don't interfere with their custom, so don't let them interfere with ours." A year later one wet broadside in Ontario added a racist twist, accusing the WCTU of:

> framing up a number of prohibition laws whereby Canadians will wear bibs and tuckers, curtsy to the Methodist Preacher, and be supervised the same as

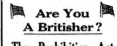

The wet forces tried to turn the wartime spirit to their advantage by suggesting that prohibition was a violation of British civil liberties. They made little headway with such arguments until after the war. From Sun *(Vancouver), 13 September 1916.*

The anti-prohibitionist campaign for greater personal liberty could take a misogynous twist. The Citizens' Liberty League in Ontario placed this message at the top of one of its 1919 newspaper ads. From Spectator *(Hamilton, Ont.), 10 October 1919.*

our Anglo-Saxon brothers supervise the inferior races of niggers, Indians and Coolies. Canadians will be officially placed on a similar footing—a nice standing for a race who proved their fighting value on the Fields of France.[15]

Concerns about state intrusion did not always have an individualist cast. Some of the leading branches of the Christian faith were opposed to using the state to impose morality. Most Anglican and Catholic churchmen insisted that education to encourage moderate consumption or abstinence, not legal coercion, was the only hope for overcoming the problems arising from drinking. Along with the Lutheran and Orthodox churches, these were both more hierarchical institutions that placed the emphasis on liturgy and ritual rather than on the personal salvation and individual responsibility for personal morality so central to evangelicalism. Each church supported active temperance societies among their flocks, but both stopped short of endorsing prohibition. "In remedying the [social] evils in one direction we must be careful lest we create others probably as great in another," the Anglican General Synod declared in 1902. "Stringent laws often defeat their purpose, and cannot be enforced unless they are supported by the hearty co-operation of all classes." Until the First World War, most Anglican clergymen stayed out of the prohibition crusades, and only the wartime atmosphere brought many of them to dry platforms. Immediately after the war, they quickly withdrew. Indeed, in Saskatchewan's 1920 plebiscite on shutting down imports, a leading churchman of the Qu'Appelle Diocese declared that "a vote for prohibition is a vote of censure on Jesus Christ." Four years later, one man's effort to present a pro-prohibition resolution was howled down in the church's General Synod.[16]

The Catholic record was similar, though more complicated. Although the Church actively promoted abstinence and, in Quebec, through the Ligue anti-alcoolique, supported local-option prohibition, across the country most Catholic clergymen continued to keep their distance from the broader prohibition crusades and often spoke against provincewide measures for state repression. Indeed, Ontario's first broad-front wet organization had the support of the Catholic bishop of London by 1915. During the run-up to the April 1919 Quebec plebiscite on allowing the sale of beer and wine, the Catholic Church made no public statements and opinion in the Ligue anti-alcoolique was divided. Of course, Catholicism was also as deeply enmeshed in ethic identities as it had been since the conquest of Quebec. As in the 1840s, the nationalist flavour of the Ligue's propaganda was unmistakable, and its spokespersons liked to identify abstinence as one of the hallowed "traditions" of French Canadians, while intemperance was "the worst enemy of our race and religion," against which the French had a long history of resistance,

comparable, it was argued, to their struggles against the English. The Catholic clergy spoke for other large minority groups in the country as well—the Acadians of the Maritimes, Franco-Ontarians, Franco-Manitobans, and numerous new European immigrant communities—who found the prohibitionists intolerant of their cultural preferences and part of the cultural imperialism of the "Anglo-Saxon race." On the eve of Quebec's 1919 plebiscite, a Quebec cabinet minister insisted that prohibition was a Methodist plot aimed at undermining the Catholic faith. Five years later, a Saskatchewan Catholic journalist similarly denounced prohibitionists:

During a turn-of-the-century hunting expedition, these two Catholic brothers had no qualms about sharing their beer with two of their students from the Collège du Sacré-coeur at Caraquet, N.B. (PANB, Eudist Fathers Collection, P38/75)

> They are in the main men filled with a virulent hatred for the Roman Catholic Church and all that belongs to it. They are those who have striven to destroy our Separate School System, who have assailed the doctrines of the Church, who have preached the "one flag, one language" doctrine from the rooftops, who class all Catholics as "foreigners," who vaunt the superiority of the Anglo-Saxon, who parade their own loyalty and insinuatingly belittle the patriotism of Catholics.

Significantly, in the provincial and national plebiscites between the 1890s and the 1920s, municipalities with large Catholic and francophone populations and those with large numbers of Anglicans registered the largest numbers of negative votes for prohibition, and the two provinces with large Catholic and Anglican populations (Quebec and British Columbia) had the weakest prohibition movements and the briefest dry spells.[17]

Although the libertarian argument would continue to run through the campaigns to repeal prohibition in the 1920s, the attempt to rally the anti-prohibitionist forces around the cry of liberty had its limitations, especially in Canada's relatively elitist political culture, in which individual rights were celebrated with less gusto than they were south of the border. With the fading away of the wartime consensus about the dire emergency that required collective restraint, the most compelling voices of doubt about prohibition came from the upper reaches of the social scale: businessmen, professionals, and their wives. Large numbers of them were clearly aghast at what they saw as the intrusiveness and fanaticism of the prohibitionists and the dangers to social and political order posed by the widespread flouting of the prohibition legislation. By 1920 urban bourgeois circles were percolating with a new anti-prohibitionist politics based on "moderation" as a third path away from the extremist experiment of prohibition or a simple return to prewar drinking regimes. This more expansive wet perspective became the common ground for the building of a social coalition to fight for repeal.

The banner of moderation reflected not only the immediate experience with prohibition but also the widening social conflicts in postwar Canada. Growing numbers of bourgeois Canadians worried that in various ways prohibition seriously threatened social order. For decades many industrialists had been arguing for a curb on alcohol consumption as means of reinforcing industrial discipline, and the demands of wartime production had convinced most business people about the connection between sobriety and efficiency. Yet many bourgeois leaders had long held grave doubts about prohibition in practice. It was bad enough that respectable businessmen would be forced to shut down without compensation—H.H. Fudger, president of the Robert Simpson Company, warned his fellow Methodists that shutting down the liquor traffic was "the ultimatum of the highwayman." But the experience of the Scott Act had also included widespread illegal marketing of alcohol and the complicity of thousands of Canadians in the process. The spectre of "lawlessness" loomed large. The Royal Commission on the Liquor Traffic heard many versions of these concerns. In 1902 the manager of the huge Dominion Iron and Steel Company in Sydney, N.S., also complained about the growth of illicit drinking under local prohibition and asked for "good regulation for the sale of liquor" rather than "the unlimited and unlicensed sale of intoxicating drinks now carried on under the supposed operation of the Scott Act." That act, he said, was "calculated to injure the efficiency of the men, affect the life and progress of Sydney, reduce the output of business and increase the cost of the product."[18]

That same year the long list of Ontario businessmen who signed the open letter against prohibition similarly worried that prohibition would "merely transfer the drinking of intoxicants from licensed and well-regulated places to unlicensed and disreputable resorts, and to the homes of the people," and would therefore be "detrimental to the best interests, both moral and commercial, of this province." A decade later, thirty-one Hamilton industrialists announced, "The experience of the manufacturer is that there is more danger in the blind pig than the open bar." The members of a large delegation of B.C. businessmen were blunt in a meeting with the premier in 1915: "Prohibition will stimulate crime. No one will think it an immoral act to smuggle liquor."[19]

The highest circles of Canadian society were not of one mind on how to handle alcohol consumption, but by the early 1920s large numbers of them agreed with Ontario's Citizens' Liberty League that prohibition had "brought the law into contempt, thus tending to destroy our national life as sober, law-abiding citizens." This was a fearful development in the wake of the shockingly powerful workers' and farmers' "revolts" immediately after the war. The League told the public that the dry regime was breeding "dissatisfaction and discontent among our workers, returned men and a large section of the citizens generally." The choice, it asserted, was between "Compromise and Harmony, or Intolerance and Widespread Resentment." A letter to the Hamilton *Spectator* was blunt in its criticism of the Ontario Temperance Act:

> The issue is sanity versus bolshevism. There is no better propaganda than present conditions under the O.T.A. Open, flagrant and continuous violations of the law; corruption of public servants, without whose connivance such violations would not take place; enormous profits obtained by breaking the law; injustice as between rich and poor—these are the results of the O.T.A., which are patent to every one who has eyes to see or ears to hear. And the effect of these things is certain—they destroy respect for the law; they undermine confidence in government; they loosen the very foundation of society. Are you in favor of well-ordered liberty and the stability of our institutions, or are you in favor of present conditions, which are a hot-bed for bolshevism?[20]

As the reference to creeping bolshevism suggests, the moderationist position found itself caught up in the rough seas of postwar politics. The elite circles that produced the leadership of the anti-prohibition campaigns by 1920 feared the challenge of more radical agendas for collectivist politics, whether liberal, labourist, or socialist, that had flowed out of the war and animated so many social movements of the period. They wanted to deflect these political concerns into channels of what one British historian has called "social liberalism"—the right to be left alone, to be freed of the incursive social engineers of all kinds, including prohibitionists. Canadians had to reduce their sense of social entitlement and their demands on the state and be encouraged to move in more self-reliant directions. Building a popular coalition that tied together personal liberty and a rollback of state intervention would help to redirect politics into safer channels. "We call it stabilized democracy, which is the broad highway up the centre of the road of just, ordinary, clean decent Anglo-Saxon living," the president of Ontario's Citizens' Liberty League announced in 1920. "On the one hand are the uplifters . . . on the other are the Reds."[21]

That perspective undoubtedly lay behind the concerns expressed by businessmen and their political allies about the loss of tax revenues under prohibition. Liquor had always provided a large chunk of excise and custom revenues, and taxation of incomes, first introduced during the war, loomed as the only alternative source of revenues to meet the rising demands on provincial government treasuries for roads, social welfare measures, and more. The state should not be allowed to appropriate bourgeois wealth when the more broad-based excise taxes could be used instead. Much like right-wing political movements at the end of the twentieth century, one moderationist rallying cry was high taxes. The Moderation League of Alberta pitched this concern to voters in the province's 1923 plebiscite:

> Are you willing to permit the revenue which would come to this province under a properly regulated government control of the sale of alcoholic beverages—and help relieve the large burden of taxation and debt which rests in this province—go into the pockets of a vicious ring of bootleggers, a menace to the law and order and the very life of this community?[22]

"Moderation," then, represented a careful packaging of resentments about an interventionist state at many levels of society. Besides making a case for the return of alcohol, it became an effective way of building social and political coalitions to steer public policy-making away from dangerously radical paths. The leadership of the new Moderation Leagues active in most provinces in the early 1920s consisted of men and women of power and wealth who wanted the return of deference, respect, and restraint among the mass of the population.

Booze and the Body

Underlying this overt political agenda were seismic shifts in bourgeois culture more generally that helped to fuel resistance to the anti-drink cause. Specifically, by the turn of the century there were clear signs of a growing disillusionment with the restrained, self-disciplined behaviour expected of bourgeois masculinity and femininity. Men and women in the middle and upper classes were creating new forms of bourgeois cultural practice in which abstention and prohibition had less and less place.

By the early twentieth century, many more upper- and middle-class men were prepared to stake out and publicly defend a new, more passionate and vigorous version of bourgeois culture that incorporated what some scholars have called a "hypermasculinity"—an approach less confined by the personal restraint and denial of the body.[23] One source of the change was the steady secularization of society, in which faith in divine causation gave way to science as a way of understanding the world. Prohibitionists made an effort to accommodate this deep cultural shift by regularly invoking scientific evidence to prove how dangerous alcohol could be, but in English Canada the movement never shook its evangelical Protestant fervour. Meetings typically opened and closed with hymns and prayers, and many of the key spokespersons and regular platform speakers were Methodist or Presbyterian clergymen whose arguments and rhetorical devices drew heavily from their theological arsenal. It was not simply that religion could no longer provide certainty, but that many men (and some women) began to find its heavy-handed moralism stifling, especially its insistence on protecting the soul by exercising maximum constraint on the evils of the flesh. Religion began to appear too feminine. As some bourgeois men got steadily wealthier in the late nineteenth and early twentieth century, the asceticism demanded by evangelicalism may well have seemed an impediment to enjoying the self-indulgent luxuries that they could now easily afford.

Other forces in their lives had also led them to deny their bodies. While wage-earners who worked with their hands might be concerned that their craft skills and workplace independence were being undermined in the industrial-capitalist workplace, bourgeois men worried that the new division of labour left them behind desks in white collars and business suits, out of touch with the productive physical labour that had helped to define "manhood" for so many generations of men. By the turn of the century they were often becoming imbedded in corporate hierarchies with severely restricted autonomy. They would have more difficulty exercising power and authority over others if they could not prove that their superior, class-based manhood sustained their assumed right to rule. Large movements of angry farmers and workers in the late nineteenth and early twentieth centuries brought home to these men of the urban elites the pressing need to buttress public confidence in their authority.

Many men were also deeply troubled by the new assertiveness of the women they lived with—women who argued for their rights to their own property, stretched the bounds of the "domestic sphere" with demands for access to higher education and professional or white-collar work, and insisted on the right to intervene in debates on public policy through their new clubs and societies—insisted even on the right to vote. These men were no happier that, in their absence from the home, their sons had to spend so much time in the exclusive care of women, whether mothers or school teachers. Boys could end up being too "effeminate"—"pussyfoots" or "sissies," or even "pansies" in the homosexual networks just beginning to open up in Canada in the pre-world war period. The line dividing masculinity from femininity seemed to be blurring.

Beyond the domestic circle, bourgeois men also watched the rising tide of new immigrants from allegedly "primitive" and "uncivilized" parts of the world, and they muttered grimly about "race suicide" for the British. Anglo-Canadian culture seemed too enervated and overrefined to stand up to these apparently more virile "races." A new "disease" of weakness and fatigue known as "neurasthenia" was traced to the airlessness and inactivity of the bourgeois lifestyle. Rethinking manhood thus became both a personal quest for meaning and fulfilment and a larger social project of relegitimizing their hegemony in class, gender, and racial hierarchies.

In the face of all these new challenges, many bourgeois men found little confidence in the prim, restrained formality and decorum and soft sentimentality of bourgeois masculinity that had been propagated for more than half a century—and had included teetotalism as a centrepiece of its prescription. Some of them had been quietly enjoying the disreputable pleasures of saloon, brothel, gambling den, or race track for many years, but the new sense of "crisis" in their masculine identities at the close of the nineteenth century brought the issues out into the open. From the literary sidelines, poet and journalist Bliss Carman wrote in 1894: "We had become so over-nice in our feelings, so restrained and formal, so bound by habit and use in our devotion to the effeminate realists, that one side of our nature was starved."[24]

Many men in elite circles had never accepted the temperance message of complete abstinence. Like these men in Calgary in the 1890s, they incorporated drinking (and smoking) into a mannered bourgeois masculinity, apart from women, in either private drawing room or exclusive club. (MM, MP-0000.538.38)

With applause from such "anti-modern" cultural ideologues, men from middle- and upper-class families began in the late nineteenth century to reconstruct their notion of appropriate manhood and simultaneously to revitalize their class and race positions. Rather than challenging social structures, they reached into the realm of leisure, recreation, and popular culture to construct a new validation of their gender, class, and racial identities through a generalized cult of vigorous bodily exertion, heroism, and "manliness." They sought more invigorating, physically demanding pursuits aimed at giving the body and its emotions more range for expression. Men's "primitive" desires for pleasure and passion, previously seen as sources of evil to be brought under the iron control of wilful self-discipline, were now to be constructed as positive forces to be unleashed and adapted to the development of a forceful new manhood. The best-known practitioner of this new lifestyle, Theodore Roosevelt, called it "the strenuous life."[25]

The body became a fixation for bourgeois men. They came to see the state of their muscles as a reflection of the state of their character and often linked the physical and the moral under the banner of "Muscular Christianity." Towards the end of the nineteenth century, a veritable explosion of new bourgeois male leisure-time pursuits accented vitality, health, strength, strenuous activity, and direct contact with "nature." Young men flocked into gymnasiums and amateur athletic clubs. In a search for adventure and heroism in defence of the Empire and the "Anglo-Saxon race" that controlled it, many men were also swept up into the Boer War and then the military preparedness and recruitment campaigns for what became the First World War.[26]

Boys got new kinds of training under male supervision: "manual training" to cultivate physical dexterity, cadet training to stimulate the martial arts, team sports to promote athletic skills (not only in schools, but also in churches and new voluntary associations such as the Young Men's Christian Association). The paramilitary Boy Scouts organized youth programs to teach the art of survival in the wild. In church, Sunday school, and popular literature, a vigorous, muscular, tough-minded carpenter replaced the soft, sentimental Jesus of the mid-nineteenth century. A cult of the wilderness grew up around hunting and fishing clubs, canoeing and camping excursions, family vacations in Muskoka, and "wild" urban parks (like Toronto's High Park, Montreal's Mount Royal, or Vancouver's Stanley Park). Even a whole new school of painting that celebrated wilderness—the Group of Seven—had drawn in enthusiastic bourgeois patronage by the 1920s.[27]

The celebration of the "primitive" by no means meant uncontrolled libertarian behaviour. Men were still expected to exercise personal restraint (notably in not wasting bodily fluids through masturbation, lest they lose vigour and vitality). But, most often, giving rein to boys and men to fight and play hard required a careful system of regulation—close supervision or military discipline. In their different ways, the YMCA and the Boy Scouts provided fine examples.

The emerging advertising industry also caught hold of this new search for "real experience" among bourgeois men and opened it up still further by encouraging them to believe that they could find some of the satisfaction and self-fulfilment they sought through consuming a wider array of products. Men learned that to participate in the more adventurous sports they had to buy the prescribed equipment. They could purchase a bicycle or later an automobile to pursue more outdoor thrills. They could buy barbells to build up muscles at home. Specialized magazines such as *Rod and Gun in Canada* linked the "strenuous life" to such products. If men had doubts about their virility, they found a market glutted with tonics and contraptions like electric belts that promised manly renewal. Health-food fads proliferated—Sylvester Graham's crackers, C.W. Post's grape-nuts, and J.H. Kellogg's corn flakes, among many others. An entertainment industry that included spectator sports, vaudeville shows, and amusement parks eliminated "rough" proletarian culture and assured class-specific spaces by introducing higher admission fees. Bourgeois men had the opportunity to get their thrills vicariously, watching spectacles of physical strength, power, and accomplishment from professional baseball or hockey

games and boxing matches to displays of feats of strength by celebrated mus-
clemen. All of these commercialized venues were tidied up to make bourgeois
participants more comfortable. In contrast to the mid-nineteenth-century
focus on asserting manhood through productive labour, men found it ever
more acceptable to buy the pleasures, intense experiences, and, ultimately, self-
fulfilment connected to the new masculine identity.[28]

Booze was marketed in ways that connected with the new bourgeois
manhood. Some of the new concern with well-regulated, healthy virility was
certainly turned against drinking, but within this new masculine celebration
of the body it was only a short step to argue that the effects of alcohol could
once again be enjoyed within the "strenuous life" if consumption was moderate and closely monitored. Canada's leading booze manufacturers shrewdly
picked up on themes of health and virility in slick new advertising campaigns.
In 1916 the Personal Liberty League in Ontario published testimonies from
several prominent athletes and trainers who considered beer "a great
upbuilder." Alfred Shrubb, champion middle-distance runner and Harvard
University coach, proclaimed that he always drank beer during his running
career and believed that "any men in training would be benefited by a glass of
beer occasionally." Similarly, Bob Dibble, champion sculler (and at that point a

*By the end of the nineteenth
century, for men who were
turning to the great outdoors
to express a more vigorous
masculine identity, it was not
unusual to bring along booze
on hunting and fishing trips.*
(GA, NA-2831-6)

soldier overseas), asserted, "I have always taken a bottle or two of beer while in my course of training, and have found it to be a big advantage to me."

Others insisted that ale "tones the system and keeps one on edge through a long training spell and prevents the running down of one's system" and that it was "a stimulant and a preventive against the constant strain and overwork." Big-game hunters in British Columbia made sure to pack plenty of alcohol for their expeditions. "I forgot all about the liquors," one wrote to a guide in 1907. "You had better buy us about 3 dozen quarts of good rye whisky if you have it there. . . . Also a bottle of the best brandy." By the end of the war many of the men who served overseas had learned to integrate regular tots of rum into their practice and conceptions of such "manliness" as courage and physical endurance.[29]

By the 1930s Hiram Walker would be making the connection between vigorous male exertion and drinking explicit in advertisements in *Life* and other magazines. The ads featured a cartoon story of some exotic adventure in a far-off, "primitive" land and always ended with a drink of Canadian Club. Suppressing consumption of these products through legal prohibition became far less popular among people attracted to this new, more consumerist variant of vigorous bourgeois masculine culture.[30]

The New Woman

By the early 1920s many bourgeois women were also rebuilding their gender identities and reconsidering the place of alcohol within their lives. The Vancouver *Sun* concluded, "The women cannot be counted upon for an instinctively prohibition vote."[31]

Bourgeois femininity was supposed to be rooted in the home, where women were expected to exercise moral guardianship over their families. Yet there is no reason to assume that all women had expelled alcohol from their lives. For half a century before the 1920s, the only public female voice on the drink question had been the WCTU, but it did not speak for all women of the middle and upper classes. Indeed, the elite National Council of Women refused to endorse prohibition until the First World War (and, as a result, the militant WCTU refused to affiliate). A less polemical form of female discourse— the mass-distribution cookbook—suggests that many women of the middle and upper classes were comfortable with a moderate consumption of alcohol in their households. Between the 1870s and the First World War, these domestic manuals continued to advise housewives on how to make alcohol-based medicinal cures and a huge variety of alcoholic beverages, including, by the turn of the century, cocktails. Indeed, Lucy Maud Montgomery's famous fictional heroine, Anne of Green Gables, once got her friend Diana drunk on Marilla's homemade currant wine, in the heart of prohibitionist Prince Edward Island.[32]

Moreover, reading materials intended to instruct bourgeois women on the intricate etiquette of entertaining gave detailed instructions about the alcohol to be served with each course, the expectations of servants pouring the drinks, and the appropriate glassware to grace the dinner table. According to *The Home Cook Book, Compiled by Ladies of Toronto and Chief Cities and Towns in Canada* (published in 1878 and 1888 editions): "Mixed drinks, like Regent's punch, or claret cup, with ale and beer, are more in keeping at lunch than wines." The matter of dinnertime beverages could be more daunting:

> The order of wines is sometimes perplexing, and the novice should remember that Chablis or Sauterne comes with the small oysters before soup, and that Sherry is drank after soup. Claret may be taken by those who prefer it during a whole dinner with entire propriety. Champagne comes with the roast, and Burgundy with the game. The French and Germans reserve champagne for a dessert wine, but we drink it with both roast and dessert.

The book advised ladies to "take but a single glass of any wine at most, having their glasses half-filled with champagne a second time."[33]

Comments on "Wines at Dinners" in an 1883 etiquette manual suggest that sometimes women would find moral minefields to negotiate on these occasions. Author John H. Young warned abstaining guests that "a dinner party is by some not regarded as complete, unless it includes one or more varieties of wine," and advised his readers that it was perfectly acceptable to decline politely. He then gave hosts and hostesses a pointed lecture about the potential risks:

> If the guests should include one or more people of well-known temperance principles, in deference to the scruples of these guests, wines or liquor should not be brought to the table. People who entertain should also be cautious as to serving wine at all. It is impossible to tell what harm you may do to some of your high-esteemed guests. It may be that your palatable wines may create an appetite for the habitual use of wines or stronger alcoholic liquors; or you may renew a passion long controlled or entombed; or you may turn a wavering will from seemingly steadfast resolution to forever abstain.

The shimmering crystal glassware facing each guest at Mrs. Yates's Montreal dinner party in 1900 testifies to the considerable amounts of alcohol consumed in upper-class households on such occasions. Cookbooks and advice manuals guided the hostess both to the correct wine, champagne, or sherry to accompany each course and to the appropriate stemware for the servants to set out on the table. Photo by William Notman. (MM, II-132676)

In 1904 Mary Arnold's *Century Cook Book* also tackled the question of teetotalling head on, but her advice hints that moderate drinking may have been more common than abstaining: "To-day there are some people who exclude wine entirely from their table, and many others who serve it only in moderation," she pointed out. Hosts, she said, typically offered their guests only "three kinds, such as sherry, claret and champagne, and sometimes only one. In this respect therefore, one may follow one's own conviction without being considered peculiar." She followed this observation with three pages of instructions on serving wines, ending with the observation that "a man's wine merchant should stand in as close relation to him as his lawyer or his physician." But she also cautioned, "The servant should name the wine offered, so that it may be refused if not wanted; the glasses should not be filled entirely full."[34]

Ten years later, Grace Denison, a widely read *Saturday Night* columnist known as "Lady Gay," was less circumspect in her *Canadian Family Cook Book*. "Wines are a feature of the greatest importance in dinner-giving," she wrote. "For a dinner of more than eight persons, a white wine, sherry, claret, Burgundy and champagne are provided, one wine, preferably claret, for a small dinner." She provided details on just when in the meal each of these drinks should be served. Like Denison's book, another manual published just before the war, *The Real Home-Keeper*, coached new brides on what to serve with what. For each guest it recommended a total of eight glasses of different wines over the course of the meal, followed by liqueurs and brandies. Since wealthy Canadians often attended a number of dinner parties each week, they may well have been consuming at least as much alcohol per person as the heavily maligned working men did in their saloons.[35]

Cookbooks merely set standards and do not report actual behaviour, but given the wide circulation of this kind of advice, the consumption of alcohol in upper- and middle-class households must have been common and acceptable. A photograph of the dinner table at Ottawa's Rideau Hall in 1898 certainly reveals the glitter of wine glasses, and Manitoba's Chief Justice T.G. Mathers confided to his diary in 1916 that his private cellar contained "5 gallons Scotch, 1 case Sparkling Burgundy, 1 case Saturne [sic], ½ case Sparkling Mouselle, 2 bottles brandy, [and] two bottles sherry." The emphasis was certainly on restraint and decorum. Flora McCrea Eaton, wife of the head of the T. Eaton Company, later recalled afternoon receptions in Toronto's poshest gardens with men in frock coats and ascot ties and women decked out in velvet gowns, assorted jewellery, feather-trimmed hats, and white kid gloves: "A fruit punch was often served, and sometimes it was flavoured with brandy, but liquor and cocktails were never offered to afternoon guests in Toronto homes at that time. The only exception was made during the Christmas season when trays

These advertisements from the Cosgraves, Cascade, and O'Keefe breweries were typical of the strong visual identification of drinking and domesticity that booze producers attempted to convey. Women were encouraged to believe that providing beer for their families and themselves was perfectly acceptable. From Saturday Night *(Toronto), 8 February 1913;* World *(Toronto), 28 February 1915;* Sun *(Vancouver), 21 October 1920.*

of Madeira or sherry would be passed to accompany the traditional Christmas cake."[36]

As long as the prohibitionists targeted the public drinking of working-class men and left home consumption alone, these women would probably not be unduly perturbed. But when the postwar thrust to cut off all importation of alcohol threatened to leave their wine cellars empty (the Dominion Alliance was talking about "the menace of the private cellar"), they finally felt the pinch of state intervention on their own households. During the two-year interval between the end of federal import controls late in 1919 and their reimposition at the request of the Ontario government, the head of Ontario's Citizens' Liberty League resigned in disgust at the indifference of those who "had participated in the work when their cellars were near depletion; however, the moment the restrictions on importation were removed by the federal government, nothing seemed to matter."[37]

Small wonder, then, that in the Ontario plebiscite on ending the importation of booze in 1921, a new organization known as the Women's League for Temperance and Government Control came out against prohibition and in favour of government control. "We don't believe in totally abstaining from a glass of beer or wine, yet eating up a pound of sweets in an hour or so and regarding that sort as temperance," one spokeswoman explained. In the 1924 and 1926 votes on rolling back prohibition, the Moderation League of Ontario had active provincial and local women's committees made up of the wives of prominent businessmen and professionals, whose names were published in newspaper ads. Little is known about these organizations, which do not seem to have been as large or powerful as their U.S. counterpart, the huge Women's Organization for National Prohibition Reform (formed in 1929 and ultimately four times larger than the WCTU), but their willingness to take such a public stand underlines the discomfort that many bourgeois women felt about the prohibition regime.[38]

As with men, women's anti-prohibitionist activism also grew out of major shifts in women's behaviour outside the home and in concepts of acceptable female comportment. The nineteenth century's patriarchal cult of domesticity had assumed that women would not participate in the public realm beyond their churches and some voluntary associations devoted to charity and moral uplift. By the turn of the century, many bourgeois women had already pushed back the confines of those expectations by joining activist organizations with broad social agendas—missionary societies, child-saving groups, historical or musical societies, the local branches of the National Council of Women, even the Woman's Christian Temperance Union—as well as pushing for independent careers before (and sometimes even after) marriage. Most of this female ferment was framed as an extension of women's domestic, mothering role into the public sphere—including the right to vote and hold office—and did not challenge women's alleged moral purity.[39]

Well before the war, however, Canadians were learning to come to terms with a so-called "New Woman"—the middle-class female who seemed to be bending gender boundaries to the breaking point. She might be found scribbling lecture notes in a university classroom, pounding away on typewriter keys in an office, riding a bicycle through a city park, handing out leaflets for women's suffrage, sitting with friends in the expensive seats of vaudeville or movie houses, or enjoying the thrills of dance halls, roller rinks, and amusement parks. Young, unmarried women from middle-class households entered the workforce in much larger numbers after the turn of the century, and when looking for pleasure after work they were ever more likely to follow the path blazed by working-class women—heading to the new commercialized spaces operated by leisure entrepreneurs as respectable, morally sound places for outings with friends. Unlike the saloon, poolroom, and other single-sex haunts of men, these new leisure arenas were sites of heterosexual mixing and socializing. Indeed, single women rarely ventured into them on their own and generally needed the companionship of a "beau" to ensure their good reputation. More and more young women were nonetheless detaching themselves from the prim, restrained model of Victorian femininity.[40]

By the end of the First World War, young women's public appearance was becoming more sexually charged. Many of them wore makeup, bobbed their hair, raised the hems of their dresses, and sometimes even smoked cigarettes. Even the less adventurous snapped up the widening range of beauty products—from cosmetics to ready-made clothing—that promised personal fulfilment and attractiveness. When the Montreal Local Council of Women fought back against the new elements of femininity in 1929 by organizing a "True Womanhood League," the members' pledge itemized the forms of behaviour that had emerged among young women:

I will NOT
Smoke,
Drink Intoxicating liquors,
Attend public dance halls,
Motor with strange men,
Permit familiarities,
Accept expensive gifts from any man to whom I am not either engaged or related,
Allow a man with whom I am not acquainted to accompany me anywhere,

Drink Cosgraves Mild (Chill-Proof) Pale Ale with your dinner and give tea and coffee a rest.

Try a glass of Cosgraves Mild (Chill-Proof) Pale Ale with your dinner. It is better for you. It aids digestion, is a food as well as a beverage and is much better for you.

Cosgraves
Mild (Chill-Proof)
Pale Ale

Made from the best malt and hops and pure filtered water. An economical and healthful beverage.

On sale at all dealers, hotels and licensed cafés.

"This is the Beer My Mistress Always Orders—She knows the Best."

For your health's sake you, too, should order Cosgraves Mild (Chill-Proof) Pale Ale—as well as for the pure enjoyment of it.

Cosgraves
Mild (Chill-proof)
Pale Ale

is a wonderful body-builder. The most nutritious as well as the most delightful.

In pint and quart bottles. On sale everywhere — dealers and hotels.

For over half a century the Cosgrave label has meant the best in malt and hop beverages.

> Accept any attention from a man I know to be married,
> Read demoralizing literature.
> AND I WILL attend church at least once a month.

Advertisers, with their carefully prepared ad content, helped to spread the appeal of self-expression through consumption for bourgeois women of all ages. The appearance of new Canadian magazines aimed at them—*Canadian Homes and Gardens* in 1924, *Mayfair* in 1927, and *Chatelaine* in 1928—signalled the consolidation of this large market of bourgeois consumers. For women with access to substantial incomes, shopping, especially in such lavish new department stores as Eaton's College Street store (opened in Toronto in 1930), became central to the new definition of their femininity.[41]

As the Montreal Local Council's list of "don'ts" suggests, women's consumerist pleasures could also involve alcohol. The booze industry's pre-prohibition advertising often featured women consuming alcohol. Just before the war, for example, Labatt produced a calendar image with two proper young women attempting to steal beer from the picnic basket of a tweedy middle-class sport fisherman. Although they were not welcome in the pre-prohibition saloons, many young bourgeois women must have learned to drink at their parents' dinner tables or at the balls and parties in private homes, hotels, and exclusive clubs. In the larger cities, some apparently found their way to licensed restaurants, as the Toronto licence commissioners discovered on their tour of drinking places in 1905. The commissioners were disturbed by "the demoralization of young women, married and unmarried" that they observed at the city's famous McConkey's Restaurant: "Young girls have frequently been brought home in carriages intoxicated, to the distress and heart-breaking trouble of the parents." With the connivance of servants a cabby had quietly whisked one "daughter of one of the most respected citizens of Toronto" safely upstairs without her parents' knowledge. "With the increasing wealth which has come to many homes, and the increasing desire to be a bit smart on the part of many young girls whose heads have been turned," the commissioners concluded, "McConkey's has grown into a place where they can play the smart and defy ordinary conventionalities."[42]

For many young women, the First World War was a watershed. One who grew up in the highest circles of Montreal's Anglo elite recalled how drinking increased after the war:

> Before that, if there was drinking at all, it was controlled. You might be served one cocktail by the butler and that was that. You weren't offered another. There might be wine at dinner, but you would get maybe two or

By the 1920s some young women, especially the so-called "flappers," were reported to be enjoying liquor from flasks when they were out socializing with friends. (GA, NA-3217-2)

three glasses all evening—not much. But after the war, men began to carry hip flasks and at dances at the Mount Royal or the Ritz there would be private rooms hired and some people would just stay there and drink all evening. It caused a lot of trouble—young men and even some girls having regularly to be carted off home from parties.

Another Montrealer remembered that footmen passed through these parties "with inexhaustible supplies of champagne." In other parts of the country where prohibition lasted longer, some adventurist young women seem to have found their way to the illegal blind pigs and speakeasies that sprang up after 1920. If the sensationalist press reporting had any basis in reality, these women would readily share a flask of bootleg liquor with friends. The Hollywood movies women watched in the 1920s showed plenty of social drinking (one 1930 study found two-thirds of the 115 films surveyed included scenes of drinking, most often including the heroes and heroines).[43]

After 1920, when they had the vote in all provinces except Quebec (and the still independent Dominion of Newfoundland), female voters were drawn much more directly into the various postwar plebiscite campaigns. In some cases, special meetings and debates were arranged for them, and newspapers reported heavy turnouts of women at the polls. In British Columbia one paper concluded after the wet victory in 1920 that "the women's vote was particularly large and the decision to try Temperance instead of Prohibition was undoubtedly greatly due to the influence which they exerted." A leading dry campaigner in the province blamed his side's defeat, in part, on the "immaturity of girl voters without sufficient age and experience to judge the problems of life." Voting for the return of retail sales of alcohol could be intimately connected with rejecting an older version of bourgeois femininity and opting for one that accented greater self-expression through consumption.[44]

The "liquor interests," then, had increasing success in getting bourgeois men and women to step forward to provide the public face and much of the energy for the wet campaigns of the various moderation leagues that appeared in all provincial fights over alcohol in the 1920s—just as they had done at the turn of the century in the United States in the business-led Committee of Fifty (an anti-saloon think-tank) and in the 1920s in the Association Against the Prohibition Amendment, which was headed by Pierre du Pont of Du Pont Chemicals and John J. Raskob of General Motors, and the equally elite-led Women's Organization for National Prohibition Reform. In Quebec the president of the Committee of Moderation was Joseph Quintal, president of the Montreal Chamber of Commerce, and the honorary presidents included Lord Shaunessey and Sir Alexandre Lacoste, former chief justice of the Quebec Court of Appeal. In British Columbia moderation league leaders included Henry O. Bell-Irving, fish-canning magnate, and Charles Wilson, a prominent Vancouver lawyer.[45]

Not only were these people appalled at the immediate impact of prohibition on their own lives and communities, but they also found this experiment in moral repressiveness running against the grain of the new bourgeois culture that they were in the process of constructing. Their communities were far from united on this question, as many still clung to a faith in the virtues of hard work, thrift, and moral restraint. If Prime Minister William Lyon Mackenzie King is any indication, many were deeply conflicted and even hypocritical on this issue. King recorded in his diary in April 1921 that he voted against the importation of liquor, but also noted, "The two boxes of whiskey that I had asked Lemieux to purchase for me in Montreal came today."[46]

Yet many more men and women in these affluent social circles, especially among the younger generations, were ready to give freer rein to their bodies and their passions than the prudish teetotaller allowed. To an unprecedented extent, they pursued personal fulfilment through various kinds of consumerism. The regular voice of respectability and taste, *Saturday Night*, must have spoken for a good number of them when it declared in 1919: "The people are getting a little fed up with the anti-horse race, anti-smoke, anti-drink, anti-anything movements, as well as the sin hounds who keep people from enjoying themselves in a legitimate manner on the Sabbath day." Once the alternative to prohibition became careful state regulation of alcohol sales and not the wide-open saloon, legalized drinking in moderation in tasteful, respectable settings—preferably the home—could be incorporated comfortably into the new bourgeois culture. On the first day of renewed alcohol sales in Toronto in 1927, the Toronto *Star*'s reporter noted limousines showing up at government liquor stores all morning, as the "upper classes" decided "to dive into the drink with leisurely dignity."[47]

In contrast to nineteenth-century conventions, a wine company had no difficulty in 1940 in associating drinking wine with sophisticated bourgeois femininity. From La revue moderne *(Montreal), February 1940. (YUA, 1893)*

Labour and Liquor

Although plenty of drinking men in working-class communities opposed prohibition, the most articulate voices of the labour leadership at the turn of the century were far more likely to be abstainers. The shift in the larger temperance movement to legislated coercion made these workers uneasy, however, and gradually labour drifted away from the dry alliance. By the end of the First

World War, after many years of deep division, the Canadian labour movement ultimately became one of the leading forces in opposition to prohibition.

Reaching that position had been a tortuous path. In the last third of the nineteenth century, many working-class leaders were committed teetotallers who, in their search for working-class respectability, worried about the impact of alcohol and alcoholism on working-class family households and on a drinker's ability to join in any collective working-class struggle. Some craft unions had actively promoted sobriety. The Brotherhood of Locomotive Engineers had staked out what was perhaps the most militant position with its motto of "Sobriety, Truth, Justice and Morality" and constitutional provisions for expelling habitual drunkards, whose names were published in its monthly journal. In 1892 the railway brotherhoods went a step further and organized a "white-button" movement in parallel with the WCTU's white-ribbon campaign, to encourage railway workers to display their sobriety with pride. To discourage their members' drinking and raise their organizations' respectability in middle-class eyes, many labour groups moved their meetings out of taverns and thus turned their backs on the European practice of linking organized workers' movements and working-class popular culture in cafés and taverns. Instead, early in the twentieth century, Canada's city-based unions would begin to pool their money to build their own halls, known as "Labour Temples."[48]

These concerns had reached their highest form of expression in the Knights of Labor. In 1884 the Knights' weekly newspaper in Hamilton, the *Palladium of Labor*, had summed up that movement's perspective on "The Fight for Temperance":

> The working classes do not probably drink more than others, but they experience its effects more. The expense of drink that would not be appreciably felt by a merchant or professional man will keep the laborer destitute and rob his family of all the comforts and sometimes of the necessaries of life. The habit is fatal to independence and self-control. The workingman who spends a large portion of his wages in liquor is obliged to live from hand to mouth, and often to go into debt. He is absolutely at the mercy of his employer who, knowing that he has no savings to fall back upon, often takes advantage of his necessities and compels him to accept low wages. Drinking fosters habits of irresolution and instability. It has been the cause of the ignominious failure of many a movement on the part of workingmen which otherwise had fair prospect of success. It is in every way bad and any movement which tends to its suppression should have the cordial sympathy of Labor Reformers.

The temperance movement reached out for working-class support with cartoons like this one by J.W. Bengough. From Pioneer *(Toronto), 8 August 1902.*

The Knights officially supported temperance as part of their effort to promote a new culture of assertive, collective working-class respectability (in contrast to middle-class individualism), and barred from membership any "person who either sells or makes his living by the sale of intoxicating drink"—meaning, primarily, saloon-keepers (bankers, lawyers, stockbrokers, and professional gamblers were the only others on the prohibited list). Sobriety could be a goal for those wanting to change the direction of the new capitalist economy as much as for those who directed it. In 1886 the Knights' Grand Master Workman, Terence V. Powderly, penned a pledge for the Order's members, which he claimed some 100,000 members took within six months:

I am a Knight of Labor. I believe that every man should be free from the
curse of slavery, whether that slavery appears in the shape of monopoly, usury
or intemperance. The firmest link in the chain of oppression is the one I
forge when I drown my manhood and reason in drink. No man can rob me
of the brain God has given me unless I am a party to the theft. If I drink to
drown grief, I bring grief to my wife, child and sorrowing friends. I add not
one iota to the sum of human happiness when I invite oblivion over the rim
of a glass.[49]

Nevertheless, the Order entered the fray with great caution. Around its members swirled demeaning middle-class discourses about working-class degradation that made them uncomfortable. The *Palladium* warned, "The attempt of
employers to dictate as to the personal habits of their workmen so long as the
latter do not incapacitate themselves for work by excess ought to be sternly
resisted." In his testimony before the Royal Commission on the Liquor
Traffic, a Knights leader in Montreal bristled at the disparaging comments of a
witness who had preceded him: "I do not like to see such prejudice shown
against the working class and their organizations." Moreover, temperance was
a divisive issue within working-class communities, because so many working
men scoffed at the prospect of giving up their glass of beer and their social life
in the saloon. Even teetotalling wage-earners worried that state repression of
drinking violated fundamental personal liberties.[50]

Rather than merge into existing temperance groups, then, the Knights
developed their own angle on temperance. In contrast to the individualism of
the middle-class temperance cry, they argued that a strong organization of
temperate working men could establish independence and dignity for workers
and usher in a new oppositional culture of working-class respectability. In the
pages of the *Palladium of Labor*, Phillips Thompson looked forward to "the
new direction" that abstinence "would give the thoughts and aspirations of
the toilers. They would have more time and more inclination for mental culture." According to Thompson, the workers "would learn to place their hopes
in the future, and to take their share, well and worthily in the struggle for
equal chances." Temperance thus became only part of a larger vision of the
"nobler and holier" place of working people in a reformed industrial society.
The issue had been appropriated and recast as a tool in the battle for working-class emancipation.[51]

In practical terms the Knights demanded a high standard of deportment
among their members. As one Montreal Knight explained, the Order insisted
that members:

Prohibitionists often presented working men as victims of the liquor traffic and vulnerable to its attacks on family life. From Pioneer *(Toronto), 26 December 1920.*

WATCHING FOR PREY

must be dressed neat and tidy, must not be seen on the streets drunk or they are liable to be expelled, and the result is that men get into the habit of coming to our meetings, they dress better, and the fact of spending money to get dress prevents them from going to the saloons, and their families are better off. Thousands of women . . . say that their husbands were never so good as since they joined the order of the Knights of Labour.

The Knights also organized their own wholesome entertainment to bring both men and women into booze-free settings, from picnics and dances to public lectures. This, they hoped, would appeal to working-class wives and daughters and strengthen the men's cultural ties to their households, rather than to saloons.[52]

The Knights leadership also took tentative steps towards an alliance with the mainstream temperance movement. By the mid-1880s, their local newspapers were promoting the benefits of taking the pledge and giving verbal support to efforts to limit saloon licences and even to full-fledged prohibition under the Scott Act. The fledgling Trades and Labor Congress of Canada, in which the Knights played a leading role, attempted to bridge the divide in the labour movement with a resolution in 1883 that "any practical legislation tending to reduce the consumption of intoxicating liquor" would meet with its "hearty approval." Officers of the Dominion Alliance made a pitch to the 1886 Congress convention and saw the 1883 resolution renewed. Behind these moves lay an effort in the mid-1880s to build an electoral coalition of Labour Reformers and prohibitionists, which the Congress also endorsed. This brief, fragile alliance brought a reformist mayor, William Howland, to office in Toronto in 1886, and a Labour-Prohibitionist candidate, William Garson, won a seat in the Ontario legislature the next year. Otherwise there was little to show for this collaboration in Ontario, and the same was apparently true in British Columbia.[53]

Nor was there any clear sign that the prohibitionists had much interest in labour's wider goals. The WCTU's U.S. leader, Frances Willard, had made a well-publicized claim that workers needed to learn to manage their wages better rather than demanding higher wages. Willard eventually retracted her comment and worked hard in the late 1880s and early 1890s to cement an alliance between her organization and the labour movement, though no such overtures came from the Canadian WCTU. The Knights' alternative vision of temperance seemed to have been sacrificed to narrow electoralism. In the 1890s some labour figures attempted to work with shifting clusters of social "regenerators," which included radical prohibitionists such as W.W. Buchanan, editor of the *Templar*, and many of whom would merge into the new Canadian Socialist League in 1899. But these new political currents lacked the Knights' numerical strength and distinctive working-class perspective.[54]

For much more complex reasons than their views on alcohol, the Knights had declined after the late 1880s, and a new North American labour movement based more narrowly on craft unionism slowly coalesced around the new American Federation of Labor (AFL) and its smaller, weaker Canadian counterpart, the Trades and Labor Congress of Canada. Although many former Knights moved over into it, this new labour movement never tried to rearticulate the same coherent vision of working-class temperance. Indeed, the AFL told the WCTU in 1897 that it did not see prohibition as essential to workers' emancipation, and a year later the Trades and Labor Congress of Canada voted down a prohibition resolution (that same year Winnipeg's unions apparently kept a temperance float out of their Labour Day parade, but made room for some brewery wagons). According to a 1901 survey, a block of nine of the thirty-nine leading international craft unions (including railwaymen, sailors, tailors, and typographers) still strongly opposed the saloon, and several more were at least somewhat negatively inclined. But those craft unionists whose livelihood was tied to the liquor traffic (especially brewers, bartenders, coopers, cigarmakers, musicians, and teamsters) and those who believed that their heavy labour required beer as a refreshment (such as the glassworkers) were staunch opponents of prohibition.[55]

The Federation tried to respect this division of opinion by avoiding any clear policy statements on booze. Similarly, when the Dominion Alliance pushed Toronto's Independent Labor Party to take a stand in 1911, a prominent labour man urged the party to steer clear: "We have in our party men who are utterly opposed to any restriction on the liquor traffic," he said, "and we cannot give the Alliance a favorable reply without antagonizing a large body of our members."[56]

Deepening Ambivalence

Few labour leaders in Canada spoke out in defence of drinking or of saloons before the war. Even though some unions had made it clear that they wanted nothing to do with prohibition, the dominant craft-union movement in the prewar period had set a public course of responsible action to win acceptance by employers and the state, and it had no intention of risking its credibility or respectability by openly allying with the liquor traffic. This position represented more than pure opportunism; many union activists were still cast in the earnest, morally upright mould of the late nineteenth century. Indeed, like Hamilton's Allan Studholme, the lone labour member of the Ontario legislature from 1906 to 1919, several individuals responded positively to the overtures of Social Gospellers to participate in reform alliances, notably in the various provincial Social and Moral Reform Councils launched after 1907, where they rubbed shoulders with prohibitionists for a few years (but generally and eventually drifted away). For the drys, the most prominent voice within international unionism was the widely read Reverend Charles Steltzle, a former machinist turned independent Presbyterian minister, whose writings on a labour-oriented Social Gospel appeared regularly in Canadian labour newspapers. In 1909, when the AFL's annual convention met in Toronto, Steltzle called a mass meeting to launch an anti-saloon fellowship within the Federation, where some prominent international union leaders defended prohibition. Thanks to the efforts of AFL president Samuel Gompers, no such organization emerged. Nonetheless, before leaving home in Britain, some recent immigrants might also have come into contact with the Trade Union and Labour Officials' Temperance Fellowship, organized in 1905 to rally the considerable number of teetotallers in the British labour movement.[57]

Even on the far left, teetotalism was remarkably common, as it was on the European and British left in the early twentieth century. To be sure, socialists typically blamed capitalism for drunkenness and saw no need for special organization or public policy to deal with this issue because it would disappear under socialism. As socialist Colin McKay wrote in 1901:

> The clergy inveigh, halfheartedly, against the liquor traffic. They ought to see that it is a necessity concomitant of the profit-mongering system, which will continue just as long as the motive principle of industry is private profit, because it affords an easy method of amassing wealth. Under the system of socialism, where industry was carried on for public welfare, not individual aggrandizement, the liquor traffic would disappear, because nobody would have any interest in prosecuting it.

In a similar vein, the socialists' leading Canadian mouthpiece, the *Western Clarion*, argued two years later: "Provide the workingmen with clean, cheerful homes and the means of intellectual culture and they will stop drinking bad whiskey in filthy and malodorous saloons." In the B.C. legislature, Socialist MLA James Hawthornthwaite proposed a popular socialist alternative to the liquor traffic in the form of municipal ownership of the drink trade modelled on the Scandinavian "Gothenburg System," but no government was prepared to go near that approach in the prewar period.[58]

Many men in the Socialist Party of Canada not only rejected temperance as a reformist middle-class ploy that deflected attention from the anti-capitalist cause, but also linked a tough version of working-class masculinity to the struggle for a new world. They objected in particular to the WCTU's multi-pronged attack on masculine amusements. Their scorn for prohibition was as searing as for any other threats to gender privilege, including women's suffrage. Yet some socialist women spoke out for controls on men's drinking, including British Columbia's widely read socialist journalist Merrill Burns, and many in the growing Finnish socialist community, which organized its own temperance societies. Once the Social Democrats had split away from the Socialist Party of Canada, their newspaper, *Cotton's Weekly*, regularly published sympathetic views of prohibition penned by the editor, William Cotton, or his sister Mary Cotton Wisdom. One of the country's most prominent socialists (and vice-president of the Trades and Labor Congress of Canada), Toronto's Jimmy Simpson, appeared on many dry platforms before and during the war.[59]

The women among these anti-booze socialists tended to rest their case on the plight of neglected or abused wives and children. The men more often argued that alcohol undermined collective working-class struggle. By the end of the war, British Columbia's R.P. ("Parm") Pettipiece was thundering:

> Drink will break a strike sooner than anything else except hunger. . . . The wage slave that tries to drown the misery of daily toil and poverty in "booze" is hopeless. He can be neither organized or educated and it will require a sober, organized and educated working class to emancipate itself from wage slavery.[60]

Organized labour was nonetheless caught in a deepening dilemma in the early twentieth century. Most of the North American labour movement (outside the socialist organizations) had shifted their discourses around wage labour away from a condemnation of "wage slavery" based on the ideal of the independent producer. In doing so they had moved to demands for "fair" wages, or "a living wage," that would permit breadwinners to provide for their families all necessities and at least some luxuries. By insisting on a high-wage economy and shorter hours of labour (in contrast to the "degraded" workers among "uncivilized races" elsewhere in the world), Canadian and U.S. labour leaders made a case for a kind of working-class consumerism, including spending on leisure pursuits. Yet they also expressed more than a whiff of disapproval of the commercialized mass culture on which workers were spending their spare change. Both labour and socialist spokespeople often seemed troubled that the saloon, roller rink, or vaudeville house appealed to baser, more hedonistic instincts and failed to uplift the worker.[61]

The leadership's view of culture was more rooted in long-standing notions of working-class self-improvement through prudent, educational forms of recreation: reading, attending lectures or debates, listening to musical concerts, and participating in the collective social life of workers' movements. When they undertook to organize an annual workers' festival on Labour Day (first celebrated in the 1880s and then as a legal holiday beginning in 1894), they emphasized sober, orderly respectability in their parades and earnest, wholesome fun in their public lectures, sports programs, band concerts, and picnics—all within the range of what has come to be known as "rational" recreation. The country's first May Day celebrations, which began in Montreal in 1906, were even more sober versions of parading and speech-making.[62]

Many labour leaders apparently still shared the earlier concerns of craft unionists and Knights of Labor that the increased leisure resulting from their demands for shorter hours posed problems as well as opportunities for workers. Unionists who showed up drunk to the Labour Day parade might be fined by their local, and beer was often officially banned from the annual picnics. Some locals supplied it nonetheless, and unionists got their own supplies from private flasks and nearby saloons, until tighter provincial liquor laws had put an end to these public pleasures by the middle of the First World War. The discomfort of some of the labour leadership—and the widening gulf between their notions of appropriate leisure activities and the real world of working-class popular culture—was evident in an interview with an unnamed "prominent laborite" standing amid the bustle of activity outside a bar on Yonge Street in 1913. It was a shame that the authorities were allowing the bars to remain open on Labour Day, this man declared, "in view of the weakness of many who might better have been with their families spending the nickels on innocent and educative entertainment at the [Canadian National] Exhibition." The steady decline of labour-sponsored Labour Day festivities in the decade before the war reflected in part how working men were voting with their feet and seeking out their own amusements.[63]

Still, the scepticism about booze and its place in a rapidly emerging world of commercialized mass culture did not push these labour and socialist figures comfortably into the arms of the prohibition movement. Ever since the days of the Knights of Labor several key points of disagreement in analysis and strategy had lingered on. They hinged on the extent to which working men should bear the brunt of blame and repressive public policy. These were fundamental class issues that pitted the narrowly focused middle-class prohibitionists against the generally more flexible working-class temperance advocates. One central issue was coercion. As far back as 1877, a prominent Toronto labour leader, John Hewitt, had "strongly advocated the use of moral suasion, but was opposed to coercive legislation in any movement that would rob a man of his rights." Several years later a Montreal Knight had a similar concern: "I do not think that any particular body of men should say what the other should take." Another had insisted that prohibition would not work: "I believe people have to be educated up to anything before they can receive it quickly, quietly and satisfactorily. Whenever too much restriction is forced on them they will rebel against it, and naturally seek other channels in order to secure what they think they have been improperly and unfairly deprived of."[64]

Many labour voices, preferring persuasion to compulsion, concentrated on promoting moderation and providing alternatives (such as meetings of the Knights of Labor or local unions, or the public libraries that the labour movement was backing in this period). Eventually many were drawn to the antiprohibitionist campaign's emphasis on individual rights—an emphasis, ironically, most often proclaimed by Conservative politicians whom labour rarely supported—and bristled at the middle-class WCTU's rhetoric as attacks on their manhood and male privileges.

There was also a key disagreement about cause and effect. While the Dominion Alliance or the WCTU saw the core of the problem in the individual weakness of the drunkard, unionists were increasingly more likely to see drunkenness as resulting from poverty rather than causing it. A Montreal Knight told the Royal Commission on the Liquor Traffic that "long hours and poverty do more than anything else to cause drunkenness." A decade later, Southern Ontario's regional labour paper, the *Industrial Banner*, explained:

> The best substitute for the saloon is the home, and a better one cannot be proposed. The trade union aims to make the home beautiful and attractive through improving the environment of the toiling masses, by shortening the work-day and obtaining a wage that will enable the husband and father to clothe his wife and children decently, have pictures on the wall, carpets on the floor and music in the home.

In 1911 an Independent Labor Party member in Toronto insisted: "Give the workingman sufficient money to enable him to make his house a home and then he will stop drinking." Labour leaders resented the indifference or hostility of prohibitionists to this larger struggle. At the same meeting in 1911, one speaker stated, "The Dominion Alliance has done nothing to strike at the social and industrial evil which in a great measure causes intemperance." Another argued, "If they came over to our side and advocated industrial reform they would do more for temperance than if they sought any amount of legislation."[65]

More and more often, even dedicated temperance supporters within the labour movement were also critical of the class bias involved in shutting down working men's saloons but leaving the rich men's private clubs and well-stocked wine cellars untouched. Studholme denounced any legislation that kept "the glass from the workingman," but allowed "the rich man to have his highball." Nor was it fair that "the rich man could get drunk and be taken home in an auto or put to bed until he sobers up at the club, while the workingman when he got a little too much was thrown out on the street to be picked up by a patrol wagon."[66]

The ever narrower focus of the post-1900 prohibitionists on the evils of the working-class saloon and their relative indifference to the older temperance approaches of moral suasion and mutual support left the dry voices in working-class communities with no comfortable space in the anti-booze crusade. Ultimately, there were far more abstainers than prohibitionists in working-class communities, but they were soon drowned out by the rising chorus of wet voices in working-class Canada.

The Rise of the Wets

As the debate over prohibition intensified at the beginning of the First World War, some prominent labour leaders expressed support. The Brotherhood of Locomotive Engineers, the bedrock of dry unionism, endorsed it in 1915. The same year, the Saskatoon Trades and Labor Council unanimously supported the Saskatchewan government's move to close barrooms and introduce government dispensaries. The editor of *Alberta Labor News*, Elmo Roper, insisted, "From an economic or humanitarian standpoint, progressive Labor's stand must be uncompromisingly against booze in any shape or form." In keeping with printers' union teetotalism, Halifax's typographical union declared prohibition would be of "inestimable benefit to the working class and to society."[67]

For the first time, however, the wet unions mobilized an outspoken resistance movement. Since well before the war, the brewery workers' union in the United States had been leading the charge. Generally (and ironically, considering that they had a staunchly socialist leadership), the U.S. union worked in close alliance with the brewing companies, whose national organization funded full-time organizers to work with labour and supplied a steady stream of articles for the labour press. Through the national organization the companies also provided funds for anti-prohibition campaigns, often waged under the banner of Trade Union Liberty Leagues or Wet Leagues. With the threat of prohibition in Canada rising by 1915, the brewery workers rallied others, such as bartenders and cigar-makers, whose jobs were at risk, and reached out to other unions, which began to show public support.

Some six hundred bartenders, brewery workers, cigar-makers, and restaurant and hotel employees gathered in Toronto's Labor Temple that year to proclaim their opposition to restrictions. Several months later they put their support behind the Personal Liberty League. In March 1916 Ontario's *Industrial*

Banner reported, "During the past few weeks several of the most influential central labor bodies in the province have voiced the sentiment that it would be detrimental to the best interests of the general public to put prohibition into effect at the present time." In Manitoba the bartenders' union took the lead in forming an alliance with brewers and hotel-owners in the oddly named Manitoba Prohibition League, and they brought in the well-known U.S. civil rights lawyer, Clarence Darrow, to highlight civil libertarian arguments. During Alberta's referendum campaign in 1915, both the Lethbridge and Calgary trades and labour councils denounced prohibition. The Alberta Federation of Labor proclaimed its almost unanimous opposition to the measure. Darrow also did a speaking tour around that province for labour.[68]

A few months later Vancouver's brewery workers pulled together a British Columbia Workers' Equal Rights Association to resist that province's new legislation, and trades and labour councils in all the leading cities formally denounced the law. A delegation from the Cumberland miners' union local arrived at the B.C. premier's door carrying a petition with six thousand signatures and insisted that they needed beer to be able to endure their work. Nationally, delegates to the 1915 convention of the Trades and Labor Congress of Canada voted to end its affiliation with the Social Service Council of Canada (formerly the Moral and Social Reform Council), in part because of the council's pro-prohibition position. The sprinkling of labour men who appeared on prohibitionist platforms—such as Vancouver printer R.H. Neelands and Toronto socialist Jimmy Simpson—could not counterbalance the general impression of growing labour opposition.[69]

With prohibition in place, the main councils and federations of the labour movement across the country moved cautiously on a potentially divisive issue in a time of national emergency. In some places, disagreements were too sharp for labour bodies to take any position.[70] Yet the campaigns of resistance to prohibition never completely stopped. By the end of the war, labour's anti-prohibition coalition was broadening out to include many more unionists. The mainstream of the Canadian labour movement began to lobby governments for the return of the working men's favourite beverage—beer with a stronger alcoholic content than the "near beer" available in hotels under prohibition. They also argued for the return of light wine, which few Anglo-Celtic workers drank but would no doubt have been appreciated by many European immigrants and some Québécois. They abandoned the liquor drinker—indeed, worried out loud about the increasing consumption of liquor once the saloons closed—and sidestepped the issue of public drinking. The whole focus of the subsequent campaign was on bringing back a heartier beer.

Ontario unions took the lead. In September 1916 the Toronto District
Trades and Labor Council brought to the national Trades and Labor Congress
convention a resolution that called on the TLC's Ontario executive to ask the
province's government to permit the retail sale of light wines and beers, to
hold a referendum on such beverages, and to allow local option for municipalities that voted for them. After lengthy debate, in which labour's dry voices
fought back forcefully, the resolution was carried "by a large majority." That
Ontario had not conducted a plebiscite before imposing prohibition gave a
sharper edge to the province's labour leaders' concerns. In December and
again in January 1918, the Ontario executive took this message into their
annual meeting with Premier William Hearst and his cabinet, but got a bluntly
unsympathetic response. The following spring, a much more substantial mobilization got underway. Trades and labour councils in Windsor, London, Brantford,
Hamilton, Toronto, Kingston, and Ottawa brought large delegations to a rally
at the Toronto Armouries on 2 March 1918, where they agreed to a resolution demanding 2.5 per cent beer. The campaign slogan was to be: "If you are
going to make it, make it fit to drink." A parade of some five thousand working men and war veterans then formed up behind a pipe band and banners
(which included the shipbuilders' threat of "No Beer—No Boats") and
marched through the streets to the provincial legislature to meet the premier
and his cabinet. When Hearst again rejected the men's request, he was greeted
with "hoots and shouting" and had to beat a hasty retreat behind police barri-
cades as angry workers surged forward.[71]

Meanwhile the New Brunswick and Alberta federations of labour were
making no more headway with their respective governments. Early in 1919, a
labour delegation's pro-beer arguments did help to convince the Quebec premier to hold a referendum on beer and wine.[72]

By this point the momentum had reached Ottawa. The issue was raised
when the new Unionist government headed by Sir Robert Borden summoned
fifty-four labour leaders for a conference on "war problems" in January 1918.
Avoiding "the merits or demerits of beer as an ordinary beverage," those in
attendance eventually decided "that inasmuch as some men considered it a
necessity, and it did not need any food grains to produce, and that it might
possibly prevent some men from freely changing their place of employment,"
they asked the government to reconsider its recently announced order-in-
council aimed at shutting down the liquor traffic as a wartime emergency.[73]

On 15 April the country's leading unionists were back in Ottawa for the
annual presentation of the Trades and Labor Congress resolutions to the federal
cabinet. This time they requested that the government amend the wartime
prohibition measure to allow 2.5 per cent beer to be made, imported, and sold

across the country. They noted that "twenty-five large labor organizations" had endorsed the measure. The cabinet minister assigned to respond was none other than the staunch "banish-the-bar" crusader from the prewar Ontario Liberal Party, Newton W. Rowell, who had joined the Unionist government in Ottawa a few months earlier. He made it clear that the alcohol content had been established by the wartime provincial legislation, and that the government had no intention of interfering with standards set by the provinces. The next fall, with only "about forty dissenting votes," the Congress endorsed the action of the Ontario executive and for the first time called on all federal and provincial governments to legalize the production and sale of stronger beer. The Congress executive presented this proposal to the federal government in February 1919, along with a petition signed by thousands of workers from across the country, but returned home empty-handed. They were no more successful a month later in a special meeting with the cabinet to consider the resolution.[74]

South of the border Sam Gompers, a former cigar-maker who liked saloons, had been speaking out against prohibition. Gompers, the head of the international labour movement to which most Canadian unionists were connected, carefully distinguished his personal views from those of the American Federation of Labor, which was still officially neutral on the question. Once the prohibitionist Eighteenth Amendment to the U.S. Constitution had been approved, he urged President Woodrow Wilson to exempt beer and wine, but, despite the president's personal support, neither Congress nor the Democratic Party would co-operate. The Volstead Act, which was passed over Wilson's veto as the enabling legislation for the Eighteenth Amendment, included beer and wine as unacceptable intoxicating beverages. Soon thousands of workers in and around New York City were actively considering staging a national general strike for their beer. In June 1919 the AFL convention finally passed a resolution opposing the Eighteenth Amendment.[75]

By the time nearly a thousand delegates arrived in Hamilton for the annual convention of the Trades and Labor Congress in Hamilton in September 1919, 1,500 labour organizations across the country (out of some 1,900) had endorsed the Congress leadership's demand for stronger beer (even the Winnipeg Women's Labor League had expressed support). At that meeting, Congress president Tom Moore reviewed the many efforts made to convince federal and provincial governments to make the beer available, and delegates passed a new resolution demanding government action. This labour campaign became a prominent feature of the wet advertising campaign in the Ontario prohibition plebiscite underway that fall.[76]

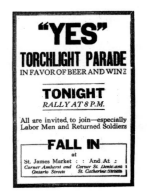

At the end of the First World War the new organizations formed to fight prohibition reached out for support from working men and war veterans. In Montreal they organized a large parade just before the referendum that turned back the ban on beer and wine. From Gazette *(Montreal), 9 April 1919.*

Arguably, Ontario workers had the best chance of getting back their lost rights, since in October 1919 a new Farmer-Labour government swept to power in the provincial election. Ontario's provincial federation of labour, then known as the Labor Educational Association of Ontario, passed a resolution the following spring in support of "a good palatable beer of sufficient alcoholic strength." Hamilton's labour member, George Halcrow, was a consistent "wet" voice in public discussions. Yet on this issue (as on the question of the eight-hour working day), Ontario's labour movement got no help from the dominant Farmer element in the coalition. Farmer leaders were committed temperance men and prohibition supporters. The one effort to get the government to hold a referendum on making beer and wine available was defeated in the house. Labour organizations in other provinces were no more successful in their lobbying with their provincial governments.[77]

Then again, the demand for alcohol was not on the agendas of the more left-wing unionists and radical working-class organizations emerging at the end of the war. The left still insisted that prohibition was not a central issue in the workers' struggle for emancipation from capitalist exploitation. "We realize that the two old parties, the Siamese twins of capitalism, will continue to make the liquor question a paramount issue to the exclusion of more fundamental matters being pressed by Labor," the manifesto of Toronto's Labour Representation Political Association proclaimed in 1923. "But we warn the workers not to be divided and side-tracked." It was more in keeping with Tom Moore's more cautious, anti-radical leadership that he kept a high public profile in the mixed-class Citizens' Liberty and Moderationist campaigns, pushing for the stronger beer that he said had been endorsed by many labour conventions as a realistic demand within the existing social system.[78]

Arguing for Beer

The arguments raised in this campaign for the working man's beer had a familiar ring, but also some new twists. Initially, much of the labour objection to the wartime prohibition crusade centred on the economic consequences, especially the unemployment that would result. The country was in the grips of a severe depression from 1913 to 1915, and labour leaders later told provincial and federal governments that the new legislation had forced "thousands engaged in the brewing and allied industries" out of work. This was one of the key arguments in the Toronto unionists' arsenal used to win over support for their resolution at the Trades and Labor Congress convention in 1916. It appealed to the labour movement's traditions of mutual support: "Now that the positions of these workers were in jeopardy it was the duty of the Congress to go to their assistance." The bartenders' union itself made an impassioned pitch for help in saving their livelihood.[79]

Once prohibition was in place and the campaign shifted to bringing back the working man's beer, the focus became the beverage and its importance, not the saloons where it had long been consumed. B.C. miners argued that "men who had to labor for the most part under ground were called upon to endure the strain of the most arduous and strenuous nature," and that "the solid properties of beer to a large extent counter-balanced loss of energy from the physical tax endured." The quality of the "near beer" on sale in hotels under prohibition legislation was roundly denounced. From the steps of the Ontario legislature, speakers declared it was "horrid, sickening and damaging" to the constitution and "unhealthy, unwholesome, indigestible and nauseating to the drinker." A month later Moore told the federal cabinet that "men who take two or three drinks detrimentally affect their stomachs." Labour spokespersons and the labour press continued to complain that former beer drinkers were turning to whisky when they could not get their favoured brew. Moore attempted to shock the Ontario government with the claim that "deaths were resulting through drinking of wood alcohol and other stimulants." Moreover, the most likely source of this booze was a medical doctor, who was "apparently making a fortune at 'one dollar per.'"[80]

The message could also take a patriotic, imperialist turn. In 1918 the Alberta Federation of Labor reminded the provincial government that the strength of beer requested was "similar to the war beer of Great Britain." The TLC delegation to Ottawa early in 1919 even gave their concerns a racist twist when they argued that "if Canada is to attract British immigration, instead of the unsatisfactory alien immigration of the past, the laws of the Dominion must be such as commend themselves to possible immigrants." They warned that "the tide of immigration would turn to Australia, where prohibition has not been spoken of, unless the palatable beer is conceded to the workers of this Dominion." B.C. miners even argued that the "physical inferiority of the Asiatic races" could be explained by the lack of alcohol in their diet.[81]

Labour journalists reminded working-class readers that prohibition had little to offer any workers. "Life and death to the working class is not a question of beer or no beer," the *BC Federationist* thundered. Repeatedly, moreover, labour spokespersons denounced what they believed to be a glaring class bias in regulations that cut off a working man's glass of beer but allowed a rich man to import his liquor—"class legislation pure and simple." The *Citizen* noted that working people could not stock their cellars with booze as the wealthy had, and that they were being treated as though they could not be trusted to drink in moderation. According to a leader of the Ontario brick-layers, it was "a direct attempt to take away the comfort and pleasure of the worker more than of the leisured and privileged class." An Ontario electrical worker saw even more sinister designs behind the new legislation:

> Prohibition is affirmed in general by those who have reason to continue the exploitation of the masses. No thought is given to the matter as to the right or wrong of it, but it is urged—and it is urged in general—because of eco-nomic efficiency. In other words, because if enacted it will bring greater profits to the manufacturer, the financier, and the capitalist generally. Prohibitory legislation as to what one eats or drinks is the earmark of a servile State and therefore in antagonism to working-class interests.

The *BC Federationist* argued that prohibition "merely voices the material aspi-rations of one group of capitalists as opposed to another. . . . One group believes workers will be rendered more productive—therefore more prof-itable—by being denied opportunity to consume alcoholic liquors. The mate-rial interest of the other group lies in the profit to be derived from the sale of alcoholic liquor."[82]

Increasingly, to justify their demands for an end to the dry regime, labour leaders used the same language of "democracy" that was fuelling so many other parts of the workers' "revolt" that spread across the country in the years after 1917. The agitation for the right to a particular kind of leisure activity was part of the expansive working-class agenda for a fuller social citizenship in postwar society. As they were doing with so many other issues, labour's wet voices took the wartime rhetoric and recast it for a working-class agenda. Fred Craig, a plumber, rose in the Nova Scotia Federation of Labor convention and explained:

> My reasons for enlisting in the cause of temperance reform is chiefly to endeavour to bring back to Nova Scotia that birthright that is mine; the liberty to think and the freedom to enjoy the privileges that were my fore-father's and have been denied to me and the rest of liberty loving Nova Scotians, under legislation placed on the statute books of this province due to the hysteria of war so prevalent during the dark days of 1915–1916.

Clifford Dane, a radical metalworker from New Glasgow, made a similar argu-ment: "It was not constitutional to take away a man's right without giving him a voice in the matter." The Charlottetown Laborers' Protective Union declared prohibition "a violation of British fair play." At the 1919 Trades and

Labor Congress convention, an American visitor had delegates cheering when he denounced prohibition as "an infringement on the rights of the men and contrary to the very idea of democracy."[83]

All these efforts by organized labour to end the bone-dry regime seemed to resonate among much larger numbers of Canadian working men and women. The prim, teetotalling working-class masculinity of the prewar years had apparently been largely eclipsed by a version that had quietly taken root in working-class saloons in that same period, and that was finally ready to defend publicly their right to drink responsibly and moderately. The plebiscite results in 1919-21 revealed solid wet majorities in working-class communities in Canadian cities. As Ontario's new Farmer premier, E.C. Drury, settled into office at the end of 1919, he was reminded of this fact in private correspondence from many people, including the following:

> You may think other matters will overshadow the question of prohibition, that the talk about it will die out, if you have that idea, dismiss it. The people are discontented at so many prohibition laws, possibly in the country around which you farm ideas may be different, but get the ideas of the workers in the Cities, in the Towns, get the ideas of the great majority and you will see that prohibition of the People's liberty is not favoured.

When William Ivens, the popular Labour MP, called a meeting to convince workers at the Canadian Pacific's Weston Shops not to vote down prohibition in 1923, only two hundred of the two thousand workers showed up, and even these heckled him heavily. When the U.S. dry orator "Pussyfoot" Johnson tried to speak in Windsor, he was shouted down and retreated to the Detroit ferry under police escort and a hail of rocks and eggs.[84]

The return of thousands of soldiers from overseas had swelled the ranks of the wet camp considerably. Alcohol consumed in sociable spaces had been central to their military experience. In England their free time had been filled with drunken binges in nearby pubs until the army set up wet canteens inside their camps. Behind the front lines in France, both officers and enlisted men had become accustomed to gathering in bars in the mess or in neighbouring towns, where some inevitably developed a serious alcohol dependency. Back in Canada, veterans' organizations had jumped into the thick of the fight for beer. The largest, the Great War Veterans' Association, sent delegations to provincial governments to demand the return of the "real stuff," in place of near beer, and they gave active support to the Citizens' Liberty and Moderation leagues, in which their leading officers were often prominent.[85]

Canada's working men, then, had struggled hard to fit their concerns into the great debates over booze in the late nineteenth and early twentieth centuries. Given that overwhelmingly the labour leaders who spoke out were male wage-earners, the perspective of working-class housewives and daughters was rarely heard. The issue was highly divisive in working-class Canada and consequently, after the decline of the Knights of Labor, was generally avoided by labour councils at all levels, just as they kept religion out of their business. On the one hand, there was a strong current of teetotalism, especially among labour leaders, which, despite its concerns about the evils of drinking, was increasingly estranged from mainstream prohibitionism. On the other hand were the drinkers, who generally remained silent before the war but found their voices once prohibition was in place.

Windsor's Robert Potts was undoubtedly right when he told the large crowd outside the Ontario legislature in 1918 that "workers resented the imputation that there was no difference between the drunkard and the man who wanted to refresh himself at the end of the day's work with a glass of beer." By the end of the war, the great majority of unions and the bulk of working-class voters, both men and women, had marginalized the dry voices among them and loudly rejected prohibition as a form of unjust, class-biased legislation. Working-class drinkers were finally coming out of the closet.

They undoubtedly felt more confident to take a stand as broader moderationist and libertarian campaigns, led by highly respectable upper-class figures, for the first time defended the right to drink in moderation, but the campaign for the working man's beer had its own momentum flowing from indignation at yet another affront to workers' rights and aspirations. This was as close as labour would come at any point after the 1880s to articulating a distinctive agenda for a public policy on alcohol consumption—an admittedly limited one at that, which never broached the possibility of public ownership, as some labour activists and socialists were doing on the other side of the Atlantic. Booze was thus swept up in the class politics of the workers' revolt in Canada at the end of the war. The difficulties that working-class leaders had in getting governments to respond to their concerns about stronger beer reflected the defeat of that wider class mobilization by the early 1920s. After that point, the workers' perspective was submerged in the more bourgeois moderationist campaigns, and the political initiative fell to the old parties, especially the Tories.[86]

Prohibition had always had its enemies. As dry islands opened through local option and then as whole provinces opted to shut down retail outlets for buying and consuming drinks, that opposition became louder and more focused. By the end of the war, substantial coalitions had emerged under the banners of liberty and moderation. The brewers seemed to have been key actors behind the scenes, but by the early 1920s the public face of the wet campaigns was highly respectable and bourgeois. Prominent businessmen, professionals, and their wives took leading public roles in attacking prohibition. They objected to the impact of dry regimes on law and order and on public finance, but, implicitly, were also making a case for a new version of bourgeois culture, including appropriate masculine and feminine identities, that found the cultural straightjacket of moral prudery too confining. In some communities they stood at the centre of a project in social reconciliation, at the end of a period of profound challenges to their hegemony over Canadian society. In the moderationist alliances, these people undertook to speak for many more Canadians of other social classes, including workers and veterans, who were independently denouncing prohibition as an unfair attack on the leisure activities of working men. The wet counterattack, then, was an important part of the "reconstruction" of Canadian society in the 1920s on a more stable, law-abiding, less conflict-ridden basis.

ENFORCING THE C.T.A.
AT MONCTON, N.B.

seven

One Hell of a Farce

UNDOUBTEDLY THE HISTORIAN OF the future will describe the body blow to the drink traffic . . . as a social revolution. It is nothing less. For it is a far-reaching change in our habits as a people—one might almost say as a race. It is a drastic break with the past in popular behavior. It is a drastic revision of our social economy . . . it is an inevitable revolution.[1]

OPPOSITE PAGE: As local-option votes brought more dry zones to many parts of the country, police forces were expected to shut down bootlegging. Disposing of booze seized in raids often became a highly ceremonial event at a prominent spot in the centre of town. Here Moncton, N.B., police empty barrels of the illicit beverage down the sewer in front of the courthouse. (AUCC, 93.004 P/7N)

Many Canadians shared with the editor of Winnipeg's *Manitoba Free Press* the expectation that a dramatically new social order would dawn once John Barleycorn had finally been banished from the land. That optimism was short-lived. Provincewide prohibition in Canada was in many ways a deeply flawed project from the start, just as it had been in its earlier local-option version. Enforcement was a policing nightmare. Despite majority support in plebiscites, prohibition became one of the most widely flouted laws on the statute books. Drinking continued as a huge underground economy opened up to supply the booze. It got more surreptitious and probably more expensive. Indeed, if consumption levels fell, that was largely because of the deep economic slump that the country settled into after 1920.

Thousands of Canadians would have agreed with Clifford Rose, a Nova Scotia official charged with enforcing prohibition. Late in the fall of 1929, he noted in his diary that the local plebiscite campaign over ending the province's dry regime had been particularly bitter. "We are living in a tight corner," he wrote. "God, I hope government control wins for this is one hell of a farce."[2]

Legal Loopholes

What had gone wrong with the great experiment in public purity? The problems rested partly in the loopholes in the legislation, but even more in the process of enforcement, which revealed a massive resistance. These obstacles to prohibition's success had been evident since the arrival of the first local-option legislation half a century earlier. The more complete shutdown that began in 1916 simply made them larger.

From its earliest days, prohibition in practice had been an attack on the trafficking of booze—that is, on retail sales. At no point did local-option or provincial legislation ban the right of individuals to have alcohol in their possession in their own homes for private consumption—unlike later laws dealing with illegal drugs.[3] As critics had forewarned, the thirst for alcohol did not disappear, and new channels of commerce soon opened up to supply the demand.

For the first few years of the dry regime, most booze reached Canadian customers through perfectly legal channels. Only as the net was tightened after 1920 did the illicit trade take off on a major scale. For one thing, except for the brief period of federal intervention in 1918–19, brewing and distilling remained legal—in sharp contrast to the United States, where all production was shut down along with retailing under the Eighteenth Amendment. As the Montreal *Gazette* explained to readers, "There are large Canadian interests engaged legitimately in an export trade, and it is not desirable that any restrictions should be imposed which may interfere with that trade as long as it is carried on lawfully." Breweries could also sell weak "near beer" to hotels that decided to stay open (more than 1,200 of these so-called "standard hotels" were still operating in Ontario in the early 1920s). They could also sell to other retail outlets not previously able to sell booze, such as cafés and poolrooms. Although a large number of the smaller breweries closed their doors forever at that point, the bigger firms brought out new labels for 2.5 per cent drinks—Labatt's "Old London Brew" ale and "Comet" lager, for example—although the new drinks did not prove to be popular.[4]

The full-strength products of the Canadian booze industry could not be sold in a province that had banned sales, but they could be exported, either to a foreign country or to a Canadian destination outside the dry province. Under local-option and initially under provincial legislation, booze could still be legally ordered from a wet district and delivered quietly to homes of drinkers. This loophole in the North-West Territories prohibition legislation between 1873 and 1891 had opened a flood of alcohol onto the Prairies, and the Royal Commission on the Liquor Traffic had heard many accounts of how liquor was shipped into dry municipalities covered by the Scott Act. Similarly, for many years before the war, Halifax had remained a regular source of alcohol for drinkers in the rest of province, as had many larger wet cities in other regions.[5]

Once full-scale prohibition began during the war, manufacturers advertised the addresses from which their products were shipped (prepaid to guarantee profits). Booze wholesalers, as well as breweries and distilleries, were also quick to establish "export warehouses" across the border in another dry province, so that, say, a resident in Calgary could legally order booze from Fernie, B.C., or Maple Creek, Sask., and have Dominion Express deliver it to his or her home. In Manitoba two-thirds of the existing liquor stores simply converted themselves into "warehouses." These export houses appeared across the country, but the biggest were located in Montreal, the wettest outpost in Canada. Both Quebec and British Columbia had legalized the sale of alcoholic beverages by 1921, and, until January 1920, when U.S. prohibition finally kicked in, importing from wet states south of the border was also possible.[6]

Early on Canada had a well-developed system of mail-order business pioneered by the large department stores. When Sam Bronfman opened his liquor importing and distribution operation in Montreal in 1916, his model was the Hudson's Bay Company. The irony that the federal postal service was used to circumvent provincial prohibition was not lost on prohibitionists. The express companies also did a booming business, eventually having to create special new warehouses for booze.

Despite the constitutional straitjacket that constrained them, some provinces tried to block this new flow of booze by banning advertising or otherwise impinging on its functioning. The federal order-in-council stopped all imports during wartime in the spring of 1918, but after that restriction expired on 1 January 1920 the export houses sprang back to life. Under new federal legislation, the provinces could hold plebiscites to determine whether importation should be banned. Within a year, most of the seven dry provinces had taken this step, winning majorities that triggered federal protection. Provincial governments also moved to close export houses. By the middle of 1922, Bronfman later recalled, the mail-order business was dead. Getting the products of Canadian breweries and distilleries by these circuitous but legal routes thus became almost impossible.[7]

Beyond the availability of mail-order services, almost every neighbourhood had two other perfectly legal outlets: the doctor's office and the drugstore. Long before the war, local prohibition measures had loopholes that allowed some alcohol to be sold for "medicinal, mechanical, scientific, and sacramental purposes." The faith in liquor as a medicine was clearly still powerful.

Under prohibition legislation, doctors could issue prescriptions for alcohol to be used as medicine. Prohibitionists like cartoonist J.W. Bengough were not alone in worrying that some doctors compromised their professional integrity by supplying prescriptions, for a fee, to perfectly healthy drinkers. (AO, F 834-3-0-1, B-893)

Doctors could write prescriptions for it, and druggists could dispense it. Before the war, in the absence of any government dispensaries, licensed drugstores were the only places that people could get alcohol within the municipalities where local-option prohibition prevailed. The system was ripe for abuse. "Men go there with a certificate of their own manufacture, with an imaginary doctor's name on it, and get as much liquor as they want," a Charlottetown newspaper complained in 1882. Ten years later, after a visit to nearby Summerside, a British writer reported, "'Prescriptions' were given for various amounts, from a bottle up to ten gallons, some practically unlimited, the liquor being taken by instalments, as required." Quebec's comptroller of provincial revenue told the royal commission a similar story: in one parish under local option in January 1889, the "medicine" dispensed amounted to 279 bottles of whisky, 217 of gin, 28 of brandy, 11 of wine, 6 pints of whisky, a pint of beer, and a half-pint of brandy.[8]

Under the post-1915 provincewide legislation, doctors were again permitted to prescribe liquor (often by the quart), and long lineups formed outside the doors of opportunistic practitioners, who might charge a fee of two or three dollars for this service. By no means were all doctors involved, but there were enough of them to supply a good many drinkers. In 1920 Alberta's doctors issued more than 500,000 prescriptions for bottles of alcohol, and Ontario's practitioners wrote more than 650,000, a figure that climbed to over 800,000 in 1924. "Patients" simply took their "prescriptions" to an authorized drugstore or one of the new provincial liquor dispensaries. "Towards Christmas especially," a B.C. civil servant later recalled, "it looked as if an epidemic of colds and colic had struck the country like a plague. In Vancouver queues a quarter of a mile long could be seen waiting their turn to enter the liquor store to get their prescriptions filled." In Ontario the monthly total of prescriptions written in December typically jumped by 50 per cent.[9]

Criticism of these practices poured into newspaper editorials and government letter boxes. "Imagine, Mr. Premier, an honest, busy doctor specifically prescribing Kilmarnock's Scotch or Thompson's Grand Highland, strictly for medical purposes," one angry prohibitionist wrote to Ontario premier Drury, who for his own part muttered grimly that the medical profession had become simply "a thin cloak for bootlegging." Deeply divided over the use of alcohol, doctors themselves expressed resentment that they had been caught in this twist of public policy. Alberta and British Columbia tried using numbered forms to be sent to specific doctors, but forgeries soon appeared. Some provincial boards restricted the number of prescriptions a doctor could write per month, and a small number of medical men were eventually prosecuted. But booze by doctors' prescription continued to be available throughout the prohibition period in Canadian provinces.[10]

Some provinces required all purchases to flow through the government dispensaries, but some left retailing to licensed vendors, most often drugstores. Druggists could also order alcohol in bulk for filling prescriptions. In Yorkton, Sask., former hotel-men Harry and Sam Bronfman had already made good use of a wholesale druggist licence to import and distribute large quantities of alcohol. Ontario's Board of License Commissioners believed that some drugstores were "little better than bar-rooms, but the proprietors display great cunning in covering up their guilt." By 1923 the Board concluded that a "very considerable number" of drugstores had opened across the province "apparently for the purpose of carrying on an illegal traffic in liquor." According to Stephen Leacock, it was only necessary to lean against a drugstore counter "and make a gurgling sigh like apoplexy. One often sees these apoplexy cases lined up four deep."[11]

In Alberta authorities discovered that some druggists hired former bartenders to handle their liquor business and then shifted legal blame to them if they were caught selling illegal booze. Provincial governments did what they could to regulate this traffic, as well as to curb consumption of so-called "medicated wines" and various extracts available in grocery stores.[12] They probably succeeded in restraining this legal flow.

Bootlegging   *Define*

If it was getting harder to buy the legitimate products of breweries and distilleries, enterprising people were ready to supply homebrew. Federal authorities
allowed anyone to brew beer for home consumption, and nearly 75,000
Ontario residents had a permit in 1927. Many of them undoubtedly sold
some of their production. Making spirits remained illegal, although in rural
areas illegal stills of "moonshine" or "swamp whisky" appeared to satisfy the
local thirst. Manitoba's collector of Inland Revenue told the Royal Commission
on the Liquor Traffic that illicit stills were common across the Prairies in the
last decades of the nineteenth century. Across the country the total number of
stills seized rose from 191 in 1917 to 985 in 1920 and over 1,100 in 1923. The
larger stills were uncovered in such unlikely places as an abandoned Methodist
church in Ranchville, Sask., a stable in Drumheller, Alta., and the organ loft of
a Baptist church in Calgary.[13]

In city and country, many of these "moonshiners" were the Canadian-
born farmers or more recent immigrants who had long been accustomed to
making homebrew—whisky or wine or beer—for their own consumption.
Some no doubt grasped the opportunity to expand their production considerably, but most probably cobbled together a makeshift distilling operation out
of available farm equipment (such as a cream separator), just turning out enough
for themselves and a few of their neighbours. One Alberta moonshiner reputedly told police as he was led away: "Yes, I voted for prohibition, and I'd vote
for it again. I went broke farming."[14]

Enforcement officers made a point of targeting the immigrants. The Ontario
Board of License Commissioners reported in 1921 that "of those who commit
offences against the Act there is a disproportionately large number of foreigners, and of these a still more disproportionately large number are Jews from
Poland and Western Russia." A year later the same body noted that licensed
wine sellers were mostly "foreigners," and that "the wine cellars of these foreigners are situated in the midst of neighbourhoods chiefly inhabited by
foreigners. . . . Consequently, particular attention has to be paid by our officers
to conditions in such communities."[15]

Before the early 1920s, local "moonshiners" probably filled only a small
part of the illicit booze market alongside the Canadian brewers and distillers,
but, once access to the legally produced beverages was choked off, illicit stills
found more customers. Much larger illicit distilling operations also began to
appear, often masquerading under such names as the Regina Vinegar Company
or Canada Drugs Limited (the Bronfmans' operation in Yorkton).

Simple stills like this one uncovered near Hamilton, Ont., provided moonshine to determined drinkers in all parts of the country. The product was unpredictable and potentially dangerous. (HPL)

Whatever the source, booze found its markets thanks to the efforts of the growing legions of bootleggers. Everywhere that prohibition was tried, both before and after the war, bootlegging flourished as small-scale entrepreneurship in dry communities. In the depressed economic times that set in across the country after 1920, it became one of the most promising survival strategies for impoverished workers, farmers, and others with limited income. Bootlegging was a business with two branches—smuggling and retailing—which might be handled by separate people or combined in the same operation. Initially bootleggers might simply be hoarding legal booze to sell at inflated prices. Then they might organize regular expeditions into wet territory to bring back alcohol in their cars or concealed under their clothes. But as the direct flow from export houses and doctors' offices came under closer government regulation, they were quickly drawn into large networks of illegal distribution within the country and across the forty-ninth parallel—the rough-and-tumble world of "rum-running."

Here lay the drama immortalized in Hollywood movies and family legends. There was no single rum-running experience, but rather a huge variety across the country. The central thread uniting those experiences was that alcohol production remained legal in Canada and illegal in the United States. Canadian producers supplied a large proportion of prohibition-era alcohol that found its way into U.S. homes and illegal drinking places. Supplying thirsty Canadians with bootleg booze was most often part of the lucrative business of smuggling huge quantities of liquor and beer into the United States. (Generally, rum-runners preferred to handle liquor rather than beer, which was bulkier and had a much lower profit margin.)

Smuggling required daring and ingenuity. During prohibition in the North-West Territories, as the royal commissioners had learned:

> Contraband liquor was brought into the country by all available avenues and by every conceivable means. It was brought in secreted in packages of merchandise; in tins specially prepared and labelled "bibles"; as canned fruits, a single peach, perhaps, floating in alcohol valued at $5; in casks of sugar and rice; in packages of bottles, supposed to contain nothing but temperance drinks; in carloads of hogs or lumber, or as eggs. Almost innumerable other devices were likewise resorted to. In some cases casks of liquor were attached to the cars or suspended in front of the engine, to be dropped off at a convenient spot. In other cases liquor was carried by the smugglers in the stateroom of sleeping cars, and even the mattresses and pillows were used to secrete it.

Similar forms of imaginative concealment proliferated after 1920. Petty smugglers might find clever ways of hiding bottles under clothing or in baby carriages, suitcases, or lunch boxes so that they could walk across the international border. When in 1929 the U.S. customs department put its first female officer on a border point (in Rouses Point, a small town in northern New York state) to do body searches of women entering from Canada, she uncovered 670 bottles of liquor in three months. An official in the Maritimes later wrote about concealment in trains:

> I saw six dozen bottles of liquor packed into barrels covered with fish gut and consigned to a glue factory in Toronto. I know of another large consignment of grain alcohol shipped in coffins. Another as Bible tracts, and still another shipment worth $100,000 was covered with Christmas trees and shipped as such. Many a boxcar was loaded at both ends with liquor and in the doorway with lumber or laths.[16]

Bootleggers put considerable effort into adapting cars and boats for carrying big shipments. Strong springs and hidden compartments throughout a car would help move alcohol over the back roads of Eastern or Western Canada. On the St. Lawrence, Lake Champlain, the Great Lakes, and the coastlines of the Atlantic and Pacific oceans, operators made use of more powerful, better designed speedboats and schooners with false bottoms under which the booze would be stowed and over which fish was piled. On land or water, devices were sometimes installed to create clouds of smoke to obscure the escape from enforcement officers.

This woman in Windsor, Ont., was engaged in the kind of small-scale smuggling that was common in most border towns, from which after 1920 Canadian booze was bootlegged into the dry United States. (WS)

The scale of smuggling operations ranged from a man who ran his own car or boat to a self-styled regional "king" of the bootleggers who ran a complex empire with numerous employees. Whatever their status in this underground economy, smugglers were typically men of modest backgrounds. Many on the East and West coasts and on the Great Lakes were fishers and sailors trying to cope with the economic crises of their local economies. In 1925 half of the one-hundred-boat Lunenburg fishing fleet was reputedly involved in smuggling. On his first trip to St. Pierre on board a rum-running schooner, for instance, one young man was surprised: "It was like going into harbour at home as every second boat there was from Lunenburg." Some boat-owners leased or sold their vessels to rum-runners. On the West Coast a discharged soldier named Johnny Schnarr later recalled: "After the war I did some more logging and this and that. And then Prohibition came along in the United States. For a young fellow with a sense of adventure, getting involved in the rumrunning seemed like a pretty good way to make a living." In their small boats and cars, these people became the daring middlemen between the producers' offshore agents and the local bootleggers.[17]

Although in a time of mass unemployment rum-running was probably more lucrative than sporadic wage-earning or going on the dole, working in pitch blackness on cold seas or in rural backwoods was no one's idea of an easy road to wealth. Work at this level of the smuggling operations also involved the ever-present risk of being caught or shot at by law officers. Or perhaps the smugglers might be robbed by some form of booze "pirates"— which became a growing problem as independent operators, squeezed out by the bigger businessmen, turned to theft and hijacking of booze in transit or in such secret storage places as barns, garages, railway cars, attics, basements, haystacks, holes in the ground. As a Toronto *Star* reporter learned from a major bootlegger in 1924, "There is so much cut-throat competition. The little bootleggers, they try to get protection by telling on each other. They are stools. . . . They have no principles, they will sell anything, they will do anything to get the business of their competitor. That makes more crime."[18]

Yet the markup on bootlegged liquor was so high that it was possible to start small and get bigger quite quickly. A Windsor policeman later explained: "The biggest majority of the poor people used to buy one case of whiskey, and when they had sold that case of whiskey they had enough to buy twelve or fifteen more. That's how they made their money so fast, and you could sell every case you wanted." A Saint John taxi driver told the same story to a writer for the *Ladies Home Journal* in 1923:

> It's easy money. I've run many a load over. I've bought it here for sixty dollars a dozen, all duty paid and all done up in burlap sacks. An ordinary touring car will carry forty dozen and I've sold it for a hundred dollars a dozen across the line, a profit of sixteen hundred dollars on a load. Even if you get knocked off every fourth load and lose your car, you're ahead of the game.[19]

Not surprisingly, in many parts of the country smuggling was a road to riches for enterprising men from rural or working-class backgrounds and sometimes from ethnic groups—Jews, Italians, French Canadians, and others—facing discrimination in local labour markets. They all began as small-time entrepreneurs who competed fiercely and often violently for greater control of the trade. In each region, dominant figures emerged to organize smuggling and bootlegging on a grander scale. They eventually hired many of the former independents as drivers, labourers, or security guards—invariably described in the press as their "gangs"—and invested in the fastest boats and land vehicles and the most intricately concealed warehousing systems. In New Brunswick's Madawaska County, Albenie J. Violette, a flamboyant French-Canadian woodsman who styled himself "Joe Walnut," pulled together a rum-running, bootlegging, and distilling empire, sustained by gun-toting gangs of former lumberjacks and sailors who rode about the backwoods in fast cars and trucks. Hundreds of miles inland Hamilton's Rocco Perri had worked as a construc-

Bootlegging became a dangerous business as large underground empires confronted each other. In 1930 the so-called "King of the Bootleggers" in Southern Ontario, Hamilton's Rocco Perri, was devastated when his beloved partner, Bessie Starkman, was gunned down in their garage, apparently by members of Al Capone's gang. (HPL)

tion labourer and a grocer before building up a solid business empire of boot-legging in South-Central Ontario. In the same city Ben Kerr, a former plumber and boat-builder, developed the most daring and successful rum-running business across Lake Ontario, while Harry Low, a former skilled toolmaker, started out as a small-time bootlegger and quickly organized perhaps the biggest whisky exporting business from Montreal through Windsor to Detroit and beyond (his huge mansion in Walkerville was later the home of Windsor MP Paul Martin). In Blairmore, Alta., Emilio Picariello, once a construction worker, shopkeeper, and factory hand, built up a large business importing contraband liquor into Southern Alberta (his meteoric career came to an end in 1923 when he was executed for his involvement in the fatal shooting of a local policeman). From their base hotel-keeping in Yorkton, the Bronfman brothers knit together an even bigger, coast-to-coast network of smuggling and bootlegging on both sides of the Canadian-U.S. border. Men like these became millionaires overnight and flaunted their new-found wealth in expensive clothing, fancy cars, lavishly furnished mansions, and extravagant luxuries—although most of them would eventually lose much of that wealth as quickly as they had acquired it.[20]

For the major operators in this illegal trade, making money from bootleg liquor involved daring escapes from authorities in pursuit and ingenious hoodwinking (or bribing) of municipal and provincial police, liquor inspectors, and temperance "spotters." The biggest bootleggers were also drawn into intense, sometimes violent competition for territory. Carrying and using guns became a regular part of rum-running and bootlegging. It was this organized violence that got them labelled "gangsters" or "mobsters." By the mid-1920s their names were linked to a number of bloody murders, especially in Southwestern Ontario. The Bronfmans' brother-in-law died from a shotgun blast in Bienfait, Sask., in 1922, and in a particularly brutal incident, Bessie (Starkman) Perri, Rocco's wife and shrewd business partner, was gunned down in 1930 in an ongoing, all-out war with the U.S. mobster Al Capone. Perri himself would eventually disappear without a trace in 1944. On the whole, though, Canada never saw the huge rash of gangland slayings that hit the United States during prohibition. Indeed, writer James Gray suggested that the Canadians were more likely to rush to court to sue each other.[21]

The Underground Economy

The transportation routes used by the rum-runners and bootleggers were shaped in part by federal policies. The Canadian government not only allowed brewing and distilling to continue, but, until 1930, also refused to take any responsibility for where the booze was shipped outside Canada. The authorities required an export duty if the booze was bound for the United States, but not if it was headed for other foreign territories. Manufacturers therefore sold their products to shipping agents who took responsibility for transporting them. Large shipments of alcohol left Canadian factories for bonded warehouses, ostensibly bound for Cuba, Mexico, St. Pierre and Miquelon (the islands off Newfoundland owned by France), or some other prohibition-free country, only to be immediately smuggled quietly across the U.S. border or simply redirected within Canada for illicit sales (a practice known as "short-circuiting").[22]

On the Great Lakes and the Detroit River, Canadian customs officials calmly watched boats that could never stand the Atlantic swell leave the Canadian shoreline ostensibly bound for "Havana." The rum-runners would then either wait for the most propitious moment to dash over to the U.S. side or slip into a dark, isolated cove on the Canadian side, where bootleggers waited to unload the cargo. Some boats on lakes Erie and Ontario and the Detroit River would make the trip to "Cuba" several times a week (one reputedly did it four times in one day). Shippers could retrieve the bond they had posted for such trips by presenting forged landing certificates. Rum-runners caught in the act of smuggling on the water would hastily heave the bottles overboard—the booze was almost always packed in burlap sacks for these runs—and later return to try dredging them up. They would often tie boxes of salt to the sacks so that once the salt had dissolved the boxes would float to the surface to mark the submerged treasure.

A large quantity of booze found its way to one of the so-called "Rum Rows" of vessels that lay at anchor just outside the territorial waters on each coast. These flotillas of as many as one hundred larger crafts were basically floating warehouses of alcohol from all over the world. Their cargoes were off-loaded bit by bit into small boats, to be whisked ashore in Canada or the United States in the dead of night.

Rum-running was organized along the entire 4,000-mile border with the United States, but a few nodes were particularly important. On the Atlantic coast smuggling had a long history, especially across the New Brunswick border into the dry state of Maine. The full-scale prohibition in the United States opened up a lucrative business for a new generation of rum-runners. "Probably nowhere along the international border boundary from the Atlantic to the Pacific is booze-running so rampant and so open as it is from New Brunswick to Maine," the Toronto *World* reported in 1921, and the *Ladies Home Journal* called Saint John "one of the headwaters of the Niagara of booze that flows southward over the border." When the U.S. Coast Guard belatedly fitted up a large "Dry Navy" to combat smuggling in 1924, the "Rum Row" moved into the Bay of Fundy and began funnelling the product through New Brunswick, via enterprising local operators. Under federal law,

This schooner was at anchor off St. Pierre, one of the French islands near Newfoundland that became the hub of East Coast rum-running in the 1920s. Countless men gave up fishing and worked in this underground economy, which supplied booze to the dry Canadian provinces and the United States. (NAC, PA-056748)

moreover, exports ostensibly bound for "Havana" could legally leave the provincially licensed export warehouses in Halifax, Saint John, and Charlottetown, even though everyone knew that virtually all that alcohol would then be smuggled into U.S. or Canadian outports. Eventually, when the three Maritime provinces closed these licensed facilities in 1923–24, the centre of the traffic headed north to St. Pierre and Miquelon, where the major Canadian distillers established export warehouses. From there booze continued to be unloaded on Maritime coastlines in the dead of night, and shipped south or distributed through the region's bootleggers.[23] Some vessels, such as the famous *Nellie J. Banks*, which served Prince Edward Island's drinkers for twelve years, worked these routes regularly.

The New Brunswick–Maine border remained a porous line that government officials on both sides never managed to seal off. In 1921 a reporter made a conservative estimate that "about a hundred cars pass daily over the line into Maine from New Brunswick containing the produce of Quebec distilleries, English and Scotch distilleries and the bootleggers' stills of New Brunswick and Quebec," in all amounting to "hundreds of thousands of gallons" per year. For similar reasons, Vancouver was a centre of smuggling on the west coast.[24]

Ultimately, given the concentration of distilleries in Southern Ontario and the proximity of the heavily populated U.S. Midwest, especially Chicago, the most important route was through Windsor and Detroit. One estimate suggests that four-fifths of smuggled booze entered the United States through this "Detroit-Windsor Funnel." The two cities were only about a mile apart

The heaviest smuggling went across the Detroit River at Windsor, Ont. Here a boxcar of Canadian booze is being unloaded into a speedboat before being conveyed to the U.S. side, where complete prohibition was in force. (WS)

across the Detroit River. The riverfront was lined for miles with export ware-houses, and, laden with booze, water vehicles of all kinds, from canoes and sailboats to sleek speedboats, plied the waters separating the cities. In winter cars slithered across the frozen surface or along wooden planks thrown over thin ice. Railway cars with false labels and fraudulent seals, perhaps ostensibly bound for Mexico, moved large quantities over the river to an unloading place outside Detroit, Chicago, or some other Midwestern city. One enter-prising rum-runner even ran a cable along the bottom of the river to drag a sled loaded with cases of liquor across the border. More dramatically, planes began to haul this cargo between farmers' fields in Ontario and small airstrips in Michigan—although this was the most visible way of moving booze and therefore the most vulnerable to police interception.[25]

Elaborate networks to organize all this smuggling took shape quickly on both sides. Canadian supplies were feeding the mushrooming empires of pow-erful U.S. bootleggers, such as the so-called Purple Gang in Detroit and the infamous Al Capone of Chicago. Capone, who occasionally visited Canada, allegedly quipped to reporters: "Do I do business with Canadian racketeers? Why, I don't even know what street Canada is on." The biggest U.S. operators did not necessarily wait for Canadians to send booze to them. Some organ-ized their own fleets of boats and planes to cross over and pick up whisky and beer from their Canadian contacts.[26]

Distillers and brewers were complicit in this illegal traffic. Indeed, their survival as profit-making enterprises required that their products continue to find a market, especially in the United States. "We have no knowledge of or interest in the prohibitory laws of the United States," the vice-president of

Windsor's British-American Brewery Company told a writer for *Ladies Home Journal* in 1923. "We believe we are privileged to fill orders for shipment of beer to the United States, even if it is illegal for citizens of the United States to have beer." They established export warehouses in convenient locations for smuggling. In the early 1920s, for example, Labatt's shrewd new general manager organized export operations at Port Stanley on Lake Erie, Ford City in Windsor, and Sarnia on Lake Huron and hired special staff to handle business with the smugglers. A year later eleven Ontario breweries agreed to price-fixing and quotas for the cross-border sales, and in 1926 they created a formal cartel under the name of the Bermuda Export Company to rationalize the flow of beer southward. The large distilleries maintained export offices in a Montreal hotel, where orders could be submitted and then telegraphed to warehouses on St. Pierre or along the St. Lawrence and Great Lakes and loaded onto rum-runners' boats. In 1921 the Canadian Industrial Alcohol Company, which had bought the Corby and Wiser distilleries on the St. Lawrence, hired a former hotel-owner turned liquor retailer, Harry Hatch, as sales manager to develop business with U.S. bootleggers. He contracted with smugglers, organized his own rum-running fleet (eventually dubbed "Hatch's Navy" as it came to dominate water traffic on lakes Ontario and Erie), and soon had revived the flagging fortunes of the distilleries. Corby's plant underwent a massive expansion in 1924, making it one of the largest distilleries in the world.[27]

Sales and profits in brewing and distilling soared. When the Royal Commission on Customs and Excise began its cross-country hearings and investigations in 1926, it found that many brewers and distillers had kept much of this activity off their books, or hidden or destroyed records that might incriminate them. In 1932 Sam Bronfman revealed privately that his company sold 750,000 gallons a year in Canada, but exported 1.7 million, almost all to the United States. Some three years later the Bronfman brothers were marched into court to face federal charges for defrauding the government of custom duties by smuggling liquor into the United States and illegally "short-circuiting" it back into Canada. They were acquitted.[28]

The links between the legal and illegal parts of the industry got closer as the huge profits from bootlegging allowed some entrepreneurs to buy up well-established production facilities. In 1924 Windsor rum-running magnates Harry Low, Charles Burns, and Marco Leon bought up the Carling brewery in London (which had been closed for four years) and organized the production of lager almost exclusively for export to the United States, where Al Capone was one of their biggest customers. A year earlier, the upstart Harry Hatch left Canadian Industrial Alcohol, bought the ailing Gooderham and

Worts plant in Toronto, and convinced the Canadian government to let him start exporting whisky before it had aged two years, as required by law. Given Hatch's bootlegging connections, the company's profits climbed steeply. Three years later Hatch took the bold leap of buying the Hiram Walker operations in Windsor as well. The Toronto *Star* promptly dubbed him "King of Canadian Distillers."[29]

The Bronfman brothers made a similar move into the mainstream of the industry. Like many other bootleggers, they had begun with an illicit operation in Saskatchewan, blending alcohol to make fake Scotch and other high-class spirits. In 1924 they transferred their operations to a new distillery in Montreal, which opened the next year as Distillers' Corporation Limited with substantial financial backing from Scottish distillers and an exclusive importing agreement for prestigious Scotch whiskies. Two years later, just as the first batches of the new firm's liquor were reaching legal maturity (and in the wake of Ontario voters' decisive rejection of prohibition), Distillers Corporation bought majority control of the venerable Seagram company in Waterloo, and a new holding company took over the two large distilling corporations, with Sam Bronfman as vice-president.[30]

Despite the regular supply of factory-made beer and spirits, the quality of the alcohol that flowed along all these routes to Canadian and U.S. customers became steadily more unreliable. Bootleggers regularly watered and adulterated the real liquor they sold, or simply coloured, flavoured, and watered down pure alcohol to make it resemble rum or whisky. Some, such as New Brunswick's Joe Walnut, reprocessed denatured alcohol, and with appropriate additives, sealed it in bottles with the illegally produced labels of well-known brands of liquor. They then sold it as the real stuff, at a whopping great profit. A journalist described how three farmers just outside Saint John made this kind of concoction in two days and had it in the hands of drinkers in Bangor on the third day. Their production costs were fifteen cents a bottle, while market value in Maine was three dollars (unless the liquor was resold, for five dollars a bottle, to Boston bootleggers, who would make their customers pay seven or eight dollars a bottle).[31]

This "hooch" could be quite hard on the unsuspecting drinker. One Saskatchewan man remembered the effects of a bottle of bootleg liquor that he consumed with friends in a Model T Ford one night: "About an hour later all of us were paralysed to a certain degree, and by Sunday noon the ends of my fingers were still numb." In Southern Ontario in 1926, forty-five deaths followed from the distribution of liquor made from denatured alcohol. It is no small wonder that moonshine was often called "lightning." Most bootleggers would have avoided such junk, however, recognizing that providing palatable, non-toxic booze was essential to business success.[32]

Blind Pigs

Few drinkers would ever encounter the big-time operators. To get bootleg liquor, most enthusiasts simply found their way to the back doors of particular houses or shops in their neighbourhoods, places where they could either buy booze by the bottle to be taken away or slip inside to enjoy it on the premises. These illegal blind pigs offered, in a more clandestine way, some of the conviviality of the saloon. Before the war, former taverns sometimes operated quite openly in local-option areas, although customers usually entered by side doors or back staircases and enjoyed their drinks behind closed blinds in dimly lit rooms. Under full-fledged prohibition, a bit more caution was usually necessary, but the number of bootleggers appears to have increased enormously. Vancouver police raided 108 of these illegal premises in December 1920 alone. Most often, a blind pig was simply a carefully guarded room in a family household. A bootlegger in the Windsor area remembered:

> The blind pigs were in ordinary homes. There would be some people in the living rooms and some in the kitchen. You would have to be a friend of a friend before they would sell you a drink. . . . I'd go into a blind pig and buy a drink for everyone there, maybe twenty or thirty people, and it would come to a lot of money, but you didn't care. The blind pigs were well run. They didn't allow any riff-raff, they were good clean people. Some were run a lot better than some of the hotels now.[33]

Large numbers of illegal drinking spots, though never anything like a majority, were run by women, typically single mothers trying to support their children. They could be tough-minded businesswomen. In 1888 Mrs. Margaret Wallace, a determined Moncton bootlegger, used a horsewhip to drive her temperance-movement prosecutor from the courtroom. In Saint John Mrs. Donnie Hart was hauled into police court at least once a year between 1916 and 1924, but apparently escaped prison sentences because she was supporting three children. A few years later Nova Scotia temperance inspector Clifford Rose found several wily, resourceful women running bootleg operations in and around New Glasgow. The women in these places were often given the title of "Ma" or "Mother" ("Mother" Robertson and so on). The daughter of one such woman read Rose's reflections half a century later and published a defence of her mother, saying she had been one of nine children in a miner's

family, was widowed with two children, and had "a job to do and did it the only way she knew how."[34]

Small-scale bootlegging also operated through drugstores, hotels, restaurants, grocery stores, barber shops, boarding houses, the trunks of taxis—any place where an operator could do business. In 1922 Alberta police estimated that 40 per cent of the province's pool halls and 30 per cent of the cafés were involved in the trade. Many hotel managers kept the real thing under the counter in jugs, which would be quickly dumped or watered down if police arrived. These services sometimes got the nickname of "jitney bars." Years later a former Nova Scotia hotel-keeper described how easy it was to run his business:

Every neighbourhood had well-known bootleggers to whom drinkers turned for booze. This woman in east-end Fort William apparently provided the service for her Italian neighbours in the 1920s. (AO, F 1405-21-46, MSR 2541-12)

As far as I was concerned I had a respectable business. I had a hotel here in Sydney. I started bootlegging in 1922. By 1923 the rum runners started coming. We'd buy rum in 10 gallon kegs and scotch was in 12 bottles to a case. I'd serve it by the drink or by the bottle. You'd sit at a table. Oh, yes, it was open enough. The law didn't want to stop it no more than we did. They come up and every now and then you'd pay a fine . . . and that was it. They never cleaned you out. . . . It was practically wide open.

An Ontario hotel-keeper had a two-way tap that allowed him to switch quickly between kegs of weak and full-strength beer. "Your drink depended on whether you were known or not," a family member recalled. "All hotels boot-legged in those days."[35]

Brewers across the country kept local operators well supplied with full-strength beer. The Royal Commission on Customs and Excise discovered that, like so many others, the Kuntz Brewery in Waterloo and the Hamilton Brewing Association sold full-strength beer out the door on the "cash and carry system," while Toronto's Cosgrave Brewery delivered it directly to the city's hotels. New Brunswick's Oland's and Ready's breweries admitted to supplying the stronger stuff to local retailers and to paying half or more of the fines that the operators faced for violating the law, just to keep the outlets for their product in business. By 1927, when Ontario finally legalized retail sales of booze, 90 per cent of Labatt's production in London was already full-strength beer, and its staff was quietly supplying reliable bootleggers.[36]

Many dives offered additional entertainment, often gambling casinos in an upstairs room. The most elaborate drinking places were the roadhouses near the U.S. border, especially around Windsor, where Americans in large numbers came over for dining, dancing, gambling, and drinking. A few speakeasies were also sprinkled along the road out of Hull, across the river from Ottawa in the shelter of Quebec's looser liquor laws. In all the illicit drinking spots, the pro-prietors would never stray far from the bottle or the pitcher from which the booze was being dispensed, so that it could be quickly hidden, dumped, or smashed in the event of a raid. For the bigger places, spies would be stationed along the road to warn the owner if the police were in sight, and if so all incriminating drinks and gaming tables could be whisked away to be placed behind false walls or in secret compartments or hideaway cupboards.[37]

Prohibition had been intended to kill off the liquor traffic, but in practice it merely forced a restructuring. Countless Canadians were still lucratively engaged in supplying a continuing large market in booze.

The Enforcers

Why could the laws against selling alcohol not be better enforced? Part of the answer lies in the long-term confusion about and resentment over who should be enforcing prohibition. All three levels of government had some responsibility, but there was, at best, limited co-operation among them, and often icy distancing. Part of the answer too rests in the breakdown of effective policing.

In practice, before the war, most enforcement came at the local level. Municipal governments and their police forces were expected to bear the brunt of the work, but some provincial governments appointed local boards of licence commissioners, who in turn hired their own liquor inspectors. Town constables sometimes resented this intrusion onto their turf and were unco-operative. The liquor inspectors often had to hire outside detectives to assist them. Where this extra inspectorate was not imposed, towns might hold back from prosecution to avoid the costs involved. When Prince Edward Island passed its 1901 law to extend complete prohibition to Charlottetown, for example, the city council was furious about not being consulted and refused to assist in any prosecutions. After the war, cash-strapped municipalities were reluctant to enforce the legislation, especially (as in New Brunswick) if revenues from fines went to the province rather than the city.[38]

Beyond the issue of cost, the local police had good reasons for resentment. Dealing with violations of prohibition legislation distracted them from other important work and risked embroiling them in troubling conflicts between political factions in the town. Most municipal police forces were also poorly paid and susceptible to bootleggers' influence. They could become enmeshed in local loyalties and suspicious of outside authorities. In many cases the officers were all too fond of having a drink themselves. Indeed, in most jurisdictions the leading category of police misbehaviour on the job was drinking. "We had one provincial policeman here in town, and he knew me, and he knew what I was doing," a hotel-owner and bootlegger from Southwestern Ontario explained. "But he didn't bother me." Only in larger cities were police departments likely to tackle bootlegging more aggressively, sometimes even with their own "dry squads." Even there, though, enthusiasm for enforcement could be lacking.[39]

In some dry communities, notably in the Maritimes, municipal officials often came to terms with the local bootleggers and blind pigs by regularly imposing fines as substitutes for licence fees, rather than completely closing the places down. The patterns of resistance to enforcement were strongest in towns that had been outvoted by their rural neighbours—for example, such

Enforcement officers often had little enthusiasm for upholding prohibition legislation, partly because many of them, like these Mounties in their canteen at Fort Macleod, Alta., were drinkers themselves. (GA, PA-3481-5)

industrial centres as Sydney, Glace Bay, Stellarton, Springhill, Truro, or Amherst in Nova Scotia, or a larger centre like Charlottetown (where in the 1880s 146 illegal outlets operated in defiance of the Scott Act). Moncton's mayor said in 1901 that, despite local-option prohibition, "Many bar-rooms in the city are practically wide open night and day the whole week and no attempt is made to stop this state of affairs." In Ontario Owen Sound's mayor complained in 1907 that sixty-one "liquor places" were still in operation in defiance of the law.[40]

With the arrival of full-fledged prohibition, provincial governments took on more responsibility for battling bootleggers. Most empowered the new liquor commissioners to hire their own special temperance enforcement officers, often pure patronage appointments that could prove to have limited effectiveness (or worse, as in British Columbia, where the first prohibition commissioner ended up behind bars in 1918 for bootlegging). But the board and staff overseeing the prohibition legislation in some provinces were die-hard temperance men whose zeal got them into trouble. At various points, evangelical ministers filled the position of chief inspector in Alberta, Manitoba, Ontario, New Brunswick, and Nova Scotia, and clergymen took up all the seats on the liquor commission board in Prince Edward Island.[41]

The most celebrated clergyman in the battles with bootleggers was the Reverend J.O.L. Spracklin, a Methodist minister from Sandwich, Ont., who was hired in 1920 to head a special new squad in his province's western border region of Essex County, not far from busy Windsor. Taking his cue from his boss, Ontario's righteous, crusading attorney-general William E. Raney, Spracklin launched into his assignment with overzealous fervour and loose regard for established procedure. His work included aggressive searches and daring raids that ranged along the outer edges of the law. In November 1920 he shot and killed a Sandwich roadhouse owner, "Babe" Trumble. Although Spracklin was acquitted of manslaughter a few months later, the whole country was swept up in discussions about the appropriateness of such fanaticism in pursuit of bootleggers. Shortly afterward Spracklin was fined $500 for trespass on a yacht, and he finally resigned his job as enforcer (soon after that he lost his pulpit—this time on charges of sexually propositioning women in his congregation). "If the law is to be respected and properly enforced, the enforcement of it must never be committed to such persons as the defendant," Ontario's appeal court justices ruled when the trespass case went before them. "It must be left to trained, experienced, and impartial officers of the law." For their part, Windsor's bootleggers responded to Spracklin's departure with a jubilant, highly publicized "Bootleggers' Ball."[42]

Not surprisingly, the other option for enforcement was to establish new provincial police forces or resuscitate old ones. Alberta, Saskatchewan, and Manitoba organized new forces in 1917, followed by New Brunswick in 1927 and Nova Scotia and Prince Edward Island in 1930 (by 1932 all six provincial units had been folded into the RCMP). After the Spracklin affair, Ontario brought the Ontario Provincial Police much more directly into the enforcement of prohibition, while British Columbia reorganized its provincial force in 1924. A special unit staffed with plain-clothes detectives might then be created within the provincial police to deal with infractions of the prohibition law.[43]

Both forms of provincial enforcement did bring many lawbreakers to court and in many cases resulted in convictions. In 1920 more than 10,000 convictions were brought down under liquor control acts across the country, and by 1929 over 19,000. But typically the policing units were plagued by insufficient staff and equipment. While some officers may have found the job exciting, the work was not likely to attract and hold many first-rate policing agents. Often the provincial units had to resort to part-time "spotters" to sniff

out illegal selling or drinking, and many of those helpers proved to have disreputable backgrounds themselves.[44]

Constitutionally, cracking down on stills and cross-border rum-running
remained in federal hands—meaning the RNWMP (and after 1919 the new
Royal Canadian Mounted Police) and officers and patrol boats of the Preventive
Service of the Department of National Revenue (created in 1919 out of a
merger of the Customs and Inland Revenue departments). Until it was reorganized in 1925 the Preventive Service was tiny and ineffective, but even with
the 35 cruisers and patrol boats, 50 cars, and 350 men on land that it had by
the end of the 1920s, it was woefully understaffed and underequipped for its
massive task. Its officers operated independently of other customs officials and
could not possibly patrol all the roads that crossed the international border or
watch the innumerable islands and bays along the coastlines. To apprehend
many of the moonshiners and bootleggers, the Preventive Service officers
often had to rely on the provincial and municipal police, who resented that
the fines levied went to the federal government.[45]

Across the border, U.S. federal enforcement forces were equally inadequate. A former customs official at the Rouses Point border crossing in northern New York state later recalled that staff at his post often had to hire taxis to
carry out night patrols along the border. The Detroit and Michigan police
forces had only one patrol boat each in 1920, and they managed to expand
their fleet primarily by seizing rum-runners' speedboats and arming the vessels for police work. Until the tiny, antiquated Coast Guard was substantially
beefed up in the mid-1920s, its polyglot workforce, with a well-developed
fondness for drink themselves, scarcely made a dent in the illicit trade on the
coasts. Only after that point did rum-runners face much more aggressive
policing backed by heavy firepower and more often end up in court and
behind bars.[46]

Because so much of the underground economy operated under the cover
of darkness, enforcement officers worked in a gloom of uncertainty and
potential danger. Catching rum-runners and bootleggers red-handed often
resulted in hair-raising chases as the men being pursued simply took off in
their high-powered cars or boats or, if necessary, abandoned the booze and
vanished into the night on foot. In 1923 an Alberta policeman died after
jumping onto (and falling off) the running board of a bootlegger's speeding
car. Enforcement officers got into the habit of freely firing their guns at cars
or across the bows of boats in attempts to intimidate their prey. In 1923 the
Alberta Provincial Police proudly showed off its six new motorcycles, two of
them equipped with machine guns and four with submachine guns in their
sidecars. In 1929 the U.S. Coast Guard fired on and sank a Canadian schooner

known as *I'm Alone*, killing one sailor and raising eyebrows at the violence of the attack. In all cases, the increased firepower only raised the stakes of danger. Furthermore, if these officers managed to seize some contraband liquor, there was a good chance that it would subsequently be stolen from them. If they caught the culprits and tried to make charges stick, they frequently faced the popular resistance to giving evidence or testifying.[47]

Local police magistrates did not always co-operate in cracking down on violations of prohibition legislation, especially when the case hinged on the testimony of a "spotter," and they often dismissed cases or levied light sentences. "In some few instances," Ontario's licence commissioners reported in 1922, "the Judge displays so great a tendency to quash [Ontario Temperance Act] convictions that people and officers who desire proper enforcement quite lose heart and regard it as useless to prosecute." Lawbreakers were therefore "encouraged to set the law at defiance." In rural areas in particular, these magistrates might be tied into local patronage networks and they would deal lightly with political friends in the bootlegging business. The fines imposed rarely shut the bootleggers down for good. One hotel-keeper in a small Southwestern Ontario town "just paid the fine and opened up as soon as they [liquor inspectors] left," while Windsor's leading blind-pig owner, Bertha Thomas, would never let raids shut her down for more than ten minutes. "A fine was nothing to her," a policeman said. "It was part of the operating expenses for Bertha." In other cases, even a brief stay in jail did not stop determined operators from picking up the business again on their release.[48]

To further complicate the enforcement picture, throughout the history of local-option and provincewide prohibition teetotallers felt no qualms about undertaking vigilante action. Trying to unearth the threats to the new moral order, temperance enthusiasts frequently assumed the role of unofficial policemen, often as self-styled law and order leagues. Besides volunteering as spies and snitches, they paid out-of-town "spotters" to visit hotels and determine whether alcohol was being served illegally. They even took the offenders to court themselves. In Amherst, N.S., the Moral Reform League once used a fire engine to flood a restaurant that was allegedly serving liquor. But both the outside snoops and their prohibitionist sponsors could face popular outrage in many communities, as well as the resistance to testifying.[49]

In the face of such obstacles to effective enforcement, many policing officials at all levels developed a nod-and-wink, live-and-let-live relationship with bootleggers and rum-runners. Considerable numbers of officers were prepared to skim off a small bribe from the huge profitable traffic that passed under their gaze. When a new police constable arrived at a post in Southern Alberta, he was offered $2,000 to "shut his eyes for a month or so." A Windsor bootlegger admitted in 1921 to paying more than $96,000 in bribes. New Brunswick's Joe Walnut even undertook to get his hand-picked candidate appointed as provincial liquor inspector for his district. When the former carpenter Clifford Rose took up his Conservative patronage appointment as New Glasgow's temperance inspector in 1925, he discovered the many ways in which "enforcement" had become merely accommodation with bootlegging. "Rum dives are thick as bees," he recorded in his diary. Although bootleggers dispersed free rum to campaign workers in both parties at election time, it was clear that Rose's raids on blind pigs were not supposed to embarrass political friends of the ruling Conservative Party. A Saskatchewan royal commission (whose lawyer was the young John G. Diefenbaker) learned in 1929 that a similar political bias had been shown in local enforcement under a Liberal government. Moreover, because fines were intended to be in effect licence fees and important revenues for the town coffers, heavy-handed prosecution to drive out the bootleggers was completely out of the question.[50]

Many staff in the Customs, Inland Revenue, and, after 1919, National Revenue departments were likewise on the take. "When one considers that these men are very poorly paid, it seems astonishing that they could afford the luxurious homes they possessed," a 1921 visitor to the households of three customs officers in St. Leonard, N.B., later wrote. In Lunenburg the men hired by the department's local official to guard barrels of liquor were recommended by a local rum-runner.[51]

A little bootlegging on the side was also possible. Years later a demolition crew tearing down a customs house in Quebec found in the basement a huge vat with a pipe from the upstairs sink into which all the seized booze had ceremoniously been poured, and from which it could later be tapped. Montreal's chief preventive officer was found to be regularly bootlegging the booze he seized. Higher officials in the department not only failed to stop such practices, but also often encouraged local officers to keep their hands off some illicit traders. When the high-minded inspector Cyril Knowles decided to tackle the Bronfman brothers in Saskatchewan, his superior ordered him to confine his work to Winnipeg.[52]

A lengthy parliamentary inquiry in 1926 and then a full-scale royal commission in 1926–27 discovered widespread bribery and collusion among the customs officials who were supposed to be monitoring the international flow of alcohol. At that point the Preventive Service was reorganized, and in 1932 it was absorbed into the RCMP.[53]

Popular Collusion

In the end, prohibition did not fail simply because the police were ineffective, incompetent, or corrupt. In essence, the rule of law broke down. Large numbers of Canadians refused to accept the legitimacy of either the idea of clamping down on alcohol consumption or the heavy-handed administration of the law, and many saw an economic opportunity in subverting the state measures.

Enforcement officers most often found themselves enmeshed in community relationships that were more powerful than the new anti-booze laws. A former Customs Department administrator later explained:

> In those days, all members of the Preventive Service were appointed by the minister of Customs as part of the spoils of office. It was part of my job to find these people. You can imagine what this meant in all the small towns and villages. The preventive officer couldn't be expected to inform on his brother or cousin for rum running and that kind of thing. Our whole Preventive Service was too close to home, so to speak.

Although plenty of citizens were ready to inform on their neighbours, identifying lawbreakers frequently required overcoming the community collusion in their nefarious activities. A retired Ontario policeman observed:

> It wasn't a very popular law in Amherstburg. For instance, there was an awful lot of people who made their money through that, and they paid good wages. Nearly every family in that area had somebody connected with the family involved in the rumrunning business. They didn't feel too bad about it. The stores and restaurants did good business from people who came over with their boats and in the course of a day there would be quite a few of them.

In 1924 the RCMP reported from Southern Saskatchewan that the telephone was "a great hindrance" to the work. "When our patrols leave certain points or are seen on the trails, farmers warn each other of our presence in their district." Similarly, an enforcement officer in Nova Scotia recalled: "We had to be careful not to let the people know that we were searching for something, because I had been warned that if news got around that we were searching for liquor, everyone would be against us." In New Brunswick neighbours would fire a warning shot if inspectors approached illegal stills. In one attempt to arrest a bootlegger in Westmoreland County, N.B., police had to face an angry crowd that attacked them and unleashed their dogs on them. Calgary's police chief stated that "under prohibition 75% of the population broke the law, 20% did not care whether it was observed or not, and only 5% were concerned about its enforcement."[54]

This pattern of resistance to unpopular laws had bubbled up at points in the nineteenth century—against the imposition of mandatory schooling in the 1840s or compulsory smallpox inoculation in the 1880s (though these involved more overt, collective challenges)—but it is difficult to find any other moment in modern Canadian history when such conscious, wilful, defiant lawbreaking took place on such a mass scale. The bootleggers and rum-runners operated on a solid basis of popular support, confident that the communities they served would usually close ranks to protect them. A Windsor rum-runner later described how blue-collar workers would take their pay to Montreal, buy twenty-five cases of alcohol, and then bring it home and ferry it across the Detroit River—all as a community-based way of getting a bit ahead. "They never thought there was nothing criminal about it," he said. Rocco Perri operated on the same assumption. "The law, what is the law?" he scornfully told the Toronto *Star* in 1924. "They don't want it in the cities. They voted against it. It is forced upon them. I have a right to violate it if I can get away with it. . . . Am I a criminal because I violate a law which the people do not want?" (Al Capone made a similar case in the United States.) Perri also admitted that bootleggers had their own system of justice, also outside the state's legal system. If a man "squealed" on him, he said, "I would not kill him, I would punish him. That is the law of the Italians. We do not go to the police and complain. That is useless. We take the law into our own hands. . . . We believe we have the right to inflict our own penalties."[55]

In this sense, these men and women were much like the "social bandits" and "primitive rebels" of other periods and in other parts of the world. Some of those who rose from humble origins to leadership of the gangs were minor heroes, admired for their dash and daring, their flashy suits, and their generosity. Emilio Picariello, locally known as "Emperor Pick," was recognized in Southern Alberta as an open-handed patriarch. He helped out miners' families during a 1918 strike, donated mounds of groceries and carloads of flour to feed the poor at Christmas, and sponsored a free movie night for children on Christmas Eve in Blairmore, where he lived. Similar stories abounded about the big-time operators in the Windsor region, where roadhouse owner Bertha Thomas paid off mortgages for friends and held Halloween parties for children. Hamilton's Perri had no qualms about inviting a Toronto *Star* reporter into his sumptuous living room in the posh south end of Hamilton in November 1924 and freely admitting to being "king" of the bootleggers. "I am a bootlegger. I am not ashamed to admit it. And a bootlegger I shall remain."

The interview filled half of the paper's front page on 19 November 1924, alongside a large formal portrait of Perri that conveyed a strong sense of respectability. It must have done much to embellish the public image of bootleggers as legitimate folk heroes battling against an unpopular legal regime. Hollywood quickly latched onto this theme and sent scores of gangster movies out to eager audiences in movie houses across North America (much to the chagrin of Canadian movie censors).[56]

So, thanks to doctors, druggists, moonshiners, rum-runners, and bootleggers of all kinds, booze was still widely available by the mid-1920s. The Regina *Leader* reported its findings on Winnipeg in December 1922:

> The breweries in Manitoba are working at capacity upon the 6 to 11 percent beer which makes its appearance at hotel bars, grocery stores, refreshment booths, and at convivial gatherings. . . . The illegal sale of beer and more potent drinks is being conducted in no underground, concealed or devious manner. The hotels vending strong drink are located in many parts of the city. Clubs are well stocked with drinks. The open bar is an actuality in Winnipeg.

Three years later Nova Scotia's inspector-in-chief submitted a similar report:

> So much liquor is now smuggled and distributed throughout the Province in motor cars and by bootleggers that the closing of bars and blind pigs does not have much effect on the total consumption. It is beyond the power of local inspectors to control smuggling or even check it to any appreciable extent. Dominion officers, whose duty it is to deal with smuggling, are few in number and quite unable to keep an effective watch on all parts of the coast where liquor may be landed. . . . Owing to the prevalence of home manufacture, the consumption of intoxicating beer in some country districts, probably, has been greater in recent years than it was under the old license law.

In 1927 New Brunswick's Board of Liquor Commissioners reported, "After close observation and careful inquiry, your Commission have no hesitation in asserting that 75 per cent of the liquor handled in the province passes through the hands of the bootlegger through underground channels."[57]

Prohibition's Impact

The remarks of these officials suggest that, despite statements of prohibitionists to the contrary, prohibition was a complete failure; but given the opaque, undocumented business practices of providing alcoholic drinks it is not easy to determine the actual extent of that failure.

Certainly, the country's well-established distillers and brewers were still producing large quantities of alcohol during the legally dry years. Statistics from the Department of National Revenue indicate that the total output of legally regulated liquor for domestic consumption steadily rose to 4.6 million gallons in 1918, slipped to 2.8 million in 1921, and dropped off abruptly to only 730,000 in 1922 and 1923, but then was back to over one million by 1926. Beer production slumped from nearly 35 million gallons in 1917 to 26.5 million in 1919, but was back to nearly 36 million by 1921 and up to 52.5 million by 1926. A good deal of this production must have been destined for the United States. Department staff nonetheless calculated that those figures translated into a dramatic drop in per capita liquor consumption (including imports) from .703 gallons in 1917 to only .225 by 1925, while per capita beer consumption changed scarcely at all, starting at 4.3 gallons in 1917, bottoming out at just over 3 in 1919, but hovering between 4 and 5 in the first half of the 1920s.[58]

Yet moonshiners and bootleggers sold so much beverage alcohol that official statistics tell only part of the story; and we will never have a precise sense of how large a part. On their side, the prohibitionists liked to trumpet that consumption had dropped and that the impact of alcohol on society had diminished. Some three-quarters of the manufacturers that Ontario's Board of License Commissioners surveyed in 1922 reported "increased production of goods," increased "regularity of attendance immediately after pay day," and improved "capacity for work and . . . ability to perform their duties." Crime was down, school registration was up, a prohibition leader crowed the same year. The drys most often highlighted the huge drop in convictions for public drunkenness across the country. Especially in the first flush of the dry era at the end of the war, commentators regularly claimed that drunks were rarely seen in the street.[59]

Again, though, the statistics allow a slightly different reading. The number of cases of public drunkenness in any year after 1916 was certainly lower than the prewar peak of nearly 61,000 in 1913. But there was more than a hint of older patterns that had at least something to do with the business cycle and disposable income. The 1922 survey of manufacturers might have reflected more about the devastating depression that gripped the country at that point than about the impact of prohibition. For most working-class families, the 1920s and 1930s were a long period of severe depression in Canada, broken only by a short spell of fuller employment from 1926 to 1929. After reaching a low of 21,000 across the country in 1918, the total convictions for drunkenness almost doubled to just under 40,000 in 1920—the last year of the war-induced boom and a moment of intense social activity among returned soldiers, probably the most militant of the wets.

The sharp decline to under 27,000 convictions between 1922 and 1925 corresponded with the postwar economic slump, when, as in the past, drinking was a luxury that many could not afford. The rise in the number of convictions to nearly 39,000 in 1929, the peak of the renewed prosperity of that decade, followed by a new tumble to half that level in the early 1930s, suggests that the much-discussed decline in drunkenness was at least as much a result of poverty as of repressive legislation. In 1929, looking over the consumption statistics for the 1920s, Ontario's Liquor Control Board concluded, "The results plainly show that economic conditions, rather than laws, influence the gross sale of liquor." The act of drinking enough to get drunk was still usually connected to having regular wages.[60]

Drunkenness had never been a good indicator of overall drinking habits in any case. During prohibition the widespread disappearance of the drunk in city streets could be traced in a different direction. Public drunkenness had most often been a ritualized performance rooted in the customs of the "working man's club." Closing the barrooms simply removed the stage and the audience for these outlandish acts of masculine bravado, which had, in any case, never involved more than a small proportion of the saloons' customers. Excessive drinking was now more likely to take place at home, where enforcement officers were less likely to intervene. Given the new legal constraints, many Canadian drinkers—and the vigilant bootleggers and blind-pig operators who supplied them—may have made greater efforts to conceal their intoxication from public scrutiny. Or perhaps policemen were simply more comfortable with dealing with public drunkenness informally rather than marching drunks into court.

Yet it does seems possible that some Canadians, especially the working men who had made up the hard core of the saloon culture before the war, were drinking less booze. For one thing, they found it much harder to drop casually into an open, friendly, boisterous space on the way home from work. Drinking had to become more secretive and surreptitious. However friendly the blind pigs may have been, they were simply not as accessible for casual visits as the prewar saloons. The legal but unpopular "near beer" never did draw as many men together in hotel beverage rooms. In 1922 prohibitionist leader

Ben Spence said he found only four men sipping near beer in a former Toronto barroom where 128 had been tallied up before the war.[61]

Alcohol had also become much more expensive, partly because so much of it was illicit, partly because doctors willing to help a thirsty man charged a two-dollar fee on each prescription, and partly because liquor was the most common drink available (given that beer was bulkier for bootleggers to transport). The Ontario Liquor Control Board noted in 1929 that high prices made a big difference: "The fact that whiskey, which cost 75 cents [a bottle] in 1913, sold for $2.75 in 1928, has much and very much to do with a consumption per capita of only .425 gallons in 1928, as against a consumption of 1.136 gallons in 1913." The old era of enjoying a few shots at ten cents each was gone.[62]

It is impossible to know whether these conditions resulted in more permanent teetotallers. By 1943 two out of every five Canadians aged eighteen and over surveyed in a Gallup poll would say that they did not drink. Certainly, the producers of so-called "soft drinks" found a growing market for their ginger ales and colas. More likely, the moderate drinkers of the prewar saloons were now swallowing far less—perhaps none at all for long stretches. Prohibition may have helped to curb the minority experience of excessive drunkenness, but for much larger numbers of drinkers it probably reinforced an already existing pattern of only moderate and occasional consumption.[63]

That, of course, was far from what the anti-booze legislators had intended to accomplish. By the early 1920s it was hard to make a convincing argument that prohibition was doing what the dry forces had claimed for it. Arguably, it was the mass civil disobedience of Canadians that crippled this radical experiment in repressive public policy. Too many people were taking the opportunity to keep the flow of alcohol moving through an underground economy that allowed thousands to continue buying and drinking the beverages that were supposed to be banned from commerce. Too few enforcement officers had the resources or the will to clamp down on this new version of the liquor traffic. To those who had opposed prohibition in theory were now added large numbers who were disgusted with it in practice. Disappointed prohibitionists continued to call for better policing, but now found themselves struggling to keep the wet forces from winning support for the dismantling of what they had managed to put in place. Whatever public support the drys had won during the war quickly drained away as a new vision of state regulation gathered momentum. As the Saint John *Standard* argued in 1920, "It is rapidly becoming apparent that there are greater evils than moderate drinking."[64]

eight

Trying Again

AFTER A CENTURY OF CAMPAIGNING, Canada's teetotallers had to confront failure. They watched their dry utopia collapse in most parts of the country in less than a decade after 1920. The temperance movement, which had been thrown onto the defensive almost as soon as provincewide prohibition was launched, now found itself fighting the less draconian regulatory model of "government control" as a more workable alternative. State policy-makers, however, were not willing simply to turn back the clock to the freewheeling days of the prewar era. Instead, they set in place new administrative measures to accomplish some of the same old goals of curbing consumption and controlling behaviour. If full-scale prohibition had failed, there was no reason to give up on the project of moral regulation.

Opposite page: Quebec was the first province to introduce new public drinking legislation after the First World War. Some key features, evident in this photo of a Montreal tavern in the 1920s, were eventually carried to other provinces, notably the banning of a stand-up bar and the requirement that waiters bring drinks to customers at their tables. (MM, MP-0000.587.125)

The new watchword was "moderation." It captured the yearning of bourgeois Canadians for refined drinking occasions, an end to lawlessness, and a new era of less politically destabilizing extremism. It embraced the proletarian desire for the right to respectable imbibing and an end to class-biased legislation. It was an appeal to greater personal freedom for sensible, orderly behaviour, under the still watchful eyes of the state. It was an acceptable compromise for the brewing and distilling interests, and it made sense to the majority of the thousands of Canadians who were asked to express an opinion on the continuation or repeal of prohibition between 1919 and 1929.

The Many Roads to Repeal

In the United States prohibition lasted from 1920 to 1933, but it had a much shorter life in most of Canada and in Newfoundland. Quebec's ban on spirits

THE PROHIBITION ERA IN CANADA			
	DRY	GOVERNMENT CONTROL	
		Stores	Public Drinking
Prince Edward Island	1901	1948	1964
Manitoba	1916	1923	1928
Nova Scotia	1916	1930	1948
Alberta	1916	1924	1924
Ontario	1916	1927	1934
Saskatchewan	1917	1925	1935
New Brunswick	1917	1927	1961
British Columbia	1917	1921	1925
Newfoundland	1917	1925	1925
Yukon	1918	1921	1925
Quebec	1919	1919	1921

lasted only two years. The completely dry regime lasted only three years in the Yukon, four in British Columbia, seven in Manitoba, and eight in Alberta, Saskatchewan, and Newfoundland. The provinces of New Brunswick (ten years), Ontario (eleven), and Nova Scotia (thirteen) held out a little longer, while Prince Edward Island remained officially dry for almost half a century.

The successful plebiscites to stop imports of booze into the dry provinces, along with the many simultaneous legislative measures to tighten up prohibition—restraints on doctors and druggists, stiffer penalties for bootlegging, stronger police forces—marked the high-water mark of prohibition. But by that time, in the face of flagrant failures, an alternative had worked its way onto the political agenda—a push to allow for the re-legalizing of booze without the return of the prewar saloon.

The idea of some form of government-run retailing of alcoholic beverages had been bandied about in Canada since the turn of the century. The Scandinavian experiment with the Gothenburg System of a municipally guided, non-profit operation of tightly regulated drinking establishments, introduced in the mid-nineteenth century, was often cited as one option, and the Royal Commission on the Liquor Traffic had mulled it over (without enthusiasm). In North America, the self-styled Committee of Fifty, a group of powerful U.S. businessmen and professionals, had laid the groundwork for some such alternative with a series of investigations and multiple publications between 1893 and 1905. Their work examined the saloon and alcohol consumption in general and recommended that governments, not saloons, sell booze. In the early twentieth century some Canadian politicians and journalists showed an interest in greater state regulation as an alternative to prohibition, but the notion did not catch fire until Saskatchewan introduced a version of government "dispensaries" in 1915 as its first step towards complete prohibition of retail sales (a step taken only after an investigation of South Carolina, the one state that had implemented the system). Other provinces also ran dispensaries for filling doctors' prescriptions or providing sacramental wine or alcohol for industrial uses during the dry years. By 1920 "governmental control" had become the new rallying cry of the wet campaigners.[1]

Many politicians had their own reasons for finding this option attractive. They knew that millions of dollars of untaxed revenues were pumping through the bootlegging and rum-running networks, while provincial economies were slumping into depression. Enforcement costs for prohibition were rising, and new demands were crowding in on governments to provide more roads and highways and social-welfare measures, eventually including the provincial share of the old-age pensions that the federal government launched in 1926. Taxation of legalized alcoholic beverages could help to once again solve the financial problems of provincial administrations. The Eastern governments were soon eyeing with envy the soaring revenues from legalized sales of booze in Western Canada and Quebec.

The route for undoing prohibition was much the same as that taken in its making—via plebiscites and/or simple majorities in legislatures. A pattern emerged in which a provincial Moderation League appeared, amassed large petitions (often circulated by veterans, who apparently were sometimes paid ten cents per signature), and eventually convinced the provincial government to hold a vote. Prohibitionist organizations rallied to the defence of the existing dry regime, but now without their earlier spirit of optimism and triumph. Their organizations lacked fresh recruits or, in many cases, vital funds for campaigning.

With the exception of Quebec and, for idiosyncratic reasons, Alberta, government control arrived in two distinct, widely separated steps. Government-run cash-and-carry liquor stores appeared to be the easiest policy shift to sell to voters, and most provinces started with that measure alone. There was much more hesitation about reopening public drinking places. That possibility resurrected the menacing image of the prewar saloon, and usually only brewing interests and working-class wets were willing to champion the barroom. Except for Ontario, the sale of near beer in hotels, pool halls, and lunch counters came to an end with government-control legislation. Full-strength beer in government stores was available only in take-home bottles and, in

GOVERNMENT
BOOZORIUM

LIQUOR SELLER

Citizens of B.C., Don't Impose
This Job on Your Premier

Saskatchewan Tried It!

If the people of British Columbia were to encourage
good and capable men to enter their government, they
should not saddle them with the responsibility of run-
ing on a liquor business. — *(reduce time) staffers, Directors*
of Municipal Affairs (see footnote no. 10).

Profit by Saskatchewan's Experience and

Vote for Prohibition

In British Columbia's 1920
referendum on continuing
prohibition, the dry forces
urged voters not to turn the
government into a saloon-
keeper. They lost. From Sun
(Vancouver), *12 October 1920.*

Ontario and British Columbia at least, only a dozen at a time. Draft beer could not be sold.[2]

The liquor stores alone proved unsatisfactory. "A great many workingmen don't care to or have not the means and opportunity, to take a carton of beer home," the Hamilton *Labor News* complained in 1927. "In any event they prefer to have a glass, or perhaps two, along with friends in congenial surroundings." Manitoba's veterans agreed: "What the ordinary man wants is some place where he can lawfully get a glass of beer in decent surroundings." In his 1928 study of government control in Canada (before most provinces had licensed premises), the British writer Reginald Hose observed, "It is evident that people who perpetuate the prohibition-time habits of drinking surreptitiously in any convenient meeting place will not be satisfied with store facilities for their buying, and when two or three foregather in a back-room where treating and some sort of service of the kind they like is offered, there will continue to be secret drinking."[3]

In the end the growing evidence that moonshining and bootlegging continued to exist in full force alongside government-controlled outlets helped to convince governments and voters to make booze accessible in controlled public settings. In most provinces licensed drinking establishments arrived a few years after liquor stores as a result of renewed wet campaigning, especially by labour and war veterans' organizations and the brewing interests. The dynamics of change were somewhat different in each province, and the new experiences under government control increasingly became part of the debate in the other still-dry provinces.

The first three jurisdictions to roll back prohibition were the ones that had historically been least enthusiastic about the legislated coercion: Quebec, British Columbia, and the Yukon. Quebec moved first. The province had never been completely dry. When its government announced in 1918 that it would implement a full-fledged shutdown of sales on 1 May 1919, Montreal's august brewing families descended from their mansions on the hill to convince the administration to hold a plebiscite on legal sales of light beers, ciders, and wines. In April 1919 a landslide of voters bought the new Moderation League's arguments that these drinks should be available in hotels, taverns, cafés, clubs, and corner stores. As a result, only spirits were cut off. Some two years later, in the face of large-scale bootlegging of hard liquor, the government decided to replace this limited version of prohibition with government sales of all alcoholic beverages. Grocery stores and other outlets could apply for a licence to sell beer.[4]

British Columbia moved along a similar path. On 20 October 1920 voters registered a clear preference for government control over the existing prohibition act. They got government-owned liquor stores, but no public drinking places. Increased lobbying, especially from the veterans' groups, which had been defiantly serving beer in their clubs, resulted in a second referendum on 20 June 1924, in which the wets narrowly lost. But in a reversal of the old local-option policy, the enabling legislation for the vote had allowed constituencies that voted wet (twenty-three out of forty) to have licensed places for beer drinking. The first such place opened in March 1925. Yukon residents also got government control on 15 September 1921 after endorsement through a plebiscite the previous July, and in 1925 they got beer by the glass.[5]

The three Prairie governments were the next to act, under pressure from residents of their urban and industrial regions. The Manitoba Moderation League emerged early in 1921 and soon claimed a paid-up membership of 16,000. Their petitions with large numbers of signatures eventually convinced the provincial government to hold a plebiscite on 22 June 1923 on what it called the "Moderation League Bill," which provided only for government liquor stores. That step was not enough for the brewers and hotel-keepers, who presented their own petition and got a separate plebiscite on selling beer by the glass scheduled for 11 July 1923. In other provinces the moderationists were allies of the booze producers, but in this case they adopted a middling posture and publicly criticized the industry's campaign organization, the Beer and Wine League. The result was a split in the two provincewide votes. Government liquor stores were endorsed by a large majority, but licensed hotels were soundly defeated. Still, the tight controls on sales did not eliminate bootlegging, and working-class agitation for beer by the glass continued. A more proletarian Joint Veterans' Committee eventually presented a petition with 128,000 signatures to the provincial legislature and thus convinced the Liberal government to hold another plebiscite on 28 June 1927. In a complicated three-part ballot, voters agreed to extend the range of facilities in which beer could be sold and to allow beer to be sold by the glass. On 15 February 1928 the first beer parlours opened in the province's hotels, and customers were allowed to purchase the drink by the glass or the bottle.[6]

Meanwhile the wet forces in Alberta had decided to activate the 1915 plebiscite legislation that had been used to bring in prohibition. During 1922 the province's Moderation League collected thousands of signatures on a petition for government control, while the Hotel-keepers' Association did the same for sales of beer by the glass. Both petitions landed on the floor of the legislature, and after an extensive investigation of signatures and windy debate—the silver-tongued prohibitionist Nellie McClung was now a member of the legislature—the government agreed to hold a plebiscite with a preferential ballot. Voters would have to rank four options in order of preference:

continuation of prohibition, licensed beer sales in hotels, government sale of beer only (liquor to be available only via doctor's prescription), and sale of all alcoholic beverages through government-owned liquor stores. The United Farmers of Alberta government took no official position during the subsequent campaign, partly as a tacit recognition of how revenues from government-controlled booze could help carry the province out of the sinkhole of debt. Despite backing for prohibition from most newspapers, on 5 November 1923 the great majority of voters endorsed government liquor stores, while a somewhat smaller majority favoured sales of beer by the glass. Within a month the government was meeting with various parts of the wet forces for advice on the specifics of the new legislation, which finally became effective on 10 May 1924. The unusual decision to allow the beer-by-the-glass option on the ballot, the use of preferential voting, and the unity of the wet forces made Alberta only the second province in the country to permit public drinking, well before most other jurisdictions in Canada.[7]

Saskatchewan's Liberal government held out against moderationist petitioning until December 1923, when it agreed to hold a plebiscite the following 16 July. Voters had three options: prohibition, liquor stores only, or liquor stores along with beer drinking on licensed premises. The campaign rippled with tensions. Catholics angrily linked the issue to Protestant manoeuvres against their religion and language. Prohibitionists themselves were in a fractious mood as a result of the large Protestant churches' simultaneous debates about church union. Even the "Liquor Traffic" split: the distillers supported prohibition and the brewers public drinking. The outcome was a substantial majority for government liquor stores, but rejection of beer by the glass. Booze was back on sale on 16 April 1925. Some nine years later, on the eve of an election, the government agreed to a plebiscite on public drinking, which carried narrowly. The first licensed establishments opened on 2 May 1935.[8]

Ontario moved along a different path that eventually turned booze into a partisan political issue—something that it had not been since before the war. As elsewhere, a Moderation League emerged with growing support and in 1922 presented the legislature with a petition bearing over 200,000 signatures and calling for government control. Unlike their Independent Labour Party partners, the members of the United Farmers of Ontario in the province's ruling Farmer-Labour coalition were deeply committed prohibitionists. Across the house the leader of the Opposition, Conservative Howard Ferguson, was no lover of prohibition, but his party was divided on the issue. In 1922 he had promised vaguely "to find some reasonable means that will allow our people to exercise their God-given freedom under reasonable restriction," and in subsequent statements before and during the 1923 provincial election campaign he tried to convince both wets and drys that he was their man. Although he was particularly critical of Attorney-General Raney's "fanatical" enforcement policies, he made no promises about bringing in changes to the dry legislation. Premier E.C. Drury fought a determined campaign in defence of prohibition as his government's greatest accomplishment in social reform, even publishing his own booklet, *Temperance: The Vital Issue* (though he was thunderstruck to discover that some members of the United Farmers had been among those caught drinking whisky in a private end-of-session party at Queen's Park). The wets took heart from the Conservatives' crushing victory on election day, but Ferguson moved cautiously, assuring the public that his government would enforce the existing dry legislation without the previous government's excesses. Partly in response to Moderation League lobbying and partly to settle the feud within the Tories' own ranks, the government announced a plebiscite on government control for 23 October 1923. Although three provinces and the Yukon had already opted for the measure and another would be added to that column early the next month, Ontario broke the momentum and upheld prohibition by the slenderest of margins (and with a much lower voter turnout). Voters had shifted considerably towards government control since the 1919 and 1921 votes, but were still split sharply along urban-rural lines. In an all-too familiar echo from earlier temperance agitation, one dry correspondent even suggested to Ferguson that he should disregard the urban wet vote because it was "largely made up by Jews, Foreigners and Roman Catholics."[9]

Searching for some kind of compromise, Ferguson's government decided to allow the sale of slightly stronger "temperance beer"—4.4 per cent proof spirits, up from 2.5 per cent—which the government claimed was not intoxicating, and which disgruntled drinkers quickly dubbed "Fergie's Foam." Hamilton's *Labor News* reported that this brew was still found "unsatisfying by people who appreciate and relish a decent glass of beer." The paper's editor noted, "What the people need is an opportunity to buy and drink palatable beer of fair strength, made from pure malt and hops, and devoid of chemicals."[10]

By the time Ferguson mounted the hustings for the 1926 provincial election, booze had become the overriding issue. The premier seemed confident that the widely discussed lawlessness under the dry regime and the need to eliminate provincial deficits had shifted enough public opinion towards support for government control that he could now tie his party's fortunes to this change in public policy. Both the Farmers and the Liberals ran on flat-out prohibitionist platforms. During the campaign, Ferguson strengthened his position with moderates by ostentatiously withdrawing the promise of beer by the glass. With a significant jump in voter turnout, he won handily, and wasted no time in introducing a new law.[11]

Ontario's new liquor stores opened on 1 June 1927, and six months later the government announced its first budgetary surplus in living memory, thanks to the infusion of $2 million in booze-related revenues. The Tories resisted beer by the glass until 1934, when, against the backdrop of the U.S. decision to repeal prohibition the year before, and with a nudge from the floundering brewing industry—and in a desperate act to stave off electoral defeat—they passed the necessary legislation, which was proclaimed by Mitchell Hepburn's new Liberal government a few months later (Labatt's general manager immediately held an elaborate celebratory party for Hepburn in Lambeth, Ont.). On 24 July the province's beer drinkers flocked into the new licensed "beverage rooms."[12]

On the East Coast a new Conservative administration that took office in the Dominion of Newfoundland in 1924 carried through quickly on its campaign promise to repeal prohibition. Government liquor stores opened, and drinking beer and wine with meals was permitted in hotels, clubs, railways, and steamships (in 1935 spirits also became permissible). The governments of the three Maritime provinces moved much more cautiously. New governments in Nova Scotia and New Brunswick in 1925 and in Prince Edward Island in 1927 all promised to try to make the existing legislation work. All of them were also quickly disillusioned and sceptical that prohibition was appropriate. All three premiers also felt the heat of anti-prohibition lobbying.[13]

Given his province's large Acadian population, New Brunswick's premier J.B.M. Baxter decided to avoid a divisive plebiscite campaign and, in the wake of Ontario's decision, simply introduced government control through a bill on 6 April 1927. The first government liquor stores opened on 6 September 1927. In August of that year, Nova Scotia's Premier Edgar Rhodes bluntly asserted, "Prohibition by statute in my judgement is on all fours with the attitude of the Russian Soviets who believe in rule by force rather than rule by reason." But he waited two more years before scheduling a plebiscite for 31 October 1929. The province's Moderation League, active since 1924, rechristened itself the Temperance Reform Association and managed to convince a solid majority of Nova Scotians to endorse government control. Liquor stores opened for business in September 1930.[14]

Only Prince Edward Island bucked the trend, voting to preserve its dry regime in plebiscites in 1929 and 1940. In practice, however, successive Island governments simply used the system of doctors' prescriptions for liquor as an indirect version of government control—the legendary "medical script racket"—

and raked in substantial revenues. In 1948 another vote finally brought in government liquor stores.

By 1930, then, eight of the nine provinces, as well as the Yukon and Newfoundland, had government-owned liquor stores, which contributed over $30 million to provincial coffers each year. By that same year only four jurisdictions were licensing public drinking places, but two more were added to that column in 1934 and 1935. Public drinking places came relatively late to the Maritime provinces: 1948 in Nova Scotia, 1961 in New Brunswick, and 1964 in Prince Edward Island.[15]

Under Watchful Eyes

The new regimes of government control that all these provinces established were considerably less "wet" than what had been tolerated before the war. They were also openly designed to make access to alcoholic beverages difficult and to educate the drinker in moderation. As the Edmonton *Bulletin* suggested when Alberta introduced its government-control legislation, "While declaring the sale of beer and wine and liquor to be legal, the bill brands both seller of beer and the user of liquor as doing something that is either morally wrong or publicly dangerous or both."[16]

Although provincewide prohibition had been repealed, some kind of local-option provision, either provincial law or the old Scott Act, survived in each province to allow municipalities to keep out liquor stores, brewers' warehouses, and/or beer parlours. Even in Quebec in the mid-1920s, for example, 91 per cent of people living in cities and 58 per cent of those in towns had access to licensed premises, but 85 per cent of the rural population did not, so that only half of the province's population lived in wet municipalities. As in the prewar version of local prohibition, booze could legally be sent into these dry areas by mail or express order, and transportation by automobile now allowed drinkers to travel longer distances to government liquor stores. A 1928 study of government control in Canada concluded, "The belief in local option is losing weight as a means of arresting excessive drinking." Although there was little expansion of dry zones, most withstood referendum challenges and held on for many more years.[17]

Each provincial liquor control act also created a powerful provincial regulatory commission of between one and five members, usually known as a liquor control board (or commission), with sweeping powers to set policy for alcohol consumption. Like a growing number of regulatory agencies (such as labour-relations boards), these bodies made and enforced law in their own ad hoc fashion, largely outside the purview of legislatures or courts. They were headed by high-profile, widely respected men (such as Ontario's Sir Henry Drayton, a former federal railways minister, and Manitoba's R.D. Waugh, a former League of Nations commissioner). In Quebec they reported to the treasurer, in Saskatchewan and British Columbia they reported directly to the legislature, and elsewhere to the provincial cabinet. The sweeping powers of these boards or commissions took many of the details of public policy around booze out of the hands of legislators and away from close public scrutiny. As a result, most of the related issues gradually faded away from the vortex of political controversy and fell off the agendas of political parties. Politicians were happy to let the new administrators handle the problems.[18]

Each board employed a large, widely scattered but rigidly controlled staff to monitor drinkers and inspect drinking places. Neither the board members nor the staff was rooted in any particular profession, such as medicine, psychiatry, public health, or even the law; their political connections were generally far more important than any kind of professional expertise. The dynamics of this new regulatory regime primarily involved moral policing. The boards saw their role as much more than administering retail outlets and issuing licences; they were moral guardians whose policies and procedures were intended to encourage sobriety and discourage alcohol abuse. As Ontario's Liquor Control Board indicated in its first annual report, "The Board has endeavoured always to keep in mind that the Act under which it was organized was a control act, and that therefore a proper control of the purchase and sale of liquor should be its aim." The Ontario board was proud of its initial accomplishments:

> A marked cutting down of the bootlegging evil; a lessening of youthful temptations to break prohibitory laws; the bringing about of greater respect for all law; a decrease if not an elimination of the making of "home brew" with its dangerous poisonous tendencies; and, it is hoped, a real stimulation to temperance in all things by education and home training rather than by prohibiting which does not prohibit.

Board policies tried not only to curb consumption but also to nudge drinkers towards less alcoholic beverages—beer and wine—which were generally made easier to obtain and less expensive than spirits. As the secretary of the Quebec Liquor Commission put it in 1922, "The Board is much more anxious to push the sale of beer and wine than of whisky and is importing French wines in large quantities and selling them at small profit to encourage their consumption." Five years later Alberta's board reported that beer made up nearly 93 per cent of alcohol sales, wines only 3.4 per cent, and spirits only 3.9 per cent. Liquor control boards also kept tight controls over advertising for alcoholic beverages, which was banned outright in Ontario, Nova Scotia, and New Brunswick and closely monitored elsewhere.[19]

The liquor control boards had a monopoly on the wholesale purchase and retail sale of most alcoholic beverages. Building on the much more limited experience of the "dispensaries" that some provinces had operated during prohibition, each board ran a chain of stores that were the only places in which drinkers could buy booze by the bottle, domestic or imported—and at uniform prices fixed by the board. Beer (and, in Ontario, wine) got special treatment, and could often be sold through other outlets. In Quebec grocers and other retailers were allowed to sell beer (and nothing else) purchased directly from brewers, and several provinces (Quebec, Manitoba, Saskatchewan, Alberta, and British Columbia), as well as Newfoundland, eventually permitted hotels to sell beer in cases for off-premise consumption. In some provinces brewers were permitted to pool their wholesaling in one warehousing operation, and to deliver beer directly to customers. Ontario permitted the breweries, brewers' warehouses, and wineries to sell directly to the public from their own government-inspected retail outlets, a practice later introduced by only half the provinces.[20]

Compared to prewar retail outlets, the government stores themselves were less numerous and convenient. In 1930 there were only 27 across Nova Scotia, 32 in Alberta, 109 in Quebec (85 of them in Montreal), and 124 in Ontario (compared to 211 private shops in 1915, as well as nearly 1,300 taverns and clubs). The outlets were also open for shorter hours. By 1933 stores in six of the eight wet provinces were closed in the evenings, and two provinces closed their stores at 1:00 p.m. on Saturdays. All of them shut down on Sundays, public holidays, and election days.[21]

Customers entering government liquor stores found them to be coldly austere places, more like banks than retail stores. No advertisements or displays adorned the windows or walls. The booze was kept out of reach behind counters, and customers had to hand their written requests to board employees behind wickets. Until 1928 Manitoba required bottles purchased to be delivered directly to the purchasers' homes, but most provinces allowed customers to carry bottles, wrapped discreetly in brown paper, out the door. "The fact that the sale is confined to sealed packages and that there are no opportunities for 'tasting and sampling' has rid the stores of a certain loafing element which frequented the wine and spirit shops of the past," wrote one commentator in 1928. In Saskatchewan's small towns and villages, only beer was available in the government stores; liquor was delivered to homes by mail order. In places where taverns had not been legalized, drinking outside households remained illegal, and even in places where beer was available by the glass, spirits had to consumed out of sight at home. Some provinces established specific limits on the amount of booze an individual could buy: one bottle of spirits at a time in Quebec and New Brunswick; one case of spirits or two dozen quarts of beer per week in Manitoba; one quart of spirits, one gallon of wine, or two gallons of beer in Saskatchewan. Prices were kept high to discourage drinking (but also, ironically, to help provincial revenues). Even well-paid steelworkers and autoworkers who brought home $25 to $30 in their pay packets each week in 1925 would think twice about laying out $3.50 and up for a "twenty-sixer" of rye or gin or $5 for Scotch.[22]

In all wet provinces except Quebec and New Brunswick drinkers had to get an annual permit to buy alcohol from these stores, at a cost of one or two dollars. Generally the permits were booklets that had to be presented for each purchase, when the clerk would enter the date and amount obtained. They were, in the words of one commentator, "a constant if somewhat irksome reminder to the public that the purchase of liquor, like other drugs, requires proper supervision." Tourists could get special, short-term permits.[23]

Issuing these permits turned liquor store staff into social workers who had to determine whether a customer should for any reason be denied a permit and whether he or she was consuming too much. Police, municipal welfare authorities, and charity officers could intervene to prevent individuals from getting permits if they were on the dole or otherwise in economic or moral trouble (as in the pre-prohibition era, people could be put on a permanent interdiction list). In 1931 Ontario's board staff co-operated in nearly 27,000 special investigations of relief applicants; the number climbed to over 59,000 in 1932. Few of those investigated had permits, it turned out. Sometimes a permit would be returned to the wife or mother, or to the original male, with a limitation on purchasing power. Aboriginal peoples on or off reserves were to be denied permits categorically. The liquor store staff was expected to watch for excessive consumption and to turn away such bibulous customers (or potential bootleggers).[24]

In its 1928 report, Ontario's board noted that the "social side" of its work had been largely extended and that many permits had been cancelled—more than 5,000 out of some 400,000. The board believed that cancellation should happen "not only in cases where liquor has been abused, not only in cases where liquor may be purchased for resale, but also in all cases where the purchases of liquor are made at the expense of the home." Customers should be allowed to purchase booze only after they had taken care of "the necessities of life" and paid "adequate duty to dependents." Liquor store staff had therefore been instructed "to render co-operation in the putting down of abuses of the permit privilege, to apply their local knowledge, to collect doubtful permits, and from time to time to invoke Head Office assistance in dealing therewith." They were regularly reminded that "the keynote of the law is 'control,' not sale, that moderation is the best way to support the law, and that satisfactory service by a store is best proved, not by volume of sales, but by prevalence of good social conditions in the surrounding community and absence of drunkenness and of complaints from neglected dependents." In 1949 the federal government weighed in with a request that liquor stores refuse to cash the new family allowance cheques.[25]

Given that staff positions were all patronage appointments in the local constituency, these front-line workers must have faced a daily challenge in balancing such an earnest moral agenda with their continuing relationships with friends and neighbours. To keep them on their toes, the boards' chief administrators bombarded them with memoranda stipulating rules and procedures to be followed and demanding detailed reporting.

After beer by the glass was legalized, liquor control boards used their power to license "beverage rooms" or "beer parlours" to create a rigidly structured drinking environment. (Only Quebec allowed the public drinking of beer in cafés, and Nova Scotia, Ontario, and the four Western provinces eventually issued one-occasion banquet permits.) Even the labelling was significant: the terms "bar" or "saloon" were forbidden, and only in Quebec could the word "tavern" be used. Most provinces initially required that the rooms be attached to hotels (or, in some cases, set up in railway cars or steamboats) or, to satisfy the veterans, housed in military messes and social clubs with limited memberships. Would-be proprietors went through rigid screenings to determine that they were fit to run an orderly, respectable operation. "Tied houses" connected to breweries were explicitly forbidden in some cases, actively discouraged in others, but tolerated in a few. Most beer parlours were former hotel saloons, but hotel-keepers got licences only if they had a minimum number of rooms for rent and adequate dining-room facilities for guests or longer-term residents. The boards' supervision of spatial design and interior decor established a kind of moral architecture to shape customers' (and owners') behaviour. Before opening their doors to the public, the proprietors had to meet stringent architectural requirements, and all alterations had to be approved by the board. New renovations might be demanded at any time if the flow of customers revealed particular problems (such as the location of washrooms). The businesses were not allowed to advertise what they were selling on signs on the street or to accept most forms of advertising from breweries. There was no consensus about whether these places should be concealed from public view: some provinces demanded uncovered windows so that people passing by could see what was going on, while others insisted on blinds or curtains to prevent the innocent from being shocked.[26]

In parts of the United States the post-prohibition regime of public drinking was tied to restaurants, but in Canada, although beer or wine with meals might be permitted in hotel restaurants, the regulations for the main drinking sites moved in the opposite direction. Proprietors of beer parlours could sell nothing but beer (and in some cases wine, though few stocked it), and could offer no food, soft drinks, or tobacco. Customers were forbidden to play games (even checkers or cards) or gamble. Except in Montreal, where licensed nightclubs offered dancing and exotic floor shows under Quebec's more permissive legislation, patrons could see no entertainment and were not even able to amuse themselves by dancing, singing, or playing musical instruments. Even the sound of music from other rooms in the hotel had to be blocked. The idea was that without these extra services and amenities, customers would have less interest in lingering.[27]

The stand-up bar was banished. Customers had to be seated at small tables in clusters of four drinkers (presumably, four men could treat each other without getting too drunk or using up too much of the family income). Glasses or bottles of beer had to be served at these table one or two at a time, and only the waiter could move drinks between tables. The law forbade someone to stand up with a drink in hand (it was harder to pick fights from a sitting position). The more tightly restricted hours included, in some cases, a compulsory closing at supper time (curiously, although they never had prohibition, pubs in England, Australia, and New Zealand had much more restrictive hours of operations imposed on them). No credit or cheque-cashing was permitted. Lighting was often dim, the decor was simple and utilitarian, and (as in the liquor stores) little adorned the walls.

These new watering holes, then, were purposely made as stark, austere, and unattractive as possible, not just to discourage patrons from lingering and to encourage them to drink less, but also to prevent the places from becoming the freewheeling, boisterously interactive places of the past. The rules were intended to discipline drinkers to act in a decent, orderly fashion while socializing in this public space. Beer parlours soon took on the characteristic shape and texture that would last for four or five decades in most parts of the country. In the words of one British Columbia waiter, you had to "sit down, shut up, and drink your beer." A disgusted Protestant clergyman thought the new drinking place was "more of an evil than the old saloon, for men will drink more, and more men will get drunk sitting down at a table than uncomfortably standing at a bar." Many years later a government commission in Manitoba agreed that "beer parlors are places where men may drink and drink and may do nothing else" and worried that they tended "rather to encourage than to discourage drinking."[28]

Regular coercion was built into the dynamics of the beer parlours. Ironically, the immediate impact was not on the individual drinker in a beer parlour but on the proprietor and his staff. In Ontario the term applied to the licence issued to a hotel-keeper was the "authority," which suggests a legal responsibility to carry out liquor board policy. Bartenders and waiters were the front-line enforcers, regulating the flow of booze and controlling drunks when they got out of control. Inspectors visited the places frequently to check for infractions, watching out for too much drunkenness and assessing the waiters' treatment of customers. The inspectors reported on the number of glasses in front of each drinker and counted heads to see if the room had more bodies than officially designated. They measured the head in the beer glasses and checked to see that the glasses were filled to the regulation line. They looked hard at young customers to see if they were under the legal drinking age of twenty-one. They evaluated how the proprietor and his staff handled fights. Negative reports on any of these issues would lead to written reprimands from the liquor control board and even temporary suspension of the owner's licence—in effect, an indirect fine in the form of lost revenue. The new liquor control acts said nothing, though, about how much an individual could drink. Although owners could eventually lose their licences if excessive drunkenness was reported, provincial authorities left local police forces to deal with the effects of drunken behaviour—fights, family violence, too much noise, general disturbances. Interdiction of problem cases was also once again an option.[29]

Alongside the beer parlours were a variety of licensed clubs that ranged from the poshest businessmen's meeting places to the far more common veterans' clubs, eventually known in popular parlance as "Legion Halls." To qualify for these special licences, the associations had to prove that they had a closed membership and were non-profit, and they were not allowed to sell drinks to non-members (nonetheless, some would try to do so). In Quebec and British Columbia the clubs were initially supposed to be only storing members' alcohol in lockers so that they could enjoy it on the premises, for a small service fee. In practice, especially in the posher clubs, members took to "pooling" their booze, which allowed them to order individual drinks from the club staff—a legal fiction that the B.C. board finally regularized in 1940. The liquor control boards generally permitted these clubs to operate on a looser leash. They could have music and entertainment, and the more proletarian of them often got rowdier than the beer parlours. In some cases (such as Manitoba in 1931), revised regulations allowed some clubs to admit guests or

"associate" members, who paid a nominal fee. In practice those places operated as little more than another form of beer parlour.[30]

Beer Parlour Patrons

The new legal regime of "government control" thus had two distinct forms of
regulation. The liquor stores served a mixed population of people who liked
to take their booze home, which was certainly the choice of most bourgeois
drinkers who could afford to stock a liquor cabinet or maintain a wine cellar.
The beverage rooms or beer parlors and the great majority of the clubs, however, were understood to have a more specifically working-class clientele.
Outside the hushed gentility of the businessmen's clubs, the only publicly
accessible places to drink had been opened in response to working-class pressure and were designed to be spartan, unattractive sites where only working
men, for the most part, would want to gather for a glass of beer. The middle
and upper classes would find little to their taste there, and liquor control
boards made their decisions about where and to whom to grant licences on
that basis. The great majority of beverage rooms were in hotels in the downtown core or in, or near, working-class neighbourhoods.[31]

Workers wasted no time in making use of these new drinking places, and
the rooms quickly found a place as part of the overall pattern of working-class
life and leisure. But the extent of that place depended, as always, on the level
of living standards of Canadian working people and the material resources at
their disposal for leisure pursuits. Although the cost of living levelled off in the
1920s and even dropped in the 1930s, working-class incomes remained
chronically insecure. The interwar decades were particularly difficult because
the deep depression that hit the country late in 1920 did not lift until 1926
and then returned with a vengeance after 1929. As in past business downturns,
working-class families might have little or no disposable income for participating in the commercialized leisure that was expanding during those years.
People with young, growing families would also have felt more constraint.

Within this context, working men did what they had always done: they
either restrained their leisure-time expenditures or, in a small minority of
cases, indulged their patriarchal privilege to drink, with the risk of pushing
their families to the edge of abject poverty. Most probably did not need a
liquor store clerk to remind them that their booze was a luxury that their
families could not afford. Among Canadians over fourteen years of age, per
capita consumption rose from half a gallon of absolute alcohol in 1923 to .87
gallons in 1930, then tumbled to .46 in 1933 and 1934 and slowly returned to

.74 in 1937, the most prosperous year of the depression decade. Total beer consumption, which made up between 52 and 62 per cent of the absolute alcohol consumed in the 1920s and 1930s, followed a parallel course—from nearly 41 million gallons in 1924 to 62 million in 1930, down to just over 40 million in 1934 and up again to well over 60 million by the end of the decade. The number of liquor permits issued also rose and fell in the same pattern. Drinking was a cheap pleasure, but one that must have been sacrificed often in these years. In contrast, full employment at better wages during the Second World War brought soaring consumption and sales of liquor permits.[32]

There is no question, however, that working men moved into the new public drinking places in large numbers and, within the legal and structural constraints imposed on those rooms, made every effort to use them as the multipurpose social centres that the old-time saloons had been. Prohibitionists had too often failed to understand that the thirst to be slaked among wage-earners was at least as much a yearning for male conviviality as it was for alcoholic beverages (though many workers certainly thought they needed the latter to get the former). So, once again these rooms became spaces in which workers could relax together, talk politics, gossip, and generally reaffirm their identities as manly working men. For the many single men who rented rooms upstairs in the hotels to which so many drinking places were attached, or in nearby boarding houses, beer parlours were a communal living room shared with other bachelors. As in the past, many drinking spots took on the flavour of the nearest group of workers—longshoremen, loggers, railwaymen, steel-workers, miners, for instance. Others drew the bulk of their clientele from a specific neighbourhood. As a former Québécois bushworker, Gérard Fortin, remembered, taverns in Quebec City in the 1930s could still be places to pick up news about jobs or meet a recruiter. In some neighbourhoods they were also once again good places to talk about unions or conduct union business.[33]

Workers soon pushed the limits of the liquor control board regulations. They wandered about the room, bursting into loud choruses of popular songs in defiance of the ban on singing, breaking into fights to defend offended honour. "They were the same old saloons, with the exception that the men sat at tables instead of standing at a bar; and they drank beer instead of whiskey," a *Ladies Home Journal* writer reported after visiting several Montreal taverns. "There were the same old smells, same old maudlin songs and laughter, same old vulgarity, same old quarrelling and wrangling, same old drunks."[34]

Once again it was younger men who seemed to set the tone of these places. "In these taverns we saw few old men," a Quebec writer noted after visiting fifteen taverns. "Eighty per cent, at least, were young men between the ages of 18 and 30." The rituals of violence that unfolded echoed the displays

By 1946, when this photo was taken in a beer parlour in Standard, Alta., working men had pushed the limits of the regulations to make these places comfortable for male socializing, far from work and home responsibilities. (GA, NA-3271-11)

of masculine identity that had erupted around taverns and saloons for generations. When the young Gérard Fortin ended up working in a West Coast pulp and paper mill in the 1930s, drinking became the occasion for settling scores over ethnic tensions in the local workforce. "We had spent the evening drinking in the workers' club, and now one fellow who was always trying to provoke us was blasting off on all cylinders," he recalled. "I just wasn't ready to put up with it. I jumped him, but before I had a chance to hang one on him, a whole bunch of English guys jumped me."

Like the prewar drinking places, beer parlours ranged from the rough and rowdy to the more sedate and affable. In the mid-1920s Sir John Willison found the ones he visited in Calgary and Edmonton "without exception quiet and orderly" and saw "no evidence of drunkenness or heavy drinking." On the whole workers seemed to treat these gathering places as spaces in which they could "have a quiet beer and tell a few good jokes." In their reports inspectors might well designate such places as "decent."[35]

In his 1950 painting, "Talking Union," artist Frederick B. Taylor presented the beer parlour as a setting for union organizing, in this case the Canadian Seamen's Union. (MMFA)

If these new drinking places had familiar features held over from the saloon era, in some parts of the country they also had a major new element—women. Public drinking was no longer an exclusively male experience, as growing numbers of female drinkers settled into chairs in beer parlours to enjoy a beer. This was not an entirely surprising development, because the prohibition period had coincided with a considerable change in the standards of acceptable public behaviour for women, especially those from working-class families. Even before the war, young women had been staking out more public space within popular culture, showing up in much larger numbers at the various sites of leisure and entertainment, both in groups of single women and in the company of boyfriends. By the 1910s and 1920s young women were challenging conventions about feminine propriety in their appearance and behaviour—including smoking cigarettes in public. They found new role models on the movie screens: women like Mary Pickford or Theda Bara who stepped outside conventional models of femininity in their performances and highly publicized private lives. During the war most women had been granted the right to vote for the first time, and during the 1920s many young women no doubt voted to end prohibition.[36]

Many young women were eager to participate in public drinking. The new sections of beer parlours for "Ladies and Escorts" became popular wherever they were introduced, especially during the Second World War. (GA, NA-3579-1)

Since most provinces waited a few years between opening government liquor stores and licensing public drinking, they forced most drinking into the home, where, according to the moderationist argument, women's power in the domestic sphere would restrain their menfolk from drinking too much. Inadvertently, government policy may have had quite a different effect by breaking down the male near-monopoly on drinking and giving wives easier access to the bottle that their husbands brought home. As *Saturday Night* argued in 1934, when these legal regimes pushed drinking into private spaces, "It was obviously difficult to exclude women from participation when once they had decided that they were the equals of the lords of creation."[37]

In Edmonton the first person out the door of the new government liquor store in 1924 was a woman with six bottles of Guinness under her arm. Several women were also spotted in the lineups outside liquor outlets in Ontario cities on opening day in 1927. "In the days of the saloon only men drank," Halifax's labour paper, the *Citizen*, argued in 1929. "But now the women are drinking." Many women no doubt shared the widespread belief that beer in particular was a healthy food and tonic, but they also seemed to want to join in the social life around drinking. Courtship and long-term relationships with men had a new glow of romantic heterosexual companionship, beamed out most powerfully in the Hollywood movies to which thousands of Canadians were flocking in the 1920s. Married couples were spending more leisure time together at home and some no doubt shared a drink, probably most often with friends or kin on special or celebratory occasions—birthdays, seasonal holidays, card parties, or summer outings, for example.[38]

By no means would all these women risk the possible attack on their reputations that visiting a beer parlour might bring, particularly those in non-Anglo-Canadian households, but many evidently saw nothing indecent or disreputable about quiet socializing with female friends or male companions over a glass or two in such places. No feminist organization or women's groups took up this cause, but informally women were asserting a new demand for equal treatment. As the first beer parlours opened up, however, hotel-owners were strongly inclined to exclude women, on the assumption that a female in a public drinking place had loose morals and was probably a prostitute. The liquor control boards reinforced that patriarchal concern by consistently refusing to let women serve drinks (in Ontario, even if they were hotel-owners). In the face of such resistance, some young women may well have found it easier to visit blind pigs or speakeasies with their dates. A staff writer with the *Ladies Home Journal* said he had seen many such places when he visited Montreal:

> Between midnight and morning, in a cabaret and in a half-dozen bootleg-ging clubs and joints I saw hundreds of women drinking; many of them were mere girls; and fully one third of them were drunk. A newspaper woman I met that night in a "blind pig" club where three hundred men and women were drinking, told me she had seen a thousand women drunk in such places in Montreal.

Again, many illicit drinking places were run by women, most often in the informal, less commercial atmosphere of their own homes, where women drinkers probably felt more comfortable. These places were most likely an important lever for prying open a wider, perhaps grudging social acceptance of women amidst the beer glasses.[39]

As more women insisted on their right to participate in the new public drinking culture, space for them eventually opened up in the beer parlours in a few provinces in the interwar period. Quebec, Saskatchewan, and Manitoba shut the door on them completely, but a version of heterosocial public drink-ing was gradually worked out in the 1920s in British Columbia and was even-tually extended to the two other jurisdictions with licensed beer parlours. Initially, with some hesitation, British Columbia's Liquor Control Board allowed women in. They showed up in much smaller numbers than the men, as another group of evangelical snoops discovered when they descended on Vancouver's beer parlours on two weeknights in 1926 to count noses and tallied up only

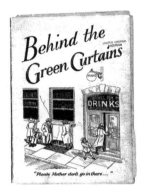

Women's plunge into public drinking provoked familiar commentaries—a celebration by breweries and earnest expressions of concern by the now marginal temperance movement. From Canadian Hotel Review, *15 April 1935. (UACC)*

284 women alongside 2,396 men in 54 establishments one night and 143 mixing with 766 in five parlours on another night (a somewhat smaller proportion than investigators found in British pubs at the end of the 1930s). On the one hand, the disparity in numbers is not surprising, considering that the still pitifully low wages earned by women left them dependent on their beaus or husbands to pay for an evening's entertainment. Most wives and mothers also still had far too much work and responsibility for running the family household to have the time (or the independent income) to take an evening off to visit a beer parlour, and many husbands did not like to see their wives in such a place. On the other hand, the proportions are so much larger than they were in the 1913 surveys that there can be little doubt that many more women wanted some space in the new arenas of public drinking.[40]

By mid-1925 many B.C. hotel-keepers were nonetheless refusing to serve women, and the next year their provincial association voted unanimously to keep women out. Although the government was sympathetic to the owners, especially because it wanted to deflect some of the heavy criticism pouring down on the beer parlours from moral reformers, it advised the hotel-men that the law was not likely to allow this kind of overt discrimination. With the Liquor Control Board's consent, a gentlemen's agreement among the proprietors led to signs warning female customers that they were not welcome. The Vancouver *Province* liked this move: "There is no doubt that the presence of women makes it more difficult to conduct beer parlors in a decent and orderly manner." The paper argued that "whatever an odd woman here or there may say about it, public opinion and particularly that part of it contributed by women, is strongly averse to women frequenting beer parlors."[41]

In their quiet, persistent ways, some women nonetheless continued to show up for a drink. Then, in 1927, after one hotel lost its licence briefly for serving them, the B.C. Liquor Control Board agreed to a compromise that allowed a completely separate section for women and any men who accompanied them—that is, for "ladies and escorts" (this was the informal division of space in British pubs at the time, and some version of it had existed in parts of the United States before the war). Men could not enter that side of the beer parlour on their own. This arrangement was not entrenched in law or formal regulation, but other hotels began to follow suit, sometimes simply reserving a part of the main parlour for women and their male friends (only in 1942, in the heat of hysteria about venereal diseases being spread by prostitutes in beer parlours, did the B.C. Liquor Control Board begin to insist on partitions between the sections).[42]

Next door in Alberta a similar story unfolded. Women drinkers were admitted for two years until the provincial board decided to turn Calgary and

Provincial governments also
began to license social clubs in
addition to beer parlours.
Here a group of unionists
and their spouses were
photographed in the
Mine-Mill Local 598 union
hall in Sudbury, Ont.
(AO, F 1280-10-1, Box B 795,
File 4 (1), 25-EAC-4:19)

Edmonton beer parlours into male-only enclaves, but then, two years later, it allowed proprietors elsewhere in the province to open women-only rooms within their establishments. Apparently few did. Nonetheless, by the time Ontario licensed its first "beverage rooms" in 1934, the presence of women was so non-controversial that the Liquor Control Board made these specially designated areas for "Ladies and Escorts" a requirement in almost all licensed hotels. These spaces typically took up half the beverage-room area, had their own separate entrances and washrooms, and were heavily patronized from the beginning. Informally, some proprietors allowed only one or two men to accompany each woman. Early on, the licensed clubs also wanted to be able to have female guests, but the board made them submit specific requests for "ladies' nights," which could not be held more than once or twice a month. Small, independently organized clubs of married couples often rented space in the hotels or clubs to enjoy monthly card games or other social activities along with their beer.[43]

Women drinkers had found a new space within working-class culture, but the authorities who regulated public drinking did not lose their suspicions about shady morality. Not only did they agree to co-operate with public health campaigns against venereal disease, but proprietors could also be much less tolerant of women who they believed drank too much than they were of men on the other side of the partition. Gendered constructions of drunkenness lived on. Women excluded from public drinking could nonetheless be deeply resentful. In May 1945 the Victory-in-Europe celebrations saw hundreds of women storm into Winnipeg beer parlours to demand service. Some of them were served, and some were thrown out, and two days later these places were once again male-only bastions.[44]

Clearly, new feminine identities—particularly among single women, but apparently also with many wives—had been worked out in working-class communities in these early decades of the twentieth century; and these identities incorporated booze as part of a more public, less domestically focused lifestyle. Of course, this process had also included the construction of new masculinities that did not require the exclusion of women from male-only environments and allowed for regular heterosexual socializing in leisure time, yet did not fundamentally disrupt patriarchal authority. After all, women still needed the protection of an "escort."

Interestingly, though, this mingling of the sexes co-existed with the renewed booze-based solidarities of male-only drinking spaces on the other side of the beer parlour partition. As in the past, many working-class men still preferred to enjoy the experience without women; as one B.C. observer noted, "There are many men who can not be happy unless they are telling or listening to lewd stories or punctuating their conversation with a series of oaths, and such men do, no doubt, find their liberty of action circumscribed by the presence of ladies in the parlor." This tendency was more than a question of personal comfort or individual liberty. Male-only drinking was an important symbol and reinforcement of male privilege in the working-class household and beyond.[45]

Post-prohibition public drinking had thus allowed for the crystallization of two versions of working-class masculinity side by side in the state-regulated beer parlour: one that replicated the "boys-only," often misogynistic, bachelor-driven form that had roots all the way back to the earliest days of tavern-going; and the newer form based in public courtship in commercialized spaces and companionate socializing with spouses after marriage.

Women were not the only outcasts from this male social space. People of colour were not always made to feel welcome either. Aboriginal peoples faced the harshest treatment, since the federal legislation governing their lives would continue to deny them legal access to alcohol until 1951. Those who had entered beer parlours might get the same service as whites, particularly if they could "pass" and drew no attention to themselves, but in practice waiters in some hotels were likely to refuse to serve anyone with recognizably "Indian" features. Native women might also be more readily targeted as prostitutes. Aboriginal drinkers also had to watch out for the RCMP officers who occasionally showed up to check for violators of the Indian Act. Native people deeply resented the inequitable treatment they faced.[46]

For other groups there was no formal process of exclusion, and, especially by the 1940s, Blacks and Asians could usually sit down in the same beer parlours as white drinkers (though Japanese customers were barred during the war). Yet, as in the prewar saloons, men who gathered in these public drinking places might have distinct ideas about who belonged in their little community, and racially based tensions could erupt, particularly if the non-white drinkers were sitting with white women. Hotel-keepers could arbitrarily refuse to serve mixed-race couples or particular people of colour, and liquor control boards generally refused to intervene to stop such racist practices.[47]

Lingering Shadows

Allowing alcoholic beverages to be legally sold undoubtedly undercut the business of rum-running, certainly after the end of U.S. prohibition in 1933, but the rigidity of the new regulatory regime left plenty of room for small-scale bootleggers. Most survived in the shadows, alongside the legal outlets. As a Canadian political economist observed in 1932, "While bootlegging is as prevalent as before, it is not quite so centralized in gangs." Now bootleggers could obtain their supplies at government liquor stores and resell them after hours at inflated prices. Astute operators used false permits under different names to buy far more than their legal limit. Liquor control boards warned their staffs to watch for anyone buying unusually large quantities of booze. Some bootleggers still had other sources of supply and sold much cheaper booze. Police kept up their half-hearted efforts at prosecuting them.[48]

Across the country, drinkers looking for alcohol outside the time constraints and watchful eye of liquor stores and beer parlours could easily locate the neighbourhood bootlegger or the more sociable blind pigs (increasingly known as "booze cans"). In 1925 the Montreal *Standard* reported that there were dozens of such establishments in the heart of the city, and four years later the Quebec government passed legislation allowing police to arrest people found in a blind pig. Over the next twenty years, according to a retired union leader in Welland, Ont., workers often found their way to such places, especially when they came off a shift after hotel closing hours. "In order to buy a drink after work, they would sometimes end up at a friend's place," he wrote. "There were few larger commercial bootleggers; most were family-run places." He explained that they were known as "social clubs." The proprietors and customers, he said, "were mainly workers who, in most cases, worked together. The price was reasonable, and the bootlegger's wife usually made sandwiches for the customers." In rural areas especially, moonshine also continued to bubble away in backyard stills, which provincial authorities could not touch (that phenomenon remained a federal responsibility).[49]

Whatever the source of the booze, the bootlegger was probably closer to home than were the widely scattered government liquor stores. It might take several days for an express order from a government store to arrive, while bootleggers could deliver quickly, right to the door. Taxi drivers were often reliable suppliers. A former worker at Toronto's huge Inglis plant recalled how bootleg booze came right into the factory:

> People had taken out a brick. It was a double brick because it was a double wall, and you just went to the phone. If you wanted a bottle in the daytime, you would just phone the cab number and just say, "The hole in the wall," and you stood there with your money and you passed your money out to the cab driver. He used to drive up to it, roll down the window, and pass the bottle through. And we had a lot of bottles. That was a pretty hot little corner, at times. We had a lot of wine come through that hole.

This worker's account was not an isolated story of alcohol in the workplace. Despite managerial efforts to prevent drinking on the job, foremen in non-union plants still expected to receive bottles of liquor as tribute from fearful employees, especially recent immigrants. If there was a labour shortage the flow could be in the other direction as well: a Saint John dry-dock worker remembered some supervisors during the Second World War using booze as a bribe to keep workers on the job. He knew of cases "where fellows would be given a crock by the general manager if they'd stay all night and the next day." Workers also brought their own booze onto the job site: "A lot of times you'd drink a pint of liquor during your shift just to keep warm. You'd be so cold that you wouldn't even feel the effect of booze."[50]

What the rigid new regime of government control had created was a dual system of alcohol consumption: one stream flowed through state-regulated stores and public drinking outlets; the other went through the illicit channels that had appeared decades earlier, matured during the prohibition era, and continued to thrive as a result of the strictness of the new laws and regulations. These two systems—the government policies intended to remind customers of liquor stores and beer parlours that they were engaged in a somewhat disreputable activity, and the furtive practices of the illicit underground economy in booze—combined to cast drinking as a disreputable pleasure to be enjoyed quietly and secretively. In the tradition of the speakeasy, patrons of the unlicensed cabarets (outside Quebec) got accustomed to enjoying their booze from a bottle hidden under the long tablecloths, with no objections from the staff of these so-called "bottle clubs."[51]

Just how profoundly public policy and popular attitudes had changed became clear after the outbreak of the Second World War. The temperance movement's continued lobbying for tighter controls convinced Mackenzie King to take action, but in the face of his cabinet's considerable resistance the prime minister announced, late in 1942, no more than a program to restrain consumption. Beyond requiring the dilution of spirits to 70 proof, he merely called on the provinces to reduce sales (spirits by 30 per cent, wine by 20 per cent, and beer by 10 per cent), ban advertising, and restrict hours for stores and beer parlours. The provincial governments, angry at not being consulted and concerned about the potential loss of revenue, pointed out the administrative difficulties posed by the measure and railed against the unpopularity of the rationing that was soon necessary. Working men needed their beer to keep them contented, they argued. Indeed, some workers were soon sporting buttons with the slogan "No Beer—No Bonds." The restrictions on beer were withdrawn fifteen months later after making no appreciable dent in the public's thirst for booze.[52]

Yet prohibition did not discredit all roles for the Canadian state in shaping the moral environment. The repeal campaign was carried in large part on a promise that government control would be more effective in regulating drinking practices than was the uncontrolled behaviour that had emerged in the dark shadows of the illicit underground economy in booze. With governments haunted by the memories of prewar saloons, the new system of control was explicitly designed to deter easy or heavy consumption of alcohol by regulating both time and space in which drinking was to take place, the activities that were permissible while drinking, and the company people could keep in public drinking places. In many ways the new drinking regime was not so much a completely new approach to moral regulation as a vastly expanded version of what had been evolving before prohibition was introduced. It was a model that U.S. policy-makers examined closely as the campaign for repeal in that country reached its peak in 1933. Some U.S. states borrowed the Canadian version of government liquor stores, though many more simply licensed private retailers. Most states initially allowed public drinking only where food was available, but more of them gradually took up the Canadian beer parlour model of selling drinks only.[53]

A new legal regime had thus set the boundaries of drinking cultures for the next half-century. Although the diversity of public drinking places would increase in most provinces after the Second World War, the fundamentals of this structure of regulation would not begin to change until the 1970s. Within these limits, the working men and women who filled up most of the licensed establishments made them work as effectively as possible as oases of pleasure and sociability. In some cases, when the legally regulated facilities proved inadequate, they turned back to the underground economy that prohibition had brought to life and that continued to thrive. However they got their booze, many working-class men still treated public drinking places as exclusive bastions of collective male privilege that validated their dominance over women and children in their own families and in society more generally. At the same time, this gendered solidarity operated against a still substantial wall of widespread social disapproval of their behaviour, which was disparaged as a disreputable low-class excess. Class identities hardened in the heat of such scorn.

nine

The Recreational Drug

GOVERNMENT CONTROL SHARED WITH prohibition a profound distrust of John Barleycorn. If drinking was to take place, it had to be under tight rein. Yet the forces that had opened the carefully controlled flow of alcohol had a momentum behind them that was not so easily contained. The association of consumerism and pleasure created pressure for increased consumption under looser regulation. By the mid–1930s, selling booze only from government liquor stores for use in private homes had already given way to the return of public drinking in two-thirds of the provinces. After the Second World War, Canadians wanted still easier contact with John Barleycorn.

Between the 1930s and the 1970s, more and more Canadians in all social classes embraced alcohol as they had not done in more than a century. Booze was once again a respectable part of the mainstream of Canadian social life. This was in reality three interwoven stories of capitalist triumph, popular culture, and state intervention. Beverage alcohol producers reorganized the three main branches of the liquor traffic—spirits, beer, and wine—into huge, mass-production marvels, and consumers drank up more and more of their output. To accommodate this new attitude to drinking, governments eventually agreed to fund specialized programs for the minority of drinkers afflicted with the "disease" of "alcoholism" and, for all others, gradually made booze easier to get and to enjoy.

Yet, by the end of the 1970s, a reaction against the new permissiveness had set in. Many Canadians began to put on the brakes, to drink less and to worry more about excessive drinking. Some age-old questions about alcohol still swirled around the public arena and the private conscience. For considerable numbers of Canadians, booze nonetheless remained the drug of choice.

OPPOSITE PAGE: In 1961 government liquor stores, like this one in Calgary, were still starkly austere places where customers continued to fill out request slips for bottles stored out of reach behind the counters. (GA, NA-5093-1006)

The Hard Stuff

Prohibition had not required brewers and distillers to shut down, but it certainly had a significant impact on their sales. While brewers and vintners could continue to sell less alcoholic versions of beer, cider, and wine, the full-strength product of their factories, along with the spirits turned out by distillers, had to flow through the illegal channels of the underground economy in Canada, or out to the risky export markets, mainly in the United States. Although some booze producers had risen to the challenge, it was hard for many of them to hold on in the face of such rough-and-tumble instability. Dry legislation rolled back slowly and unevenly in the interwar period, and the severe economic depressions of much of the 1920s and all of the 1930s hampered the sales of luxury goods, which included alcoholic beverages.

As in the past, survival and expansion took different paths in the distinct industrial sectors of liquor, beer, and, for the first time on a substantial scale, wine. Between the 1930s and 1970s, these industries were thoroughly transformed through a massive consolidation of ownership, much bigger, more concentrated production facilities, and a completely new range of products for changing markets. Only a few die-hard temperance activists still called them the "Liquor Traffic," but the leading brewing and distilling corporations had an economic power that earlier booze producers could only dream of.

Most of the large, well-established distilleries had weathered prohibition by regrouping as larger corporate units. Toronto's Gooderham and Worts merged with Windsor's Hiram Walker in 1926, and in the same year the Bronfmans bought up Waterloo's Seagram operations and linked them to their new Distillers Corporation in Montreal. The Bronfmans poured in new capital to expand production enormously, until by the end of the decade their Montreal plant was one of the largest in the world. These two corporate giants alone controlled close to two-thirds of the Canadian market by the early 1930s. Still, the future looked grim. Consumption of spirits had plummeted, and liquor-control-board pricing policies and government duties made liquor an expensive item for consumers. Profits were sliding precipitously downward. The five leading distillers tried to work out marketing quotas among themselves in 1931, but that deal soon fell apart. A disastrous price war was looming.

The distillers' great hope for recovery lay south of the border, where Canadian liquor was widely sold during the prohibition era, and where production had been shut down for fourteen years. When the dry era ended in the United States in 1933, the two biggest Canadian firms took an optimistic plunge into that market. Hiram Walker built a huge new distillery in Illinois that year and launched an aggressive marketing campaign to promote its ever-popular Canadian Club Whisky, which soon paid off with a jump in sales. Sam Bronfman also began buying up existing U.S. distilleries and promoting his new, "lighter-tasting" blended whiskies with aggressive advertising that aimed to make Seagram a "national" brand—a status no U.S. whisky had ever before achieved. By 1935 U.S. customers were buying a million cases a year across the country, and the new Five Crown and Seven Crown whiskies had become national best-sellers.[1]

The companies now focused on a small number of mass-produced brands that were distilled with new scientific precision in massive technologically sophisticated plants, guaranteeing a reliable, standardized product for the committed consumer. Despite the curtailment of liquor production during the Second World War, by the late 1940s Seagram still held 20 per cent of the U.S. market, ahead of all leading U.S. distillers. After absorbing three regional competitors, the Canadian operations of what had become the world's biggest distiller were rechristened The House of Seagram Limited in the 1950s. To convey the impression of competition, the Bronfmans (and eventually other firms) set up nominally independent but wholly owned companies—notably Thomas Adams Company and Calvert—to produce their own lines and compete for customers with Seagram's products.[2]

By the 1970s a handful of companies ran twenty-two distilleries spread over seven provinces (twelve of them in Ontario and Quebec, four in British Columbia). Of these distilleries, five (Seagram, Hiram Walker, Gilbey, Schenley, and McGuiness) supplied three-quarters of the Canadian market. The output of the country's distillers was preponderantly Canadian rye whisky, though they also made rum, gin, vodka, and brandy (aside from gin, a much larger proportion of these other drinks was imported). All of this success was accomplished in the face of heavy federal and provincial government taxation and tight regulation over production and marketing, conditions that no other industry had to face (and about which distillers repeatedly complained).[3]

Canadian customers had become far less important to these firms. Whisky had become the largest fully manufactured export item from Canada by the late 1950s, and ranked fifteenth among all exports. After the war 90 per cent of Seagram's distribution was outside Canada, covering some 114 countries, though concentrated in the United States. Canadian firms also established overseas production facilities. In 1950 Seagram also bought the old Chivas Brothers distillery in Scotland, and two years later began selling a new remarkably successful product, Chivas Regal, for a high-end market. Bronfman also pushed the company in new directions in the 1950s by buying up rum distilleries in Jamaica, Puerto Rico, the Bahamas, Venezuela, and elsewhere, and opening Canada's first rum plant in living memory (by the 1960s rum was the second most popular liquor in Canada after whisky and ahead of gin and vodka, two drinks that Bronfman personally disliked). In the early 1940s Bronfman had also moved into California wines, and over the next decade absorbed two Canadian wine companies (Jordan and Danforth), the world-famous French champagne company G.H. Mumm, and wine firms in France and Italy, including the well-known French vintner Barton et Guestier. In 1956 this huge, sprawling global empire was brought under the single umbrella of Seagram Overseas Corporation. By that point Hiram Walker had already absorbed Ontario's Bright's Wines, bought a Scottish company, and established a distillery in Argentina to serve the Latin American market. Canadian distillers had become major players in international markets for booze.[4]

Beer and Wine

Brewing in Canada would follow a similar course to corporate consolidation, but the industry started out in the 1920s in a much more fragmented and fragile state. Breweries were typically much smaller operations than distilleries, and before prohibition scores of them were sprinkled across the country. In 1915 the federal government licensed 115 breweries. A few of these had been absorbed into larger corporations, such as National Breweries in Quebec, and some ran huge plants, but far more continued to operate as small family-run firms serving local or regional markets. These small operations became the casualties of the dry era, so much so that by 1924 civil servants tallied up only sixty-four licensed breweries. Carling's closed in 1920, the Labatt family came close to shutting down at the same point, and the Molsons were uneasy about their future.[5]

Bootlegging helped to keep many operations afloat, and in 1924 eleven Ontario breweries formed a cartel known as the Bermuda Export Company to stabilize prices and streamline sales to the United States. As prohibition receded, many of the old family firms changed hands, and the new owners invested heavily in new equipment to meet the expected demand. But beer sales were not buoyant enough to sustain all the producers in the industry, and in 1930 the *Financial Post* noted that Ontario's brewing industry in particular was "in a state of considerable chaos, due to overexpansion." Like the distillers, some brewers looked for recovery through mergers.[6]

The numerous regional consolidations paled alongside a bold scheme on the part of Ontario's E.P. Taylor, whose kin owned the Brading Brewery in Ottawa and had made him a director. In 1928, although working for a Toronto investment firm, Taylor undertook a thorough study of the thirty-seven breweries operating in Ontario. Most of them, he concluded, were producing far below capacity. He then convinced the Brading board to reach out to other companies with a merger plan. After absorbing the Kuntz Brewery in Waterloo, he got a helpful boost from a partnership with a U.S. investment broker who represented substantial British interests looking to invest in brewing. In 1930 they launched the Brewing Corporation of Ontario (renamed the Brewing Corporation of Canada a few months later and Canadian Breweries in 1938). As Taylor admitted privately in 1934, "The object I have been working for the last four years has been one of bringing about in Ontario a similar situation to that which exists in the Province of Quebec, where the industry is virtually controlled by two companies." He wanted a deal with Molson and Labatt to pool resources to buy up smaller breweries, but they refused to cooperate.[7]

By 1938 the new corporation had nonetheless acquired sixteen Ontario plants on its own. Taylor tried to create a guaranteed market for his company's beer by buying into hotels, but the province's Liquor Control Board squashed that move. He nonetheless used his involvement in the Brewers' Warehousing Company (the collective marketing arm of Ontario brewers) to try to impose order and discipline on his competitors' relationship with hotel-keepers through a "Code of Ethics," particularly to avoid price-cutting.[8]

Taylor's corporate vision soon had national dimensions. In 1943 he explained, "Having been successful in Ontario, we have now raised our sights and plan to repeat the process in the four Western Provinces so that we will become a truly national concern." Since most provincial regulations required that beer sold in a province had to be produced there, his new continentalist strategy involved acquiring and running a string of regional breweries. By 1953 he had netted seven more firms, including Western Canada Breweries and Quebec's National Breweries.[9]

Taylor was a capitalist bulldozer who ruthlessly pursued the companies he wanted. Most often the owners of the older firms agreed to share exchanges, but when he encountered resistance he fought them through buying shares until he won control, most notably in the case of National Breweries. Two decades later, a study for the Royal Commission on Corporate Concentration concluded that some of his tactics had been "at best . . . questionable by today's standards." But they had worked: by the mid-1950s Canadian Breweries controlled half of the Canadian beer market.[10]

The firm's major competitors were now the Labatt and Molson companies. Each of them had followed the different route of expanding their existing facilities. Only much later, in the 1950s, did they open large new plants in

Montreal and Toronto and buy up regional breweries in the West (Labatt took over Lucky Lager in 1957, and Molson bought Sick's the next year) and Newfoundland (each of the "Big Three" bought a brewery there in 1962). The industry had shaken down into three huge corporations, each gearing its production to the whole Canadian market—with the exception of the Maritimes, where the Oland family would hold out until the 1970s, and Northern Ontario, where a regional independent, Doran's, held out. Each recognized the need to establish decentralized production facilities, because beer was too bulky to produce in one central location and they also had to adapt to distinctive provincial regulations and local tastes (such as Western Canadians' overwhelming preference for lager and the equally strong Québécois taste for ales). At first they found some provinces (Newfoundland, Manitoba, Alberta, British Columbia) willing to tolerate brewery ownership or financial subsidy of hotels—and thus beer parlours—through which they could expect to market their products more or less exclusively. By the 1950s, liquor boards were less willing to sanction this connection, and brewers were selling a rapidly rising percentage of their output in packaged form for home consumption and thus becoming less dependent on licensed establishments for their sales (except in the provinces that allowed hotels to sell packaged beer to be carried home).[11]

All three corporations were also looking for wider markets beyond Canadian borders. Exports of Canadian beer were still less than 4 per cent in 1977, but the purchase of production facilities in other countries allowed Canadian brewers to expand into new markets. In 1944 Taylor went after the U.S. consumer by buying up and expanding the Brewing Corporation of America. Some eight years later he also arranged a reciprocal deal with a British brewer to get Carling's Black Label into the United Kingdom, and in 1959 he undertook to repeat his Canadian consolidation strategy with British breweries. By the end of the following year he had brought together eight breweries in the new United Breweries Limited, which also owned some 1,500 pubs, and two years later added Charrington. In 1967 his entrepreneurial daring brought about an even larger merger to create Bass-Charrington, at that point Britain's largest brewing company. To the horror of many lovers of traditional British ales, the new firm began pushing North-American-style beer as "national" brands in their eleven thousand pubs.[12]

By that point Taylor's Canadian brewing operations were slumping as a result of difficulties in both the Canadian and U.S. markets—not at all helped by a sensationalized story in 1964 that some heavy beer drinkers in Quebec had died as a result of consuming large quantities of the firm's Dow beer. In 1970 Canadian Breweries slipped to second place in national market share behind Labatt, which had also acquired U.S. brewing capacity. Molson had also tried, but failed, to break into the highly corporatized U.S. beer market in the 1960s.[13]

The goal of all this corporate activity was to rationalize the industry by closing smaller plants, reducing the number of brands competing for customers, and promoting the sale of a small number of "national" brands. During the 1930s Taylor had quickly reduced his sixteen plants to six, and only five of the next seven acquisitions survived the axe. At the end of the Second World War there were still sixty-one brewing plants operated by thirty-one independent companies, but by the mid-1960s ten companies ran all of the fifty-one breweries across the country. Of those plants, twelve were in the hands of Canadian Breweries, seven were owned by Molson, and six by Labatt. Together these three controlled 90 per cent of production, and one by one the remaining independents were absorbed. Notably, Labatt reduced the competition in 1971 by buying up the Oland breweries in Nova Scotia and New Brunswick, while in the same year Canadian Breweries took over Doran's Northern Ontario Breweries. Three years later, Molson's absorbed the large new Formosa Brewery plant in Barrie, Ont. By 1976 six companies controlled the remaining forty-three breweries across the country—with three of the six controlling 97 per cent of the market.[14]

From the beginning of this consolidation process, brewing was concentrated and expanded at each of the remaining plants, where much larger facilities and new technology created a vastly greater brewing capacity. The country's breweries produced two and a half million barrels of beer in 1929, three million in 1940, seven million in 1950, and over ten million in 1960. Not only was more beer flowing, but also much more of it was made up of the same few brands. In 1945 Taylor boasted, "We have reduced the number of brands from several hundred to only nine today." In place of the rich diversity of local brews, a small number of standard brands were produced at plants across the country. Canadian Breweries organized all its plants into three multiplant operating groups that each made the same beers—Brading, Carling, and O'Keefe. When Canadian Breweries took over National Breweries in Quebec in 1952, for example, the former Frontenac Brewery became Carling Brewery (Quebec) Limited. Similarly, eight years later, Labatt acquired the Saskatoon Brewing Company and shifted the plant's output to a familiar Labatt brand. The Big Three promoted a small number of new "national" brands and de-emphasized local and regional labels. Along with its old favourite, IPA, Labatt launched its Fiftieth Anniversary Ale (soon known as "50") in 1950 and the next year its new Pilsener Ale (eventually dubbed "Blue" because of its label). Molson introduced Golden Ale in 1954 and Canadian

*After the Second World War
Canada's leading breweries
began to shut down production
of many local beers and to
push "national" brands.
Labatt's launched an
anniversary brew that
quickly became known as
"50," and sent free cases to
Canadian troops in Korea.
(NAC, PA-132059)*

Lager in 1959. Canadian Breweries concentrated on Black Label, Old Vienna Lager, O'Keefe's Ale, Dow Ale, Black Horse Ale, and Red Cap. By the 1960s there was even a hope that the number of brands would be reduced internationally. For a time Labatt participated in a consortium of firms in Scandinavia, Belgium, Austria, Italy, Portugal, and England to produce a "world beer" known as "Skol."[15]

The brewing industries of most Western countries were going through the same process of consolidation in the postwar period. The power of these corporations over the beer market was nonetheless unsettling for some Canadians. The country's social democratic party, the Co-operative Commonwealth Federation, tried to push public ownership of the industry onto the political agenda, without any success. Instead, in 1953 the federal Restrictive Trades Practices Commission launched an investigation into the most powerful of the Big Three, Canadian Breweries. Its report two years later concluded that there were grounds to proceed with a prosecution against the firm for unduly restricting trade in the industry. Charges were not laid until 1959, and a long court battle eventually resulted in a judgment by the chief justice of Ontario's Supreme Court, which acquitted the company the next year. He argued that the extensive regulation of the industry through provincial liquor control boards both explained the level of consolidation and price-fixing and guaranteed that the public interest was served (even though, as an economist later pointed out, the breweries jointly set the prices, which the boards then simply rubber-stamped, and used their provincial warehousing organizations to discipline independents and to keep out foreign competition, particularly from the United States). The judge also ruled that neither buying

up and closing breweries to eliminate competition nor discontinuing the production of many brands constituted a violation of Canada's Combines Act.
The brewing corporations had been given a green light to continue merger
and expansion plans.[16]

Recognizing that the Canadian beer market would not expand infinitely,
all the major brewing corporations had already begun to become conglomer-
ates with diverse lines of business. E.P. Taylor had run the Orange Crush soft
drink company since the 1930s as an offshoot of his brewery acquisitions, and
during the war had drawn together numerous food-processing and retailing
companies into a holding company known as Canadian Food Products. He
had also entered into the forest-products and chemical industries (eventually
consolidated into Domtar). In 1945 Canadian Breweries became a cornerstone of Taylor's powerful new holding company Argus Corporation, which
brought together his scattered holdings and soon included major corporations
in several sectors (by 1972 those were Massey-Ferguson, Hollinger Mines,
Standard Broadcasting, Dominion Stores, Domtar, and British Columbia
Forest Products). In 1952 Taylor moved into real-estate development by launch-
ing Canada's most famous suburb, Don Mills, on the edge of Toronto. In similar moves, Labatt purchased Ogilvy Flour and Laura Secord, and in 1967
Molson began acquiring retail merchandising companies (including the multi-
store chains Beaver Lumber and Aikenhead Hardware) and diverse production
and service companies. Perhaps the most telling moment for this new pattern
of multi-industry control came in 1968, when Taylor's Argus Corporation sold
Canadian Breweries to the South African tobacco giant Rothmans of Pall
Mall, which immediately had to fend off a takeover bid by the U.S. tobacco
producer Philip Morris (which had tried unsuccessfully to get into Labatt the
year before and a few years later merged with the U.S. giant Miller Brewing).
Rothmans renamed the brewing firm Carling-O'Keefe in 1973 in deference
to the surging Canadian nationalism of the period. It sold off its shares in
Bass-Charrington, but, in a now familiar pattern, it proceeded quickly to buy
up Canadian producers of wine, oil and gas, plastics, soft drinks, another small
Canadian brewing company (Doran's four-plant Northern Ontario operation), and a large U.S. brewer (National Brewing).[17]

Corporate consolidation was only part of the story of beer production in
Canada between the 1930s and 1970s. Standardization and mass production
also became central goals of Canadian brewers after the war. Technological
changes to introduce more automation were aimed at eliminating labour-
intensive labour processes wherever possible and speeding up and cheapening
production. Experiments on new processes known as "continuous fermentation" and "continuous brewing" also promised to increase output and reduce

By 1951, when this photo was taken in the Canadian Breweries analytical laboratory, the old-time shop-floor know-how of the brewmaster had been replaced with the careful scientific analysis of white-coated chemists. Their work gradually gave most beers a similarly bland taste. (YUA, Telegram Collection, 1816)

labour and transportation costs. Workers in the industry often found themselves watching gauges and other monitoring devices. Each firm also developed large scientific laboratories, and industrial chemistry played an enhanced role in production. Not surprisingly, the much smaller number of mass-produced "national" brands began to taste more and more alike. Symbolically, in 1961, all the breweries agreed to adopt a new standardized twelve-ounce amber-coloured bottle. Developed after considerable research, the "brown stubby" was durable, hence easily recyclable, and easy to store and carry. Canadians would buy virtually all their bottled beer in these now mythical containers until 1983.[18]

Alongside the meteoric successes of the liquor and beer producers, the makers of Canadian wine remained a distant third. Yet, after prohibition, this branch of the booze industry emerged from severe marginality in the early twentieth century to command the attention of a much larger proportion of the country's drinkers half a century later. Before the 1920s only a handful of small wineries existed, almost all of them in Southern Ontario. They had been unable to make much of a dent in the wine-drinking market, despite the supportive work of the government-funded Horticultural Research Institute of Ontario, established in 1913 at Vineland, Ont. That province's prohibition legislation in 1916 made a significant gesture to agricultural interests by allowing vintners to continue selling wine when beer and spirits were banned. Getting a licence to sell out the winery door was not difficult, and the number of producers rose from twenty in 1919 to fifty-one in 1925. Some of these new producers were no doubt little more than low-skill moonshiners running primitive, makeshift operations and hoping to send some product across the U.S. border, but many of them were recent European immigrants who made wine in basements, sheds, and storefronts to serve their own communities. The flood of cheap local wine that hit the beverage market during the 1920s was variable in the extreme, frequently adulterated, and often dreadful. Under government control established in 1927, Ontario continued to encourage grape cultivation and wine production but also, through its Liquor Control Board, set more rigid standards through regular testing and inspection. The board refused to issue any new licences (a policy that lasted, with only one exception, until the 1970s), and, in a now familiar pattern, the larger vintners, such as Bright's, Barnes, and London, began buying up existing licences and shutting down the smaller operations, though keeping their retail outlets.[19]

Before the Second World War the Ontario industry produced mainly sweet, fortified wines, especially port and sherry. Although the big producers were able to sell through both government liquor stores and their own retail outlets, they had little success in getting drinkers to buy their lighter or sparkling wines. But after the war, as wineries were expanded, new varieties of European grapes were planted, and more scientific approaches to production were introduced, wine sales boomed. By the 1970s the nine large companies producing in Ontario had diversified into several more lines. Bright's alone had fifty different products in 1977. Ontario producers were now facing new competition from B.C. wineries, most notably the upstart Andrés Wines company. With branches in six provinces, Andrés had become the biggest wine producer in Canada by the 1970s. The country's vintners supplied two-thirds of the volume of wine sold in 1970–71, although the overall quality still left them decidedly at the low end of the market (symbolized by Andrés' best-selling bubbly, "Baby Duck," launched in 1971) and unable to match the finer imported wines or, perhaps, the huge quantity of wine made in Canadian households, estimated in the mid-1960s to be nearly six million gallons—an amount equivalent to three-quarters of the quantity sold in Ontario liquor stores.[20]

All too many Canadian wine connoisseurs agreed with the actor Christopher Plummer, who reportedly said of Canadian wines in 1974: "My God, they're terrible! I had a glass on the train from Montreal, and my hand nearly fell off." The volume of imported wine, mostly from France, Italy, and Germany, was, not surprisingly, rising.[21]

Union-Made

Making spirits, beer, or wine in the postwar period involved not only large-scale investment in new technology and marketing, but also new working relationships with the workforce still needed to run the plants. So too did selling booze, whether in licensed outlets or government liquor stores. In all cases, the workers in these various branches of the liquor traffic joined thousands of other Canadian wage-earners in insisting on their rights to be represented by unions. Starting in the 1940s, collective bargaining between the corporate employers and the newly certified unions extended throughout the industry, first under special wartime legislation passed in 1944 (P.C. 1003) and later under postwar provincial and federal labour codes. The paternalism of past labour-relations practices did not disappear, nor did close identification between workers and the products of their industries; although from time to time, when lengthy strikes cut off the flow of booze, Canadian drinkers were forced to find other beverages.[22]

Prohibition had been hardest on the strongest of the industry's old unions, the brewery workers. In 1919 they scrambled to find a new footing by extending their jurisdiction to become the International Union of United Brewery, Flour, Cereal, Soft Drink, and Distillery Workers, but the number of their Canadian locals nonetheless dropped from twenty-four in 1915 to only ten in 1923. When the Brewers and Maltsters Association of Ontario announced in 1923 that the breweries would no longer sign contracts with the union, workers at Toronto's O'Keefe Brewery struck in protest, but found their places filled by scabs. The "open shop" had arrived in the industry. In 1930 the union revived at O'Keefe's, and during the Depression other union locals slowly got back on their feet, although numerous plants were closing in the merger mania of that decade.[23]

By the late 1940s most brewery workers in Canada were covered by regular collective agreements with the local breweries, including for the first time employees at Quebec breweries (though Molson workers continued in the paternalistic tradition, with an independent employees' association). A few groups of brewery workers faced bitter opposition (notably those at National Breweries in Quebec in 1946), but most did not require the convulsive regional or national strikes that hit many other industries in the mid-to-late

1940s. They soon nailed down better wages and shorter hours, along with group insurance, pension plans, welfare plans, paid vacations, and many more benefits—the tradeoffs for the speedups and productivity increases being introduced by the brewing corporations.[24]

Although fewer workers were needed in relation to output in the huge new breweries, and many more of those needed were semi-skilled machine-minders, employment in the industry was generally regular and secure, thanks to their employers' willingness to promote from within. By 1960 brewery workers were the highest paid industrial workers in Canada. While they could make few claims to significant skills, these men (there were still no women) took manly pride in producing a popular beverage (which, unlike distillery workers, they were allowed to enjoy themselves during the working day). As in the distant past, the "union-made" label on all beer bottles—one of the last union-label products of any kind—helped to guarantee sales in the much more highly unionized working-class communities of postwar Canada. The union also eventually extended its reach to workers in some wineries and distilleries.[25]

Meanwhile, the first four Canadian locals of the Distillery, Rectifying, Wine and Allied Workers International Union of America had been organized in 1941, including one each in Windsor and Waterloo. By 1960 that union had fourteen locals in Canada with 3,500 members and a much more cautious, accommodating approach to labour relations. The booze-making corporations found smooth-running labour relations an important feature of the stability and efficiency of their booming operations. In the mid-1970s, in the midst of the largest wave of wage-earner militancy in Canadian history, Carling-O'Keefe went so far as to overhaul its management schemes in the hopes of promoting worker satisfaction—removing time clocks, increasing worker involvement in managerial decision-making, and enhancing its contract offers.[26]

On the retail side, prohibition had destroyed the old bartenders' union, the Hotel and Restaurant Employees (HRE), and, in the 1920s, that union began reaching out for the first time in Canada to cooks, waiters, and other staff in the hospitality industry. By 1938 the union had thirty-two Canadian locals with 4,500 members, including many waiters in the new beer parlours. Although later on the locals representing beer parlours would worry about the impact of the new category of "lounges" on their employment, their fears proved groundless. With only beer and wine allowed in the post-prohibition licensed drinking establishments, there was no work for bartenders until the lounges opened after the Second World War, and the men who flocked into these more skilled jobs readily joined the union. In Toronto the HRE was so

THE BUTTON THAT SERVICES YOU

LOCAL 168
LOCAL 7
LOCAL 299

HOTEL and RESTAURANT EMPLOYEES
BARTENDERS INTERNATIONAL UNION AND A.F of L.

After the war, workers in taverns and hotels signed on with the Hotel and Restaurant Employees and Bartenders International Union in much larger numbers. Here Toronto bartenders display their occupational skills for the crowds watching the 1949 Labour Day parade. (CTA, Globe and Mail, 136368)

effective that, by the late 1940s, a union card was essential for getting a job behind a hotel bar. By 1953 the union's Canadian membership reached nearly 12,500. The Toronto local alone had 2,174 members—more than the entire Canadian membership before 1936. This status was not always easily maintained, and bartenders in Quebec City and Calgary ended up in long, bitter strikes in 1950 and 1951. Three years later bartenders in Alberta's main cities suffered a humiliating defeat after lengthy strikes. But beer parlour employees in several cities hit the bricks many times in the 1940s and 1950s with considerable success, including the five hundred unionists in Toronto's taprooms, taverns, and public houses who won a strike in 1958 against the hotel-owners' association. Only in the 1960s did the organization begin to lose its hold on the Canadian hotel industry, signalled by a bitter, eleven-month strike at Toronto's Royal York Hotel in 1961. That long strike proved unable both to stop major rollbacks in wages and hours of work and to prevent layoff notices.[27]

(BHC)

The men who sold alcohol across counters for home consumption had a more mixed history. The brewery workers' union had organized the men in the brewers' warehouse and retail outlets, who proved themselves ready to flex their militancy. In the summer of 1958, all 1,400 workers in these jobs across Ontario shocked the province's beer drinkers by walking out for eight long, dry weeks and precipitating the lockout of almost all brewery workers as well. Some ten years later, as part of a rising wave of labour militancy in Canada, a similarly large strike began with Molson workers, then spread to the other two major brewing corporations and the brewers' warehousing and transportation workers. The strike lasted twenty-six days before a highly favourable settlement was reached.[28]

In contrast the government liquor store employees were tied into the complex workplace relations of the civil service. Not only were their jobs part of the patronage system presided over by the ruling political parties in each province, but also many were former servicemen, whose bosses liked to remind them that working for the board was being in the "service." In Ontario this was a racially and ethnically homogeneous workforce that had no African-Canadian employee until 1965. Generally, like other civil servants, the employees were forbidden to unionize, and most had some version of a relatively powerless employees' association. In 1944, for example, the workers at Ontario's board formed a primarily social organization with close ties to a strong, paternalist management and engaged in no formal collective bargaining. It operated out of the liquor board's head office, and its newsletter was jointly produced with management. Many of its executive officers were managers, and it was hard not to see the organization as a classic "company union." Only in 1953 did the association begin to discuss industrial relations, though not formal collective bargaining (and then only because the Teamsters and the Civil Servants' Association of Ontario had been trying to organize the board's workers over the previous two years). Finally, in 1968, the association transformed itself into a full-fledged union with its first full-time staff, its own newsletter, and its first collective agreements. Nine years later it affiliated with the National Union of Provincial Government Employees, and in 1979 for the first time it joined other unions in Toronto's annual Labour Day parade.[29]

Let the Good Times Roll

The corporations that came to dominate each of the three major sectors of beverage alcohol production built their new empires on big changes in economic and social life in Canada after 1940. The buoyant economy of the

Ontario beer drinkers were shocked to discover that their supplies were cut off in the summer of 1958 when unionized workers at the Brewers Warehousing Company walked out on strike for eight long weeks. Brewery workers were also eventually locked out. (YUA, Telegram Collection, 1819)

war years continued for most of the next three decades, and Canadians enjoyed a more generalized level of prolonged prosperity than they had ever known. Working people in particular were able to take advantage of the much more regular employment ensured by the federal government's Keynesian economic policies, as well as the leverage of widespread collective bargaining through much larger unions, all added to the social safety net of a limited welfare state. As industrial and service sectors boomed, cities made room for thousands of new immigrants and for the sons and daughters of Canadian farm families, who left the countryside on a scale never before seen, leaving the rural population drastically and permanently reduced. For the first time in the history of Canadian capitalism, a large majority of the population had the disposable income to participate in consumer pleasures, including a lot more booze. Leisure time also expanded, as the eight-hour day, five-day week, long weekend, and paid vacation were nailed down in union contracts and then guaranteed in new government employment-standards legislation. Alcohol actually got cheaper in relation to income in the quarter-century after the war. Equally important, drinking became socially acceptable among a much wider range of Canadians, including more middle-class consumers and many more women.[30]

The story can be traced through statistics. The Canadian Institute of Public Opinion, the new Gallup polling agency, learned through its surveys that a larger proportion of the population was drinking. From 1943—when six out of ten adults had occasion to consume alcoholic beverages—the numbers rose quickly, to two-thirds by 1950 and more than seven in ten by 1955. A 1970 poll reported that only one out of five Canadians was an abstainer. Within this general pattern there were sharp generational differences. Younger Canadians aged eighteen to twenty-nine were much more likely to integrate alcohol into their lifestyles. Canadians over fifty drank much less than the average amount, perhaps for health reasons, perhaps constrained by insecure family budgets before the introduction of the Canada Pension Plan in 1965,

As in the previous world war, the much increased number of men in the Navy got daily rum rations. (NAC, PA-166428)

perhaps as a product of their growing up in the anti-booze atmosphere of the interwar years. Men were also more likely than women to be drinkers, and big-city residents were more likely than rural folk to drink. So too were the wealthier more likely to indulge than the poor. Indeed, in a reversal of a century of bourgeois cultural formation, many more of those with college or university education were drinkers than were those with less than high-school education.[31]

People who drank were also imbibing much more. In the pinched period between 1930 and 1939 Canadians had each consumed roughly five gallons of beer a year and less than a third of a gallon of spirits. During the war higher incomes helped to double per capita consumption of both beverages by 1945. Indeed, demand frequently outstripped supply, and quotas for particular outlets were sometimes necessary. Servicemen in this war, as in the previous one, found that alcohol was a prominent feature of social life in and around their camps. Thousands of residents of Halifax provided the most dramatic symbol of the new enthusiasm for alcohol when they broke into liquor stores during celebrations of the Allied victory in Europe in May 1945 and staged a huge drunken party in the city streets. Perhaps twice as many Canadians had liquor permits by that point as at the outbreak of the war, and Gallup polls found that a majority of Canadians kept alcohol in their households.[32]

When the news of victory in Europe reached Halifax in May 1945, local authorities decided to batten down the hatches to avoid riotous celebrations. All liquor outlets were closed. Large crowds of soldiers, sailors, and civilians defiantly broke into these stores and held a huge, rowdy street party—an indication of the widespread acceptance of celebratory drinking that wartime prosperity had helped to stimulate. (NAC, C-079571)

The postwar imagery of the "good life" promoted in particular by the U.S. films and television programs that filled so much Canadian cultural space was awash in alcohol. The consumption trend continued sharply upward. During the 1950s each Canadian averaged 13.28 gallons of beer and .78 of spirits a year, figures that by 1965 had reached 14.25 and 1.03 respectively. Wine drinking increased as well, though more slowly until the 1960s, when it became much more popular. Regional differences persisted. In 1970, compared to the national average, Atlantic Canadians consumed considerably less absolute alcohol per adult aged fifteen and over (reflecting the much lower incomes of the region and perhaps the fewer outlets for consumption). The country's heaviest consumers were found in British Columbia and Ontario (not including drinkers in the Yukon and the Northwest Territories, who were far out in front). A survey of Ontario drinkers in 1977 found more than half of them drinking at least once a week and a third more than once. To symbolize the new attitudes, St. Catharines launched an annual grape and wine festival and Kitchener-Waterloo initiated an event dedicated to beer, the Oktoberfest.[33]

Postwar Canada was largely a nation of beer drinkers, although the consumption of high-priced spirits and wine (especially imported varieties) rose quickly as drinking took deeper roots in the middle class. By 1970, of their consumer dollar directed to alcohol, Canadians were spending forty-seven

cents on spirits, about forty-four cents on beer, and nearly ten cents on wine. Roughly half the alcohol consumed in most provinces (three-fifths in Newfoundland and two-thirds in Quebec) came in the form of beer; only in Prince Edward Island did drinkers get half their alcohol in spirits. Within these broad patterns, booze producers also became aware of a shift in drinking tastes towards more diversity (for example, the rising popularity of rum, Scotch, vodka, and imported wines) and a preference for "lighter" drinks—blended whisky, lager beer, lighter table wines (notably the less alcoholic "sparkling" kinds), and mixed drinks ("cocktails") of myriad varieties. These new trends did not so much displace older patterns of beer drinking as add new layers of drinkers and drinking practices.[34]

In 1945 Toronto's drinkers readily lined up in the August heat to get their beer before the liquor store closed for the Civic Holiday. Despite ongoing instructions from Liquor Control Board officials to keep children away from these stores, several youngsters waited to earn some cash carting booze to customers' homes. (YUA, Telegram *Collection, 1822)*

Booze manufacturers did their best to promote the new, more positive climate for drinking. Indeed, given the price-fixing through liquor control boards, their main arena of competition was advertising (although the Big Three breweries made agreements to use mutually acceptable, "fair trade" promotional

Since the advertising of booze was either banned or tightly controlled, distillers and brewers found ways of promoting their products indirectly by associating them with some kind of public service or cultural activity. In the late 1930s Seagram's launched a series of ads promoting responsible drinking. These ads would extend well into the postwar period. (UWL, Seagram Collection)

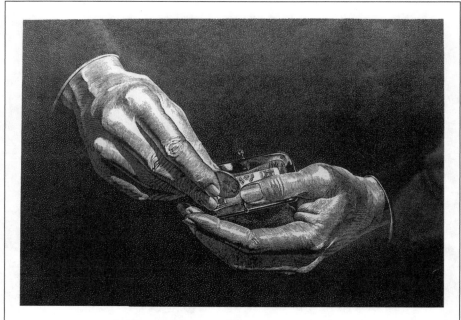

PAY YOUR BILLS FIRST

No person should spend a cent for liquor until the necessities of living are provided—and paid for. Bills for groceries...clothes...shoes...rent...light...heat...doctors... bills such as these have the first call on America's payroll.

We don't want to sell whiskey to anyone who buys it at a sacrifice of the necessities of life.

Whiskey is a luxury and should be treated as such. Fine whiskey can play a pleasing part in the scheme of gracious living...but only when taken in moderation and only after the bills are paid.

This statement may seem contrary to our self interest. Actually it is not. As one of America's leading distillers we recognize a definite social responsibility. The very existence of legalized liquor in this country depends upon the civilized manner in which it is consumed. In the long run, we believe, it is good business for us to say "pay your bills first."

··· THE HOUSE OF SEAGRAM ···
Fine Whiskies Since 1857

practices), and their expenditures on ads began to climb steeply in the 1950s. Their goal was countrywide advertising to promote their "national" brands. But they had to tread carefully. Aside from messages beamed across the border in U.S. magazines or on U.S. television, advertising still had to conform to provincial liquor control board standards, which could range from controls on the message that could be delivered to outright bans. In the mid-1950s, Alberta, Saskatchewan, and Prince Edward Island still forbade all advertising of alcohol. Five more provinces severely restricted the size and content of ads and their location—mostly in newspapers and magazines, not on outdoor signs or billboards, and in Ontario or Manitoba not on radio. Ontario, New Brunswick, and Nova Scotia allowed no product advertising, but firms could promote their so-called "institutional" identity and attach their name to some form of public service. This practice had become generalized during the Second World War, when companies had to restrict themselves to sponsoring ads for such noble ends as higher production or war bond drives. Perhaps the shrewdest version of such marketing was launched across North America by Seagram in 1934 as an invocation to "moderation." The little homilies on thrift and responsibility were remarkably popular and would continue for many years after the war. Eventually booze companies would sponsor sporting activities as indirect forms of advertising, such as Oland's support for the revival of the *Bluenose II* in Nova Scotia. Similarly, until 2001, the Molsons owned the Montreal Canadiens and the Montreal Forum, and advertised their beer on *Hockey Night in Canada*.[35]

Since Quebec had the least restrictive regulations (though still not permitting the display of bottles or glasses containing alcohol or scenes of drinking), booze manufacturers had freer range there to devise enticing but wholesome imagery. In 1936, for example, Labatt started comic-strip advertisements featuring an endearing delivery boy, who also appeared in radio ads on a news program broadcast by Montreal English-language station CKAC. The firm also used stars of sports and entertainment to endorse their products. In 1938 it sponsored a half-hour francophone program broadcast to four Quebec cities, and a variety show on a Buffalo station beamed at the Southern Ontario audience. To reach out to other provinces, Labatt took out ads in magazines published in Montreal, but sold across the country. In these ads the company liked to emphasize the deep historic roots of its various operations. "We didn't sell beer," one of Labatt's ad men later recalled. "We just told a picturesque historical story." Regulatory bodies were frustrated that they could control only the forms and content of advertising generated within particular provinces while the newsstands and airwaves were full of material sent in from the United States, where advertising was less restrained.[36]

Governments sensed the new postwar mood and slowly adjusted their regulatory regimes. At the national level the most glaring residue of prohibitionist (and racist) thinking was the complete ban, built into the Indian Act, on Aboriginal peoples' access to alcohol. After the Second World War Ottawa faced a barrage of civil-rights arguments, both from Aboriginal men who had enjoyed drinking rights as servicemen during the war and from the increasingly vocal Native organizations. Following a major legislative investigation of Native issues in 1946, the federal government finally amended the Indian Act in 1951 to allow Aboriginal people to consume alcohol in public drinking establishments, though not to buy booze to take home—a curious half-measure that another government inquiry a few years later rightly noted was an incentive to binge drinking during the limited hours of beer parlour operation. Consequently, the Indian Act was again amended in 1956 to permit provinces to grant Native peoples full drinking rights once each band had voted in favour of having alcohol on its reserve. Action to bring provincial legislation into line stretched out over the next decade.[37]

Provincial governments were also getting the message that other changes in regulatory policies were necessary. Ontario's attorney-general argued in 1947 that it was time to legitimize what was already happening—"to legalize, and bring to the light of day, drinking practices that have grown up illegally in every large municipality." A few years later the Manitoba Liquor Enquiry Commission similarly noted the public's "reaction against certain restrictive doctrines of the past." The shiny image of government control had become tarnished over the quarter-century since it had arrived in most provinces—the allocation of licences and inspection of premises got tangled in patronage practices (and abuses), and many beer parlours were allowed to deteriorate into what a 1952 B.C. royal commission called "slum" conditions. Middle-class drinkers wanted more attractive surroundings. Recognizing the still powerful anti-booze current among many voters (their wrath helped to defeat Ontario's premier George Drew in his own riding in the 1948 provincial election), governments moved cautiously, in some cases waiting for reports from commissions of inquiry (in British Columbia, Manitoba, Nova Scotia, and New Brunswick) or special legislative committees (in Alberta and Saskatchewan). In the end, they all eventually gave liquor control boards authority to license new kinds of public drinking establishments.[38]

Quebec's already more permissive regime was broadened in 1941 by allowing the sale of spirits as well as wine and beer on licensed premises. Ontario set the postwar pace with a new act in 1946, and Newfoundland followed three years later, as did the Yukon in 1952 and each of the Western provinces between 1953 and 1959. Nova Scotia, which had opened beer parlours only in 1946, waited until 1961 to legalize other kinds of drinking places. When New Brunswick finally allowed public drinking of any kind the next year and Prince Edward Island in 1964, each authorized all the public drinking options that had been set up in the other provinces. For some time, in a time-worn pattern of local political patronage, both provinces had been allowing Canadian Legion branches and many other "private" clubs—with some 35,000 members in New Brunswick by the early 1960s—to purchase alcohol from government liquor stores for resale on their own premises to members and their many guests.[39]

After the Second World War the federal government finally recognized that Aboriginal peoples should not be denied the same right to drink held by other Canadians. Drinking on reserves, however, remained a matter for the First Nations to settle themselves. Here members of the Six Nations reserve near Brantford, Ont., are casting ballots in a referendum to decide whether they will allow liquor in their homes. (NAC, PA-123914)

In all cases, licensed spaces for public drinking got permission to expand the range of products sold and activities allowed. The old-style beer parlours (now known as "public houses" in Ontario and British Columbia) were gradually allowed to add snack foods, recorded music in jukeboxes, and television sets. In the new category of licensed taverns called "lounges" (popularly dubbed "cocktail lounges" and, for meals, "dining lounges"), men and women could sit together, order spirits as well as beer and wine, have food with their drinks, and enjoy recorded or live entertainment—which included, by the mid-1960s, "go go" dancers. They could even drink at a bar, albeit seated on stools. Some of these taverns developed into "night clubs."

These changes did not entail any slide back into turn-of-the-century saloon culture, however, and regulation of the establishments was as rigid as ever. Applications to open such drinking spots were scrutinized rigorously, and the number of the new kinds of drinking places was kept small. Women were still forbidden to serve alcoholic beverages (even at the same tables where they served food). Liquor board inspectors not only continued to watch for loose management, sloppy service, inadequate lighting, underage drinkers, and excessive drunkenness, but also assessed the moral content of live performances and warned the owners to curb any lewd gestures or off-colour jokes.

More liberal attitudes to drinking brought new pressure to roll back the remaining zones of local-option prohibition and to allow more "cocktail lounges" to open. Referenda like this one in Kitchener, Ont., in 1957 began to proliferate. (YUA, Telegram Collection, 1817)

Televised entertainment was under scrutiny as well. In British Columbia, as the Manitoba Liquor Enquiry Commission discovered in 1955, "programs tending to encourage noisy or boisterous conduct on the part of drinkers" were forbidden. The moral harness had been loosened slightly, but the regulatory environment was far from permissive.[40]

Feelin' Alright

After the Second World War, Canadian social scientists began for the first time to turn their investigative lenses on these public drinking places. Beginning with a pioneering study of Toronto establishments in the early 1950s, a handful of Canadian sociologists, anthropologists, and psychologists joined academics in the United States and elsewhere in investigating what went on in taverns. Sometimes their projects got support from new addiction research foundations set up by provincial governments, and they reflected those agencies' concerns with the personal and social problems of excessive consumption and alcoholism. In all cases their methodology was drenched with the "scientific" apparatus of their disciplines, but in many ways it was not far removed from the work of the evangelical snoops who had skulked around saloons just before the First World War (except that these new researchers were generally willing to drink alcohol in the process of gathering their data).[41]

Some projects openly interviewed or surveyed drinkers and staff. Some hired researchers to sit against a wall sipping beer and jotting down observations or counting drinks and sips per customer as surreptitiously as possible. Some of these research assistants were sent in to gather information by chatting casually with patrons and staff without letting on that a study was underway. Some scholars simply turned their regular visits to a particular watering hole into "participant observation" and, after months or even years of sharing the company of drinkers and staff, put their insights on paper in scholarly journals. One frequently cited article was based on what the author frankly called a "systematic pub-crawl" on two nights during the Calgary Stampede.[42]

Typically the projects focused on a small number of establishments or a small population sample in one city. (Canadian researchers apparently never followed their U.S. counterparts in running experiments in simulated barrooms in "laboratories.") The results of the research were always consciously situated within an international (primarily U.S.) field of intellectual discussion about taverns and alcohol consumption. The volume of Canadian publications from all these projects was not large, at least compared to U.S. research, but they do open a few small windows on the changing world of public drinking in Canada down to the 1970s.

The new Canadian postwar liquor legislation had created two basic types of drinking places, with slight variations: the beer parlour and the lounge. Customers, owners, and staff then shaped more subtle distinctions within these categories. Researchers across North America struggled with the challenge of categorizing the "taverns" they found according to use rather than by their legal designations, but no consensus emerged.[43] Clearly, what the new organization of drinking places offered, beyond the different drinks and food available, was a diversity of possible experiences, with largely distinct social groups making use of each possibility in their own ways.

Outside Quebec, beer parlours remained by far the most numerous drinking spots, and still drew a clientele that was predominantly male and working-class. In Ontario 55 per cent of men and only 27 per cent of women in a 1946 survey indicated that they "definitely visited" beer parlours six or more times a year. Among that group of public drinkers, three-quarters were male, and two-thirds of those men were in skilled, semi-skilled, or unskilled occupations. Nearly three-fifths of the women were wives of such men or workers in the same sectors. The new postwar regulations did not fundamentally alter the culture of the existing beer parlours, beyond letting women into the previously all-male enclaves from which they had been legally barred in more than half the provinces—and typically the women got access only to the segregated facilities for "ladies and escorts." Surveys in Toronto and Winnipeg in the mid-1950s found patrons still showing up in heaviest numbers for an hour or two right after work and in slightly smaller numbers later in the evening, mostly on Fridays and Saturdays in the warmer months of the year. Attendance dropped off in the winter.[44]

Researchers also discovered that, like the taverns and saloons that had preceded them, beer parlours still functioned primarily as informal clubs for

Few changes occurred in beer parlours before the 1970s. These drinkers were photographed in Toronto in 1963. (YUA, Telegram Collection, 0-0233)

customers in search of relaxed sociability, especially for the core of "regulars" in a particular establishment (one estimate from the 1950s put this number at around half the patrons). Again and again across North America, social scientists concluded that drinking in such places was only incidental to finding good company with friends or compatible people. "The atmosphere is nearly always friendly, and it appears that most of the patrons either come into the parlor with friends or plan to meet friends there," said five researchers working for the Manitoba Liquor Commission in the mid-1950s. "It seemed that many of these friendly meetings were more important to the patrons than the actual drinking of beer." Treating was still central to group interaction.[45]

People who came alone seldom stayed long. They drank less, and often expected to join others during their visit. Men either came to spend time with other men without any women, in the time-honoured form of male privilege, or arrived in a separate space with female friends or spouses. It was difficult for men to use beer parlours to strike up new relationships with women because the men were not allowed to enter the women's side on their own. Intimate tête-à-têtes were much less common than larger, more gregarious gatherings, although the liquor board requirement that everyone remain seated at small tables limited the extent of social interaction. Men typically each drank about four or five eight-ounce glasses of draught beer in their one-to-two-hour visits (in most cases not enough to make them seriously inebriated); women drank considerably less and more slowly. People got noticeably drunker on special occasions, but regular drunks often found themselves isolated and excluded from socializing.

Each beer parlour had its own special flavour and attracted people who felt comfortable

Across North America, as social scientists began to research tavern life, they discovered that most drinkers seemed to be attracted primarily by the sociability of these places. This National Film Board still, taken in Dawson's Creek, B.C., in 1942, captures the intensity of this experience for men in an all-male setting. (NAC, PA-113191)

with each other. That flavour could be based on some combination of occupational experience, income level, neighbourhood proximity, and ethnic mix, but it could also, as investigators noted, depend on the active role of the owner and staff in shaping the social environment through their concern for their regulars, or their role as confidents and counsellors. With support from gay waiters, for example, gays and lesbians in Toronto and Montreal first began to use a few beer parlours in the postwar period as community gathering places and pickup zones. In a 1970–71 survey of drinking practices in three Vancouver cities, seven out of ten respondents said they chose a particular establishment because they could expect to find their friends there and the surroundings were pleasant. By that point, far across the country in London, Ont., the York Hotel had become a magnet for a fascinating collection of artists, intellectuals, and musicians, who rubbed shoulders with the blue-collar regulars.[46]

As in the 1920s and 1930s, beer parlours could vary a good deal. At one end of the scale were the shabby, dirty, rough-edged "dives" filled with what social scientists liked to call "skid-row" types—poorer workers, heavy drinkers, and chronic alcohol abusers (including those from upper classes who were trying to hide their drinking from their peers)—and where husky waiters could be expected to be curt with customers, push more beer at them, and tolerate no hint of violence, though fights erupted regularly. Most other beer parlours were less grim. Sometimes they brought together groups of industrial workers employed nearby (including, on occasion, a band of female workers interested in talking about shared problems, such as the women at Oshawa's General Motors plant in the late 1960s). Sometimes they drew in residents from the local neighbourhood, including perhaps some lower middle-class as well as working-class patrons. A U.S. researcher referred to both of these kinds of establishments as "home territory" places. They tended to be cleaner, and sometimes were more comfortably furnished and warmly decorated. Patrons could wear their work clothes or clean sports outfits, and the atmosphere was casual. They tended to monitor each other's moral standards and curbed sexual aggression or excessive drunkenness. "The noise increased with the crowd," researchers reported after visiting forty-five Winnipeg beer parlours. "But even at their noisiest there seemed to be little rowdiness."[47]

Customers could now munch potato chips and listen to canned music while they drank, but continuing liquor board prohibitions on live entertainment and dancing meant that conversation was still the most likely social activity (by contrast, U.S. taverns usually had card playing, shuffleboard, billiards, or other forms of amusement). In any case, conversation was probably why people came in the first place. Sports and sex were popular topics of discussion, but a Toronto researcher concluded after nearly five years of observations that "it may be the *act* of talking and the *fact* of companionship within the tavern environment which are significant rather than the specific content of what is said or done." Despite the difficulties of "meaningful communication between patrons" when the place was "a chaos of sound and movement," he noted, "patrons *do* talk, drink, and sit with other patrons." This he labelled "ritual behaviour." In the 1950s a resident of the solidly working-class "Lower Ward" in downtown Toronto summed up the attraction of these places in familiar language:

> I believe the pubs have real social functions; they are the poor man's club, the equivalent of the rich man's Granite Club. They're treated well there. Going there may help solve problems, domestic or job difficulties. Also they get a sense of importance there, perhaps in ordering the beer, or showing off in talk with the guys. They do band together to meet emergencies, for instance sickness. . . . The poor have to find people on their level; this is so in the pub.[48]

Patrons of cocktail lounges wanted a much wider variety of drinks than had generally been served in the old-time saloons. Bartenders now had to know how to mix a multitude of alcoholic beverages. Some entered the competitions that their union held. (YUA, Telegram Collection, 0-0321)

The cocktail lounges were much fewer in number and quite different. Some had the quality of neighbourhood or work-related hangouts, with their groups of regulars and a socially mixed clientele. Sometimes lounges catered to more affluent members of ethnic minority groups, but middle-class residents made sure that few of those were located in or near their neighbourhoods. Most lounges operated in downtown business districts (sometimes a hotel was licensed to run both a lounge and a beer parlour) and had many fewer regulars. Customers tended not to stay as long as those at the beer parlours. Lounges were generally much more lavishly decorated and furnished, and patrons often had to meet stringent dress codes, including shirt and tie for men and skirts for women. Waiters and bartenders treated them with more formality and deference and expected good tips. Customers could choose from a much wider range of drinks, but, because beer was available there only in bottles, all drinks were more expensive than in beer parlours (where most people drank draft beer). All of these qualities made cocktail lounges less appealing to working-class patrons. Investigators saw mostly white-collar workers, professionals, middle-managers, and others of the middle and upper-middle classes. By the 1960s live entertainment was bringing younger crowds to some lounges.[49]

In many parts of the business community, a lunchtime meeting at such an establishment could be the occasion to make deals, plot corporate manoeuvres, or solve management problems (and might later be charged as a legitimate business expense for tax purposes). Later in the day visits probably filled

Les Voyageurs bar in Montreal's Queen Elizabeth Hotel typified the postwar cocktail lounge. The decor is modern and tasteful, customers are well dressed and tend to be paired off in couples, and a whiff of sexual intimacy hangs over the place. (CSTMC, CN001181)

more personal needs. "Cocktail lounges are quieter, less brightly lit, and the seating arrangements are more conducive to privacy," researchers in Vancouver reported in 1975. Clusters of drinkers were typically smaller than in beverage rooms, perhaps one or two couples, and solitary drinkers were more common—although sometimes many more people would arrive together for a party. Since men and women could enter the lounges on their own, the rooms became much more active sexual marketplaces. Singles found cocktail lounges convenient for dating or finding new partners, and married men for meeting mistresses. In Toronto, as a researcher discovered in the 1950s, a few lounges attached to hotels became easier locales for commercial sex, because the prostitutes could sit alone waiting for customers and then take them upstairs to complete their business. The more awkward structure of beer parlours required either that men bring streetwalkers into the ladies and escort section, or that waiters co-operate in linking a prostitute and her potential customers on the men's side. While some middle-class Canadians used lounges as extensions of their workplace relations, they were less likely to integrate them into their casual neighbourhood life, and had to make more formal plans for a session of sociable drinking in a public place. They probably also saw these outings as fitting more individual needs than did the patrons of beer parlours.[50]

Outside these public watering holes, booze could still be marketed and purchased only through government liquor stores, brewers' warehouses, and, in a few provinces, hotels (Quebec remained the exception, with alcohol available in corner stores). And, despite the somewhat more pleasant atmosphere of the beer parlours and taverns, there seemed to be a decided trend by the 1960s towards taking booze home to drink, as part of a general turn towards more household-based leisure. After the war, a larger-than-ever proportion of working-class Canadians were able to afford better housing, sometimes in new suburbs, with more amenities like refrigerators and televisions (both of which became universal for the first time in Canada by the end of the 1950s) and more space for family relaxation and entertaining friends and kin. In Ontario the percentage of all beer consumed in licensed premises dropped from 51 to under 40 between 1949 and 1963, and in Manitoba from 58 to under 48, during the same period in which the vast majority of Canadian households got their first TV sets. By the mid-1970s, only about one-sixth of all alcohol was consumed in public places (though beer drinkers downed 27 per cent of their beverage of choice in licensed premises).[51]

While moralists might have applauded the move from bar to home, it was soon clear that the household was a much less easily regulated space, where drinkers undoubtedly enjoyed much more booze alone or with only one or two others—drinks before dinner, in front of a televised hockey game, at the backyard picnic table, and so on. Once again, men were much more likely than women to engage in this more private drinking. One study of a Toronto working-class neighbourhood in the 1960s also reported that, unless they were kin, men and women at these home-based gatherings sat in separate rooms. Consumption could now be spread out over the week in smaller quantities, instead of (or often in addition to) bigger celebratory binges. Little research was undertaken on this sphere of alcohol consumption, but the heaviest drinking probably took place in family households, often in parties. In a 1975 survey, more than a third of Ontario drinkers had been drinking in at

Like these Toronto consumers in 1958, many more drinkers were taking their booze home. (YUA, Telegram Collection, 1818)

least one party in the previous week. These events took on diverse shapes—from formal cocktail parties, to ritualized family celebrations of birthdays or weddings, to loosely structured gatherings of young men around open cases of beer. Meanwhile, as other studies would reveal, by the 1960s teenaged members of the family were highly likely to be drinking with friends discreetly out of sight of parents.[52]

Of course, still other more disreputable forms of privatized drinking existed. Some people still drank on the job, out of sight of supervisors (anecdotes about these practices abound, but there has been little systematic research in Canada).[53] In the heart of most large cities could also be found the so-called "winos," "alkies," "rubbies," or "skid-row bums"—the loose communities of alcohol abusers, mostly older men without jobs and cut off from families, who gathered in back alleys or parks to share bottles of cheap wine, shaving lotion, or rubbing alcohol, or perhaps, in less respectable beer parlours, watery beer. These were communal events, in which men each contributed to the purchase of a bottle and then passed it around in well-understood rituals of sharing, often but not always to the point of heavy intoxication. They told investigators that these sociable drinking sprees were the bright spots in a marginal existence broken by only occasional part-time employment and mostly lived out in "flops," city missions, hostels, and, frequently, jail cells, because being drunk in a public place was still a punishable offence whether or not any disturbance resulted. Many of these men did not mind being sent to jail, where they could dry out, get more nutritious food, put on weight, and generally improve their health.[54]

Some of them, especially in Western Canada, were Aboriginal peoples, who were less enthusiastic about white jail-keepers. After more than three centuries of colonization and marginalization, they faced the worst forms of systemic discrimination in urban labour markets and social relations more generally. Their drinking patterns carried over from the reserves, where occasional but lengthy binges were almost the only form of drinking, thanks in

In 1961, when breweries wanted to raise customers' awareness of their new "stubby" bottles, they used a setting in which much more alcohol was then being consumed—at home in front of the television set. (YUA, *Telegram* Collection, 1820)

part to the poverty and legal constraints that encouraged Aboriginal peoples to enjoy booze while they were able to get it, and, according to some anthropologists, thanks in part to a desire to celebrate in a distinctively "Indian" way in defiance of paternalistic white expectations. However defiant, drunken Aboriginals inflicted serious damage to their own bodies and destructive violence on their communities. Compared to other Canadians, First Nations people were far more likely than other Canadians to die from accident, suicide, or homicide, often with high blood–alcohol levels.[55]

By the end of the 1960s, then, John Barleycorn strode confidently across the country. Booze manufacturers had enormously increased both their capacity to produce and their corporate power within the market. More and more Canadians made alcoholic beverages a regular part of their lives and swallowed as much per capita as drinkers had in the early twentieth century, before prohibition, though now it was much more often at home than in licensed establishments. Women were drinking publicly and privately without the moral outrage they once would have created. Most Canadians were becoming accustomed to relaxing with alcohol, which, along with caffeine and nicotine, was their favourite recreational drug by the 1970s. Governments had made modest gestures towards this shift in attitudes, but the rigid structures of regulation introduced four decades earlier remained firmly in place to discourage excessive consumption.

By the end of the 1960s, however, the consensus about the appropriateness of that regulatory regime had disintegrated. A new order was in the making.

Becoming European

Booze regulations in Canada after prohibition had been solidly grounded in a stern commitment to restraint and probity in private and public morality. Expressiveness of all kinds, it was assumed, should be governed by moderation. But on many fronts those assumptions had melted away by the late 1960s and early 1970s. A large generation of postwar baby boomers led a cultural challenge to deeply entrenched notions of personal expression and democratic rights.

Authoritarianism and inequalities in human relationships came to be seen as intolerable, and a highly publicized counterculture of sexual experimentation, drug use, fanciful body adornment, communitarian living, and social protest took shape as a vibrant critique of the received morality. Movements for student power, women's and gay liberation, environmental protection, rank-and-file unionism, tenants' rights, and much more brought new challenges to marriage and the family, educational institutions, electoral politics, and the waged workplace. The traditional bastions of moral authority, the churches, saw attendance and membership go into decline. In 1968–69 liberalized laws governing divorce and homosexuality implicitly sanctioned a so-called "sexual revolution," and the author of this new legislation, Canada's new prime minister, Pierre Elliott Trudeau, borrowed the language of the new movements by promising "participatory democracy."[56]

If, as Trudeau asserted, the state had no business in the bedrooms of the nation, what right, many began to ask, did it have to keep such a tight rein on the consumption of alcoholic beverages? Why not give individuals the right and the personal responsibility to govern their own moral behaviour? Why not emulate some European cultures where booze was more integrated into daily life from an early age? Going in that direction would certainly please the large number of postwar immigrants to Canada from countries such as Italy, Greece, and Portugal, whose communities were self-confidently promoting a more tolerant "multiculturalism" as state policy in Canada. Policy-makers also took a lot more interest in the drinking patterns of North American Jewish communities, where drinking typically began in family rituals at a young age and remained moderate and restrained through adulthood.[57]

These percolating liberal and radical critiques undermined many of the props of the old regulatory regime, and a new ideology took shape suggesting that moderate drinking could be encouraged—and problems of alcohol abuse thus discouraged—through less restrictive measures. Within the scholarly research community, a new interest in a "sociocultural" approach to alcohol was gathering steam and providing new comparative studies of drinking practices in diverse cultures. If moderate drinking could be taught from an early age and integrated more casually and less restrictively into daily life, the problems of excessive, harmful drinking would fade away. B.C. Premier Dave Barrett called this the "European approach to drinking." The widely accepted consensus that alcoholism was a disease, and that therefore alcoholics were a distinct group from social drinkers, helped to undermine lingering notions that taking a drink was to enter onto a slippery slope to perdition. So did pressure from the hospitality industry to make Canada more attractive to tourists. One after another, provincial governments authorized liquor boards to loosen up many of the controls (once again, often after hearing from commissions of inquiry). All provinces had abandoned the personal permit for liquor purchases by 1970. Public drunkenness was partially decriminalized to allow police to refer "public inebriates" to non-medical detoxification centres rather than laying a criminal charge.[58]

Perhaps the most celebrated, and soon most controversial, change in public policy was the lowering of the legal age for drinking from twenty-one to eighteen or nineteen in all provinces and territories between 1970 and 1972, generally at the same time as the age of majority and voting was also lowered. Despite the assertion of the chair of the Brewers' Association of Canada that beer on university campuses might steer young people away from other drug use, Ontario and Saskatchewan had second thoughts and raised the age a notch to nineteen a few years later, alleging much more trouble from teenaged drunks; similarly the U.S. federal government pushed all states to return to twenty-one by threatening to cut off highway funds. Bringing older teenagers into the legalized community of drinkers was credited with helping to push up per capita consumption levels among adults to a peak of 11.28 litres of absolute alcohol in the late 1970s (more than 80 per cent of those aged eighteen to twenty drank).[59]

Buying booze got easier, as government liquor stores proliferated—in 1970 there were 1,233 across the country, and in 1991, 2,605—and began to function more like other retail operations. British Columbia opened its first self-serve stores in 1962 (a significant factor in rising consumption rates,

All provinces lowered the legal age for drinking in the early 1970s. These eighteen-year-olds took advantage of Ontario's new law to enjoy a pint in downtown Toronto's Colonial Tavern in 1971. (YUA, Telegram Collection, 1814)

according to Ontario researchers). Ontario and New Brunswick followed in 1969, and had phased out almost all of the old-style stores by the late 1980s. In an effort to attract customers rather than discourage them, these outlets got entirely new decors to make them attractive and pleasant. In sharp contrast to the earliest administrative policies, customers could expect to find knowledge-able staff who would offer advice about wines or liquors, and even industry representatives offering free samples. Indeed, as liquor stores lost more and more of their social-control functions and became overtly more similar to regular businesses (and cash cows for provincial treasuries), debates opened up about privatizing them, a step vigorously opposed by the unions that repre-sented the stores' employees. Privately owned "agency stores" were allowed to sell some beverage alcohol in remote areas. British Columbia's hotels and pubs got to open beer and wine stores on their premises, and, in addition to their own independent outlets, local wineries in Ontario and British Columbia got permission to set up kiosks in supermarkets. Yet only Alberta, in 1994, carried through a complete dismantling of government liquor stores (although that direction remained a policy option actively discussed in other provinces with neo-liberal governments).[60]

Liquor control boards also loosened the controls on licensed drinking places. They no longer had to close for dinnertime in the early evening, and got the right to stay open later and on Sun-

In the 1960s and 1970s provincial governments made it possible for shoppers to serve themselves in government liquor stores. These discriminating Toronto consumers benefited from Ontario's 1969 legislation. (YUA, Telegram *Collection, 1813)*

days, public holidays, and after the polls closed on election days. The sharp distinction between beer parlours and lounges broke down, as did the segregation of women from men (many drinking places nonetheless remained male-dominated, especially the large number of licensed social clubs). Licensed establishments could also hire female servers, who were expected to raise the tone and lower the level of violence of such places. Licences were granted to many more places, including such hitherto unacceptable spots as outdoor patios, sidewalk cafés, beer gardens, sports arenas, baseball parks, theatres, and university student centres. Inside these establishments, customers could now stand up with their drinks, even at the bar, and move about more freely. They could also get food, play pool or video games, watch sports on huge TV screens, dance to pre-recorded music, or enjoy live entertainment—even strippers. In this process of loosening up, the old beer parlour gradually disappeared as the cheap, working-class hangout that it had been for more than half a century, and public drinking places became more diverse and more expensive. Students and young workers, especially men, flocked to these places.[61]

As in the past, public drinking places continued to develop particular clienteles. A mid-1980s study of drinking behaviour in Toronto had no difficulty

In the 1960s regulations governing public drinking began to loosen up. These two women were the first "bar maids" hired in Winnipeg's beer parlours in 1961. Their boss reported that he had never seen the place so quiet and orderly. (YUA, Telegram Collection, 1821)

finding five bars with distinct groups of patrons: one filled with those "employed in white-collar occupations," another "predominantly university-aged students and older individuals," another "largely lower middle-class" (mostly "small-shop owners"), another "young and well-dressed office workers," and another "typically working-class and retired individuals." Around the same time an anthropologist noted that the young working-class men he was studying in Thunder Bay frequented a range of bars but preferred those where they could "feel the atmosphere is relaxed and unpretentious, yet where symbols of poverty do not exist." He described his time in one packed with beer-company insignia and sports paraphernalia that seemed, unconsciously, to

*New liquor control regulations
in the 1970s allowed for more
variety in public drinking
establishments. Montreal's Le
Carrefon was the country's
first "wine bar," a specialized
kind of tavern intended to
draw in middle-class
consumers, but that never
really caught fire across the
country. (NAC)*

echo a turn of the century saloon. Across Canada, this kind of "sports bar" seemed to become the preferred hangout for working-class men. Clearly people were still using bars and pubs as places to spend their "free time" with their own kind.[62]

The booze industry responded energetically to these new opportunities. The large corporations that controlled virtually all production struggled to maintain or increase their market share, both among producers of the same kind of beverage and among the three distinct sectors of brewing, distilling, and wine-making. They recognized that the much larger population of drinkers was fragmented in many different ways—by age, gender, class, and region in particular—and, turning their back on their history of trying to reduce their customers' options to a handful of national brands, began a remarkable diversification of products, following a trend towards segmenting markets that hit most consumer-goods industries. Despite continuing controls on advertising (a federal ban on all commercials for liquor on radio and television, a continuing ban in a few provinces, and tight restrictions in most others), which remained more heavy-handed than those in most Western countries, the beverage alcohol industries also poured millions into associating their products with the "good life" in advertisements in newspapers and magazines and on radio and television. Not surprisingly, after watching slick, upbeat depictions of friends relaxing immediately after work, or on weekend and holiday time, hundreds of people replied to a classified advertisement placed by some young adults in the early 1980s inviting responses from people who would like to "live in a beer commercial" (one of the respondents ended up finding a husband this way). In a similar vein, tavern-owners reached out for customers through improved interior decor, more live entertainment, and after-work "happy hours" offering cheaper drinks and snacks (later banned in Ontario and British Columbia). Theme bars began to appear, from the western-American saloon to the Victorian or Edwardian British pub to the sports bar. Starting in 1971 a completely new kind of drinking place called a "wine bar" also arrived in the larger cities.[63]

The 1970s thus saw a remarkable opening up to alcohol. State policies got much more liberal, corporate producers and local retailers marketed their goods with new enthusiasm, and thousands of drinkers bellied up to the bar. Consumption reached a new post-prohibition peak.

Second Thoughts

Consumers were not easily manipulated, though, and starting in the late 1970s they began to drink less for the first time since the war. Across the country annual per capita consumption of absolute alcohol among those fifteen and over dropped from just over eleven litres in the late 1970s to under nine in the early 1990s (that is, by about 22 per cent). All provinces and territories saw the same trend, although the decline was steeper in the East than in the West. The slide over the past quarter-century was most noticeable for spirits—more than a quarter of the volume of Canadian sales—but the volume of beer marketed also remained flat, and in the late 1980s wine sales started to decline. The estimated number of standard drinks per week consumed by an adult in Canada fell from nearly thirteen to ten from the late 1970s to the early 1990s, and between 1985 and 1995 the percentage of those telling surveys that they were drinkers fell from 82 per cent to 73 per cent (among those aged eighteen to twenty-nine the decline was from 90 to 77 per cent). People in Ontario who described themselves as "daily drinkers" tumbled from 13.4 per cent in 1977 to 8.3 per cent in 1991. Most of these trends were evident in almost all Western industrialized countries in the same period, although Canada's decline was steeper than most others.[64]

That sharp decline came about first of all, and perhaps most importantly, because Canadians faced a much less economically secure way of life after the mid-1970s. Two deep economic depressions in the early 1980s and early 1990s threw thousands out of work and frightened many more. Many jobs also disappeared in the private sector through economic restructuring and managerial and technological innovation, and governments at all levels down-sized and shed employees. Many workers could find only casual or part-time work. Young workers entering the labour market faced much more limited job opportunities than did most of their parents. State policy also shifted to give workers less protection from economic dislocation, as the already limited welfare state was steadily dismantled, labour legislation was weakened, and the postwar Keynesian policies aimed at sustaining incomes were abandoned.[65]

Many Canadians found the purchasing power of their wages declining over the 1980s and 1990s. A large majority of families came to depend on two adult incomes in order to survive. Under these circumstances, many people once again had to treat alcoholic beverages as luxuries to be enjoyed less frequently, especially since the cost of packaged booze was no longer dropping. By the end of the 1980s, the price of beverage alcohol in constant dollars, which had dropped by 25 per cent of the 1950 level by the late 1970s, had almost returned to its earlier peak. The cost of drinking in bars and pubs was also rising. With both heads of household working and, to some extent at least, sharing domestic labour, the time that a man had to get out to a tavern each week became more constrained.[66]

Lower alcohol consumption also reflected major demographic shifts. The overall population was aging as people had fewer children. In the wake of the baby boom, the birth rate in Canada dropped in the 1970s to about half of what it had been in the late 1950s, and it stayed low. The postwar demographic bulge of young adult consumers thus shrank, and older adults drank less as they aged and directed more resources into raising families and caring for their own health.[67]

The Canadian population mix was also changing after 1970, largely as a result of a major shift in the source of immigrants. People were now coming from parts of the Third World that had never sent so many people to this country before—particularly Asia, Africa, and Latin America and the Caribbean. Many of these newcomers, especially those from Asia, brought drinking cultures that limited alcohol beverages to mealtimes and rarely involved heavy drinking. Some, such as the Moslems, were expected to be complete abstainers. In a 1993 national survey, groups who spoke neither English nor French had by far the highest levels of abstainers. Only half said they were "current drinkers" and nearly one in five had never drunk alcohol. This was a sharp contrast with the impact on overall drinking patterns of earlier immigrants from Southern and Eastern Europe.[68]

Against the background of these broad social changes, working-class and middle-class Canadians admitted alcohol into their lives in different ways. Workers found their empty wallets pushing them to cut back on their drinking.

In a 1990 Health and Welfare Canada survey only 62 per cent of the "very poor" and 69 per cent of the "poor" said they were currently drinkers (14 and 11 per cent in each case had never been)—a finding similar to other such cases in the distant past—while 78 per cent of the "lower middle," 88 per cent of the "upper middle," and 92 per cent of the "rich" admitted to being drinkers. Fewer women in all these categories declared themselves drinkers, although the gender difference was greater at the lower levels than at the top. Drinkers among managers and professionals were also somewhat more numerous than among blue-collar and other white-collar workers. Yet working-class men who drank were much more likely to consume in greater quantity. In 1990 blue-collar workers still reported the highest average consumption every week (6.77 drinks), compared to nearly four and a half drinks among other white-collar workers, just over four among managers and professionals, and less than two among those "keeping house." Proportionally more blue-collar drinkers still got their booze in taverns, which also suggests the survival of older class and gender identities.[69]

Over the same quarter-century period, middle-class Canadians re-created their cultural moorings and the place of alcohol therein in quite different ways. To some extent these conditions reflected the new political economy. Middle-class jobs were also disappearing, and the work experience was often deteriorating, while incomes were squeezed by a sharpening polarization of wealth between rich and poor. Many in the middle class had good reason to turn away from the more acquisitive consumer habits of the postwar boom time towards more constraint. Self-reliance and personal responsibility also became more important in the face of the retreat of welfare-state provisions for looking after people. The consumer practices of these people began to respond to the marketing of new programs and products of self-help and self-governance, from RRSPs to health clubs to various psycho-therapies. Health consciousness became almost a badge of class identity. Besides taking up regular exercise with unaccustomed enthusiasm, middle-class Canadians showed more concern about the food and other substances that entered their bodies, including most dramatically a massive rejection of tobacco. They also turned a sharper eye on the alcohol they consumed.

A concern with healthiness slid easily into an obsession with quality. Building on much older middle-class conceptions of how to participate "tastefully" in consumer culture, they now turned their scorn on the synthetic, conformist, mass-produced consumer goods that corporations had geared up to make available in so many sectors since the Second World War (and which the first postwar generation of the middle class had initially embraced). High quality, authenticity, purity, and natural ingredients became watchwords for new patterns of middle-class consumption, especially among the loosely defined "yuppies" (young urban professionals). They wore pure cotton or wool next to their skin, ate granola for breakfast and fresh vegetables for dinner, searched out the rich tastes of non-Anglo cuisine, and reached out for more flavour in their alcoholic beverages. In the mid-1970s the leading Canadian mouthpiece of this new consumer sensitivity, *Harrowsmith* magazine, published a hard-hitting critique of Canadian beer:

> All the big breweries are making virtually the same product, with different names and labels. Accompanying this trend is a shift of power from the hands of the brewmaster to the marketing, accounting, and advertising men. Like tasteless white bread and the universal cardboard hamburger, the new beer is produced for the tasteless common denominator. It must not offend anyone, anywhere. Corporate beer is not too heavy, not too bitter, not too alcoholic, not too malty, not too yeasty and not too gassy. In other words, corporate beer reduces every characteristic that makes beer beer.

Imported wines were the first beneficiaries of the search for quality, but this segment of drinkers was open to new appeals to their discriminating palates. While only a minority of the population became caught up in these new trends (and professionals were one of the two most likely occupational groups to drink), the wave was nonetheless unsettling enough to give the beverage alcohol industry plenty of concern.[70]

Within working-class Canada, then, drinking was curtailed because of tighter family budgets, though still enjoyed by many men as the centre of their celebration of class and gender identities. Within middle-class Canada, drinking fitted into a new class culture of individual constraint, self-awareness, and creative expression through consumption. On these parallel paths, both classes moved towards drinking less in general.

What had also become sharply clear was that a small number of drinkers consumed far more than everyone else. Gender and age made the difference. In 1990 men over fourteen told surveyors that they had an average of 6.4 drinks per weeks, while women reported having only 2.3. In the same survey, 28 per cent of male drinkers said they consumed more than seven drinks a week compared to only 6 per cent of female drinkers. As had been true during the four centuries of European settlement, single men in their early twenties were still far and away the heaviest drinkers. Those aged 20–24 averaged over eight drinks a week in 1990, those 25–34 nearly seven (compared to only 2.55 and 2.24 among women at those ages), and a third of the men in this second age bracket drank more than seven per week.[71]

People were also starting to drink at a much younger age, often initially in the company of parents, but quickly moving to peer-group gatherings out of parental oversight, usually in bars or taverns. Many researchers across the country turned their lens on high-school-aged drinkers in the 1970s and 1980s and highlighted the expanding role of alcohol in youth culture. By their mid-teens, the great majority of teenagers had tasted alcohol, and large numbers, especially boys, were drinking frequently. A national survey in 1978–79 found that 30 per cent of the fifteen- to seventeen-year-old males who drank consumed more than six drinks a week. By the early 1990s, 95 per cent of university students were drinking alcohol, and three out of ten had more than fifteen drinks a week. Indeed, convivial drinking for many young people in their teens and early twenties, especially males, came to mean intentionally swallowing enough to get drunk. No doubt the relentless enthusiasm of younger men for binge drinking together was related to the new uncertainties of masculine identity sparked by the success of feminist critiques of patriarchy and the insecurities of jobs in a restructuring economy.[72]

In the 1980s and 1990s, these heavy drinkers faced a lot more heat. Their drinking patterns were framed by two critical discourses that attacked the direct damage they caused others. From their considerably different vantage points, policing authorities and women's groups converged on the need for a new public policy to curb excessive drinking. The large new feminist movement that had grown up since the 1970s helped to sensitize many Canadians to the harm that men's heavy drinking could inflict and its role in male violence, especially sexual assault. They targeted the role of alcohol in courtship rituals and sexual interplay. When in 1994 the Supreme Court of Canada upheld a man's claim that he was too drunk to be responsible for his actions, Parliament responded to the loud public outcry with a new law in 1995 affirming that intoxication "could not be used socially and legally to excuse violence, particularly violence against women and children," and that "people who, while in a state of self-induced intoxication, violate the integrity of others are blameworthy in relation to their harmful conduct."[73]

Women with a less feminist perspective launched a highly successful campaign on another front—drunk driving. In the 1960s policing authorities long concerned about road safety and traffic accidents had seen a need for stricter legislation. A federal Criminal Code amendment in 1969, patterned on a much-discussed British law two years earlier, set the acceptable blood-alcohol content at .08 per cent, made breath testing mandatory if police had "reasonable and probable cause" to suspect serious intoxication, and established serious fines for driving above this limit. The new law proved to have only a limited deterrent effect, and drivers impaired by heavy alcohol consumption still left a large trail of serious accidents and deaths without provoking much public debate. Eventually the victims of that carnage sparked a North-American-wide grassroots movement to support victims in the judicial process and to agitate for tougher laws and enforcement and better public-education programs. In the early 1980s movement activists created independent provincial groups in Ontario, Manitoba, Alberta, and British Columbia, the last of which affiliated in 1984 with the large U.S. organization Mothers Against Drunk Driving (MADD), founded four years earlier. A national Canadian body soon drew together the provincial units into MADD Canada, as an arm of the U.S. body. By the turn of the century it had five thousand members spread through fifty-five local chapters (alongside six hundred chapters in the United States) and a ten-million-dollar budget. Hugely successful fundraising campaigns enabled the organization to advertise widely through direct mails and in all the major media.[74]

As the name suggests, women launched and sustained this movement, though, unlike the much older WCTU, men were eventually centrally active. In a throwback to that earlier women's movement, chapters promoted the wearing of red ribbons by members and supporters and poured energy into youth education programs. Yet aside from the emotional tales of "broken-hearted mothers," MADD made little use of the older maternalist rhetoric. Nor did its propaganda attack alcohol or drinking, or target the modern "Liquor Traffic" (which actually contributed money to the campaign) or the lifestyle promotion of slick advertising. In an age of liberalized attitudes to alcohol consumption, the organization might well have been no more effective than the tiny remnant of the WCTU if it had attacked booze itself. Instead, it put the individual drinking driver at the centre of its moralistic analysis and demonology. This was a victims-rights movement that laid blame squarely on the personal irresponsibility of "killer drunks," who were constructed as dangerous deviants and criminals, not as typical drinkers. In this way MADD paralleled the widespread rightward turn in North American politics in the 1980s and indeed had early and consistent support from conservatives who liked to unleash "law and order" campaigns as solutions to social problems.[75]

MADD's focus on drunk driving was the cutting edge of a wider, ideologically more diverse "neo-temperance" activism that intervened in public debate and lobbied for public policy to curb excessive drinking. Some of it was based in addiction research institutes across the country, places that wanted to frame alcohol abuse as a public-health problem. In the face of such agitation, penalties for drunk driving were made tougher across the country, and police forces set up more vigilant surveillance, especially in the period around Christmas and New Year, in the form of well-publicized Check-Stop

As this Toronto man knew in
1958, Breathalyzer tests had
been around for some time
before new legislation in 1969
gave them more legal potency
in dealing with drunk drivers.
By the 1980s the threat of
breath tests encouraged
more drivers to reduce their
drinking, especially during
intensive police surveillance in
the Christmas season. (YUA,
Telegram Collection, 1815)

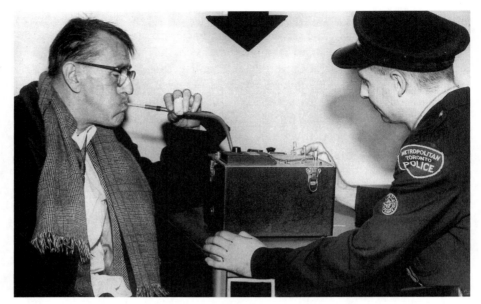

or RIDE (Reduce Impaired Driving Everywhere) programs. The risk of a negative Breathalyzer test soon had many drivers watching their intake. Those
caught were now likely to be forced into some kind of addiction treatment
program. These neo-temperance activists also helped to forestall the privatization of alcohol sales, which, they argued, would make more available and thus
push up consumption levels and then alcohol abuse. They also convinced
some provincial governments to increase public awareness about the hazards
of drinking too much, including public-service advertising and training programs for serving staff in drinking establishments. The effect of all of this
heightened awareness and state intervention on drinking cannot be easily
measured, but it seems clear that many more drinkers at parties or in taverns
recognized the need to curb their drinking if they planned to drive home, or
to make sure that there was a "designated driver" among them.[76]

Multiplying Markets

The convergence of factors that led many Canadians to restrain their drinking
in the last quarter of the twentieth century was not good news for the beverage alcohol industry, and the country's powerful booze producers scrambled
to meet the challenge. The name of the game was market share. In a highly
concentrated industry that had billions of dollars in revenues each year, winning over even one per cent of the market could net millions in profits. The

trend towards market segmentation accelerated enormously. Young consumers were targeted more directly, as were more "upscale" middle-class tastes. In the process new players, both tiny and gigantic, entered the beverage alcohol industry.

Not surprisingly in a country whose drinkers preferred beer, the three major breweries were particularly aggressive in trying to snatch loyal drinkers away from each other in what one commentator dubbed an ongoing "beer war." Provincial regulation and a long tradition of quiet price-fixing among the companies ruled out price-cutting; to attract consumers they simply had to make their products, new and old, seem more appealing than that of their main competitors. In the mid-1970s each of the Big Three companies copied the U.S. industry in bringing out the first "light" beers since prohibition— beers expected to please both younger drinkers and women. The light beers were not instant hits, because Canadian drinkers tended to scorn the weaker brews they associated with U.S. beer, but during the 1980s they took off. Between 1981 and 1983, in hopes of drawing in more drinkers, each of the Big Three also began producing, under licence in Canada, well-known brands of American beer (Budweiser, Miller, Coors), as well as a few from Europe (Carling-O'Keefe's deal with Carlsberg in the 1970s set the pattern). By the end of the decade, U.S. brands produced in Canada had taken some 15 per cent of the Canadian beer market. In 1983 the companies also abandoned the pact that had them all selling their beer in the "stubby." They began filling bottles of a variety of shapes and colours in their separate bids to win over customers in different market niches.[77]

During the 1980s the brewing corporations also gradually became aware of a new pack of small-scale competitors snapping at their heels. For the first time in decades new breweries were appearing in an outgrowth of what was dubbed the "Real Ale" movement in Britain. In 1971 British drinkers had started mobilizing against the bland, standardized product of mass production and in support of beer conditioned in casks with no additives or preservatives. In 1982 the Troller Pub, Canada's first "brew pub," opened in Vancouver, offering customers the beer brewed across the road in its tiny Horseshoe Bay Brewery. Over the next year a handful of brew pubs opened across Western Canada, and in 1984 Vancouver's Granville Island Brewery became the country's first free-standing cottage brewery, or "microbrewery," dedicated to producing more flavourful beer in the old-fashioned way. More microbreweries followed in quick succession—a total of fifty-four by 1990, although twenty of them were short-lived. With a high-tech production process, a handful of staff (many of them part-time), and no unions, each struggled valiantly for more customers. More of these alternatives appeared over the next decade, and through mergers and increases in production, a few of them (notably Brick, Sleeman, and Pacific Western) became significant regional brewers that reached out across the country (by 2001 Sleeman would be the third-largest brewing company in Canada).[78]

Molson and Labatt fought back, first by producing their own "premium" beers and then in the early 1990s with so-called "ice beers" with higher alcohol content. Meanwhile, the West Coast independent Pacific Western pushed Molson and Labatt into the production of bottled draft beer and low-alcohol "dry" beers, while an upstart in Hamilton, Lakeport, began producing a line of cheaper beers, including some U.S. brands. Molson and Labatt brought out their own versions in 1993.[79]

Many more brands, independent and otherwise, came and went over the 1990s. But the Achilles heel of the independents was their relatively limited resources for advertising, and the dominant corporations made full use of the media to sell their new lines. They also recognized that the best way to appeal to the discerning drinker who wanted stronger flavour was to become the importing agents for beers from Europe, Mexico, and elsewhere (even though these remained a tiny part of the market), which started to enter Canada in much larger quantities. Meanwhile, drinkers in Ontario and British Columbia were learning to make their own beer through some three hundred "U Brew" outlets.[80]

The domestic market could not contain the ambitions of Canada's leading corporations, and each of them had been producing and selling abroad, especially in the United States. Molson Golden, Moosehead, and Labatt's Blue were among the leading imports in the U.S. market. During the 1980s a handful of transnational brewing companies reached out to consolidate their hold on production in many countries. From the mid-1980s on, public policy in Canada encouraged this kind of business activity, first with the inauguration of the Free Trade Agreement in 1989 and the country's adherence to the continuing General Agreement on Tariffs and Trade, which aimed at eliminating all obstacles to global free trade. In the mid-1990s provincial trade barriers were completely dismantled, and all the provincial preferences that liquor control boards had imposed for decades came to an end. The Canadian industry first felt the shock of the new global strategizing in 1987 when the huge firm from down under, Elders IXL bought Carling-O'Keefe and introduced Canadian production of Foster's Lager, the Australian company's leading product. Two years later the stakes got even bigger when that company merged with Molson to operate under the name Molson Breweries Canada and to market Carling and Molson brands separately. Molson was suddenly the sixth-largest brewery in North America, controlling more than half the beer market in Canada. In a major rationalization of production, it closed seven plants and laid off two thousand brewery workers. Over the next decade Molson would spend large amounts of money, first bringing in the big U.S. brewery Miller as a minority partner and later buying out both that company and the Elders interest.[81]

In 1995 the other Canadian brewing giant, Labatt, was swallowed up by the mammoth Belgian firm Interbrew, which became the second largest brewer in the world. By the winter of 2001–2, the union representing its Canadian workers was protesting that the corporation was trying to undermine their long-established job security with more part-time labour and outsourcing.[82]

Looking over their shoulders at the rest of the beverage alcohol industry, the brewers could take heart from a decrease in the consumption of spirits, but they were less pleased with the rising popularity of wine, especially white wine, and notably of imported products, which by the 1990s were making up over half the market (and each of the major breweries had invested in Canadian wineries). A new generation of small-scale vintners looking to develop higher-quality wines with different grapes had sprung up in Ontario and British Columbia since the 1970s to try to reach the same kind of customers as the microbreweries were finding, but their overall impact was limited. In the mid-1980s, moreover, both the distillers and the vintners began to compete more directly for a mass market with a new drink called a "cooler," a beverage with about 5 per cent alcohol and combining liquor or wine with soft drinks or fruit juice. Young drinkers in particular liked these sweet, cold beverages, although the drinks did not seriously challenge the hegemony of beer. Indeed, it seems that they were add-ons to the alcohol consumer's diet rather than substitutions.[83]

Despite these efforts, the late twentieth century remained a period of relative sobering up. The great majority of Canadians still drank, but despite the undying efforts of the new liquor traffic to keep them knocking back great quantities of booze, a larger number of people were abstaining, and those who imbibed were consuming considerably less than they had on average in the previous three decades. They might occasionally drink enough (or more than enough) to feel the full effects of the alcohol in their bloodstreams, but the heavy drinkers among them were still a decidedly small minority—in 1990 only 18 per cent admitted to drinking more than seven drinks a week, and only 7 per cent more than fourteen a week.[84]

Producers, consumers, and governments had thus engaged in an intricate half-century dance around John Barleycorn. Brewers, distillers, and vintners successfully convinced most adult Canadians that drinking their products was part of participating in the good life. Governments were eventually convinced to make alcohol more accessible. Drinkers were not dupes, and they negotiated their own versions of pleasure, with the highlight on sociability. They welcomed the gradually more relaxed atmosphere of pubs and taverns, but also happily brought more alcohol into their homes for private socializing. Still, what once appeared to be increasing libertarianism abruptly reversed course after the 1970s, as consumption levels fell and excessive drinking faced new scorn. Moderation once again became compelling.

Despite the postwar changes in marketing and regulation, drinking patterns retained at least some of their long-standing distinctions. Men still drank much more than women—often mainly with other men—and tied their consumption to masculine identities. Most women joined drinking cultures in which they typically remained subordinated to their male partners, though more young women struck out on their own with female friends. Working-class and middle-class drinkers still tended to part company, both in the places where they drank and the products that they consumed. Cheap, mass-produced beer remained the most common alcoholic beverage among working men (and probably most working-class women), while drinkers from the middle and upper classes turned to an ever wider array of spirits, mixed drinks, wines, and specialty beers. Ethnic differences also multiplied, though the oldest cultural gulf, between the European colonizers and Canada's First Nations, continued, in part, through divergent drinking patterns.

THE 12 STEPS

WE ADMITTED WE WERE POWERLESS OVER AL...
...OUR LIVES HAD BECOME UNMANAGEA...

...LIEVE THAT A *POWER* GREATE...
...ULD RESTORE US TO SANI...

...ON TO TURN OUR WILL A...
...RE OF *GOD AS WE UNDE*...

...HING AND FEARLESS MORA...

...OD. TO OURSELVES AND T...
...E EXACT NATURE O...

...Y TO HAVE...

ten

Rediscovering the Alcoholic

⨭In the decades after the Second World War, people who liked to consume moderate amounts of alcohol in a relaxed fashion with family, friends, neighbours, or workmates became known as "social drinkers." Public policy had been redesigned to give these people plenty of leeway to buy and consume their favourite drinks in many more places with fewer constraints on their behaviour, aside from making sure that they were not slipping behind the wheel of an automobile with too much alcohol in their systems or otherwise endangering the lives of others.

Alongside this liberalization of the regulatory regime lingered a continuing concern about "problem drinkers." The term was exceedingly loose, blurring the line between, on the one hand, people who indulged in occasional binges with few long-term consequences and, on the other, heavy drinkers who got drunk often enough to disrupt their own lives and health and the lives of others around them. Although a wide range of people might indulge in binge drinking, most often heavy drinking remained a ritual of masculine identity among young bachelors. In postwar discussions about heavy intoxication, two groups loomed large: Aboriginal men and, as the legal drinking age fell, young men at high school, college, and university. Yet although there was plenty of public concern about binge drinking, especially when it came to drunk driving, it was no longer as widely assumed that this kind of heavy drinking was evidence of, or would inevitably create, a "craving for drink." Instead the focus shifted from the nature of the drink itself to the characteristics of the drinker.

From the 1940s onward, the people whom temperance activists would have pointed to as "habitual drunkards"—for decades denounced as living proof of the inevitable consequences of any contact with booze—were now labelled

Opposite page: *Alcoholics Anonymous was the largest organization that had ever existed in Canada for mutual support among self-declared alcoholics. Members like these ones attending the Ontario Regional Conference in 1957 united around a set of principles known as "The Twelve Steps."* (YUA, Telegram Collection, 1812) "alcoholics," and tended to be seen more as an atypical group apart from other drinkers. They compulsively drank large amounts every day, were chronically dependent on (some said, addicted to) alcohol, and needed special attention. Nor were they any longer primarily the extremely poor, marginal working-class men and women of the inner city, the so-called "skid-row types," who had dominated the public imagination for the previous century; they were also to be found in the comfortable and affluent households of the middle class.

This new focus seeped into public consciousness as Hollywood regularly splashed the image of white-collar problem drinkers across the silver screen in the postwar years, starting with the 1945 hit *The Lost Weekend*. The precise meaning of what was now regularly called "alcoholism" would remain as elusive as ever. Ironically, the postwar solutions proposed for dealing with alcoholics involved dusting off and refurbishing some old approaches to treating drunkards pioneered back in the nineteenth century.[1]

In the 1940s the only regular "treatment" that most severe alcoholics could expect was still a jail sentence. The Salvation Army soldiered on, and there were a few private sanatoria, such as the Homewood Sanitarium in Guelph and the tiny Glenmaple clinic east of Toronto (opened in 1946 and reopened as Shadow Brook two years later), though apparently far fewer than in the United States and much too expensive for most of the population (Shadow Brook charged $400 for three to four weeks of residential treatment). Public hospitals generally refused to deal with drunks, and general practitioners were not much more interested in them. "This disgraceful conduct wasn't considered a disease at all—just cantankerous no-good people," a former Ontario cabinet minister later recalled. Soon enough, though, two distinct, though closely allied, movements emerged in Canada, as in many other Western countries, with new solutions for their problems.[2]

Helping Hands

The first movement was a remarkably successful practice of mutual support. A therapy based on drunkards helping each other to overcome their patterns of heavy drinking was certainly not new. Experiments among Dashaways, Washingtonians, and Gospel Reformers, for instance, dated back a century, although most of those efforts had collapsed under the torrent of prohibitionism. In the early part of the twentieth century a few local organizations in the United States—notably the Emmanuel Clinic in Boston—had begun using mutual support groups, along with counselling and education. One graduate of that program, Richard R. Peabody, a troubled drinker from a rich Boston family, became an alcoholism counsellor in New York and in 1931 published *The Common Sense of Drinking*, a popularly written treatise that was widely used in treatment programs well into the 1950s. The approaches of these groups leaned away from heavy-handed moral suasion towards helping people find ways of dealing with their alcohol abuse. Rather than turning to medical theories and practices, lay counsellors drew on their own mixtures of the Social Gospel and new Freudian psychology to help "diagnose" the deeper moral and psychological problems that appeared to lie behind the heavy drinking.[3]

Although these counsellors also encouraged reformed drinkers to meet regularly in clubs, a different kind of meeting was also starting to happen. In 1935 two men with serious drinking problems, New York stockbroker Bill Wilson and Akron medical doctor Robert Smith, met and began to work out a program for helping alcoholics to stay sober. Earlier, in an effort to find the incentive to stop their own drinking, the two of them had each separately joined a branch of the Oxford Group, a far-flung, non-denominational evangelical Protestant fellowship. At its regular meetings, members discussed and promoted their own spiritual renewal. Wilson and Smith recruited alcoholics to attend these gatherings, but realized that they had the most success when the drinkers were able to talk directly to each other. They began to set up separate meetings of alcoholics, and came under criticism from other Oxford Group members for doing so. As a result, Wilson's group in New York left the Oxford Group in 1937 and Smith's in Akron in 1939. They carried on the spiritual emphasis in their new groups, which had no name until Wilson and Smith decided to publish a book to make their approach to alcoholism more widely known. The book's title, *Alcoholics Anonymous*, gave the roughly one hundred members a handy label, which was regularly shortened to "AA."[4]

Stories about the new organization in the mass media over the next two years brought a flood of new recruits, and AA groups soon began to function in Canada. The Reverend George A. Little, editor of Sunday School publications at the United Church of Canada headquarters, launched the first group in downtown Toronto in January 1943. An AA clubroom opened a few months later. Each local group was autonomous, and there was little central organization beyond a newsletter, regional and national "service" centres (to handle inquiries), and, beginning in 1951, an annual conference of North American members. By the mid-1950s more than one hundred thousand members were spread through some five thousand groups, a growing number of them outside the United States and Canada (by 1990 adherents in Europe, Latin America, Asia, and the British dominions made up 45 per cent of the nearly two million members). Given that the organization sent out no paid organizers, this is a stunning pattern of expansion. In the words of a recent study, "AA has for the most part spread from drunkard to drunkard as an authentic grass-roots movement."[5]

The AA approach to alcoholism owed less to theory than to trial and error. At the beginning the founders paid little attention to any psychoanalytic theory, but drew on some of the communitarian Protestantism of the Oxford Group and the philosophical pragmatism of William James. Far more input came from their own discoveries in their meetings. The decision to publish an accessible book-length exposition in 1939 (often referred to as the "Big Book") encouraged Bill Wilson to try to codify what had been learned in four years of experience. After careful consultation with the membership, he wrote up the organization's famous "Twelve Steps," which became its guiding principles. A decade later he would similarly publish the "Twelve Traditions" to encapsulate the basic operational procedures developed within the organization's loose, decentralized structure. The "Big Book" was recommended as a regular source of help and inspiration. It became the central text of the widening movement and helped to provide its coherence.

AA members operated on the assumption that alcoholism was a "malady" or even an "allergy," but drew little from medical notions of "disease." Unlike temperance activists, they were not prepared to blame alcohol itself, or alcoholics for getting into that state, unless they failed to do something about the "sickness" that made them different from other drinkers. Within AA thinking, there was no cure ("Once an alcoholic, always an alcoholic," the "Big Book" said), but life-long sobriety in a perpetual state of recovery was a realizable goal. In practice, the groups devoted little time to alcoholism and more to the individual alcoholic and his or her recovery, which, they believed, involved the body, mind, and spirit.[6]

The process began when drinkers "hit bottom"—that is, admitted they were powerless to overcome their condition on their own. They then surrendered completely to "a Power greater" than themselves (a God "as we understand Him," which could encompass a religious deity or, for agnostics and atheists, the collective power of the AA membership) to guide their future actions. They thus accepted their need for some kind of sudden or gradual conversion or "spiritual awakening" that would engender new hope.

Despite the evangelical overtones and later criticisms that it was a cult, AA always insisted that it was a "spiritual" and not a "religious" organization. In practice, following the "Steps" after conversion involved using simple daily rituals of self-evaluation, meditation, or prayer. It involved making restitution to anyone the practitioners may have harmed with their drunkenness, and performing service to other alcoholics—encouraging others to join, helping them "dry out," bringing them to meetings and attending regularly, relating his or her personal narrative and listening to others' (storytelling was always a key element, and much of the "Big Book" was taken up with personal histories). It involved discovering the power of mutual support through example, not advice or criticism, in staying sober.

At no point did any doctor or professional therapist intervene. The "healing" power was peer pressure and support. To sustain their commitment, AA provided a host of simple slogans as tools for following the program: "One day at a time," "Let go and let God," "Keep it simple," "Keep the plug in the jug," "I'm only one drink away from a drunk." What distinguished the AA program from most of its predecessors was the lack of emphasis on personal willpower ("taking the pledge") as the key to recovery and its adamant refusal to link up with any larger project of social reform, particularly temperance organizations. This was a fellowship, not a movement for social change, and the focus remained entirely on the individual alcoholic.[7]

New AA members might find their way to the organization by calling an answering service, attending a weekly meeting with a member (a "sponsor" who would continue to serve as a mentor), or being referred through a professional treatment centre or program. They would most likely find a casual, welcoming atmosphere. Membership was open to anyone who professed a desire to stop drinking, and all participants were considered equals. Group decisions were made democratically, and leadership was expected to rotate regularly. In recognition of the painful personal process at work, meetings were not public events, though visitors were usually welcome, and members retained their anonymity (even the co-founders' full names and photographs were not allowed into the media until after their deaths). Because each local branch was self-governing and self-sustaining financially, and because there were no unifying rituals or rigid rules of conduct (such as fraternal societies imposed), each local meeting had a distinctive flavour.

To be sure, there were subtle pressures on new recruits to shape their own stories into the well-worn AA narrative structure and to adopt the styles of speech expected in meetings (one writer has called the speaker texts "highly structured cultural performances"). Yet the spirit of tolerance meant that members were never allowed to interrupt, judge, or criticize each other, or to suggest specific remedies or treatments for their situations. A Canadian doctor who began sitting in on meetings in Toronto in 1946 noticed "their laughter, their easy friendliness, and their general freedom from embarrassment." AA offered a new way of life with a new community of like-minded people. The intimacy and sense of community in these gatherings were a powerful substitute for the social life of the tavern, and some local groups even organized their own clubhouses. Conflicts and tensions might surface and become the basis for breaking up a local group or starting a new one, but that was considered a perfectly acceptable organizational development.[8]

In practice, AA typically drew in specific parts of the population. Certainly far more men than women joined, and initially women were not always welcome, partly no doubt because of the male bonding and the implicitly patriarchal and perhaps even overtly misogynist discourse that could be at work in many of these meetings, and partly because of the still widespread association of female alcoholism with loose morals. As a product of the Depression era, the organization's program was also premised primarily on the need to get male breadwinners back into shape to meet the needs of their families. Some women fought back by forming their own all-female groups. In 1968 less than a quarter of the U.S. and Canadian AA members were female. Although wives of male AA members were sometimes allowed to attend meetings with their husbands, they tended to be steered into women's auxiliaries and then into their own organization, known as Al-Anon, founded in 1951 (the children of alcoholics could join Alateen by 1957).[9]

Membership had other tendencies: more older people than young, more middle-class drinkers than working-class, and far more whites than people of colour, who were seldom made welcome in the early years (in North America, at least). Whatever their background, at least half the participants tended to drop out within three months. The longer they hung in the more likely they were to stay, and stay sober. In the 1970s the ranks of AA members began to swell with more conscripts—people who had been caught in alcohol-induced run-ins with the law, especially drunk driving, and had chosen the option of treatment over jail. As a method, the AA program was eventually adopted by more than four hundred other organizations dealing with various "addictions" and problems other than alcoholism.[10]

The Doctors Take Charge

The non-hierarchical, non-professional features of Alcoholics Anonymous contrasted sharply with the other major new current of interest in alcoholism taking shape in the 1940s, a current eventually dubbed the "alcoholism movement." Once again, the inspiration was American. Medical researchers in the United States had responded to demands from legal authorities for more information on the metabolic and psychological impact of alcohol (for dealing with drunk drivers in particular) and gradually developed a renewed interest in the causes of alcoholism. They were adamant that their work was "scientific" and rejected the overt moralism of the moribund temperance movement. A key research centre was Yale University's Laboratory of Applied Physiology. The national Research Council on the Problems of Alcohol, founded in 1937, turned its attention more narrowly to an exclusive focus on alcoholism. With a small Carnegie Foundation grant, the Council launched a research project on the effects of alcohol on the body, but, ultimately, it showed less interest in new research than in a public-health agenda of disease prevention. Council propaganda set out to build public acceptance for the notion that problem drinkers had a particular illness that could be helped by medical intervention.[11]

When the Council's grant ran out in 1941, the leading researchers moved to Yale to continue their studies and two years later helped to launch the Center of Alcohol Studies, headed by the physiologist Elvin M. ("Bunky") Jellinek. This new unit drew in researchers from several disciplines, published the *Quarterly Journal of Alcohol Studies* and an increasing number of educational books and pamphlets, and in 1943 began staging an annual Summer School on Alcohol Studies. These gatherings brought together researchers and practitioners from varied backgrounds—hospitals, churches, social work institutions, schools, courts—for lectures, seminars, and courses on specific issues in handling problem drinking. In 1944 the centre also opened Yale Plan Clinics in Connecticut, staffed with diverse professionals, to counsel alcoholics and refer them to treatment programs, especially AA, and eventually to offer treatment themselves. The Yale researchers then convinced the state legislature to set up the country's first Commission on Alcoholism, a model soon followed elsewhere, to take over its clinics. In 1944 the Yale centre also spun off a National Committee for Education on Alcohol (renamed the National Committee on Alcoholism in 1954) to promote public education around these issues. The centre was not popular in its own academic setting, however, and in 1962 was forced to relocate to Rutgers University.[12]

A leading voice of this new movement was Jellinek, whose lectures, articles, and books helped to give the work its intellectual core. He began with the assumption that the problem was not alcohol, but rather what drove the alcoholic to drink compulsively. He insisted that such an individual was sick and worthy of treatment, not a moral degenerate. By the late 1940s he was talking about alcoholism as a disease and elaborating distinct stages of its development. He also provided a formula for calculating the number of alcoholics in a given population, based on the incidence of cirrhosis deaths, and in 1951 the World Health Organization (where he served as a consultant from 1950 to 1955) adopted that approach. Jellinek eventually consolidated these ideas into *The Disease Concept of Alcoholism*, published in 1960—a pivotal text

for the postwar alcoholism movement and a much more tentative and carefully qualified statement than many critics in the field acknowledged.

Jellinek's definition of the illness he was studying was extremely general—
"any use of any alcoholic beverages that causes any damage to the individual
or society or both"—but he itemized five specific types of alcoholism (each
labelled with a Greek letter). The most important of these in the United
States, Canada, and other predominantly Anglo-Celtic countries, he argued,
was "gamma alcoholism," which included increasing tolerance to alcohol,
physical dependency, withdrawal stress, and loss of control over the intake of
alcohol, and which was progressively degenerative over time. This was alcohol
"addiction," affecting fewer than 10 per cent of the population. Although he
admitted that the condition had its ambiguities (he had more success describ-
ing the progression of the disease than its origins), explanations lay more
within "psychiatric, psychopathological, and physiopathological" frameworks
than in economic or sociocultural realms. Numerous researchers and writers
elaborated their own adaptations of the "theory" in the 1950s and 1960s,
including the old turn-of-the-century belief that the disease was inherited
(weak versions of this research were directed at Aboriginal peoples to explain
their alleged inability to "hold their liquor"). Although medical science had
yet to provide irrefutable evidence for a "disease concept," that term carried
immense metaphoric weight as an easily understood slogan for those working
in the field and their audiences.[13]

To deal with this "disease," Jellinek and his colleagues advocated a variety
of treatments depending on the patient. All of their approaches shared with
Alcoholics Anonymous the nineteenth-century assumptions that the main
symptom was loss of control, that there was no permanent cure, and that
complete lifelong abstention was essential. This orientation made them sympathetic to AA (whose members to some degree shared the disease concept),
but they were far more likely to recommend the guiding hand of the professional, especially a doctor. Practitioners in the hospitals and specialized clinics
where most of the work was concentrated between the 1940s and 1960s
experimented with aversion therapies (including the later controversial drug
Antabuse and the Canadians' widely hailed alternative, Temposil), a huge variety of mood-modifying drugs (including LSD), and even prefontal lobotomies,
as well as the mutual-support process of AA and other group therapies.
Treatment could involve public-health workers, social workers, psychologists,
and other professionals, but medical practitioners remained central.[14]

To an extent not possible in the nineteenth century, the problem of compulsive drinking had been medicalized. The distilling and brewing industries
liked this new trend in alcohol studies because it took the focus off beverage

alcohol and concentrated on the problem drinker. The companies were prepared to help fund such research.

The Center of Alcohol Studies became a fountainhead of ideas that spread
quickly across North America and framed public discussion and public policies aimed at alcohol problems for at least the next three decades. Alcoholism
treatment, like retail sales, remained primarily a provincial responsibility in
Canada, and Canadians from nine provinces were participating in the Summer
School by the end of the 1940s. The participants included temperance leaders,
women's groups, clergymen, and educators (the Brewers' Association of
Ontario provided scholarships for Canadians to attend). Among them was
David Archibald, a young academic in the University of Toronto's School of
Social Work, who in 1949 was hired as the first research director of the
province's Liquor Control Board, with a mandate to develop an agency to
deal with alcoholism. Later that year the Ontario government created the
country's first such body, the Alcoholism Research Foundation (ARF), within
the Ministry of Health. Since the government's primary concern was clinical
treatment, this agency was initially responsible simply for a new hospital for
alcoholics in Toronto (branches gradually opened in other cities over the next
twenty years), but in 1950 new legislation expanded its terms of reference to
include ongoing research, rehabilitation, and education programs, as well as
community work with various voluntary organizations.[15]

Two developments in the start-up phase of this body showed the direction for the future of such work. First, although AA had been a major force in
lobbying for the hospital as a detoxification centre for members starting their
program, the organization was sidelined in the treatment work, which was
placed securely in the hands of doctors, nurses, and psychiatrists (although AA
members were encouraged to visit patients they had sent to the hospital). The
Alcoholism Research Foundation appointed a medical advisory board, and
most research over the first decade was contracted to faculty in the province's
research hospitals and medical schools. Gradually the Foundation's research
staff expanded through short-term contracts, scholarships, secondments, and
cross-appointments to include other professionals—social scientists and social
workers, in particular, including the eminent sociologist John R. Seeley, who
became research director in 1957. Like the worldwide field of "alcohol studies," its research became increasingly multidisciplinary. Yet, as Seeley later
recalled, the medical advisory group "couldn't quite distinguish between giving advice and giving orders," and in clinical work a physician headed every
treatment centre and the treatment teams within centres. Although the medical profession as a whole was slow to accept this new specialized field, doctors
remained solidly in the saddle of the movement. This was also true at

Ontario's leading privately owned treatment centre, eventually known as the Bell Clinic.[16]

The second step was to look southward for ideas and inspiration. The new foundation was explicitly modelled on the new institutions for dealing with alcoholism that were appearing in the United States at the time. Archibald spent two weeks with Jellinek getting plenty of help in designing the new agency. "We worked together setting out the general structure of the proposed Foundation, its major responsibilities, its major lines of investigation and study, and the kind of people required to develop and work in the organization," he later wrote. "All during the Foundation's early growth and development, we were in regular contact with Jellinek, both by visit and by letter." Archibald also took fifteen people from various Ontario agencies and organizations to Yale for a special conference with Jellinek and his associates. A few years later the Manitoba Liquor Enquiry Commission also invited Jellinek up to Winnipeg for an extended visit, and in 1959 the esteemed American would take up a three-year position as research consultant with Ontario's Foundation, where, according to its staff, he was "of very great benefit to many research undertakings." Ontario's premier Leslie Frost reputedly wanted ARF to get the most from this connection: "Don't get into a big research program," he advised. "You can take the results we get from Yale and you can divide them by 10."[17]

The U.S. influence was evident in a background paper that laid out the Foundation's initial view of alcoholism:

a. Alcoholism is a disease and the alcoholic is a mentally and physically ill person, not an amoral being.

b. The alcoholic can be effectively treated and helped by modern therapeutic procedures.

c. The alcoholic, economically and socially, is worth helping.

In 1954 a researcher at ARF published its first article using the Jellinek formula for calculating the alcoholic population, and by the end of the 1960s ARF was confidently announcing that there were 125,000 alcoholics in Ontario. The Foundation's staff knew that the public needed to be convinced of this radical break with prevailing conceptions of drunkards, and that alcoholics themselves had to learn about the nature of their "disease" before it was too late. Among its many educational efforts, the Foundation hired writer Ted Allan to produce fifteen-minute radio programs entitled "A Sickness Everyone Hates—But Few Understand" and "A Secret Illness." It also worked with the National Film Board on three films that demonstrated Jellinek's theory of alcoholism, and sponsored "It's Best to Know," a comic book aimed at school children that eventually sold millions of copies across North America. In 1961, again with Jellinek's advice, ARF also started its own Summer School for professionals in the field, which rotated to a different university campus each year. In 1978 this training program got permanent status at the University of Toronto as the School for Addiction Studies, which would provide courses for nearly four thousand people by the end of the 1980s. By the early 1970s the Foundation was distributing thousands of copies of publications, making and distributing films, and producing radio spots to raise the profile of alcohol (and drug) abuse. The impressive output of its research staff had brought international recognition and respect.[18]

Differential Treatment

People arriving for help at the ARF clinic (modelled on the Yale Plan Clinics) encountered a heavily psychiatric therapeutic program. After an initial diagnostic interview with a doctor or social worker, the individual could choose two-to-three-week in-patient treatment in the Foundation's small hospital or an ongoing out-patient program. Those who moved in got a steady diet of lectures, films, and discussion groups, some individual sessions with a psychiatrist, social worker, or physician, and, most likely, aversion-therapy and/or psychoactive drugs. Out-patients had some combination of individual interviews, group psychotherapy, and drugs. The Foundation saw its research and treatment programs as being closely linked, using its clinical work to expand the knowledge about alcoholism. It consequently tried to deflect most chronic alcoholics to hospitals and other out-patient and detoxification services. This orientation culminated in the opening of a hundred-bed teaching hospital known as the Institute for the Study of Addiction in 1971.[19]

In practice the "alcoholism movement" in Canada, as in the United States, treated alcoholics differently on the basis of their gender and class. An implicit operating assumption was that those with the "disease" at the heart of this project were men (in his early research, Jellinek had rejected data gathered from women because the information diverged so much from that of men). Far less was written about female alcoholics. Treatment programs rarely acknowledged the particular experience of women in a patriarchal society and women's probable responses to particular therapies, and relatively few facilities made space for women. New Brunswick, for example, had nothing available until 1974. (Then, too, women with heavy domestic responsibilities might find a prolonged stay in an institution difficult, if not impossible.) Indeed, the analytical construction of "alcoholism" focused on the disintegration of acceptable masculinities in the face of various anxieties. Men needed to be rescued from their "un-masculine" dependency on alcohol, their "immature" neediness, and their overly "feminine" emotionalism, because "good men" should be as self-reliant and stoic as possible. Some of the alcohol studies literature even hinted at suppressed homosexuality among alcoholics. The goal of treatment was to make alcoholic men capable of filling the stereotypic roles of responsible breadwinner.[20]

Within the new medico-moral analytical framework, moreover, researchers and practitioners began to discuss the "alcoholic marriage." The wives of alcoholics were cast as "co-dependents" who had to share responsibility for their husbands' dilemmas and had to be exhorted to help them grapple with their disease—which was a throwback to the suggestion of the Royal Commission on the Liquor Traffic that working men would spend less time in saloons if their wives were better cooks and housekeepers, although this time the wives' alleged failings were mostly psychological. In contrast to earlier temperance ideology, the alcoholic's family was not so much threatened as threatening, the source of the social problems flowing from excessive drinking.[21]

Among the men, the blue-collar working class tended to get specific treatment. Heavy drinkers from the upper and middle classes would be more likely to find their own way to private clinics, Alcoholics Anonymous, or other treatment services. But many male wage-earners found themselves pushed coercively towards institutional treatment programs. One group came from the ranks of "public inebriates," many of them part of the "skid-row" population of men in the heart of large cities. These men put heavy demands on social-welfare agencies and city jails. Starting in 1951, inmates in the Mimico Reformatory on the edge of Toronto could spend their last month in custody in a voluntary treatment and rehabilitation program. In 1968 ARF started a pilot project in non-medical detoxification, which soon became the basis of much wider public policy in the province.[22]

Besides those in the clutches of the police and courts, some workers also faced pressure from their bosses to overcome disruptive habits resulting from drinking, such as absenteeism. Otherwise they risked losing their jobs. In the 1940s and 1950s, aside from Bell Telephone and Eastman Kodak, few Canadian companies seemed interested in alcoholism programs as part of their expanding "human resources" and personnel work, in contrast to some large U.S. corporations such as Du Pont and Allis Chalmers. The alcoholism movement approached them nonetheless. In 1950 the North American organization of company doctors, the American Association of Industrial Physicians and Surgeons (later renamed the American Occupational Medical Association), established a Committee on Problem Drinking, whose goal was to encourage company doctors to treat alcoholic employees more sympathetically. It was chaired by Dr. Gordon Bell, who ran a private alcoholism treatment clinic in Toronto and served as company doctor for four local firms, and included Dr. Harvey Cruickshank, who since 1947 had used his position as medical director of Bell Telephone to develop a company-wide policy for managers to deal with problem drinkers.[23]

Like its counterparts at Yale, who launched the "Yale Plan for Business and Industry" and put an "Industrial Consultant" on the road to visit corporate offices, Ontario's Alcoholism Research Foundation also sought out major companies to convince them that alcoholics were largely full-time wage-earners, not "skid-row" derelicts, and to urge them to adopt workplace-based treatment programs, eventually known as "employee assistance programs." A two-day conference in Ottawa in 1953 drew 140 personnel officers and other industrial executives, and in the following year a newsletter on alcoholism was produced for personnel managers. But few employers responded. In 1962 two industrial consultants were hired away from other corporate jobs to organize a more systematic pitch to small groups of chief executive officers about the value of introducing treatment programs, but four years later the Foundation decided that it needed to open a demonstration treatment unit if industrialists were going to be convinced. It still failed to make much of dent in Canadian management policies, though the Canadian Armed Forces proved interested. Alberta's Alcoholism Foundation organized similar conferences and workshops and worked with individual companies. All these efforts involved appealing to top-down paternalism, with the hope of using managerial threats to coerce heavy drinkers. "Job probation is often an effective motivation in getting the alcoholic into treatment," the executive director of the Alcoholism Foundation of Alberta wrote in 1959. There is no evidence that activists in the alcoholism movement put much effort into bringing unions into the process, despite a growing interest on the part of some of the larger international unions. Not surprisingly, the language used by the labour movement played on industrial efficiency rather than human rights.[24]

A study of patients at the ARF clinic between 1958 and 1960 (sponsored by the Foundation itself) highlighted the class differences at work in even the "voluntary" programs. In the late 1950s one in six working-class drinkers came to the clinic after being nudged to do so by various social agencies, generally as a result of unemployment. Staff at general hospitals sent a slightly larger proportion of working-class drinkers, often people who had been recuperating from devastating drinking binges (compared to much lower percentages of middle- and upper-class patients). Far more often than the records of those from affluent backgrounds, the files of working-class patients contained such judgments as "having low intelligence, being impatient, lacking insight, lacking motivation, suffering from loneliness, being retiring, being quiet, and having social defects." The researchers concluded, "The recorded class patterns in behaviour and personality were at least in part due to the difficulties that some therapists had in establishing intimate relationships with patients of low social status." Only a quarter of the working-class alcoholics entered the in-patient program (compared to closer to half of the other classes), perhaps because they could not afford to. Those that did encountered strong staff biases. Nurses tended to observe that they did not "fit well" into ward populations because their behaviour was allegedly "'uncouth,' 'crude,' 'abusive,' 'disrespectful,' 'inter-fering,' and so forth." In either treatment stream, working-class patients were more likely to see physicians than psychiatrists, and they thus got exposed to "less uncovering techniques" and more simple support and advice. Clinic staff tended to assume that these people were not good candidates for psychother-apy, because "persons in the lower social classes are less likely to have the capacity for verbalization than the better educated classes." Instead they directed them to "protective" drugs (Antabuse and Temposil), and, to a lesser extent, group therapy. They also got sedatives and anti-depressants far less often than the upper- and middle-class patients did. These workers, it seemed, were "poor treatment risks," and "individual treatment was not warranted." The investigators were blunt: "A first step towards a more equitable distribu-tion of therapies would be the realization among those who treat alcoholics that current clinical practice favours patients from the higher classes." They might also have made more of their own casual observation about ethnicity and race—that 97 per cent of the patients in these programs were Anglo-Celtic, "and only a fraction of one per cent was non-white."[25]

By the early 1970s, Ontario's high-profile, internationally respected Founda-tion was not alone. Every province and the federal government had created some kind of government-sponsored institution to study and treat alcoholics and their problems. Many of the provinces had moved much more slowly than Ontario and devoted far fewer resources to research, and there was con-siderable variation in the administration of treatment programs among the provinces. Quebec, for example, eventually dissolved its separate commission and integrated its work into other health services. Therapeutic methods also varied considerably. New Brunswick's new Lonewater Farm treatment centre used mainly the fresh air and physical labour that nineteenth-century propo-nents of "inebriate asylums" had recommended. Yet the highly medicalized "alcoholism movement" had become well entrenched in Canada. In 1980 the country had 340 specialized agencies, two-thirds of which had appeared since 1970, at a total cost of $70 million (up from $14 million a decade earlier). A high proportion of the treatment staff at all of these centres were recovered alcoholics.

New Paradigms

By 1980 the alcoholism field was becoming more and more difficult to describe as anything like a unitary movement. The theory and practice that were borrowed so liberally from the United States had already begun to unravel, and the next decade would see it spin off in many new directions.

The theory that had carried alcoholism studies out of the 1940s was the first to collapse. From the start the term "alcoholism" had conveyed multiple meanings. Did its meaning relate to the physiological evidence of excessive drinking, especially cirrhosis of the liver, or the social behaviour of the heavy drinker? The "disease concept" had taken hold with relatively little empirical evidence to sustain it. Jellinek himself had built much of his theoretical edifice on a seriously flawed study of ninety-eight AA members who responded to a questionnaire printed in the organization's newsletter in 1946. The concept of the illness lacked the clearly identifiable source of other diseases: a germ, or a virus, perhaps. Nor did it have a regular, predictable form. By the 1960s researchers were reporting many versions of alcoholic behaviour, drawn from both clinical studies and large national surveys, that did not fit Jellinek's tight model of progressive deterioration, particularly the alleged "loss of control" that "gamma" alcoholics in particular were supposed to experience. International connections among researchers also brought to light significantly different patterns of alcohol abuse and dependency. It became clear that a complex variety of drinking sequences and associated effects existed, not a uniform set of symptoms that could add up to a single disease. Jellinek's rejoinder in 1960 that "a disease is what the medical profession recognizes as such" did not clear away the confusion.[26]

And then there was the thorny question of what caused alcoholism (its "etiology"). Why did some people get the "disease" but not others? The community of researchers, doctors, clinicians, and other professionals in this field could not agree on this crucial issue and frequently muddled the causes with the consequences. Their answers tended to fall into two broad categories with numerous variants: the cause was either something unique in alcoholics' bodies (brain lesions, nutritional deficiencies, endocrine dysfunction) or something in their minds (the "alcoholic personality") that predisposed them to alcoholism. Often some mixing of the physiological and the psychological occurred, but ultimately no single entity could be labelled satisfactorily as the triggering force for heavy drinking. If alcoholics were not a homogeneous group with a single identifiable disease, the implications for treatment were obviously profound, including the hotly debated possibility that alcohol abusers could at some point return to more "normal" levels of drinking. The confusion was evident in surveys in the 1960s, which tended to show that the general population had absorbed the disease concept to a remarkable extent, but still rooted it in a moralist framework. Most of the public believed that alcoholics were responsible for their own "illnesses." Perhaps "Once an alcoholic, always an alcoholic" was not at all true.[27]

Hard-core disease theorists relabelled the condition as "alcohol dependency syndrome," but by the 1980s many practitioners and researchers shared a new consensus that heavy drinking was a behavioural disorder that had many different causes, produced many different results, and could not be traced to a specific "disease," especially not one with clear biological or psychological roots. Some researchers used the term "biopsychosocial" for this new, looser analytical framework. With the help of the LeDain Commission on the Non-Medical Use of Drugs, many researchers in the field in Canada had also come to see alcohol as only one of a number of problematic "recreational" drugs, which were often combined, and began to redefine heavy use as "substance abuse." In a sharp turn away from the postwar consensus, these practitioners were shifting the focus back onto the alcohol, rather than the alcoholic. Ontario's anti-alcoholism agency had already renamed itself the Alcoholism and Drug Addiction Research Foundation in 1961, and simplified that to the Addiction Research Foundation in 1969. The very concept of "addiction" itself—increasingly loosely applied to a host of other compulsive behaviours (gambling, overeating, television-watching, shopping, working, to name a few)—was fraught with problems, because so many "addicts" were apparently able to move in and out of the compulsion without complete loss of control. The word "dependency" quietly slipped in to replace addiction.[28]

Many practitioners were also concerned that the medical model of "treatment" had few positive results to report. As an indication of the sense of drift that had set in, one physician told a conference that he relied on "the SHAG method . . . a 'Scientifically Half-Assed Guess.'" Medical treatment frequently had no permanent effect, and often those who had no regular, continuing contact with professional supervision apparently did as well (or as poorly) as those in treatment. Even the success rate of AA methods appeared to be extremely limited (to the extent that it could even be measured).[29]

In this context of critical debate and practical experimentation within the now vastly larger field of "alcohol studies," new approaches to helping heavy drinkers break the habit continued to proliferate. Many of them were non-medical, community-based services, rather than help given in hospital settings. Many made alcohol abusers voluntary, active players in the process, without the simple, old-style, moralistic exhortation to renewed willpower (the "pledge"), and attempted to deal with a complex amalgam of issues and behavioural adaptations that prompted people to make alcohol so central to their lives. Each case had its own inner momentum and its own process for helping an alcohol abuser develop a less destructive and more satisfying life.

Specialized programs or treatments targeted women, youth, Aboriginal peoples, and others. Unions promoted new programs for their members, usually spearheaded by recovered alcoholics who wanted to confront fellow workers with the need to get help with drinking problems. Some unions ran their own counselling programs, but more often they negotiated jointly run programs with employers. Progress was evidently slow; only a third of workplaces in Ontario had an "employee assistance program" in 1993, a doubling over 1989. Similarly, and on an even wider scale, Aboriginal peoples took hold of their own treatment programs and based them on the spiritual healing practices of their communities, such as sweat lodges, presided over by band elders. By the 1990s the federal government was funding fifty-one residential programs for Aboriginal peoples and addiction counsellors in their communities. Many bands imposed complete prohibition on their own reserves, though enforcement remained a huge problem. At the close of the decade, a few were experimenting with "harm-reduction" policies to regulate (rather than ban) alcohol use on the reserves.[30]

Many researchers grew increasingly uncomfortable with the narrow focus on "alcoholics," which ignored what they believed was a much wider array of problems arising from excessive drinking. Some people engaged with the issue began to use the term "problem drinking" or "alcohol abuse" in preference to "alcoholism" as a way of recognizing the huge diversity of behaviour and its impact across the whole society, and to propose "a continuum of care." At Ontario's Alcoholism Research Foundation, what soon became a distinctively Canadian contribution to the debate began with John Seeley's 1960 study of cirrhosis rates in the general population across time. Seeley found that the rates declined as people constrained their spending on alcohol. Along with other empirical studies, the conclusion reached was that, across the Western world, heavy drinkers were the problem, that their numbers increased and they drank more when per capita consumption rose and less if booze was less easily available, and that the key therefore was to restrain per capita consumption. This notion was eventually labelled the "single distribution model." It shifted the blame back to alcohol itself and away from the notion that the source of the alcoholism lay in the "sickness" of particular individuals.

Indeed, the individual alcoholic became much less important in this new line of thinking. The public-policy package for controlling per capita consumption that would flow from these findings would include higher prices, heavier taxation, fewer retail outlets, restricted advertising, and more public education—that is, an emphasis on prevention—rather than focusing on experiments in medical science. The Rutgers school resisted such a proposition. Clinical psychologists and psychiatrists were sceptical, and the alcohol beverage industries greeted it with horror and began funding research to debunk such a model. The remnants of the temperance movement were much happier with the approach. It was also a theory that ran against the grain of the libertarian expressiveness that had taken hold across so much of the culture. It had nonetheless become the central thrust of ARF ideology by the 1970s and won considerable international acceptance, including from the World Health Organization.[31]

Within Canada politicians generally ignored this new argument in setting their alcohol pricing policies, although the debates about therapeutic directions in treatment programs played into the hands of government budget-trimmers in the 1980s and 1990s. More generally, many more activists in the alcoholism movement embraced this new conceptualization of drinking problems because it shifted some blame back onto the shoulders of the heavy drinkers and connected with the concerns of the "neo-temperance movement" about the social costs of drunkenness, notably drunk driving. Unfortunately, it was a theory that could not easily explain what was actually happening in Canada in the 1980s and 1990s. Not only was there evidence that making booze more accessible through new taverns or banning "happy hours" had made no appreciable difference to alcohol-related accidents and impaired driving, but there were also indications that restraining the flow of booze was not co-related to bringing down consumption levels and the incidence of the whole range of drinking problems (such as cirrhosis and drunk driving). Those problems had declined on their own despite the exploding numbers of retail outlets and licensed establishments and the longer hours of operation in both.

At the close of the twentieth century, the whole treatment "industry" managed to touch only a small percentage of heavy drinkers directly. The estimated rates of "alcoholism" had dropped from 4,200 per 100,000 population aged twenty and over in 1976 to 2,600 in 1989, but the great majority of those people must have overcome their drinking problems on their own. When 11,000 people across Canada were surveyed by telephone in 1989, only 8.5 per cent of those who admitted to drinking problems had reached out to any services, and more than three-quarters of those had turned to Alcoholics Anonymous. Although other evidence from Ontario suggests that many more people were attending AA meetings or trying other treatment programs, the more than one thousand specialized treatment agencies across the country still served a tiny market within the drinking population.[32]

Since the 1930s, then, attitudes to the "problem drinker" had evolved and changed considerably. The moralistic condemnation of the "habitual drunkard" had gradually given way to a concept of an illness, "alcoholism," which was believed to be beyond individual control and could be tackled either by mutual support from fellow alcoholics or by medical intervention (or both). Governments had eventually responded with new research and treatment programs, and public opinion had slowly absorbed some version of the disease concept as a new understanding of heavy drinking. Yet any consensus about appropriate therapies for alcoholics had broken down by the 1970s, and in any case the treatments seemed to be having an extremely limited impact on the "problem." Amidst a new diversity of approaches to helping alcohol abusers came a rising chorus of experts insisting that prevention was at least as important as treatment—creating, ironically, a faint echo of the concern about too much drinking that had animated the old temperance movement.

A by-product of this new direction in thinking about alcohol abuse was to leave any scientific definition of "alcoholism" in tatters. By the close of the twentieth century, "alcoholics" in popular parlance were simply people who drank enough to endanger their own lives and the lives of those around them. While this meaning was not much different from the older usage of "drunkard," especially since it might assume the alcoholic's personal responsibility for his or her problem, it was more likely to be applied more sympathetically—an important legacy of the "disease concept" and its promoters.

eleven

The Elusive John Barleycorn

Opposite page: *Reading the Bible versus enjoying a bottle of booze: around the the turn of the twentieth century these Alberta cowboys gave a playful performance of the extremes of morality that would rage through Canadian society for generations.* (GA, NA-1130-15)

THE STORY OF BOOZE HAS been different everywhere alcohol has been consumed, and for some four hundred years those of us occupying the northern half of the North American continent have dealt with John Barleycorn in our own ways. That is not to say that our drinking cultures and general attitudes to alcoholic beverages do not have parallels in other societies. But the particular configuration of peoples, economies, cultures, and state policies that evolved in what became Canada shaped a particular experience with alcoholic beverages that sets us apart from the equally distinctive stories elsewhere. Looking back, we can see those patterns more clearly.

The first Europeans who settled in what is now Canada brought attitudes to and practices of alcohol consumption that were common across Europe and throughout many rural, pre-industrial societies around the world. In both French and British settlements, beverage alcohol was imported and locally produced, and was regularly integrated into daily life as a food and medicine, a tonic for heavy labour, and the main lubricant of celebrations in family, workplace, and community among all social classes. Alcohol was a relatively cheap luxury that gave short-term gratification, but most people were too poor to indulge in frequent heavy drinking and they limited their consumption mainly to clearly demarcated occasions. Sometimes this drinking involved drunken binges, particularly among men, but intoxication was rarely perceived as a grave social problem, except, to some degree, among First Nations peoples, who, like their counterparts in the South Pacific, Africa, and other colonized areas, learned to place alcohol at the centre of their trading relations with the European newcomers.[1]

In many parts of the world, those patterns continued well into the nineteenth and twentieth centuries. But around 1830 British North America first began to diverge, as broad-based social movements sprang up to challenge the place of alcohol in colonial society. The timing was far earlier than in most European countries and the new colonies of the future Commonwealth dominions of Australia and New Zealand, and reflected a particular convergence of economic, social, and cultural forces. The most visible change may have been the wider availability and rapidly increasing consumption of alcohol in the many new taverns that opened up in city and country. But heavy drinking was common in many other countries and regions—Australia and New Zealand, for example—without provoking any significant moralistic backlash. The burning issue more specifically was the decided preference for spirits, as thousands of Upper Canadian farmers turned their surplus grain into whisky (much like British farmers and German and Eastern European peasants in the same era) and new commercial distilleries in the colonies cranked up production. The Atlantic region too welcomed the steady flow of West Indian rum that British mercantilism brought to that area.[2]

As in many other places—Germany, England, Ireland, Australia, New Zealand, Finland, Iceland, Norway, the Netherlands, Switzerland, and later France, Italy, and Russia—the first attacks on alcohol in British North America took aim specifically at the rising tide of liquor, and not beer, cider, and wine. The increasing consumption of spirits may have generated concern that drinking often led to drunken binges, which tended to be the pattern in spirits-drinking countries. Yet something more must have been needed, because Russia and Poland also experienced heavy drinking of hard liquor in the nineteenth century without sparking a major temperance movement.[3]

Rather than looking primarily to a dramatic change in drinking practices, we need to focus on how and why particular groups in colonial society constructed fairly old drinking practices in a new framework of "social problems." In part, the search for an explanation for the reaction against spirits has to take into account the emerging social structure of British North America. Like the United States and some parts of Europe, British North America was home to large numbers of small-scale producers, especially farmers and artisans, people looking increasingly for commercial success and political and religious independence. They placed an emphasis on personal responsibility and self-discipline and, initially, were at the forefront of those turning a critical eye on heavy drinking. Only gradually during the 1830s and 1840s did the leadership of the anti-drink forces become more bourgeois. Many of those leaders and plebeian activists wove this concern about sobriety into their new commitment to democracy and liberalism, but, in contrast to the experience of plebeian radicalism in France or Italy during the same period, in British North America it was often the preachers of evangelical Protestantism, particularly

Methodists, Baptists, and Presbyterians, who were delivering the message. These men made the connections between self-discipline, sobriety, and personal improvement as a way of understanding and ordering human life. International and regional comparisons indicate that evangelicalism—and not merely Protestantism—was the crucial cultural variable that explains the strength of temperance sentiment. Lutherans in Denmark, Catholics in Ireland or Quebec, and Anglicans everywhere might urge restraint in personal behaviour, including moderation in alcohol consumption, but, as liturgical, ritualistic faiths, their brand of Christianity generally did not promote as much of a sense of individual responsibility for moral perfection as the evangelicals demanded.[4]

The idea of moving from faith to social action came from the American temperance pioneers, also steeped in evangelicalism, who made the case for a separate, non-denominational movement to fight booze. By mid-century they were also providing the new strategic model of statutory prohibition, which had undoubtedly drawn inspiration from the large and powerful movement to abolish slavery in the United States. The message of the American teetotallers soon spread across oceans to other countries. Organizations such as the Good Templars and the Woman's Christian Temperance Union amassed supporters in the British Isles and dominions, and many parts of Western and Northern Europe, but the impact was uneven and rarely as great as in Canada, where the particular mix of class and culture would give life to this movement for the next century. Temperance was a specific cultural project that had to win over supporters. It was no more inevitable and necessary to capitalist development than fascism would be later on, and, although bourgeois constraint of some kind spread throughout the emerging capitalist world in the nineteenth century, the focus on suppressing all beverage alcohol from daily life was quite specific to North America, where the idea had much more appeal than almost anywhere else outside the Islamic world.[5]

Canada's early temperance movements did not manage to completely transform public and private morality, but their impact was considerable nonetheless. Temperance ideology was woven into large parts of the new bourgeois culture of individualism and self-control among men and serene domesticity among women that was taking shape by the 1840s—around the time when the British North American colonies were lurching into a more commercial and, eventually, industrialized and urbanized era of capitalist development. "Respectable" people withdrew from the arenas of celebratory binges and regular public drinking that their predecessors had so comfortably visited, and retreated into more privatized domestic spaces or more refined, morally sound, and sometimes exclusive public venues—churches, mechanics' institutes, concert halls, posh hotels, and social clubs, among others. Taverns were left to the more disreputable—primarily male urban wage-earners—and soon evolved into cornerstones of working-class bachelor cultures. Simultaneously, public drunkenness was more aggressively repressed as part of the general campaigns to reduce the disorder of the streets, and working-class drunks became by far the most numerous criminals in police courts across the country. As in many other colonial contexts, Aboriginal peoples (whose drinking had generally been shaped by white traders and state paternalism) found themselves legally barred from drinking.

To reinforce the link between sobriety and industry, employers banned drinking on the job, probably more aggressively than in many European (and Third World) industrial settings, and, although some workers would continue to sneak a swig of their favourite booze at the workplace, most drinkers could enjoy alcohol only in the more sharply demarcated time after work—the evening and particularly the weekend. In the late nineteenth and early twentieth centuries, moreover, North American industry came to have a much more heavy-handed managerial system than in many other parts of the industrializing world. The practice, much more rigid, authoritarian, and intensified, allowed less room for sociability on the job, and wage-earners consequently had a greater need for reaching out and relaxing after work.

Most of these changes in drinking practices and occasions were taking place in other Western industrializing countries over the nineteenth and early twentieth centuries, though, in contrast to French, Italian, or some Latin American drinking practices, Canadians probably consumed more of their alcohol outside the home and separately from meals. The Canadian brewing and distilling industries, now demonized as the "Liquor Traffic," expanded their productive capacity and marketing systems to supply this growing leisure-time market, and beer rapidly overtook spirits as the most popular drink among urban workers. The controversy over drinking henceforth raged over its status as a leisure activity, especially among working men, and the potential disruption of family life when the breadwinner joined his mates and John Barleycorn in a nearby saloon. Critics of the new leisure-time drinking practices demanded that work and play not be radically counterposed activities, but rather that the sobriety and industriousness of the work world should extend into "free time" and govern how people spent money for pleasure.

This new configuration of drinking led to three overlapping but competing discourses, all of them focusing on heavy drinking and drunkenness and looking to state intervention. All of them hoped to use a mix of overt coercion and the inculcation of self-regulation. Legal authorities addressed the issues of public order on the streets, specialized medical men promoted new therapies for the "disease" they had identified as "inebriety," and moral reformers highlighted the destructive power of the "Liquor Traffic" on individual willpower. The courts clamped down on drunkards and some doctors struggled to get public (and professional) support for their programs, and by the 1870s new temperance movements had taken shape to demand prohibition. For the next half-century, these movements targeted retail sales of alcohol, especially public drinking. Displaying a diversity of motivations and goals within their ranks, the proponents formed broad coalitions under their prohibition umbrella. In the cities the prohibitionist project brought together businessmen, professionals, middle-class women, and, to a decreasing extent, working men. By the early twentieth century the movement had an unmistakable flavour that expressed the optimistic aspirations of middle- to upper-class, English-speaking, evangelical Protestants for a solidly British, morally sound, economically "efficient" nation. In contrast to the Northern European countries with strong prohibitionist movements—Finland, Norway, Sweden, Iceland—where suppressing alcohol was a part of the program of the labour movement and the left, Canada's urban prohibition movement had a decidedly bourgeois and petty-bourgeois cast.[6]

A different note was sounded in rural Canada, where prohibition became part of the arsenal of many farmers and their rural allies against the allegedly destructive forces of a centralizing, increasingly urbanized national economy (and, in the Quebec countryside, Anglo jingoism). The earliest and most consistent prohibitionist victories were in the rural areas of Eastern Canada, where arguably temperance (and its evangelical parents) became a central part of a culture of resistance and survival.[7] The burgeoning farmers' movements of the early twentieth century all incorporated prohibition into their potent political challenge to the direction of the Canadian economy and public affairs. Spanning small town and big city were the women organized independently in the WCTU, whose focus was much more on gender relations and the problems faced by women.

All of these groups incorporated a ban on alcohol into their larger visions of a reordered Canadian society. Rather than simply imposing behavioural expectations on drinkers (through some kind of "social control"), they all expected conformity with their own values and lifestyle choices.

Tactically, the campaigns that these movements launched emphasized mass mobilization, open public debate, and popular politics: huge petitions, mass lobbying, and plebiscites, in particular. But the idea of shutting down alcohol sales proved to be far from universally popular, and politicians dodged the issue as often as possible. The first great campaign for national prohibition in the mid-1870s gave birth only to the quickly discredited local-option approach of the 1878 Scott Act, and the second mobilization in the 1890s led only to a royal commission and an inconclusive national plebiscite. Provincial governments everywhere but in Prince Edward Island similarly refused to move decisively against the liquor traffic. Certainly, by the turn of the century, the booze producers represented a substantial bloc of corporate power that governments were rarely willing to antagonize (and on whom they relied for substantial state revenues), but opposition went far beyond such narrow self-interest.

From the 1850s through the 1920s, prohibition generated stiff resistance from many parts of Canadian society and eventually pitted classes (and class factions), ethnic groups, and regions against each other. Non-evangelical Christians denied the need for heavy-handed state intervention in moral reform. French Canadians deplored the association of the temperance cause with attacks on their language and religion, as did new European immigrants. Men and women from bourgeois circles worried about the threat that prohibition posed to the rule of law, state finances, and their evolving cultural and recreational preferences. Many working-class men resented how their drinking habits were being placed at the centre of the prohibitionist critique and how their off-the-job social life and neighbourhood recreational centres, the saloons, were being targeted. Those areas of the country with fewer evangelical Protestants, more francophones and continental European immigrants, more city dwellers, and proportionally more men—notably Quebec, British Columbia, and non-English communities in New Brunswick, Ontario, and the Prairie provinces—refused to vote themselves dry. Wherever prohibitory laws were passed, secretive drinking continued—including in the bedrock of temperance allegiance in the countryside—thanks to a flourishing underground economy of smuggling and illicit sales. Indeed, one major long-term impact of the temperance campaigns was to turn an appreciation of alcohol into a naughty, disreputable pleasure.

The prohibitionist project thus proceeded by fits and starts. By the early twentieth century, hopes for national prohibition had been crushed by the political resistance of French Canada and by court decisions that awkwardly divided constitutional jurisdiction over this issue and forced the battles over "banishing the bar" onto the provincial level. Only tiny Prince Edward Island was prepared to implement a provincewide shutdown. Elsewhere, provincial governments would go no further than tightening up the licensing system, notably closing badly managed saloons and limiting hours of sales. To choke off alcohol consumption more completely, the dry forces had to fight a myriad of battles over "local option," which eventually produced a large patchwork of dry outposts, mainly in rural areas. It took the special conditions of wartime mobilization after 1914 to convince many more Canadians that closing down the liquor traffic was appropriate. By 1918 the whole country outside

Quebec was finally, if briefly, dry. Enforcement in both the local-option and provincewide phases of prohibition, however, was not only fragmented by jurisdictional divisions, but also often only half-hearted. In frustration, prohibitionists in many communities took the law into their own hands and created vigilante committees to attack, root out, and prosecute bootleggers. Generally they were no more successful in these endeavours than were state officials in theirs.

Internationally Canada was at the most repressive end of the anti-booze policy spectrum, joined by only four other Western nations. From 1920 to 1933 the United States had national prohibition (in contrast to Canada's provincial patchwork) through a constitutional amendment. Iceland also banned booze from 1915 to 1921, as did the new Soviet Union from 1917 to 1925 and Finland from 1919 to 1932. Like the Americans, Canadian prohibitionists were uncompromising in their attacks on all beverages containing ethanol. Several countries (including Norway and initially Russia) clamped down on spirits but left beer and wine alone. Belgium, Brazil, the Netherlands, Switzerland, and France banned only absinthe. Strong prohibitionist sentiment in Sweden suffered an irreparable defeat in a national referendum in 1922, and had to be content to accept the new "Bratt" system of state-controlled liquor sales, some version of which was also eventually adopted in Poland, Finland, Norway, and the Soviet Union. Several countries retained some version of local option. Britain and the other dominions also stopped short of a full-scale shutdown (New Zealand voters defeated prohibition by a razor-thin margin in 1919) and concentrated instead on drastically curtailing the hours of sale—introducing the notoriously rowdy "six o'clock closing."[8]

Canada's prohibition experiment had to be filtered through the oddly divided constitutional division of powers between federal and provincial governments. Given the great unevenness of support between regions and the deep-seated opposition of francophone Quebec, it is unlikely that any national government would have made a different decision from Laurier's Liberals in 1898. Fighting province by province probably gave the prohibitionists a greater chance of success, but not until they could recast their struggle as part of the European war to which the country was committed after 1914. The immediate postwar victories to continue prohibition into peacetime rested in part on the surge of moral fervour for renewal and reconstruction that flowed out of the war period in many parts of the country, and also in part on the abstention of growing numbers of voters from the plebiscites called to judge public opinion. By the early 1920s, large numbers of Canadians were voting with their feet by visiting doctors' offices or bootleggers' dives to get the alcohol they wanted.

The unpopularity of prohibition was soon evident, partly in the massive popular resistance to the legislation, partly in the quick return of legalized drinking in Quebec and Western Canada in the early 1920s. Vigorous anti-booze sentiment persisted nonetheless in Ontario and the Maritimes, especially in rural areas. The depth of that opinion across the country meant that none of the provincial governments simply rolled back prohibition. Instead they replaced it with rigid new regulatory regimes known as "government control," aimed at limiting consumption and shaping drinking habits, and under the direct administration of powerful new state agencies called liquor control boards. Initially, in most provinces, alcohol was available only in austere, widely scattered government stores and had to be taken home to be consumed. Outside Quebec public drinking in beer parlours got legal sanction much more slowly, and remained tightly regulated until well after the Second World War (an interesting parallel with the beer halls set up in the same period in Southern Africa). In contrast to some Northern and many Eastern European countries, the Canadian provincial governments were never willing (or, probably, constitutionally able) to challenge the private ownership of booze production. As a result they operated only retail stores, often as a state monopoly (as Sweden and Switzerland had done since well before 1900). Post-prohibition regulatory regimes in the United States varied widely, from the Canadian model of repressive tolerance to much looser arrangements that allowed for less severely restrained public drinking environments (with food, music, games, dancing). Canadian practice did match many other countries' efforts to divert consumption from spirits to beer and wine: after the repeal of prohibition, brewers and vintners were often allowed to run their own retail outlets (and in Quebec to sell their products to corner grocers), and until the 1940s only fermented drinks could be sold in public drinking establishments.[9]

Outright victory over "King Alcohol" may have eluded the prohibitionists, but for close to seven decades after the turn of the century the relentless grip of many of their key assumptions on public policy helped to reshape Canadian popular culture and leisure patterns profoundly. Constraints on public drinking were the cutting edge of a moral-reform juggernaut that brought Sunday closings for everything from toboggan slides to ice-cream parlours to sporting events, as well as strict censorship of books and movies. The range of acceptable public activities was steadily curtailed in the relentless efforts to clear the streets, especially in evenings and on Sundays and public holidays, and to push social activities into the presumably more orderly private spaces of family and household. In English Canada, both before and after prohibition, the isolation of public drinking from music and other forms of entertainment undoubtedly undercut the potential for popular music and popular theatre that took off in British music halls and Montreal night clubs (not surprisingly, Canada's most vigorous jazz scene developed in Montreal). Canada's booze legislation, then, contributed to the country's international reputation as a coldly austere, culturally repressed country whose public cultural life matched its often forbidding climate.[10]

However tempting it might be to argue that the post-prohibition control measures curbed alcohol consumption and shaped drinking customs to a significant extent, the reduced drinking of the 1920s and 1930s had far more to do with the empty pockets of consumers, who faced prolonged economic uncertainty through so much of the interwar period and had trouble finding extra cash for a luxury such as drinking. This was a trend throughout the industrialized world. Then, despite the strict regulatory regime, fuller employment at wartime wages soon had the cash register bells ringing in booze outlets, and alcohol consumption began to soar in postwar years, until it had reached pre-prohibition levels by the 1970s. Stimulated and shaped by powerful, aggressive beverage-alcohol industries, drinking at home or in licensed establishments became a popular form of participation in the new consumer society for both the middle and the working classes and for both men and women. The corporate producers tried to make the most of these mushrooming markets by producing a handful of relatively bland "national" drinks and thus eliminating the earlier diversity of brands and tastes. Drinking nonetheless expanded across the three main categories of booze, and came to include more wine and spirits, although they never did supplant the supremacy of beer.

By the 1970s governments in all provinces and territories were loosening the controls on alcohol. Contributing to this liberalization was the postwar influence of both a mass movement of mutual support (Alcoholics Anonymous) and small groups of doctors and other professionals (loosely linked in an "alcoholism movement"). Compulsively heavy drinking was redefined as a legitimate disease and not merely a moral failing, and governments were convinced to fund professional intervention and treatment. In the 1960s and 1970s state support for such programs expanded enormously, and most drinkers relaxed about enjoying their booze safe in the knowledge that they were not "alcoholics." These too were patterns evident throughout the drinking populations of the world after the Second World War.[11]

Then, fairly abruptly in the 1970s and 1980s, many drinkers began to pull back. Aside from the clampdown on drunk driving and new warnings from research agencies (which had changed their tune about "alcoholism"), the shift came with little push from any branch of the state. Perhaps people were once again worried about spending too much on luxuries in the uncertain economic climate of the 1980s and 1990s, or perhaps they were showing new concern for public safety and their own health. In any case, some of them became complete abstainers, while many others drank less and shifted towards drinks with lower alcohol content. The main exceptions were young, single men, who were still the hard-core drinkers they had been for generations and were now making drunken binges a leading part of their social lives.

In all of these postwar trends, the Canadian experience had parallels in most countries where alcohol was regularly consumed, although Canadians remained among the more moderate consumers: twenty-second on a list of thirty-one (in 1990 adults in Canada consumed nine litres of absolute alcohol per capita, just behind the United Kingdom and the United States, but far above the roughly five litres in the USSR, Norway, and Mexico). Like the peoples of most Western countries and a growing proportion of the developing world, Canadians were still getting the largest proportion of their alcohol from beer.[12]

Over four centuries, then, Canadians have approached alcoholic beverages with sharply contrasting attitudes and practices. Nonetheless some common threads run through this complex, often tumultuous history. One thread is certainly the resurgent interest in drinking in some form that could never be stamped out. Again and again, large numbers of people in this country expressed a desire to have access to booze. They subverted efforts to stop them, and justified their desire with arguments ranging from health and nutrition to personal liberty to pure frivolity. The once-central notion that booze is food has noticeably faded over the past half-century with the decline in the nutritional quality of mass-produced alcohol and the increased separation of consumption from eating. At the same time the assertion that booze forms an important part in the exuberant play needed to compensate for the intensity and authoritarianism of the paid workplace has grown steadily. Throughout the twentieth century, booze producers reinforced and reshaped these popular conceptions with their advertising and marketing campaigns.[13]

Then too, most consumers have enjoyed their booze in moderation. Since the late nineteenth century many Canadian drinkers have apparently recognized that drinking is a luxury they can afford only when they have surplus earnings, and that heavy consumption can undermine their social and familial obligations. Across Canadian history, incomes and living standards tended to lag behind some other industrialized countries, especially the United States; so it is not surprising that the recorded levels of alcohol consumption were considerably lower. Generally, therefore, patrons of drinking establishments from colonial taverns to pre-prohibition saloons to dingy beverage rooms to late-twentieth-century sports bars exercised more constraint in their drinking habits than the outcries of shocked moralists might suggest. Many male drinkers made an effort to make their behaviour a somewhat respectable pastime within industrial capitalist society.

National averages tell us little about the patterns and distribution of drinking across a population, and there has certainly been plenty of unevenness in enthusiasm for booze among Canadians. As in virtually every society, drinking was always, and still is, a preponderantly male activity. Social constructions of womanhood regularly invoked a judgment that women drinking (especially those drinking in public) were women out of control, with loose morals and insufficient concern for domestic and maternal responsibilities. Women have had at least limited access to the arenas of drinking since pre-industrial times (far less from the mid-nineteenth to the mid-twentieth centuries), and since the Second World War they have participated much more regularly in public and private drinking—a parallel experience to their expanding participation in the paid workforce and public life in general. Until quite recently, however, they usually had to participate in spheres of public drinking only with male companions and on terms set by men. There were always proportionately fewer of them, they typically drank far less and less often (and still do), and in recent surveys they have been more likely than men to express negative attitudes about drinking. In the last quarter of the twentieth century, many more women plunged into public drinking, often in all-female groups, as part of the broader redefining of acceptable feminine behaviour. Yet at the turn of the millennium, shifting gender roles had still not significantly reduced the income gap between men and women (and thus the availability of disposable income for drinking). Nor had they released women from the bulk of responsibility for domestic labour and child-rearing. Women who drink heavily can still face the lingering stigma of "the fallen woman."[14]

In contrast, men have always used drinking as a focus for gathering together away from the authority structures and responsibilities of family and work, for building solidarities with other men in the same occupation, status, or class, and for asserting their patriarchal right to enjoy the public sphere in ways generally denied to women. Drinking was woven into the language and practices through which men constructed their masculine identities. Men most regularly made intimate contact with John Barleycorn in their late teens and twenties, generally in taverns, followed by a tapering off of the connection over the remainder of their life cycles—a pattern evident in most societies. The place of alcohol in the lives of young men changed over the course of the twentieth century. In the early twentieth century, heavy drinking in saloons was a male-only activity, a central part of vigorous bachelor culture. A century later young men still turn in large numbers to that kind of homosocial drinking, but with women now welcomed into bars and taverns, men also now use binges as occasions for finding sexual partners. Indeed, many young men see drinking with a woman (or man) as a direct route to casual sex, and alcohol has figured prominently in many late-twentieth-century cases of sexual abuse and date rape.[15]

All males did not use alcohol in the same ways. In New France and the early years of British North America, it could be the means of bonding among men of the same class or, when a figure of power and wealth provided the booze, a part of the process of maintaining patriarchal class rule. During the nineteenth century, however, the classes parted company in their recreational life. In the cities, many men of the dominant classes gave up drinking entirely, and those who refused to take the pledge most often drank together in socially exclusive spaces. Within the emerging working class, some men also embraced sobriety as part of a strategy for surviving (and, in the case of labour organizations such as the Knights of Labor, even transcending) the insecurities of the capitalist labour market, while many held onto older drinking habits in the now predominantly working-class saloons. By the early twentieth century, most of these proletarian drinkers had tamed their barroom culture to make a generally quieter, more respectable alternative to teetotalling, and in the face of prohibition they mobilized to defend their beer. In the countryside, a similar split gradually seemed to develop between male abstainers and imbibers.[16] There were also persistent ethnic and racial differences in consumption patterns. Generally those with continental European backgrounds and Catholic upbringing were more likely to drink than those from the Anglo-Canadian, African Canadian, Asian, and/or evangelical Protestant households. First Nations people were officially denied access to alcohol but many found their way to the bottle.

There has therefore never been a single Canadian drinking experience or drinking pattern. Rather we have created a diversity of drinking cultures. The abstainers and occasional drinkers stand at one extreme. In the middle is a great number of moderate drinkers. According to medical research, these are the imbibers who enjoy the greatest health benefits from booze. On the other extreme is the much smaller group of people who drink often and regularly end up drunk. A small fraction of them become compulsive drinkers dependent on alcohol to a degree that seriously interferes with their ability to function "normally" as workers, husbands, and parents. Far more of the heavy drinkers engage in binges on weekends or other moments of "time out." They may or may not drink more in total than the moderate drinkers, but they guzzle their drinks down quickly on single occasions (and thus get none of the physiological advantages of drinking alcohol).

Heavy drinking in Canada, as in other societies, has been related to identities of class, gender, and age, but arguably some parts of the Canadian context have encouraged drinking sprees. The heavy concentration on resource
extraction in our economy has brought together a large number of young
male workers in industrial jobs (logging, mining, construction, long-distance
transportation, for example) located far outside the main urban centres. Both
the intensity of the work experience and the tight regulation of public drinking undoubtedly encouraged drinking as much as possible as quickly as possible, often on an empty stomach (or perhaps doing the same at one of the many
unregulated bootleggers' dives after hours). It may be that the tight restrictions
on drinking increased its appeal for young men, or at least cast the activity
into the realm of illicit pleasures to be enjoyed in defiance of convention. A
widespread pattern of binge drinking thus became deeply rooted among
young male drinkers in Canada, much as in the United States and some
Nordic countries. By international standards, Canadians may appear to drink a
moderate amount per capita, but a small proportion of binge drinkers actually
consume the great bulk of the booze. Certainly binges have long been much
more common here than in countries such as France, Spain, Italy, or parts of
South America, where the drinking of smaller amounts a number of times a
day is more typical.

These structuring factors in the Canadian experience may help us to
understand part of our drinking history, but for explanations as to why, when,
and how people drank (or abstained), we have to follow them into the cultures they were attempting to create or defend. It is not too helpful to consider the individual drinker in isolation. As in all parts of the world, Canadians
generally used their decisions to consume or not to consume as a means of
sustaining a sense of community within particular social groups and of pursuing a larger vision of the kind of world they wanted to live in. For most
drinkers, the attraction of booze was far less the kick of the ethanol than the
anticipated social experience of drinking with others. Upper-class club members, working-class tavern-goers, and back-alley "rubbies" made drinking the
occasion for reaffirming social bonds that provided mutual support and
immediate pleasure. The need for that experience undoubtedly changed over
four hundred years—from the isolation that early European settlers tried to
overcome in their taverns and community drinking, to the harsh indignities
and strains of the industrial-capitalist workplace from which wage-earners
sought relief, to the mounting challenges and social conflict that encouraged
bourgeois men to adopt a more robust version of their manhood, to mounting uncertainties about masculine identities that pushed many young men
into boisterous binges at many points in the past. After the Second World War,

members of all social classes plunged more eagerly into drinking as part of living the "good life" through consumerism. By that point too, the choice to drink could be bound up in more private practices, including rituals of courtship and sexual engagement.

At the other extreme, many people in Canada became militant teetotallers as a strategy of liberation from destructive forces in their lives—the Aboriginal peoples from the early nineteenth to the late twentieth centuries who pushed alcohol off their reserves to help buttress their indigenous cultures, the African Canadians who saw sobriety as the road to respectability and acceptance, the skilled working men (including many radical socialists) who argued that sobriety was necessary for united class action, the maternal feminists who insisted that women and children would benefit from men giving up the bottle, the fundamentalist Moslems who wanted to resist the degrading impact of Western culture, and the rural folk in many parts of the country, especially in Atlantic Canada, who staked out a moral high ground in opposition to the alleged iniquities of the urban, capitalist world. Alcohol in Canadian society has long been rooted in conflictual social relationships.

So too has drunkenness. It was drinking too much that always brought the constantly shifting identification of "social problems" and a whole arsenal of solutions. The responses began by promoting individual self-control and self-denial, evolved into coercive repression of both drunkards and their booze, emerged out of prohibition as closely repressive tolerance, and then returned to an emphasis on inculcating personal responsibility and self-discipline. Popular attitudes have often incorporated two different views of heavy drinking: on the one hand, tolerance of some degree of intoxication when it is occasional and celebratory, and does little or no harm, and, on the other, condemnation of excessive and repeated ("habitual") drunkenness that is destructive to oneself and others (in the late twentieth century, the popular usage of the term "alcoholic" became simply, and vaguely, someone who drank too much too often).

The temperance movement refused to accept those distinctions, and insisted that all "inebriety" was unacceptable, and that all drinking would ultimately make the drinker a drunkard. The measure of that movement's legacy has been the depth and persistence of the ideology of individual self-control in North American society. Even within the more liberalized drinking regimes after the Second World War, Canadians still constructed excessive drinking as "losing control." Medical attempts to define a distinct illness known as "alcoholism" in the nineteenth century and then again in the post-Second World War period also never escaped making it a "disease of the will."

Both the non-professional Alcoholics Anonymous and the medicalized treatment programs implicitly accepted this premise.

What most Canadian discussions of drunkenness have lacked (like their American counterparts) has been the notion imbedded in other cultures—and probably widely experienced, but rarely acknowledged, in North American practice—that a heavy intake of alcohol may not be a weakness or a vice, or a step along the road to "addiction," but a consciously chosen pleasure. Although intoxication is common in virtually all societies around the world, relatively few cultures have fixated on it as a major social problem. In most African towns and villages, drinking has almost invariably been expected to lead to drunkenness. As one writer says of Kenyans, "Drinkers did not mind losing control; in fact, they relished it." A Chinese scholar has explained how within Chinese culture, alcoholic beverages were thought to "stimulate one's mind and stir one's sentiments" and were often combined with an appreciation of music or art. A Danish writer notes that most English words for intoxication have negative connotations, and wonders at the difficulty of expressing "the primary exhilarating effect of drinking alcohol" and the desired effect of "coziness." A French anthropologist similarly explains how the French word *ivresse* conveys possibilities of "ecstasy, rapture, and exhilaration" that are lost in the English word "intoxication" (with its connotations of poisoning).

In contrast, in Canadian society the enjoyment of alcohol was, for a long time at least, something furtive and illicit. The lure of John Barleycorn is the stirring of passions and desire, and, in cultures such as ours that have long encouraged delayed gratification in pursuit of longer-term goals (schooling, careers, marriage, parenting, mortgages, the afterlife), turning to his company can implicitly become a tiny act of rebellion or subversion—a moment of immediate, celebratory pleasure that provides some "time out" from (or, for some drinkers, alternatives to) those relentless demands. By international standards, many Canadians have long seemed remarkably uneasy about that kind of appeal to the senses. The collective public uncertainty about the appropriateness of getting drunk or otherwise breaking loose and letting our hair down is central to the lingering public personality that has been labelled the "polite Canadian."[17]

In practice, however, public and private morality continued to diverge. The old hegemonic discourses of danger and disgust still prevail in public discussions about alcohol, alongside private rebellions against such prudery. A British writer who came to Canada to investigate our liquor legislation in the early 1890s was struck by this divergence. "I have repeatedly been informed that people voted for the Act who never intended to observe it," he explained. "And a case was related to me of several such voters in Simcoe country

[Ontario] who, shortly after they had helped to carry the [Scott] Act, were discovered drinking in an illicit rum shop."[18] Mackenzie King was just as hypocritical in voting to tighten prohibition in 1921 and the same day receiving a new shipment of whisky from Montreal. My father's late companion liked to tell the story of arriving in Bowmanville, Ont., as a war bride in 1945 and moving in with her husband's family. After growing up with English pubs, she was horrified to discover that her mother-in-law would not allow alcohol in the household. Yet her father-in-law and other menfolk would disappear into the outside root cellar, turn off the light, and talk in whispers while trying to muffle the sound of snapping beer caps. Across the country, local bootleggers helped to keep such clandestine practices alive.

After trying outright repression, Canadians struggled to resolve the moral dilemma by integrating alcohol into their lives "moderately." In this new century they still do, though with the proliferating literature on the healthful qualities of ethanol and the lack of consensus on appropriate levels of consumption, "moderation" is a term as fluid and ephemeral as "alcoholism" and "addiction." The premier of British Columbia provided a sharp reminder of our persistent doubts early in 2003. When a public uproar erupted over his arrest for drunk driving in Hawaii, he felt called upon to make a tearful public statement about his need to curb his drinking, rather than promising to stop driving, which was the dangerous act that he had been apprehended for committing. His statement came only two days after media reports of the study of 38,000 adults undertaken by Harvard University's School of Public Health showing the highly beneficial health effects of drinking one to three drinks a day seven days a week. For countless Canadians, beverage alcohol is still "booze" in both the sternly dismissive and the deliciously naughty senses.[19]

State policy towards alcohol has grown out of this ambivalence. On the assumption that alcoholic beverages were morally suspect luxuries but nonetheless widely popular, governments in the early colonies and then in the Dominion of Canada leaned heavily on drinkers for tax revenues. Until the rise of the welfare state half a century ago, that ready source of income for the public treasury allowed them to avoid stiffer taxes on wealth and property, and getting those revenues back was a major motivation in repealing full-scale prohibition in the 1920s. Indeed, politicians and state officials were often hard-pressed to see the increasingly large and powerful distilling and brewing corporations as enemies of the public good. Governments had to balance that view against ever louder demands for anti-booze measures to promote public order (by locking up drunks or prosecuting bootleggers), public and private morality (by curbing consumption), and public health (by submitting "alcoholics" to treatment programs). There was never a clear consensus about whether excessive drinking was a vice or a disease, or whether the response should be punitive or therapeutic, though most state measures tilted towards the former.

From the late nineteenth century onward, then, ambivalence became official hypocrisy, wherein governments raked in taxes from alcohol, sanctimoniously maintained a legal regime of tight controls, but in practice tolerated a remarkable level of illicit marketing and drinking of booze (in themselves, small acts of rebellion against intrusive government). The most dramatic examples were on display in the Maritime provinces, where prohibition and then rigid government control lasted longer than anywhere else, but where rum-running, bootlegging, and vote-buying with liquor were deep-rooted and widespread.

The gulf between public and private morality was still evident in the early 2000s when, at different points, the premiers of Alberta and British Columbia and a federal cabinet minister faced public scrutiny and stern criticism for the kind of heavy drinking that is actually commonplace in Canada. At the same time, the state's public-health officials are still reluctant to proclaim loudly the health benefits of moderate drinking that are widely acknowledged within the medical research world. There is now no temperance movement of any size left to throw these issues into the public arena. Despite decades of permissiveness that have largely undone what the old teetotallers fought for, the impulse to check undue expressiveness still seems so deeply ingrained in the dominant discourses of public morality that the WCTU is no longer needed. Most Canadians now seem to respect the regulatory regime that at least partially contains our collective appetites and thirsts, and most Canadians deplore the transgressions of public figures who violate the acceptable norms of that regime. Or, perhaps, more precisely, we have remained stubbornly unwilling to let personal indulgence and hedonism, however enjoyable, undermine our sense of mutual responsibilities.[20]

Nowadays, then, Canadians are still not at all certain as to what they should do with their ambivalence towards alcohol. In the past, relying purely on exhortations to individual morality rarely worked for long—since the earliest days of temperance agitation, "backsliding" has been far too common. Heavy-handed repression was never successful in either eliminating or dramatically reducing alcohol consumption—it merely pushed much of it underground and encouraged more furtive, probably less healthy drinking practices. Trying to marginalize alcohol consumption proved to be no solution either. There is actually plenty of evidence from other parts of the world that societies in which drinking is more thoroughly integrated within the daily lives of people have seldom constructed anything like our notions of "drinking problems."[21] Shifting the responsibility for these problem drinkers to "experts" and treatment programs has been no more successful.

Looking back, we might well conclude that most often cultures of mutual support and collective constraint have been the most successful in monitoring and curbing abusive and destructive behaviour related to drinking—whether it was the helping hands of family members or fellow drinkers who talked drunks out of drinking any more or sent them home in cabs; or the deeply committed groups of teetotallers—from the Washingtonians and Dashaways in the 1840s, to the Salvation Army, to Alcoholics Anonymous, to the labour-sponsored programs and Aboriginal support groups of recent years—who were prepared to work with heavy drinkers in reducing the influence of John Barleycorn in their lives.

Ambivalence towards drinking has a long, long history. It falls into the polarities of hedonism and asceticism, of pleasure and danger, of expressiveness and control, that have run through public discourses and social confrontations for centuries.[22] Ultimately, in keeping with a general political culture that tolerates ethnic and racial diversity and unconventional sexual preferences, it seems that a grudging mutual tolerance of the diverse drinking customs and practices in Canada has become our predominant response to this dilemma. The teetotallers and occasional drinkers simply ignore the more bibulous or the drunks. Still, our particular history of repression and restraint, combined with resistance and subversion, has left us uneasy not only about openly acknowledging that diversity but also about reconciling our differences. Instead we have privatized this vice and now seem to have a simple message for drinkers: enjoy your booze, but please try to keep quiet about it.

Abbreviations Used
in the Captions

ACJ	Archives de la Compagnie de Jésus (St-Jérôme, Que.)
AO	Archives of Ontario (Toronto)
ASL	Alaska State Library (Juneau)
AUCC	Archives of the United Church of Canada (Toronto)
BCA	British Columbia Archives (Victoria)
BHC	Bradbury-Heron Collection (Toronto)
BNQ	Bibliothèque nationale du Québec (Montreal)
CSTMC	Canadian Science and Technology Museum Corporation (Ottawa)
CTA	City of Toronto Archives
GA	Glenbow Archives (Calgary)
HPL	Hamilton Public Library, Special Collections (Hamilton, Ont.)
MM	McCord Museum (Montreal)
MMFA	Montreal Museum of Fine Arts
NAC	National Archives of Canada (Ottawa)
NLC	National Library of Canada (Ottawa)
NSM	Nova Scotia Museum (Halifax)
PANB	Provincial Archives of New Brunswick
RHMA	Rossland Historical Museum and Archives (Rossland, B.C.)
TG	*Tavistock Gazette*, Lemp Studio Collection (Tavistock, Ont.)
TPL	Toronto Public Library, Baldwin Room
UTL	University of Toronto Libraries, Thomas Fisher Library
UWL	University of Waterloo Libraries, Doris Lewis Rare Book Room
WAHC	Workers' Arts and Heritage Centre (Hamilton, Ont.)
WS	*Windsor Star*
YUA	York University Archives and Special Collections (Toronto)

Notes

Preface

1. Two years later Will Heron apparently put in some time in support of the temperance campaign in a referendum to stop the importation of alcohol into the province, and in 1924 he turned out again for a temperance rally before yet another referendum, this time on the issue of government control of alcoholic beverages. The day before that event, he recorded in his diary that he was at Scarborough Junction "getting in votes for O.T.A. [Ontario Temperance Act]." William Heron's Diaries, 5 August, 15 September, 6, 20 October 1919, and 16, 18 April 1921, 17 September, 10, 23 October 1924 (in author's possession).

2. The list of topics that deserve further research includes the following: distinctive drinking patterns and cultures in various parts of the country; the particular patterns among men, women, and specific racial and ethnic groups; the changing contours of tavern life and its relationship to other forms of leisure activity; the experience of drinking on the job; the business of producing and marketing beer, wine, and spirits; the political activities of the booze industries and the industry-wide organizations that sustained them; the mutual-support organizations for teetotallers and compulsive drinkers; the social composition, discourses, cultural products (music, plays, poetry, visual imagery, and so on), and internal politics of the temperance and prohibition movements; the regional variation in support for those movements, notably their remarkable strength in Atlantic Canada; the role of the courts in dealing with booze issues; the operation of bootlegging and rum-running networks and their relationship to particular communities; the drinking cultures that developed in illicit blind pigs and speakeasies; the development of administrative policy by the provincial liquor control boards; partisan politics involved in administration of government control; and medical views of and therapies for alcohol abusers.

one ➤ In Search of John Barleycorn

1. Austin, *Alcohol in Western Society*; Heath, "Critical Review" and *Drinking Occasions*; Peel and Grant, eds., *Alcohol and Pleasure*; Courtwright, *Forces of Habit*; Schivelbusch, *Tastes of Paradise*; Walton, *Out of It*.

2. Braun, *Buzz*; Walton, *Out of It*, 223–6; Heath, *Drinking Occasions*, 73, 123–5 and "Critical Review," 24–7; Nadeau, "Gender and Alcohol." Medical researchers disagree about many aspects of the impact of ethanol on the body; see Roach, "Biochemical and Physiological Effects."

3. Braun, *Buzz*; Klatsky, "Is Drinking Healthy?"; Nestle, "Alcohol Guidelines"; Daube, "Pleasure in Health Promotion"; Camargo, "Gender Differences"; and several other essays in Peele and Grant, eds., *Alcohol and Pleasure*.

4. The *Oxford English Dictionary* tells us that "booze" is a variant of the Middle-English "bousen," the Middle-Dutch "busen," and the German "bausen," all of which by the sixteenth century were slang and colloquial terms for "to drink; to drink to excess or for enjoyment or goodfellowship; to swill, guzzle, tipple." The word was also applied to alcoholic drinks themselves and sometimes to "a drinking bout, a carouse."

5. Dietler, "Driven by Drink," 353–8; Phillips, *Short History of Wine*, 1–28; Bennett, *Ale, Beer, and Brewsters*; Park, "Sketches Toward a Political Economy" and "Supply Side of Drinking"; Austin, *Alcohol in Western Society*, xxi–xxiii.

6. Blocker, "Consumption and Availability"; Van Onselen, "Randlords and Rotgut"; Partanen, *Sociability and Intoxication*; Sulkunen, "Drinking Patterns"; Heath, *International Handbook*, 364.

7.   Mathias, "Brewing Industry, Temperance, and Politics"; Dingle, "Truly Magnificent Thirst";
      Moreira, "Rum in the Atlantic Provinces"; Burnett, *Liquor Pleasures*, 111–78; Marshall and
      Marshall, "Holy and Unholy Spirits"; Kudlick, "Fighting the Internal and External Enemies,"
      137 (quotation).

8.   Dietler, "Driven By Drink"; Ambler and Crush, "Alcohol in Southern African Labor
      History"; Mills, "Cape Smoke"; Partanen, *Sociability and Intoxication*, 107–8; Rorabaugh,
      Alcoholic Republic; Roberts, "Drink and Industrial Discipline"; Vogt, "Defining Alcohol
      Problems," 555–7; Way, *Common Labour*; Eriksen, "Making of the Danish Liberal Drinking
      Style," 10; Sonnenstuhl, *Working Sober*, 2–6; Warner, "Historical Perspectives." An interesting
      discussion about drinking on the job began on <H-LABOR@H-NET.MSU.EDU> at the
      end of May 2002, in which contributors reported the twentieth-century work-related drink-
      ing practices of shoe workers, railroad workers, steelworkers, construction workers, auto-
      workers, and, of course, brewery workers.

9.   Heath, *Drinking Occasions*; Mandelbaum, "Alcohol and Culture"; Douglas, "Distinct Anthro-
      pological Perspective"; Jellinek, "Symbolism of Drinking"; Gusfield, "Passage to Play"; Karp,
      "Beer Drinking"; Austin, *Alcohol in Western Society*; Tlusty, *Bacchus and Civic Order*; Brennan,
      Public Drinking and Popular Culture; Clark, *English Alehouse*. The concept of "sociability" that
      runs through so much writing on communal drinking practices is heavily indebted to the
      theorizing of the German sociologist Georg Simmel in the early twentieth century; see
      Partanen, *Sociability and Intoxication*, 217–35.

10.   Australian writer Oscar Mendelsohn has produced a list of more than 1,400 synonyms in
      English for the word "drunk"; *Nicely, Thank You*, 24–45.

11.   The classic study of drunken behaviour in different societies that established the cultural
      structuring of these occasions was MacAndrew and Edgerton, *Drunken Comportment*, which
      argues convincingly that "the way people comport themselves when they are drunk is deter-
      mined not by alcohol's toxic assault upon the seat of moral judgment, conscience, or the like,
      but by what their society makes of and imparts to them concerning the state of drunken-
      ness" (165). On drunkenness in mitigating guilt, see Tlusty, *Bacchus and Civic Order*, 80–102.

12.   Sherratt, "Alcohol and Its Alternatives," 17.

13.   Austin, *Alcohol in Western Society* (quotation at 148); Heath, "Critical Review," 12–13, and
      Drinking Occasions, 97–8; Xiao, "China," 42–3; Shinfuka, "Japanese Culture and Drinking";
      Sharma and Mohan, "Changing Sociocultural Perspectives"; Courtwright, *Forces of Habit*, 72
      (quotation); *Holy Bible* (King James Edition), Psalm 104.15, 1 Timothy 5.23 (quotations);
      Tlusty, *Bacchus and Civic Order*, 74 (quotation); Sherratt, "Alcohol and Its Alternatives"; De Silva,
      "Buddhist Attitude to Alcoholism"; Baasher, "Use of Drugs"; Partanen, *Sociability and Intoxication*,
      193–4. The Bible contains 165 references to wine; Courtwright, *Forces of Habit*, 10.

14.   Levine, "Discovery of Addiction," 145–51, and "Good Creature of God and the Demon
      Rum," 115–26; Tlusty, "Defining 'Drunk,'" 434–45; Spode, "First Step Toward Sobriety";
      Porter, "Drinking Man's Disease"; Warner, "Resolv'd to Drink No More"; McCandless,
      "Curses of Civilization"; Woiak, "A Medical Cromwell"; Sournia, *History of Alcoholism*; Warsh,
      "Because There Is Pain"; Trainor, "Towards a Genealogy of Temperance," 94–181; Jaffe,
      "Reform in American Medical Science"; Bynum, "Chronic Alcoholism" and "Alcoholism
      and Degeneration"; McCandless, "Curses of Civilization"; Jellinek, *Disease Concept*; White,
      Slaying the Dragon; Valverde, *Diseases of the Will*.

15.   Austin, *Alcohol in Western Society*; Harrison, *Drink and the Victorians*; Barrows, "Parliaments of
      the People"; Roberts, "Tavern and Politics."

16.   For a classic statement of the "social control" perspective, see Boyer, *Urban Masses and Moral
      Order*; for critiques, see Hunt, *Governing Morals*; Valverde, *Age of Light, Soap, and Water*; Strange
      and Loo, *Making Good*; Muraskin, "Social-Control Theory"; Thompson, "Social Control."

17.   For an influential alternative perspective, see Rumbarger, *Profits, Power, and Prohibition*.

18.   For a wide-ranging review of the Canadian literature that situates alcohol in the interna-
      tional field, see Warsh, "John Barleycorn Must Die."

19.   See, for example, MacAndrew and Edgerton, *Drunken Comportment*; Marshall, ed., *Beliefs,
      Behaviors, and Alcoholic Beverages*; Douglas, ed., *Constructive Drinking*; Gefou-Madianou, ed,
      Alcohol, Gender, and Culture; Heath, *Drinking Occasions*; McDonald, ed., *Gender, Drink, and*

Drugs. In 1984 sociologist Robin Room sparked a debate in *Current Anthropology* by raising questions about anthropologists' apparent indifference to problem drinking; see "Alcohol and Ethnography" and various responses.

20. In the 1970s the large body of American literature on the temperance movement turned away from disparaging the teetotallers as fanatical, cranky, and anti-modern (see Hofstadter, *Age of Reform*; Spence, *Prohibition*) towards a much more sympathetic treatment of their construction of drinking problems and their idealistic solutions (see, in particular, Clark, *Deliver Us from Evil*). Most Canadian writing on temperance, which began to appear for the most part only in the 1970s, fell into this more sympathetic framework.

two ✒ The Water of Life

1. Proulx, *Between France and New France*, 106–11; Pack, *Nelson's Blood*; Kopperman, "Cheapest Pay"; Jaenen, "Amerindian Views of French Culture," 116; Vachon, "L'eau-de-vie dans la société indienne," 22; Howay, "Introduction of Intoxicating Liquors," 157–61; Mancall, *Deadly Medicine*, 67, 138–9; Heath, "Alcohol Use," 346–7, and *Drinking Occasions*, 61–2; MacAndrew and Edgerton, *Drunken Comportment*, 100–15. Andrew Sherratt suggests that, before the development of alcoholic beverages, Bronze-Age Europe may well have had the kind of smoking culture that the first European newcomers found in North America; see Sherratt, "Alcohol and Its Alternatives," 27–9.

2. Brennan, "Social Drinking in Old Regime Paris," and *Public Drinking and Popular Culture*; Barr, *Drink*; Harrison, *Drink and the Victorians*, 37–63; Rorabaugh, *Alcoholic Republic*; Baron, *Brewed in America*; Malcolm, *"Ireland Sober, Ireland Free"*, 1–11; Barrett, "Why Paddy Drank."

3. Greer, *Peasant, Lord, and Merchant* and "Wage Labour and the Transition to Capitalism"; Bitterman, "Farm Households and Wage Labour"; Palmer, *Working-Class Experience*, 35–80.

4. Clark, *English Alehouse*, 95–6, 239–42; Malcolm, *"Ireland Sober, Ireland Free,"* 1–6; Roberts, *Drink, Temperance, and the Working Class*, 2–3.

5. Sournia, *History of Alcoholism*, 16–19; Clark, *English Alehouse*; Pope, "Historical Archaeology and the Demand for Alcohol"; Gosselin, "Boissons douces et boissons enivrantes"; Vaillancourt, *History of the Brewing Industry*, 4–12; Prévost, Gagne, and Phaneuf, *L'histoire de l'alcool*, 14–30; Greer, *Peasant, Lord, and Merchant*, 157–9; Harrison, *Drink and the Victorians*, 87–90; Shipkey, "Problems in Alcohol Production and Controls."

6. Pope, "Fish into Wine"; Gosselin, "Boissons douces et boissons enivrantes"; Malchelosse, "Ah! mon grand-per'," 141–5; Head, *Eighteenth Century Newfoundland*, 100–32, 151–5, 159, 169, 234; Moreira, "Rum in the Atlantic Provinces"; Gwyn, "Rum, Sugar, and Molasses"; Park, "Supply Side of Drinking."

7. Gosselin, "Boissons douces et boissons enivrantes," 101–5; Sneath, *Brewed in Canada*, 20–4; Baron, *Brewed in America*, 3–51, 95–100; Saracino, "Household Production of Alcoholic Beverages"; Park, "Supply Side of Drinking." A recipe for the popular spruce beer can be found in Hunter, *Molson*, 96–7. Peter Kalm, the Swedish botanist who visited New France in the 1740s, reported that the local population did not make malted beer; Benson, ed., *Peter Kalm's Travels*, vol. 2, 535.

8. Vachon, "De l'abitation de Québec à l'hostellerie de Jacques Boisdon," 99; Vaillancourt, *History of the Brewing Industry*, 4–35; Prévost, Gagne, and Phaneuf, *L'histoire de l'alcool*, 24–5.

9. Prévost, Gagne, and Phaneuf, *L'histoire de l'alcool*, 14–51; Brewers Association of Canada, *Brewing in Canada*, xii; Denison, *Barley and the Stream*, 11–55, 101–2; Hunter, *Molson*; Bowering, *Art and Mystery of Brewing*, 17–18, and *Brewing in Formosa*, 5–8; Phillips, *On Tap*, 49–64; Dorion, *La brasserie Boswell*; Sneath, *Brewed in Canada*, 27–36; Garceau, *Chronique de l'hospitalité hôtelière*, 13–16. The Kingston brewers and Joseph Boswell in Quebec City built up equally prosperous businesses supplying local garrisons.

10. The first of two rum distilleries opened in Halifax in 1751, two years after the settlement was established. With access to West Indian molasses, it did a booming business for several years. A similar operation at Quebec City in 1767 was less successful, though twenty years later there were three in that city and one in Montreal. By 1849 Halifax still had the only four rum

distilleries in Nova Scotia, since the steady flow of cheap West Indian rum discouraged local enterprise, and one of these closed four years later. Moreira, "Rum in the Atlantic Provinces," 19; Gwyn, "Rum, Sugar, and Molasses."

11.   Rannie, *Canadian Whisky*, 26–31; Greer, *Peasant, Lord, and Merchant*, 148; Malchelosse, "Ah! Mon grand-per'," 145; Denison, *Barley and the Stream*, 119–37; 160, 186–7; Hunter, *Molson*, 377–8; Shuttleworth, *Windmill and Its Times*; McCalla, *Planting the Province*, 98–100; Brown, *Two Hundred Years of Tradition*, 1–20; Rorabaugh, *Alcoholic Republic*, 61–9; Park, "Supply Side of Drinking"; Craig, ed., *Early Travellers in the Canadas*, xxxi (quotation). The Molsons abruptly closed their distillery forever in 1866.

12.   Phillips, *On Tap*, 21–6, 36; Bowering, *Art and Mystery of Brewing*, 15–17; Denison, *Barley and the Stream*, 37–48, 140, 165, 180–2; Hunter, *Molson*, 95, 113, 177, 215–28, 305; Tucker, "Labatt's," 13; Monckton, *History of English Ale and Beer*; Baron, *Brewed in America*.

13.   Brown, *Two Hundred Years of Tradition*, 7–8 (quotation at 8); Denison, *Barley and the Stream*, 121–35, 140, 152, 165, 169–75, 180–84, 189, 221–2, 231–2; Rannie, *Canadian Whisky*, 28–32; Rorabaugh, *Alcoholic Republic*, 69–76. The striving for improvement in technique and quality of output was evident in the Molson firm when in 1836 Thomas Molson set off on a lengthy trip to visit U.S. and British distilleries to learn about the most up-to-date production methods and then returned to experiment in the family's Montreal enterprise.

14.   Mancall, *Deadly Medicine*, 29–61; Ray, "Hudson's Bay Company Fur Trade in the Eighteenth Century," 131–4; Stanley, "Indians and the Brandy Trade"; Riddell, "First Canadian Bishop"; Munro, "Brandy Parliament"; Schilz, "Brandy and Beaver Pelts"; Vachon, "L'eau-de-vie dans la société indienne"; Bédard-Lévesque, "La tempérance au Québec," 4–13; Ferland, "Thémis contre Bacchus"; Hamer and Steinbring, "Introduction," in Hamer and Steinbring, eds., *Alcohol and Native Peoples*, 3–15; Dempsey, *Firewater*, 7–16.

15.   Denison, *Barley and the Stream*, 191–3; Prévost, Gagne, and Phaneuf, *L'histoire de l'alcool*, 35–43; Davis, "Rum and the Law," 40–5.

16.   Ferland, "Thémis contre Bacchus"; Vachon, "De l'abitation de Québec à l'hostellerie de Jacques Boisdon," 101–3; Johnston, *Control and Order*, 144–50; Royal Commission on Liquor Traffic, *Report*, 766, 776, 955, Spence, *Prohibition*, 27–33; Clark, *English Alehouse*, 3, 260–3, 278; Rannie, *Canadian Whisky*, 73–6.

17.   In early-nineteenth-century Montreal, booze was often served illegally in brothels. In 1845 there were five unlicensed grog shops per mile along the construction sites of the Welland Canal—124 in all. As late as 1863 a Toronto municipal committee claimed that innumerable "groggeries" were "selling without license with the greatest impunity." At the same point the Quebec countryside was still littered with illicit inns. Royal Commission on Liquor Traffic, *Report*, 955 (quotation); Way, *Common Labour*, 182; Poutanen, "To Indulge Their Carnal Appetites," 136–9; Barry, "Shades of Vice," 10–11; Barron, "Genesis of Temperance," 193; McBurney and Byers, *Tavern in the Town*, 5–6; Trainor, "Towards a Genealogy of Temperance," 50–4, 77; Weaver, "Crime, Public Order, and Repression," 30; McGahan, *Crime and Policing*, 15–21; Rousseau, "Boire ou ne pas boire," 116–18. David Conroy has traced how Puritan efforts to curb the tavern culture of colonial Massachusetts were ineffective; see *In Public Houses*. For the Irish story, see Malcolm, *"Ireland Sober, Ireland Free,"* 11–18.

18.   Greer, *Peasant, Lord, and Merchant*, 157–8; McCalla, *Consumption Stories*; Bowering, *Art and Mystery of Brewing*, 9–11; Whitfield, *Tommy Atkins*, 43–58; Fingard, "A Great Big Rum Shop," 90–2; De Lottinville, "Joe Beef"; Johnson, *Ontario County*, 216 (quotation); Hughes, "Inns and Taverns," 104; Barry, "Shades of Vice," 19–20; Clark, "Professional Aspirations," 46; McBurney and Byers, *Tavern in the Town*, 42, 130–1.

19.   The English distinction between an inn, whose services included accommodation, and a tavern, which merely served food and drink, did not take hold in North America, where a variety of terms were used interchangeably. Merritt, "Early Inns and Taverns," 187.

20.   By the early eighteenth century, Quebec City had 24 taverns (one for every 88 residents) and Montreal 19 (one for every 132). Right after the Conquest, the new English governor of Quebec quickly licensed the colony's 208 existing taverns. When Halifax was founded in 1749, the governor immediately granted seventeen licences for the town's 3,000 residents. A visitor to Newfoundland's rudimentary outports in the same period found many "tippling

houses," another name for the English alehouse (of which there were 55,000 to 60,000 in England by the end of the seventeenth century). Vachon, "Cabarets de la Nouvelle-France," 329; Gosselin, "Boissons douces et boissons enivrantes," 105; Pope, "Fish into Wine," 261; Massicotte, "L'industrie hôtelière," 206; Garland and Talman, "Pioneer Drinking Habits," 172–3; Guillet, *Pioneer Inns and Taverns*; McBurney and Byers, *Tavern in the Town*; Hildebrand, "Les débuts du mouvement," 13–18; Merritt, "Early Inns and Taverns," 198–204; Hughes, "Inns and Taverns"; Roberts, "Taverns and Tavern-goers," 303; Clark, *English Alehouse*, 45; Royal Commission on Liquor Traffic, *Report*, 766.

21. Poutanen, "To Indulge Their Carnal Appetites," 138–9; Roberts, "Taverns and Tavern-goers," 42–5.
22. Roberts, "Taverns and Tavern-Goers"; Christie, "Function of the Tavern"; Brennan, *Public Drinking and Popular Culture*; Clark, *English Alehouse*; Wrightson, "Alehouses, Order, and Reformation"; Malcolmson, *Popular Recreations*, 71–4; Conroy, *In Public Houses*; Thompson, *Rum Punch and Revolution*.
23. Roberts, "Taverns and Tavern-goers," 76–84; Garland and Talman, "Pioneer Drinking Habits," 172–3; Guillet, *Pioneer Inns and Taverns*; McBurney and Byers, *Tavern in the Town*; Merritt, "Early Inns and Taverns," 188–95; Barry, "Shades of Vice," 17–18.
24. This paragraph relies heavily on Julia Roberts's careful reconstruction of taverning in the colonial period; see "Taverns and Tavern-Goers." On female tavern-keepers, see Errington, *Wives and Mothers, School Mistresses and Scullery Maids*, 189–99. In England it had been common to allow impoverished widows to have tavern licences as a means of survival other than poor relief, but that practice was in decline by the eighteenth century; women were nonetheless still active in the business; see Clark, *English Alehouse*, 73–82, 205–6. For parallels with U.S. tavern-keeping, see Thompson, *Rum Punch and Revolution*, 52–74; Conroy, *In Public Houses*, 103. French practices are discussed in Brennan, *Public Drinking and Popular Culture*, 76–134.
25. Hildebrand, "Les débuts du mouvement," 12–13; Fingard, "A Great Big Rum Shop."
26. Roberts, "Taverns and Tavern-Goers" and "Harry Jones and His Cronies"; Denison, *Barley and the Stream*, 109–15, 149; Garceau, *Chronique de l'hospitalité hôtelière*, 18–20. This kind of hierarchy of taverns had appeared earlier in England and in the American colonies; see Clark, *English Alehouse*, 10, 307, 337–8; Thompson, *Rum Punch and Revolution*, 145–204; Conroy, *In Public Houses*, 119.
27. Austin, *Alcohol in Western Society*, 133, 153, 198, 282, 310; Goubert, *French Peasantry*, 90–2; Barrows, "Worlds of Drink," 8; Burnett, *Liquid Pleasures*, 8–12; Clark, *English Alehouse*, 112–4; Benson, ed., *Peter Kalm's Travels*, vol.2, 575 (quotation); Pope, "Historical Archaeology and the Demand for Alcohol," 76.
28. Roland, "Health, Disease, and Treatment," 235–8 (quotation at 239); Hughes, "Eating on the Move," 38, 40, and "Inns and Taverns," 102–3.
29. By this point, pensions arranged between elderly French-Canadian parents and their children regularly included rum. Greer, *Peasant, Lord, and Merchant*, 35–6, 68, 206, 284 (quotation); Fyson, "Du pain au madère," 79–81, 87–8; Bédard-Lévesque, "La tempérance au Québec," 12; Noel, *Canada Dry*, 156; Abrahamson, *God Bless Our Home*, 56–67; Rorabaugh, *Alcoholic Republic*, 95–122; Harrison, *Drink and the Victorians*, 37–45.
30. In eighteenth-century Britain, doctors might recommend from two to six glasses of wine a day to raise the spirits of the middle-aged or elderly. Pope, "Fish into Wine," 271; Decarie, "Something Old, Something New," 156–7; Barry, "Shades of Vice," 13 (quotation); Marble, *Surgeons, Smallpox, and the Poor*; Porter, "Drinking Man's Disease," 387–9; Tlusty, "Defining 'Drunk,'" 428–34; Barron, "Genesis of Temperance," 242; Trainor, "Towards a Genealogy of Temperance," 98; Hildebrand, "Les débuts du mouvement," 13, 20–3.
31. Thompson, "Time, Work, and Industrial Capitalism"; Gutman, "Work, Culture, and Society"; Roberts, "Drink and Industrial Discipline."
32. Wilson, "Reciprocal Work Bees"; Craig, ed., *Early Travellers*, 140–1 (quotation by clergyman); Barry, "Shades of Vice," 13; Barron, "American Origins," 75; Garland and Talman, "Pioneer Drinking Habits," 175; Smart and Ogborne, *Northern Spirits*, 7–8 (quotation by Moodie). There is a long history of using alcohol in rural societies to stimulate communal labour in a

community; on pre-industrial societies, see, for example, Dietler, "Driven by Drink"; for twentieth-century Africa, see Karp, "Beer Drinking," 88–9.

33.   Clark, *English Alehouse*, 24–5, 213; Stivers, *Hair of the Dog*, 26–33; Proulx, *Between France and New France*, 107–9; Pack, *Nelson's Blood*; Moreira, "Rum in the Atlantic Provinces," 17; Reid, "Rum and the Navy"; Sager, *Seafaring Labour*, 227.

34.   The custom of fortifying men for battle, which would also last into the twentieth century, threatened to trigger a military crisis in 1813–14 during the war with the United States, when, to conserve grain for flour, Upper Canada's chief administrator prohibited distilling. Kopperman, "Cheapest Pay" (quotation at 468); Whitfield, *Tommy Atkins*, 43–52; Rioux, *British Garrison*, 39–41; Carter-Edwards, "Supplying Military Posts," 52; McDonald, "Defending the Finest Wine Cellar"; Braudel, *Capitalism and Material Life*, 173; Riddell, "First Canadian War-Time Prohibition Measure." The sheet music for General James Wolfe's drinking song, "How Stands the Glass Around: A Favorite Soldiers Song," is in the National Library of Canada (Amicus No. 23329090).

35.   Vachon, "Cabarets de la Nouvelle-France," 327 (quotation by Jesuits, translated by author); Samson, *Les Forges du Saint-Maurice*, 308–10; Moreira, "Rum in the Atlantic Provinces," 21; Lender and Martin, *Drinking in America*, 47; Barry, "Shades of Vice," 11; Young, *Reminiscences*, 68–9; Craig, ed., *Early Travellers*, 8; Burley, *Servants of the Honourable Company*, 35, 134 (quotation by HBC official); Noel, *Canada Dry*, 13–14, 47, 221 (quotation about Montreal workers); Kilbourn, *Elements Combined*, 25–6; Way, *Common Labour*, 181–7; Wylie, "Poverty, Distress, and Disease," 20; Cross, ed., *Workingman in the Nineteenth Century*, 47–8; Moyles, *"Complaints Is Many and Various"*, 158; Davis, "I'll Drink to That," 28; Barron, "Genesis of Temperance," 14–15; Rosenzweig, *Eight Hours for What We Will*, 36; Roberts, "Drink and Industrial Work," 28.

36.   Winkler, "Drinking on the American Frontier," 419–20 (quotation by British military officer). A 1770 ordinance in Prince Edward Island proved useless in preventing employers from paying their men with booze. Bumsted, *Land, Settlement, and Politics*, 34. These were practices common in Britain and the United States as well; see Harrison, *Drink and the Victorians*, 39–40; Rorabaugh, *Alcoholic Republic*, 14–16; Barrett, "Why Paddy Drank," 160. David Courtwright argues that, like other drugs, alcohol was used in many parts of the world to keep workers on a "treadmill"; see *Forces of Habit*, 135–51; see also Van Onselen, "Randlords and Rotgut"; Ambler and Crush, "Alcohol in Southern African Labor History."

37.   Tlusty, "Gender and Alcohol" and *Bacchus and Civic Order*; Clark, *Struggle for the Breeches*; Eisenberg, "Artisans' Socialization at Work"; Weisner, "*Wandervogels* and Women"; Thompson, *Rum Punch and Revolution*, 96; Benson, "American Workers and Temperance Reform," 95–3.

38.   Roberts, "Taverns and Tavern-goers," 89–102; Vachon, "Cabarets de la Nouvelle-France," 328; Moyles, *"Complaints Is Many and Various"*, 52, 80, 158; Neary and O'Flaherty, eds., *By Great Waters*, 46; Eddington, "Whooping It Up," 44; McDonald, "Defending the Finest Wine Cellar"; Fyson, "Du pain au madère," 87–8; Connell, *Masculinities*, 190–1.

39.   Clark, *English Alehouse*, 127–8, 230–1, 236, 307–8; Clark, *Struggle for the Breeches*, 13–87; Leeson, *Travelling Brothers*, 132–47; Clawson, "Early Modern Fraternalism"; Wiesner, "*Wandervogels* and Women"; Wamsley and Kossuth, "Fighting It Out."

40.   Rorabaugh, *Alcoholic Republic*, vii (quotation).

41.   Roberts, "Taverns and Tavern-goers," 221–89, 299.

42.   Roberts, "A Mixed Assemblage of Persons."

43.   Clark, *English Alehouse*, 131–2, 225, 311–12; Brennan, *Public Drinking and Popular Culture*, 146–51; Thompson, *Rum Punch and Revolution*, 111–44.

44.   McBurney and Byers, *Tavern in the Town*, 71–2 (quotation); Trainor, "Towards a Genealogy of Temperance," 54–5; Lockwood, "Temperance in Upper Canada as Ethnic Subterfuge"; Poutanen, "To Indulge Their Carnal Appetites," 109–10, 128, 136, 152–5; Fingard, *Dark Side of Life*, 64–6, 100–2; Roberts, "Taverns and Tavern-goers," 257–61.

45.   Brennan, *Public Drinking and Popular Culture*, 154; Clark, *English Alehouse*, 124; Barron, "Genesis of Temperance," 16, 33 (quotation by traveller); Smart and Ogborne, *Northern Spirits*, 6–7 (quotations by Traill and Moodie); Roberts, "Taverns and Tavern-Goers"; Denison, *Barley and the Stream*, 114; Eddington, "Whooping It Up."

46. Vernette, *Domestic Life*, 106–9; Burley, *Servants of the Honourable Company*, 42, 76, 131–4; Noel, *Canada Dry*, 192; Chapman, "Mid-Nineteenth-Century Temperance Movement," 46; Bumstead, *Land, Settlement, and Politics*, 128; Riddell, "First Canadian War-Time Prohibition Measure," 189; Rorabaugh, *Alcoholic Republic*, 149–54.

47. Harrison, *Drink and the Victorians*, 42; Adler, "From Symbolic Exchange to Commodity Consumption"; Clark, *English Alehouse*, 212; Tlusty, "Gender and Alcohol," 254–9; Roberts, "Taverns and Tavern-goers," 134–8; Thompson, *Rum Punch and Revolution*, 93–105; Conroy, *In Public Houses*; Brennan, *Public Drinking and Popular Culture*, 218–27; Barrett, "Why Paddy Drank," 162; Barron, "Genesis of Temperance," 33 (quotation). James Epstein has explored how important toasts could be in celebrating shared political values among England's early-nineteenth-century radicals; see "Radical Dining, Toasting, and Symbolic Expression."

48. Roberts, "Taverns and Tavern-goers," especially 132–67; Tlusty, "Defining 'Drunk,'" 433, and *Bacchus and Civic Order*, 2–9; Clark, *English Alehouse*, 297; Thompson, *Rum Punch and Revolution*, 1.

49. Tlusty, "Gender and Alcohol," 252–3. The available sources do not provide a clear picture of how women and children participated in community-wide drinking binges, but it seems that, although some may certainly have ended up inebriated, women probably drank less than men (as they still do today).

50. Goubert, *French Peasantry*, 91–2; Wallot, "Religion and French-Canadian Mores," 83; Vernette, *Domestic Life*, 107; Lachance, *La vie urbaine en Nouvelle-France*, 56–8; Johnston, *Religion in Life at Louisbourg*, 20, 77; Proulx, *Between France and New France*, 125–6; Kopperman, "Cheapest Pay"; Rioux, *British Garrison*, 42–4; Senior, *British Regulars*, 145–51; McBurney and Byers, *Tavern in the Town*, 29–42; Perry, "Gender, Race, and the Making of Colonial Society," 96; Merritt, "Early Inns and Taverns," 198–9; Fingard, *Jack in Port*, 96–8, 103–6, 130–1, and "'A Great Big Rum Shop,'" 90–3; Dunnigan, "Military Life at Niagara," 92; Way, "Evil Humors and Ardent Spirits"; Burley, *Servants of the Honourable Company*, 132; Colombo, ed., *Colombo's Canadian Quotations*, 392 (quotation).

51. Kealey, *Toronto Workers*, 54, 68; Palmer, *Culture in Conflict*, 21, 125; Reid, "Decline of Saint Monday."

52. Pope, "Fish into Wine," 273–8; Clark, *English Alehouse*, 114.

53. Tlusty, "Gender and Alcohol," 254–6; Errington, *Wives and Mothers, School Mistresses and Scullery Maids*; MacAndrew and Edgerton, *Drunken Comportment*; Roberts, "Taverns and Tavern-goers," 151–66; Brennan, *Public Drinking and Popular Culture*, 20–75; Wamsley and Kossuth, "Fighting It Out"; Cross, "Shiners' War"; Way, "Evil Humors and Ardent Spirits"; Kaplan, "New York City Tavern Violence"; Barrett, "Why Paddy Drank," 162; Haliburton, *Old Judge* (quotation).

54. De Belmont, "History of Brandy"; Vachon, "L'eau-de-vie dans la société indienne"; Howay, "Introduction of Intoxicating Liquors"; MacAndrew and Edgerton, *Drunken Comportment*, 100–63; Rich, *Fur Trade and the Northwest*, 43, 103, 141, 157, 158, 164, 194, 240; Ray and Freeman, *"Give Us Good Measure"*, 128–44, 194–6; Ray, *Indians in the Fur Trade*, 142–6, 197–8, 214; Mancall, *Deadly Medicine* and "Men, Women, and Alcohol in Indian Villages"; Barron, "Alcoholism, Indians, and the Anti-Drink Cause," 191–2; Thomas, ed., *Prairie West*, 22–6; Grant, *Moon of Wintertime*, 56–7; Dickason, *Canada's First Nations*, 469–70; Miller, *Skyscrapers Hide the Heavens*, 48–50; Medick, "Plebian Culture," 96–108; Way, "Evil Humors and Ardent Spirits."

55. Mancall, *Deadly Medicine* (quotation at 68); Carpenter, "Alcohol in the Iroquois Dream Quest"; Maher and Steinbring, "Introduction," in Hamer and Steinbring, eds., *Alcohol and Native Peoples*, 16–23 (quotation at 17); MacAndrew and Edgerton, *Drunken Comportment*, 100–63.

56. De Belmont, "History of Brandy" (quotation at 52); Mancall, "Men, Women, and Alcohol in Indian Villages"; Dickinson, "C'est l'eau-de-vie."

57. Some writing on Aboriginal drinking suggests that it may have been empowering for peoples facing devastating disease, extensive warfare, and growing marginalization in the fur trade. The problem with this hypothesis is that Native peoples incorporated alcohol into their lives in these ways long before their societies were anywhere near crisis. For a critical review

of literature that looks for Aboriginal drinking patterns in social disorganizsation or deprivation, see Hill, "Ethnohistory and Alcohol Studies."

58.   Burley, *Servants of the Honourable Company*, 131. A few women in each community might develop reputations as heavy drinkers, but by the 1830s and 1840s they would rarely be seen in barrooms (as they were at the turn of the nineteenth century) unless they were prostitutes; see Roberts, "Taverns and Tavern-goers," 281–7; Poutanen, "To Indulge Their Carnal Appetites," 153–4.

59.   Shuttleworth, *Windmill and Its Times*, 24; Fingard, *Jack in Port*, 96–100, 103–6; Burley, *Servants of the Honourable Company*, 131–9 (quotation at 135).

60.   Roberts, "Taverns and Tavern-goers," 141–51; Barbeau, *Jongleur Songs*, 87–9.

61.   Vachon, "De l'abitation de Québec à l'hostellerie de Jacques Boisdon," 99–100; Ferland, "Thémis contre Bacchus"; Way, *Common Labour*, 184–7; Burley, *Servants of the Honourable Company*, 138–9; Pack, *Nelson's Blood*, 47, 57–66; Payne, "Sports, Games, Recreations, and Pastimes," 63; Tlusty, "Gender and Alcohol"; Whitfield, *Tommy Atkins*; Barry, "Shades of Vice," 21–3; Oliver, *"Terror to Evil-Doers"*; Baehre, "From Bridewell to Federal Penitentiary," 164–8; Wrightson, "Alehouses, Order, and Reformation," 16–17; Brennan, *Public Drinking and Popular Culture*, 187–227; Martin, "Violence, Gender, and Intemperance."

62.   Levine, "Discovery of Addiction," 145–51, and "Good Creature of God and the Demon Rum," 115–26; Tlusty, "Defining 'Drunk,'" 434–45, and *Bacchus and Civic Order*, 48–79; Spode, "First Step Toward Sobriety"; Roy Porter, "Introduction," to Sournia, *History of Alcoholism*, xi; Bynum, "Chronic Alcoholism," 160–2; Clark, *English Alehouse*, 115; Jaenen, *Role of the Church*, 154; Austin, *Alcohol in Western Society*, 329. Rush's book, *An Inquiry into the Effects of Ardent Spirits on the Human Mind and Body*, was published in 1784. In "Drinking Man's Disease," Porter argues that Trotter's writings reflected long-standing views among medical writers in eighteenth-century Britain that habitual drunkenness had the qualities of a disease, and that there was less of a dramatic paradigm shift in the nineteenth century than is asserted in much of the history of alcoholism. He does not argue, however, that this early recognition of alcohol dependence had the kind of popular resonance in the eighteenth century that it would have a hundred years later, or that it resulted in new social programs or institutions for dealing with chronic drunks. In "Resolv'd to Drink No More," Jessica Warner insists that, in England, it was not the doctors, but the clergy who propagated a "disease" concept of drunkenness from at least the early seventeenth century. She admits, however, that these were moralistic admonitions against a spiritual rather than a physical addiction, and that, despite references to bodily harm, they incorporated the language of "addiction" in highly ambiguous ways.

63.   Royal Commission on Liquor Traffic, *Report*, 769 (quotation). For a view of the drunkard as a recognized fool or jester in a Mexican village, see Dennis, "Role of the Drunk."

three Taking the Pledge

1.   Malchelosse, "Ah! mon grand-per,'" 142–5; Greer, *Peasant, Lord, and Merchant*, 157–9; Barry, "Shades of Vice," 9–10, 39; Noel, "Temperance Campaigning and Alcohol Consumption," 408–11; and *Canada Dry*, 14–15, 156; Denison, *Barley and the Stream*, 154; McCalla, *Planting the Province*, 98–100.; Hildebrand, "Les débuts du mouvement," 19; McBurney and Byers, *Tavern in the Town*, 103–4; Park, "Supply Side of Drinking"; Tyrrell, *Sobering Up*, 25–8; Lender and Martin, *Drinking in America*, 34–40, 46–58; Roberts, *Drink, Temperance, and the Working Class*, 16–18; Royal Commission on Liquor Traffic, *Report*, 957. France provides a later example of the anxiety that distilled liquor could prompt: no temperance movement appeared there until the 1870s, when the wine industry was crippled by a widespread blight on French grapes and French drinkers swung massively towards consumption of absinthe; see Marrus, "Social Drinking"; Prestwich, *Drink and the Politics of Social Reform*. Italy's temperance movement similarly arose much later than in North America, and focused its concern on the rising consumption of distilled grappa.

2. Acheson, *Saint John*, 139–40; Clark, "'Mother Gin' Controversy"; Warner, "In Another City, In Another Time"; Malcolm, *"Ireland Sober, Ireland Free"*, 38–55; Rorabaugh, *Alcoholic Republic*, 149–51, 167–9; Blocker, *American Temperance Movements*, 10. Peter Clark notes that, in a context of major social and economic change, increasing drunkenness in sixteenth- and seventeenth-century England may have resulted from the shift away from household consumption "towards alehouse drinking, often just with other males, frequently (as in the case of the tramping poor) with complete strangers"; "Alehouse and the Alternative Society," 59. David Conroy also suggests that, as looser licensing laws brought many more taverns to eighteenth-century Massachusetts, "The popular culture of drink traditionally invoked to express fellowship and interdependence, now contributed to the self-destruction of some troubled individuals with only tenuous ties to the community. . . . The social foundations of traditional drinking habits had weakened." *In Public Houses*, 145, 156. The least convincing explanation of the apparent rising consumption and drunkenness in the early nineteenth century is W.J. Rorabaugh's use of a now discredited anthropological theory of the 1940s that highlighted personal stress and anxiety (*Alcoholic Republic*, 125–83). His psychological theorizing floats too freely over the material lives of North Americans in the period, and flies in the face of well-established drinking practices, in which binge drinking was joyful, not anxious.

3. Levine, "Temperance Cultures."

4. Barry, "Shades of Vice," 14; Barron, "Genesis of Temperance," 190; Lockwood, "Temperance in Upper Canada as Ethnic Subterfuge," 46; Smart and Ogborne, *Northern Spirits*, 6–7.

5. The ensuing discussion leans heavily on Jan Noel's excellent study of the early temperance movement, *Canada Dry: Temperance Crusades before Confederation*.

6. The first temperance society in British North America seems to have been one functioning in Russelltown in the Eastern Townships of Lower Canada in 1822. Others appeared at Gloucester, N.B., in 1826, at West River, N.S., and Bedeque County, P.E.I., in 1827, and in Beaver River, N.S., Bastard Township in Upper Canada, and Montreal the next year. The only faint echo of the much earlier, patriarchal U.S. temperance work in these colonies seems to have been a public declaration by twelve employers in Hants County, N.S., not to provide liquor to employees; nothing further was heard from them (or anyone else), it seems. New Brunswick's inaugural temperance organizations had elite patronage, but that had drained away by the late 1830s. Harrison, *Drink and the Victorians*, 87–106; Quinn, *Father Mathew's Crusade*, 46–51; Roberts, *Drink, Temperance, and the Working Class*, 20–1; Levine, "Temperance Cultures"; Noel, *Canada Dry*; Barron, "Genesis of Temperance," 36–79, 104–32, and "American Origins"; Royal Commission on Liquor Traffic, *Report*, 770; Acheson, "Evangelicalism and Public Life," 55.

7. Noel, *Canada Dry*; Acheson, "Evangelicalism and Public Lie," 56.; Hildebrand, "Les débuts du mouvement"; MacLeod, "Dryness of the Liquor Dealer."

8. Noel, *Canada Dry*, 109 (quotation; for similar pledges in the Maritimes, see Barry, "Shades of Vice," 57–8, 80–1).

9. Acheson, *Saint John*, 142–4; Miller, "Unfermented Wine"; Tyrrell, *Sobering Up*, 135–58; Blocker, *American Temperance Movements*, 23–5; Olsen, "From Parish to Palace." The origin of the term "teetotal" seems to have been in the mouth of a English temperance enthusiast with a stammer, but it spread across the Atlantic to both Canada and the United States during the 1830s. Harrison, *Drink and the Victorians*, 126; Tyrrell, *Sobering Up*, 135. In contrast, the German temperance movement of the 1830s and 1840s never embraced complete abstention, concentrating simply on spirits; see Roberts, *Drink, Temperance, and the Working Class*, 24–5.

10. Noel, *Canada Dry*, 3; Barry, "Shades of Vice," 24–30, 85–95; Barron, "Genesis of Temperance," 44–79, 116–18, 160–9, 198–201; Davis, "I'll Drink to That," 73–87; Dick, "From Temperance to Prohibition," 530–1, 534–5; Dannenbaum, *Drink and Disorder*, 16–23; Spence, *Prohibition*, 37–45; Sturgis, "Beer under Pressure," 85; Allen, *Forty Years' Journey*.

11. Barry, "Shades of Vice," 55 (quotation); Noel, *Canada Dry*; Levine, "Good Creature of God and the Demon Rum," 128–47; Tyrrell, *Sobering Up*, 54–86; Harrison, *Drink and the Victorians*, 127–37; Bretherton, "Against the Flowing Tide," 153–5.

12. Barron, "Genesis of Temperance," 40; Noel, *Canada Dry*; Shiman, "John B. Gough."

13.   In 1845 a wealthy tanner, Jesse Ketchum, created a symbolic oasis for the cause in the heart
        of Toronto. He laid a public road through his garden that he dubbed "Temperance Street,"
        and inserted in the deed to the property a restriction against constructing any buildings for
        making or selling alcohol on the site (the street still exists in the heart of downtown
        Toronto). He also set aside another lot for the construction of a public meeting place to be
        known as Temperance Hall. Acheson, *Saint John*, 142–5; Huskins, "From *Haute cuisine* to Ox
        Roasts"; Barry, "Shades of Vice," 62, 98, 143, 204–38; Barron, "Genesis of Temperance,"
        99–103, 149–50, 203–4; Hildebrand, "Les débuts du mouvement," 82–99; McBurney and
        Byers, *Tavern in the Town*, 73, 111, 133; Spence, *Prohibition*, 46–60; Holman, *Sense of Their Duty*,
        132.
14.   Noel, *Canada Dry*, 37–40, 144–7, 207; Acheson, *Saint John*, 149–51; Ferry, "To the Interests
        and Conscience"; Spence, *Prohibition*, 46–56; Barron, "Genesis of Temperance," 202; Davis,
        "I'll Drink to That," 106–9; Graham, *Greenbank*, 75–7; Fahey, *Temperance and Racism*, 23–31,
        and "How the Good Templars Began"; Dannenbaum, *Drink and Disorder*, 32–68; Hampel,
        Temperance and Prohibition, 129–43.
15.   Noel, *Canada Dry*, 32–4, 89–102; Morgan, *Public Men and Virtuous Women*, 167, 208–11;
        Cook, *"Through Sunshine and Shadow"*, 22–9, 38–40; Tyrrell, *Woman's World, Woman's Empire*,
        18.
16.   Marks, "No Double Standard?"
17.   The Methodists banned all alcohol as a "deleterious drug" in 1830. Barron, "Genesis of
        Temperance," 195. See also Semple, *Lord's Dominion*, 67–70; Davis, "I'll Drink to That," 60–80;
        Hildebrand, "Les débuts du mouvement," 42–7; Marks, "Religion, Leisure, and Working-Class
        Identity," 281–92; Harrison, *Drink and the Victorians*, 93–4; Boyer, *Urban Masses and Moral
        Order*, 12–21.
18.   Davis, "I'll Drink to That," 55–93; Grant, *Profusion of Spires*, 76, 108–9, 112–3; Olsen, "From
        Parish to Palace"; Tyrrell, *Sobering Up*, 54–86; Harrison, *Drink and the Victorians*, 97–8.
19.   Greer, "Wage Labour and the Transition to Capitalism"; Palmer, *Working-Class Experience*,
        35–80; Heron and Storey, "On the Job in Canada," 5–7. Barron somewhat exaggerates the
        impact of waged employment in Upper Canada before the 1840s; "Genesis of Temperance,"
        83–4.
20.   Barry, "Shades of Vice," 54 (quotation); Johnson, *History of the County of Ontario*, 223–52.
21.   Morgan, *Public Men and Virtuous Women*; Holman, *Sense of Their Duty*, 132–4; Davidoff and
        Hall, *Family Fortunes*; Johnson, "Drinking, Temperance, and the Construction of Identity";
        Blumin, *Emergence of the Middle Class*; Ryan, *Cradle of the Middle Class*; Tyrrell, *Sobering Up* and
        "Temperance and Economic Change"; Harrison, *Drink and the Victorians*, 147–78; Barry,
        "Shades of Vice"; Barron, "Genesis of Temperance," 81–97, 255–67; Rotundo, "Learning
        about Manhood." In *Symbolic Crusade*, sociologist Joseph Gusfield presented the most influ-
        ential (and misleading) analysis of the U.S. temperance movement as a backward-looking,
        symbolic defence of the social status of the rural, Protestant middle class in the face of threats
        from below, and later from urban industrial society more generally.
22.   Barry, "Shades of Vice," 42 (quotation). Jan Noel sees this as two distinct steps in the develop-
        ment of the movement, but it seems equally likely that the identities of evangelical and inde-
        pendent producer/citizen were being forged simultaneously. See Davidoff and Hall, *Family
        Fortunes*, 25–7.
23.   See, in particular, Clark, *Church and Sect*, 266–7; Clemens, "Taste Not; Touch Not; Handle
        Not"; Barron, "Genesis of Temperance," 94–6; Hildebrand, "Les débuts du mouvement";
        Rumbarger, *Profits, Power, and Prohibition*; Faler, *Mechanics and Manufacturers*. Brian Harrison
        finds some of the English support for temperance based on this desire to discipline workers,
        especially in the textile districts, but sees this as an insufficient explanation for the success of
        the movement; *Drink and the Victorians*, 95–7.
24.   Noel, *Canada Dry*, 7–9; Acheson, *Saint John*, 138–59; Barry, "Shades of Vice," 152–60; Barron,
        "Genesis of Temperance," 136–40; Hildebrand, "Les débuts du mouvement," 30; Tyrrell,
        Sobering Up, 125; Blumin, *Emergence of the Middle Class*, 192–206; Harrison, *Drink and the
        Victorians*, 107–26.

25. Barron, "Genesis of Temperance," 140 (quotation); Noel, *Canada Dry*, 117–18, 160; Acheson, *Saint John*.

26. Noel, *Canada Dry*, 28–33, 63–76, 133–5, 217–20; Tyrrell, *Sobering Up*, 87–134; Holman, *Sense of Their Duty*, 133–4.

27. Morgan, *Public Men and Virtuous Women*, 164 (poem); Barron, "Genesis of Temperance," 95–6 (quotation from temperance manual).

28. McKay, "Liberal Order Framework"; Greer and Radforth, eds., *Colonial Leviathan*; Fecteau, *Un nouvel ordre des choses*; Curtis, *Building the Educational State*; and *True Government by Choice Men?*

29. Greer and Radforth, eds., *Colonial Leviathan*. Temperance forces in Ireland made the same case in this period; see Bretherton, "Against the Flowing Tide," 151–2.

30. Barron, "Genesis of Temperance," 229 (quotation; author's translation of "le mal capitale de ce pays, qui menace la fortune et la religion").

31. Barron, "Genesis of Temperance," 135 (quotation); Clemens, "Taste Not; Touch Not; Handle Not"; Hildebrand, "Les débuts du mouvement," 24.

32. The Toronto Temperance Society reported in 1841 that most of those who had joined in the previous year were from "laborious classes—men who earn their support by the sweat of their brow." Six years later, in 1847, the officers of the Toronto Reformation Society included two blacksmiths, a saddler, a mason, a watchmaker, a tailor, a printer, and a carpenter. Similarly, in the second half of the nineteenth century, master artisans and skilled workers made up the bulk of the membership in local anti-alcohol societies in Goderich, Galt, Thorold, Campbellford, and North Toronto. Toronto's Catholic temperance groups also had many working-class members. Noel, *Canada Dry*, 31–2, 105–6; Acheson, *Saint John*, 141–4; Barron, "Genesis of Temperance," 136; Burnet, "Urban Community," 310–11; Ferry, "To the Interests and Conscience," 3–4 (quotations), 18; Holman, *Sense of Their Duty*; Marks, *Revivals and Roller Rinks*, 249–50; Clark, *Piety and Nationalism*, 141–2; Palmer, *Culture in Conflict*; Newbury, "No Atheist, Eunuch, or Woman." See also Laurie, *Working People*, 120–4, and "Nothing on Impulse"; Faler, "Cultural Aspects of the Industrial Revolution," 390–4; Dodd, "Working Classes and the Temperance Movement"; Harrison, "Teetotal Chartism"; Benson, "American Workers and Temperance Reform," 5–34; Fahey, *Temperance and Racism*, 21–3.

33. In 1841 a new society modelled on the Washingtonians was formed in Montreal and another in Quebec the next year. Large crowds also attended Washingtonian meetings in New Brunswick. At the end of the next decade, similar groups began to appear in white settlements on the West Coast, one of whose members styled themselves "Dashaways." Noel, *Canada Dry*, 7–9; Morgan, *Public Men and Virtuous Women*, 152; Hildebrand, "Les débuts du mouvement," 95–6; Chapman, "Mid-Nineteenth-Century Temperance Movement," 47–8; Trainor, "Towards a Genealogy of Temperance," 185–8; Clemens, "Taste Not; Touch Not; Handle Not," 146; Perry, *On the Edge of Empire*, 80; Birrell, "D.I.K. Rine and the Gospel Temperance Movement"; *Advocate* (Toronto and Montreal), 1 March 1894, 81–2; Baumohl, "Confessions of Balder Hartpole"; Royal Commission on Liquor Traffic, *Report*, 782; Tyrrell, *Sobering Up*, 159–224; Blocker, *American Temperance Movements*, 39–47, 69–70; Hampel, *Temperance and Prohibition*, 103–28; Alexander, "We Are Engaged as a Band of Sisters"; Wilentz, *Chants Democratic*, 306–14; Decarie, "Prohibition Movement in Ontario," 13; Johnson, "Drinking, Temperance, and the Construction of Identity," 525–6; Baumohl, "Inebriate Institutions," 93–5, 97–100; Baumohl and Room, "Inebriety, Doctors, and the State," 138–41, 146–9. The Gospel Temperance movement deserves a good deal more scholarly attention than it has received to date.

34. Morgan, *Public Men and Virtuous Women*, 141–82; Trainor, "Towards a Genealogy of Temperance," 43–93; Barry, "Shades of Vice," 204–38; Hildebrand, "Les débuts du mouvement," 67; Levine, "Temperance and Women," 35–43; Davidoff and Hall, *Family Fortunes*; Ryan, *Cradle of the Middle Class*; Johnson, "Drinking, Temperance, and the Construction of Identity," 523–6; Kimmel, *Manhood in America*, 43–78; Rotundo, "Learning about Manhood"; Carnes, "Middle-Class Men and the Solace of Fraternal Ritual." Anna Clark has traced the evolving class and gender identities in working-class England; see *Struggle for the Breeches*; see also McClelland, "Masculinity and the 'Representative Artisan.'" On this side of the Atlantic,

Bettina Bradbury's *Working Families* shows that, by the last third of the nineteenth century, working-class family economies in Montreal assumed that the breadwinner had crucial domestic responsibilities, which became a cornerstone of his masculinity. Christina Burr also notes that by 1872 the country's first independent labour newspaper, the *Ontario Workman*, was articulating a distinctly working-class version of domesticity and masculinity; see *Spreading the Light*, 127–35.

35.   Morgan, *Public Men and Virtuous Women*; Noel, *Canada Dry*, 89–102; Nadelhafdt, "Alcohol and Wife Abuse."

36.   Montreal had a society modelled on Mathew's work in 1840 and Halifax in 1841. In New Brunswick the Irish Abstinence Society had several branches at the same point, and in Newfoundland an Irish disciple of Father Mathew spearheaded a widely supported temperance society in St. John's. Father Thomas Fitzhenry similarly built a large following of teetotallers among his parishioners in Toronto. Townend, *Father Mathew*; Malcolm, "Catholic Church and Irish Temperance Movement," 1–6; and *"Ireland Sober, Ireland Free"*, 101–50; Bretherton, "Against the Flowing Tide," 155–62, and "Battle between Carnival and Lent"; Quinn, *Father Matthew's Crusade*; Barry, "Shades of Vice," 169, 184, 260–71; Barron, "Genesis of Temperance," 2–12; Davis, "I'll Drink to That," 36–7; Acheson, *Saint John*, 146–8; Chapman, "Mid-Nineteenth-Century Temperance Movement," 49; Grant, *Profusion of Spires*, 164; Burnet, "Urban Community," 303.

37.   Clarke, *Piety and Nationalism*, 132–51.

38.   Bernard, "Deux phases de l'antialcoolisme," 135–55 (quotation at 151).

39.   Noel, "Dry Patriotism" and *Canada Dry*, 27–8, 153–82; Hildebrand, "Les débuts du mouvement," 48–54; Ares, "Les campagnes de tempérance"; Trudel, *Chiniquy*; Bédard-Lévesque, "La tempérance au Québec"; Rousseau, "Boire ou ne pas boire."

40.   Voisine, "Mouvements de tempérance" (quotation at 70; author's translation of "l'ivrognerie [est] reparue plus hideuse et plus hardie que jamais"); Rousseau and Remiggi, eds., *Atlas historique de pratiques religieuses*; Miller, "Anti-Catholicism in Canada." The church had not been alone in these efforts. During the same period, in a more secular vein, French Canada's left-liberal *rouges* also supported the dry cause as part of their concern for moral and intellectual self-improvement. A Catholic-nationalist temperance movement also emerged in Poland; see Moskalewicz and Zielinski, "Poland," 225.

41.   Law, "Self-Reliance Is the True Road to Independence"; Winks, *Blacks in Canada*, 217; Spray, *Blacks in New Brunswick*, 50; Ferry, "To the Interests and Conscience," 5–6; Kitossa, "Criticism, Reconstruction, and African-Centred Feminist Historiography," 96–8; Herd, "Paradox of Temperance"; Fahey, *Temperance and Racism*, 30–1, 58–80, 105–25; Barron, "Alcoholism, Indians, and the Anti-Drink Cause."

42.   Canada, House of Commons, *Journals*, 1873, Appendix 3, 13–15; McBurney and Byers, *Tavern in the Town*, 40–1; Burley, *Servants of the Honourable Company*, 133–4; Way, *Common Labour*, 185; Cross, "Lumber Community," 229–30; Grant, *When Rum Was King*, 6–7; Noel, *Canada Dry*, 120, 221; Heron, "Factory Workers"; Pack, *Nelson's Blood*, 77–80; Wilson, "Reciprocal Work Bees," 444; Roberts, "Drink and Industrial Discipline"; Barrows, "Worlds of Drink," 16; Rodgers, *Work Ethic*; Pollard, *Genesis of Modern Management*. There is still far too little research on the effectiveness of these workplace bans in Canada, but research on Germany, France, Denmark, and Wales suggests that European employers may have been slower to crack down on drinking on the job; Roberts, *Drink, Temperance, and the Working Class*; Barrows, "Worlds of Drink"; Schioler, "Denmark"; Lambert, "Drink and Work-Discipline."

43.   Noel, "Temperance Campaigning and Alcohol Consumption"; *Canada Dry*, 120; Hartlen, "From a Torrent to a Trickle"; Christie, "Function of the Tavern"; Smart and Ogborne, *Northern Spirits*, 8; Butsch, "Introduction: Leisure and Hegemony." For a discussion of the development of the new "laws of etiquette" to regulate social relations with more personal restraint, see Kasson, *Rudeness and Civility*.

44.   Denison, *Barley and the Stream*, 217–18, 229, 232–3; Phillips, *On Tap*, 58, 65–70, 74–5; Tucker, "Labatt's," 48–9; Sneath, *Brewed in Canada*, 36–62.

45.   Denison, *Barley and the Stream*, 198–200, 217–18, 229, 232–3; Harrison, "Pubs," 162–3; and *Drink and the Victorians*, 334–6, 353–64. The Molsons' decision to close their distillery in 1867

seems to have been the result of the much steeper government excise duties that cut deeply into profits; Denison, *Barley and the Stream*, 244.

46. Roberts, "Taverns and Tavern-goers," 74; Barron, "Genesis of Temperance," 17. In 1874 Ontario had the relatively low ratio of one tavern for every 338 residents, and one licence (including retail shops) for every 262; Drummond, *Progress without Planning*, 294.

47. McKeon and McKeon, *Oakville*, 53 (quotation; my thanks to Steve Penfold for this reference); Barron, "Genesis of Temperance," 135–6, 172–3; Holman, *Sense of Their Duty*, 132.

48. Fingard, "A Great Big Rum Shop"; DeLottinville, "Joe Beef"; Thompson, "Prohibition Question," 8 (quotation).

49. Johnston, *Drury*, 157; Kristofferson, "Craft Capitalism," 242, 260 (quotation).

50. Houston and Smyth, *Irish Emigration and Settlement*; Way, *Common Labour*; Tyrrell, *Sobering Up*, 269–78.

51. Roberts, "Harry Jones and His Cronies" (quotation), and "Taverns and Tavern-goers," 189–218.

52. Acheson, *Saint John*, 151–9; Chapman, "Mid-Nineteenth-Century Temperance Movement"; Canada, Department of Inland Revenues, *Report*, 1917, xvi; Waite, "Sir Oliver Mowat's Canada" and *Man From Halifax*, 81, 222; Colombo, ed., *Colombo's Canadian Quotations*, 380 (quote); Gwyn, *Private Capital*, 51, 148; Campbell, "'Smashers' and 'Rummies'"; Walden, *Becoming Modern*, 65; Tyrrell, *Sobering Up*, 95–110; Blocker, *American Temperance Movements*, 37, 70–1; Harrison, *Drink and the Victorians*, 135–46; Lawrence, "Class and Gender." On the spread of bourgeois cultural exclusivist distance from the lower classes, see Levine, *Highbrow/Lowbrow*; and Kasson, *Rudeness and Civility*.

53. Noel, *Canada Dry*, 46–54, 117–22; Garland and Talman, "Pioneer Drinking Habits," 186; Decarie, "Something Old, Something New," 157; Dick, "From Temperance to Prohibition," 539–41; Sturgis, "Spectre of a Drunkard's Grave"; Clark, *Of Toronto the Good*, 144; *Montreal by Gaslight*; *Toronto by Gaslight*; Huggins, "More Sinful Pleasures?" As a medical student at McGill University in 1871, the young William Osler (later Canada's most prominent doctor) boarded with other students from Ontario who, together, consumed several gallons of whisky a week. Bliss, *William Osler*, 65.

four≈The Reign of King Alcohol

1. Frances Willard, quoted in Levine, "Temperance and Women," 61.

2. Royal Commission on Liquor Traffic, *Minutes of Evidence*, vol.2, 385; Bradbury, "Pigs, Cows, and Boarders"; Blocker, *American Temperance Movements*, 65–6. In 1878 the federal Department of Inland Revenue's *Annual Report* began including an annual table of "illicit stills" seized during the year (in 1890 the term was changed to "illicit manufactures"). When, starting in 1897, the "residences" of those charged were included, rather than simply the departmentally defined district in which they were charged, it was immediately clear that virtually all the moonshiners were located in rural villages and townships.

3. Excise duties on Canadian production doubled to 60 cents a gallon at Confederation and then shot up to 90 cents in 1875, $1 in 1879, $1.30 in 1885, and $1.50 in 1891, while custom duties on imported gin, rum, and whisky jumped from 80 cents to $2 per gallon over the same period. Brown, *Two Hundred Years of Tradition*, 12, 21; Canada, Department of Inland Revenue, *Annual Reports*, 1870–1916 (calculations of averages are mine); Royal Commission on Liquor Traffic, *Report*, 736, 738.

4. Denison, *Barley and the Stream*, 233; Royal Commission on Liquor Traffic, *Report*, 16–24; Blocker, *American Temperance Movements*, 64–6; Burnett, *Liquid Pleasures*, 126–7; and *Plenty and Want*, 26–7; Harrison, *Drink and the Victorians*, 311–14; Artibise, *Winnipeg*; Taylor, "Fire, Disease, and Water"; Warfe, "Search for Pure Water"; Baldwin, "But Not a Drop to Drink"; Cain, "Water and Sanitation Services." Jack Blocker suggests that two distinct patterns of alcohol consumption can be seen in the United States over the nineteenth century (patterns parallelled in Canada): first, one rooted in a predominantly rural commercial economy where widely scattered independent commodity producers were supplied with distilled liquor,

which was less bulky and less prone to spoiling in transport than beer; then, after the Civil War, the more concentrated populations of urban drinkers who could be supplied with locally produced beer or the heavily marketed products of the largest brewers, available through a smaller number of retail outlets. Blocker, "Consumption and Availability of Alcoholic Beverages."

5. Canada, Department of Inland Revenue, *Annual Reports*, 1870–93.
6. Royal Commission on Liquor Traffic, *Report*, 75; Rowntree and Shadwell, *Temperance Problem and Social Reform*, 435–6; Marrus, "Social Drinking"; Blocker, *American Temperance Movements*, 67, 109–10.
7. In 1903 a Catholic scholar at Laval University undertook a detailed investigation of a respectable typographer's family budget in Quebec City (a rare study in Canada in the period) and, while saying nothing about alcohol consumption outside the house, noted that at the end of social evenings, "il est d'habitude de présenter à ses hôtes un verre de bière, de vin ou de spiritueux, avec des gâteaux et des fruits." Lortie, "Compositeur typographe," 96.
8. Kilbourn, *Elements Combined*, 25–6 (quotation by historian), 120 (quotation by foreman); Royal Commission on Liquor Traffic, *Minutes of Evidence*, vol.4, part 1, 181, 209; Ajzenstadt, "Medical-Moral Economy," 92–3; Benson, "American Workers and Temperance Reform," 27–31; Rosenzweig, *Eight Hours for What We Will*, 38.
9. Cook, "More a Medicine Than a Beverage" (quotations at 8, 11, 12).
10. Heron, "Factory Workers" and "Second Industrial Revolution."
11. Heron, "Factory Workers"; Kealey, "Work Control, the Labour Process, and Nineteenth-Century Canadian Printers"; Bailey, *Leisure and Class*. Labour Day arrived in many communities in the 1880s and was declared a national holiday in 1894, alongside Christmas, New Year, Easter, the Queen's Birthday (later Victoria or Empire Day), Dominion Day, and, in many places, Thanksgiving; Heron and Penfold, *Workers' Festival*.
12. Gusfield, "Passage to Play," 80; Gray, *Booze*, 35–47, 63–70; Clark, *Of Toronto the Good*, 143–4; Strople, "Prohibition and Movements of Social Reform," 20; Hiebert, "Prohibition in British Columbia," 17; Methodist and Presbyterian Churches, *St. Catharines Survey*, 22–3; Men's Federation of London, *City of London*, 73.
13. Royal Commission on Liquor Traffic, *Report*, 72–6; Gagan and Gagan, "Working-Class Standards of Living," 178–80; Baskerville and Sager, *Unwilling Idlers*; Burnett, *Liquid Pleasures*, 125–30; Marks, *Revivals and Roller Rinks*; Rosenzweig, *Eight Hours for What We Will*, 48–9; Dingle, "Drink and Working-Class Living Standards"; Swiencicki, "Consuming Brotherhood"; Norcliffe, *Ride to Modernity*. A U.S. Bureau of Industry study of some three thousand working-class families in textile communities surveyed between 1888 and 1890 found that all discretionary expenditures (as opposed to those on necessities) across all these households were never much more than 6 per cent of total family income, an amount that could easily disappear in times of financial crisis; only a minority of families reported any expenditures on liquor. Clubb, Austin, and Kirk, *Process of Historical Inquiry*, 51–7; Blocker, *American Temperance Movements*, 69.
14. Royal Commission on Liquor Traffic, *Report*, 6.
15. Canada, Department of Inland Revenue, *Annual Reports*, 1870–1916 (calculations of averages are mine); Brown, *Two Hundred Years of Tradition*, 22–41; Rannie, *Canadian Whisky*, 31–8, 89–116, 125–30, 133, 137–8; <www.canadianclubwhisky.com/legacy>. Although a few eventually well-known companies such as Bright's, Barnes, and Turner's emerged in the late nineteenth century, what little wine-making was undertaken in Canada before prohibition was centred in Ontario (chiefly on the Niagara Peninsula and Point Pelee), often merely a farmer's by-product of grape-growing, limited to local consumption, undistinguished in quality, and prone to shutdowns; Rowe, *Wines of Canada*, 25–46; Rannie, *Wines of Ontario*, 12–35, 47–63; Aspler, *Vintage Canada*, 7–12; Diston, "Our Changing Tastes." John and Joseph Meagher started a gin distillery in Montreal in 1873, and two years later Jan Melcher, a Dutch immigrant, did the same at Berthierville in Quebec; both men intended to serve the province's growing taste for that beverage.
16. Canada, Department of Inland Revenue, *Annual Reports*, 1870–1916 (calculations of averages are mine).

17. Ibid.

18. Tucker, "Labatt's," 103–4.

19. Denison, *Barley and the Stream*, 243, 255; Phillips, *On Tap*, 65–84; Tucker, "Labatt's," 103–8, 122–34; Rudy, "Sleeman's"; Bowering, *Brewing in Formosa*; Dorion, *La brasserie Boswell*; Haliburton, *What's Brewing*, 11–22; Sneath, *Brewed in Canada*, 63–83, 93–100; Watson and Watson, *Pioneer Breweries of British Columbia*. These growth patterns parallelled those in the United States in the late nineteenth and early twentieth centuries, though the scale of the Canadian industry remained smaller; see Kerr, "American Brewing Industry."

20. *Globe* (Toronto), 7 February 1862, 1; see also Somerville, "Description of the Distillery."

21. *Globe*, 7 February 1862, 1; Somerville, "Description of the Distillery"; Bloomfield and Bloomfield, *Industrial Leaders*, 60–6; Heron, "Factory Workers"; Rannie, *Canadian Whisky*, 43–57.

22. *Spectator* (Hamilton), 9, 11, 14, 17 September 1863 (I am grateful to Rob Kristofferson for these references); Tucker, "Labatt's," 62, 77; Phillips, *On Tap*, 26–34; Rudy, "Sleeman's."

23. Denison, *Barley and the Stream*, 226, 258–60, 276–81; Tucker, "Labatt's," 89–95.

24. Denison, *Barley and the Stream*, 260, 274, 285–90; Tucker, "Labatt's," 163; *Advocate* (Toronto and Montreal), 22 March 1894, 156; 10 May 1894, 323; Baron, *Brewed in America*, 228–46; Heron, "Second Industrial Revolution."

25. Denison, *Barley and the Stream*, 25–56, 281, 305; Phillips, *On Tap*, 11–12; Heron, "Factory Workers," 516–20.

26. Lager was first brewed in Ontario in 1847 in Berlin (Kitchener) and Hamilton, and local German-owned breweries brought it to many more communities. Carling's London brewery began producing it in 1869 and O'Keefe's Toronto factory ten years later. By the late 1890s Reinhardt's brewery in Toronto and the Montreal Brewing Company were specializing solely in lager beer. Labatt won medals at international exhibitions for his IPA, which would be the main product of his brewery until the end of the Second World War. Much like today's beers, the alcohol content in all these beers ranged from roughly 4 to 8 per cent. Phillips, *On Tap*, 36–8, 93–120; Tucker, "Labatt's," 77–80, 155; Denison, *Barley and the Stream*, 258–60, 299; Bowering, *Brewing in Formosa*, 9–37; Sneath, *Brewed in Canada*, 78; *Spectator*, 25 January 1878 (thanks to Rob Kristofferson for this reference); *Advocate*, 22 March 1894, 156; Royal Commission on Liquor Traffic, *Minutes of Evidence*, vol.4, part 1, 71, 165; Walden, *Becoming Modern*, 59–65; Gutzke, *Protecting the Pub*, 2–4; Baron, *Brewed in America*, 175–90, 228.

27. Denison, *Barley and the Stream*, 262, 299–300; Rannie, *Canadian Whisky*, 98–102; Tucker, "Labatt's," 234–40; Men's Federation of London, *City of London*, 73 (quotation); Strasser, *Satisfaction Guaranteed*, 29–57; Lears, "From Salvation to Self-Realization."

28. Phillips, *On Tap*, 94, 114–5, 118, 135–58 (quotation at 137); Rudy, "Sleeman's" (quotation at 57); *Advocate*, 22 March 1894, 156.

29. Royal Commission on Liquor Traffic, *Minutes of Evidence*, vol.4, part 1; Denison, *Barley and the Stream*, 305.

30. Phillips, *On Tap*; Rudy, "Sleeman's"; Tucker, "Labatt's," 56–7, 101–2, 109–15.

31. Royal Commission on Liquor Traffic, *Minutes of Evidence*, vol.4, part 1, 111, 165–7, 201; *Canadian Annual Review*, 1907, 528–30; Marrus, *Mr. Sam*, 47–8; Spence, *Prohibition*, 383; Sendbuehler, "Battling 'The Bane of Our Cities'"; Rannie, *Canadian Whisky*, 96; Phillips, *On Tap*, 141–52; Baron, *Brewed in America*, 257–64, 272–73; Duis, *Saloon*, 15–45; Blocker, "Artisan's Escape"; Gutzke, *Protecting the Pub*. In Britain, where three-quarters of the pubs were "tied" to brewers by the end of the nineteenth century, retailers frequently protested the terms of the relationship; that few complaints of this kind surfaced in Canada suggests that the "tied house" may well have been much less common here.

32. Brown, *Two Hundred Years of Tradition*, 30–5; Fraser, *Hiram Walker Remembered*; <www.canadi-anclubwhisky.com/legacy>.

33. Bowering, *Art and Mystery of Brewing*; Denison, *Barley and the Stream*, 255–6; Tucker, "Labatt's," 95–7; Rudy, "Sleeman's"; Bowes, "George Sleeman"; Haliburton, *What's Brewing*, 20, 22; *Advocate*, 22 March 1894, 156; 10 May 1894, 323; Schneider, "German Brewery Workers." For a parallel workplace experience in woodworking, see Parr, *Gender of Breadwinners*, 123–42.

34.   Forsey, *Trade Unions*, 283, 321, 323, 339; *75 Years of Progress*, 1–9; Tucker, "Labatt's," 134–41; Canada, Department of Labour, *Labour Organization in Canada*, 1911–15; *Labour Gazette*, March 1904, 937; June 1904, 1248; July 1904, 84; November 1905, 577; December 1905, 690; May 1906, 1268; Canada, Department of Labour, *Strikes and Lockouts in Canada*, 1902–14; Schneider, "German Brewery Workers.".

35.   Josephson, *Union House, Union Bar*,131–2; *100 Years of Service*.

36.   Kealey, *Toronto Workers*, 183; Mittelman, "A Conflict of Interest"; Schluter, *Brewing Industry and Brewery Workers' Movement*; Josephson, *Union House, Union Bar*, 3–128.

37.   Royal Commission on Liquor Traffic, *Report*, 6–29 (quotation at 29).

38.   McIntosh, *Collectors*, 133; Perry, *Taxes, Tariffs, and Subsidies*, vol.1, 69–73, 104–7, vol. 2, 624–5, 628–30; for discussions of the U.S. federal government's close relationship with the liquor traffic as a result of tax revenues derived from distilling and brewing, see Hamm, "Convoluted State"; and Mittelman, "Who Will Pay the Tax?" See also Gerritsen, *Fuddle and Flash*, 87–115.

39.   Phillips, *On Tap*, 79–80; *Dictionary of Canadian Biography*, vol.14, 185–9, 916–17; Brown, *Two Hundred Years of Tradition*, 24–37; Fingard, "Great Big Rum Shop," 96; Rudy, "Sleeman's"; Hiebert, "Prohibition in British Columbia," 53; Evans, *Sir Oliver Mowat*, 110 (quotation); *History of the Vote in Canada*; Marrus, *Mr. Sam*, 62. A disgruntled hotel-keeper who was denied a licence complained to Manitoba's premier in 1891 that the proprietor of another, allegedly inferior, drinking establishment got one because he had voted the right way in the last election: "White has as good as said the reasons he got his license was because he knew how to work the party." Thompson, "Prohibition Question," 44. Among the booze-producers in politics, George Sleeman was mayor of Guelph, Henry Corby was mayor of Belleville and a member of the Ontario legislature, J.P. Wiser sat in the House of Commons as a Liberal MP, John Carling was a prominent cabinet minister in the Macdonald Conservative regime in Ottawa in the last quarter of the nineteenth century, and Corby's son Harry joined the Tory caucus there in 1888, as did Joseph Seagram in 1896.

40.   Legally, the term "saloon" was most often used to refer to the drinking establishments not attached to hotels, but critics and drinkers alike used it more loosely.

41.   Powers, *Faces along the Bar*; Blocker, "Tidy Pictures."

42.   Fingard, "Great Big Rum Shop," 90, 95; Couturier, "Prohibition or Regulation?" 157, 159–60; *A Few Facts Bearing on the Social and Civic Character of Montreal*, 4–5; Royal Commission on Liquor Traffic, *Minutes of Evidence*, vol.4, part 1, 124, 156, 187, 191; Gray, *Booze*, 1–18. Mark Davis identified three female bootleggers in Nova Scotia and ten in New Brunswick, among many more; see "Ill Drink to That," 205–6.

43.   DeLottinville, "Joe Beef"; *Montreal by Gaslight*, 22 (quotation by journalist); Methodist and Presbyterian Churches, *Vancouver*, 15 (quotation by social survey); Benson, "American Workers and Temperance Reform," 118–20.

44.   DeLottinville, "Joe Beef"; *Montreal by Gaslight*, 66–79, 94–120; Marks, *Revivals and Roller Rinks*, 85; Perry, "Gender, Race, and the Making of Colonial Society" (quotation); Gray, *Booze*, 1–18.

45.   Kinsdale, "Poor Man's Club"; Harrison, "Pubs"; Girouard, *Victorian Pubs*; Powers, *Faces along the Bar*. In the absence of many detailed descriptions of saloons in Canada, the many surviving photographs in archives across the country provide the best evidence of the interiors of these establishments. The brewing and distilling companies provided many of the images that appeared on saloon walls.

46.   Ennals and Holdsworth, *Homeplace*, 213–31; Doucet and Weaver, *Housing the North American City*, 436–7; McBurney and Byers, *Tavern in the Town*, 37–8, 45, 60–1; DeLottinville, "Joe Beef"; Benson, "American Workers and Temperance Reform," 112–18; Porsild, *Gamblers and Dreamers*, 82, 158, 173, 186; Hiebert, "Prohibition in British Columbia," 13–18; Kingsdale, "Poor Man's Club"; Sendbuehler, "Battling 'The Bane of our Cities'"; Gray, *Booze*, 64–7; Campbell, *Demon Rum or Easy Money*, 17–18; Methodist and Presbyterian Churches, *Vancouver*, 15; *Report of a Preliminary and General Social Survey of Fort William*, 17; *Report of a Preliminary and General Social Survey of Port Arthur*, 12; Sobel and Meurer, *Working at Inglis*, 21.

47.   Gray, *Booze*, 33 (quotation).

48. Fowke, *Penguin Book of Canadian Folk Songs*, 96–7 (quotation); Christie, "Function of the Tavern"; DeLottinville, "Joe Beef"; Walden, *Becoming Modern*, 250.

49. Walmsley and Kossuth, "Fighting It Out"; McBurney and Byers, *Tavern in the Town*, 29–30, 51–2; Marks, *Revivals and Roller Rinks*, 85–6; Fingard, "Great Big Rum Shop," 93, 98; Burr, "Roping in the Wretched," 88; Porsild, *Gamblers and Dreamers*, 186.

50. *Montreal by Gaslight*, 94–105; Guillet, *Pioneer Inns and Taverns*, vol.1, 35, 41–4, 125; Lenton-Young, "Variety Theatre," 186–90; *Spectator*, 4 October 1919, 29 (quotation); Harrison, "Pubs," 174–5; Bailey, *Leisure and Class*, 147–68; Snyder, *Voice of the City*; Jones, *Languages of Class*, 179–238.

51. Weaver, *Crimes, Constables, and Courts*, 229–30. Madelon Powers' study of U.S. saloons is by far the most sensitive discussion of this saloon culture; see *Faces along the Bar*; see also Kinsdale, "Poor Man's Club"; Ade, *Old-Time Saloon*; Popham, "Social History of the Tavern," 277–89; Lockwood, "Music and Songs," 180–206. For the competitive edge of barroom behaviour; see Walmsley and Kossuth, "Fighting It Out"; Parsons, "Risky Business"; and Archer, "Men Behaving Badly?"

52. Royal Commission on Liquor Traffic, *Minutes of Evidence*, vol.2, 531.

53. McBurney and Byers note that there were some female entrances to taverns, and they provide vignettes of female tavern-keepers, many of them widows; see *Tavern in the Town*, 7, 60–1, 93, 100, 132, 202; Marks, *Revivals and Roller Rinks*, 85–7; Perry, "Gender, Race, and the Making of Colonial Society," 91–104, 111–76; Porsild, *Gamblers and Dreamers*, 100–1, 110; Warsh, "Oh, Lord, Pour a Cordial in Her Wounded Heart"; Gray, *Booze*, 5; Powers, *Faces along the Bar*, 32–5, Bailey, "Parasexuality and Glamour"; Girouard, *Victorian Pubs*, 17–18; Kirby, *Barmaids*; Hey, *Patriarchy and Pub Culture*, 13–22; Royal Commission on Liquor Traffic, *Minutes of Evidence*, vol.2, 362–3, vol.4, part 1, 138; Methodist and Presbyterian Churches, *St. Catharines Survey*, 23, and *Report of a Preliminary and General Social Survey of Hamilton, Report of a Preliminary and General Social Survey of Fort William, Report of a Preliminary and General Social Survey of Port Arthur, Report of a Preliminary and General Social Survey of Regina*; and *Vancouver*; Men's Federation of London, *City of London*, 68, 70, 76; *Spectator*, 29 March 1910, 14, 13 June 1910, 12; Tyrrell, *Woman's World, Woman's Empire*, 15; *Toronto by Gaslight*, 28. The Ontario and Quebec governments formally banned the employment of women in taverns in 1907; Humphries, *"Honest Enough to Be Bold,"* 132; Spence, *Prohibition*, 363. It may well be that tighter regulations on Canadian saloons excluded women more completely than in the United States; see Peiss, *Cheap Amusements*, 28. U.S. prohibitionists were shocked at the number of women they saw in public drinking places in Britain, France, and Germany.

54. Powers, *Faces along the Bar*, 31. Photographs of the barrooms in both the New Western Hotel in Ladysmith, B.C., and the Vendome Hotel in downtown Toronto reveal these troughs in front of the bars. AO, F 1505-15-127, MSR 8361, File 73, Photo 1790; CTA, SC 653-3.

55. Powers, *Faces along the Bar*, 26–47; Parsons, "Risky Business," 284–8; Marks, *Revivals and Roller Rinks*, 85–6 (quotation at 86); Ripmeester, "Mines, Homes, and Halls," 106; Methodist Church and Presbyterian Church, *Report of a Preliminary and General Social Survey of Hamilton*, 19, and *Report of a Preliminary and General Social Survey of Regina*, 47; Chudacoff, *Age of the Bachelor*, 75–105. The history of saloon architecture in Canada remains an unexplored terrain, but arguably the absence of women (reinforced by legislation in some provinces) and the departure of more affluent drinkers may have discouraged hotel owners from creating the numerous, highly differentiated drinking spaces available within turn-of-the-century British pubs, and encouraged the pattern of the single large barroom more common across North America. See Girouard, *Victorian Pubs*.

56. Bradbury, *Working Families*; Heron, "High School and Household Economy"; Coulter, "Working Young."

57. Marks, *Revivals and Roller Rinks*, 82–5; *Montreal by Gaslight*, 148–59; *Toronto by Gaslight*, 1–2, 6–7, 19–22, 48–9; Forestall, "Bachelors, Boarding-Houses, and Blind Pigs"; Chan, "Bachelor Workers"; McDonald, "Lumber Society," 94–5; Harney, "Men without Women"; Bradwin, *Bunkhouse Man*; McCormack, "Wobblies and Blanketstiffs"; Leier, *Where the Fraser River Flows*; Avery, *Reluctant Host*, 20–81; Porsil, *Gamblers and Dreamers*; Chudacoff, *Age of the Bachelor*, 107–14; McLean, "Most Effectual Remedy," 42–3; Gray, *Booze*, 63–7; Mark, *Revivals*

and Roller Rinks, 85–91; Methodist Church and Presbyterian Church, *Report of a Preliminary and General Social Survey of Hamilton*, 19; Royal Commission on Liquor Traffic, *Report*, 171. The U.S. writer Jack London, writing about his experiences as a young transient worker in the West Coast of the United States in the early twentieth century, emphasized that, outside the saloons where he regularly got drunk, there was no place for young men to socialize; see London, *John Barleycorn*.

58. Forestall, "Bachelors, Boarding-Houses, and Blind Pigs"; Chan, "Bachelor Workers"; Powers, *Faces along the Bar*, 43–4; Heron, "Boys and Their Booze." The Chinese were an exception to this general pattern: other workers shunned them, and they turned to their own bachelor culture, which did not include specialized drinking places.

59. Royal Commission on Liquor Traffic, *Minutes of Evidence*, vol.4, 376, 506 (quotation by working man); *Toronto by Gaslight*, 2 (quotation by journalist); DeLottinville, "Joe Beef."

60. Ade, *Old-Time Saloon*, 26(quotation).

61. Methodist and Presbyterian Churches, *Vancouver*, 15, *Report of a Preliminary and General Social Survey of Regina*, 46, *Report of a Preliminary and General Social Survey of Fort William*, 15, 17, *Report of a Preliminary and General Social Survey of Port Arthur*, 11–12, *Report of Preliminary and General Social Survey of Hamilton*, 20, *St. Catharines Survey*, 22; Men's Federation of London, *City of London*, 66–7(calculations of averages are mine). In 1901 a U.S. writer described four distinct kinds of drinking places: the rough "waterfront" saloon, the lavishly furnished "American" saloon (catering to a more respectable, downtown clientele), the "immigrant" saloon (serving a particular working-class neighbourhood and ranging from dingy back-alley places to more comfortable beer gardens, cafés, or restaurants), and "political" saloons (centres of local political organizing and patronage). It seems likely that in Canada, as in the United States, there was more shading and overlap between these types. Benson, "American Workers and Temperance Reform," 102–11. For some men, "pub-crawling" might blur these distinctions.

62. *Montreal by Gaslight*, 68–79, 94–120, 154–6.

63. Benson, "American Workers and Temperance Reform," 112 (quotation by Gompers), 139–42; Perry, "Gender, Race, and the Making of Colonial Society," 96 (quotation by visitor to B.C.); McBurney and Byers, *Tavern in the Town*, 116–7 (quotation from later reminiscence); Rosenzweig, *Eight Hours for What We Will*, 58–64; Barrows, "Parliaments of the People"; Haine, "Priest of the Proletarians"; Roberts, "Tavern and Politics"; Harrison, "Pubs," 185.

64. Marks, *Revivals and Roller Rinks*, 86 (quotation).

65. The informal culture among working men on the shop floor remains an opaque world that scholars have had difficulty penetrating; on the experience of craftworkers, see (for Canada) Kealey, *Toronto Workers*; Palmer, *Culture in Conflict*; (for the United States) Montgomery, *Workers' Control*, 9–31; (for Germany) Luedtke, "Cash, Coffee Breaks, Horseplay"; on the twentieth-century experience, see Meyer, "Work, Play, and Power"; Collinson, "Engineering Humour."

66. Crouse, "They 'Left Us Pretty Much as We Were'"; Forestall, "Bachelors, Boarding-Houses, and Blind Pigs," 266–7, 269–70; Chudacoff, *Age of the Bachelor*, 106–45; Carnes, *Secret Ritual and Manhood*; Clawson, *Constructing Brotherhood*; Marks, *Revivals and Roller Rinks*; Peiss, *Cheap Amusements*; Strange, *Toronto's Girl Problem*. Madelon Powers argues that in the United States saloons were "decaying from within," as a result of these counterattractions, rising living standards, enhanced ethnic tensions, and withdrawal of union support. My reading is that none of these factors had seriously dislodged the saloon from its central place in urban working-class life, certainly not in the Canadian context. See Powers, "Decay from Within."

67. Dingle, "Drink and Working-Class Living Standards"; Lees, "Getting and Spending," 182–3; Byington, *Homestead*, 84; Roberts, "Drink and Working Class Living Standards"; Kingsdale, "Poor Man's Club," 482; Chapin, *Standard of Living among Workingmen's Families*; Bevans, *How Workingmen Spend Their Spare Time*; Horowitz, *Morality of Spending*.

68. Burr, "Roping in the Wretched," 90 (quotation); Royal Commission on Liquor Traffic, *Report*.

69. As a proportion of husbands in any community, the number of names on the "Indian List" remained relatively small (only seventy in London in 1908, for example), although the great

majority of delinquent husbands were never taken to court. At the turn of the century the Montreal businessman Herbert Ames had researchers knocking at the doors of the city's working-class population asking many questions; he learned that drunkenness was "at the bottom of the trouble" in no more than 7 per cent of the cases in the poorest group (Charles Booth's famous contemporary study of workers in London, England, found 14 per cent). A recent study of non-support cases in turn-of-the-century Ontario found only about a quarter of them rooted in alcohol abuse. Davies, *Leisure, Gender, and Poverty*, 31–54; Bradbury, *Working Families*, 152–81; Harvey, "To Love, Honour, and Obey"; Fingard, "Prevention of Cruelty"; Hiebert, "Prohibition," 17; Golz, "If a Man's Wife Does Not Obey Him"; Lepp, *Dis/Membering the Family*, chapter 5; Marks, *Revivals and Roller Rinks*, 91–2; Burr, "Roping in the Wretched," 90 (quotations); Gray, *Booze*, 42–4; Peiss, *Cheap Amusements*, 27–8; Royal Commission on Liquor Traffic, *Report*, 152, 186, 209, 789, 797–8, 822; Ames, *City below the Hill*, 75; Harrison, *Drink and the Victorians*, 404; Parsons, "Risky Business"; Roberts, *Classic Slum*, 49–50. With the exception of Lortie's 1903 study of a relatively prosperous typographer's family ("Compositeur typographe"), the historical studies of working-class living standards in Canada in the late nineteenth and early twentieth centuries are all forced to rely on "average" family budgets rather than real family expenditures; see, for example, Gagan and Gagan, "Working-Class Standards of Living"; Copp, *Anatomy of Poverty*, 30–43. In 1907 U.S. social investigator Margaret Byington surveyed the discretionary expenditures of various income groups in working-class Homestead, a steel town in Pennsylvania, and discovered that weekly spending on "liquor" averaged only 20 cents for those spending under $12 a week, 14 cents for those spending $12 to $14.99, and a whopping 63 cents for those spending $15 to $19.99. Byington, *Homestead*, 84. Since the Canadian rate of alcohol consumption was consistently lower than the American, we can speculate that the proportion of working-class income spent on booze might have been even lower.

70.   Gray, *Boy from Winnipeg*, 20–34.

71.   Canada, Department of Agriculture, *Statistical Yearbook of Canada*, 1890–1915.

72.   Royal Commission on Liquor Traffic, *Minutes of Evidence*, vol.4, 364, 376–81; Benson, "American Workers and Temperance Reform," 28–9, 129–38; Leacock, *Wet or Dry?* 2–3 (quotation).

73.   Methodist Church and Presbyterian Church, *Report of Preliminary and General Social Survey of Hamilton*, 19, *Report of a Preliminary and General Social Survey of Port Arthur*, 12, and *St. Catharines Survey*, 22–3; Men's Federation of London, *City of London*, 66–8; Leacock, *Wet or Dry?* 2–3 (quotation). The social surveys are discussed in Hunt, "Measuring Morals"; and Christie and Gauvreau, *Full-Orbed Christianity*, 17–87.

74.   McLean, "'Deserving' Wives and 'Drunken' Husbands, 64–5"; Golz, "If a Man's Wife Does Not Obey Him"; Harvey, "Amazons and Victims"; and "To Love, Honour, and Obey"; Heron, "Boys and Their Booze"; Snell, "Marital Cruelty," and *In the Shadow of the Law*, 97–192; Weaver, *Crimes, Constables, and Courts*, 225–32; Gordon, *Heroes of Their Own Lives*, 264–71; Hammerton, *Cruelty and Companionship*, 13–67; Clark, "Domesticity and the Problem of Wifebeating"; Rowbotham, "Only When Drunk."

75.   Bailey, "Will the Real Bill Banks Please Stand Up?"; Roberts, *Drink, Temperance, and the Working Class*, 109–27. In the late nineteenth and early twentieth centuries, the North American craft-union movement was making a strong case for a "living wage" that would sustain a respectable, comfortable lifestyle; see Glickman, *A Living Wage*.

76.   *Toronto by Gaslight*, 28–34; Royal Commission on Liquor Traffic, *Minutes of Evidence*, vol.4, 362 (quotation by labour leader); Spence, *Prohibition*, 383 (quotation by licence commissioners); Thompson, "Prohibition Question," 55–6; Stage, *Female Complaints*, 32, 183–4; Young, *Toadstool Millionaires*.

77.   See, for example, *Times* (Hamilton), 21 December 1912; Heron, "Boys and Their Booze."

78.   Dingle, "Drink and Working-Class Living Standards," 616.

five⟩The Long Arm of the Law

1. *Christian Guardian*, 26 May 1841, quoted in Barron, "Genesis of Temperance," 208.
2. Bailey, *Leisure and Class*; Jones, *Languages of Class*, 179–238; Horowitz, *Morality of Spending*; Wright, *Urban Parks*; Martin and Segrave, *City Parks*. Significantly, in the same period the "social purity" movement shifted its focus from such individual moral failings as adultery or seduction to another kind of commercialized leisure—prostitution. Hunt, *Governing Morals*, 77–191.
3. Vachon, "L'eau-de-vie dans la société indienne"; Howay, "Introduction of Intoxicating Liquors"; Rich, *Fur Trade and the Northwest*, 43, 103, 141, 157, 158, 164, 194, 240; Ray and Freeman, *"Give Us Good Measure"*, 128–44, 194–6; Ray, *Indians in the Fur Trade*, 142–6, 197–8, 214; Mancall, *Deadly Medicine*, and "Men Women, and Alcohol in Indian Villages"; Thomas, ed., *Prairie West*, 22–6; Grant, *Moon of Wintertime*, 56–7; Dickason, *Canada's First Nations*, 469–70; Miller, *Skyscrapers Hide the Heavens*, 48–50.
4. Lutz, *Makuk*, chapter 3B; Dempsey, *Firewater*.
5. Tobias, "Protection, Civilization, Assimilation"; Grant, *Moon of Wintertime*, 45, 56–7, 59, 64, 92–3, 110, 138–9; Miller, *Skyscrapers Hide the Heavens*, 100, 221; Dickason, *Canada's First Nations*, 251, 331; Roberts, "Taverns and Tavern-goers," 226–36; Barron, "Genesis of Temperance," 5; Perry, *On the Edge of Empire*, 40; Royal Commission on Liquor Traffic, *Report*, 766, 800, 802, 805, 807, 809–13, 956, 959.
6. Valverde, "Symbolic Indians."
7. Mawani, "In Between and Out of Place"; Ajzenstadt, "Medical-Moral Economy," 44–54, 61–6; Lutz, *Makuk*, chapter 3B; Ray, *Canadian Fur Trade in the Industrial Age*, 149, 150.
8. Barron, "Genesis of Temperance," 37–9.
9. Cross, "Laws Are Like Cobwebs"; Burnet, "Urban Community," 307; Rogers, "Serving Toronto the Good"; Marquis, "History of Policing," 86–8, "'Machine of Oppression,'" "Enforcing the Law," and *Policing Canada's Century*, 12–53; McCulloch, "Most Assuredly Perpetual Motion"; Fecteau, "Between the Old Order and Modern Times"; Oliver, *Terror to Evil-Doers*; Weaver, *Crimes, Constables, and Courts*, 50–63. France and Italy passed their first laws against public drunkenness in 1873 and 1887 respectively, in both cases in response to growing fears of proletarian violence. Barrows, "After the Commune"; Prestwich, *Drink and the Politics of Social Reform*, 59; Morgan, "Industrialization, Urbanization, and the Attack on Italian Drinking Culture," 615.
10. Weaver, *Crimes, Constables, and Courts*, 23–63; Oliver, *Terror to Evil-Doers*, 3–85; Barry, "Shades of Vice," 116.
11. Nearly one-third of those committed to Ontario's jails between 1875 and 1899 had been convicted on those charges. The Royal Commission on the Liquor Traffic collected statistics on arrests for drunkenness from several Canadian cities; the figures revealed that, from 1880 to 1893, nearly two out of five people arrested in Montreal faced drunkenness charges, roughly half in Toronto, Ottawa, and Guelph, three out of five in Quebec City and Saint John, and almost three-quarters in Charlottetown. Across the country, a third of all criminal convictions between 1882 and 1891 were for drunkenness. Royal Commission on the Liquor Traffic, *Report*, 504, 706–7, 719–29 (calculations of percentages are mine); Oliver, *Terror to Evil-Doers*, 355–98; Craven, "Law and Ideology," 263; Homel, "Denison's Law"; Katz, Doucet, and Stern, *Social Organization*, 201–41; Burr, "Roping in the Wretched"; Weaver, *Crimes, Constables, and Courts*, 53–8; 68–79; Fingard, *Dark Side of Life*, and "Jailbirds"; Marquis, "'Machine of Oppression'"; Rogers, "Serving Toronto the Good," 133–5; Warsh, "Oh, Lord, Pour a Cordial in Her Wounded Heart"; Phillips, "Poverty, Unemployment, and the Administration of the Criminal Law"; Wodson, *Whirlpool*, 102–15; Boritch and Hagan, "Crime and the Changing Forms of Class Control"; Ajzenstadt, "Medical-Moral Economy." See also Smith, "Drinking and Imprisonment"; Lender, "Special Stigma." Harry Gene Levine notes that the U.S. temperance movement had such deeply etched notions of feminine virtue that it could scarcely ever acknowledge female drunkards as a problem; see "Temperance and Women," 33–5.

12. Katz, Doucet, and Stern, *Social Organization*, 233–4 (quotation by police reporter); Royal Commission on the Liquor Traffic, *Report*, 504 (quotation by Commission).

13. Harvey, "To Love, Honour, and Obey," and "Amazons and Victims"; Burr, "Roping in the Wretched," 98–102; Fingard, *Dark Side of Life*, and "Jailbirds"; Weaver, *Crimes, Constables, and Courts*; Bradbury, *Working Families*, 102–5, 194–5; Lepp, *Dis/Membering the Family*, chapter 5; Ajzenstadt, "Medical-Moral Economy," 55–7; Clarkson, "Remoralizing Families?" 206, 301–3.

14. Levine, "Discovery of Addiction"; McCandless, "Curses of Civilization"; Woiak, "A Medical Cromwell"; Sournia, *History of Alcoholism*, 70–5; Tyrrell, *Sobering Up*, 89–90.

15. Decarie, "Something Old, Something New," 160–1; Spence, *Prohibition*, 66–8; Cook, *"Through Sunshine and Shadow"*, 116–30; Trainor, "Towards a Genealogy of Temperance," 153–9 (quotation at 158 from student essay); Sheehan, "National Pressure Groups and Provincial Curriculum Policy," 78 (quotation from textbook); and "WCTU and Educational Strategies," 102–7; Veer, "Feminist Forebears," 95–153; Strople, "Prohibition and Movements of Social Reform," 7–18, 27–9; Timberlake, *Prohibition and the Progressive Movement*, 40–56; Canada, House of Commons, *Journals*, 6 (1873), appendix 3, 15–16; 8 (1874), appendix 8, 11; Royal Commission on Liquor Traffic, *Report*, 773.

16. The country's most illustrious medical practitioner, Dr. William Osler, strongly recommended alcohol as a stimulant and preventive of heart failure. "You cannot do any harm by giving a few ounces of whiskey in a day," he wrote. In the same vein, he suggested, "Pin your faith, if to nothing else, to alcohol, in pneumonia." In the 1890s one of the country's first female doctors, Emily Stowe, supplied a medical remedy for "very weak invalids" to a popular cookbook, in which eggs, lemon juice, and rock candy were combined with a pint of rum to make an "excellent and very nourishing" tonic. Similarly, the young Dr. Elizabeth Smith left the Women's Christian Temperance Union in part over the issue of medicinal alcohol, and well into the 1920s she used whisky and other alcoholic drinks to relieve her own arthritic pain. Canada, House of Commons, *Journals*, 8 (1874), appendix 8, 11 (quotations by doctors); Warsh, *Moments of Unreason*, 145–6, and "Oh, Lord, Pour a Cordial in Her Wounded Heart"; Bliss, *William Osler*, 51, 108 (quotations by Osler); Taylor and McNaught, *Galt Cook Book*, 411 (quotation); McLaren, "Becoming Indispensable," 175; Murray, "Road to Regulation."

17. Warsh, "Because There Is Pain,"6 (quotation by asylum superintendent); Shortt, *Victorian Lunacy*, 129–30; O'Neill, "Temperance Movement," 48–55; Williams, "Use of Beverage Alcohol"; Cassedy, "Early American Hangover"; Warner, "Physiological Theory and Therapeutic Explanation"; Zimmerman, "When Doctors Disagree," and *Distilling Democracy*; Pauly, "Struggle for Ignorance about Alcohol"; Spence, *Prohibition*, 68; Royal Commission on Liquor Traffic, *Report*, 53–5 (calculations are mine). After 1900, scientific temperance instruction in Ontario was cut back to Grades 2, 3, and 4 and ceased to be a subject on high-school entrance examinations.

18. Warsh, "Because There Is Pain," 13–17; Valverde, *Diseases of the Will*, 43–95; Levine, "Discovery of Addiction"; Trainor, "Towards a Genealogy of Temperance," 94–181; Jaffe, "Reform in American Medical Science"; Bynum, "Chronic Alcoholism."

19. Trainor, "Towards a Genealogy of Temperance," 122 (quotation).

20. Valverde, *Diseases of the Will*; Jellinek, *Disease Concept*, 2 (quotation).

21. Warsh "Because There Is Pain," 13–19; Baumohl, "Inebriate Institutions," 92–114; Trainor, "Towards a Genealogy of Temperance," 110–27; Valverde, *Diseases of the Will*, 69–75; Warsh, *Moments of Unreason*, 15, 17, 144–54, 192; MacLeod, "Edge of Hope"; White, *Slaying the Dragon*, 21–50.

22. Trainor, "Towards a Genealogy of Temperance," 110–27; Royal Commission on Liquor Traffic, *Report*, 504; Baumohl and Room, "Inebriety, Doctors, and the State," 146–67; Baumohl and Tracy, "Building Systems to Manage Inebriates." *The Journal of Inebriety* folded in 1914, and inebriate institutions in all countries had mostly closed their doors by the 1920s, even before the arrival of prohibition.

23. Royal Commission on Liquor Traffic, *Report*, 86–7, 94–5, 133–4, 142; Warsh, "Because There Is Pain," 19; Trainor, "Towards a Genealogy of Temperance"; Valverde, *Diseases of the Will*, 87; McLaren, *Our Own Master Race*; Ajzenstadt, "Medical-Moral Economy," 143–50, 181–92;

White, *Slaying the Dragon*, 88–90; Bynum, "Alcoholism and Degeneration"; McCandless, "Curses of Civilization," 55–6; Sournia, *History of Alcoholism*, 98–114; Berridge, "Society for the Study of Addiction," 999–1015; Jaffe, "Reform in American Medical Science"; MacLeod., "Edge of Hope," 240, 244–5; Jellinek, *Disease Concept*, 2–7; Comacchio, *Nations Are Built of Babies*; Gutzke, "Cry of the Children."

24.   Warsh, "Adventures in Maritime Quackery"; Trainor, "Towards a Genealogy of Temperance," 162–5; Baumohl, "Inebriate Institutions," 100; Valverde, *Diseases of the Will*, 62–5, 72–4; Warsh, *Moments of Unreason*, 148–50; White, *Slaying the Dragon*, 50–63.

25.   Warsh, "Adventures in Maritime Quackery"; White, *Slaying the Dragon*; *Advocate* (Toronto and Montreal), 1 March 1894, 81–2.

26.   Valverde, *Diseases of the Will*; Burr, "Roping in the Wretched," 87 (quotation by medical superintendent). As late as 1925, British Columbia's Royal Commission on Mental Hygiene was still presenting a muddled medical analysis: "Many drink excessively because of their mental condition. In others the mental condition is to some extent at least, the result of the alcoholic habit." Ajzenstadt, "Medical-Moral Economy," 148 (quotation), 153–60.

27.   In 1906 doctors in the new Ontario Society for the Reformation of Inebriates proposed a medically controlled diagnostic test to identify alcoholics brought to court and special institutional treatment for such cases, but such procedures were never implemented. Ajzenstadt, "Medical-Moral Economy," 156–7. Scott Haine uses careful research into legal and medical records in Paris to conclude: "On the drink question, the police, the courts, and the doctors did not form one integrated system of coercion or 'normalization' in the interests of social order and public health." See "Spectrum of Cultural Constructs," 536. On the Salvation Army, see Moyles, *Blood and Fire*, 66–72; Valverde, *Diseases of the Will*, 88–91. For an example of the use of criminal statistics, see W.F. Burgess, "Liquor and Crime," in Rutherford, ed., *Saving the Canadian City*, 93–101.

28.   Popham, *Legislative History*, 1–2; Barron, "Genesis of Temperance," 209–14; Fingard, "A Great Big Rum Shop," 96–7. The only instance of more aggressive state intervention had come in Upper Canada during the War of 1812–14, when the government had briefly prohibited distilling in order to economize on grain needed for bread—an unpopular measure with the army, which doled out daily rations of booze to maintain morale. Riddell, "First Canadian War-Time Prohibition Measure."

29.   *Montreal by Gaslight*, 71 (quotation); Davis, "I'll Drink to That," 168, 198–9, 256; Decarie, "Prohibition Movement," 11–13, 102, 267; Holman, A *Sense of Their Duty*, 139–45; Anstead, "Hegemony and Failure"; Spence, *Facts of the Case*; Davis, "Small Town Reformism"; Blocker, *Retreat from Reform*, 8. Just as the drunkard was now seen as the victim of the liquor traffic, so too did the "social purity" movement reconfigure the prostitute as a victim of the brothel-keepers and others in the so-called "white-slave trade." Hunt, *Governing Morals*, 118–21.

30.   Ferry, "To the Interests and Conscience"; Fahey, *Temperance and Racism*, 12–14; Spence, *Prohibition*, 55; Royal Commission on Liquor Traffic, *Report*, 971–2; *Canadian Annual Review*, 1901, 461 (quotation), 465, and 1909, 471; Thompson, "Prohibition Question," 96.

31.   Harrison, *Drink and the Victorians*, 29–96; Dominion Alliance for the Total Suppression of the Liquor Traffic, *Liberty Question* (quotations). Richard Hamm examines the implications of temperance ideology for legal challenges in U.S. courts, which appeared to be much more important in prohibitionist battles in the United States than in Canada; *Shaping the Eighteenth Amendment*, 33–44.

32.   Hamm, *Shaping the Eighteenth Amendment*, 25–33; Blocker, *American Temperance Movements*, 90–1, 102; Kazin, *Populist Persuasion*, 79–86.

33.   Jack Blocker has suggested that in the United States prohibitionists shared a sense that sobriety was connected to "worldly success." Blocker, *Retreat from Reform*, 16–18. See also Ferry, "To the Interests and Conscience."

34.   Youmans, *Campaign Echoes*, 94 (quotation).

35.   Ibid., 184–205 (for the text of "Haman's License"); Lockwood, "Music and Songs"; Gray, *Booze*, 48–50; Strople, "Prohibition and Movements of Social Reform," 30–1. Bengough's cartoons appeared first in *Grip* and then regularly in the Ontario movement's weekly paper, the *Pioneer*, after the turn of the century. On the issue of social-scientific research into alcohol

in this period, Thomas Babor and Barbara Rosenkrantz surveyed all that was undertaken in Massachusetts between 1880 and 1916 and concluded the studies were deeply biased by the ideological positions of the researchers; see "Public Health, Public Morals, and Public Order."

36. Barry, "Shades of Vice," 70–1; Barron, "Genesis of Temperance," 214–20; Fingard, "A Great Big Rum Shop," 91–2; Hildebrand, "Les débuts du mouvement," 30–1. The inspiration for these measures were undoubtedly the parallel U.S. initiatives for reform of licensing; see Hampel, *Temperance and Prohibition*, 55–94.

37. Spence, *Prohibition*, 77–91; Noel, *Canada Dry*, 43–5, 147–9; Chapman, "Mid-Nineteenth-Century Temperance Movement"; Dick, "From Temperance to Prohibition," 537–41; Waite, "Fall and Rise of the Smashers"; Campbell, "'Smashers' and 'Rummies,'" and "Disenfranchised but Not Quiescent," 87–92; Holman, *Sense of Their Duty*, 136–7; Tyrrell, *Sobering Up*, 225–315. British teetotallers had also been drawn to the politics of the "Maine Law"; see Harrison, *Drink and the Victorians*, 196–218.

38. Blocker, *"Give to the Wind Thy Fears"*; Youmans, *Campaign Echoes*; Cook, *"Through Sunshine and Shadow"*; Mitchinson, "WCTU."

39. Youmans, *Campaign Echoes*; Tyrrell, *Woman's World, Woman's Empire*.

40. Marks, *Revivals and Roller Rinks*, 95–101; Sheehan, "National Pressure Groups and Provincial Curriculum Policy," "WCTU and Educational Strategies," "WCTU on the Prairies," and "Women Helping Women"; Malleck, "Priorities of Development"; Valverde, *Age of Light, Soap, and Water*, 58–61; Spence, *Prohibition*, 61–72; Gough, *As Wise as Serpents*; Strople, "Prohibition and Movements of Social Reform," 99; Decarie, "Something Old, Something New," 169 (poem); Bordin, *Women and Temperance*; Epstein, *Politics of Domesticity*; Levine, "Temperance and Women," 52–63; Zimmerman, *Distilling Democracy*; Tyrrell, "Women and Temperance," and *Woman's World, Woman's Empire*; Blocker, *American Temperance Movements*, 79–85.

41. In 1863 the United Canadian Alliance for the Suppression of the Liquor Traffic (later renamed the Ontario Temperance and Prohibitory League) brought together prohibitionists in the Province of Canada. New provincial groups emerged in Ontario, Quebec, and New Brunswick after Confederation. Spence, *Prohibition*, 105–18; Ferry, "To the Interests and Conscience," 7–8; Magney, "Methodist Church and National Gospel"; Allen, *Social Passion*.

42. Royal Commission on Liquor Traffic, *Report*, 48–52, 81–2, 92–3, 146, 498–503; *Canadian Annual Review*, 1901, 462, 467 (quotation); Decarie, "Prohibition Movement," 20–33; O'Neill, "Temperance Movement," 147–53; Forbes, "Prohibition and the Social Gospel," 64–8; Davis, "I'll Drink to That," 173–84; Thompson, "Prohibition Question," 13–20, 26–7; Sturgis, "Beer under Pressure," 87; Decarie, "Something Old, Something New," 163–7; McCann, "1890s: Fragmentation and the New Social Order," 145–6; Gray, *Booze*, 72–3; Hamm, *Shaping the Eighteenth Amendment*, 22; Bordin, *Women and Temperance*, 82–8; Mattingly, *Well-Tempered Women*.

43. Royal Commission on Liquor Traffic, *Report*, 48–52, 115, 498; Decarie, "Prohibition Movement," 30–33; Forbes, "Prohibition and the Social Gospel," 68; Spence, *Quebec and the Liquor Problem*, 29–32.

44. Spence, *Prohibition*, 119–22, 125–6, 219–21, 266–8; Saywell, *Lawmakers*, 86–107, 133–42; Romney, *Mr Attorney*, 259–74; Evans, *Mowat*, 162–75, 262–7; Waite, *Man from Halifax*, 393–4; Vipond, *Liberty and Community*, 153–6, 164–9. U.S. prohibitionists got entangled in similar constitutional uncertainties; see Hamm, *Shaping the Eighteenth Amendment*.

45. In 1875 Ontario had 4,794 licensed taverns and 1,307 licensed shops; by 1900 the numbers had dropped to only 2,611 and 308, and by 1914 to only 1,371 and 218—despite the huge increase in population over that period (from 1.6 million to over 2.5 million). Nova Scotia would not authorize any saloon licences at all by the 1890s. In contrast, Quebec had roughly the same number in the mid-1870s as in the early 1890s (around 2,500), and British Columbia's total nearly doubled during the 1880s. Evans, *Mowat*, 105–10; Holman, *Sense of Their Duty*, 137–8; Graham, *Greenbank*, 93; Noel, *Canada Dry*, 143; Burr, "Roping in the Wretched," 88–9; Spence, *Prohibition*, 587–8; Youmans, *Campaign Echoes*, 148; Royal Commission on Liquor Traffic, *Report*, 87, 123, 136–7, 151, 210, 214, 738–49.

46. Sendbuehler, "Battling 'The Bane of Our Cities'"; Men's Federation of London, *City of London*, 66–9.

47.   Fanshawe, *Liquor Legislation*; Graham, *Greenbank*, 76–82; Gray, *Booze*, 9; Cook, *"Through Sunshine and Shadow"*, 42, 131–3; Sendbuehler, "Battling 'The Bane of Our Cities,'" 30; Strople, "Prohibition and Movements of Social Reform," 5–7; Ajzenstadt, "Medical-Moral Economy," 96–7; Royal Commission on Liquor Traffic, *Report*, 766–7, 779–81, 790–1, 797–8, 960–2; Blocker, *American Temperance Movements*, 75.

48.   For an example of weak enforcement, see Couturier, "Prohibition or Regulation?"

49.   Barron, "Genesis of Temperance," 226–9; Decarie, "Prohibition Movement," 20–44; Thompson, "Prohibition Question," 8–9; Youmans, *Campaign Echoes*, 112–21, 153–66, 174–83; Romney, *Mr Attorney*, 264. The text of the Canada Temperance Act can be found in Royal Commission on Liquor Traffic, *Report*, 750–2.

50.   Fanshawe, *Liquor Legislation*, 383.

51.   Magney, "Methodist Church and National Gospel," 16–17; Sendbuehler, "Battling 'The Bane of Our Cities'"; Bliss, *Canadian Millionaire*, 19–22; Rudy, "Sleeman's," 64.

52.   Royal Commission on Liquor Traffic, *Report*, 753–5, 759, 768; Decarie, "Prohibition Movement," 87–93, 109; Davis, "I'll Drink to That," 135–9; Holman, *Sense of Their Duty*, 145–7; McGahan, *Crime and Policing*, 39–46.

53.   Fanshawe, *Liquor Legislation*, 374–400 (quotations at 376–7 and 385); Royal Commission on Liquor Traffic, *Report*, 80, 91–2, 97–115, 128–9, 147, 759; Rowntree and Sherwell, *Temperance Problem and Social Reform*, 207–12.

54.   Dempsey, *Firewater*; Horrall, "Policeman's Lot"; Spence, *Prohibition*, 183–90; Gray, *Booze*, 19–34; McLean, "Most Effectual Remedy," 12–15, 27–30; McLeod, "Liquor Control"; Mawani, "In Between and Out of Place"; Royal Commission on Liquor Traffic, *Report*, 154–206 (quotation at 167).

55.   Horrall, "Policeman's Lot"; McLeod, "Liquor Control."

56.   Brown and Cook, *Canada, 1896–1921*, 1–107; Avery, *Reluctant Host*.

57.   Brown and Cook, *Canada, 1896–1921*, 1–107; Heron, "Second Industrial Revolution."

58.   Brown and Cook, *Canada, 1896–1921*, 108–87; Bliss, *Living Profit*; Rutherford, ed., *Saving the Canadian City*; Valverde, *Age of Light, Soap, and Water*.

59.   Hamm, *Shaping the Eighteenth Amendment*, 2–6; Allen, *Social Passion*; McKay, "The 1910's"; Timberlake, *Prohibition and the Progressive Movement*; Blocker, *Retreat from Reform*, 192–4; Boyer, *Urban Masses and Moral Order*, 195–204.

60.   Thompson, "Prohibition Question," 38 (quotation); Ajzenstadt, "Medical-Moral Economy," 204–9; Timberlake, *Prohibition and the Progressive Movement*, 67–80; *Canadian Annual Review*, 1909, 440.

61.   Tyrrell, "Prohibition, American Cultural Expansion, and the New Hegemony," 440; *Canadian Annual Review*, 1913, 391 (quotation).

62.   Spence, *Prohibition*, 105–38; Sendbuehler, "Battling 'The Bane of Our Cities'"; Sturgis, "Beer under Pressure," 91; Decarie, "Prohibition Movement," 87–93; and "Something Old, Something New," 156; O'Neill, "Temperance Movement," 180–6; Davis, "I'll Drink to That," 114–5, 135–9, and "Small Town Reformism"; Strople, "Prohibition and Movements of Social Reform," 99–100, 155; Thompson, "Prohibition Question," 21–25; Hallowell, *Prohibition in Ontario*, 11–12 (quotation at 12); Gray, *Booze*, 60. Rural support for temperance was parallelled in the United States, where local-option campaigns closed booze retailing in much of the countryside in the South and West; Blocker, *American Temperance Movements*, 89–90, 107–9.

63.   Shortt, "Social Change and Political Crisis"; Hann, *Farmers Confront Industrialism*; Wood, *History of Farmers' Movements*; McLean, "Most Effective Remedy," 77–80; Bate, "Prohibition and the U.F.A."

64.   Bate, "Prohibition and the U.F.A.," 3 (quotation); McLean, "Most Effective Remedy," 77 (quotation).

65.   Chambers, "Referendum and Plebiscite"; Boyer, *Direct Democracy*, 78–95; Adamson, "We Were Here Before"; Thompson, "Prohibition Question," 38, 58–61, 67 (quotation); *Canadian Annual Review*, 1913, 391, 398. All four Western provinces passed direct-legislation acts in the 1912–19 period.

66. Decarie, "Paved with Good Intentions," 20 (quotation); Sendbuehler, "Battling 'The Bane of Our Cities,'" 48 (quotation); Cook, *"Through Sunshine and Shadow"*, 105–8 (quotation at 108); Woodsworth, *My Neighbour*, 88, and *Strangers within Our Gates*, 92; Smart and Ogborne, *Northern Spirits*, 48; Ajzenstadt, "Medical-Moral Economy," 62–72.

67. Bernard, "Deux phases de l'antialcoolisme," 163 (quotations, author's translation of "l'une des pires ennemis de la religion et de la patrie" and "un véritable fléau national").

68. Spence, *Prohibition*, 141–58, 292–7; Cook, *Regenerators*, 177–9; Thompson, "Prohibition Question," 10–12; Bédard-Lévesque, "La tempérance au Québec"; *Canadian Annual Review*, 1902, 381; Decarie, "Spence," 957; Blocker, *Retreat from Reform*, 39–153, and *American Reform Movements*, 85–111; Kerr, *Organized for Prohibition*.

69. Spence, *Prohibition*, 293–7; *Star* (Toronto), 22 September 1898, 4 (quotation).

70. Palmer, *Working-Class Experience*, 155–213; Blocker, *American Temperance Movements*, 117; Kazin, *Populist Persuasion*, 86–96. In a parallel move to this focus on the saloon, the "social purity" movement turned its guns on the brothel. Hunt, *Governing Morals*.

71. O'Neill, "Temperance Movement," 207–11; Forbes, "Prohibition and the Social Gospel"; Couturier, "Prohibition or Regulation?"; Sturgis, "Beer under Pressure," 96; Marks, *Revivals and Roller Rinks*, 104–6; Cook, *"Through Sunshine and Shadow"*, 3–6; Spence, *Prohibition*, 576–7; Decarie, "Prohibition Movement," 46–8, 94 (quotations by Laurier); Humphries, "*Honest Enough to Be Bold*," 44 (quotation by cabinet minister). On the strength of wet sentiment in Conservative ranks, see Heron, "Working-Class Hamilton"; Lawrence, "Class and Gender."

72. Spence, *Prohibition*, 161–79 (quotation); Waite, *Man from Halifax*, 392–3; Canada, Royal Commission on Liquor Traffic, *Report*. Prohibitionists nonetheless dipped into the testimony heard before the royal commission for their own propaganda; F.S. Spence extracted supportive testimony to produce a widely used handbook, misleadingly entitled *Facts of the Case*. The anti-regulationist stance of the prohibition movement was an echo of the abolitionist campaign against slavery in North America and was parallelled in the "social purity" movement, which refused to countenance any compromise with prostitution. Hunt, *Governing Morals*, 101–3.

73. Decarie, "Prohibition Movement," 50–93; Spence, *Prohibition*, 183–228; Evans, *Mowat*, 301–4.

74. Spence, *Prohibition*, 231–58; Boyer, *Direct Democracy*, 16–26, 90–1.

75. Canada, Department of Agriculture, *Statistical Year Book*, 1900, 572; Decarie, "Prohibition Movement," 94–112; Davis, "I'll Drink to That," 144–8; McLean, "Most Effectual Remedy," 37; Campbell, *Demon Rum or Easy Money*, 12–13; Gray, *Booze*, 51–4.

76. Hamm, *Shaping the Eighteenth Amendment*; Spence, *Prohibition*, 261–342; Decarie, "Prohibition Movement," 125–42.

77. Davis, "I'll Drink to That," 215–18; Gray, *Booze*, 57–62; *Canadian Annual Review*, 1901, 461–8 (quotation at 462), 475–83, and 1902 (369–92), 1904 (296–302), 1906 (329–34), 1908 (314–20, 418–20, 468–9), 1909 (383, 439–42, 469–71, 509–10, 537–8).

78. *Canadian Annual Review*, 1901, 463.

79. Davis, "I'll Drink to That," 168–9; Strople, "Prohibition and Movements of Social Reform," 119–20, 200; Forbes, "Prohibition and the Social Gospel," 70; Gray, *Booze*, 59, 71; McLean, "Most Effectual Remedy," 39–56, 61–2; Hiebert, "Prohibition in British Columbia," 48.

80. Bédard-Lévesque, "La tempérance au Québec," 32–52; Bernard, "Deux phases de l'antialcoolisme," 153–65; Spence, *Quebec and the Liquor Problem*, 31 (quotation).

81. Ontario and Manitoba also banned the links between the producers and retailers that had created the so-called "tied" saloons. British Columbia restricted the establishment of saloons not connected to hotels. Alberta barred any licensing of premises within 200 yards of schools and churches. Ontario eliminated all licences across the north between Kenora and Fort William in the path of Grand Trunk Pacific railway construction. Decarie, "Prohibition Movement," 197–217; Humphries, "*Honest Enough to Be Bold*," 116–19, 129–34, 168–9; Davis, "I'll Drink to That," 214–20; Strople, "Prohibition and Movements of Social Reform," 120–32; Forbes, "Prohibition and the Social Gospel," 63, 68–74; Thompson, "Prohibition Question," 54–74; McLean, "Most Effectual Remedy," 59–61; Ajzenstadt, "Medical-Moral Economy," 105–6, 125; *Canadian Annual Review*, 1906, 329–30, and 1907 (527), 1908 (419, 469, 588 [quotation about singing]), 1909 (471), 1910 (435), 1912 (349–55 [quotation at 352

by Ontario's premier]), 1913 (391–8), 1914 (470–1, 598), 1915 (535–6, 667); Spence, *Prohibition*, 323–478; Gray, *Booze*, 51–2, 55–62; Campbell, *Demon Rum or Easy Money*, 19–20; Cook, *"Through Sunshine and Shadow"*, 43–4.

82.   Humphries, *"Honest Enough to Be Bold,"* 132; Davis, "I'll Drink to That," 219; *Canadian Annual Review*, 1909, 537, and 1912 (436–7).

83.   Between 1900 and 1914, Hamilton lost 18 licenses, Ottawa 25, Toronto 41, and Halifax 24. Spence, *Prohibition*, 329–478; O'Neill, "Temperance Movement," 69–86; Decarie, "Prohibition Movement," 194–221, 235–8; Humphries, *"Honest Enough to Be Bold,"* 131–4; *Canadian Annual Review*, 1908, 469, and 1909 (383–6), 1910 (434), 1912 (349–55), 1914 (597–9, 642–3, 669–70); Ontario, Board of License Commissioners, *Report on the Operation of the Liquor License Acts*, 1916, 48–50, 119–25 (calculations are mine); Hiebert, "Prohibition in British Columbia," 46–62; Campbell, *Demon Rum or Easy Money*, 19–20; Bliss, *Flavelle*.

84.   Prang, *Rowell*, 142–4; *Canadian Annual Review*, 1912, 350–5, 463, and 1913 (391–8), 1914 (439–41); Spence, *Prohibition*, 387; Pinno, "Temperance and Prohibition," 39–42. The increase in consumption was parallelled in the United States; Blocker, *American Temperance Movements*, 115–6.

85.   Decarie, "Prohibition Movement."

86.   *Canadian Annual Review*, 1914, 599 (quotation by Manitoba Methodists), and 1916 (516 [quotation by review]).

87.   Canada, Department of Inland Revenues, *Report*, 1917, part I, xvi.

88.   Heron and Siemiatycki, "Great War, State, and Working-Class Canada"; Thompson, *Harvests of War*, 98–101, "Prohibition Question," 68–71 (quotation at 70), and "Beginning of Our Regeneration"; Decarie, "Prohibition Movement," 278–80; Davis, "I'll Drink to That," 222–7; McLean, "Most Effective Remedy," 127–8; Hiebert, "Prohibition in British Columbia," 62–5; Pinno, "Temperance and Prohibition," 48–58 (quotation at 51); *Canadian Annual Review*, 1914, 643.

89.   O'Neill, "Temperance Movement," 233 (quotation).

90.   Davis, "I'll Drink to That," 227 (quotation).

91.   Thompson, "Prohibition Question," 69 (quotation by Prairie newspaper); Pinno, "Temperance and Prohibition," 51 (quotation by temperance paper).

92.   Decarie, "Prohibition Movement," 278–301; Pinno, "Temperance and Prohibition," 58–129; Hiebert, "Prohibition in British Columbia," 63–91.

93.   McLean, "Most Effective Remedy," 91–139; Gray, *Booze*, 74–7; Hiebert, "Prohibition in British Columbia," 63–91; Thompson, "Prohibition Question," 72–4; Pinno, "Temperance and Prohibition," 58–129.

94.   Spence, *Prohibition*, 321–492; Decarie, "Prohibition Movement," 278–301; O'Neill, "Temperance Movement," 160–1; Hallowell, *Prohibition in Ontario*; Davis, "I'll Drink to That," 222–30; Doyle, *Front Benches and Back Rooms*, 101–3; *Canadian Annual Review*, 1914, 642–3, 670, and 1915 (538, 665–73, 694–5, 734–5), 1918 (638).

95.   The federal government trod carefully around the powerful distillers and brewers; although production was officially to cease on 1 April 1918, according to the *Canadian Annual Review* (1918, 575), "prohibition of manufacture . . . was not put into formal operation—the restriction of sale and transportation and import making it perhaps unnecessary."

96.   Spence, *Prohibition*, 323–478; Campbell, *Demon Rum or Easy Money*, 21–2; Hallowell, *Prohibition in Ontario*, 34–6; Grant, *When Rum Was King*, 94; *Canadian Annual Review*, 1916, 521, 633, 678–9, 741, and 1917 (682, 690, 706–7, 716, 798). An even more heavy-handed crackdown on drug use followed; see Solomon and Green, "First Century"; Carstairs, "Innocent Addicts, Dope Fiends, and Nefarious Traffickers."

97.   Campbell, *Demon Rum or Easy Money*, 23; Hallowell, *Prohibition in Ontario*, 7–8, 11; Davis, "I'll Drink to That." 254–5, 325; Spence, *Prohibition*, 381, 493–566.

98.   Hallowell, *Prohibition in Ontario*, 37–72; Grant, *When Rum Was King*, 178; Thompson, "Prohibition Question," 80; Pinno, "Temperance and Prohibition," 143–183; *Canadian Annual Review*, 1920, 778, 802; Ontario, Board of License Commissioners, *Report on the Operation of the Ontario Temperance Act*, 1920–21, 6, 22.

99.   Tyrrell, "Prohibition, American Cultural Expansion, and the New Hegemony" (quotation at 429).
100.   *Canadian Annual Review*, 1922, 590 (quotations). The popular support behind the U.S. prohibitionist Eighteenth Amendment has been the subject of some dispute; see Kyvig, "Sober Thoughts," 10–12.

six ⁓ Wet Voices

1.   Bob Edwards, 17 March 1904, quoted in Colombo, ed., *Colombo's Canadian Quotations*, 178.
2.   Perry, *On the Edge of Empire*, 42; Lockwood, "Music and Songs," 236.
3.   Sendbuehler, "Battling 'The Bane of Our Cities'"; *Yeas and Nays*.
4.   Burley, *Particular Condition*, 227; Decarie, "Prohibition Movement," 299–300; Marks, *Revivals and Roller Rinks*, 105; Bliss, *Canadian Millionaire*, 23–4; Phillips, *On Tap*, 129–30; *Spectator* (Hamilton), 8 April 1921, 19, 9 April 1921, 15, 11 April 1921, 3, 13, 12 April 1921, 15.
5.   Toronto had a Licensed Victuallers' Association in the 1870s, as did Halifax by 1884. In 1894 eight hundred of Ontario's retailers gathered in Toronto to form a provincewide Licence Holders' Protective Association, which co-ordinated the anti-prohibition campaign for the 1898 plebiscite and could still draw 250 delegates to a convention in 1902. These organizations and their alleged (and certainly exaggerated) political influence deserve a great deal more research; in the meantime, see *Yeas and Nays*; Romney, *Mr Attorney*, 265; Tucker, "Labatt's," 9 (quotation), 108, 154–5; *Canadian Annual Review*, 1901, 479, 483, and 1902 (371, 375, 385), 1903 (551), 1909 (509), 1912 (436–7), 1915 (672, 695); *Spectator*, 22 September 1898, 5; *Star* (Toronto), 3 September 1898, 1; Denison, *Barley and the Stream*, 317–23; *Spectator*, 10 October 1919, 36, 15 October 1919, 19, 16 October 1919, 3; Stretch, "From Prohibition to Government Control," 33.
6.   *Herald* (Hamilton), 26 September 1898, 6, 12 February 1910, 8; *Sun* (Vancouver), 14 September 1916, 4; *World* (Toronto), 18 September 1912, 5, 21 September 1912, 4, 3 March 1918, 7; Spence, *Prohibition*, 365; Royal Commission on Liquor Traffic, *Report*, 6; *Advocate* (Toronto and Montreal), 1894–95; *Canadian Annual Review*, 1902, 377–8, 385, and 1908 (318), 1909 (509), 1912 (436), 1915 (672, 695); Saywell, *Lawmakers*, 87, 135; Pinno, "Temperance and Prohibition," 38, 82–91; *Sun*, 14 September 1916. The United States Brewers Association dated back to 1862. U.S. booze interests had considerable difficulty co-operating across industry lines; the brewers refused to join the distillers and dealers in the National Model License League, formed in 1908 for self-regulation and political action. Brewers and distillers did sometimes co-operate at the state level and for a while after 1913 in the National Association of Commerce and Labor, but remained uncomfortable bedfellows. Baron, *Brewed in America*, 211–18; Kerr, *Organized for Prohibition*, 24–43, 160–84, 201; Hamm, *Shaping the Eighteenth Amendment*, 44–55; Blocker, *American Temperance Movements*, 113, 115, and *Retreat from Reform*, 242. The British experience was similar; see Gutzke, *Protecting the Pub*; Fahey, "Brewers, Publicans, and Working-Class Drinkers"; and Weir, "Obsessed with Moderation."
7.   *Star*, 3 September 1898, 1; Denison, *Barley and the Stream*, 235, 263; Fingard, "Great Big Rum Shop," 99; Holman, *Sense of Their Duty*, 146; Decarie, "Prohibition Movement," 82, 85, 107–8, 140–2, 232, 234, 269; Strople, "Prohibition and Movements of Social Reform," 108–9, 142; McLean, "Most Effective Remedy," 34–5, 52–3, 87–8, 100, 108–9, 122, 127–8, 130–4; Spence, *Prohibition*, 170–5, 298–9; Gray, *Booze*, 74, 77; Hiebert, "Prohibition in British Columbia," 45, 52–3, 76, 84; Humphries, "*Honest Enough to Be Bold*," 133; Stretch, "From Prohibition to Government Control," 14–16; Pinno, "Temperance and Prohibition," 84–5; Ajzenstadt, "Medical-Moral Economy," 110–13; *Advocate*, 12 April 1894, 235; *Canadian Annual Review*, 1914, 472, and 1915 (537). In contrast to the limited public face of the Canadian liquor traffic, the British brewers sent out vans with lecturers to counter temperance propaganda; Gutzke, *Protecting the Pub*, 219–20; Fahey, "Brewers, Publicans, and Working-Class Drinkers," 91, 101.
8.   Spence, *Prohibition*, 348 (quotation); *Canadian Annual Review*, 1914, 472 (quotation).

9. *World*, 21 September 1912, 5; *Spectator*, 9 October 1919, 14; *Sun*, 16 August 1916, 7; *Herald* (Hamilton), 12 February 1910, 3.

10. Davis, "I'll Drink to That," 100, 192–5, 205; Hiebert, "Prohibition in British Columbia," 57; McLean, "Most Effectual Remedy," 118; Strople, "Prohibition and Movements of Social Reform," 139–40. Invoking medical authority became common in ads for many products in the early twentieth century; see Lears, "From Salvation to Self-Realization," 24.

11. These organizations' state of preparedness varied—in Quebec and Ontario, they seemed well organized for the 1919 votes, but far less so for the 1920 plebiscites in the three Prairie provinces. Denison, *Barley and the Stream*, 318–23; Hallowell, *Prohibition in Ontario*, 37–58; Stretch, "From Prohibition to Government Control," 13–15; Thompson, "Prohibition Question," 79–80; Pinno, "Temperance and Prohibition," 157–9.

12. Davis, "I'll Drink to That," 104, 205 (quotation by MacNeill), 260–1; Grant, *Principal Grant's Letters*; Decarie, "Prohibition Movement," 232, 295; *Star*, 14 January 1916, 7 (quotation from Personal Liberty League); *Canadian Annual Review*, 1902, 387–9, and 1916 (518 [quotation by Fallon]), 1920 (614), 1921 (556).

13. Leacock, "Tyranny of Prohibition," 301 (quotations).

14. *Industrial Banner* (Toronto), 3 March 1916, 6; *Sun*, 13 September 1916, 7; Hallowell, *Prohibition in Ontario*, 81, 82–3; Davis, "I'll Drink to That," 260–1; Pinno, "Temperance and Prohibition," 162; Hiebert, "Prohibition in British Columbia," 107 (quotation); Aaron and Musto, "Temperance and Prohibition," 150–1; Murphy, "Societal Morality and Individual Freedom." As in the controversial B.C. plebiscite in 1916, returned soldiers in Toronto cast 70 to 75 per cent of their ballots for the wet options in the 1919 Ontario plebiscite.

15. Hallowell, *Prohibition in Ontario*, 5 (quotation), 10; Campbell, *Demon Rum or Easy Money*, 47 (quotation); *Spectator*, 24 September 1919, 14, 26 September 1919, 28; Blocker, *American Temperance Movements*, 113.

16. Hiebert, "Prohibition in British Columbia," 24 (quotation by Synod), 49, 66; Strople, "Prohibition and Movements of Social Reform," 65–8; Davis, "I'll Drink to That," 184–7; Forbes, "Prohibition and the Social Gospel," 67–8; *Canadian Annual Review*, 1901, 462, and 1908 (316, 419), 1909 (386), 1909 (510), 1912 (354, 436), 1913 (400), 1915 (538), 1916 (632); Pinno, "Temperance and Prohibition," 159 (quotation by Saskatchewan churchman); *Spectator*, 25 September 1924, 1.

17. Bédard-Lévesque, "La tempérance au Québec," 32–52; Bernard, "Deux phases de l'antial-coolisme," 153–65 (quotation at 163, author's translation of "ce pire ennemi de la race et de la religion"); Spence, *Prohibition*, 357–81, and *Quebec and the Liquor Problem*, 29–32; Pinno, "Temperance and Prohibition," 162–3; Thompson, "Prohibition Question," 25–32; Davis, "I'll Drink to That," 135–9, 144–8, 184–90, 266–67; Forbes, "Prohibition and the Social Gospel," 69; O'Neill, "Temperance Movement," 189–92; Pinno, "Temperance and Prohibition," 15–20, 21 (quotation), 121–3; Hallowell, *Prohibition in Ontario*, 16–17; *Canadian Annual Review*, 1914, 471. The Catholic *Casket* in Antigonish, N.S., eventually gave qualified support to prohibition in 1917; Strople, "Prohibition and Movements of Social Reform," 70. For similar ethno-religious divisions in the United States, see Wasserman, "Prohibition and Ethnocultural Conflict." Anglicans and Catholics held similar views about prohibition of tobacco or constraints on smoking; see Rudy, "Manly Smokes," 154–61.

18. In 1898 a massive study of U.S. employers' attitudes to the liquor traffic included in a report by U.S. Commissioner of Labor Carroll D. Wright had revealed considerable concern among industrialists about how prohibition would merely increase the thirst for alcohol. The Winnipeg Board of Trade weighed in with the same concerns during the 1902 referendum campaign in Manitoba, as did thirty-one Hamilton industrialists in an open letter in 1913. Magney, "Methodist Church and National Gospel," 55 (quotation); Davis, "I'll Drink to That," 100, 204–5 (quotation at 204).

19. *Spectator*, 3 December 1902, 1 (quotation by Toronto and Hamilton businessmen), 27 December 1910, 5, 28 December 1910, 5, 29 December 1910, 5, 30 December 1910, 4, 4 January 1913, 1 (quotation by Hamilton industrialists); *Canadian Annual Review*, 1902, 373, 378, 384, 392, and 1915, (733 [quotation by B.C. businessmen]).

20. Hallowell, *Prohibition in Ontario*, 70 (first quotation by League), 80–3; *Spectator*, 13 September 1919, 2, 7 October 1919, 4 (second quotation by league), 24 March 1921, 8, 26 March 1921, 11, 8 October 1924, 4 (quotation from letter to newspaper; Hiebert, "Prohibition in British Columbia," 108; Stretch, "From Prohibition to Government Control," 18–19; Ajzenstadt, "Medical-Moral Economy," 208–9; Spence, *Prohibition*, 381; Oliver, *Howard Ferguson*, 271; Kerr, *Organized for Prohibition*, 14; Levine, "Birth of American Alcohol Control"; Aaron and Musto, "Temperance and Prohibition," 161–70. In a similar vein, Stephen Leacock warned: "The drinkless workman, robbed of the simple comforts of life, will angrily demand its [sic] luxuries. A new envy will enter into his heart. The glaring inequalities of society will stand revealed to him as never before. See to it that he does not turn into a Bolshevik." A military officer carried the same alarmist message to a Moderationist rally in British Columbia, arguing that, thanks to prohibition, "'Reds' and revolutionaries were being made of formerly quiet workers who now found time to dwell upon troubles, real and imaginary, and who were becoming sulky and grouchy." Campbell, *Demon Rum or Easy Money*, 30; Leacock, *Wet or Dry?* 3.

21. Lawrence, "Class and Gender," 646.

22. *Gazette* (Montreal), 26 September 1898, 8; *Herald* (Calgary), 25 October 1923, 8 (quotation), 27 October 1923, 7, 30 October 1923, 13, 1 November 1923, 22; *Herald* (Halifax), 30 October 1929, 12; Bumsted, *Documentary Problems*, 203–4.

23. The following four paragraphs draw on Lears, *No Place of Grace*; Kimmel, *Manhood in America*, 81–188; Bederman, *Manliness and Civilization*; Parr, *Gender of Breadwinners*, 140–64; Kasson, *Houdini, Tarzan, and the Perfect Man*; Griffen, "Reconstructing Masculinity."

24. Huggins, "More Sinful Pleasures?"; Lears, *No Place of Grace*, 106 (quotation).

25. Bederman, *Manliness and Civilization*, 170–216.

26. Moss, *Manliness and Militarism*; Kimmel, *Manhood in America*, 81–188; Rotundo, *American Manhood*, 222–46; Kasson, *Houdini, Tarzan, and the Perfect Man*; Mangan and Walvin, eds., *Manliness and Morality*.

27. McLeod, *Building Character*; Dawson, "That Nice Red Coat"; Loo, "Of Moose and Men"; Jessup, "Prospectors, Bushwackers, Painters"; Janen, *Wild Things*; Curtis, "Son of Man and God the Father."

28. Lears, "From Salvation to Self-Realization," and *Fables of Abundance*; Kimmel, "Consuming Manhood"; Breward, *Hidden Consumer*; Hardy, "Adopted By All the Leading Clubs"; Swiencicki, "Consuming Brotherhood"; Rudy, "Manly Smokes," 75–113; Blocker, *American Temperance Movements*.

29. *Star*, 22 January 1916, 14 (quotations by athletes); Loo, "Of Moose and Men," 311 (quotation by hunter); Zuehlke, *Scoundrels, Dreamers, and Second Sons*, 104–6; Cook, "More a Medicine Than a Beverage."

30. Brown, *Two Hundred Years of Tradition*, 108; Warsh, "Smoke and Mirrors," 203–5.

31. *Sun*, 20 October 1920, 2, 21 October 1920, 1 (quotation); *Tribune* (Winnipeg), 19 June 1923, 6 (reporting on a packed meeting of 1,400 women in Winnipeg).

32. Strong-Boag, *Parliament of Women*, 96–7, 185, 312, 381; Black and Brandt, "Alcohol and the First Canadian Women's Movement," 100–3; Montgomery, *Anne of Green Gables*, 120–30.

33. *Nouvelle cuisinière canadienne*, 227–37; *Mrs. Clarke's Cookery Book*, 309–26; *Home Cook Book*, 22–3 (quotation), 28 (quotation), 30 (quotation), 346–52; *Common Sense Recipe Book*, 223–6, 237; Taylor and McNaught, *Galt Cook Book*, 379–82, 411–13, 420–1, 424–5.

34. Young, *Our Deportment*, 100 (quotation); Nitouche, *L'Ami des salons*, 50; Humphrey, *Etiquette*, 135–6; Arnold, *Century Cook Book*, 11 (quotation), 555–62 (quotations at 560, 562).

35. Denison, *Canadian Family Cook Book*, 450–6, 521, 522–3 (quotation at 522), 525–6, 528; Sauvalle, *Mille questions*, 254–6, 260; *Real Home-Keeper*, 30.

36. Gwyn, *Private Capital*, 286; Thompson, "Prohibition Question," 83 (quotation from diary); Eaton, *Memory's Wall*, 107–8 (quotation by Eaton); Westley, *Remembrance of Grandeur*, 35, 101.

37. Hallowell, *Prohibition in Ontario*, 80 (quotation).

38. Hallowell, *Prohibition in Ontario*, 82 (quotation); *Canadian Annual Review*, 1921, 556; Murdock, *Domesticating Drink*; Rose, *American Women and the Repeal of Prohibition*; Blocker, *Retreat from Reform*, 243. There were, of course, still many women who campaigned against

repeat of prohibition; see, for example, the personal statements of twenty and the list of several dozen more in Winnipeg in a dry advertisement during the 1923 Manitoba plebiscite campaign, *Tribune*, 20 June 1923, 7.

39.   Strong-Boag, *Parliament of Women*.

40.   Smith-Rosenberg, "New Woman as Androgyne"; Norcliffe, *Ride to Modernity*; Peiss, "Commercial Leisure and the 'Woman Question,'" *Cheap Amusements*, and "Making Up, Making Over"; Strange, *Toronto's Girl Problem*; Lenton-Young, "Variety Theatre," 198–211; Lever, *Histoire générale du cinéma*, 25–76; Morris, *Embattled Shadows*, 1–26; Snyder, "Big Time, Small Time," and *Voice of the City*; Gomery, "Movie Palace."

41.   Nasaw, *Going Out*; Erenberg, *Steppin' Out*; Strong-Boag, *Parliament of Women*, 425 (quotation), and *New Day Recalled*; Wright, "Feminine Trifles."

42.   Bliss, *Canadian Millionaire*, 162–3 (quotations); Tucker, "Labatt's," 240.

43.   Westley, *Remembrance of Grandeur*, 107, 133, 150–1 (quotations); *Star Weekly* (Toronto), 26 December 1925, 1; Gervais, *Rumrunners*, 101; Warsh, "Smoke and Mirrors," 207–11.

44.   *Sun*, 20 October 1920, 2, 21 October 1920, 1; *Tribune*, 19 June 1923, 6; *Canadian Annual Review*, 1920, 830 (quotation by temperance spokesperson); Campbell, *Demon Rum or Easy Money*, 31 (quotation by B.C. newspaper); Kyvig, "Sober Thoughts," 12. In New Zealand, where women got the vote in 1893, A.R. Grigg calculated that their voting patterns did not show considerably more support than those of male voters, and therefore "that the prohibition movement had not attracted as much support from women as had been expected in the early 1890s." Grigg, "Prohibition and Women," 165.

45.   Levine, "Committee of Fifty," and "Birth of American Alcohol Control"; Kyvig, *Repealing National Prohibition*; Campbell, *Demon Rum or Easy Money*, 28–9; Thompson, "Prohibition Question," 85.

46.   In the 1919 Quebec plebiscite, for example, the affluent St. George and Westmount areas voted 65 per cent in favour of allowing the sales of beer, cider, and wines, compared to 94 per cent in six predominantly working-class wards, while in Manitoba in 1923, only 61 per cent of the affluent South Winnipeg voted wet, compared to 78 per cent in the working-class North End. Denison, *Barley and the Stream*, 322 (percentages are mine); *Tribune*, 23 June 1923, 1; Campbell, *Demon Rum or Easy Money*, 32; Oliver, *Ferguson*, 161 (quotation).

47.   Oliver, "New Order," 70 (quotation from magazine); *Star*, 1 June 1927, 1 (quotation from newspaper). This interpretation, based on long-range developments in bourgeois culture, is clearly at odds with John Burnham's idiosyncratic reading of repeal agitation in the United States, which he presents as the cynical machinations of "bohemians," "sophisticates," and the media who marshalled "lower-order parochialism" (that is, the working class) to make the formerly disreputable now respectable; see Burnham, *Bad Habits*, 23–49.

48.   *Yeas and Nays*, xi, xv, xvi–xvii; Benson, "American Workers and Temperance Reform," 35–94; Burr, *Spreading the Light*, 14–31; Haine, *World of the Paris Café*; Barrows, "Parliaments of the People"; Roberts, "Tavern and Politics."

49.   *Palladium of Labor* (Hamilton), 12 January 1884, 1 (quotation by labour paper); Royal Commission on Liquor Traffic, *Minutes of Evidence*, vol.2, 359–61; Kealey and Palmer, *Dreaming of What Might Be*; Sendbuehler, "Battling 'The Bane of Our Cities,'" 31–3; Benson, "American Workers and Temperance Reform," 150–86 (quotation by Powderly at 163); Walker, "Terence V. Powderly, the Knights of Labor, and the Temperance Issue." Nova Scotia's leading labour movement, the Provincial Workmen's Association, incorporated the same principles into its ideological framework. McKay, "By Wisdom, Wile, or War."

50.   *Palladium of Labor*, 12 January 1884, 1 (quotation by paper); Canada, Royal Commission on Liquor Traffic, *Minutes of Evidence*, vol.2, 360, 369 (quotation by Knight); Trainor, "Towards a Genealogy of Temperance"; Kealey and Palmer, *Dreaming of What Might Be*; Walker, "Terence V. Powderly, the Knights of Labor, and the Temperance Issue"; Brundage, "The Producing Classes and the Saloon."

51.   *Palladium of Labor*, 12 January 1884, 1 (quotation). In Finland in the late nineteenth century, the emerging labour movement similarly used temperance as a unifying force in working-class struggle and actually organized a "drinking strike" in 1898; workers were numerically dominant in the country's temperance movement; see Sulkunen, "Temperance as a Civic

Religion." Similarly, in Sweden, where drinking was associated with bourgeois immorality, the temperance movement was overwhelmingly proletarian and closely linked to labour, socialist, and universal-suffrage movements; Hurd, "Liberals, Socialists, and Sobriety."

52. Royal Commission on Liquor Traffic, *Minutes of Evidence*, vol.2, 374; Palmer, *Working-Class Experience*, 127–32; Weir, *Beyond Labor's Veil*.

53. *Palladium of Labor*, 12 January 1884, 1; Trainor, "Towards a Genealogy of Temperance," 190–250 (quotation); Ferry, "To the Interests and Conscience"; Morton, *Mayor Howland*; Schwantes, *Radical Heritage*, 34.

54. Walker, "Terence V. Powderly, the Knights of Labor, and the Temperance Issue"; Homel, "Fading Beams"; Heron, "Working-Class Hamilton," 588–93.

55. Benson, "American Workers and Temperance Reform," 253–6; Drescher, "Organized Labor and the Eighteenth Amendment"; Davis, "I'll Drink to That," 206; Bordin, *Women and Temperance*, 104–8; *Star*, 19 September 1898, 1.

56. *Globe* (Toronto), 4 December 1911, 8 (quotation).

57. Christie and Gauvreau, *Full-Orbed Christianity*, 208–10; Heron, "Studholme"; Trades and Labor Congress of Canada, *Proceedings*, 1907, 37, 1908, 9–10, 1909, 62–8, 1911, 95–6, 1914, 94–6, 1915, 78, 84, 105–6, 1916, 117–18; Drescher, "Organized Labor and the Eighteenth Amendment," 288–9; Jones, "Labour, Society, and the Drink Question," 114–19; Brown, "The Pig or the Stye," 389–95.

58. Waters, *British Socialists and the Politics of Popular Culture*; Roberts, "Alcohol, Public Policy, and the Left"; and *Drink, Temperance, and the Working Class*, 83–108; De Lint, "Anti-Drink Propaganda"; McKay, ed., *For a Working-Class Culture*, 19, 34–8, 66 (quotation by McKay), 101; Ajzenstadt, "Medical-Moral Economy," 94 (*Western Clarion* quotation); Hiebert, "Prohibition in British Columbia," 54.

59. Newton, *Feminist Challenge*, 22–4, 29–36, 145; Lindstrom-Best, "Finnish Socialist Women," 211; Sulkunen, "Temperance as a Civic Religion"; Sariola, "Finnish Temperance Movement"; Hurd, "Liberals, Socialists, and Sobriety"; Homel, "James Simpson."

60. Campbell, *Demon Rum or Easy Money*, 30 (quotation). Toronto's John W. Bruce, the socialist plumber, had similar concerns: "A sober and studious working class are the best asset of the nation, and if the workers ever hope to liberate themselves from the bonds of wage slavery, it will only be when they themselves are strong and free from the destructive influence of intoxicating liquor." *Pioneer* (Toronto), 3 October 1919, 1. Out on the East Coast, the radical leader of Cape Breton's coal miners, J.B. McLachlan, was equally caustic: "I hate the liquor traffic with a whole hearted hatred because I have seen it used over and over again to dash the hopes of working men when they are on the eve of doing something for themselves." He fought hard against an effort to pass a resolution in favour of abolishing prohibition at the first Nova Scotia Federation of Labor convention in January 1919 and continued to carry his concerns into the pages of his popular newspaper, the *Maritime Labor Herald*, in the early 1920s. Davis, "I'll Drink to That," 206–9 (quotation at 207); see also Strople, "Prohibition and Movements of Social Reform," 155–6; Frank, *McLachlan*.

61. Glickman, *Living Wage*; Weir, *Beyond Labour's Veil*; Waters, *British Socialists and the Politics of Popular Culture*.

62. Heron and Penfold, *Workers' Festival*.

63. Ibid. (quotation).

64. *Yeas and Nays*, xv (quotation by Hewitt); Royal Commission on Liquor Traffic, *Report*, 376–7 (quotation by Knights); *Herald* (Hamilton), 6 March 1913, 5.

65. *Palladium of Labor*, 12 January 1884, 1, 31 May 1884, 1; Royal Commission on Liquor Traffic, *Minutes of Evidence*, vol.2, 360–1, 371, 373 (quotation by Knight), 744–5; *Industrial Banner*, January 1906, 2 (quotation), April 1912, 1; *Herald* (Hamilton), 4 April 1912, 13, 31 March 1914, 5; *Globe*, 4 December 1911, 8 (quotations by Labourists).

66. *Labor News* (Hamilton), 19 June 1914, 4 (quotations); Decarie, "Something Old, Something New," 158, 167; David, "I'll Drink to That," 208; Benson, "American Workers and Temperance Reform," 260–1. For similar tensions between prohibitionists and labour in New Zealand, see Grigg, "Prohibition, the Church and Labour." In a parallel development, Black temperance supporters in the United States felt increasingly uncomfortable linked to a

movement that became overtly racist in the U.S. South; see Herd, "Ambiguity in Black Drinking Norms."

67.   Strople, "Prohibition and Movements of Social Reform," 156 (quotation by printers); Benson, "American Workers and Temperance Reform," 270–3; Bumsted, ed., *Documentary Problems*, 195 (quotation by Roper); Morton, *Ideal Surroundings*, 71.

68.   Decarie, "Prohibition Movement," 294–5; *Industrial Banner*, 10 March 1916, 2 (quotation); Thompson, "Voice of Moderation"; McLean, "Most Effectual Remedy," 122–3; Gray, *Booze*, 79; *Canadian Annual Review*, 1916, 519; Forbes, "Prohibition and the Social Gospel," 76.

69.   Hiebert, "Prohibition," 74–6; Campbell, *Demon Rum or Easy Money*, 28–33; Hallowell, *Prohibition in Ontario*, 19; Pinno, "Temperance and Prohibition," 64–5; Trades and Labor Congress of Canada, *Proceedings*, 1915, 106–7; Benson, "American Workers and Temperance Reform," 261–2, 274–81; Drescher, "Organized Labor and the Eighteenth Amendment."

70.   The trades and labour councils in Hamilton in 1916 and Vancouver in 1920 voted to remain neutral. When Nova Scotia unionists took up the question early in 1919, a bitter two-hour debate ensued before a compromise resolution emerged. In New Brunswick a stalemate developed when Moncton's labour council refused to allow the provincial federation of labour to endorse a partial repeal of prohibition. And some labour figures continued to appear on prohibitionist platforms—notably a few prominent B.C. socialists who had abandoned the wet camp. *Sun*, 8 October 1920, 5; Davis, "I'll Drink to That," 261; Allen, *Social Passion*, 267–9.

71.   Trades and Labor Congress of Canada, *Proceedings*, 1916, 148–52 (quotation at 152), 1918, 49, 58; *Globe*, 30 September 1916, 7, 4 March 1918, 1, 9; *Telegram* (Toronto), 4 March 1918, 14; *Herald* (Hamilton), 4 March 1918, 10; *Labor News*, 8 March 1918, 1.

72.   *Gazette*, 9 April 1919, 4.

73.   Trades and Labor Congress of Canada, *Proceedings*, 1918, 18.

74.   Trades and Labor Congress of Canada, *Proceedings*, 1918, 26–7, 30, 112–3 (quotation at 113), 1919, 32–3; *Globe*, 16 April 1918, 13; *Spectator*, 6 February 1919, 1.

75.   Drescher, "Organized Labor and the Eighteenth Amendment," 292–9; Benson, "American Workers and Temperance Reform," 286–95.

76.   Trades and Labor Congress of Canada, *Proceedings*, 1919, 32–3, 60, 73, 81, 1924, 57, 1925, 71, 73, 158, 1926, 77, 156, 1927, 74, 76, 167; Newton, *Feminist Challenge*, 82.

77.   Hallowell, *Prohibition in Ontario*, 101, 148–9 (quotation); *Canadian Annual Review*, 1922, 590–1. At least one of Halcrow's ILP colleagues in the legislature had doubts about this issue and objected to "any man adopting the beer keg as an emblem, and he didn't believe that the people would vote for the man with the beer keg on his shoulder. 'The beer and wine question should not be brought into the Labor movement,'" he argued in 1923. *Labor News*, 23 February 1923, 1.

78.   Hallowell, *Prohibition in Ontario*, 148–9 (quotation).

79.   Trades and Labor Congress of Canada, *Proceedings*, 1916, 148–52; 1918, 26–7 (quotation), 58 (quotation).

80.   *Star*, 5 December 1916, 17; *Labor News*, 8 March 1918, 1 (quotations by Ontario labour speaker), 21 June 1918, 2, 18 October 1918, 2; Trades and Labor Congress of Canada, *Proceedings*, 1918, 27 (quotation by Tom Moore). Halifax's labour weekly, the *Citizen*, ran a series of articles by C.E. Popplestone, a French and German professor at the University of New Brunswick, who hammered away at the ineffectiveness and hypocrisy of prohibition and the growth of illicit production and bootlegging.

81.   *Spectator*, 6 February 1919, 1 (quotation by TLC delegation); Ajzenstadt, "Medical-Moral Economy," 212 (quotation by B.C. miners' union).

82.   Hiebert, "Prohibition in British Columbia," 75 (quotations by B.C. paper); *Free Press* (London), 18 October 1919, 12 (quotation by bricklayer); Davis, "I'll Drink to That," 259–62; Strople, "Prohibition and Movements of Social Reform," 156–9, 173; Campbell, *Demon Rum or Easy Money*, 29–31, 52; Thompson, "Voice of Moderation," 183, and "Prohibition Question," 89; Trades and Labor Congress of Canada, *Proceedings*, 1916, 148; *Globe*, 30 September 1916, 7; *Herald* (Hamilton), 2, 4 March 1918, 10; *Spectator*, 6 February 1919, 1; *Labor News*, 8 March 1918, 1, 21 June 1918, 2, 18 October 1918, 2; *New Democracy*

(Hamilton), 29 April 1920, 2; *Industrial Banner*, 28 May 1920, 4; *Star*, 5 December 1916, 1, 17; *Canadian Annual Review*, 1916, 523; Benson, "American Workers and Temperance Reform," 274–6.

83. Heron, "National Contours"; Davis, "I'll Drink to That," 259–62 (quotations by Craig, Dane, and Charlottetown union); *Spectator*, 24 September 1919, 11 (quotation by U.S. visitor).

84. Hiebert, "Prohibition in British Columbia," 107; Stretch, "From Prohibition to Government Control," 18; Pinno, "Temperance and Prohibition," 159; Johnston, *Drury*, 155 (quotation by letter-writer); Thompson, "Prohibition Question," 100; Gervais, *Rumrunners*, 59.

85. Morton, *When Your Number's Up*, 26, 109, 239.

86. *Telegram*, 4 March 1918, 14 (Potts quotation); *Gazette*, 9 April 1919, 4; Jones, "Labour, Society and the Drink Question."

seven ⤳ One Hell of a Farce

1. *Manitoba Free Press* (Winnipeg), 11 March 1916, quoted in Thompson, "Prohibition Question," 23.

2. Rose, *Four Years with the Demon Rum*, 79.

3. Solomon and Green, "First Century."

4. In 1920 New York City's Department of Health reported the results of a survey on the new beverage, results evidently shared in Canada: "It is the general consensus that near beer is utterly useless as a beverage, that it affords no pleasure whatsoever and that it is a waste of time to bother with it. The consumption of six to eight bottles gives [drinkers] a sense of nauseated fullness with none of the stimulated sense of well-being that the old-time beer gave after two or three bottles." *Canadian Annual Review*, 1924–5, 88 (quotation); Bowering, *Brewing in Formosa*, 46–7.

5. Royal Commission on Liquor Traffic, *Report*, 197; McLeod, "Liquor Control"; Davis, "I'll Drink to That," 216–18, 221–2; Strople, "Prohibition and Movements of Social Reform," 97.

6. Grant, *When Rum Was King*, 59–60; Hallowell, *Prohibition in Ontario*, 35; Thomson, "Prohibition Question," 76; Pinno, "Temperance and Prohibition," 125–6; Gray, *Booze*, 118–38; Marrus, *Mr. Sam*, 65–79,101–2. Booze delivered across borders was most often liquor. At the outset of prohibition, Labatt was troubled to see how few beer drinkers were interested in waiting for express deliveries; Tucker, "Labatt's," 166.

7. Gray, *Booze*, 118–38; Marrus, *Mr. Sam*, 65–79,101–2.

8. McGahan, *Crime and Policing*, 44 (quotation by Charlottetown newspaper); Fanshawe, *Liquor Legislation*, 381 (quotation by British writer); Royal Commission on Liquor Traffic, *Report*, 125 (quotation by Quebec official).

9. In Quebec City physicians wrote over 15,000 prescriptions in the seven months after 1 May 1919. In Prince Edward Island they handed out over 34,000 over a nine-month period. British Columbia's doctors signed over 181,000 during 1919, and one Vancouver doctor issued 4,000 in a month. A Winnipeg doctor-pharmacist team sold 5,800 prescriptions in August 1920 alone. Hiebert, "Prohibition in British Columbia," 111 (quotation); Thompson, "Prohibition Question," 76–7; Stretch, "From Prohibition to Government Control," 20; *Canadian Annual Review*, 1922, 588–9, 746, 764, 794–5.

10. Johnston, *Drury*, 162 (quotations). There is no Canadian research on the attitudes of the medical community to the use of alcohol as medicine in this period, but for a review of the U.S. debates (and the American Medical Association's about-face on its 1917 rejection of alcohol's therapeutic possibilities), see Jones, "Prohibition Problem."

11. Campbell, *Demon Rum or Easy Money*, 24; Thompson, "Voice of Moderation," 173; Gray, *Booze*, 92; Hiebert, "Prohibition in British Columbia," 111 (quotation by Leacock); Hallowell, *Prohibition in Ontario*, 107–10; Ontario, Board of License Commissioners, *Report on the Operation of the Ontario Temperance Act*, 1917–18, 7, 1919–20, 9–10, 1920–1, 8, 1921–2, 13, 1922–3, 6–7, 8 (quotations by Ontario board), 1923–4, 6–8, 1924–5, 6–8, 1925–6, 6–8; Davis, "I'll Drink to That," 258; Stretch, "From Prohibition to Government Control," 36; Marrus, *Mr. Sam*, 68–70; Newman, *Bronfman Dynasty*, 79; Grant, *When Rum Was King*, 85–92;

Anderson, *Rum Runners*, 12–13, 30–1; Tucker, "Labatt's," 165; *Canadian Annual Review*, 1920, 657, 697, 1922, 747, 832–3.

12. In 1920 British Columbia limited the amount of alcohol that druggists could sell to any one person. Alberta also intervened to set prices and then quotas and then in 1922 transferred all liquor sales to new government dispensaries. In 1924 Ontario required drug stores to obtain liquor licences.

13. Ontario, Liquor Control Board, *Report*, 1928, 8; *Spectator* (Hamilton), 25 November 1926, 14; Royal Commission on Liquor Traffic, *Report*, 155; Canada, Department of Inland Revenue/National Revenue, *Reports*, 1917–23.

14. Stretch, "From Prohibition to Government Control," 12; Grant, *When Rum Was King*, 103–114; Doyle, *Front Benches and Back Rooms*, 237–8; Gray, *Booze*, 97–8; *Canadian Annual Review*, 1921, 661, and 1922 (763, 833); Stretch, "From Prohibition to Government Control," 11–12; Davis, "I'll Drink to That," 272; Anderson, *Rum Runners*, 7–18, 34, 36–43, 53 (quotation); Thompson, "Prohibition Question," 82; Morton, *Ideal Surroundings*, 78; Calder, *Booze and a Buck*, 82–3; Royal Commission on Customs and Excise, *Interim Reports*, 16, 52–3; Marrus, *Mr. Sam*, 79–83.

15. Ontario, Board of License Commissioners, *Report on the Operation of the Ontario Temperance Act*, 1920–1, 7, 1921–2, 9–10 (quotations).

16. Horrall, "Policeman's Lot"; Royal Commission on the Liquor Traffic, *Report*, 197 (quotation by Commission); Doyle, *Front Benches and Back Rooms*, 238 (quotation by Maritime official); Gervais, *Rumrunners*, 45; Everest, *Rum across the Border*, 26–34, 60; Andrieux, *Prohibition and St. Pierre*, 102; Hennigar, *Rum Running Years*, 10, 13, 42, 108–9.

17. Forbes, "'Rum' in the Maritimes Economy"; Hennigar, *Rum Running Years*, 8, 39–43, 104 (quotation by Lunenburg man); Calder, *Booze and a Buck*; Everest, *Rum across the Border*, 23, 53–5; Parker and Tyrrell, *Rumrunner*, 4 (quotation by Schnarr); Miles, *Slow Boat*; Andrieux, *Prohibition and St. Pierre*, and *Over the Side*.

18. Dubro and Rowland, *King of the Mob*, 139 (quotation).

19. Gervais, *Rumrunners* (quotation by policeman at 111); Doyle, *Front Benches and Back Rooms*, 237–8 (quotation by taxi driver at 235).

20. Grant, *When Rum Was King*, 37–45, 135–72; Hunt, *Booze, Boats, and Billions*, and *Whiskey and Ice*; Dubro and Rowland, *King of the Mob*; Marrus, *Mr. Sam*, 102–5; Anderson, *Rum Runners*, 19–23, 33–6, 39, 45–51; Gray, *Booze*, 139–43; Allsop, *Bootleggers*. As they were squeezed out by the bigger players and their better-organized networks, the small-time bootleggers turned to robbing each other and, in a few cases, kidnapping. In the early 1930s a few gangs snatched major figures in booze production and marketing: Sam Low, brother of the major owner of Carling's; Mo Nathanson, a Windsor agent for the Bronfmans; and, most sensationally, John Labatt, head of the family firm. A similar plot to snatch Sam Bronfman fell apart at the last minute. Tucker, "Labatt's," 195–212; Marrus, *Mr. Sam*, 172.

21. Gray, *Booze*, 134; Dubro and Rowland, *King of the Mob*, 254–79.

22. Campbell, *Demon Rum or Easy Money*, 23–6; Dubro and Rowland, *King of the Mob*; Grant, *When Rum Was King*, 99; Newsome, *Pass the Bottle*, 19; Engelmann, *Intemperance*, 70–121; Gervais, *Rumrunners*, 16, 50–1, 111–18; Parker and Tyrrell, *Rumrunner*; Waters, *Smugglers of Spirits*; Royal Commission on Customs and Excise, *Interim Reports*, 15.

23. Davis, "I'll Drink to That," 274–7; Doyle, *Front Benches and Back Rooms*, 233–38 (quotations at 237); Grant, *When Rum Was King*, 11–36; McIntosh, *Collectors*, 254, 271–2; Marrus, *Mr. Sam*, 131–43; Kottman, "Volstead Violated."

24. Geoff and Dorothy Robinson, *Duty-Free, It Came By the Boatload*, and *Nellie J. Banks*; Grant, *When Rum Was King*, 20 (quotation).

25. Gervais, *Rumrunners*; Mason, *Rum Running and the Roaring Twenties*.

26. Gervais, *Rumrunners*, 55 (quotation).

27. Hallowell, *Prohibition in Ontario*, 122 (quotation); Royal Commission on Customs and Excise, *Interim Reports*, 13, 44–116; and *Final Report*.

28. Marrus, *Mr. Sam*, 107–31, 135; Newman, *Bronfman Dynasty*, 125–31.

29. Hunt, *Booze, Boats, and Billions*, 73–107, 202–15; Andrieux, *Prohibition and St. Pierre*, 43–53; Hennigar, *Rum Running Years*, 90–9; Anderson, *Rum Runners*, 29–20; Tucker, "Labatt's," 173–9,

187–8; McIntosh, *Collectors*, 269–81. Despite prohibition, Labatt was able to expand its production facilities considerably, and it increased its staff from 68 in 1922 to 127 in 1927 and 194 in 1930. Tucker, "Labatt's," 190–1.

30. Newman, *Bronfman Dynasty*, 104–8; Haller, "Bootleggers as Businessmen."
31. Grant, *When Rum Was King*, 115–25; Gervais, *Rumrunners*, 68–70.
32. Newman, *Bronfman Dynasty*, 74–131 (quotation at 85); Dubro and Rowland, *King of the Mob*, 153–67.
33. Couturier, "Prohibition or Regulation?"; Grant, *When Rum Was King*, 115–25; Calder, *Booze and a Buck*, 65–71 (quotation at 66), 77–83.
34. Burr, "Roping in the Wretched," 88–9; Couturier, "Prohibition or Regulation?" 160; Rose, *Four Years with the Demon Rum*, 20–1, 27, 30, 33–4, 42, 60, 64–6, 78; Grant, *When Rum Was King*, 72, 73, 76, 77, 79, 80, 81; Forbes, "'Rum' in the Maritimes Economy," 106 (quotation); Hennigar, *Rum Running Years*, 63–4.
35. Campbell, *Demon Rum or Easy Money*, 23; Couturier, "Prohibition or Regulation?" 157, 159–60; Calder, *Booze and a Buck*, 66 (quotation by hotel-keeper); Bowering, *Brewing in Formosa*, 47 (quotation by Ontario family member); Ontario, Board of License Commissioners, *Report on the Operations of the Ontario Temperance Act*, 1917–1819, 22–3; Hiebert, "Prohibition in British Columbia," 101–2, 113; Gray, *Bacchanalia Revisited*, 36; Everest, *Rum Across the Border*, 115–16.
36. Royal Commission on Customs and Excise, *Interim Reports*; Grant, *When Rum Was King*, 71–83, 93–101; Tucker, "Labatt's," 181–20.
37. Miller, *Such Melodious Racket*, 70–1, 73, 122; Gervais, *Rumrunners*, 42, 46, 52–3 (quotation), 101–7, 112.
38. Royal Commission on Liquor Traffic, *Report*, 78–9, 91–2, 97–115, 816; Spence, *Prohibition*, 345; Couturier, "Prohibition or Regulation?"; Bliss, *Canadian Millionaire*, 23–4; Forbes, "Prohibition and the Social Gospel," 63; Davis, "I'll Drink to That," 139, 159–60; and "Small Town Reformism," 134; Strople, "Prohibition and Movements of Social Reform," 97–9, 164–5; Gray, *Bacchanalia Revisited*, 38–9; McIntosh, *Collectors*, 148.
39. Marquis, "Canadian Police and Prohibition," 2–8, and "Vancouver Vice," 261–6; Gervais, *Rumrunners*, 23 (quotation).
40. Couturier, "Prohibition or Regulation?"; *Canadian Annual Review*, 1901, 481 (quotation by Moncton mayor), and 1907 (527 [quotation by Owen Sound mayor]); Ajzenstadt, "Medical-Moral Economy," 230–1.
41. Marquis, "Canadian Police and Prohibition," 14–19, "History of Policing," 88–92, and *Policing Canada's Century*; Davis, "I'll Drink to That," 250–1; Stretch, "From Prohibition to Government Control," 8–12, 37–8; Hiebert, "Prohibition in British Columbia," 114; Anderson, *Rum Runners*, 28–9; Hunt, *Booze, Boats, and Billions*, 168–70.
42. Hallowell, *Prohibition in Ontario*, 119–21 (quotation at 121); Oliver, "New Order"; Johnston, *E.C. Drury*, 157–65; Gervais, *Rumrunners*, 119–29.
43. Marquis, "Canadian Police and Prohibition," 14–19, "History of Policing," 88–92, and *Policing Canada's Century*; Phyne, "Prohibition's Legacy"; Davis, "I'll Drink to That," 250–1; Stretch, "From Prohibition to Government Control," 8–12, 37–8; Hiebert, "Prohibition in British Columbia," 114.
44. Marquis, "Vancouver Vice," 263–5.
45. McIntosh, *Collectors*, 148–52, 253–88; Blake, *Customs Administration*, 142–54.
46. Royal Commission on Customs and Excise, *Interim Reports*, and *Final Report*; Gray, *Booze*, 154–76; Marrus, *Mr. Sam*, 87–90; Andrieux, *Prohibition and St. Pierre*, 99–100; Everest, *Rum across the Border*, 6–7; Hunt, *Booze, Boats, and Billions*, 128–39; Newsome, *Pass the Bottle*, 21–5; Stretch, "From Prohibition to Government Control," 11–12; Newman, *Bronfman Dynasty*, 89–91, 93–5; Engelman, *Intemperance*, 70–121; Mason, *Rum Running and the Roaring Twenties*, 103–12; Waters, *Smugglers of Spirits*; Calder, *Booze and a Buck*, 17–35; Kottman, "Volstead Violated."
47. Marquis, "History of Policing," 88–92; Hiebert, "Prohibition in British Columbia," 104.

48. Ontario, Board of License Commissioners, *Report*, 1921–2, 14 (quotation); Thorner and Watson, "Keeper of the King's Peace," 48; Homel, "Denison's Law"; Gervais, *Rumrunners*, 10 (quotation by hotel-keeper), 52 (quotation by policeman).

49. *Canadian Annual Review*, 1901, 477, 481 (quotation), and 1907 (527 [quotation]).

50. Hallowell, *Prohibition in Ontario*, 112–16; Davis, "I'll Drink to That," 249–51, 257–8; Strople, "Prohibition and Movements of Social Reform," 166–8; Doyle, *Front Benches and Back Rooms*, 238; Grant, *When Rum Was King*, 47–69, 179–82; Gervais, *Rumrunners*, 23, 25, 46; Rose, *Four Years with the Demon Rum* (quotation by Rose at 64); Anderson, *Rum Runners*, 9–12, 17–18, 25–7, 52 (quotation by Alberta policeman); McIntosh, *Collectors*, 280. The young social scientist Escott Reid discovered in 1931 that electioneering in dry Nova Scotia throughout the 1920s had included liquor at campaign rallies and whole bottles of liquor for voters on election day. Henderson, "Provincial Liberal," chapter 1.

51. McIntosh, *Collectors*, 256 (quotation); Royal Commission on Customs and Excise, *Interim Reports*.

52. McIntosh, *Collectors*, 253–88; Royal Commission on Customs and Excise, *Interim Reports*, and *Final Report*; Gray, *Booze*, 162–8. In Windsor a local brewer admitted to bribing a customs officer "for extra services performed by this officer in attending to his office before and after office hours and facilitating the shipments made by the British American Brewing Company to the United States, in giving clearances after hours, and other work of a like nature," and breweries and liquor exporters fended off prosecutions under the Customs and Excise Acts with regular payments to the department's solicitor in the city. Royal Commission on Customs and Excise, *Interim Report, no.10*, 48. All levels of U.S. enforcement also suffered from the bribing of officials, which rum-runners and bootleggers came to see as a standard business expense.

53. McIntosh, *Collectors*, 253–88; Royal Commission on Customs and Excise, *Interim Reports*, and *Final Report*.

54. McIntosh, *Collectors*, 149 (quotation by customs official); Gervais, *Rumrunners*, 52 (quote by Ontario policeman); Allen, ed., "Triumph and Decline," 207 (quotation by Saskatchewan police); Hennigar, *Rum Running Years*, 72 (quotation by Nova Scotia enforcement officer); Grant, *When Rum Was King*; Willison, "Liquor Control in Western Canada," 8 (quotation by Calgary police chief); Stretch, "From Prohibition to Government Control," 8–12, 30–1, 53–4.

55. Dubro and Rowland, *King of the Mob*, 140–1 (quotations).

56. Hobsbawm, *Primitive Rebels*, 13–56; Dubro and Rowland, *King of the Mob*, 137–42 (quotations at 140, 141); Anderson, *Rum Runners*, 19–23, 33–6, 39, 45–51; Gervais, *Rumrunners*, 97, 105; Nelli, "American Syndicate Crime," 127.

57. Thompson, "Voice of Moderation," 173 (quotation by Regina paper); Forbes, "Prohibition and the Social Gospel," 77 (quotation by Nova Scotia official); David, "I'll Drink to That," 308 (quotation by New Brunswick board).

58. *Canada Year Book*, 1931, 849.

59. Ontario, Board of License Commissioners, *Report*, 1922, 15 (quotations); Spence, "Prohibitory Legislation," 259–64.

60. Popham and Schmidt, *Statistics*, 37–8; Dominion Bureau of Statistics, *Control and Sale of Alcoholic Beverages*, 1933, 30, 98; Ontario, Liquor Control Board, *Report*, 1929, 10 (quotation); Miron and Zwiebel, "Alcohol Consumption during Prohibition." The percentage of deaths attributed to alcoholism followed precisely the same pattern over this period (rising from .12 per cent in 1921 to .28 in 1929, then falling to .16 in 1931).

61. Spence, "Prohibitory Legislation," 259.

62. Gray, *Booze*, 83–93; Ontario, Liquor Control Board, *Report*, 1929, 10 (quotation); Valverde, *Diseases of the Will*, 183–9. In the United States a 1932 study commissioned by the anti-prohibition forces reported: "The working class is consuming not more than half as much alcohol per capita as formerly," and a survey of social workers reached similar conclusions. Warburton, *Economic Results of Prohibition*, 202; Burnham, "New Perspectives," 63–4; Kyvig, *Repealing National Prohibition*, 23–5; Blocker, *American Temperance Movements*, 120.

63. Smart and Ogborne, *Northern Spirits*, 66.

64. Grant, *When Rum Was King*, 173 (quotation).

eight Trying Again

1. Prévost, Gagne, and Phaneuf, *L'histoire de l'alcool*, 73; Davis, "I'll Drink to That," 279–80, 300–1; Levine, "Committee of Fifty."
2. Hose, *Prohibition or Control?* 32–43, 66–9.
3. *Labor News* (Hamilton), 29 July 1927, 2 (quotation by Hamilton labour paper); Thompson, "Prohibition Question," 102 (quotation by veterans); Hose, *Prohibition or Control?* 30 (quotation by Hose); Hallowell, *Prohibition in Ontario*, 138; Campbell, *Demon Rum or Easy Money*, 47, 52–3, and *Sit Down and Drink Your Beer*, 20.
4. Denison, *Barley and the Stream*, 317–23; Sneath, *Brewed in Canada*, 114–16; *Canadian Annual Review*, 1921, 660–6; Prévost, Gagne, and Phaneuf, *L'histoire de l'alcool*, 66–8; Vigod, *Quebec before Duplessis*, 82–3; Spence, *Prohibition*, 375–81; Spence, *Quebec and the Liquor Problem*, 26; Molson, *Molsons*, 343–4.
5. *Canadian Annual Review*, 1922, 853–4, and 1923 (765–6); Campbell, *Demon Rum or Easy Money*, 26–55.
6. *Canadian Annual Review*, 1923, 706–9, and 1924 (765), 1926–27 (407–9), 1927–28 (485–7); Thompson, "Prohibition Question," 82–105; Gray, *Booze*, 192–3.
7. *Canadian Annual Review*, 1923, 744–5; Stretch, "From Prohibition to Government Control," 28–78; Gray, *Booze*, 193–4.
8. *Canadian Annual Review*, 1922, 795–6, and 1924–25 (415–16); Gray, *Booze*, 195–6.
9. Hallowell, *Prohibition in Ontario*, 131–57 (quotation by Ferguson at 134); Johnston, *Drury*, 196–206; Oliver, *Ferguson*, 82–3, 95, 106, 138–9, 143, 159–64 (quotation by dry correspondent at 163); *Canadian Annual Review*, 1922, 594–6, and 1923 (541), 1924–25 (337–9, 341).
10. Oliver, *Ferguson*, 164–9; *Labour News* (Hamilton), 29 May 1925, 2 (quotation).
11. Oliver, *Ferguson*, 265, 269–80.
12. Saywell, *Just Call Me Mitch*, 45–6, 60–1, 119–22, 140–4, 170; *Canadian Annual Review*, 1926–27, 313–16, and 1927–28 (389–90), 1934 (148); Rohmer, *Taylor*, 68–70; Tucker, "Labatt's," 227.
13. Noel, *Politics in Newfoundland*, 180; Brewers Association of Canada, *Brewing in Canada*, 101.
14. Davis, "I'll Drink to That," 297–330 (quotation at 314); Grant, *When Rum Was King*, 185–97; *Canadian Annual Review*, 1927–28, 461–2, and 1928–29 (414–15), 1929–30 (423, 451); Marquis, "Civilized Drinking," 177–8.
15. Davis, "I'll Drink to That," 330–5.
16. Moffit, "Control of the Liquor Traffic," 192; Stretch, "From Prohibition to Government Control," 76 (quotation).
17. Fosdick and Scott, *Toward Liquor Control*, 166–77; Hose, *Prohibition or Control?* 12–21 (quotation at 20); Moffit, "Control of Liquor Traffic," 191–2; Gray, *Bacchanalia Revisited*, 59; Marquis, "Canadian Temperance Movement," 10–11.
18. Moffit, "Control of the Liquor Traffic," 189–90; Prévost, Gagne, and Phaneuf, *L'histoire de l'alcool*, 73–83; Surprenant, "Une institution québécois."
19. Valverde, *Diseases of the Will*, 145–53; Ontario, Liquor Control Board, *Report*, 1927, 5, 7 (quotations by Ontario board); *Canadian Annual Review*, 1922, 706 (quotation by Quebec official), and 1924–25 (388), 1927–28 (532). In 1922 the Quebec government opened its own plant for bottling foreign wine to help reduce prices for consumers. Prévost, Gagne, and Phaneuf, *L'histoire de l'alcool*, 89–93. On his fact-finding tour of the Western provinces in the mid-1920s, Sir John Willison met several officials who were convinced that less hard liquor was being consumed under government control. Willison, "Liquor Control in Western Canada."
20. Fosdick and Scott, *Toward Liquor Control*, 166–77; Hose, *Prohibition or Control?* 22–31, 44–54; Dominion Bureau of Statistics, *Control and Sale of Liquor*, 1934, 4–13; Manitoba Liquor Enquiry Commission, *Report*, 304–27.
21. *Canadian Annual Review*, 1930–31, 171, 195, 284; Fosdick and Scott, *Toward Liquor Control*, 166–77; Dominion Bureau of Statistics, *Control and Sale of Liquor*, 1934, 4–13.

22. Hose, *Prohibition or Control?* (quotation at 23); Prévost, Gagne, and Phaneuf, *L'histoire de l'alcool*, 78; Gray, *Bacchanalia Revisited*, 65; Heron, *Working in Steel*, 92.

23. Fosdick and Scott, *Toward Liquor Control*, 166–77; Gray, *Bacchanalia Revisited*, 40–3; Hose, *Prohibition or Control?* 24–6 (quotation at 26), 62–5; Willison, "Liquor Control in Western Canada"; *Canadian Annual Review*, 1922, 853, and 1923 (708–9), 1924–25 (434).

24. Ontario, Liquor Control Board, *Report*, 1931, 8, and 1932, 8.

25. Ontario, Liquor Control Board, *Report*, 1928, 9–10 (quotations), and 1929 (11–13), 1930 (9–13), 1931 (7–8), 1932 (7–8); Moffit, "Control of the Liquor Traffic," 191; Valverde, *Diseases of the Will*, 166–7; Campbell, *Sit Down and Drink Your Beer*, 67; Heron, "Boys and Their Booze."

26. Brewers Association of Canada, *Brewing in Canada*, 41, 49; Campbell, *Sit Down and Drink Your Beer*; *Canadian Hotel Review*, September 1934, 7, 22–8; Heron, "Boys and Their Booze."

27. Hose, *Prohibition or Control?* 32–43; Willison, "Liquor Control in Western Canada"; *Canadian Annual Review*, 1924–25, 433–4; Campbell, *Demon Rum or Easy Money*, 54–5, "Managing the Marginal," and *Sit Down and Drink Your Beer*, 15–27; Prévost, Gagne, and Phaneuf, *L'histoire de l'alcool*, 94; Gilmore, *Swinging in Paradise*; Weintraub, *City Unique*, 23, 33, 52, 121–30; Heron, "Boys and Their Booze"; Rohmer, *Taylor*, 73–4.

28. Campbell, *Demon Rum or Easy Money*, 54 (quotation by B.C. waiter); Spence, *Quebec and the Liquor Problem*, 48–9 (quotation by clergyman); Manitoba Liquor Enquiry Commission, *Report*, 398–412 (quotation by Commission at 404). In the mid-1920s, Judge Emily Murphy worried about the seating arrangements of the beer parlours: "Personally, I would like to see the table abolished in favor of a standing bar," she told Sir John Willison. "It would prevent people sitting down easefully [sic] and ordering glass after glass of beer." Willison, "Liquor Control in Western Canada," Edmonton, 8.

29. Valverde, *Diseases of the Will*, 145–62; Forbes, "Prohibition," 81; Spence, *Quebec and the Liquor Problem*, 39–46, 135–44; Moffit, "Control of the Liquor Traffic," 190–1; Campbell, "Managing the Marginal," 115–6, and *Sit Down and Drink Your Beer*, 29–49; *Canadian Annual Review*, 1934, 149; Prévost, Gagne, and Phaneuf, *L'histoire de l'alcool*, 95; Willison, "Liquor Control in Western Canada."

30. *Canadian Annual Review*, 1922, 708, and 1924–25 (434, 449, 500), 1929–30 (523); Willison, "Liquor Control in Western Canada"; Campbell, *Demon Rum or Easy Money*, 48, 83–6, and *Sit Down and Drink Your Beer*, 19–20, 112; Heron, "Boys and Their Booze"; Manitoba Liquor Enquiry Commission, *Report*, 417–26.

31. Heron, "Boys and Their Booze"; Popham, *Working Papers on the Tavern, 3*, 19. In a 1946 survey in Ontario, two-thirds of those who identified themselves as fairly regular patrons of beverage rooms were skilled, semi-skilled, or unskilled workers; Popham, *Working Papers on the Tavern*, 22. The major exception to the working-class dominance of beer parlours was in the grander hotels, which generally had well-appointed beer parlours for affluent guests or businessmen; the *Canadian Hotel Review* featured some of these in the 1930s. By refusing to serve draught beer and offering only bottled beer (which at twenty cents a bottle was twice the price of beer by the glass), hotel managers kept out the riff-raff; in this way, the manager of Toronto's posh King Edward Hotel "restricts his guests to the quieter, more refined type who want to enjoy a good drink in peaceful surroundings." *Canadian Hotel Review*, September 1934, 10–11; see also May 1934, 13, August 1934, 10, 27.

32. Popham and Schmidt, *Statistics*, 24; *Canada Year Book*, 1941, 533; Gray, *Bacchanalia Revisited*, 66–7, 76–92; Campbell, *Demon Rum or Easy Money*, 86–96.

33. Fortin and Richardson, *Life of the Party*, 46; Sobel and Meurer, *Working at Inglis*, 125; Bosnich, *One Man's War*, 71, 81. For a detailed description of using a tavern in union organizing by structural steelworkers in 1950–51, see Popham, *Working Papers on the Tavern, 3*, 106–8.

34. Spence, *Quebec and the Liquor Problem*, 162–3 (quotation).

35. Ibid., 463–4 (quotation by Quebec writer); Fortin and Richardson, *Life of the Party*, 43–4, 46, 55, 58–9 (quotation by Fortin), 79; Willison, "Liquor Control in Western Canada," 9 (quotation by Willison); Campbell, "Managing the Marginal," 117 (quotation by inspector); *Canadian Annual Review*, 1932, 226; Heron, "Boys and Their Booze"; Rosenfeld, "It Was a Hard Life," 262–3.

36. Strange, *Toronto's Girl Problem*; Peiss, *Cheap Amusements*; Strong-Boag, *New Day Recalled*.

37. *Saturday Night* (Toronto), 3 November 1934, 2 (quotation).

38. Gray, *Bacchanalia Revisited*, 43, 54–7; Morton, *Ideal Surroundings*, 85 (quotation); Davies, *Leisure, Gender, and Poverty*, 55–81; Murphy, *Mining Cultures*, 42–70; Wexman, *Creating the Couple*. For the arrival of working-class women in British pubs during the First World War, see Gutzke, "Gender, Class, and Public Drinking."

39. Spence, *Quebec and the Liquor Problem*, 131–2 (quotation); *Star* (Toronto), 1 June 1927, 1–2; *Globe* (Toronto), 2 June 1927, 1–2. Our view of the inside of prohibition-era drinking places in Canada remains opaque, because there has been little systematic study of the rooms in Canada.

40. Campbell, *Demon Rum or Easy Money*, 55–8.

41. Ibid., 57 (quotation).

42. Ibid., 55–8; Manitoba Liquor Enquiry Commission, *Report*, 315, 322, 424; Gutzke, "Gender, Class, and Public Drinking."

43. Campbell, "Ladies and Escorts," *Sit Down and Drink Your Beer*, 51–77, and "Managing the Marginal," 114–17, 125; Willison, "Liquor Control in Western Canada"; Heron, "Boys and Their Booze." Women were kept out of taverns in New Brunswick until 1971, when the first ladies and escorts sections were finally approved. Marquis, "Civilized Drinking," 191.

44. Gray, *Bacchanalia Revisited*, 88–9.

45. Ibid., 44–5; Campbell, "Managing the Marginal," 116–17 (quotation at 117); Heron, "Boys and Their Booze."

46. Campbell, *Sit Down and Drink Your Beer*, 93–105.

47. Ibid., 79–88; Valverde, *Diseases of the Will*, 162–70; Heron, "Boys and Their Booze."

48. Moffit, "Control of the Liquor Traffic," 196 (quotation). As late as the 1990s, the Liquor Control Board of Ontario estimated that 15 per cent of the alcohol consumed in the province was sold illegally.

49. Spence, "Prohibitory Legislation," 243; *Canadian Annual Review*, 1928–29, 389; Gray, *Booze*, 197–207; Grant, *When Rum Was King*, 71; Stretch, "From Prohibition to Government Control," 85–7; Manitoba Liquor Enquiry Commission, *Report*, 308–9; Mann, "Lower Ward"; Smart and Ogborne, *Northern Spirits*, 64; Bosnich, *One Man's War*, 99 (quotations); *Canadian Hotel Review* (Toronto), February 1934, 19.

50. Sobel and Meurer, *Working at Inglis*, 127 (quotation by Inglis worker); Heron, *Working in Steel*, 95–6; Spence, *Quebec and the Liquor Problem*, 138–9; Prévost, Gagne, and Phaneuf, *L'histoire de l'alcool*, 119; Bosnich, *One Man's War*, 67; Calhoun, *"Ole Boy"*, 21–2 (quotations by *Saint John* worker).

51. Campbell, *Demon Rum or Easy Money*, 93–4, 127–9.

52. Pickersgill, ed., *Mackenzie King Record*, 460–4, 485–8, 652–4; Campbell, *Demon Rum or Easy Money*, 86–90; Marquis, "Canadian Temperance Movement," 11–13; Gray, *Bacchanalia Revisited*, 76–92; Rohmer, *Taylor*, 133–8, 152–3; Marrus, *Mr. Sam*, 311–13.

53. Kyvig, *Repealing National Prohibition*, 187–9.

nine ∽ The Recreational Drug

1. Marrus, *Mr. Sam*, 131, 161–4, 180–200, 302–8, 321–6, 368–80; Newman, *Bronfman Dynasty*, 132–41; Rannie, *Canadian Whisky*, 58–70, and *Wines of Ontario*, 38; Brown, *Two Hundred Years of Tradition*, 98–103, 108, 110–12. Sam Bronfman brought a passion for royalty to the naming of his brands—in 1939 he launched the famous "Crown Royal" whisky in honour of the visit of King George VI and Queen Elizabeth to Canada.

2. In 1941 Bronfman bought the British Columbia Distillery and in 1953 added that province's other producer, United Distillers, and in 1955 a smaller Quebec company. The only new firms in the distilling industry after 1930 were the U.S. Schenley branch plant (opened in Valleyfield in 1945), the British Gilbey distillery (established at Toronto in 1933, then at Lethbridge in 1973, producer of the widely popular "Black Velvet" brand), and three smaller

operations in Calgary (1946), Vancouver (1958), and Collingwood, Ont. (1966, producing a hit in the U.S. market, "Canadian Mist").

3. Rannie, *Canadian Whisky*, 83–141, 168.

4. Petrie, *Handbook on Beverage Distilling Industry*, and *Some Economic Facts*.

5. Canada, Department of Inland Revenue, *Reports*, 1900–26; Sneath, *Brewed in Canada*, 95–100; Tucker, "Labatt's," 173.

6. Sneath, *Brewed in Canada*, 95–100; Tucker, "Labatt's," 187–8; Bowering, *Brewing in Formosa*, 49–62; Restrictive Trades Practices Commission, *Report Concerning an Alleged Combine*, 14–17. During the 1920s, British Columbia Breweries, Quebec's National Breweries, and the Oland family in Halifax and Saint John each absorbed smaller competitors. In 1926 the new Canadian Brewing Corporation began accumulating breweries in Toronto, Hamilton, Brandon, and St. Boniface. The next year, five breweries in Manitoba and Saskatchewan joined hands as Western Breweries (renamed Drewry's Limited five years later, and in 1950 merged with the old British Columbia Breweries, newly renamed Western Canada Breweries); in 1928 Associated Breweries of Canada Limited began to integrate a series of producers in Saskatchewan, Alberta, British Columbia, Washington, and Oregon (renamed Sick's in 1944). A similar merger began when four B.C. firms joined hands as Coast Breweries in 1927; a quarter-century later, after buying three West Coast U.S. operations, it renamed itself Lucky Lager Breweries Limited.

7. Trades Practices Commission, *Report Concerning an Alleged Combine*, 14 (quotation).

8. Rohmer, *Taylor*, 39–63, 71–84; Tucker, "Labatt's," 215, 246–7, 258–60, 271; Restrictive Trades Practices Commission, *Report Concerning an Alleged Combine*, 13–42.

9. Rohmer, *Taylor*, 177–9, 203–6; Restrictive Trades Practices Commission, *Report Concerning an Alleged Combine*, 13–42 (quotation at 39); Dorion, *La brasserie Boswell*.

10. Shoniker, *Rothmans*, 41–50 (quotation at 50).

11. Manitoba Liquor Enquiry Commission, *Report*, 531–9; Fogarty, "From Saloon to Supermarket."

12. Denison, *Barley and the Stream*, 344–73; Sneath, *Brewed in Canada*, 96, 99, 183–6.

13. Tucker, "Labatt's," 231, 260, 291, 312–19, 337–49, 362–5, 374–7, 390–4; Brewers Association of Canada, *Brewing in Canada*, 38–9; Shoniker, *Rothmans*, 379; Conference Board of Canada, *Canadian Brewing Industry*, 37. Canadian Breweries' new owners sold the British investment in 1970, but promptly linked up with Carlsberg Breweries of Copenhagen to brew that firm's beer in Canada.

14. Perreault, *Molson Companies*, 49.

15. Restrictive Trades Practices Commission, *Report Concerning an Alleged Combine*, 20–1 (quotation at 21), 42; Tucker, "Labatt's," 334–6, 369–70, 374–7, 414–19; Rohmer, *Taylor*, 157, 177; Brewers Association of Canada, *Brewing in Canada*, 116; Bowering, *Brewing in Formosa*, 78–9; Sneath, *Brewed in Canada*, 181–2.

16. Gourvish, "Concentration, Diversity, and Firm Strategy"; Millns, "British Brewing Industry"; Ronnenberg, "American Brewing Industry"; Merrett, "Stability and Change"; Jones, "New Zealand Brewing Industry"; Campbell, *Demon Rum or Easy Money*, 80; Manitoba Liquor Enquiry Commission, *Report*, 18–19; Conference Board of Canada, *Canadian Brewing Industry*, 7–8, 34; McLaughlin, *Story of Beer*, 69–79; Restrictive Trades Practices Commission, *Report Concerning an Alleged Combine*; Jones, "Mergers and Competition."

17. Rohmer, *Taylor*, 139–44, 165–75, 206–10, 212–14; Shoniker, *Rothmans*, 37, 48–58; Tucker, "Labatt's," 371–2, 401–7; Perreault, *Molson Companies*; Sneath, *Brewed in Canada*, 188–94. In 1970 Philip Morris's Canadian subsidiary, Benson and Hedges, bought the much smaller Formosa Brewery, which was undergoing a major expansion. When the company's profits failed to satisfy the tobacco interests, they sold it to Molson in 1974.

18. Tucker, "Labatt's," 377–9; Brewers Association of Canada, *Brewing in Canada*, 36, 43–46, and *Supplement to Brewing in Canada*, 34; Dorion, *La brasserie Boswell*; Sneath, *Brewed in Canada*, 205. Quart bottles were still available in the Maritimes, Quebec, and Eastern Ontario in the 1960s, but declined from 30 per cent of packaged beer in 1953 to less than 9 per cent in 1966. Two Canadian breweries had begun packaging beer in cans in 1948, and the product first went on the market in Quebec only. Canned beer still made up only 1 per cent of the

market in the late 1960s, compared to 39 per cent in the United States. *Canadian Food Industries*, August 1948, 33, August 1949, 30–3 (I am grateful to Steve Penfold for these references).

19.   A merger of six firms in 1928 created Canadian Wineries Limited (renamed Chateau-Gai in 1940). Distillers showed some interest as well: in 1933 Hiram Walker's Harry Hatch acquired Bright's, and fifteen years later Sam Bronfman snapped up Jordan's. Rannie, *Wines of Ontario*; Aspler, *Vintage Canada*, 13–92.

20.   Dominion Bureau of Statistics, *Control and Sale of Alcoholic Beverages*, 1970, 16–17 (calculations of proportions of market share are mine); Single and Giesbrecht, *Rates of Alcohol Consumption*, 20; Single, Giesbrecht, and Eakins, "Alcohol Policy Debate," 131–2.

21.   Rannie, *Wines of Ontario*, 156 (quotation).

22.   For the new consolidation of unionism in large-scale, blue-collar industries in Canada in the 1940s, see Heron, *Canadian Labour Movement*, 58–84.

23.   National Archives of Canada (hereafter NAC), RG 27 (Department of Labour Records), T-2706, no.267 (Brewery Workers, Lethbridge, Alta., 2–5 July 1920); T-2713, no.23 (Brewery Workers, Toronto, 16 April–1 June 1923); *Union with a Heart*; *Canadian Hotel Review*, 15 July 1935, 4.

24.   NAC, RG 27, T-4077, no.44 (Brewery Workers, Montreal, 28 March–21 May 1946); T-4103, no.124 (Brewery Workers, Regina, 9–19 November 1949); *Union with a Heart*; Denison, *Barley and the Stream*, 366–8, 375–9; Tucker, "Labatt's," 294–303, 322, 350–7. After a falling out with the craft-unionist American Federation of Labor and Trades and Labor Congress of Canada in 1941, the brewery workers went independent before affiliating with the Congress of Industrial Organizations (CIO) and Canadian Congress of Labour five years later.

25.   Brewers Association of Canada, *Brewing in Canada*, 70; Dorion, *La brasserie Boswell*.

26.   NAC, RG 27, T-3001, no.340 (Winery Employees, Toronto, 3–6 November 1936); T-3007, no.174 (Winery Employees, 3 October–? 1938); Canada, Department of Labour, *Labour Organization in Canada*, 1941, 1961; Shoniker, *Rothmans*, 28.

27.   NAC, RG 27, T-4092, no.235 (Tapmen and Waiters, Timmins, Ont., 7 November–? 1947); T-4099, no.13 (Hotel Barmen and Waiters, Quebec, 7 March–13 April 1949); T-4103, no.9 (Beverage Room Tapmen, Calgary, 4 February–4 March 1950); *100 Years of Service*; Canada, Department of Labour, *Labour Organization in Canada*, 1920–70, *Strikes and Lockouts in Canada*, 1951–61; Campbell, *Demon Rum or Easy Money*, 95, 103, 115, 151, 154; Strong, *My Life*, 9–13. In some provinces, beer-parlour employees benefited from the new "industrial standards" legislation introduced in the 1930s; Fudge and Tucker, *Labour before the Law*, 188–204; *Canadian Hotel Review*, 15 October 1935, 5, 16, 24; 15 August 1937, 5, 19; 15 January 1938, 5, 11. Some bartenders and waiters organized in Catholic unions in Quebec and an independent union in Newfoundland, while in Sudbury they were members of a General Workers' Union.

28.   Bowering, *Brewing in Formosa*, 62–5, 69–72; Tucker, "Labatt's," 157, 186–7; Canada, Department of Labour, *Strikes and Lockouts in Canada*, 1951, 1952, 1955, 1956, 1958;

29.   Dalys, *No Longer a "Two-Bit" Union*.

30.   Li, *Making of Post-War Canada*; Finkel, *Our Lives*; Holmes, *Demand for Beverage Alcohol*; Weintraub, *City Unique*, 159–60.

31.   Smart and Ogborne, *Northern Spirits*, 65–7, 73–4.

32.   Popham and Schmidt, *Statistics*, 3–12; Single and Giesbrecht, *Rates of Alcohol Consumption*, 3–27; Manitoba Liquor Enquiry Commission, *Report*, 245–6, 267–73; Brewers Association of Canada, *Brewing in Canada*, 118–19, and *Supplement to Brewing in Canada*, 23; Petrie, *Handbook on Beverage Distilling Industry*, 10; Redman, *Open Gangway*; Kimber, *Sailors, Slackers, and Blind Pigs*.

33.   The absolute alcohol content of the three main beverages rose from .760 gallons in 1931 to 1.373 in 1951 (of which beer comprised 65 per cent, spirits 29 per cent, and wine 6 per cent) to 2.063 in 1971 (57 per cent of which was in beer, 33 per cent in spirits, and 10 per cent in wine). Dominion Bureau of Statistics, *Control and Sale of Alcoholic Beverages*, 1970, 15 (percentage calculations are mine); Brewers' Association of Canada, Alcoholic Beverage Study Committee, *Beer, Wine, and Spirits*, 16, 23; Smart, *New Drinkers*, 4; Bowering, *Brewing in Formosa*, 72; Sulkunen, "Drinking Patterns."

34.   Dominion Bureau of Statistics, *Control and Sale of Alcoholic Beverages*, 1970, 15.

35.   Jones, "Mergers and Competition," 559–62; Dominion Bureau of Statistics, *Control and Sale of Alcoholic Beverages*, 1949, 6–14; Manitoba Liquor Enquiry Commission, *Report*, 545–57; Sneath, *Brewed in Canada*, 129. Brewery salesmen also regularly visited individual drinking establishments to promote their company's products, sometimes illegally offering samples to customers. *Canadian Hotel Review*, 15 July 1938, 23.

36.   Tucker, "Labatt's," 248–57 (quotation at 249–50).

37.   Campbell, "Fantastic Rigmarole"; Schlase, "Liquor and the Indian"; Gray, *Bacchanalia Revisited*, 116–18.

38.   Archibald, *Addiction Research Foundation*, 2 (quotation by Ontario attorney-general); Manitoba Liquor Enquiry Commission, *Report*, 266 (quotation by Manitoba Commission), 312, 316, 325–7; Campbell, *Demon Rum or Easy Money*, 115–20 (quotation by B.C. Commission); Henderson, "Provincial Liberal," chapter 6; Marquis, "Civilized Drinking"; Graham, *Old Man Ontario*, 118–21, 252–8; Brewers Association of Canada, *Brewing in Canada*, 42–3, 102–10.

39.   Marquis, "Civilized Drinking."

40.   Manitoba Liquor Enquiry Commission, *Report*, 327 (quotation). The individual establishment files of the Liquor Control Board of Ontario, now at the Archives of Ontario, are full of moralistic reports on live performances.

41.   The main studies were Popham, *Working Papers on the Tavern, 3*; Manitoba Liquor Commission, *Report*, 412–15; Mann, "Lower Ward"; Dewar, *Consumption of Alcohol*; Sommer, "Isolated Beer Drinker"; Ossenberg, "Social Class and Bar Behavior"; Listiak, "Legitimate Deviance"; Cutler and Storm, *Drinking Practices*; Storm and Cutler, "Observations of Drinking"; Ratcliffe et al., "Drinking in Taverns." For reviews of this literature, see Single, "Studies of Public Drinking"; and Clark, "Contemporary Tavern."

42.   Ossenberg, "Social Class and Bar Behavior," 30 (quotation).

43.   U.S. classifications posed problems for Canadian researchers because most U.S. taverns operated under more liberal regulatory regimes than did their Canadian counterparts, outside Quebec.

44.   Popham, *Working Papers on the Tavern, 3*, 23; Manitoba Liquor Commission, *Report*, 412–15.

45.   Popham, *Working Papers on the Tavern, 3*, 21–30, 37–41, 54–72, 86 (quotation); Manitoba Liquor Commission, *Report*, 412–15 (quotation at 413); Sommer, "Isolated Drinker"; Ossenberg, "Social Class and Bar Behavior"; Listiak, "Legitimate Deviance"; Cutler and Storm, *Drinking Practices*, 86–96; Storm and Cutler, "Observations of Drinking," and "Functions of Taverns"; Graham et al., "Aggression and Barroom Environments"; Macrory, "Tavern and the Community"; Gottlieb, "Neighborhood Tavern and Cocktail Lounge"; Richards, "City Taverns"; Clark, "Demographic Characteristics"; Cavan, *Liquor License*; Dumont, "Tavern Culture"; Kessler and Gomberg, "Observations of Barroom Drinking"; LeMasters, *Blue–Collar Aristocrats*; Thomas, "Class and Sociability"; Clark, "Contemporary Tavern"; Oldenburg, "Augmenting the Bar Studies."

46.   Churchill, "Coming Out"; Chamberland, "Remembering Lesbian Bars"; Kinsman, *Regulation of Desire*, 144–7; Israelstam and Lambert, "Gay Bars"; Cutler and Storm, *Drinking Practices*; Gusfield, Kotara, and Rasmussen, "Bar as a Context"; Johnston, *At the York*.

47.   Popham, *Working Papers on the Tavern, 3*, 26–40; Sugiman, *Labour's Dilemma*, 159; Manitoba Liquor Commission, *Report*, 412–15 (quotation at 413).

48.   Popham, *Working Papers on the Tavern, 3*, 86 (quotation by researcher); Mann, "Lower Ward," 58 (quotation by "Lower Ward" resident).

49.   Campbell, *Demon Rum or Easy Money*, 118–20; Popham, *Working Papers on the Tavern, 3*, 30–6, 42–54; Ossenberg, "Social Class and Bar Behavior."

50.   Storm and Cutler, "Observations of Drinking" (quotation at 975); Single, "Public Drinking," 145.

51.   Owram, "Canadian Domesticity"; Parr, "Household Choices"; and *Domestic Goods*; Single and Giesbrecht, *Rates of Alcohol Consumption*, 46–8.

52.   Crysdale, "Family and Kinship," 109; Heath, *Drinking Occasions*, 179–80; White, Fallis, and Pickett, *Investigation into the Effects of Alcohol Use in Ontario Schools*, 44–5. Another Addiction Research Foundation study published suggested that "the number of incidents involving

intoxications has increased in absolute terms but decreased as a proportion of the number of drinking occasions. Thus, drinkers may be less likely to become intoxicated when they drink, but the number of drinking occasions has increased." Single and Giesbrecht, *Rates of Alcohol Consumption*, 53.

53. One summer in the 1960s I worked for a moving company, one of whose drivers kept beer in his truck and took a swig from time to time as we loaded or unloaded, though I never saw him anywhere close to what, in my innocence, I could identify as intoxication. One of my colleagues at York University described to me how the garment workers on Spadina Avenue in Toronto with whom her father worked kept a bottle behind the counter at a local restaurant for lunchtime consumption. Students in my labour studies courses have occasionally related their experiences of drinking on the line at General Motors in Oshawa. For scholarly studies of the role of alcohol in occupational cultures in the United States in the 1980s, see Sonnenstuhl, *Working Sober*; Ames and Janes, "Heavy and Problem Drinking."

54. Giffen, *Alienation of the Skid Row Drunkenness Offender*; Rubington, "Bottle Gang"; Spradley, *You Owe Yourself a Drunk*.

55. Leland, *Firewater Myths*; Maracle, *Crazywater*; Lithman, "Feeling Good and Getting Smashed"; MacAndrew and Edgerton, *Drunken Comportment*; Fisher, "Alcoholism and Race"; Whitehead and Hayes, *Insanity of Alcohol*; Smart and Ogborne, *Northern Spirits*, 101–10.

56. Owram, *Born at the Right Time*; Li, *Making of Post-War Canada*, 129–32.

57. Valverde, *Diseases of the Will*, 115–19; Snyder, *Alcohol and the Jews*.

58. Frankel and Whitehead, "Sociological Perspectives," 13–25; Sulkunen, "Drinking Patterns," 258–9; Marquis, "Public Drunkenness."

59. Smart, *New Drinkers*; Whitehead, *Young Drinkers*.

60. When the country's biggest liquor store opened in a renovated train station in Toronto in early 2003, it offered, in addition to the five thousand brands on the shelves, a room of party ideas and a testing room, where customers could buy one-ounce shots of 120 different products. *Globe and Mail*, 5 February 2003, A8.

61. Campbell, *Demon Rum or Easy Money*, 130–82; Marquis, "Civilized Drinking," 184–91, 198–9; Single, Giesbrecht, and McKenzie, "Alcohol Policy Debate," 140, 146, 148; Smart and Ogborne, *Northern Spirits*, 72, 85, 143–50, 176–7; Archibald, *Addiction Research Foundation*, 65–72; Single and Giesbrecht, *Rates of Alcohol Consumption*, 45–9; Smart and Goodstadt, "Effects of Reducing the Legal Alcohol-Purchasing Age"; Vingilis and Smart, "Effects of Raising the Legal Drinking Age"; Smart and Adlaf, "Banning Happy Hours," 257.

62. Ratcliffe et al., "Drinking in Taverns," 874 (quotation by Toronto researchers); Dunk, *It's a Working Man's Town*, 69 (quotation by anthropologist), 77–8.

63. Cohen, *Consumer's Republic*, 292–344; Smart, "Happy Hours Experiment." The booze producers can take cold comfort from the inability of various studies in "alcohol studies" circles to prove that the advertising has any effect on consumption. See Smart, "Does Alcohol Advertising Affect Overall Alcohol Consumption"; Smart and Ogborne, *Northern Spirits*, 163–7. I heard the story about the classified ad on CTV's *W5* in the early 1980s.

64. Statistics Canada, *Control and Sale of Alcoholic Beverages*, 1980–96; Smart and Ogborne, *Northern Spirits*, 61–78, Single, Williams, and McKenzie, *Canadian Profile*, 37.

65. Heron, *Canadian Labour Movement*, 126–32. The role of the business cycle in shaping drinking patterns became clear when consumption levels began to rise slightly again in the new economic boom of the late 1990s.

66. Jackson et al., *Falling Behind*; Smart, "Is the Postwar Drinking Binge Ending?" and "Socio-Economic, Lifestyle, and Availability Factors"; Smart and Ogborne, *Northern Spirits*, 167–8; Campbell, *Demon Rum or Easy Money*, 166–8, 199; Ratcliffe, "Drinking in Taverns," 874. In Alberta, by the late 1970s, draft beer in taverns had become twice as expensive as bottled beer from the retail stores, and bottled beer in taverns two and a half times higher. Similarly, the ten-cent price for a glass of beer that had survived in British Columbia beer parlours since the 1920s suddenly became twenty-five cents in the early 1970s, and in 1979 the Social Credit government removed all price controls on on-premise drinking and, two years later, on beer sold in government liquor stores. The cost of a case of twenty-four bottles was soon twice what it had been in 1975.

67.   Chui, "Canada's Population"; Smart, "Is the Postwar Drinking Binge Ending?" and "Socio-Economic, Lifestyle, and Availability Factors"; Smart and Ogborne, *Northern Spirits*, 90, 93–8.

68.   Avery, *Reluctant Host*, 170–91.

69.   Single, Williams, and McKenzie, *Canadian Profile*, 21, 31–2. A similar income-based spread was reported for "mean number of drinks per week"; ibid., 40.

70.   Sneath, *Brewed in Canada*, 214–15 (quotation); Smart and Ogborne, *Northern Spirits*, 89.

71.   Single, Williams, and McKenzie, *Canadian Profile*.

72.   Smart and Ogborne, *Northern Spirits*, 85–9. In the mid-1990s, according to Statistics Canada, a quarter of young men aged 15–19 had five or more drinks on one occasion twelve or more times a year; by the end of the decade, the proportion had reached 40 per cent. The percentage of females aged 15–19 doing so rose from only 11 per cent to 26 per cent, while, for young men aged 20–24, the numbers rose from about a third to nearly a half; <www.statscan:80/english/freepub/82-221-XIE/01002/tables/html/2151>.

73.   Valverde, *Diseases of the Will*, 192–204 (quotations at 200); for a fuller discussion of the issues in this case, see Bondy, ed., "Intoxication as a Legal Defence."

74.   Reinarman, "Social Construction of an Alcohol Problem"; <http://www.madd.ca>.

75.   Reinarman, "Social Construction of an Alcohol Problem," 105 (quotation about drunks); Gusfield, "Control of Drinking-Driving"; <www.madd.org> (quotation about mothers).

76.   Ross, "Deterrence-Based Policies"; Campbell, *Demon Rum or Easy Money*, 164–6; Smart and Ogborne, *Northern Spirits*, 179–80; Single, Giesbrecht, and McKenzie, "Alcohol Policy Debate," 134–5; Archibald, *Addiction Research Foundation*, 117–20; Bell, *Special Calling*, 149–55; Johnson, Gibson, and Linden, "Alcohol and Rape"; Single, "Public Drinking," 146–50.

77.   Conference Board of Canada, *Canadian Brewing Industry*, 6, 9; Sneath, *Brewed in Canada*, 199–207, 252–76, 286–303 (quotation at 207). In 1992 the major brewers returned to a standard shape of bottle but not the "stubby." Sneath, *Brewed in Canada*, 410.

78.   Sneath, *Brewed in Canada*, 210–51, 263–71, 277–302, 316–24; *Star* (Toronto), 12 March 2003, D1–D3.

79.   Sneath, *Brewed in Canada*, 288–302.

80.   Smart and Ogborne, *Northern Spirits*, 133.

81.   Conference Board of Canada, *Canadian Brewing Industry*, 10; Campbell, *Demon Rum or Easy Money*, 176–9; Sneath, *Brewed in Canada*, 252–5; Gourvish, "Concentration, Diversity and Firm Strategy"; Ronnenberg, "American Brewing Industry"; Merrett, "Stability and Change";

82.   Sneath, *Brewed in Canada*, 255–6; *Excalibur* (Toronto), 31 January 2002, 10.

83.   The Brewers' Association of Canada used every opportunity to distance itself from the other two branches of booze production and to promote the "healthy" qualities of their beverage; see, for example, the major study sponsored by their association: Brewers' Association of Canada, Alcoholic Beverage Study Committee, *Beer, Wine, and Spirits*.

84.   Heavy drinkers undoubtedly gave low estimates of their consumption, because the per capita consumption among adults over age fourteen based on actual government sales figures was ten drinks of 1.7 cl., or .6 oz., of absolute alcohol each in 1990, compared to an average of only 4.4 drinks in the self-reporting surveys. Single, Williams, and McKenzie, *Canadian Profile*, 21–2, 37–8; Single and Wortley, "Drinking in Various Settings"; Single, "Public Drinking"; Cosper, Okraku, and Neumann, "Tavern Going"; Smart and Ogborne, *Northern Spirits*, 83–99; Dunk, *It's a Working Man's Town*, 69.

ten ⟨Rediscovering the Alcoholic

1.   Herd and Room, "Alcohol Images in American Film"; Room, "Alcoholism and Alcoholics Anonymous in U.S. Films."

2.   Bell, *Special Calling*, 81, 115–16; Archibald, *Addiction Research Foundation*, 3–5 (quotation at 5). Many doctors had moved only slowly away from prescribing alcohol for their patients after the end of prohibition; see Jones, "Prohibition Problem."

3.   McCarthy, "Early Alcoholism Treatment."

4.   Kurtz, *Not-God*; White, *Slaying the Dragon*, 96–108.

5.   Kurtz, *Not-God*; White, *Slaying the Dragon*, 96–108, 127–43; Makela et al., *Alcoholics Anonymous*, 19–39 (quotation at 33); Bell, *Special Calling*, 77–8.

6.   White, *Slaying the Dragon*, 143–55; Makela et al., *Alcoholics Anonymous*, 117–32, 153–69.

7.   Valverde and White-Mair, "One Day at a Time"; Valverde, *Diseases of the Will*, 120–42. Paul Antze has drawn a fascinating parallel between AA and tribal cults of affliction and possession, as well as placing the organization solidly in the evangelical Protestant tradition of sin and salvation; see Antze, "Symbolic Action."

8.   Makela et al., *Alcoholics Anonymous*, 52–84, 96–114, 133–52, 170–82; White, *Slaying the Dragon*, 156–63, 220–2; Bell, *Special Calling*, 78 (quotation); Rodin, "Getting on the Program."

9.   Rotskoff, *Love on the Rocks*, 105–48, 162–93.

10.   Ogborne and Glaser, "Characteristics of Affiliates"; Valverde and White-Mair, "One Day at a Time," 402–6. After visits to a dozen AA groups interviews with seventeen members in Southern Ontario, Valverde and White-Mair concluded that working-class men formed a majority of the membership by the 1990s, a contrast with most other findings about AA members in earlier periods.

11.   White, *Slaying the Dragon*, 178–87.

12.   Ibid.; Milgram, "Summer School of Alcohol Studies."

13.   Jellinek, *Disease Concept* (quotation at 190).

14.   White, *Slaying the Dragon*, 188–98, 223–49; Valverde, *Diseases of the Will*, 94–119; Archibald, *Addiction Research Foundation*, 9; Room, "World Health Organization and Alcohol Control"; Fisher, "Alcoholism and Race"; Popham and Schmidt, *Decade of Alcoholism Research*, 7–8. Gordon Bell, the director of a succession of highly respected pioneering treatment centres in and near Toronto starting in 1946 (Glenmaple, Shadow Brook, Willowdale, Bell, and Donwood), experimented with insulin injections and chemical sedatives, and was the enthusiastic sponsor of the arrival of Antabuse in Canada from Denmark in 1949, apparently ahead of U.S. practitioners. He used it as a central part of his therapeutic arsenal for many years, and then participated in the development of a new drug for aversion therapy, Temposil, patented by the Alcoholism Research Foundation of Ontario in 1955 and used at least to the end of the 1980s. Bell, *Special Calling*, 64–5, 79, 87–8, 90–101, 119.

15.   Archibald, *Addiction Research Foundation*.

16.   Ibid. (quotation at 31); Popham and Schmidt, *Decade of Alcoholism Research*. Gordon Bell asserted that his 1952 address to the Canadian Medical Association on his work at the Shadow Brook clinic (published in the association's journal the next year) was "the first paper on alcoholism to be presented in general session of that august body," and that during the 1950s "We were still not widely accepted in medical circles." Bell, *Special Calling*, 102, 161.

17.   Archibald, *Addiction Research Foundation* (quotations at 15, 16).

18.   Ibid., 169 (quotation); Popham and Schmidt, *Decade of Alcoholism Research*, 2–4 (quotation at 4); Gibbins, "Alcoholism in Ontario."

19.   Schmidt, Smart, and Moss, *Social Class*, 20–1, 53–5. Therapy at the private Shadow Brook and Donwood clinics was similar. Bell, *Special Calling*, 162–3, 172–5, 210–14.

20.   Valverde, *Diseases of the Will*, 104–10; Rotskoff, *Love on the Rocks*; Plant, *Women and Alcohol*, 174–214.

21.   Rotskoff, *Love on the Rocks*.

22.   Bell, *Special Calling*, 102–29; Marquis, "Civilized Drinking," 193–4, 200, and "Public Drunkenness."

23.   Trice, "History of Job-Based Alcoholism Programs"; Archibald, *Addiction Research Foundation*.

24.   Trice, "History of Job-Based Alcoholism Programs"; Archibald, *Addiction Research Foundation*; Strachan, "Industry Discovers Alcoholism" (quotation at 43); Fingarette, *Heavy Drinking*, 21.

25.   Schmidt, Smart, and Moss, *Social Class* (quotations at 47, 52, 60, 86, 88, 92, 95).

26.   Marquis, "Civilized Drinking," 195–201; Rush and Ogborne, "Alcoholism Treatment"; MacAndrew, "On the Notion" (quotation at 499).

27.   Room, "Sociological Aspects"; Fingarette, *Heavy Drinking*; Miller, "Controlled Drinking."

28.   Rush and Ogborne, "Alcoholism Treatment"; Valverde, *Diseases of the Will*, 8–9; Fingarette, *Heavy Drinking*, 70–95; Peele, *Diseasing of America*.

29.   Rush and Ogborne, "Alcoholism Treatment" (quotation at 258); Bell, *Special Calling*, 131, 176 (quotation), 183 (where Bell notes that roughly half his patients had not met his criteria of successful recovery).

30.   Johnson, "Union Responses"; Smart and Ogborne, *Northern Spirits*, 57, 110–11, 191; Saggers, "Dry Damp and Wet Revisited."

31.   Archibald, *Addiction Research Foundation*, 121–6; Rush and Ogborne, "Alcoholism Treatment" (quotation at 258); Bruin et al., *Alcohol Control Policies*; Moore and Gerstein, eds., *Alcohol and Public Policy*; Fingarette, *Heavy Drinking*; Peele, *Diseasing of America*; Smart and Docherty, "Effects of the Introduction of On-Premise Drinking"; Smart and Mann, "Treatment, Health Promotion, and Alcohol Controls." Eleven of the world's largest brewing, distilling, and wine-making corporations fund the International Center for Alcohol Policies, which produced an edited collection in 1998 to debunk the notion that limiting per capita consumption would solve alcohol problems; see Grant and Litvak, eds., *Drinking Patterns and Their Consequences*.

32.   Single, Williams, and McKenzie, *Canadian Profile*, 43–4; Smart and Ogborne, *Northern Spirits*, 171–94; Smart and Mann, "Treatment, Health Promotion, and Alcohol Problems," 341.

eleven ✍ The Elusive John Barleycorn

1.   For other experience in rural settings, see Netting, "Beer as a Locus of Value"; Doughty, "Social Uses of Alcoholic Beverages"; Masden and Masden, "Cultural Structure of Mexican Drinking Behavior"; Marshall and Marshall, "Holy and Unholy Spirits"; Lemert, "Forms and Pathology"; Hutchinson, "Alcohol as a Contributing Factor"; Mills, "Cape Smoke"; Honigmann, "Dynamics of Drinking"; Karp, "Beer Drinking"; Crush and Ambler, eds., *Liquor and Labor*; Xiao, "China"; Oshodin, "Nigeria."

2.   Austin, *Alcohol in Western Society*, xxi–xxiv; Tlusty, "Water of Life, Water of Death"; Park, "Sketches Toward a Political Economy"; Vogt, "Defining Alcohol Problems"; Hall and Hunter, "Australia"; Dingle, "Truly Magnificent Thirst"; Eldred-Grigg, *Pleasures of the Flesh*, 178–88.

3.   Townend, *Father Mathew*, 10; Osterberg, "From Home Distillation to the State Alcohol Monopoly"; Pinson, "Temperance, Prohibition, and Politics"; Cahannes and Mueller, "Alcohol Control Policy in Switzerland"; Brun-Gulbrandsen, "Drinking Habits"; Prestwich, *Drink and the Politics of Social Reform*; Morgan, "Industrialization, Urbanization, and the Attack on Italian Drinking Culture." In considering the apparent rise in German alcohol consumption in the sixteenth century, Ann Tlusty argues that it is more fruitful to examine changing perspectives on drinking; see Tlusty, *Bacchus and Civic Order*, 2–6.

4.   Levine, "Temperance Cultures"; Eriksen, "Making of the Danish Liberal Drinking Style."

5.   Aaron and Musto, "Temperance and Prohibition"; Harrison, *Drink and the Victorians*; Lambert, *Drink and Sobriety*.

6.   Sariola, "Prohibition in Finland"; Roberts, "Alcohol, Public Policy, and the Left."

7.   That Atlantic Canada's rural communities stood out as the earliest and most persistent supporters of temperance across the country deserves closer examination than has been possible here. Because the region was facing a serious erosion of its status within the Canadian economy and national state from the late nineteenth century onward, it might be useful to see prohibitionist sentiments as part of a distinctive regional consciousness, based partly in the material realities of widespread poverty and deprivation and partly in the sense of moral purpose among many of the region's numerous primary producers (there are hints of this possibility in Forbes, "Prohibition and the Social Gospel," which remain undeveloped). Prohibitionism has certainly been part of the arsenal of subordinate groups in many societies, including urban workers, Black Canadians, and Americans, and some Aboriginal groups, and of some colonized peoples in European empires. Ann Pinson notes that the regions of Scandinavia that imposed prohibition were the "colonial" areas—Finland, Iceland, and the Fargoes—in contrast to the independent states—Denmark, Sweden, and Norway—which

did not. Perhaps the Atlantic region's "colonial" status within the Canadian nation-state helps to explain the strength of the region's commitment to temperance. See Pinson, "Temperance, Prohibition, and Politics," 249; and other articles in the special issue of *Contemporary Drug Problems*, Summer 1985, including the introduction by Robin Room, "Liquor Question and Formation of Consciousness"; also his "Drink, Popular Protest, and Government Regulation."

8. Room, "Formulation of State Alcohol Monopolies and Controls"; Herlihy, *Alcoholic Empire*; Kudlick, "Fighting the Internal and External Enemies"; Brun-Gulbrandsen, "Drinking Habits"; Osterberg, "From Home Distillation to the State Alcohol Monopoly"; Sariola, "Prohibition in Finland"; McLauchlan, *Story of Beer*, 91–109.
9. Makela, Osterberg, and Sulkunen, "Drink in Finland"; Moskalewicz, "Alcohol"; Osterberg, "From Home Distillation to the State Alcohol Monopoly"; Sariola, "Prohibition in Finland"; Ambler and Crush, "Alcohol in Southern African Labor History."
10. Burnet, "Urban Community"; Armstrong and Nelles, *Revenge of the Methodist Bicycle Company*; Dean, *Censored!*; Homel, "Sliders and Backsliders"; Gilmore, *Swinging in Paradise*; Miller, *Such Melodious Racket*.
11. Sulkunen, "Drinking Patterns."
12. Heath, ed., *International Handbook*, 365; Heath, *Drinking Occasions*, 135–58.
13. Gusfield, "Benevolent Repression"; and "Passage to Play."
14. Marshall, ed., *Beliefs, Behaviors, and Alcoholic Beverages*; Heath, ed., *International Handbook*; Plant, *Women and Alcohol*; Nadeau, "Gender and Alcohol"; *Globe and Mail* (Toronto), 12 February 2003, A7.
15. Heath, *Drinking Occasions*, 81–2; Single and Pomeroy, "Drinking and Setting."
16. Rural patterns of drinking remain poorly researched and analyzed. On the one hand, numerous studies of farmers' movements have underlined the commitment of the men in those movements to sobriety. On the other, a wealth of popular literature points to the persistence of illicit selling and drinking of alcohol in the countryside.
17. Levine, "Temperance Cultures"; Valverde, *Diseases of the Will*; Walton, *Out of It*, 1–17, 195–238; Partanen, *Sociability and Intoxication* (quotation at 171); Xiao, "China," 46; Schioler, "Denmark," 55; Naboum-Grappe, "France," 79–80.
18. Fanshawe, *Liquor Legislation*, 386 (quotation).
19. *Globe and Mail*, 11 January 2003, F7, 13 January 2003, A1, A4, A12, 15 January 2003, A7, R1, R3, 16 January 2003, A1, A9.
20. Nestle, "Alcohol Guidelines"; Peele, ed., *Alcohol and Pleasure*. The Alberta and Ottawa politicians were observed to be intoxicated in public, while the B.C. premier took more flak for the more serious crime of drunk driving during a holiday in Hawaii. But, even in this case, journalist commentators and phone-in callers repeatedly noted that the man had only done what many other Canadian drinkers had done at some point of their lives.
21. To be sure, scholars are now raising questions about the notion of "integrated drinking" that has dominated anthropological studies for so long; see, for example, Partanen, *Sociability and Intoxication*, 199–216.
22. Heath, "Critical Review," 47–50. I am not using "ambivalence" as a form of individual psychology (see Room, "Ambivalence as Sociological Explanation"), but rather as the cultural product of confrontations and struggles through time, consolidated in complex ways in institutions, public discourses, and popular practices.

Bibliography

Abbreviations

BJA	British Journal of Addiction
CDP	Contemporary Drug Problems
CHR	Canadian Historical Review
CIHM	Canadian Institute of Historical Materials
HP	Canadian Historical Association, Historical Papers
HS/SH	Histoire sociale/Social History
JCS	Journal of Canadian Studies
JDI	Journal of Drug Issues
JSA	Journal of Studies on Alcohol
L/LT	Labour/Le Travail
OH	Ontario History
QJSA	Quarterly Journal of Studies on Alcohol

Aaron, Paul, and David Musto. "Temperance and Prohibition in America: A Historical Overview." In Moore and Gerstein, eds., *Alcohol and Public Policy*. Pp.127–81.

Abrahamson, Una. *God Bless Our Home: Domestic Life in Nineteenth Century Canada*. Toronto: Burns and MacEachern 1966.

Acheson, T.W. "Evangelicals and Public Life in Southern New Brunswick, 1830–1880." In Van Die, ed., *Religion and Public Life in Canada*. Pp.50–68.

_____. *Saint John: The Making of a Colonial Urban Community*. Toronto: University of Toronto Press 1985.

Adamson, Agar. "We Were Here Before: The Referendum in Canadian Experience." *Policy Options*, 1, no.1 (March 1980). Pp.50–4.

Ade, George. *The Old-Time Saloon: Not Wet—Not Dry, Just History*. New York: Ray Long and Richard R. Smith 1931.

Adler, Marianna. "From Symbolic Exchange to Commodity Consumption: Anthropological Notes on Drinking as a Social Practice." In Barrows and Room, eds., *Drinking*. Pp.376–98.

Advocate (Toronto and Montreal), 1894–5 (CIHM no.P04183).

Ajzenstadt, Mimi. "The Medical-Moral Economy of Regulation: Alcohol Legislation in B.C., 1871–1925." Ph.D. thesis. Simon Fraser University, 1992.

Alexander, Ruth M. "'We Are Engaged as a Band of Sisters': Class and Domesticity in the Washingtonian Temperance Movement, 1840–1850," *Journal of American History*, 75, no.3 (December 1988). Pp.763–85.

Allen, Harold Tuttle. *Forty Years' Journey: The Temperance Movement in British Columbia to 1900*. N.p. n.d.

Allen, Richard. *The Social Passion: Religion and Social Reform in Canada, 1914–28*. Toronto: University of Toronto Press 1973.

_____, ed. "The Triumph and Decline of Prohibition." In Bumsted, ed., *Documentary Problems in Canadian History*, vol. 2.

Allsop, Kenneth. *The Bootleggers: The Story of Chicago's Prohibition Era*. London: Hutchinson 1961.

Ambler, Charles and Jonathan Crush. "Alcohol in Southern African Labor History." In Crush and Ambler, eds., *Liquor and Labor*. Pp.1–55.

Ames, Genevieve and Craig R. Janes. "Heavy and Problem Drinking in an American Blue-Collar Population: Implications for Prevention." *Social Science Medicine*, 25, no.8 (1987). Pp.949–60.

Ames, Herbert Brown. *The City below the Hill: A Sociological Study of a Portion of the City of Montreal, Canada*. Toronto University of Toronto Press 1972 [1897].

Anderson. Frank W. *The Rum Runners*. Frontier Book no.11. High River, Alta.: High River Times n.d.

Andrieux, Jean-Pierre. *Over the Side: Stories from a Rum Runner's Files from Prohibition Days in Atlantic Canada and Newfoundland.* Lincoln, Ont.: W.F. Rannie 1984.

_____. *Prohibition and St. Pierre: When Distillers and Rum Runners Made France's Colony Off Newfoundland a Principal Centre for the Liquor Trade.* Lincoln, Ont.: W.F. Rannie 1983.

_____. *La Prohibition . . .: Cap sur Saint-Pierre et Miquelon.* Ottawa: Editions Lemeac 1983.

Anstead, Christopher J. "Hegemony and Failure: Orange Lodges, Temperance Lodges, and Respectability in Victoria Ontario." In Blocker and Warsh, eds., *Changing Face of Drink.* Pp.163–88.

Antze, Paul. "Symbolic Action in Alcoholics Anonymous." In Douglas, ed., *Constructive Drinking.* Pp.149–81.

Archer, John E. "'Men Behaving Badly?': Masculinity and the Uses of Violence, 1850–1900." In D'Cruze, ed., *Everyday Violence.* Pp.43–54.

Archibald, H. David. *The Addiction Research Foundation: A Voyage of Discovery.* Toronto: Addiction Research Foundation 1990.

Arès, Jean-Patrice. "Les campagnes de tempérance de Charles Chiniquy: Un des principaux moteurs de réveil religieux montréalais de 1840." Maitrise en sciences religieuses, Université de Québec à Montréal 1990.

Arès, Jean-Patrice and Louis Rousseau. "Les campagnes de Chiniquy, 1848–1851"; and "Le sens d'un geste: Faire profession de tempérance après 1840." In Rousseau and Remiggi, eds., *Atlas historique des pratiques religieuses.* Pp.71–2, 184–5.

Armstrong, Christopher and H.V. Nelles. *The Revenge of the Methodist Bicycle Company: Sunday Streetcars and Municipal Reform in Toronto, 1888–1897.* Toronto: Peter Martin Associates 1977.

Artibise, Alan F.J. *Winnipeg: A Social History of Urban Growth, 1874–1914.* Montreal and Kingston: McGill-Queen's University Press 1975.

Aspler, Tony. *Vintage Canada.* Scarborough, Ont.: Prentice-Hall 1983.

Austin, Gregory A. *Alcohol in Western Society from Antiquity to 1800: A Chronological History.* Santa Barbara, Cal.: ABC-Clio Information Services 1985.

Avery, Donald H. *Reluctant Host: Canada's Response to Immigrant Workers, 1896–1994.* Toronto: McClelland and Stewart 1995.

Baasher, Taha. "The Use of Drugs in the Islamic World." In Griffith Edwards, Awni Arif, and Jerome Jaffe, eds., *Drug Use and Misuse: Cultural Perspectives.* London: Croom Helm 1983. Pp.21–32.

Babor, Thomas F. and Barbara G. Rosenkrantz. "Public Health, Public Morals, and Public Order: Social Science and Liquor Control in Massachusetts, 1880–1916." In Barrows and Room, eds., *Drinking.* Pp.265–86.

Baehre, Rainer. "From Bridewell to Federal Penitentiary: Prisons and Punishment in Nova Scotia before 1880." In Philip Girard and Jim Phillips, eds., *Essays in the History of the Canadian Law,* vol. 3, *Nova Scotia.* Toronto: University of Toronto Press 1990. Pp.163–99.

Bailey, Peter. *Leisure and Class in Victorian England: Rational Recreation and the Contest for Control, 1830–1885.* London: Routledge and Kegan Paul 1978.

_____. "Parasexuality and Glamour: The Victorian Barmaid as Cultural Protoype." *Gender and History,* 2, no.2 (Summer 1990). Pp.148–72.

_____. "'Will the Real Bill Banks Please Stand Up?': Towards a Role Analysis of Mid-Victorian Working-Class Respectability." *Journal of Social History,* 12, no.2 (Summer 1979). Pp.336–53.

Baldwin, Douglas. "'But Not a Drop to Drink': The Struggle for Pure Water." In Douglas Baldwin and Thomas Spira, eds., *Gaslights, Epidemics, and Vagabond Cows: Charlottetown in the Victorian Era.* Charlottetown: Ragweed Press 1988. Pp.103–24.

Barbeau, Marius. *Jongleur Songs of Old Quebec.* Toronto: Ryerson Press 1962.

Baron, Stanley. *Brewed in America: A History of Beer and Ale in the United States.* Boston: Little, Brown and Company 1962.

Barr, Andrew. *Drink: A Social History.* London: Pimlico 1998.

Barrett, James R. "Why Paddy Drank: The Social Importance of Whiskey in Pre-Famine Ireland." *Journal of Popular Culture,* 21, no.1 (Summer 1977). Pp.155–66.

Barron, F.L. "Alcoholism, Indians, and the Anti-Drink Cause in the Protestant Indian Missions of Upper Canada, 1822–1850." In Ian A.L. Getty and Antoine S. Lussier, eds., *As Long as the Sun*

Shines and Water Flows: A Reader in Canadian Native Studies. Vancouver: UBC Press 1983. Pp.191–202.

—————. "The American Origins of the Temperance Movement in Ontario, 1828–1850." *Canadian Review of American Studies*, 11, no.2 (Fall 1980). Pp.131–50.

—————. "The Genesis of Temperance in Ontario, 1828–1850." Ph.D. thesis. University of Guelph 1976.

Barrows, Susanna. "After the Commune: Alcoholism, Temperance, and Literature in the Early Third Republic." In John M. Merriman, ed., *Consciousness and Class Experience in Nineteenth-Century Europe*. New York: Holmes and Meier Publishers 1979. Pp.205–18.

—————. "'Parliaments of the People': The Political Culture of Cafés in the Early Third Republic." In Barrows and Room, eds., *Drinking*. Pp.87–97.

—————. "Worlds of Drink in Nineteenth-Century France." In Barrows, Room, and Verhey, eds., *Social History of Alcohol*. Pp.6–19.

Barrows, Susanna and Robin Room, eds. *Drinking: Behavior and Belief in Modern History*. Berkeley: University of California Press 1991.

Barrows, Susanna, Robin Room, and Jeffrey Verhey, eds. *The Social History of Alcohol: Drinking and Culture in Modern Society*. Berkeley, Cal.: Medical Research Institute of San Francisco, Alcohol Research Group 1987.

Barry, Sandra. "'Shades of Vice . . . and Moral Glory': The Temperance Movement in Nova Scotia, 1828 to 1848." M.A. thesis. University of New Brunswick 1986.

Baskerville, Peter and Eric W. Sager. *Unwilling Idlers: The Urban Unemployed and Their Families in Late Victorian Canada*. Toronto: University of Toronto Press 1998.

Bate, J.P. "Prohibition and the U.F.A." *Alberta Historical Review*, 18, no.4 (1970). Pp.1–6.

Baumohl, Jim. "The Confessions of Balder Hartpole: A Note on Therapeutic Temperance in Montreal during the 1870s." *Drink and Drug Practices Surveyor*, 23 (May 1990). Pp.6–11.

—————. "Inebriate Institutions in North America, 1840–1920." In Warsh, ed., *Drink in Canada*. Pp.92–114.

Baumohl, Jim and Robin Room. "Inebriety, Doctors, and the State: Alcoholism Treatment Institutions before 1940." In Marc Galanter, ed., *Recent Developments in Alcoholism*, vol.5. New York: Plenum Press 1987. Pp.135–74.

Baumohl, Jim and Sarah W. Tracy. "Building Systems to Manage Inebriates: The Divergent Paths of California and Massachusetts, 1891–1920." *CDP*, 21, no.4 (Winter 1994). Pp.557–97.

Bédard-Lévesque, Claire. "La tempérance au Québec." M.A. thesis, Université Laval 1979.

Bederman, Gail. *Manliness and Civilization: A Cultural History of Gender and Race in the United States, 1880–1917*. Chicago: University of Chicago Press 1995.

Bell, R. Gordon with Stan Solomon. *A Special Calling: My Life in Addiction Treatment and Care*. Toronto: Stoddart 1989.

Bennett, Judith M. *Ale, Beer, and Brewsters in England: Women's Work in a Changing World, 1300–1600*. New York: Oxford University Press 1996.

Bennett, Linda A. and Genevieve M. Ames, eds. *The American Experience with Alcohol: Contrasting Cultural Perspectives*. New York: Plenum Press 1985.

Benson, Adolph B., ed. *Peter Kalm's Travels in North America: The English Version of 1770*. 2 vols. New York: Dover 1966.

Benson, Ronald Morris. "American Workers and Temperance Reform, 1866–1933." Ph.D. thesis. University of Notre Dame 1974.

Bernard, Jean-Marc. "Deux phases de l'antialcoolisme au Canada français (1840–1855 et 1905–1920): Essai d'interprétation sociologique." *Toxicomanies*, 1, no.2 (May–August 1968). Pp.135–66.

Berridge, Virginia. "The Society for the Study of Addiction, 1884–1988." *BJA*, 85, no.8 (August 1990). Pp.982–1077.

Bevan, George E. *How Workingmen Spend Their Spare Time*. New York: n.p. 1913.

Birrell, A.J. "D.I.K. Rine and the Gospel Temperance Movement in Canada." *CHR*, 58, no.1 (March 1977). Pp.23–42.

Bitterman, Rusty. "Farm Households and Wage Labour in Northeastern Maritimes in the Early 19th Century." *L/LT*, 31 (Spring 1993). Pp.13–45.

Black, Naomi and Gail Cuthbert Brandt. "Alcohol and the First Women's Movement." *Études canadiennes/Canadian Studies*, 35 (1993). Pp.95–106.

Blake, Gordon. *Customs Administration in Canada: An Essay in Tariff Technology*. Toronto: University of Toronto Press 1957.

Bliss, Michael. *A Canadian Millionaire: The Life and Business Times of Sir Joseph Flavelle, Bart., 1858–1939*. Toronto: Macmillan 1978.

_____. *A Living Profit: Studies in the Social History of Canadian Business, 1883–1911*. Toronto: McClelland and Stewart 1974.

_____. *William Osler: A Life in Medicine*. Toronto: University of Toronto Press 1999.

Blocker, Jack S., Jr. *Alcohol, Reform, and Society: The Liquor Issue in Social Context*. Westport, Conn.: Greenwood Press 1979.

_____. *American Temperance Movements: Cycles of Reform*. Boston: Twayne Publishers 1989.

_____. "Artisan's Escape: A Profile of the Postbellum Liquor Trade in a Midwestern Small Town." In *Essays in Economic and Business History*, 1994. Pp.335–46.

_____. "Consumption and Availability of Alcoholic Beverages in the United States, 1863–1920." *CDP*, 21, no.4 (Winter 1994). Pp.631–62.

_____. *"Give to the Winds Thy Fears": The Women's Temperance Crusade, 1873–1874*. Westport, Conn.: Greenwood Press 1985.

_____. *Retreat from Reform: The Prohibition Movement in the United States, 1890–1913*. Westport, Conn.: Greenwood Press 1976.

_____. "Tidy Pictures of Messy Behavior." *Journal of Urban History*. Forthcoming.

Blocker, Jack S. and Cheryl Krasnick-Warsh, eds. *The Changing Face of Drink: Substance, Imagery, and Behaviour*. Ottawa: Les publications Histoire sociale 1997.

Bloomfield, Elizabeth and G.T. Bloomfield. *Industrial Leaders: The Largest Manufacturing Firms of Ontario in 1871*. Guelph: Department of Geography, University of Guelph 1989.

Blumin, Stuart M. *The Emergence of the Middle Class: Social Experience in the American City, 1760–1900*. Cambridge: Cambridge University Press 1989.

Bondy, Susan J., ed. "Intoxication as a Legal Defence: Recent Canadian Experience with Changes in the Criminal Law." *CDP*, 23, no.4 (Winter 1996).

Bordin, Ruth. *Women and Temperance: The Quest for Power and Liberty, 1873–1900*. Philadelphia: Temple University Press 1981.

Boritch, Helen and John Hagan. "Crime and the Changing Forms of Class Control: Policing Public Order in 'Toronto the Good,' 1859–1955." *Social Forces*, 66, no.2 (December 1987). Pp.307–35.

Bosnich, Milan (Mike). *One Man's War: Reflections of a Rough Diamond*. Toronto: Lugus Productions 1989.

Bowering, Ian. *The Art and Mystery of Brewing in Ontario*. Burnstown, Ont.: General Store Publishing 1988.

_____. *Brewing in Formosa: 125 years of Tradition*. Burnstown, Ont.: General Store Publishing 1995.

Bowes, Lisa. "George Sleeman and the Brewing of Baseball in Guelph." *Historic Guelph*, 27 (1987–8). Pp.44–57.

Boyer, Patrick. *Direct Democracy in Canada: The History and Future of Referendums*. Toronto: Dundurn Press 1992.

Boyer, Paul. *Urban Masses and Moral Order in America, 1820–1920*. Cambridge, Mass.: Harvard University Press 1978.

Bradbury, Bettina. "Pigs, Cows, and Boarders: Non-Wage Forms of Survival among Montreal Families, 1861–91." *L/LT*, 14 (Fall 1984). Pp.9–46.

_____. *Working Families: Age, Gender, and Daily Survival in Industrializing Montreal*. Toronto: McClelland and Stewart 1993.

Bradwin, Edmund. *The Bunkhouse Man: A Study of Work and Pay in the Camps of Canada, 1903–1914*. Toronto: University of Toronto Press 1972 [1928].

Braudel, Fernand. *Capitalism and Material Life, 1400–1800*. New York: Harper and Row 1967.

Braun, Stephen. *Buzz: The Science and Lore of Alcohol and Caffeine*. New York: Oxford University Press 1996.

Brennan, Thomas. *Public Drinking and Popular Culture in Eighteenth-Century Paris.* Princeton, N.J.: Princeton University Press 1988.

_____. "Social Drinking in Old Regime Paris." In Barrows and Room, eds., *Drinking.* Pp.61–86.

Bretherton, George. "Against the Flowing Tide: Whiskey and Temperance in the Making of Modern Ireland." In Barrows and Room, eds., *Drinking.* Pp.147–64.

_____. "The Battle between Carnival and Lent: Temperance and Repeal in Ireland, 1829–1845." *HS/SH,* 27, no.54 (November 1994). Pp.295–320.

Breward, Christopher. *The Hidden Consumer: Masculinities, Fashion, and City Life, 1860–1914.* Manchester, U.K.: Manchester University Press 1999.

Brewers Association of Canada. *Brewing in Canada.* Ottawa: Brewers Association of Canada 1965.

_____. *Supplement to Brewing in Canada.* Ottawa: Brewers Association of Canada 1967.

_____. Alcoholic Beverage Study Committee. *Beer, Wine, and Spirits: Beverage Differences and Public Policy.* Ottawa: Brewers Association of Canada 1973.

Brown, J.B. "The Pig or the Stye: Drink and Poverty in Late Victorian England." *International Review of Social History,* 17 (1973). Pp.380–95.

Brown, Lorraine. *Two Hundred Years of Tradition: The Story of Canadian Whiskey.* Toronto: Fitzhenry and Whiteside 1994.

Brown, Robert Craig and Ramsay Cook. *Canada, 1896–1921: A Nation Transformed.* Toronto: McClelland and Stewart 1974.

Bruin, Kettil et al. *Alcohol Control Policies in Public Health Perspective.* Forssa, Finland: Finnish Foundation for Alcohol Studies 1975.

Brundage, David. "The Producing Classes and the Saloon: Denver in the 1880s." *Labor History,* 26, no.1 (Winter 1985). Pp.29–52.

Brun-Gulbransen, Sverre. "Drinking Habits in Norway." In Ole-Jorgen Skog and Ragnar Waahlberg, eds., *Alcohol and Drugs: The Norwegian Experience.* Oslo: National Directorate for the Prevention of Alcohol and Drug Problems [1988].

Bumsted, J.M., ed. *Documentary Problems in Canadian History. Vol 2. Post-Confederation.* Georgetown, Ont: Irwin-Dorsey 1969.

_____. *Land, Settlement, and Politics on Eighteenth-Century Prince Edward Island.* Montreal and Kingston: McGill-Queen's University Press 1987.

Burley, David. *A Particular Condition of Life: Self-Employment and Social Mobility in Mid-Victorian Brantford, Ontario.* Montreal and Kingston: McGill-Queen's University Press 1994.

Burley, Edith I. *Servants of the Honourable Company: Work, Discipline, and Conflict in the Hudson's Bay Company, 1770–1879.* Toronto: Oxford University Press 1997.

Burnet, J.R. "The Urban Community and Changing Moral Standards." In Michiel Horn and Ronald Sabourin, eds., *Studies in Canadian Social History.* Toronto: McClelland and Stewart 1974. Pp.298–325.

Burnett, John. *Liquid Pleasures: A Social History of Drinks in Modern Britain.* London: Routledge 1999.

_____. *Plenty and Want: A Social History of Diet in England from 1815 to the Present Day.* London: Scolar Press 1979.

Burnham, J.C. *Bad Habits: Drinking, Smoking, Taking Drugs, Gambling, Sexual Misbehavior, and Swearing in American History.* New York: New York University Press 1993.

_____. "New Perspectives on the Prohibition 'Experiment' of the 1920's." *Journal of Social History,* 2, no.1 (Fall 1968). Pp.51–68.

Burns, Thomas F. "Getting Rowdy with the Boys." *JDI,* 10, no.2 (Spring 1980). Pp.273–86.

Burr, Christina. "'Roping in the Wretched, the Reckless, and the Wronged': Narratives of the Late Nineteenth-Century Toronto Police Court." *Left History,* 3, no.1 (Spring/Summer 1995). Pp.83–108.

_____. *Spreading the Light: Work and Labour Reform in Late-Nineteenth-Century Toronto.* Toronto: University of Toronto Press 1999.

Butsch, Richard, ed. *For Fun and Profit: The Transformation of Leisure into Consumption.* Philadelphia: Temple University Press 1990.

_____. "Introduction: Leisure and Hegemony." In Butsch, ed., *For Fun and Profit.* Pp.3–25.

Byington, Margaret. *Homestead: The Households of a Mill Town*. Pittsburgh: University of Pittsburgh, University Center for International Studies 1974 [1910].

Bynum, William F. "Alcoholism and Degeneration in 19th Century European Medicine and Psychiatry." *BJA*, 79, no.1 (1984), 59–70.

_____. "Chronic Alcoholism in the First Half of the 19th Century." *Bulletin of the History of Medicine*, 42, no.1 (January–February 1968). Pp.160–85.

Cahannes, Monique and Richard Muller. "Alcohol Control Policy in Switzerland: An Overview of Political Compromise." In Single, Morgan, and De Lint, eds., *Alcohol, Society, and the State,* vol.2. Pp.61–86.

Cain, Louis P. "Water and Sanitation Services in Vancouver: An Historical Perspective." *BC Studies*, 30 (Summer 1976). Pp.27–43.

Calder, J. William. *Booze and a Buck*. Halifax: Formac Publishing 1977.

Calhoun, Sue. *"Ole Boy": Memoirs of a Canadian Labour Leader, J.K. Bell*. Halifax: Nimbus Publishing 1992.

Camargo, Carlos, A., Jr. "Gender Differences in the Health Effects of Moderate Alcohol Consumption." In Peele and Grant, eds., *Alcohol and Pleasure*. Pp.157–70.

Campbell, Gail. "Disenfranchised But Not Quiescent: Women Petitioners in New Brunswick in the Mid-Nineteenth Century." In Veronica Strong-Boag and Anita Clair Fellman, eds., *Re-Thinking Canada: The Promise of Women's History*. Toronto: Copp Clark Pitman 1991. Pp.81–96.

_____. "'Smashers' and 'Rummies': Voters and the Rise of Parties in Charlotte County, New Brunswick, 1846–1857." *HP*, 1986. Pp.86–116.

Campbell, Robert A. *Demon Rum or Easy Money: Government Control of Liquor in British Columbia from Prohibition to Privatization*. Vancouver: University of British Columbia Press 1991.

_____. "A 'Fantastic Rigmarole': Ottawa, British Columbia, and the Deregulation of Aboriginal Drinking, 1939–1962." Paper presented to the Canadian Historical Association Meeting 2002.

_____. "Ladies and Escorts: Gender Segregation and Public Policy in British Columbia Beer Parlours, 1925–1945." *BC Studies*, 105/106 (Spring/Summer 1995). Pp.119–8.

_____. "Liquor and Liberals: Patronage and Government Control in British Columbia, 1920–1928." *BC Studies*, 77 (Spring 1988). Pp.30–53.

_____. "Managing the Marginal: Regulating and Negotiating Decency in Vancouver's Beer Parlours, 1925–1954." *L/LT*, 44 (Fall 1999). Pp.109–27.

_____. "'Profit Was Just a Circumstance': The Evolution of Government Liquor Control in British Columbia." In Warsh, ed., *Drink in Canada*. Pp.172–92.

_____. *Sit Down and Drink Your Beer: Regulating Vancouver's Beer Parlours, 1925–1954*. Toronto: University of Toronto Press 2001.

_____. "Sit Down, Shut Up and Drink Your Beer." In The Working Lives Collective, eds., *Working Lives: Vancouver, 1886–1986*. Vancouver: New Star Books 1985. Pp.136–7.

Canada. Department of Agriculture. *Statistical Yearbook of Canada*. Ottawa: Government Printing Bureau 1884–1920.

_____. Department of Inland Revenues. *Reports, Returns, and Statistics*. Ottawa: King's Printer.

_____. Department of Labour. *Labour Organization in Canada*. Ottawa: King's Printer.

_____. Department of Labour. *Strikes and Lockouts in Canada*. Ottawa: King's Printer.

_____. Dominion Bureau of Statistics/Statistics Canada. *Control and Sale of Alcoholic Beverages in Canada*. Ottawa. 1933–96.

_____. House of Commons. *Journals*. Ottawa: Queen's Printer. 6 (1873), Appendix 3 ("Second Report of the Select Committee of the House of Commons Respecting a Prohibitory Liquor Law"); 8 (1874), Appendix 8 ("Third Report of the Select Committee of the House of Commons Respecting a Prohibitory Liquor Law").

_____. Restrictive Trades Practices Commission. *Report Concerning an Alleged Combine in the Manufacture, Distribution and Sale of Beer in Canada*. Ottawa: Queen's Printer 1955.

_____. Royal Commission on Customs and Excise. *Interim Reports*, and *Final Report*. Ottawa: F.A, Acland 1928.

_____. Royal Commission on the Liquor Traffic in Canada. *Report*, and *Minutes of Evidence*. Ottawa: S.E. Dawson 1895.

Canadian Annual Review of Public Affairs. Toronto: Annual Review Publishing 1901–40.

Canadian Food Industries. Toronto 1948.

Canadian Hotel Review. Toronto 1920–45.

Carnes, Mark C. "Middle-Class Men and the Solace of Fraternal Ritual." In Carnes and Griffen, eds., *Meanings for Manhood.* Pp.37–52.

——————. *Secret Ritual and Manhood in Victorian America.* New Haven: Yale University Press 1989.

Carnes, Mark C. and Clyde Griffen, eds. *Meanings for Manhood: Constructions of Masculinity in Victorian America.* Chicago: University of Chicago Press 1990.

Carstairs, Catherine. "Innocent Addicts, Dope Fiends, and Nefarious Traffickers: Illegal Drug Use in 1920s English Canada." *JCS*, 33, no.3 (Fall 1998). Pp.145–62.

Carpenter, Edmund S. "Alcohol in the Iroquois Dream Quest." *American Journal of Psychiatry*, 116, no.2 (August 1959). Pp.148–51.

Carter-Edwards, Dennis. "Supplying Military Posts in Upper Canada." In Clow et al., eds., *Consuming Passions.* Pp.45–55.

Cassedy, James H. "An Early American Hangover: The Medical Profession and Intemperance, 1800–1860." *Bulletin of the History of Medicine*, 50, no.3 (Fall 1976). Pp.405–13.

Cavan, Sherri. *Liquor License: An Ethnography of a Bar.* Chicago: Aldine 1966.

Chamberland, Line. "Remembering Lesbian Bars: Montreal, 1955–1975." In Wendy Mitchinson et al., eds., *Canadian Women: A Reader.* Toronto: Harcourt Brace and Company 1996. Pp.352–79.

Chambers, Elizabeth. "The Referendum and the Plebiscite." In Norman Ward and Duff Spafford, eds., *Politics in Saskatchewan.* Don Mills, Ont.: Longmans Canada 1968. Pp.59–77.

Chan, Anthony B. "Bachelor Workers." In Franca Iacovetta with Paula Draper and Robert Ventresca, eds., *A Nation of Immigrants: Women, Workers, and Communities in Canadian History, 1840s–1960s.* Toronto: University of Toronto Press 1998. Pp.231–50.

Chapin, Robert C. *The Standard of Living among Workingmen's Families in New York City.* New York: Charities Publication Committee 1909.

Chapman, J.K. "The Mid-Nineteenth-Century Temperance Movement in New Brunswick and Maine." *CHR*, 25, no.1 (March 1954). Pp.43–60.

Cheung, Yuet W. and Patricia G. Erickson. "Canada." In Heath, ed., *International Handbook.* Pp.20–30.

Christie, Howard Angus. "The Function of the Tavern in Toronto, 1834 to 1875, with Special Reference to Sport." M.A. thesis, University of Windsor 1973.

Christie, Nancy and Michael Gauvreau. *A Full-Orbed Christianity: The Protestant Churches and Social Welfare in Canada, 1900–1940.* Montreal and Kingston: McGill-Queen's University Press 1996.

Chudacoff, Howard P. *The Age of the Bachelor: Creating an American Subculture.* Princeton, N.J.: Princeton University Press 1999.

Chui, Tina. "Canada's Population: Charting into the 21st Century." *Canadian Social Trends.* Vol.3. Toronto: Thompson Educational Publishing 2000. Pp.6–10.

Churchill, David S. "Coming Out in a Cold Climate: A History of Gay Men in Toronto during the 1950s." M.A. thesis, University of Toronto 1993.

Clark, Anna. "Domesticity and the Problem of Wifebeating in Nineteenth-Century Britain: Working-Class Culture, Law, and Politics." In D'Cruze, ed., *Everyday Violence.* Pp.27–39.

——————. *The Struggle for the Breeches: Gender and the Making of the British Working Class.* Berkeley: University of California Press 1995.

Clark, C.S. *Of Toronto the Good: A Social Study; The Queen City of Canada as It Is.* Montreal: Toronto Publishing Company 1898.

Clark, Norman H. *Deliver Us from Evil: An Interpretation of American Prohibition.* New York: W.W. Norton and Company 1976.

Clark, Peter. "The Alehouse and the Alternative Society." In Donald Pennington and Keith Thomas, eds., *Puritans and Revolutionaries: Essays in Seventeenth-Century History Presented to Christopher Hill.* Oxford: Clarendon Press 1978. Pp.47–72.

——————. *The English Alehouse: A Social History, 1200–1830.* London: Longman 1983.

——————. "The 'Mother Gin' Controversy in the Early Eighteenth Century." Royal Historical Society. *Transactions*, 5th Series, 38 (1988). Pp.63–84.

Clark, R.J. "Professional Aspirations and the Limits of Occupational Autonomy: The Case of Pharmacy in Nineteenth-Century Ontario." *Canadian Bulletin of Medical History*, 8, no.1 (1991). Pp.43–63.

Clark, S.D. *Church and Sect in Canada.* Toronto: University of Toronto Press 1948.

Clark, Walter. "Demographic Characteristics of Tavern Patrons in San Francisco." *Quarterly Journal of Alcohol Studies*, 27, no.2 (June 1966). Pp.316–27.

Clark, W.B. "The Contemporary Tavern." In Yedy Israel et al., eds., *Research Advances in Alcohol and Drug Problems*, vol.6. New York: Plenum Press 1981. Pp.425–70.

Clarke, Brian P. *Piety and Nationalism: Lay Voluntary Associations and the Creation of an Irish-Catholic Community in Toronto, 1850–1895.* Montreal and Kingston: McGill-Queen's University Press 1993.

Clarkson, Christopher Allan. "Remoralizing Families? Family Regulation and State Formation in British Columbia, 1862–1940." Ph.D. thesis, University of Ottawa 2002.

Clawson, Mary Ann. *Constructing Brotherhood: Class, Gender, and Fraternalism.* Princeton, N.J.: Princeton University Press 1989.

_____. "Early Modern Fraternalism and the Patriarchal Family." *Feminist Studies*, 6, no.2 (Summer 1980). Pp.368–91.

Clemens, James M. "Taste Not; Touch Not; Handle Not: A Study of the Social Assumptions of the Temperance Literature and Temperance Supporters in Canada West between 1839 and 1859." *OH*, 64, no.3 (September 1972). Pp.144–60.

Clinard, Marshall B. "The Public Drinking House and Society." In David J. Pittman and Charles R. Snyder, eds., *Society, Culture, and Drinking Patterns.* New York: John Wiley and Sons 1962. Pp.270–92.

Clow, Meribeth et al., eds. *Consuming Passions.* Willowdale, Ont.: Ontario Historical Society 1990.

Clubb, Jerome M., Erik W. Austin, and Gordon W. Kirk, Jr. *The Process of Historical Inquiry: Everyday Lives of Working Americans.* New York: Columbia University Press 1989.

Coffey, T.G. "Beer Street: Gin Lane: Some Views of 18th-Century Drinking." *QJSA*, 27, no.4 (December 1966). Pp.669–92.

Cohen, Lizabeth. *A Consumer's Republic: The Politics of Mass Consumption in Postwar America.* New York: Alfred A. Knopf 2003.

Collinson, David L. "'Engineering Humour': Masculinity, Joking, and Conflict in Shop-Floor Relations." *Organization Studies*, 9, no.2 (1988). Pp.181–99.

Colombo, John Robert, ed. *Colombo's Canadian Quotations.* Edmonton: Hurtig 1974.

Comacchio, Cynthia R. *Nations Are Built of Babies: Saving Ontario's Mothers and Children, 1900–1940.* Montreal and Kingston: McGill-Queen's University Press 1993.

Common Sense Recipe Book, The, Containing All the Latest Recipes on Cooking with Economy and also Valuable Medicinal Recipes. Montreal: John Lovell and Son 1895 (CIHM no. 01519).

Conference Board of Canada. International Studies and Service Development Group. *The Canadian Brewing Industry: Historical Evolution and Competitive Structure.* Ottawa: Conference Board of Canada 1989.

Connell, R.W. *Masculinities.* Berkeley: University of California Press 1995.

Conroy, David W. *In Public Houses: Drink and the Revolution of Authority in Colonial Massachusetts.* Chapel Hill: University of North Carolina Press 1995.

Cook, Ramsay. *The Regenerators: Social Criticism in Late Victorian English Canada.* Toronto: University of Toronto Press 1985.

Cook, Sharon Anne. "'Sewing Seeds for the Master': The Ontario WCTU and Evangelical Feminism, 1874–1930." *JCS*, 30, no.3 (Fall 1995). Pp.175–94.

_____. *"Through Sunshine and Shadow": The Woman's Christian Temperance Union, Evangelicalism, and Reform in Ontario, 1874–1930.* Montreal and Kingston: McGill-Queen's University Press 1995.

Cook, Tim. "'More a Medicine Than a Beverage': 'Demon Rum' and the Canadian Trench Soldier of the First World War." *Canadian Military History*, 9, no.1 (Winter 2000). Pp.7–22.

Copp, Terry. *The Anatomy of Poverty: The Condition of the Working Class in Montreal, 1897–1929.* Toronto: McClelland and Stewart 1974.

Cosper, Ronald L., Ishmael O. Okraku, and Brigette Neumann. "Tavern Going in Canada: A National Survey of Regulars at Public Drinking Establishments." *JSA*, 48, no.3 (May 1987). Pp.252–9.

Coulter, Rebecca. "The Working Young of Edmonton, 1921–1931." In Joy Parr, ed., *Childhood and Family in Canadian History*. Toronto: McClelland and Stewart 1982. Pp.143–59.

Courtwright, David T. *Forces of Habit: Drugs and the Making of the Modern World*. Cambridge, Mass.: Harvard University Press 2001.

Couturier, Jacques Paul. "Prohibition or Regulation? The Enforcement of the Canada Temperance Act in Moncton, 1881–1896." In Warsh, ed., *Drink in Canada*. Pp.144–65.

Craig, Gerald M., ed. *Early Travellers in the Canadas, 1791–1867*. Toronto: Macmillan 1955.

Craven, Paul. "Law and Ideology: The Toronto Court, 1850–80." In David H. Flaherty, ed., *Essays in the History of the Canadian Law*. Vol.2. Toronto: University of Toronto Press 1983. Pp.248–307.

Cross, Michael S. "'The Laws Are Like Cobwebs': Popular Resistance to Authority in Mid-Nineteenth Century British North America." In Clive Emsley, ed., *Essays in Comparative History: Economy, Politics, and Society in Britain and America, 1850–1920*. Milton Keynes, U.K.: Open University Press 1984. Pp.103–23.

——————. "The Lumber Community of Upper Canada, 1815–1867," *OH*, 52 no.4 (November 1960). Pp.213–33.

——————. "The Shiners' War: Social Violence in the Ottawa Valley in the 1830s." *CHR*, 54, no.1 (March 1973). Pp.1–26.

——————, ed. *The Workingman in the Nineteenth Century*. Toronto: Oxford University Press 1974.

Crouse, Eric. "They 'Left Us Pretty Much as We Were': American Saloon/Factory Evangelists and Canadian Working Men in the Early Twentieth Century." Canadian Society of Church History. *Historical Papers*, 1999. Pp.51–71.

Crush, Jonathan and Charles Ambler, eds. *Liquor and Labor in Southern Africa*. Athens: Ohio University Press 1992.

Crysdale, Stewart. "Family and Kinship in Riverdale." In W.E. Mann, ed., *Canada: A Sociological Profile*. Toronto: Copp Clark 1968. Pp.106–15.

Curtis, Bruce. *Building the Educational State: Canada West, 1836–1871*. London: Althouse Press 1988.

——————. *True Government by Choice Men? Inspection, Education, and State Formation in Canada West*. Toronto: University of Toronto Press 1992.

Curtis, Susan. "The Son of God and God the Father: The Social Gospel and Victorian Masculinity." In Carnes and Griffen, eds., *Meanings for Manhood*. Pp.67–78.

Cutler, Ronald and Thomas Storm. *Drinking Practices in Three British Columbia Cities*. 3 vols. Vancouver: Alcoholism foundation of British Columbia 1973.

Dailey, R.C. "The Role of Alcohol among North American Indian Tribes as Reported in the Jesuit Relations." *Anthropologica*, 10, no.1 (1968). Pp.45–57.

Dalys, Beverly. *No Longer a "Two-Bit" Union: The History of the Ontario Liquor Boards Employees' Union*. N.p., n.d.

Dannenbaum, J., ed. *Drink and Disorder: Temperance Reform in Cincinnati from the Washingtonian Revival to the WCTU*. Urbana: University of Illinois Press 1984.

Daube, Michael. "Pleasure in Health Promotion." In Peele and Grant, eds., *Alcohol and Pleasure*. Pp.37–47.

Davidoff, Leonore and Catherine Hall. *Family Fortunes: Men and Women of the English Middle Class, 1780–1850*. Chicago: University of Chicago Press 1987.

Davies, Andrew. *Leisure, Gender, and Poverty: Working-Class Culture in Salford and Manchester, 1900–1939*. Buckingham, U.K.: Open University Press 1992.

Davis, C. Mark. "Atlantic Canada's Rum Running Tradition." *Acadiensis*, 14, no.2 (Spring 1985). Pp.147–56.

——————. "I'll Drink to That: The Rise and Fall of Prohibition in the Maritime Provinces, 1900–1930." Ph.D. thesis, McMaster University 1990.

——————. "Rum and the Law: The Maritime Experience." In Morrison and Moreira, eds., *Tempered by Rum*. Pp.40–52.

——————. "Small Town Reformism: The Temperance Issue in Amherst, Nova Scotia." In Larry McCann, ed., *People and Place: Studies of Small Town Life in the Maritimes*. Fredericton: Acadiensis Press 1987. Pp.125–34.

Dawson, Michael. "'That Nice Red Coat Goes to My Head Like Champagne': Gender, Antimodernism, and the Mountie Image, 1880–1960." *JCS*, 32, no.3 (Fall 1997). Pp.119–39.

Dean, Malcolm. *Censored! Only in Canada: The History of Film Censorship—the Scandal off the Screen.* Toronto: Virgo Press 1981.

De Belmont, François Vachon. "The History of Brandy in Canada." *Mid-America*, 34, no.1 (January 1952). Pp.42–63.

Decarie, Graeme. "Francis Stephens Spence." *Dictionary of Canadian Biography.* Vol.14. *1911–1920.* Toronto: University of Toronto Press 1998. Pp.956–8.

_____. "Paved with Good Intentions: The Prohibitionists' Road to Racism in Ontario." *OH*, 66, no.1 (March 1974). Pp.15–22

_____. "The Prohibition Movement in Ontario, 1894–1916." Ph.D. thesis, Queen's University 1972.

_____. "Something Old, Something New. . . : Aspects of Prohibitionism in Ontario in the 1890s." In Donald Swainson, ed., *Oliver Mowat's Ontario.* Toronto: Macmillan 1972.

D'Cruze, Shani, ed. *Everyday Violence in Britain, 1850–1950.* New York: Longman 2000.

De Grazia, Victoria with Ellen Furlough, eds. *The Sex of Things: Gender and Consumption in Historical Perspective.* Berkeley: University of California Press 1996.

De Lint, Jan. "Anti-Drink Propaganda and Alcohol Control Measures: A Report on the Dutch Experience." In Single, Morgan, and De Lint, eds., *Alcohol, Society, and the State,* vol.2. Pp.87–102.

DeLottinville, Peter. "Joe Beef of Montreal: Working Class Culture and the Tavern, 1869–1889." *L/LT*, 8–9 (Autumn 1981/Spring 1982). Pp.9–40.

Dempsey, Hugh. *Firewater: The Impact of the Whiskey Trade on the Blackfoot Nation.* Calgary: Fifth House 2002.

Denison, Grace E., ed. *The Canadian Family Cook Book: A Volume of Tried, Tested, and Proven Recipes.* Toronto: McLeod and Allen 1914) (CIHM no.80496).

Denison, Merrill. *The Barley and the Stream: The Molson Story.* Toronto: McClelland and Stewart 1955.

Dennis, Philip A. "The Role of the Drunk in a Oaxacan Village." In Marshall, ed., *Beliefs, Behaviors, and Alcoholic Beverages.* Pp.54–64.

De Silva, Padmal. "The Buddhist Attitude to Alcoholism." In Griffith Edwards, Awni Arif, and Jerome Jaffe, eds., *Drug Use and Misuse: Cultural Perspectives.* London: Croom Helm 1983. Pp.33–41.

Dewar, Robert. *The Consumption of Alcohol in a Saskatchewan Community before and after the Opening of a New Liquor Outlet.* Regina: Department of Social Welfare and Rehabilitation, Bureau on Alcoholism 1962.

Dick, Ernest J. "From Temperance to Prohibition in 19th Century Nova Scotia." *Dalhousie Review*, 61, no.3 (Autumn 1981). Pp.530–52.

Dickason, Olive Patricia. *Canada's First Nations: A History of Founding Peoples from Earliest Times.* Toronto: McClelland and Stewart 1992.

Dickinson, John A. "'C'est l'eau-de-vie qui a commis ce meutre': Alcool et criminalité amérindienne à Montréal sous le régime français." *Études canadiennes/Canadian Studies*, 35 (1993). Pp.83–94.

Dictionary of Canadian Biography. Vol.14. Toronto: University of Toronto Press 1998.

Dietler, Michael. "Driven by Drink: The Role of Drinking in the Political Economy and the Case of Early Iron Age France." *Journal of Anthropological Archaeology*, 9, no.4 (December 1990). Pp.352–406.

Dingle, A.E. *The Campaign for Prohibition in Victorian England: The United Kingdom Alliance, 1872–1895.* New Brunswick, N.J.: Rutgers University Press 1980.

_____. "Drink and Working-Class Living Standards in Britain, 1870–1914." *Economic History Review*, 2nd Series, 25, no.4 (1972). Pp.608–22.

_____. "'The Truly Magnificent Thirst': An Historical Survey of Australian Drinking Habits." *Historical Studies*, 19, no.75 (October 1980). Pp.227–49.

Diston, David. "Our Changing Tastes in Wine." In Clow et al., eds., *Consuming Passions.* Pp.227–32.

Dodd, Jill Siegel. "The Working Classes and the Temperance Movement in Ante-Bellum Boston." *Labor History*, 19, no.4 (Fall 1978). Pp.510–31.

Dollard, John. "Drinking Mores of the Social Classes." In Yale University Center of Alcohol Studies, *Alcohol, Science, and Society.* New Haven, Conn.: QJSA 1945.

Dominion Alliance for the Total Suppression of the Liquor Traffic. *The Liberty Question.* Campaign Leaflet no.7. 1898 (CIHM no.05181).

Dominion Brewers Association. *Facts on the Brewing Industry in Canada, a National Industry: A Manual Outlining the Development of the Industry and Its Place in the Canadian Economy.* Ottawa: Dominion Brewers Association 1948.

Dorion, Nicole. *La brasserie Boswell: un essai d'ethnologie industrielle.* Quebec: CELAT 1989.

_____. "L'industrie de la bière: Le cas de la brasserie Boswell." *Material History Review*, 33 (Spring 1991). Pp.1–9.

Doucet, Michael and John Weaver. *Housing the North American City.* Montreal and Kingston: McGill-Queen's University Press 1991.

Doughty, Paul L. "The Social Uses of Alcoholic Beverages in a Peruvian Community." In Marshall, ed., *Beliefs, Behaviors, and Alcoholic Beverages.* Pp.64–81.

Douglas, Mary, ed. *Constructive Drinking: Perspectives on Drink from Anthropology.* New York: Cambridge University Press 1987.

Doyle, Arthur T. *Front Benches and Back Rooms: A Story of Corruption, Muckraking, Raw Partisanship, and Political Intrigue in New Brunswick.* Toronto: Green Tree Publishing 1976.

Drescher, Nuala McGann. "Labor and Prohibition: The Unappreciated Impact of the Eighteenth Amendment." In Kyvig, ed., *Law, Alcohol, and Order.* Pp.35–52.

_____. "Organized Labor and the Eighteenth Amendment." *Labor History*, 8, no.3 (Fall 1967). Pp.280–99.

Drummond, Ian M. *Progress without Planning: The Economic History of Ontario from Confederation to the Second World War.* Toronto: University of Toronto Press 1987.

Dubro, James and Robin F. Rowland. *King of the Mob: Rocco Perri and the Women Who Ran His Rackets.* Toronto: Viking 1987.

Duis, Perry R. *The Saloon: Public Drinking in Chicago and Boston, 1880–1920.* Urbana and Chicago: University of Illinois Press 1983.

Dumont, Matthew P. "Tavern Culture: The Sustenance of Homeless Men." *American Journal of Orthopsychiatry*, 37, no.4 (October 1967). Pp.938–45.

Dunk, Thomas W. *It's a Working Man's Town: Male Working-Class Culture in Northwestern Ontario.* Montreal and Kingston: McGill-Queen's University Press 1991.

Dunnigan, Brian Leigh. "Military Life at Niagara, 1792–1796." In Merritt, Butler, and Power, eds., *Capital Years.* Pp.67–102.

Eaton, Flora McCrea. *Memory's Wall: The Autobiography of Flora McCrea Eaton.* Toronto: Clarke, Irwin and Company 1956.

Eddington, Bryan. "Whooping It up at the Beaver Club." *The Beaver*, 83, no.1 (February/March 2003). Pp.43–4.

Eisenberg, Christine. "Artisans' Socialization at Work: Workshop Life in Early Nineteenth-Century England and Germany." *Journal of Social History*, 24, no.3 (Spring 1991). Pp.507–20.

Eldred-Grigg, Stevan. *Pleasures of the Flesh: Sex and Drugs in Colonial New Zealand, 1840–1915.* Wellington, N.Z.: Reed 1984.

Elwall, Robert. *Bricks and Beer: English Pub Architecture, 1830–1939.* London: British Architectural Library 1983.

Engelmann, Larry. *Intemperance: The Lost War against Liquor.* New York: Free Press 1979.

Ennals, Peter and Deryck W. Holdsworth. *Homeplace: The Making of the Canadian Dwelling over Three Centuries.* Toronto: University of Toronto Press 1998.

Epstein, Barbara Leslie. *The Politics of Domesticity: Women, Evangelism, and Temperance in Nineteenth-Century America.* Middletown, Conn.: Wesleyan University Press 1981.

Epstein, James. "Radical Dining, Toasting, and Symbolic Expression in Early Nineteenth-Century Lancashire: Rituals of Solidarity." *Albion*, 20, no.2 (Summer 1988). Pp.271–91.

Erenberg, Lewis A. *Steppin' Out: New York Nightlife and the Transformation of American Culture, 1890–1930.* Chicago: University of Chicago Press 1981.

Eriksen, Sidsel. "The Making of the Danish Liberal Drinking Style: The Construction of a 'Wet' Alcohol Discourse in Denmark." *CDP*, 20, no.1 (Spring 1993). Pp.1–31.

Errington, Elizabeth Jane. *Wives and Mothers, School Mistresses and Scullery Maids: Working Women in Upper Canada, 1790–1840.* Montreal and Kingston: McGill-Queen's University Press 1995.

Evans, A. Margaret. *Sir Oliver Mowat.* Toronto: University of Toronto Press 1992.

Everest, Allan S. *Rum across the Border: The Prohibition Era in Northern New York.* Syracuse, N.Y.: Syracuse University Press 1978.

Fahey, David M. "Brewers, Publicans, and Working-Class Drinkers: Pressure Group Politics in Late Victorian and Edwardian England." *HS/SH*, 13, no.25 (May 1980). Pp.85–103.

_____. "How the Good Templars Began: Fraternal Temperance in New York State." *Social History of Alcohol Review*, 38–9 (1999). Pp.17–27.

_____. *Temperance and Racism: John Bull, Johnny Reb, and the Good Templars.* Lexington: University Press of Kentucky 1996.

Faler, Paul. "Cultural Aspects of the Industrial Revolution: Lynn, Massachusetts Shoemakers and Industrial Morality, 1826–1860." *Labor History*, 15, no.3 (Summer 1974). Pp.367–94.

_____. *Mechanics and Manufacturers in the Early Industrial Revolution: Lynn, Massachusetts, 1780–1860.* Albany: State University of New York Press 1981.

Fanshawe, E.L. *Liquor Legislation in the United States and Canada: Report of a Non-Partisan Inquiry on the Spot into the Laws and Their Operation, Undertaken at the Request of W. Rathbone, M.P.* London: Cassell and Company n.d. [1893] (CIHM no.02947).

Fecteau, Jean-Marie. "Between the Old Order and Modern times: Poverty, Criminality, and Power in Quebec, 1791–1840." In Jim Phillips, Tina Loo, and Susan Lewthwaite, eds., *Essays in the History of Canadian Law, vol.5, Crime and Criminal Justice.* Toronto: University of Toronto Press 1994. Pp.292–323.

_____. *Un nouvel ordre des choses: la pauvreté, le crime, l'état au Québec, de la fin du XVIIIe siècle à 1840.* Montreal: VLB Editeur 1989.

Ferland, Cathérine. "Thémis contre Bacchus: La réglementation de la circulation de l'alcool en Nouvelle-France, 1663–1760." Paper presented to the Canadian Historical Association Meeting, 2001.

Ferry, Darren. "'To the Interests and Conscience of the Great Mass of the Community': The Evolution of Temperance Societies in Nineteenth-Century Central Canada." Paper presented to the Canadian Historical Association, Annual Meeting, 2003.

A Few Facts Bearing on the Social and Civic Character of Montreal. Montreal: J.C. Becket n.d. [c.1860] (CIHM no.43077).

Fingard, Judith. *The Dark Side of Life in Victorian Halifax.* Porter's Lake, N.S.: Pottersfield Press 1989.

_____. "'A Great Big Rum Shop': The Drink Trade in Victorian Halifax." In Morrison and Moreira, eds., *Tempered by Rum.* Pp.89–101.

_____. *Jack in Port: Sailortowns of Eastern Canada.* Toronto: University of Toronto Press 1982.

_____. "Jailbirds in Victorian Halifax." In Peter Waite, Sandra Oxner, and Thomas Barnes, eds., *Law in Colonial Society.* Toronto: Carswell 1984. Pp.81–102.

_____. "The Prevention of Cruelty, Marriage Breakdown and the Rights of Wives in Nova Scotia, 1880–1900." *Acadiensis*, 22, no.2 (Spring 1993). Pp.84–101.

Fingarette, Herbert. *Heavy Drinking: The Myth of Alcoholism as a Disease.* Berkeley: University of California Press 1988.

Finkel, Alvin. *Our Lives: Canada after 1945.* Toronto: James Lorimer and Company 1997.

Fisher, A.D. "Alcoholism and Race: The Misapplication of Both Concepts to North American Indians." *Canadian Review of Sociology and Anthropology*, 24, no.1 (1987). Pp.81–97.

Fogarty, David. "From Saloon to Supermarket: Packaged Beer and the Reshaping of the U.S. Brewing Industry." *CDP*, 12, no.4 (Winter 1985). Pp.541–92.

Forbes, Ernest R. "The East-Coast Rum-Running Economy." In Warsh, ed., *Drink in Canada.* Pp.166–71.

_____. "Prohibition and the Social Gospel in Nova Scotia." In Samuel D. Clark et al., eds., *Prophecy and Protest: Social Movements in Twentieth-Century Canada.* Toronto: Gage 1975. Pp.62–86.

_____. "'Rum' in the Maritimes Economy during the Prohibition Era." In Morrison and Moreira, eds., *Tempered by Rum.* Pp.103–9.

Forbes, Ernest R. and D.A. Muise, eds. *The Atlantic Provinces in Confederation.* Toronto and Fredericton: University of Toronto Press and Acadiensis Press 1993.

Forestall, Nancy. "Bachelors, Boarding-Houses, and Blind Pigs: Gender Construction in a Multi-Ethnic Mining Camp, 1909–1920." In Franca Iacovetta with Paula Draper and Robert

Ventresca, eds., *A Nation of Immigrants: Women, Workers, and Communities in Canadian History, 1840s–1960s.* Toronto: University of Toronto Press 1998. Pp.251–90.

Forsey, Eugene. *Trade Unions in Canada, 1812–1902.* Toronto: University of Toronto Press 1982.

Fortin, Gerard and Boyce Richardson. *Life of the Party.* Montreal: Vehicule Press 1984.

Fosdick, Raymond B. and Albert L. Scott. *Toward Liquor Control.* New York: Harper and Brothers 1933.

Fowke, Edith, ed. *The Penguin Book of Canadian Folk Songs.* Harmondsworth, U.K.: Penguin 1973.

Franberg, Per. "The Social and Political Significance of Two Swedish Restrictive Systems." *CDP*, 12, no.1 (Spring 1985). Pp.53–62.

Frank, David. *J.B. McLachlan: A Biography.* Toronto: James Lorimer 1999.

Frankel, B. Gail and Paul C. Whitehead. "Sociological Perspectives on Drinking and Damage." In Blocker, ed., *Alcohol, Reform, and Society.* Pp.13–43.

Fraser, Wendy Carol. *Hiram Walker Remembered.* Windsor, Ont.: Forest Press 1992.

Fudge, Judy and Eric Tucker. *Labour before the Law: The Regulation of Workers' Collective Action in Canada, 1900–1948.* Toronto: Oxford University Press 2001.

Fyson, Donald. "Du pain au madère: l'alimentation à Montréal au début du XIXe siècle." *Revue d'histoire de l'Amérique française*, 46, no.1 (Summer 1992). Pp.67–90.

Gagan, David and Rosemary Gagan. "Working-Class Standards of Living in Late-Victorian Urban Ontario: A Review of the Miscellaneous Evidence on the Quality of Material Life." Canadian Historical Association. *Journal*, 1990. Pp.171–93.

Garceau, Henri-Paul. *Chronique de l'hospitalité hôtelière du Québec de 1880 à 1940: Les pionniers.* Montreal: Editions du Méridien 1990.

Garland, M.A. and J.J. Talman. "Pioneer Drinking Habits and the Rise of Temperance Agitation in Upper Canada Prior to 1840." In F.A. Armstrong et al., eds., *Aspects of Nineteenth Century Ontario.* Toronto: University of Toronto Press 1974.

Gefou-Madianou, Dimitra, ed. *Alcohol, Gender, and Culture.* London: Routledge 1992.

Gerritsen, Jan-Wilem. *The Control of Fuddle and Flash: A Sociological History of the Regulation of Alcohol and Opiates.* Boston: Brill 2000.

Gervais, C.H. *The Rumrunners: A Prohibition Scrapbook.* Thornhill, Ont.: Firefly Books 1980.

Gibbins, Robert J. "Alcoholism in Ontario: A Survey of an Ontario County." *QJSA*, 15, no.1 (March 1954). Pp.47–62.

Giffen, P.J. *The Alienation of the Skid Row Drunkenness Offender.* Toronto: Addiction Research Foundation Substudy 1-11-61 n.d.

Gilmore, John. *Swinging in Paradise: The Story of Jazz in Montreal.* Montreal: Vehicule Press 1988.

Girouard, Mark. *Victorian Pubs.* London: Studio Vista 1975.

Glickman, Lawrence B. *A Living Wage: American Workers and the Making of Consumer Society.* Ithaca, N.Y.: Cornell University Press 1997.

Golz, Annalee. "'If a Man's Wife Does Not Obey Him, What Can He Do?' Marital Breakdown and Wife Abuse in Late Nineteenth Century and Early Twentieth Century Ontario." In Louis Knafla and Susan W.S. Binnie, eds., *Law, Society, and the State: Essays in Modern Legal History.* Toronto: University of Toronto Press 1995. Pp.323–50.

Gomery, Douglas. "The Movie Palace Comes to American Cities." In Butsch, ed., *For Fun and Profit.* Pp.136–51.

Gordon, Linda. *Heroes of Their Own Lives: The Politics and History of Family Violence.* New York: Penguin 1988.

Gosselin, Amedee. "Boissons douces et boissons enivrantes chez les colons, 1632–1760." Royal Society of Canada, *Transactions*, 3rd series, 33 (1938), Section 1. Pp.99–108.

Gottlieb, David. "The Neighbourhood Tavern and the Cocktail Lounge: A Study in Class Differences." *American Journal of Sociology*, 62, no.6 (May 1957). Pp.559–62.

Goubert, Pierre. *The French Peasantry in the Seventeenth Century.* New York: Cambridge University Press 1986.

Gough, Lyn. *As Wise as Serpents: Five Women and an Organization That Changed British Columbia.* Victoria: Swan Lake Publishing 1988.

Gourvish, T.R. "Concentration, Diversity, and Firm Strategy in European Brewing, 1945–90." In Wilson and Gourvish, eds., *Dynamics of the International Brewing Industry.* Pp.80–92.

Graham, Kathryn et al. "Aggression and Barroom Environments." *JSA*, 41, no.3 (March 1980). Pp.277–92.

Graham, Roger. *Old Man Ontario: Leslie M. Frost.* Toronto: University of Toronto Press 1990.

Graham, W.H. *Greenbank: Country Matters in 19th Century Ontario.* Peterborough: Broadview Press 1988.

Grant, B.J. *When Rum Was King.* Fredericton: Fiddlehead Poetry Books 1984.

Grant, George Monro. *Principal Grant's Letters on Prohibition, as They Appeared in the "Globe," December, 1897, January 1898.* N.p. n.d. (CIHM no.05122).

Grant, John Webster. *Moon of Wintertime: Missionaries and the Indians of Canada in Encounters since 1534.* Toronto: University of Toronto Press 1984.

——————. *A Profusion of Spires: Religion in Nineteenth-Century Ontario.* Toronto: University of Toronto Press 1988.

Grant, Marcus and Jorge Litvak, eds. *Drinking Patterns and Their Consequences.* Washington, D.C.: Taylor and Francis 1998.

Gray, James H. *Bacchanalia Revisited: Western Canada's Boozy Skid to Social Disaster.* Saskatoon, Sask.: Western Producer Prairie Books 1982.

——————. *Booze: The Impact of Whisky on the Prairie West.* Scarborough, Ont.: New American Library of Canada 1972.

——————. *The Boy from Winnipeg.* Toronto: Macmillan 1970.

Greer, Allan. *Peasant, Lord, and Merchant: Rural Society in Three Quebec Parishes, 1740–1840.* Toronto: University of Toronto Press 1985.

——————. "Wage Labour and the Transition to Capitalism: A Critique of Pentland." *L/LT*, 15 (Spring 1985). Pp.7–22.

Greer, Allan and Ian Radforth, eds. *Colonial Leviathan: State Formation in Mid-Nineteenth-Century Canada.* Toronto: University of Toronto Press 1992.

Griffen, Clyde. "Reconstructing Masculinity from the Evangelical Revival to the Waning of Progressivism: A Speculative Synthesis." In Carnes and Griffen, eds., *Meanings for Manhood.* Pp.183–204.

Grigg, A.R. "Prohibition and Women: The Preservation of an Ideal and a Myth." *New Zealand Journal of History*, 17, no.2 (October 1983). Pp.144–65.

——————. "Prohibition, the Church and Labour: A Programme for Social Reform, 1890–1914." *New Zealand Journal of History*, 15, no.2 (October 1981). Pp.135–54.

Guillet, Edwin C. *Pioneer Inns and Taverns.* Toronto: Ontario Publishing Company 1964.

Gusfield, Joseph R. "Benevolent Repression: Popular Culture, Social Structure, and the Control of Drinking." In Barrows and Room, eds., *Drinking.* Pp.399–424.

——————. *Contested Meanings: The Construction of Alcohol Problems.* Madison: University of Wisconsin Press 1996.

——————. "The Control of Drinking-Driving in the United States: A Period of Transition?" In Michael D. Laurence, John R. Snortum, and Franklin E. Zimring, eds., *Social Control of the Drinking Driver.* Chicago: University of Chicago Press 1988. Pp.109–35.

——————. "Passage to Play: Rituals of Drinking Time in American Society." In Douglas, ed., *Constructive Drinking.* Pp.73–90.

——————. *Symbolic Crusade: Status Politics and the American Temperance Movement.* Urbana: University of Illinois Press 1963.

Gusfield, Joseph R., Joseph A. Kotarba, and Paul K. Rasmussen. "The Bar as a Context of Social Control." In Gusfield, *Contested Meanings.* Pp.147–68.

Gutman, Herbert G. "Work, Culture, and Society in Industrializing America, 1815–1919." *American Historical Review*, 78 (June 1973). Pp.531–88.

Gutzke, David W. "'The Cry of the Children': The Edwardian Medical Campaign against Maternal Drinking." *BJA*, 79 (1984). Pp.71–84.

——————. "Gender, Class, and Public Drinking in Britain during the First World War." *HS/SH*, 27, no.54 (November 1994). Pp.367–91.

——————. "Gentrifying the British Public House, 1896–1914." *International Labor and Working-Class History*, 45 (Spring 1994). Pp.29–43.

_____. *Protecting the Pub: Brewers and Publicans against Temperance.* Woodbridge, U.K.: Boydell Press 1989.

Gwyn, Julian. "Rum, Sugar, and Molasses in the Economy of Nova Scotia, 1770–1854." In Morrison and Moreira, eds., *Tempered by Rum.* Pp.111–33.

Gwyn, Sandra. *The Private Capital: Ambition and Love in the Age of Macdonald and Laurier.* Toronto: McClelland and Stewart 1984.

Haine, W. Scott. "The Priest of the Proletarians: Parisian Cafe Owners and the Working Class, 1820–1914." *International Labor and Working-Class History,* 45 (Spring 1994). Pp.16–28.

_____. "A Spectrum of Cultural Constructs: The Inter-Relationship Between Social, Legal, and Medical Constructs of Intemperate Behavior in Parisian Drinking, 1860–1914." *CDP,* 21, no.4 (Winter 1994). Pp.535–56.

_____. *The World of the Paris Café: Sociability among the French Working Class, 1789–1914.* Baltimore: Johns Hopkins University Press 1999.

Haliburton, G. Brenton. *What's Brewing: Oland, 1867–1971, A History.* Tantallon, N.S.: Four East Publications 1994.

Haliburton, Thomas Chandler. *The Old Judge; or, Life in a Colony: A Selection of Sketches.* Ottawa: Tecumseh Press 1978.

Hall, Wayne and Ernest Hunter. "Australia." In Heath, ed., *International Handbook.* Pp.7–19.

Haller, Mark H. "Bootleggers as Businessmen: From City Slums to City Builders." In Kyvig, ed., *Law, Alcohol, and Order.* Pp.139–57.

Hallowell, Gerald A. *Prohibition in Ontario, 1919–1923.* Ottawa: Ontario Historical Society 1972.

Hamer, John and Jack Steinbring, eds. *Alcohol and Native Peoples of the North.* Lanham, Md.: University Press of America 1980.

Hamm, Richard F. "Administration and Prison Suasion: Law Enforcement in the American Temperance Movement, 1880–1920." *CDP,* 21, no.3 (Fall 1994). Pp.375–99.

_____. "The Convoluted State: The Federal System, the Prohibition Movement, and the Liquor Tax, 1862–1920." *Social History of Alcohol Review,* 25 (Spring 1992). Pp.10–27.

_____. *Shaping the Eighteenth Amendment: Temperance Reform, Legal Culture, and the Polity, 1880–1920.* Chapel Hill: University of North Carolina Press 1995.

Hammerton, A. James. *Cruelty and Companionship: Conflict in Nineteenth-Century Married Life.* London: Routledge 1992.

Hampel, Robert L. *Temperance and Prohibition in Massachusetts, 1813–1852.* Ann Arbor, Mich.: UMI Research Press 1982.

Hann, Russell. *Farmers Confront Industrialism: Some Historical Perspectives on Ontario Agrarian Movements.* Toronto: New Hogtown Press 1975.

Hanson, David J. "The United States of America." In Heath, ed., *International Handbook.* Pp.300–15.

Hardy, Stephen. "'Adopted by All the Leading Clubs': Sporting Goods and the Shaping of Leisure, 1800–1900." In Butsch, ed., *For Fun and Profit.* Pp.69–101.

Harney, Robert F. "Men without Women: Italian Migrants in Canada, 1885–1930." In Franca Iacovetta with Paula Draper and Robert Ventresca, eds., *A Nation of Immigrants: Women, Workers, and Communities in Canadian History, 1840s–1960s.* Toronto: University of Toronto Press 1998. Pp.206–30.

Harrison, Brian. *Drink and the Victorians: The Temperance Question in England, 1815–1872.* London: Faber and Faber 1971.

_____. "Pubs." In H.J. Dyos and Michael Wolff, eds., *The Victorian City: Images and Realities,* vol.1, *Past and Present and Numbers of People.* London: Routledge and Kegan Paul 1973. Pp.161–90.

_____. "Teetotal Chartism." *History,* 58, no.193 (June 1973). Pp.193–217.

Hartlen, G.C. "'From a Torrent to a Trickle': A Case Study of Rum Imports and the Temperance Movement in Liverpool, N.S." In Morrison and Moreira, eds., *Tempered by Rum.* Pp.62–74.

Harvey, Kathryn. "Amazons and Victims: Resisting Wife Abuse in Working-Class Montreal, 1869–1879." Canadian Historical Association, *Journal,* New Series, 2 (1991). Pp.131–48.

_____. "To Love, Honour, and Obey: Wife-Battering in Working-Class Montreal, 1869–79." *Urban History Review,* 19, no.2 (October 1990). Pp.128–40.

Head, C. Grant. *Eighteenth Century Newfoundland: A Geographer's Perspective*. Toronto: McClelland and Stewart 1976.

Heath, Dwight B. "Alcohol Use among North American Indians: A Cross-Cultural Survey of Patterns and Problems." In Reginald Smart et al., eds., *Research Advances on Alcohol and Drug Problems*, vol.7. New York: Plenum Press 1983. Pp.343–96.

——————. "A Critical Review of Ethnographic Studies of Alcohol Use." In Robert J. Gibbins et al., eds., *Research Advances in Alcohol and Drug Problems*, vol.2. New York: John Wiley and Sons 1975. Pp.1–91.

——————. *Drinking Occasions: Comparative Perspectives on Alcohol and Culture*. Philadelphia: Brunner/Mazel 2000.

——————, ed. *International Handbook on Alcohol and Culture*. Westport, Conn.: Greenwood Press 1995.

Henderson, Stephen. "A Provincial Liberal: Angus L. Macdonald, 1890–1954." Ph.D. thesis, York University 2003.

Hennigar, Ted R. *The Rum Running Years*. Hantsport, N.S.: Lancelot Press 1981.

Herd, Denise. "Ambiguity in Black Drinking Norms: An Ethnohistorical Interpretation." In Bennett and Ames, eds., *American Experience with Alcohol*. Pp.149–70

——————. "The Paradox of Temperance: Blacks and the Alcohol Question in Nineteenth-Century America." In Barrows and Room, eds., *Drinking*. Pp.354–75.

Herd, Denise and Robin Room. "Alcohol Images in American Film, 1909–1960." *Drinking and Drug Practices Surveyor*, 18 (August 1982). Pp.24–35.

Herlihy, Patricia. *The Alcoholic Empire: Vodka and Politics in Late Imperial Russia*. Oxford: Oxford University Press 2002.

Heron, Craig. "Allan Studholme." *Dictionary of Canadian Biography*. Vol.14. *1911 to 1920*. Toronto: University of Toronto Press 1998. Pp.976–80.

——————. "The Boys and Their Booze: Masculinities and Public Drinking in Working-Class Hamilton, 1890–1946." Paper presented to the North American Labor History Conference, Detroit 2002.

——————. *The Canadian Labour Movement: A Short History*. Toronto: James Lorimer 1996.

——————. "Factory Workers." In Paul Craven, ed., *Labouring Lives: Work and Workers in Nineteenth-Century Ontario*. Toronto: University of Toronto Press 1995. Pp.479–590.

——————. "The High School and the Household Economy in Working-Class Hamilton, 1890–1940." *Historical Studies in Education*, 7, no.2 (Fall 1995). Pp.217–59.

——————. "National Contours: Solidarity and Fragmentation." In Heron, ed., *Workers' Revolt*. Pp.268–304.

——————. "The Second Industrial Revolution in Canada, 1890–1930." In Deian R. Hopkin and Gregory S. Kealey, eds., *Class, Community, and the Labour Movement: Wales and Canada, 1850–1930*. Aberystwyth, Wales: Llafur and Canadian Committee on Labour History 1989. Pp.48–66.

——————, ed. *The Workers' Revolt in Canada, 1917–1925*. Toronto: University of Toronto Press 1998.

——————. "Working-Class Hamilton, 1895–1930." Ph.D. thesis, Dalhousie University 1981.

——————. *Working in Steel: The Early Years in Canada, 1883–1935*. Toronto: McClelland and Stewart 1988.

Heron, Craig and Steve Penfold. *The Workers' Festival: A History of Labour Day in Canada*. Forthcoming.

Heron, Craig and Myer Siemiatycki. "The Great War, the State, and Working-Class Canada." In Heron, ed., *Workers' Revolt*. Pp.11–42.

Heron, Craig and Robert Storey. "On the Job in Canada." In Craig Heron and Robert Storey, eds., *On the Job: Confronting the Labour Process in Canada*. Montreal and Kingston: McGill-Queen's University Press 1986. Pp.3–46.

Hey, Valerie. *Patriarchy and Pub Culture*. London: Tavistock Publications 1986.

Hiebert, John Albert. "Prohibition in British Columbia." M.A. thesis, Simon Fraser University 1969.

Hildebrand, Ghislaine Blais. "Les débuts du mouvement de tempérance dans le Bas-Canada: 1828–1840." M.A. thesis, McGill University 1975.

Hill, Thomas W. "Ethnohistory and Alcohol Studies." In Marc Gallanter, ed., *Recent Developments in Alcoholism*, vol.2. New York: Plenum Press 1984. Pp.313–37.

History of the Vote in Canada, A. Ottawa: Minister of Public Works and Government Services Canada 1997.

Hobsbawm, Eric. *Primitive Rebels: Studies in Archaic Forms of Social Movement in the 19th and 20th Centuries*. New York: W.W. Norton and Company 1959.

Holman, Andrew C. *A Sense of Their Duty: Middle-Class Formation in Victorian Ontario*. Montreal and Kingston: McGill-Queen's University Press 2000.

The Home Cook Book, Compiled by Ladies of Toronto and Chief Cities and Towns in Canada. Saint John: R.A.H. Morrow 1878; Toronto: Rose Publishing Company 1888 (CIHM nos. 06848, 29260).

Homel, Gene Howard. "Denison's Law: Criminal Justice and the Police Court in Toronto, 1877–1921." *OH*, 72, no.3 (September 1981). Pp.171–86.

——————. "'Fading Beams of the Nineteenth Century': Radicalism and Early Socialism in Canada's 1890s." *L/LT*, 5 (Spring 1980). Pp.9–32.

——————. "James Simpson and the Origins of Canadian Social Democracy." Ph.D. thesis, University of Toronto 1978.

——————. "Sliders and Backsliders: Toronto's Sunday Tobogganing Controversy of 1912." *Urban History Review*, 10, no.2 (October 1981). Pp.25–34.

Honigmann, John J. "Dynamics of Drinking in an Austrian Village." In Marshall, ed., *Beliefs, Behaviors, and Alcoholic Beverages*. Pp.414–28.

Horowitz, Daniel. *The Morality of Spending: Attitudes Toward the Consumer Society in America, 1875–1940*. Chicago: Ivan R. Dee 1985.

Horrall, Stan. "A Policeman's Lot Is Not a Happy One: The Mounted Police and Prohibition in the North-West Territories, 1874–91." Historical and Scientific Society of Manitoba. *Transactions*, series 3, no.30 (1973–4). Pp.5–16.

Hose, Reginald E. *Prohibition or Control? Canada's Experience with the Liquor Problem, 1921–1927*. New York: Longmans, Green, and Company 1928.

Houston, Cecil J. and William J. Smyth. *Irish Emigration and Canadian Settlement: Patterns, Links, and Letters*. Toronto: University of Toronto Press 1990.

Howay, F.W. "The Introduction of Intoxicating Liquors amongst the Indians of the Northwest Coast." *British Columbia Historical Quarterly*, 6, no.3 (July 1942). Pp.157–69.

Huggins, Mike J. "More Sinful Pleasures? Leisure, Respectability and the Male Middle Classes in Victorian England." *Journal of Social History*, 33, no.3 (Spring 2000). Pp.585–600.

Hughes, Jeanne. "Eating on the Move." In Clow et al., eds., *Consuming Passions*. Pp.35–43.

——————. "Inns and Taverns." In Clow et al., eds., *Consuming Passions*. Pp.93–112.

Humphrey, Mrs. *Etiquette for Every Day*. Toronto: Musson Book Company n.d.

Humphries, Charles W. *"Honest Enough to Be Bold": The Life and Times of Sir James Pliny Whitney*. Toronto: University of Toronto Press 1985.

Hunt, Alan. *Governing Morals: A Social History of Moral Regulation*. Cambridge: Cambridge University Press 1999.

——————. "Measuring Morals: The Beginnings of the Social Survey Movement in Canada, 1913–1917." *HS/SH*, 35, no.69 (May 2002). Pp.171–94.

Hunt, Geoffrey and Sandra Satterlee. "Darts, Drink and the Pub: The Culture of Female Drinking." *Sociological Review*, 35, no.3 (August 1987). Pp.575–601.

Hunt, C.W. *Booze, Boats, and Billions: Smuggling Liquid Gold!* Toronto: McClelland and Stewart 1988.

——————. *Whiskey and Ice: The Saga of Ben Kerr, Canada's Most Daring Rumrunner*. Toronto: Dundurn Press 1995.

Hunter, Douglas. *Molson: The Birth of a Business Empire*. Toronto: Penguin 2001.

Hurd, Madeleine. "Liberals, Socialists, and Sobriety: The Rhetoric of Citizenship in Turn-of-the-Century Sweden." *International Labor and Working-Class History*, 45 (Spring 1994). Pp.44–62.

Huskins, Bonnie. "From *Haute Cuisine* to Ox Roasts: Public Feasting and the Negotiation of Class in Mid-19th-Century Saint John and Halifax." *L/LT*, 37 (Spring 1996), 9–36.

Hutchinson, Bertram. "Alcohol as a Contributing Factor in Social Disorganization: The South African Bantu in the Nineteenth Century." In Marshal, ed., *Beliefs, Behaviors, and Alcoholic Beverages*. Pp.328–41.

Israelstam, Stephen and Sylvia Lambert. "Gay Bars." *JDI*, 14, no.4 (Fall 1984). Pp.637–53.

Jackson, Andrew, David Robinson, with Bob Baldwin and Cindy Wiggins. *Falling Behind: The State of Working Canada, 2000*. Ottawa: Canadian Centre for Policy Alternatives 2000.

Jaenen, Cornelius J. "Amerindian Views of French Culture in the Seventeenth Century." In Chad Gaffield, ed., *The Invention of Canada: Readings in Pre-Confederation History*. Toronto: Copp Clark Longman 1994. Pp.110–39.

_____. *The Role of the Church in New France*. Toronto: McGraw-Hill Ryerson 1976.

Jaffe, A. "Reform in American Medical Science: The Inebriety Movement and the Origins of the Psychological Disease Theory of Addiction." *BJA*, 73, no.2 (June 1978). Pp.139–47.

Janen, Patricia. *Wild Things: Nature, Culture, and Tourism in Ontario, 1790–1914*. Toronto: University of Toronto Press 1995.

Jellinek, E.M. *The Disease Concept of Alcoholism*. New Haven, Conn.: College and University Press 1960.

_____. "The Symbolism of Drinking: A Culture-Historical Approach." *JSA*, 38, no.5 (May 1977). Pp.852–66.

Jessup, Lynda. "Prospectors, Bushwackers, Painters: Antimodernism and the Group of Seven." *International Journal of Canadian Studies*, 17 (Spring 1998). Pp.193–14.

Johnson, Leo. A. *History of the County of Ontario, 1615–1875*. Whitby, Ont.: Corporation of the County of Ontario 1973.

Johnson, Leroy. "Union Responses to Alcoholism." *JDI*, 11, no.3 (Summer 1981). Pp.263–77.

Johnson, Paul. "Drinking, Temperance, and the Construction of Identity in Nineteenth-Century America." *Social Science Information*, 25, no.2 (June 1986). Pp.521–30.

Johnson, Stuart D., Lorne Gibson, and Rick Linden. "Alcohol and Rape in Winnipeg, 1966–1975." *JSA*. 39, no.11 (November 1978). Pp.1887–94.

Johnston, A.J.B. *Control and Order in French Colonial Louisbourg, 1713–1758*. East Lansing: Michigan State University Press

_____. *Religion in Life at Louisbourg, 1713–1758*. Montreal and Kingston: McGill-Queen's University Press 1984.

Johnston, Charles M. *E.C. Drury, Agrarian Idealist*. Toronto: University of Toronto Press 1986.

Johnston, Wayne A. *At the York*. London: Ergo Productions 1990.

Jones, Bartlett C. "Prohibition and Eugenics." *Journal of the History of Medicine*, 18, no.2 (April 1963). Pp.158–72.

_____. "A Prohibition Problem: Liquor as Medicine, 1920–1933." *Journal of the History of Medicine*, 18, no.4 (October 1963). Pp.353–69.

Jones, Gareth Stedman. *Languages of Class: Studies in English Working Class History, 1832–1982*. Cambridge: Cambridge University Press 1983.

Jones, J.C.H. "Mergers and Competition: The Brewing Case." *Canadian Journal of Economics and Political Science*, 33, no.4 (November 1967). Pp.551–68.

Jones, S.R.H. "The New Zealand Brewing Industry, 1840–1995." In Wilson and Gourvish, eds., *Dynamics of the International Brewing Industry*. Pp.247–65.

Jones, Stephen G. "Labour, Society and the Drink Question in Britain, 1918–1939." *Historical Journal*, 30, no.1 (March 1987). Pp.105–22.

Josephson, Matthew. *Union House, Union Bar: The History of the Hotel and Restaurant Employees and Bartenders International Union, AFL-CIO*. New York: Random House 1956.

Kaplan, Michael. "New York City Tavern Violence and the Creation of a Working-Class Male Identity." *Journal of the Early Republic*, 15, no.3 (Winter 1995). Pp.591–617.

Karp, Ivan. "Beer Drinking and Social Experience in an African Society: An Essay in Formal Sociology." In Ivan Karp and Charles S. Bird, eds., *Explorations in African Systems of Thought*. Bloomington: Indiana University Press 1980. Pp.83–119.

Kasson, John F. *Houdini, Tarzan, and the Perfect Man: The White Male Body and the Challenge of Modernity in America*. New York: Hill and Wang 2001.

_____. *Rudeness and Civility: Manners in Nineteenth-Century Urban America*. New York: Hill and Wang 1990.

Katz, Michael B., Michael J. Doucet, and Mark J. Stern. *The Social Organization of Industrial Capitalism*. Cambridge, Mass.: Harvard University Press 1982.

Kazin, Michael. *The Populist Persuasion: An American History*. Ithaca, N.Y.: Cornell University Press 1998.

Kealey, Gregory S. *Toronto Workers Respond to Industrial Capitalism, 1867–1892*. Toronto: University of Toronto Press 1980.

_____. "Work Control, the Labour Process, and Nineteenth-Century Canadian Printers." In Craig Heron and Robert Storey, eds., *On the Job: Confronting the Labour Process in Canada*. Montreal and Kingston: McGill-Queen's University Press 1986. Pp.75–101.

Kealey, Gregory S. and Bryan D. Palmer. *Dreaming of What Might Be: The Knights of Labor in Ontario, 1880–1900*. Toronto: New Hogtown Press 1987.

Kerr, K. Austin. "The American Brewing Industry, 1865–1920." In Wilson and Gourvish, eds., *Dynamics of the International Brewing Industry*. Pp.176–92.

_____. *Organized for Prohibition: A New History of the Anti-Saloon League*. New Haven, Conn.: Yale University Press 1985.

Kessler, Marc and Christopher Gomberg. "Observations of Barroom Drinking: Methodology and Preliminary Results." *QJSA*, 35, no.4 (December 1974). Pp.1392–6.

Kilbourn, William. *The Elements Combined: A History of the Steel Company of Canada*. Toronto: Clarke Irwin and Company 1960.

Kimber, Stephen. *Sailors, Slackers, and Blind Pigs: Halifax at War*. Toronto: Anchor Canada 2002.

Kimmel, Michael. "Consuming Manhood: The Feminization of American Culture and the Recreation of the Male Body, 1832–1920." In Laurence Goldstein, ed., *The Male Body: Features, Destinies, Exposures*. Ann Arbor: University of Michigan Press 1994. Pp.12–41.

_____. *Manhood in America: A Cultural History*. New York: New Press 1996.

Kingsdale, Jon M. "The 'Poor Man's Club': Social Functions of the Urban Working-Class Saloon." *American Quarterly*, 25, no.4 (October 1973). Pp.472–89.

Kinsman, Gary. *The Regulation of Desire: Sexuality in Canada*. Montreal: Black Rose Books 1987.

Kirby, Diane. *Barmaids: A History of Women's Work in Pubs*. Melbourne, Aust.: Cambridge University Press 1997.

Kitossa, Tamari. "Criticism, Reconstruction, and African-Centred Feminist Historiography." In Njoki Nathani Wane, Katerina Deliovsky, and Erica Lawson, eds., *Back to the Drawing Board: African-Canadian Feminisms*. Toronto: Sumach Press 2002.

Klatssky, Arthur L. "Is Drinking Healthy?" In Peel and Grant, eds., *Alcohol and Pleasure*. Pp.141–56.

Kopperman, Paul E. "'The Cheapest Pay': Alcohol Abuse in the Eighteenth-Century British Army." *Journal of Military History*, 30, no.3 (July 1996). Pp.445–70.

Kottman, Richard N. "Volstead Violated: Prohibition as a Factor in Canadian-American Relations." *Canadian Historical Review*, 43, no.2 (June 1962). Pp.106–26.

Kristofferson, Robert. "Craft Capitalism: Craftworkers, Industrialization, and Class Formation in Hamilton, Ontario, 1840–1872." Ph.D. thesis, York University 2003.

Kudlick, Catherine J. "Fighting the Internal and External Enemies: Alcoholism in World War I France." *CDP*, 12, no.1 (Spring 1985). Pp.129–58.

Kurtz, Ernest. *Not-God: A History of Alcoholics Anonymous*. Center City, Minn.: Hazelden 1979.

Kyvig, David E., ed. *Law, Alcohol, and Order: Perspectives on National Prohibition*. Westport, Conn.: Greenwood Press 1985.

_____. *Repealing National Prohibition*. Chicago: University of Chicago Press 1979.

_____. "Sober Thoughts: Myths and Realities of National Prohibition after Fifty Years." In Kyvig, ed., *Law, Alcohol, and Order*. Pp.3–20.

Lachance, André. *La vie urbaine en Nouvelle-France*. Montreal: Boréal 1987.

Lambert, W.R. *Drink and Sobriety in Victorian Wales, c.1820–c.1895*. Cardiff: University of Wales Press 1983.

_____. "Drink and Work-Discipline in Industrial South Wales, c.1800–1870." *Welsh History Review*, 7, no.3 (June 1975). Pp.289–306.

Laurie, Bruce. "'Nothing on Impulse': Life Styles of Philadelphia Artisans, 1820–1860." *Labor History*, 15, no.3 (Summer 1974). Pp.337–66.

_____. *Working People of Philadelphia, 1800–1850*. Philadelphia: Temple University Press 1980.

Law, Howard. "'Self-Reliance Is the True Road to Independence': Ideology and the Ex-Slaves in Buxton and Chatham." In Franca Iacovetta with Paula Draper and Robert Ventresca, eds., *A

Nation of Immigrants: Women, Workers, and Communities in Canadian History, 1840s–1960s. Toronto: University of Toronto Press 1998. Pp.82–100.

Lawrence, Jon. "Class and Gender in the Making of Urban Toryism, 1880–1914." *English Historical Review*, 108, no.428 (July 1993). Pp.629–52.

Leacock, Stephen. *The Case against Prohibition.* N.p. n.d. (CIHM no.83352).

——————. "The Tyranny of Prohibition." In Alan Bowker, ed., *The Social Criticism of Stephen Leacock: The Unsolved Riddle of Social Justice and Other Essays.* Toronto: University of Toronto Press 1973. Pp.61–9.

——————. *Wet or Dry?* N.p. 1918 (CIHM no.85300).

Lears, T.J. Jackson. *Fables of Abundance: A Cultural History of Advertising in America.* New York: Basic Books 1994.

——————. "From Salvation to Self-Realization: Advertising and the Therapeutic Roots of the Consumer Culture, 1880–1930." In Richard Wightman Fox and T.J. Jackson Lears, eds., *The Culture of Consumption: Critical Essays in American History, 1880–1980.* New York: Pantheon Books 1983. Pp.1–38.

——————. *No Place of Grace: Antimodernism and the Transformation of American Culture, 1880–1920.* Chicago: University of Chicago Press 1994.

Lees, Lynn Hollen. "Getting and Spending: The Family Budgets of English Industrial Workers in 1890." In John M. Merriman, ed., *Consciousness and Class Experience in Nineteenth-Century Europe.* New York: Holmes and Meier 1979. Pp.169–86.

Leeson, R.A. *Travelling Brothers: The Six Centuries' Road from Craft Fellowship to Trade Unionism.* London: Granada 1980.

Leier, Mark. *Where the Fraser River Flows: The Industrial Workers of the World in British Columbia.* Vancouver: New Star Books 1990.

Leland, Joy. *Firewater Myths: North American Indian Drinking and Alcohol Addiction.* New Brunswick, N.J.: Rutgers Center of Alcohol Studies 1976.

LeMasters, E.E. *Blue-Collar Aristocrats: Life-Styles at a Working-Class Tavern.* Madison: University of Wisconsin Press 1975.

Lemert, Edwin M. "Forms and Pathology of Drinking in Three Polynesian Societies." In Marshall, ed., *Beliefs, Behaviors, and Alcoholic Beverages.* Pp.192–208.

Lender, Mark Edward. "A Special Stigma: Women and Alcoholism in the Late 19th and Early 20th Centuries." In David L. Strug, S. Priyadarsini, and Merton M. Myman, eds., *Alcohol Interventions: Historical and Sociocultural Approaches.* New York: Haworth Press 1986. Pp.41–57.

Lender, Mark Edward and James Kirby Martin. *Drinking in America: A History.* New York: Free Press 1982.

Lenton-Young, Gerald. "Variety Theatre." In Ann Saddlemyer, ed., *Early Stages: Theatre in Ontario, 1800–1914.* Toronto: University of Toronto Press 1990. Pp.166–213.

Lepp, Annalee E. *Dis/Membering the Family: Marital Breakdown, Domestic Conflict, and Family Violence in Ontario, 1830–1920.* Forthcoming.

Lever, Yves. *Histoire générale du cinéma au Québec.* Montreal: Boréal 1988.

Levine, Harry Gene. "The Birth of American Alcohol Control: Prohibition, the Power Elite, and the Problem of Lawlessness." *CDP*, 12, no.1 (Spring 1985). Pp.63–115.

——————. "The Committee of Fifty and the Origins of Alcohol Control." *JDI*, 13, no.1 (Winter 1983). Pp.95–116.

——————. "The Discovery of Addiction: Changing Concepts of Habitual Drunkenness in America." *JSA*, 39 no.1 (January 1978). Pp.143–74.

——————. "The Good Creature of God and the Demon Rum: Colonial American and 19th Century Ideas about Alcohol, Crime, and Accidents." In Robin Room and Gary Collins, eds., *Alcohol and Disinhibition: Nature and Meaning of the Link.* Washington: National Institute on Alcohol Abuse and Alcoholism 1983. Pp.111–61.

——————. "Temperance and Women in 19th-Century United States." In Oriana Josseau Kalant, ed., *Research Advances in Alcohol and Drug Problems,* vol. 5, *Alcohol and Drug Problems in Women.* New York: Plenum Press 1980. Pp.25–67.

_____. "Temperance Cultures: Concern about Alcohol Problems in Nordic and English-Speaking Cultures." In Malcolm Lader, Griffith Edwards, and D. Colin Drummond, eds., *The Nature of Alcohol and Drug Related Problems*. Oxford: Oxford University Press 1992. Pp.15–36.

Levine, Lawrence. *Highbrow/Lowbrow: The Emergence of Cultural Hierarchy in America*. Cambridge, Mass.: Harvard University Press 1988.

Li, Peter S. *The Making of Post-War Canada*. Toronto: Oxford University Press 1996.

Licensed Victuallers Gazette (Montreal), 11 November 1897 (CIHM no.P04312).

Lindstrom-Best, Varpu. "Finnish Socialist Women in Canada, 1890–1930." In Linda Kealey and Joan Sangster, eds., *Beyond the Vote: Canadian Women and Politics*. Toronto: University of Toronto Press 1989. Pp.196–216.

Listiak, Alan. "'Legitimate Deviance' and Social Class: Bar Behavior during Grey Cup Week." *Sociological Focus*, 7, no.3 (Summer 1974). Pp.13–44.

Lithman, Y.G. "Feeling Good and Getting Smashed: On the Symbolism of Alcohol and Drunkenness among Canadian Indians." *Ethnos*, 44 (1979). Pp.119–33.

Lockwood, Glenn J. "Music and Songs Related to Food and Beverages." In Clow et al., *Consuming Passions*. Pp.233–7.

_____. "Temperance in Upper Canada as Ethnic Subterfuge." In Warsh, ed., *Drink in Canada*. Pp.43–69.

London, Jack. *John Barleycorn*. New York: Century Company 1913.

Loo, Tina. "Of Moose and Men: Hunting for Masculinities in British Columbia, 1880–1939." *Western Historical Quarterly*, 32, no.3 (Autumn 2001). Pp.297–319.

Lortie, Stanislas-Alfred. "Compositeur typographe de Québec en 1903." In Pierre Savard, ed., *Paysans et ouvriers québécois d'autrefois*. Quebec: Les presses de l'Université Laval 1968. Pp.77–150.

Luedtke, Alf. "Cash, Coffee-Breaks, Horseplay: Eigensinn and Politics among Factory Workers in Germany circa 1900." In Michael Hanagan and Charles Stephenson, eds., *Confrontation, Class Consciousness, and the Labor Process: Studies in Proletarian Class Formation*. Westport, Conn.: Greenwood Press 1986. Pp.65–95.

Lutz, John Sutton. *Makuk: Work and Welfare in Aboriginal Non-Aboriginal Relations*. Forthcoming.

MacAndrew, Craig. "On the Notion That Certain Persons Who Are Given to Frequent Drunkenness Suffer from a Disease Called Alcoholism." In Stanley C. Plog and Robert B. Edgerton, eds., *Changing Perspectives in Mental Illness*. New York: Holt, Rinehart and Winston 1969. Pp.483–501.

MacAndrew, Craig and Robert Edgerton. *Drunken Comportment: A Social Explanation*. Chicago: Aldine 1969.

MacLeod, John. "The Dryness of the Liquor Dealer." In Morrison and Moreira, eds., *Tempered by Rum*. Pp.76–87.

MacLeod, Roy M. "The Edge of Hope: Social Policy and Chronic Alcoholism, 1870–1900." *Journal of the History of Medicine*, 22, no.3 (July 1967). Pp.215–45.

Macrory, Boyd E. "The Tavern and the Community." *QJSA*, 3, no.4 (December 1952). Pp.609–37.

Magney, William. "The Methodist Church and the National Gospel, 1884–1914." United Church of Canada, Committee on Archives. *Bulletin*, 20 (1968). Pp.3–95.

Makela, Klaus, Esa Osterberg, and Pekka Sulkunen. "Drink in Finland: Increasing Alcohol Availability in a Monopoly State." In Single, Morgan, and De Lint, eds., *Alcohol, Society, and the State*, vol.2. Pp.31–60.

Makela, Klaus et al. *Alcoholics Anonymous as a Mutual-Help Movement: A Study in Eight Societies*. Madison: University of Wisconsin Press 1996.

Makela, Klaus et al. *Alcohol, Society, and the State*. Vol.1. *A Comparative Study of Alcohol Control*. Toronto: Addiction Research Foundation 1981.

Malchelosse, Gérard. "Ah! mon grand-per', comme il buvait!" *Les Cahiers des dix*, 8 (1943). Pp.141–54.

Malcolm, Elizabeth. "The Catholic Church and the Irish Temperance Movement, 1838–1901." *Irish Historical Studies*, 23, no.89 (May 1982). Pp.1–16.

_____. *"Ireland Sober, Ireland Free": Drink and Temperance in Nineteenth-Century Ireland*. Syracuse, N.Y.: Syracuse University Press 1986.

Malcolmson, Robert W. *Popular Recreations in English Society, 1700–1850*. Cambridge: Cambridge University Press 1973.

Malleck, Daniel J. "Priorities of Development in Four Local Woman's Christian Temperance Unions in Ontario, 1877–1895." In Blocker and Warsh, eds., *Changing Face of Drink.* Pp.189–208.

Mancall, Peter C. *Deadly Medicine: Indians and Alcohol in Early America.* Ithaca, N.Y.: Cornell University Press 1995.

_____. "Men, Women, and Alcohol in Indian Villages in the Great Lakes Region in the Early Republic." *Journal of the Early Republic,* 15, no.3 (Fall 1995). Pp.425–48.

Mandelbaum, David. "Alcohol and Culture." In Marshall, ed., *Beliefs, Behaviors, and Alcoholic Beverages.* Pp.14–30.

Mangan, J.A. and James Walvin, eds. *Manliness and Morality: Middle-Class Masculinity in Britain and America, 1800–1940.* New York: St. Martin's Press 1987.

Manitoba Liquor Enquiry Commission. *Report.* Winnipeg 1955.

Mann, W.E. "The Lower Ward." In S.D. Clark, ed., *Urbanism and the Changing Canadian Society.* Toronto: University of Toronto Press. Pp.39–69.

Maracle, J. *Crazywater: Native Voices on Addiction and Recovery.* Toronto: Viking 1993.

Marble, Allan Everett. *Surgeons, Smallpox, and the Poor: A History of Medicine and Social Conditions in Nova Scotia, 1749–1799.* Montreal and Kingston: McGill-Queen's University Press 1993.

Marks, Lynne. "No Double Standard? Leisure, Sex, and Sin in Upper Canadian Church Discipline Records, 1800–1860." In Kathryn McPherson, Cecil Morgan, and Nancy M. Forestell, eds., *Gendered Pasts: Historical Essays in Femininity and Masculinity in Canada.* Toronto: Oxford University Press 1999. Pp.48–64.

_____. "Religion, Leisure, and Working-Class Identity." In Paul Craven, ed., *Labouring Lives: Work and Workers in Nineteenth-Century Ontario.* Toronto: University of Toronto Press 1995. Pp.278–332.

_____. *Revivals and Roller Rinks: Religion, Leisure, and Identity in Small-Town Ontario.* Toronto: University of Toronto Press 1996.

Marquis, Greg. "Brewers and Distillers Paradise: American Views of Canadian Alcohol Policies, 1919–35." *Canadian Review of American Studies.* Forthcoming.

_____. "The Canadian Police and Prohibition, 1890–1930." Unpublished paper presented to the Canadian Historical Association Annual Meeting, 1991.

_____. "The Canadian Temperance Movement: What Happened after Prohibition?" Unpublished paper presented to the Canadian Historical Association Annual Meeting, 2001.

_____. "Civilized Drinking: Alcohol and Society in New Brunswick, 1945–1975." *Journal of the Canadian Historical Society,* 2000. Pp.173–203.

_____. "Enforcing the Law: The Charlottetown Police Force." In Douglas Baldwin and Thomas Spira, eds., *Gaslights, Epidemics, and Vagabond Cows: Charlottetown in the Victorian Era.* Charlottetown: Ragweed Press 1988. Pp.86–102.

_____. "The History of Policing in the Maritime Provinces: Themes and Prospects." *Urban History Review,* 19, no.2 (October 1990). Pp.84–99.

_____. "'A Machine of Oppression under the Guise of the Law': The Saint John Police Establishment, 1860–1890." *Acadiensis,* 16, no.1 (Autumn 1986). Pp.58–77.

_____. *Policing Canada's Century: A History of the Canadian Association of Chiefs of Police.* Toronto: University of Toronto Press 1993.

_____. "Public Drunkenness and the Justice System: Canada, 1945–1980." Unpublished paper presented to the Canadian Historical Association Annual Meeting, 2003.

_____. "Vancouver Vice: The Police and the Negotiation of Morality, 1904–1935." In Hamar Foster and John McLaren, eds., *Essays in the History of Canadian Law,* vol.6, *British Columbia and the Yukon.* Toronto: University of Toronto Press 1995. Pp.242–73.

Marrus, Michael R. *Mr. Sam: The Life and Times of Samuel Bronfman.* Toronto: Penguin Books 1991.

_____. "Social Drinking in the *Belle époque.*" *Journal of Social History,* 7, no.2 (Winter 1974), 115–41.

Mars, Gerald. "Longshore Drinking, Economic Security and Union Politics in Newfoundland." In Douglas, ed., *Constructive Drinking.* Pp.91–101.

Marshall, Mac, ed. *Beliefs, Behaviors, and Alcoholic Beverages: A Cross-Cultural Survey.* Ann Arbor: University of Michigan Press 1979.

Marshall, Mac and Leslie B. Marshall. "Holy and Unholy Spirits: The Effects of Missionization on Alcohol Use in Eastern Micronesia." In Marshall, ed., *Beliefs, Behaviors, and Alcoholic Beverages.* Pp.208–37.

Martin, Linda and Kerry Segrave. *City Parks of Canada.* Oakville: Mosaic Press 1983.

Martin, Scott C. "Violence, Gender, and Intemperance in Early National Connecticut." *Journal of Social History*, 34, no.2 (Winter 2000). Pp.309–25.

Masden, William and Claudia Masden. "The Cultural Structure of Mexican Drinking Behavior." In Marshall, ed., *Beliefs, Behaviors, and Alcoholic Beverages.* Pp.38–54.

Mason, Philip P. *Rum Running and the Roaring Twenties: Prohibition on the Michigan-Ontario Waterway.* Detroit: Wayne State University Press 1995.

Massicotte, E.-Z. "L'industrie hôtelière et les premiers aubergistes du régime anglais." *Bulletin des recherches historiques*, 36, no.4 (April 1930). Pp.203–6.

Mathias, Peter. "The Brewing Industry, Temperance, and Politics." *Historical Journal*, 1, no.2 (1958). Pp.97–113.

Mattingly, Carol. *Well-Tempered Women: Nineteenth-Century Temperance Rhetoric.* Carbondale and Edwardsville: Southern Illinois University Press 1998.

Mawani, Resina. "In Between and Out of Place: Mixed-Race Identity, Liquor, and the Law in British Columbia, 1850–1914." In Sherene H. Razack, ed., *Race, Space, and the Law: Unmapping a White Settler Society.* Toronto: Between the Lines 2002. Pp.47–69.

McBurney, Margaret and Mary Byers. *Tavern in the Town: Early Inns and Taverns of Ontario.* Toronto: University of Toronto Press 1987.

McCalla, Douglas. *Consumption Stories: Customer Purchases of Alcohol at an Upper Canadian Country Store in 1808–1809 and 1828–1829.* Quebec: Centre interuniversitaire d'études québécoises 1999.

——————. *Planting the Province: The Economic History of Upper Canada, 1784–1870.* Toronto: University of Toronto Press 1993.

McCandless, Peter. "'Curses of Civilization': Insanity and Drunkenness in Victorian Britain." *BJA*, 79, no.1 (1984). Pp.49–58.

McCann, Larry. "The 1890s: Fragmentation and the New Social Order." In Forbes and Muise, eds., *Atlantic Provinces in Confederation.* Pp.119–54.

McCarthy, Katherine. "Early Alcoholism Treatment: The Emmanuel Movement and Richard Peabody." *JSA*, 45, no.1 (1984). Pp.59–74.

McClelland, Keith. "Masculinity and the 'Representative Artisan' in Britain, 1850–80." In Michael Roper and John Tosh, eds., *Manful Assertions: Masculinities in Britain Since 1800.* London: Routledge 1991. Pp.74–91.

McCormack, A. Ross. "Wobblies and Blanket Stiffs: The Constituency of the IWW in Western Canada." In W.J.C. Cherwinski and Gregory S. Kealey, eds., *Lectures in Canadian Labour and Working-Class History.* St. John's and Toronto: Committee on Canadian Labour History and New Hogtown Press 1985. Pp.101–14.

McCulloch, Michael. "Most Assuredly Perpetual Motion: Police and Policing in Quebec City, 1838–58." *Urban History Review*, 19, no.1 (October 1990). Pp.100–12.

McDonald, Maryon, ed. *Gender, Drink, and Drugs.* Oxford: Berg 1994.

McDonald, Robert A.J. "Lumber Society on the Industrial Frontier: Burrard Inlet, 1863–1886." *L/LT*, 33 (Spring 1994). Pp.69–96.

McDonald, Terry. "Defending the Finest Wine Cellar in Canada: Commodore Barry and the Royal Navy Establishment at Kingston, 1819–1834." Unpublished paper presented to the British World II Conference, Calgary 2003.

McGahan, Peter. *Crime and Policing in Maritime Canada: Chapters from the Urban Records.* Fredericton: Goose Lane Editions 1988.

McIntosh, Dave. *The Collectors: A History of Canadian Customs and Excise.* Toronto: NC Press 1984.

McKay, Ian. "'By Wisdom, Wile, or War': The Provincial Workmen's Association and the Struggle for Working-Class Independence in Nova Scotia, 1879–97." *L/LT*, 18 (Fall 1986). Pp.13–62.

——————, ed. *For a Working-Class Culture in Canada: A Selection of Colin McKay's Writings on Sociology and Political Economy, 1897–1939.* St. John's: Canadian Committee on Labour History 1996.

_____. "The Liberal Order Framework: A Prospectus for a Reconnaissance of Canadian History." *CHR*, 81, no.4 (December 2000). Pp.617–45.

_____. "The 1910s: The Stillborn Triumph of Progressive Reform." In Forbes and Muise, eds., *Atlantic Provinces in Confederation*. Pp.192–229.

McKeon, Clare and Joseph McKeon. *Oakville: A Place of Some Importance*. Burlington, Ont.: Windsor Publications n.d.

McLaren, Angus. *Our Own Master Race: Eugenics in Canada, 1885–1945*. Toronto: McClelland and Stewart 1990.

McLaren, Sheryl Stotts. "Becoming Indispensable: A Biography of Elizabeth Smith Shortt (1859–1949)." Ph.D. thesis, York University 2001.

McLaughlan, Gordon. *The Story of Beer: Beer and Brewing—A New Zealand History*. Auckland, N.Z.: Penguin Books 1994.

McLaughlin, Patrick M. "Inebriate Institutions in Scotland: An Institutional History." In Barrows and Room, eds., *Drinking*. Pp.287–314.

McLean, Lorna. "'Deserving' Wives and 'Drunken' Husbands: Wife Beating, Marital Conduct, and the Law in Ontario, 1850–1910." *HS/SH*, 35, no.69 (May 2002). Pp.59–81.

McLean, Robert Erwin. "A 'Most Effectual Remedy': Temperance and Prohibition in Alberta, 1875–1915." M.A. thesis, University of Calgary 1969.

McLeod, David I. *Building Character in the American Boy: The Boy Scouts, the YMCA, and Their Forerunners, 1870–1920*. Madison: University of Wisconsin Press 1983.

McLeod, D.M. "Liquor Control in the North-West Territories: The Permit System, 1870–1891." *Saskatchewan History*, 16 (1963). Pp.81–9.

Medick, Hans. "Plebeian Culture in the Transition to Capitalism." In Raphael Samuel and Gareth Stedman Jones, eds., *Culture, Ideology, and Politics: Essays for Eric Hobsbawm*. London: Routledge and Kegan Paul 1982. Pp.84–113.

Mellor, H.E. *Leisure and the Changing City, 1870–1914*. London: Routledge and Kegan Paul 1976.

Mendelsohn, Oscar. *Nicely, Thank You (Drunk 2000 Times): A Frolic with Some Synonyms*. Melbourne, Aust.: National Press 1971.

Men's Federation of London. *The City of London, Ontario: Report of a Limited Survey of Educational, Social, and Industrial Life*. N.p. 1913.

Methodist Church, Board of Temperance and Moral Reform, and Presbyterian Church, Board of Social Service and Evangelism. *Vancouver, British Columbia: A Preliminary and General Social Survey*. N.p. n.d. [1913].

_____. *Report of a Preliminary and General Social Survey of Fort William*. N.p. 1913.

_____. *Report of a Preliminary and General Social Survey of Hamilton*. N.p. 1913.

_____. *Report of a Preliminary and General Social Survey of Port Arthur*. N.p. 1913.

_____. *Report of a Preliminary and General Social Survey of Regina*. N.p. 1913.

_____. *Report of a Preliminary and General Social Survey of Sydney, Nova Scotia*. N.p. 1913.

Merrett, David T. "Stability and Change in the Australian Brewing Industry, 1920–1994." In Wilson and Gourvish, eds., *Dynamics of the International Brewing Industry*. Pp.229–46.

Merritt, Richard D. "Early Inns and Taverns: Accommodation, Fellowship, and Good Cheer." In Merritt, Butler, and Power, eds., *Capital Years*. Pp.187–222.

Merritt, Richard D., Nancy Butler, and Michael Power, eds. *The Capital Years: Niagara-on-the-Lake, 1792–1796*. Toronto: Dundurn Press 1991.

Metcalfe, Alan. *Canada Learns to Play: The Emergence of Organized Sport, 1807–1914*. Toronto: McClelland and Stewart 1987.

Meyer, Stephen. "Work, Play, and Power: Masculine Culture on the Automotive Shop Floor, 1930–1960." In Roger Horowitz, ed., *Boys and Their Toys: Masculinity, Technology, and Class in America*. New York and London : Routledge 2000. Pp.13–32.

Miles, Fraser. *Slow Boat on Rum Row*. Madeira Park, B.C.: Harbour Publishing 1992.

Milgram, Gail Gleason. "The Summer School of Alcohol Studies: An Historical and Interpretive Review." In David L. Strug et al., eds., *Alcohol Interventions: Historical and Sociocultural Approaches*. New York: Haworth Press 1986. Pp.59–74.

Miller, Doris. "Unfermented Wine on the Lord's Table: Origins and Implementation in Nineteenth-Century Canadian Methodism." *Methodist History*, 1990. Pp.3–13.

Miller, J.R. "Anti-Catholicism in Canada: From the British Conquest to the Great War." In Terrence Murphy and Gerald Stortz, eds., *Creed and Culture: The Place of English-Speaking Catholics in Canadian Society, 1750–1930*. Montreal and Kingston: McGill-Queen's University Press 1993. Pp.25–48.

_____. *Skyscrapers Hide the Heavens: A History of Indian-White Relations in Canada*. Toronto: University of Toronto Press 1989.

Miller, Mark. *Such Melodious Racket: The Lost History of Jazz in Canada, 1914–1949*. Toronto: Mercury Press 1997.

Miller, William R. "Controlled Drinking: A History and a Critical Review." *JSA*, 44, no.1 (January 1983). Pp.68–83.

Millns, Tony. "The British Brewing Industry, 1945–95." In Wilson and Gourvish, eds., *Dynamics of the International Brewing Industry*. Pp.142–59.

Mills, Wallace. "Cape Smoke: Alcohol Issues in the Cape Colony in the Nineteenth Century." *CDP*, 12, no.2 (Summer 1985). Pp.221–47.

Miron, Jeffrey A. and Jeffrey Zwiebel. "Alcohol Consumption during Prohibition." *American Economic Review*, 81, no.2 (May 1991). Pp.242–7.

Mitchinson, Wendy. "The WCTU: 'For God, Home and Native Land': A Study in Nineteenth-Century Feminism." In Linda Kealey, ed., *A Not Unreasonable Claim: Women and Reform, 1870s–1920s*. Toronto: Women's Press 1979. Pp.151–67.

Mittelman, Amy. "'A Conflict of Interest': The United Brewery Workmen in the Nineteenth Century." *CDP*, Winter 1985. Pp.511–40.

_____. "Who Will Pay the Tax? The Federal Government and the Liquor Industry, 1880–1933." *Social History of Alcohol Review*, 25 (Spring 1992). Pp.28–38.

Moffit, L.W. "Control of the Liquor Traffic in Canada." American Academic of Political and Social Sciences. *Annals*, 163 (September 1932). Pp.188–96.

Molson, Karen. *The Molsons: Their Lives and Times, 1780–2000*. Toronto: Firefly Books 2001.

Monckton, H.A. *A History of English Ale and Beer*. London: Bodley Head 1966.

Montgomery, David. *Workers' Control in America: Studies in the History of Work, Technology, and Labor Struggles*. Cambridge: Cambridge University Press 1979.

Montgomery, Lucy Maud. *Anne of Green Gables*. Toronto: McClelland and Stewart 1981.

Montreal by Gaslight. N.p. [Montreal] 1889 (CIHM no.11210).

Moore, Mark H. and Dean R. Gerstein. *Alcohol and Public Policy: Beyond the Shadow of Prohibition*. Washington: National Academy Press 1981.

Moreira, James. "Rum in the Atlantic Provinces." In Morrison and Moreira, eds., *Tempered by Rum*. Pp.15–29.

Morgan, Cecilia. *Public Men and Virtuous Women: The Gendered Languages of Religion and Politics in Upper Canada, 1791–1850*. Toronto: University of Toronto Press 1996.

Morgan, Patricia. "Industrialization, Urbanization, and the Attack on Italian Drinking Culture." *CDP*, 15, no.4 (Winter 1988). Pp.607–26.

Morris, Peter. *Embattled Shadows: A History of Canadian Cinema, 1895–1939*. Montreal and Kingston: McGill-Queen's University Press 1978.

Morrison, James H. and James Moreira, eds. *Tempered by Rum: Rum in the History of the Maritime Provinces*. Porters Lake, N.S.: Pottersfield Press 1988.

Morton, Desmond. *Mayor Howland: The Citizens' Candidate*. Toronto: Hakkert 1973.

_____. *When Your Number's Up: The Canadian Soldier in the First World War*. Toronto: Random House of Canada 1993.

Morton, Suzanne. *Ideal Surroundings: Domestic Life in a Working-Class Suburb in the 1920s*. Toronto: University of Toronto Press 1995.

Moskalewisz, Jacek. "Alcohol: Commodity and Symbol in Polish Society." In Single, Morgan, and De Lint, eds., *Alcohol, Society, and the State*, vol.2. Pp.9–30.

Moskalewisz, Jacek and Antoni Zielinski, "Poland." In Heath, ed., *International Handbook*. Pp.224–36.

Moss, Mark. *Manliness and Militarism: Educating Young Boys in Ontario for War*. Toronto: Oxford University Press 2001.

Moyles, R.G. *The Blood and Fire in Canada: A History of the Salvation Army in the Dominion, 1882–1976*. Toronto: Peter Martin Associates 1977.

_____. "Complaints Is Many and Various, but the Odd Divil Likes It": Nineteenth Century View of Newfoundland. Toronto: Peter Martin Associates 1975.

Mrs. Clarke's Cookery Book, Comprising a Collection of about Fourteen Hundred Practical, Useful, and Unique Receipts. . . . Toronto: Grip Publishing Company 1883 (CIHM no.01114).

Munro, William Bennett. "The Brandy Parliament of 1678." CHR, 2 no.2 (June 1921). Pp.172–89.

Muraskin, William A. "The Social-Control Theory in American History: A Critique." Journal of Social History, 9, no.4 (June 1976). Pp.559–69.

Murdock, Catherine Gilbert. Domesticating Drink: Women, Men, and Alcohol in America, 1870–1940. Baltimore: Johns Hopkins University Press 1998.

Murphy, Mary. Mining Cultures: Men, Women, and Leisure in Butte, 1914–41. Urbana and Chicago: University of Illinois Press 1997.

Murphy, Paul L. "Societal Morality and Individual Freedom." In Kyvig, ed., Law, Alcohol, and Order. Pp.67–80.

Murray, Glenn F. "The Road to Regulation: Patent Medicines in Canada in Historical Perspective." In Judith C. Blackwell and Patricia G. Erickson, eds., Illicit Drugs in Canada: A Risky Business. Scarborough, Ont.: Nelson Canada 1988. Pp.72–87.

Naboum-Grappe, Veronique. "France." In Heath, ed., International Handbook. Pp.75–87.

Nadeau, Louise. "Gender and Alcohol: The Separate Realities of Women's and Men's Drinking." In Peele and Grant, eds., Alcohol and Pleasure. Pp.305–21.

Nadelhaft, Jerome. "Alcohol and Wife Abuse in Antebellum Male Temperance Literature." Canadian Review of American Studies, 25, no.1 (Winter 1995). Pp.15–43.

Nasaw, David. Going Out: The Rise and Fall of Public Amusements. New York: Basic Books 1993.

Neary, Peter and Patrick O'Flaherty, eds. By Great Waters: A Newfoundland and Labrador Anthology. Toronto: University of Toronto Press 1974.

Nelli, Humbert S. "American Syndicate Crime: A Legacy of Prohibition." In Kyvig, ed., Law, Alcohol, and Order. Pp.123–37.

Nestle, Marion. "Alcohol Guidelines for Chronic Disease Prevention: From Prohibition to Moderation." Social History of Alcohol Review, 32–3 (1996). Pp.45–59.

Netting, Robert McC. "Beer as a Locus of Value among the West African Kofyar." In Marshall, ed., Beliefs, Behaviors, and Alcoholic Beverages. Pp.351–62.

Newbury, Darryl Jean-Guy. "'No Atheist, Eunuch, or Woman': Male Associational Culture and Working-Class Identity in Industrializing Ontario, 1840–1880." Ph.D. thesis, Queen's University 1992.

Newsome, Eric. Pass the Bottle: Rum Tales of the West Coast. Victoria: Orca Books 1995.

Newton, Janice. The Feminist Challenge to the Canadian Left, 1900–1918. Kingston and Montreal: McGill-Queen's University Press 1995.

Newman, Peter C. Bronfman Dynasty: The Rothschilds of the New World. Toronto: McClelland and Stewart 1978.

Nitouche, L. L'Ami des salons. Montreal: Librairie Ste. Henriette 1892 (CIHM no.81574).

Noel, Jan. Canada Dry: Temperance Crusades before Confederation. Toronto: University of Toronto Press 1995.

_____. "Dry Patriotism: The Chiniquy Crusade." In Warsh, ed., Drink in Canada. Pp.27–42.

_____. "Temperance Campaigning and Alcohol Consumption: A Case Study From Pre-Confederation Canada." CDP, 21, no.3 (Fall 1994). Pp.401–26.

Noel, S.J.R. Politics in Newfoundland. Toronto: University of Toronto Press 1971.

Noel, Thomas J. The City and the Saloon: Denver, 1858–1916. Lincoln: University of Nebraska Press 1982.

Norcliffe, Glen. The Ride to Modernity: The Bicycle in Canada, 1869–1900. Toronto: University of Toronto Press 2001.

Nouvelle cuisinière canadienne. Montreal: C.O. Beauchemin et Fils 1979 (CIHM no.13725).

Ogborne, Alan C. and Frederick B. Glaser. "Characteristics of Affiliates of Alcoholics Anonymous." JSA, 42, no.7 (July 1981). Pp.661–75.

Oldenburg, Ray. "Augmenting the Bar Studies." Social History of Alcohol Review, 28–9 (Fall 1993/Spring 1994). Pp.30–7.

Oliver, Peter. "The New Order: W.E. Raney and the Politics of Uplift." In Oliver, *Public and Private Persons: The Ontario Political Culture, 1914–1934*. Toronto: Clarke Irwin and Company 1975. Pp.65–90.

_____. *G. Howard Ferguson, Ontario Tory*. Toronto: University of Toronto Press 1977.

_____. *"Terror to Evil-Doers": Prisons and Punishment in Nineteenth-Century Ontario*. Toronto: University of Toronto Press 1998.

Olsen, Gerald Wayne. "From Parish to Palace: Working-Class Influences on Anglican Temperance Movements, 1835–1914." *Journal of Ecclesiastical History*, 40, no.2 (April 1989). Pp.239–52.

100 Years of Service: A History of Hotel Employees & Restaurant Employees International Union. N.p., n.d.

O'Neill, R. Dennis. "The Temperance Movement, Prohibition, and Scarcity in Ontario, 1900–1916." D.Ed. thesis, University of Toronto 1984.

Ontario. Board of License Commissioners. *Report on the Operation of the Liquor License Acts*. Toronto: Queen's/King's Printer 1876–1916.

_____. *Report on the Operation of the Ontario Temperance Act*. Toronto: King's Printer. 1917–27.

_____. Liquor Control Board. *Reports*. Toronto: King's Printer 1928–40.

Ossenberg, Richard J. "Social Class and Bar Behavior during an Urban Festival." *Human Organization*, 28, no.1 (Spring 1969). Pp.29–34.

Osterberg, Esa. "From Home Distillation to State Alcohol Monopoly." *CDP*, 12, no.1 (Summer 1985). Pp.31–51.

Oshodin, O.G. "Nigeria." In Heath, ed., *International Handbook*. Pp.213–23.

Owram, Doug. *Born at the Right Time: A History of the Baby Boom Generation*. Toronto: University of Toronto Press 1996.

_____. "Canadian Domesticity in the Postwar Era." In Peter Neary and J.L. Granatstein, eds., *The Veterans Charter and Post-World War II Canada*. Montreal and Kingston: McGill-Queen's University Press 1998. Pp.205–23.

Pack, A.J. *Nelson's Blood: The Story of Naval Rum*. Havant, U.K.: Kenneth Mason 1982.

Palmer, Bryan D. *A Culture in Conflict: Skilled Workers and Industrial Capitalism, 1860–1914*. Montreal: McGill-Queen's University Press 1979.

_____. *Cultures of Darkness: Night Travels in the Histories of Transgression*. New York: Monthly Review Press 2000.

_____. *Working-Class Experience: Rethinking the History of Canadian Labour, 1800–1991*. Toronto: McClelland and Stewart 1992.

Park, Julie. "New Zealand." In Heath, ed., *International Handbook*. Pp.201–12.

Park, Peter. "Sketches toward a Political Economy of Drink and Drinking Problems: The Case of 18th and 19th Century England." *JDI*, 13, no.1 (Winter 1983). Pp.57–75.

_____. The Supply Side of Drinking: Alcohol Production and Consumption in the United States before Prohibition." *CDP*, 12, no.4 (Winter 1985). Pp.473–509.

Parker, Marion and Robert Tyrrell. *Rumrunner: The Life and Times of Johnny Schnarr*. Victoria: Orca Books 1988.

Parr, Joy. *Domestic Goods: The Material, the Moral, and the Economic in the Postwar Years*. Toronto: University of Toronto Press 1999.

_____. *Gender of Breadwinners: Women, Men, and Change in Two Industrial Towns, 1880–1950*. Toronto: University of Toronto Press 1990.

_____. "Household Choices as Politics and Pleasure in 1950s Canada." *International Labor and Working-Class History*, 55 (Spring 1999). Pp.112–28.

Parsons, Elaine Frantz. "Risky Business: The Uncertain Boundaries of Manhood in the Midwestern Saloon." *Journal of Social History*, 34, no.2 (Winter 2000). Pp.283–307.

Partanen, Juha. *Sociability and Intoxication: Alcohol and Drinking in Kenya, Africa, and the Modern World*. Helsinki: Finnish Foundation for Alcohol Studies 1991.

Pauly, Philip J. "The Struggle for Ignorance about Alcohol: American Physiologists, Wilbur Olin Atwater, and the Women's Christian Temperance Union." *Bulletin of the History of Medicine*, 64, no.3 (Fall 1990). Pp.366–92.

Payne, Michael. "The Sports, Games, Recreations, and Pastimes of the Fur Traders: Leisure at York Factory." In Morris Mott, ed., *Sports in Canada: Historical Readings*. Toronto: Copp Clark Pitman 1989.

Peele, Stanton. *Diseasing of America: How We Allowed Recovery Zealots and the Treatment Industry to Convince Us We Are out of Control*. San Francisco: Jossey-Bass Publishers 1995.

Peele, Stanton and Marcus Grant. *Alcohol and Pleasure: A Health Perspective*. Philadelphia: Brunner/Mazel 1999.

Peiss, Kathy. *Cheap Amusements: Working Women and Leisure in Turn-of-the Century New York*. Philadelphia: Temple University Press 1986.

_____. Commercial Leisure and the 'Women Question.'" In Butsch, ed., *For Fun and Profit*. Pp.105–17.

_____. "Making up, Making Over: Cosmetics, Consumer Culture, and Women's Identity." In De Grazia with Furlough, eds., *Sex of Things*. Pp.311–36.

Perreault, Michael G. *The Molson Companies Limited: A Corporate Background Report*. Ottawa: Royal Commission on Corporate Concentration, study no.8, Supply and Service Canada 1976.

Perry, Adele. "Gender, Race and the Making of Colonial Society: British Columbia, 1858–1871." Ph.D. thesis, York University 1997.

_____. *On the Edge of Empire: Gender, Race, and the Making of British Columbia, 1849–1871*. Toronto: University of Toronto Press 2001.

Perry, J. Harvey. *Taxes, Tariffs, and Subsidies: A History of Canadian Fiscal Development*. 2 vols. Toronto: University of Toronto Press 1955.

Petrie, J.R. *A Handbook on the Beverage Distilling Industry in Canada*. Montreal: Association of Canadian Distillers 1957.

_____. *Some Economic Facts about the Beverage Distilling Industry in Canada*. Montreal: Association of Canadian Distillers 1961.

Phillips, Glen C. *On Tap: The Odyssey of Beer and Brewing in Victorian London-Middlesex*. Sarnia: Cheshire Cat Press 2000.

Phillips, Jim. "Poverty, Unemployment, and the Administration of the Criminal Law: Vagrancy Laws in Halifax, 1864–1890." In Philip Girard and Jim Phillips, eds., *Essays in the History of Canadian Law*, vol.3, *Nova Scotia*. Toronto: University of Toronto Press 1990. Pp.128–62.

Phillips, Rod. *A Short History of Wine*. London: Penguin 2000.

Phyne, John. "Prohibition's Legacy: The Emergence of Provincial Policing in Nova Scotia, 1921–1932." *Canadian Journal of Law and Society*, 7, no.2 (Fall 1992). Pp.157–84.

Pickersgill, J.W., ed. *The Mackenzie King Record*. Vol.1. *1939–1944*. Toronto: University of Toronto Press 1960.

Pinno, Erhard. "Temperance and Prohibition in Saskatchewan." M.A. thesis, University of Saskatchewan 1971.

Pinson, Ann. "Temperance, Prohibition, and Politics in Nineteenth-Century Iceland." *CDP*, 12, no.2 (Summer 1985). Pp.249–65.

Plant, Martin A. "The United Kingdom." In Heath, ed., *International Handbook*. Pp.289–99.

Plant, Moir. *Women and Alcohol: Contemporary and Historical Perspectives*. London: Free Association Books 1997.

Pollard, Sidney. *The Genesis of Modern Management: A Study of the Industrial Revolution in Great Britain*. London: Penguin 1965.

Pope, Peter. "Fish into Wine: The Historical Anthropology of Demand for Alcohol in Seventeenth-Century Newfoundland." *HS/SH*, 27, no.54 (November 1994). Pp.261–78.

_____. "Historical Archaeology and the Demand for Alcohol in 17th Century Newfoundland." *Acadiensis*, 19, no.1 (Fall 1989). Pp.72–90

Popham, Robert E. "The Social History of the Tavern." In Yedy Israel et al., eds., *Research Advances in Alcohol and Drug Problems*, vol.4. New York: Plenum Press 1978. Pp.225–302.

_____. *Working Papers on the Tavern*. Vol.2. *Legislative History of the Ontario Tavern, 1774–1974*. Substudy no.809. Toronto: Addiction Research Foundation 1976.

_____. *Working Papers on the Tavern*. Vol.3. *Notes on the Contemporary Tavern*. Substudy no.1232. Toronto: Alcoholism and Drug Addiction Research Foundation 1982.

Popham, Robert E. and Wolfgang Schmidt. *A Decade of Alcoholism Research: A Review of the Research Activities of the Alcoholism and Drug Addiction Research Foundation of Ontario, 1951–1961*. Toronto: University of Toronto Press 1962.

_____, comps. *Statistics of Alcohol Use and Alcoholism in Canada, 1871–1956.* Toronto: University of Toronto Press 1958.

Porsild, Charlene. *Gamblers and Dreamers: Women, Men, and Community in the Klondike.* Vancouver: UBC Press 1998.

Porter, Roy. "The Drinking Man's Disease: The 'Pre-History' of Alcoholism in Georgian Britain." *BJA*, 80, no.4 (December 1985). Pp.385–96.

Poutanen, Mary Anne. "'To Indulge Their Carnal Appetites': Prostitution in Early Nineteenth-Century Montreal, 1810–1842." Ph.D. thesis, Université de Montréal 1996.

Powers, Madelon. "Decay from Within: The Inevitable Doom of the American Saloon." In Barrows and Room, eds., *Drinking.* Pp.112–31.

_____. *Faces along the Bar: Lore and Order in the Workingman's Saloon, 1870–1920.* Chicago: University of Chicago Press 1998.

_____. "The 'Poor Man's Friend': Saloonkeepers, Workers, and the Code of Reciprocity in U.S. Barrooms, 1870–1920." *International Labor and Working-Class History*, 45 (Spring 1994). Pp.1–15.

Prang, Margaret. *N.W. Rowell: Ontario Nationalist.* Toronto: University of Toronto Press 1975.

Prestwich, Patricia E. *Drink and the Politics of Social Reform: Antialcoholism in France since 1870.* Palo Alto, Cal.: Society for the Promotion of Science and Scholarship 1988.

_____. "French Workers and the Temperance Movement." *International Review of Social History*, 25 (1980). Pp.35–52.

Prévost, Robert, Suzanne Gagne, and Michel Phaneuf. *L'histoire de l'alcool au Québec.* Montreal: Editions Internationales Alain Stanke 1986.

Proulx, Gilles. *Between France and New France: Life aboard the Tall Sailing Ships.* Toronto: Dundurn Press 1984.

Quinn, John F. *Father Mathew's Crusade: Temperance in Nineteenth-Century Ireland and Irish America.* Amherst: University of Massachusetts Press 2002.

Rannie, William F. *Canadian Whisky: The Product and Industry.* Lincoln, Ont.: W.F. Rannie 1976.

_____. *Wines of Ontario: An Industry Comes of Age.* Lincoln, Ont.: W.F. Rannie 1978.

Ratcliffe, William D. et al. "Drinking in Taverns: A 15-Year Comparison." *International Journal of the Addictions*, 17, no.5 (July 1982). Pp.869–77.

Ray, Arthur J. *The Canadian Fur Trade in the Industrial Age.* Toronto: University of Toronto Press 1990.

_____. "The Hudson's Bay Company Fur Trade in the Eighteenth Century: A Comparative Economic Study." In James R. Gibson, ed., *European Settlement and Development in North America: Essays in Honour and Memory of Andrew Hill Clark.* Toronto: University of Toronto Press 1978. Pp.116–35.

_____. *Indians in the Fur Trade: Their Role as Hunters, Trappers, and Middlemen in the Lands Southwest of Hudson Bay, 1660–1870.* Toronto: University of Toronto Press 1974.

Ray, Arthur J. and Donald Freeman. *'Give Us Good Measure': An Economic Analysis of Relations between the Indians and the Hudson's Bay Company before 1763.* Toronto: University of Toronto Press 1978.

Real Home-Keeper, The. Vancouver, Hamilton, Toronto: Brandow Publishing Company 1913–14 (CIHM nos. 77867, 78449, 78541).

Redman, Stanley R. *Open Gangway: An Account of the Halifax Riots, 1945.* Hantsport, N.S.: Lancelot Press 1981.

Reid, Douglas A. "The Decline of Saint Monday, 1766–1876." *Past and Present*, 71 (May 1976). Pp.76–101.

Reid, Max. "Rum and the Navy." In Morrison and Moreira, eds., *Tempered by Rum.* Pp.31–8.

Reinarman, Craig. "The Social Construction of an Alcohol Problem: The Case of Mothers Against Drunk Drivers and Social Control in the 1980s." *Theory and Society*, 17, no.1 (January 1988). Pp.91–120.

Rich, E.E. *The Fur Trade and the Northwest to 1857.* Toronto: McClelland and Stewart 1967.

Richards, Cara E. "City Taverns." *Human Organization*, 22, no.4 (Winter 1963–64). Pp.260–8.

Riddell, William Renwick. "The First Canadian Bishop and the Trade in Liquor with the Indians." Ontario Historical Society, *Papers and Records*, 27 (1931), 534–9.

_____. "The First Canadian War-Time Prohibition Measure." *CHR*, 1, no.2 (June 1920). Pp.187–90.

Rioux, Christian. *The British Garrison at Quebec, 1759–1871*. Ottawa: Parks Canada, National Historic Sites 1996.

Ripmeester, Michael. "Mines, Homes, and Hall: Place and Identity as a Gold Miner in Rossland, British Columbia, 1898–1901." *Canadian Geographer*, 38, no.2 (Summer 1994). Pp.98–110.

Roberts, H. Julia. "Harry Jones and His Cronies in the Taverns of Kingston, Canada West." *OH*, 95, no.1 (Spring 2003). Pp.1–21.

—————. "'A Mixed Assemblage of Persons': Race and Tavern Space in Upper Canada." *CHR*, 83, no.1 (March 2002). Pp.1–28.

—————. "Taverns and Tavern-Goers in Upper Canada, the 1790s to the 1850s." Ph.D. thesis, University of Toronto 1998.

Roberts, James S. "Alcohol, Public Policy, and the Left: The Socialist Debate in Early Twentieth Century Europe." *CDP*. 12, no.2 (Summer 1985). Pp.309–30.

—————. "Drink and Industrial Discipline in 19th Century Germany." *Journal of Social History*, 15, no.1 (Fall 1981). Pp.25–38.

—————. *Drink, Temperance, and the Working Class in Nineteenth-Century Germany*. Boston: George Allen and Unwin 1984.

—————. "Drink and Working Class Living Standards in Late 19th Century Germany." In Werner Conze and Ulrich Engelhardt, eds., *Arbeiterexistenz im 19. Jahrhundert: Lebensstandard und Lebensgestaltung deutcher Arbeiter und Handwerker*. Stuttgart: Klett-Cona 1981. Pp.74–91.

—————. "The Tavern and Politics in the German Labor Movement, c. 1870–1914." In Barrows and Rooms, eds., *Drinking*. Pp.98–111.

Roberts, Richard. *The Classic Slum: Salford Life in the First Quarter of the Century*. Harmondsworth, U.K.: Penguin Books 1973.

Robinson, Geoff and Dorothy Robinson. *Duty-Free: A Prohibition Special*. Summerside, P.E.I.: The Authors 1992.

—————. *It Came by the Boat Load: Essays on Rum-Running*. Summerside, P.E.I.: The Authors 1984.

—————. *The Nellie J. Banks: Rum-Running to Prince Edward Island*. Tyne Valley, N.S.: The Authors 1980.

Rodgers, Daniel T. *The Work Ethic in Industrial America, 1850–1920*. Chicago: University of Chicago Press 1978.

Rodin, Miriam B. "Getting on the Program: A Biocultural Analysis of Alcoholics Anonymous." In Bennett and Ames, eds., *American Experience with Alcohol*. Pp.41–58.

Roebuck, Julian and S. Lee Spray. "The Cocktail Lounge: A Study in Heterosexual Relations in a Public Organization." *American Journal of Sociology*, 72, no.4 (January 1967). Pp.388–95.

Rogers, Nicholas. "Serving Toronto the Good: The Development of the City Police Force, 1834–84." In Victor L. Russell, ed., *Forging a Consensus: Historical Essays on Toronto*. Toronto: University of Toronto Press 1984. Pp.116–40.

Rohmer, Richard. *E.P. Taylor: The Biography of Edward Plunket Taylor*. Toronto: McClelland and Stewart 1978.

Roland, Charles G. "Health, Disease, and Treatment in Early Upper Canada." In Merrett, Butler, and Power, eds., *Capital Years*. Pp.223–41.

Romney, Paul. *Mr Attorney: The Attorney General for Ontario in Court, Cabinet, and Legislature, 1791–1899*. Toronto: University of Toronto Press 1986.

Ronald, Mary. *The Century Cook Book*. Toronto: Copp Clark 1904 (CIHM no.78337).

Ronnenberg, Herman W. "The American Brewing Industry since 1920." In Wilson and Gourvish, eds., *Dynamics of the International Brewing Industry*. Pp.193–212.

Room, Robin. "Alcohol and Ethnography: A Case of Problem Deflation?" *Current Anthropology*, 25, no.2 (April 1984). Pp.169–78.

—————. "Alcoholism and Alcoholics Anonymous in U.S. Films, 1945–1962: The Party Ends for the 'Wet Generations.'" *JSA*, 50, no.4 (July 1989). Pp.368–83.

—————. "Ambivalence as a Sociological Explanation: The Case of Cultural Explanations of Alcohol Problems." *American Sociological Review*, 41, no.6 (December 1976). Pp.1047–65.

—————. "Drink, Popular Protest, and Government Regulation in Colonial Empires . . ." *Drinking and Drug Practices Surveyor*, 23 (May 1990). Pp.3–6.

_____. "The Formulation of State Alcohol Monopolies and Controls: Case Studies in Five Nations." *CDP*, 12, no.1 (Spring 1985). Pp.1–9.

_____. "The Liquor Question and the Formation of Consciousness: Nation, Ethnicity, and Class at the Turn of the Century." *CDP*, 12, no.2 (Summer 1985). Pp.165–72.

_____. "Sociological Aspects of the Disease Concept of Alcoholism." In Reginald G. Smart et al., eds., *Research Advances on Alcohol and Drug Problems*, vol.7. New York: Plenum Press 1983. Pp.47–91.

_____ "The World Health Organization and Alcohol Control." *BJA*, 79, no.1 (March 1984). Pp.85–92.

Roper, Michael and John Tosh. "Historians and the Politics of Masculinity." In Roper and Tosh, eds., *Manful Assertions: Masculinities in Britain since 1800.* London: Routledge 1991. 1–24.

Rorabaugh, W.J. *The Alcoholic Republic.* New York: Oxford University Press 1979.

Rose, Clifford. *Four Years with the Demon Rum: The Autobiography and Diary of Temperance Inspector Clifford Rose.* Ed. E.R. Forbes and A.A. MacKenzie. Fredericton: Acadiensis Press 1980.

Rose, Kenneth D. *American Women and the Repeal of Reform.* New York: New York University Press 1996.

Rosenfeld, Mark. "'It Was a Hard Life': Class and Gender in the Work and Family Rhythms of a Railway Town, 1920–1950." Canadian Historical Association. *Historical Papers*, 1988. Pp.237–79.

Rosenzweig, Roy. *Eight Hours for What We Will: Workers and Leisure in an Industrial City, 1870–1920.* Cambridge: Cambridge University Press 1983.

Ross, H. Laurence. "Deterrence-Based Policies in Britain, Canada, and Australia." In Michael D. Laurence, John R. Snortum, and Franklin E. Zimring, eds., *Social Control of the Drinking Driver.* Chicago: University of Chicago Press 1988. Pp.64–78.

Rotskoff, Lori. *Love on the Rocks: Men, Women, and Alcohol in Post-World War II America.* Chapel Hill: University of North Carolina Press 2002.

Rotundo, E. Anthony. *American Manhood: Transformations in Masculinity from the Revolution to the Modern Era.* New York: Basic Books 1993.

_____. "Learning about Manhood: Gender Ideals and the Middle-Class Family in Nineteenth-Century America." In Mangan and Walvin, eds., *Manliness and Morality.* Pp.35–51.

Rousseau, Louis. "Boire ou ne pas boire, se sauver ou se perdre ensemble: Le mouvement de tempérance dans le Québec du XIXe siècle." *Études canadiennes/Canadian Studies*, 35 (1993). Pp.107–21.

Rousseau, Louis and Frank W. Remiggi, eds. *Atlas historique des pratiques religieuses: Le sud-ouest du Québec au XIXe siècle.* Ottawa: Les Presses de l'Université d'Ottawa 1998.

Rowbotham, Judith. "'Only When Drunk': The Stereotyping of Violence in England, c. 1850–1900." In D'Cruze, ed., *Everyday Violence.* Pp.155–69.

Rowe, Percy. *The Wines of Canada.* Toronto: McGraw-Hill Company 1970.

Rowntree, Joseph and Arthur Shadwell. *The Temperance Problem and Social Reform.* London: Hodder and Stoughton 1899.

Rubington, Earl. "The Bottle Gang." *QJSA*, 29, no.4 (December 1968). Pp.943–55.

Rudy, Robert Jarrett. "Manly Smokes: Tobacco Consumption and the Construction of Identities in Industrial Montreal, 1888–1914." Ph.D. thesis, McGill University 2001.

_____. "Sleeman's: Small Business in the Ontario Brewing Industry, 1847–1916." Memoire de maitrise, Université d'Ottawa 1993.

Rumbarger, John J. *Profits, Power, and Prohibition: Alcohol Reform and the Industrializing of America, 1800–1930.* Albany: State University of New York Press 1989.

Rush, Brian R. and Alan C. Ogborne. "Alcoholism Treatment in Canada: History, Current Status, and Emerging Issues." In Harald Klingemann et al., eds., *Cure, Care, or Control: Alcoholism Treatment in Sixteen Countries.* Albany: State University of New York Press 1992.

Rutherford, Paul, ed. *Saving the Canadian City: The First Phase, 1880–1920, An Anthology of Early Articles on Urban Reform.* Toronto: University of Toronto Press 1974.

Ryan, Mary P. *Cradle of the Middle Class: The Family in Oneida County, New York, 1790–1865.* New York: Cambridge University Press 1981.

Sager, Eric W. *Seafaring Labour: The Merchant Marine of Atlantic Canada, 1820–1914.* Montreal and Kingston: McGill-Queen's University Press 1989.

Saggers, Sherry. "Dry Damp and Wet Revisited: Alcohol Control Policies in Indigenous Australia and Canada." *Australian-Canadian Studies*, 19, no.1 (2001). Pp.83–104.

Samson, Roch. *Les Forges du Saint-Maurice: Les débuts de l'industrie sidérurgique au Canada, 1730–1883*. Quebec: Les Presses de l'Université Laval 1998.

Saracino, Mary E. "Household Production of Alcoholic Beverages in Early-Eighteenth-Century Connecticut." *JSA*, 46, no.3 (May 1985). Pp.244–52.

Sariola, Sakari. "The Finnish Temperance Movement in the Great Lakes Area of the Midwest." *CDP*, 12, no.2 (Summer 1985). Pp.287–307.

_____. "Prohibition in Finland, 1919–1932." *QJSA*, 15, no.3 (September 1954). Pp.477–90.

Sauvalle, M. *Mille questions d'étiquette: discutées, resolues et classées*. Montreal: Librarie Beauchemin 1907 (CIHM no.66289).

Saywell, John T. *"Just Call Me Mitch": The Life of Mitchell F. Hepburn*. Toronto: University of Toronto Press 1991.

_____. *The Lawmakers: Judicial Power and the Shaping of Canadian Federalism*. Toronto: University of Toronto Press 2002.

Schilz, Thomas F. "Brandy and Beaver Pelts: Assiniboine-European Trading Patterns, 1695–1805." *Saskatchewan History*, 37, no.3 (Autumn 1984). Pp.95–102.

Schioler, Peter. "Denmark." In Heath, ed., *International Handbook*. Pp.51–62.

Schivelbusch, Wolfgang. *Tastes of Paradise: A Social History of Spices, Stimulants, and Intoxicants*. New York: Pantheon 1992.

Schlase, Megan. "Liquor and the Indian Post WWII." *B.C. Historical News*, 29, no.2 (Spring 1996). Pp.26–9.

Schluter, Hermann. *The Brewing Industry and the Brewery Workers' Movement in America*. New York: B. Franklin 1970 [1910].

Schmidt, Wolfgang, Reginald G. Smart, and Marcia K. Moss. *Social Class and the Treatment of Alcoholism: An Investigation of Social Class as a Determinant of Diagnosis, Prognosis, and Therapy*. Toronto: University of Toronto Press 1968.

Schneider, Dorothee. "The German Brewery Workers of New York City in the Late Nineteenth Century." In Robert Asher and Charles Stephenson, eds., *Labor Divided: Race and Ethnicity in United States Labor Struggles, 1835–1960*. Albany: State University of New York Press 1990. Pp.189–207.

Schwantes, Carol A. *Radical Heritage: Labor, Socialism, and Reform in Washington and British Columbia, 1885–1917*. Seattle: University of Washington Press 1979.

Semple, Neil. *The Lord's Dominion: The History of Canadian Methodism*. Montreal and Kingston: McGill-Queen's University Press 1996.

Sendbuehler, M.P. "Battling 'The Bane of Our Cities': Class, Territory, and the Prohibition Debate in Toronto, 1877." *Urban History Review*, 22, no.1 (October 1993). Pp.30–48.

Senior, Elinor Kyte. *British Regulars in Montreal: An Imperial Garrison, 1832–1854*. Montreal: McGill-Queen's University Press 1981.

75 Years of Progress. Don Mills: Canadian Union of United Brewery, Flour, Cereal, Soft Drink and Distillery Workers, Local 304 [1977].

Sharma, Hari Kesh and Davinder Mohan. "Changing Sociocultural Perspectives on Alcohol: Consumption in India: A Case Study." In Peel and Grant, eds., *Alcohol and Pleasure*. Pp.101–12.

Sheehan, Nancy. "National Pressure Groups and Provincial Curriculum Policy: Temperance in Nova Scotia Schools, 1880–1930." *Canadian Journal of Education*, 9, no.1 (Winter 1984). Pp.73–88.

_____. "The WCTU and Educational Strategies on the Canadian Prairie." *History of Education Quarterly*, 24, no.1 (Spring 1984). Pp.101–19.

Sherratt, Andrew. "Alcohol and Its Alternatives: Symbol and Substance in Pre-Industrial Cultures." In Jordon Goodman, Paul E. Lovejoy, and Andrew Sherratt, eds., *Consuming Habits: Drugs in History and Anthropology*. London: Routledge 1995. Pp.11–46.

Shiman, Lilian Lewis. "John B. Gough: Trans-Atlantic Temperance Orator." *Social History of Alcohol Review*, 15, nos. 3–4 (Spring/Summer 2001). Pp.20–9.

Shinfuku, Naotaka. "Japanese Culture and Drinking." In Peel and Grant, eds., *Alcohol and Pleasure*. Pp.113–19.

Shipkey, Robert. "Problems in Alcohol Production and Controls in Early Nineteenth-Century Ireland." *Historical Journal*, 16, no.2 (1973). Pp.291–302.

Shoniker, Robert G. *Rothmans of Canada Limited and Carling O'Keefe Limited*. Ottawa: Royal Commission on Corporate Concentration, study no.11, Supply and Services Canada 1977.

Shortt, S.E.D. "Social Change and Political Crisis in Rural Ontario: The Patrons of Industry, 1889–1896." In Swainson, ed., *Oliver Mowat's Ontario*. Pp.211–35.

——————. *Victorian Lunacy: Richard M. Bucke and the Practice of Late Nineteenth-Century Psychiatry*. Cambridge: Cambridge University Press 1986.

Shuttleworth, E.B. *The Windmill and Its Times: A Series of Articles Dealing with the Early Days of the Windmill*. Toronto: Edward D. Apted 1924.

Single, Eric. "Public Drinking." In Marc Galanter, ed., *Recent Developments in Alcoholism*, vol.11, *Ten Years of Progress*. New York: Plenum Press 1993. Pp.143–52.

——————. "Studies of Public Drinking: An Overview." In Single and Storm, eds., *Public Drinking and Public Policy*. Pp.5–34.

Single, Eric and Norman Griesbrecht. *Rates of Alcohol Consumption and Patterns of Drinking in Ontario, 1950–1975*. Toronto: Addiction Research Foundation 1979.

Single, Eric, Norman Griesbrecht, and Barry Eakins. "The Alcohol Policy Debate in Ontario in the Post-War Era." In Single, Morgan, and De Lint, eds., *Alcohol, Society, and the State*, vol.2. Pp.127–57.

Single, Eric, Patricia Morgan, and Jan De Lint, eds. *Alcohol, Society, and the State*. Vol.2. *The Social History of Control Policy in Seven Countries*. Toronto: Addiction Research Foundation 1981.

Single, Eric and Henry Pomeroy. "Drinking and Setting: A Season for All Things." In Peel and Grant, eds., *Alcohol and Pleasure*. Pp.265–76.

Single, Eric and Thomas Storm, eds. *Public Drinking and Public Policy: Proceedings of a Symposium on Observation Studies Held at Banff, Alberta, Canada. April 26–28, 1984*. Toronto: Addiction Research Foundation 1984.

Single, Eric, Bob Williams, and Diane McKenzie. *Canadian Profile: Alcohol, Tobacco, and Other Drugs*. Ottawa and Toronto: Canadian Centre on Substance Abuse and Addiction Research Foundation 1994.

Single, Eric and Scott Wortley. "Drinking in Various Settings As It Relates to Demographic Variables and Level of Consumption: Findings from a National Survey in Canada." *JSA*, 54, no.5 (September 1993). Pp.590–9.

Smart, Reginald G. "Does Alcohol Advertising Affect Overall Consumption? A Review of Empirical Studies." *JSA*, 49, no.4 (July 1988). Pp.314–23.

——————. "The Happy Hours Experiment in North America." *CDP*, 23, no.2 (Summer 1996). Pp.291–300.

——————. "Is the Postwar Drinking Binge Ending? Cross-National Trends in Per Capita Alcohol Consumption." *BJA*, 84, no.7 (July 1989). Pp.743–8.

——————. *The New Drinkers: Teenage Use and Abuse of Alcohol*. Toronto: Addiction Research Foundation 1980.

——————. "Socio-Economic, Lifestyle, and Availability Factors in the Stabilization of Alcohol Consumption in Canada." *Canadian Journal of Public Health*, 78, no.3 (May/June 1987). Pp.176–80.

Smart, Reginald G. and Edward M. Adlaf. "Banning Happy Hours: The Impact on Drinking and Impaired-Driving Charges in Ontario, Canada." *JSA*, 47, no.3 (May 1986). Pp.256–8.

Smart, Reginald G. and David Docherty. "Effects of the Introduction of On-Premise Drinking on Alcohol-Related Accidents and Impaired Driving." *JSA*, 37, no.5 (May 1976). Pp.683–6.

Smart, Reginald G. and Michael S. Goodstadt. "Effects of Reducing the Legal Alcohol-Purchasing Age on Drinking and Drinking Problems: A Review of Empirical Studies." *JSA*, 38, no.7 (July 1977). Pp.13113–23.

Smart, Reginald G. and Robert E. Mann. "Treatment, Health Promotion, and Alcohol Controls and the Decrease of Alcohol Consumption and Problems in Ontario: 1975–1993." *Alcohol and Alcoholism*, 30, no.3 (May 1995). Pp.337–43.

Smart, Reginald G. and Alan C. Ogborne. *Northern Spirits: A Social History of Alcohol in Canada*. Toronto: Addiction Research Foundation 1996.

Smith, David. "Drinking and Imprisonment in Late Victorian and Edwardian Scotland." *HS/SH*, 19, no.37 (May 1986). Pp.161–76.

Smith-Rosenberg, Carroll. "The New Woman as Androgyne: Social Disorder and Gender Crisis, 1870–1936." In Smith-Rosenberg. *Disorderly Conduct: Visions of Gender in Victorian America.* New York: Oxford University Press 1985.

Sneath, Allen Winn. *Brewed in Canada: The Untold Story of Canada's 350-Year-Old Brewing Industry.* Toronto: Dundurn Group 2001.

Snell, James G. *In the Shadow of the Law: Divorce in Canada, 1900–1939.* Toronto: University of Toronto Press 1991.

_____. "Marital Cruelty: Women and the Nova Scotia Divorce Court, 1900–1939." *Acadiensis*, 18, no.1 (Autumn 1988). Pp.3–32.

Snyder, Charles R. *Alcohol and the Jews: A Cultural Study of Drinking and Sobriety.* New Brunswick, N.J.: Yale University Center of Alcohol Studies 1958.

Snyder, Robert W. "Big Time, Small Time, All Around the Town: New York Vaudeville in the Early Twentieth Century." In Butsch, ed., *For Fun and Profit.* Pp.118–35.

_____. *The Voice of the City: Vaudeville and Popular Culture in New York.* New York: Oxford University Press 1989.

Sobel, David and Susan Meurer. *Working at Inglis: The Life and Death of a Canadian Factory.* Toronto: James Lorimer and Company 1994.

Solomon, Robert R. and Melvyn Green. "The First Century: The History of Non-Medical Opiate Use and Control Policies in Canada, 1870–1970." In Judith C. Blackwell and Patricia G. Erickson, eds., *Illicit Drugs in Canada: A Risky Business.* Scarborough, Ont.: Nelson Canada 1988.

Somerville, Alexander. "Description of the Distillery of Messrs. Gooderham and Worts, Toronto, Canada West, April 1863." *Canadian Illustrated News* (Hamilton), 25 April 1863, Supplement.

Sommer, Robert. "The Isolated Beer Drinker in the Edmonton Beer Parlor." *QJSA*, 26, no.1 (March 1965). Pp.95–110.

Sonnenstuhl, William J. *Working Sober: The Transformation of an Occupational Culture.* Ithaca, N.Y.: Cornell University Press 1996.

Sournia, Jean-Charles. *A History of Alcoholism.* Oxford: Basil Blackwell 1990.

Spence, Ben H. "Prohibitory Legislation in Canada." In American Academy of Political and Social Sciences, *Annals*, 109 (September 1923). Pp.230–64.

_____. *Quebec and the Liquor Problem.* Westerville, Ohio: American Issue Publishing Company n.d.

Spence, F.S. *The Facts of the Case: A Summary of the Most Important Evidence and Argument Presented in the Royal Commission on the Liquor Traffic.* Toronto: Newton and Treloar 1896.

Spence, Ruth Elizabeth. *Prohibition in Canada.* Toronto: Ontario Branch of the Dominion Alliance 1919.

Spode, Hasso. "The First Step Toward Sobriety: The 'Boozing Devil' in Sixteenth-Century Germany." *CDP*, 21, no.3 (Fall 1994). Pp.453–83.

Spradley, James P. *You Owe Yourself a Drunk: An Ethnography of Urban Nomads.* Prospect Heights, Ill.: Waveland Press 2000.

Spray, W.A. *The Blacks in New Brunswick.* [Fredericton]: Brunswick Press 1972.

Stage, Sarah. *Female Complaints: Lydia Pinkham and the Business of Women's Medicine.* New York: W.W. Norton and Company 1979.

Stanley, George F.G. "The Indians and the Brandy Trade during the Ancien Regime." *Revue d'histoire de l'Amérique française*, 6, no.4 (March 1953). Pp.489–505.

Stivers, Richard. *A Hair of the Dog: Irish Drinking and American Stereotype.* University Park: Pennsylvania State University Press 1976.

Storm, Thomas and R.E. Cutler. "The Functions of Taverns." In Single and Storm, eds., *Public Drinking and Public Policy.* Pp.35–47.

_____. "Observations of Drinking in Natural Settings: Vancouver Beer Parlors and Cocktail Lounges." *JSA*, 42, no.11 (November 1981). Pp.972–97.

Strachan, J. George. "Industry Discovers Alcoholism." *Industrial Canada*, February 1959. Pp.41–4.

Strange, Carolyn. *Toronto's Girl Problem: The Perils and Pleasures of the City, 1880–1930.* Toronto: University of Toronto Press 1995.

Strange, Carolyn and Tina Loo. *Making Good: Law and Moral Regulation in Canada, 1867–1939*. Toronto: University of Toronto Press 1997.

Strasser, Susan. *Satisfaction Guaranteed: The Making of the American Mass Market*. Washington, D.C.: Smithsonian Institution Press 1989.

Stretch, Dianne Kathryn. "From Prohibition to Government Control: The Liquor Question in Alberta, 1909–1929." M.A. thesis, University of Alberta 1979.

Strong, Cyril W. *My Life as a Newfoundland Union Organizer: The Memoirs of Cyril W. Strong, 1912–1987*. St. John's, Nfld.: Committee on Canadian Labour History 1987.

Strong-Boag, Veronica. *The New Day Recalled: Lives of Girls and Women in English Canada, 1919–1939*. Toronto: Copp Clark Pitman 1988.

——————. *The Parliament of Women: The National Council of Women of Canada, 1893–1929*. Ottawa: National Museums of Canada 1976.

Strople, Margaret J. (Campbell). "Prohibition and Movements of Social Reform in Nova Scotia, 1894–1920." M.A. thesis, Dalhousie University 1974.

Sturgis, J.L. "Beer under Pressure: The Origins of Prohibition in Canada." *Bulletin of Canadian Studies*, 8, no.1 (Spring 1984). Pp.83–100.

——————. "'The Spectre of a Drunkard's Grave': One Family's Battle with Alcohol in Late Nineteenth-Century Canada." In Warsh, ed., *Drink in Canada*. Pp.115–43.

Sugiman, Pamela. *Labour's Dilemma: The Gender Politics of Auto Workers in Canada, 1937–1979*. Toronto: University of Toronto Press 1994.

Sulkunen, Irma. *History of the Finnish Temperance Movement: Temperance as a Civic Religion*. Lewiston, N.Y.: Edwin Mellen Press 1990.

——————. "Temperance as a Civic Religion: The Cultural Foundation of the Finnish Working-Class Temperance Ideology." *CDP*, 12, no.2 (Summer 1985). Pp.267–85.

Sulkunen, Pekka. "Alcohol Consumption and the Transformation of Living Conditions: A Comparative Study." In Reginald G. Smart et al., eds., *Research Advances in Alcohol and Drug Problems*, vol.7. New York: Plenum Press 1983. Pp.247–97.

——————. "Drinking Patterns and the Level of Alcohol Consumption: An International Overview." In Robert J. Gibbins et al., eds., *Research Advances in Alcohol and Drug Problems*, vol.3. New York: John Wiley and Sons 1976. Pp.223–81.

Surprenant, Daniel. "Une institution québécoise: la Société des alcools du Québec." *Études canadiennes/ Canadian Studies*, 35 (1993). Pp.27–52.

Swainson, Donald, ed. *Oliver Mowat's Ontario*. Toronto: Macmillan 1972.

Swiencicki, Mark A. "Consuming Brotherhood: Men's Culture, Style, and Recreation as Consumer Culture, 1880–1930." *Journal of Social History*, 31, no.4 (Summer 1998). Pp.773–808.

Taylor, John H. "Fire, Disease, and Water in Ottawa: An Introduction." *Urban History Review*, 8, no.1 (June 1979). Pp.7–37.

Taylor, Margaret and Frances McNaught, comps. *The New Galt Cook Book . . .* Toronto: McLeod and Allen 1898 (CIHM no.38741).

Tennyson, Brian Douglas. "Sir William Hearst and the Ontario Temperance Act." *OH*, 55, no.4 (December 1963). Pp.233–45.

Thomas, Anthony E. "Class and Sociability among Urban Workers: A Study of the Bar as Social Club." *Medical Anthropology*, 2, no.4 (Fall 1978). Pp.9–30.

Thomas, Lewis G. *The Prairie West to 1905: A Canadian Sourcebook*. Toronto: Oxford University Press 1975.

Thompson, E.P. "Time, Work Discipline, and Industrial Capitalism." In Thompson, *Customs in Common: Studies in Traditional Popular Culture*. New York: New Press 1993. Pp.352–403.

Thompson, F.M.L. "Social Control in Victorian Britain." *Economic History Review*, 34, no.2 (May 1981). Pp.189–208.

Thompson, John Herd. "'The Beginning of Our Regeneration': The Great War and Western Canadian Reform Movements." *HP* 1972. Pp.227–45.

——————. *The Harvests of War: The Prairie West, 1914–1918*. Toronto: McClelland and Stewart 1978.

——————. "The Prohibition Question in Manitoba, 1892–1928." M.A. thesis, University of Manitoba 1969.

_____. "The Voice of Moderation: The Defeat of Prohibition in Manitoba." In S.M. Trofimenkoff, ed., *The Twenties in Western Canada*. Ottawa: National Museum of Man 1972. Pp.170–90.

Thompson, Peter. *Rum Punch and Revolution: Taverngoing and Public Life in Eighteenth-Century Philadelphia*. Philadelphia: University of Philadelphia Press 1999.

Thorner, Thomas and Neil B. Watson. "Keeper of the King's Peace: Colonel G.E. Sanders and the Calgary Police Magistrate's Court, 1911–1932." *Urban History Review*, 12, no.3 (February 1984). Pp.45–55.

Timberlake, James H. *Prohibition and the Progressive Movement, 1900–1920*. Cambridge, Mass.: Harvard University Press 1963.

Tlusty, Beverly Ann. *Bacchus and Civic Order: The Culture of Drink in Early Modern Germany*. Charlottesville: University Press of Virginia 2001.

_____. "Defining 'Drunk' in Early Modern Germany." *CDP*, 21, no.3 (Fall 1994). Pp.427–51.

_____. "Gender and Alcohol in Early Modern Augsburg." *HS/SH*, 54 (November 1994). Pp.241–59.

_____. "Water of Life, Water of Death: The Controversy over Brandy and Gin in Early Modern Augsburg." *Central European History*, 31, no.1–2 (1998). Pp.1–30.

Tobias, John L. "Protection, Civilization, Assimilation: An Outline History of Canada's Indian Policy." In J.R. Miller, ed., *Sweet Promises: A Reader on Indian-White Relations in Canada*. Toronto: University of Toronto Press 1991. Pp.127–44.

Toronto by Gaslight: The Night Hawks of a Great City, as Seen by the Reporters of "The Toronto News". Toronto: Edmund E. Sheppard n.d.

Townend, Paul A. *Father Mathew, Temperance, and Irish Identity*. Dublin: Irish Academic Press 2002.

Trades and Labor Congress of Canada. *Report of the Proceedings of the Annual Convention*. N.p. 1900–29.

Trainor, Brian Paul. "Towards a Genealogy of Temperance: Identity, Belief, and Drink in Victorian Ontario." Ph.D. thesis, Queen's University 1993.

Trice, Harrison M. "A History of Job-Based Alcoholism Programs: 1900–1955." *JDI*, 11, no.2 (Spring 1981). Pp.171–98.

Trudel, Marcel. *Chiniquy*. Trois-Rivières: Editions du Bien Public 1955.

Tucker, Albert. "Labatt's: A History—From Immigrant Family to Canadian Corporation." Unpublished manuscript.

Tyrrell, Ian R. *Sobering Up: From Temperance to Prohibition in Antebellum America, 1800–1860*. Westport, Conn.: Greenwood Press 1979.

_____. "Prohibition, American Cultural Expansion, and the New Hegemony in the 1920s: An Interpretation." *HS/SH*, 27, no.54 (November 1994). Pp.413–45.

_____. "Temperance and Economic Change in the Antebellum North." In Blocker, ed., *Alcohol, Reform, and Society*. Pp.45–68.

_____. "Women and Temperance in International Perspective: The World's WCTU, 1880–1920s." In Barrows and Room, eds., *Drinking*. Pp.217–40.

_____. *Woman's World, Woman's Empire: The Woman's Christian Temperance Union in International Perspective, 1880–1930*. Chapel Hill: University of North Carolina Press 1991.

Union with a Heart, 1886–1961. N.p.: International Union of United Brewery, Flour, Soft Drink, and Distillery Workers 1961.

Vachon, André. "Cabarets de la Nouvelle-France." *Toxicomanies*, 1, no.3 (September–December 1968). Pp.327–9.

_____. "De l'abitation de Québec à l'hostellerie de Jacques Boisdon (1608–1648)." *Toxicomanies*, 1, no.1 (January–April 1968). Pp.99–103.

_____. "L'eau-de-vie dans la société indienne." Canadian Historical Association. *Report*. 1960. Pp.22–32.

Vaillancourt, Emile. *The History of the Brewing Industry in the Province of Quebec*. Montreal: G. Ducharme 1940.

Valverde, Mariana. *The Age of Light, Soap, and Water: Moral Reform in English Canada, 1885–1925*. Toronto: McClelland and Stewart 1991.

_____. *Diseases of the Will: Alcohol and the Dilemmas of Freedom*. Cambridge: Cambridge University Press 1999.

_____. "'Slavery from Within': The Invention of Alcoholism and the Question of Free Will." *Social History*, 22, no.3 (October 1997). Pp.251–68.

_____. "Symbolic Indians: Domestic Violence and the Ontario Liquor Board's 'Indian List,' 1950–1990." Forthcoming.

Valverde, Mariana and Kimberley White-Mair. "'One Day at a Time' and Other Slogans for Everyday Life: The Ethical Practices of Alcoholics Anonymous." *Sociology*, 33, no.2 (May 1999). Pp.393–410.

Van Die, Marguerite, ed. *Religion and Public Life in Canada: Historical and Comparative Perspectives*. Toronto: University of Toronto Press 2001.

Van Onselen, Charles. "Randlords and Rotgut: An Essay on the Role of Alcohol in the Development of European Imperialism and Southern African Capitalism, with Special Reference to Black Mineworkers in the Transvaal Republic." *History Workshop*, 2 (Autumn 1976). Pp.33–89.

Veer, Joanne E. "Feminist Forebears: The Woman's Christian Temperance Union in Canada's Maritime Provinces, 1875–1900." Ph.D. thesis, University of New Brunswick 1994.

Vernette, Luce. *Domestic Life at Les Forges du Saint-Maurice*. Ottawa: Parks Canada, National Historic Parks and Sites Branch 1982.

Vingilis, Evelyn and Reginald G. Smart. "Effects of Raising the Legal Drinking Age in Ontario." *BJA*, 76, no.4 (December 1981). Pp.415–24.

Vigod, Bernard L. *Quebec before Duplessis: The Political Career of Louis-Alexandre Taschereau*. Montreal and Kingston: McGill-Queen's University Press 1986.

Vipond, Robert C. *Liberty and Community: Canadian Federalism and the Failure of the Constitution*. Albany: State University of New York Press 1991.

Vogt, Irmgard. "Cultural Beliefs and Government Propensities to Control or Ignore Drinking Problems: An Historical Comparison of Germany and the U.S." *Drinking and Drug Practices Surveyor*, 17 (September 1981). Pp.4–8.

_____. "Defining Alcohol Problems as a Repressive Mechanism: Its Formative Phase in Imperial Germany and Its Strength Today." *International Journal of the Addictions*, 19, no.5 (August 1984). Pp.551–69.

Voisine, Nive. "Mouvement de tempérance et religion populaire." In Benoit Lacroix and Jean Simard, eds., *Religion populaire, religion de clercs?* Quebec: Institut québécois de recherche sur la culture 1984. Pp.65–78.

Waite, P.B. "The Fall and Rise of the Smashers, 1856–1857: Some Private Letters of Manners-Sutton." *Acadiensis*, 2, no.1 (Autumn 1972). Pp.65–70.

_____. *The Man from Halifax: Sir John Thomson, Prime Minister*. Toronto: University of Toronto Press 1985.

_____. "Sir Oliver Mowat's Canada: Reflections on an Un-Victorian Society." In Swainson, ed., *Oliver Mowat's Ontario*. Pp.12–32.

Walden, Keith. *Becoming Modern in Toronto: The Industrial Exhibition and the Shaping of a Late Victorian Culture*. Toronto: University of Toronto Press 1997.

Walker, Samuel. "Terence V. Powderly, the Knights of Labor, and the Temperance Issue." *Societas*, 5, no.4 (Autumn 1975). Pp.279–93.

Wallot, Jean-Pierre. "Religion and French-Canadian Mores in the Early Nineteenth Century." *CHR*, 52, no.1 (March 1971). Pp.51–91.

Walsh, Dermot and Brendan Walsh. "Drowning the Shamrock: Alcohol and Drink in Ireland in the Post-War Period." In Single, Morgan, and De Lint, eds., *Alcohol, Society, and the State,* vol.2. Pp.103–26.

Walton, Stuart. *Out of It: A Cultural History of Intoxication*. London: Hamish Hamilton 2001.

Wamsley, Kevin B. and Robert S. Kossuth. "Fighting It Out in Nineteenth-Century Upper Canada/Canada West: Masculinities and Physical Challenges in the Tavern." *Journal of Sport History*, 27, no.3 (Fall 2000). Pp.405–30.

Warburton, Clark. *The Economic Results of Prohibition*. New York: Columbia University Press 1932.

Warf, Chris. "The Search for Pure Water in Ottawa: 1910–1915." *Urban History Review*, 8, no.1 (June 1979). Pp.90–112.

Warner, John Harley. "Physiological Theory and Therapeutic Explanation in the 1860s: The British Debate on the Medical Use of Alcohol." *Bulletin of the History of Medicine*, 54, no.2 (Summer 1980). Pp.235–57.

Warner, Jessica. "Historical Perspectives on the Shifting Boundaries around Youth and Alcohol: The Example of Pre-Industrial England, 1350–1750." *Addiction*, 93, no.5 (May 1998). Pp.641–57.

—————. "In Another City, in Another Time: Rhetoric and the Creation of a Drug Scare in Eighteenth-Century London." *CDP*, 21, no.3 (Fall 1994). Pp.485–511.

—————. "'Resolv'd to Drink No More': Addiction as a Preindustrial Construct." *JSA*, 55, no.6 (November 1994). Pp.685–91.

Warsh, Cheryl Krasnick. "Adventures in Maritime Quackery: The Leslie E. Keeley Gold Cure Institute of Fredericton, N.B." *Acadiensis*, 17, no.2 (Spring 1988). Pp.109–30.

—————. "Because There Is Pain: Alcoholism, Temperance, and the Victorian Physician." *Canadian Bulletin of Medical History*, 2, no.1 (Summer 1985). Pp.1–22.

—————, ed. *Drink in Canada: Historical Essays*. Montreal and Kingston: McGill-Queen's University Press 1993.

—————. "'John Barleycorn Must Die': An Introduction to the Social History of Alcohol." In Warsh, ed., *Drink in Canada*. Pp.3–26.

—————. *Moments of Unreason: The Practice of Canadian Psychiatry and the Homewood Retreat, 1883–1923*. Montreal and Kingston: McGill-Queen's University Press 1989.

—————. "'Oh, Lord, Pour a Cordial in Her Wounded Heart': The Drinking Woman in Victorian and Edwardian Canada." In Warsh, ed., *Drink in Canada*. Pp.70–91.

—————. "Smoke and Mirrors: Gender Representation in North American Tobacco and Alcohol Advertisements before 1950." *HS/SH*, 31, no.62 (November 1998). Pp.183–222.

Wascan, S. *Behind the Green Curtains: A True Story of the Beer Parlors*. Edmonton: Alberta Printing Company 1933.

Wasserman, Ira M. "Prohibition and Ethnocultural Conflict: The Missouri Prohibition Referendum of 1918." *Social Science Quarterly*, 70, no.4 (December 1989). Pp.886–901.

Waters, Chris. *British Socialists and the Politics of Popular Culture, 1884–1914*. Manchester, U.K.: Manchester University Press 1990.

Waters, Harold. *Smugglers of Spirits: Prohibition and the Coast Guard Patrol*. New York: Hastings House 1971.

Watson, George and Ilene Watson. *Pioneer Breweries of British Columbia*. Nanaimo, B.C.: Westward Collector Publishing 1974.

Way, Peter. *Common Labour: Workers and the Digging of North American Canals, 1780–1860*. Cambridge: Cambridge University Press 1993.

—————. "Evil Humors and Ardent Spirits: The Rough Culture of Canal Construction Laborers." *Journal of American History*, 79, no.4 (March 1993). Pp.1397–428.

Weaver, John. *Crimes, Constables, and Courts: Order and Transgression in a Canadian City, 1816–1970*. Toronto: McGill-Queen's University Press 1995.

—————. "Crime, Public Order, and Repression: The Gore District in Upheaval, 1832–1851." In R.C. Macleod, ed., *Lawful Authority: Readings on the History of Criminal Justice in Canada*. Toronto: Copp Clark Pitman 1988. Pp.22–48.

Weintraub, William. *City Unique: Montreal Days and Nights in the 1940s and '50s*. Toronto: McClelland and Stewart 1996.

Weir, R.B. "Obsessed with Moderation: The Drink Trades and the Drink Question (1870–1930)." *BJA*, 79 (1984). Pp.93–107.

Weir, Robert E. *Beyond Labor's Veil: The Culture of the Knights of Labor*. University Park: Pennsylvania State University Press 1996.

Weisner, Merry E. "*Wandervogels* and Women: Journeymen's Concepts of Masculinity in Early Modern Germany." *Journal of Social History*, 24, no.4 (Summer 1991). Pp.767–82.

Westley, Margaret W. *Remembrance of Grandeur: The Anglo-Protestant Elite of Montreal, 1900–1950*. Montreal: Libre Expression 1990.

Wexman, Virginia Wright. *Creating the Couple: Love, Marriage, and Hollywood Performance*. Princeton, N.J.: Princeton University Press 1993.

White, James, Anita Fallis, and Eric Pickett. *An Investigation into the Effects of Alcohol Use in Ontario Schools.* Toronto: Ontario Ministry of Education 1978.

White, William L. *Slaying the Dragon: The History of Addiction Treatment and Recovery in America.* Bloomington, Ill.: Chestnut Health Systems/Lighthouse Institute 1998.

Whitehead, Paul C. *Young Drinkers: A Review of Recent Canadian Studies.* Ottawa: Health and Welfare Canada, Health Promotion Directorate 1984.

Whitehead, Paul C. and Michael J. Hayes. *The Insanity of Alcohol: Social Problems in Canadian First Nations Communities.* Toronto: Canadian Scholars' Press 1998.

Whitfeld, Carol. *Tommy Atkins: The British Soldier in Canada, 1759–1870.* Ottawa: National Historic Parks and Sites Branch, Parks Canada 1981.

Wilentz, Sean. *Chants Democratic: New York City and the Rise of the American Working Class, 1788–1850.* New York: Oxford University Press 1984.

Williams, Sara E. "The Use of Beverage Alcohol as Medicine, 1790–1860." *JSA*, 41, no.5 (May 1980). Pp.543–64.

Willison, Sir John. "Liquor Control in Western Canada." In Archives of Ontario, F8 (Howard Ferguson Papers), MU1029 ("Papers Concerning the Temperance Question in Ontario, 1907–1929").

Wilson, C. Anne. "Water of Life: Its Beginnings and Early History." In Wilson ed., *"Liquid Nourishment": Potable Foods and Stimulating Drinks.* Edinburgh: University of Edinburgh Press 1993. Pp.142–64.

Wilson, Catharine Anne. "Reciprocal Work Bees and the Meaning of Neighbourhood." *CHR*, 82, no.3 (September 2001). Pp.431–64.

Wilson, R.G. and T.R. Gourvish, eds. *The Dynamics of the International Brewing Industry since 1800.* London: Routledge 1998.

Winkler, Allan M. "Drinking on the American Frontier." *Quarterly Journal of Alcohol Studies*, 29, no.2 (June 1968). Pp.413–45.

Winks, Robin W. *The Blacks in Canada: A History.* Montreal and Kingston: McGill-Queen's University Press 1997.

Wodson, Harry M. *The Whirlpool: Scenes from Toronto Police Court.* Toronto: n.p. 1917.

Woodsworth, J.S. *My Neighbour: A Study of City Conditions, A Plea for Social Service.* Toronto: University of Toronto Press 1972 [1911].

⸻⸻. *Strangers within Our Gates, Or Coming Canadians.* Toronto: University of Toronto Press 1972 [1909].

Wright, Cynthia. "'Feminine Trifles of Vast Importance': Writing Gender into the History of Consumption." In Franca Iacovetta and Mariana Valverde, eds., *Gender Conflicts: New Essays in Women's History.* Toronto: University of Toronto Press 1992. Pp.229–60.

Wright, David and Cathy Chorniawry. "Women and Drink in Victorian England." Canadian Historical Association. *Historical Papers*, 1985. Pp.117–31.

Woiak, Joanne. "'A Medical Cromwell to Depose King Alcohol': Medical Scientists, Temperance Reformers, and the Alcohol Problem in Britain." *HS/SH*, 27, no.54 (November 1994). Pp.337–65.

Wood, Louis Aubrey. *A History of Farmers' Movements in Canada.* Toronto: University of Toronto Press 1975 [1924].

Wright, J.R. *Urban Parks in Ontario. Part 2. The Public Park Movement, 1860–1914.* Ottawa: Ministry of Tourism and Recreation 1984.

Wrightson, Keith. "Alehouses, Order, and Reformation in Rural England, 1590–1660." In Eileen and Stephen Yeo, eds., *Popular Culture and Class Conflict, 1590–1914: Explorations in the History of Labour and Leisure.* Sussex, U.K.: Harvester Press 1981. Pp.1–27.

Wylie, William N.T. "Poverty, Distress, and Disease: Labour and the Construction of the Rideau Canal, 1826–32." *L/LT*, 11 (Spring 1983). Pp.7–29.

Xiao, Jiacbeng. "China." In Heath, ed., *International Handbook.* Pp.42–50.

Yamamuro, Bufo. "Notes on Drinking in Japan." In Marshall, ed., *Beliefs, Behaviors, and Alcoholic Beverages.* Pp.270–7.

The Yeas and Nays Polled in the Dunkin Act Campaign in Toronto, Carefully Prepared with the Official Returns, with Introductory Remarks and Extracts of Speeches Delivered during the Campaign. Toronto: Leader Steam Job Printing Office 1877.

Youmans, Letitia. *Campaign Echoes: The Autobiography of Mrs. Letitia Youmans.* Toronto: William Briggs 1893.

Young, James. *Reminiscences of the Early History of Galt and the Settlement of Dumfries in the Province of Ontario.* Toronto: Hunter, Rose, and Company 1880.

Young, James Harvey. *The Toadstool Millionaires: A Social History of Patent Medicines in America before Federal Regulation.* Princeton, N.J.: Princeton University Press 1961.

Young, John H. *Our Deportment; Or the Manners, Conduct and Dress of the Most Refined Society . . . .* Paris, Ont.: John S. Brown 1883 (CIHM no.34666).

Zimmerman, Jonathan. *Distilling Democracy: Alcohol Education in America's Public Schools, 1880–1925.* Lawrence: University Press of Kansas 1999.

_____. "'When the Doctors Disagree': Scientific Temperance and Scientific Authority, 1891–1906." *Journal of the History of Medicine,* 48, no.2 (April 1993). Pp.171–97.

Zuehlke, Mark. *Scoundrels, Dreamers, and Second Sons: British Remittance Men in the Canadian West.* Toronto: Dundurn 2001.

Index

public house. *See* beer parlours; taverns
public ownership, 220, 232, 306, 378
Purple Gang, 249

Quarterly Journal of Alcohol Studies, 357
Quarterly Journal of Inebriety, 141
Quebec, Diocese of, 70
Quebec, 19, 31, 41, 88, 90, 101, 157, 176, 194,
212, 239, 373, 394n17; bootlegging, 248,
254, 260; brewing, 88, 90, 101, 302, 303,
304, 305, 310, 430n6; drinking patterns, 81,
317, 404n15; government control, 237, 272,
278, 279, 280, 281, 283, 289, 320, 378;
labour, 226; plebiscites and referenda, 172,
180, 182, 194, 195, 226, 272, 376, 377, 420;
prohibition legislation, 160, 162, 180, 182,
183, 196, 269–70, 277, 377; prohibition
movements, 165, 175, 184, 196; regulatory
legislation, 157, 176; "wets," 212. *See also*
Lower Canada; New France
Quebec City, 19, 20, 26, 27, 32, 51, 285, 312,
393n9, 393n10, 394n20, 410n11, 423n9
Quebec Liquor Commission, 278
Queen's County Temperance Society (N.S.), 60
Quintal, Joseph, 212

race and racism, 11, 12, 15, 37, 43, 68, 106, 109,
163, 164, 168, 178, 191, 193, 195, 200–2,
221, 229, 293, 364, 382, 388. *See also*
Aboriginal peoples; African Canadians; Asian
Canadians
railway cars, alcohol served on, 176, 276, 281
railway workers, 72, 214, 219, 231
Ranchville, Sask., 240
Raney, William E., 257, 275
Raskob, John J., 212
Ready, James, 73
Ready Brewery, 254
"Real Ale" movement, 345
Rechabites, 56, 66
Recollets, 19
Red Deer, Alta., 155
Reformers, 61
refrigeration, mechanical, 4, 88, 93, 97
Regina, 109, 190
Regina *Leader*, 263
Regina Vinegar Company, 240
regulation. *See* state policies
Reid, Escott, 426n50
Reinhardt Brewery, 101, 405n26
religion, views of alcohol, 6, 8–9, 19, 48, 55,
155–6, 194, 199. *See also* Jews; Protestants;
Roman Catholics
Research Council on the Problems of Alcohol,
357

respectability, 12, 51, 59, 65, 77, 96, 102, 106, 107,
117, 118, 125–6, 214, 215, 219, 221, 269,
286, 289, 373, 381, 382, 384, 409n75
restaurants, 98, 253, 282
Restrictive Trade Practices Commission, 306–7
retailing. *See* liquor stores
Rhodes, Edgar, 276
Rideau Hall (Ottawa), 207
Rine, R.I.K., 66
Roberts, Julia, xi
Roblin, Rodmond P., 176
Rolph, John, 61
Roman Catholics, 6, 12, 19, 24, 53, 54, 55, 58, 62,
75, 155, 156, 160, 164, 172, 192, 194–6, 274,
373, 382, 418n17; French-Canadian, 69–71,
165, 168, 175; Irish, 68. *See also* Social
Catholicism
Rome, 8
Roosevelt, Theodore, 201
Roper, Elmer, 224
Rose, Clifford, 235, 252, 260
Ross, George, 174
Rossland, B.C., 109
Rothman's of Pall Mall, 307
"rough" culture, 75, 154, 286
Rouses Point, N.Y., 242, 258
Rowell, Newton W., 166, 227
Royal Canadian Mounted Police, 258, 260, 261,
292
Royal Commission on Corporate Consolidation,
303
Royal Commission on Customs and Excise, 250,
254
Royal Commission on the Liquor Traffic, 87, 171,
188, 189, 376; evidence presented to, 85, 96,
98, 117, 124, 163, 196, 216, 223, 230, 240,
410n11; report, 81, 102–3, 138, 142, 171,
242, 270, 362; surveys by, 141, 162
royal commissions. *See* state policies
Royal North-West Mounted Police, 109, 134,
162–3, 256, 258
Royal Templars of Temperance, 56, 146, 174, 218
Royal York Hotel (Toronto), ix, 312
rum, 5, 18, 19, 27, 31, 33, 41, 67, 317, 395n29; distilling, 4, 20, 301, 302, 393n10; importation,
20, 51, 372; military rations, 32, 72, 82–3,
180, 204, 315
rum-running, 246–51, 258, 261–2, 271, 387
Rush, Benjamin, 48, 52, 53, 139
Russell House (Ottawa), 75, 76
Russelltown, Lower Canada, 399n6
Russell v. the Queen, 156
Russia, 52, 183, 372, 377. *See also* Soviet Union
Rutgers University, 357, 368
rye whisky, 22, 81, 82, 91, 204, 280, 301

About the Author

CRAIG HERON teaches Canadian history and labour studies at York University, Toronto. He has written numerous articles and books on Canadian working-class history, including *Working in Steel: The Early Years in Canada, 1883–1935*, *The Canadian Labour Movement*, and *The Workers' Revolt in Canada, 1917–1925*. Keenly interested in public history, for fifteen years Heron has worked closely with the Workers' Arts and Heritage Centre in Hamilton, Ont. He has also been known to enjoy a glass of wine with his dinner.